Business, Government, and Society

Douglas F. Greer

San Jose State University
San Jose, California

MACMILLAN PUBLISHING CO., INC.
New York

Collier Macmillan Publishers
London

Macmillan Publishing Co., Inc.
866 Third Avenue, New York, New York 10022

Collier Macmillan Canada, Inc.

Acknowledgments

Excerpt from Jonathan Kwitny, "The Sweet Success of Smell," is reprinted by permission of *The Wall Street Journal,* © Dow Jones & Company, Inc., 1975. All rights reserved.

Excerpt from Murray L. Weidenbaum, *Business, Government, and the Public,* 2nd Ed., © 1981, p. 194. Reprinted by permission of Prentice-Hall, Inc., Englewood Cliffs, New Jersey.

Library of Congress Cataloging in Publication Data

Greer, Douglas F.
  Business, government, and society.
  Includes index.
    1. Industry and state—United States.
2. Trade regulation—United States.
I. Title.
HD3616.U47G76   338.973   82–7208
ISBN 0–02–347050–X   AACR2

Printing: 4 5 6 7 8   Year: 4 5 6 7 8 9 0

ISBN   0-02-347050-X

To Wendy, Darby, and Leah

Preface

This is a text for a first course in business and government. The titles of such courses tend to be very broad, whether they are taught in business schools or economics departments. Titles of books in this field are no less expansive. The obvious reason for this is that the government's impact on business is now enormous in weight, variety, complexity, and effect. As this impact grew with time, textbooks on the topic likewise grew—in weight, complexity, and so on. In reaction to this, some recent textbooks have retreated into brevity and simplicity.

The aim of this book is to be neither too fat nor too thin, neither too simple nor too complex. Nevertheless it is long, and in many places it is complex because government policy toward business *is* voluminous and contorted. In other words, a simple, brief book would by nature misrepresent the truth.

To soften the blow, I have tried to write good introductions and overviews. I have also been repetitious where I thought it could be helpful. Furthermore, I have made a special effort to separate things that should be separated—things like point-to-point communications and broadcast communications. These and other characteristics give the book a flexibility not otherwise attainable. If a simple survey is all that an instructor wants, he or she can get it from Part I in its entirety, plus the introductory chapters of Parts II, IV, and V, plus certain selected key chapters such as 6, 7, 15, 21, and 26. On the other hand, if a more complete tour of state and federal capital buildings is desired, the book is open to the diligent and courageous. Indeed, when combined with appropriate supplementary texts of case readings or government documents, the book could be the foundation for an entire year of study, with separate courses in the sequence on such broad topics as antitrust or economic regulation.

In ideological point of view, the book takes a middle path. It is neither "libertarian" nor "radical," neither "liberal" nor "conservative." It tries to give each view its due when it is important to do so. Moreover, the book is neither strictly economic-theoretical nor patently legal-institutional. Notions of economic efficiency are fully developed, but value judgments other than economic efficiency frequently enter the story. That is why "society" is in the title. I seriously doubt that anyone could properly explain or assess government policy without reference to a wide range of value judgments. Finally, I have also taken the middle path between the market and the government. Each is depicted in its ideal form. Each is criticized for its failures and imperfections. Indeed, the reader should be warned that this middle course fosters many of the book's complexities and details. If markets were always good and governments always bad, or conversely, if governments were always good and markets always bad, this book would have been very simple and spindly.

This book would have been nonexistent were it not for the generous and able help of others. Professors Robert E. Smith of the University of Oregon, Sanford Berg of the University of Florida, and Sidney M. Blumner of California State Polytechnic University—Pomona contributed with careful reading and wise comments. Finally, my wife Wendy, who for some mysterious reason continues to make great sacrifices as my editor and typist, was indispensable to this project.

D. F. G.

Brief Contents

Detailed Contents

Part I

Introduction and Overview

Source: The Wall Street Journal. Used by permission of Cartoon Features Syndicate.

Chapter 1

Introduction: Functions and Values

The importance of the government-business relationship to the American people cannot be overestimated. Government and business are *the* key institutions of the nation; how they interact is of profound significance to all Americans.
—Arthur Selwyn Miller

Randomly pick any day in the life of the *Wall Street Journal*. What do you find? A long parade of reports from the government and business front. Let's take the issue of June 4, 1980, for instance. An easing in auto fuel-economy standards was approved by the House of Representatives. San Diego Gas & Electric Company modified a rate increase request. A federal judge began a pretrial hearing for an antitrust suit against uranium cartel conspirators. The Food and Drug Administration reported progress in the recall of 450,000 cans of mushrooms suspected of containing deadly botulism poison. General Motors told the National Highway Traffic Safety Administration that it would meet NHTSA's 1982 passive restraint standards with automatically fastening seat belts instead of inflatable air bags. The Justice Department claimed that the Energy Department could not rightfully drop its suits against oil companies accused of overcharging customers in violation of price controls. The Equal Employment Op-

portunity Commission accused IBM of discriminating against black professionals and managers at four Maryland facilities. Government delegates to a meeting of the Organization for Economic Cooperation and Development endorsed a declaration discouraging the use of import tariffs and quotas, despite rising pressures for increasingly protectionist policies. And so it went, all on one typical day.

The purpose of this book is to give the reader a broad understanding of government policies toward business and their impact on society. Such an understanding will bring some order to the apparent chaos of government intervention. It will convert any newspaper clippings you might collect into something more than overgrown confetti.

The three main characters in this tale are business, government, and society. *Business* includes colossal corporations and small proprietorships. It encompasses manufacturing, mining, transportation, and everything in between.

Business is conducted in markets, which comprise the central nervous system of our economy and which are the real focus of government intervention. *Government* spans federal, state, and local levels. It includes commissions, agencies, courts, and committees as well as the more familiar congresses, senates, presidents, and governors. *Society* of course includes those in business and government, but the term is meant mainly to cover all of us taken together—consumers, students, employees, children, authors, whoever.

Ideally and essentially, business pursues its own self-interest by providing products and services that best satisfy the preferences of those in society, something which benefits both society and business. Profit is the incentive, the honey of this harmony. But profit can also be made in "antisocial" ways, so if for some reason business fails to meet the expectations of society, society may then call upon government to straighten things out. Ideally, government responds with policies that best serve society's interests, again measured by private personal preferences. Unfortunately, government is likewise capable of failure, just as a would-be rescuer might throw a heavy life-ring to a drowning man, inadvertently clubbing the poor fellow senseless. Stated differently, we shall attempt (1) to *explore* this interesting triangle of business, government, and society; (2) to *organize* the diverse relationships linking the triangle; (3) to *analyze* how business and government function; and (4) to *evaluate* how fully business and government satisfy the preferences and expectations of society.

Among the numerous specific issues that will be addressed along the way, the following are apt to be of greatest interest to the reader. Why do just a few firms dominate some of our markets, such as those for autos, computers, telephone service, and aluminum? What are the effects of such dominance for profits, innovation, and efficiency? What policies attempt to check the power of big firms? What does gov-

ernment hope to accomplish with measures like truth-in-lending, grade rating, and product standardization? What is false advertising? What have been the costs and benefits of auto safety regulation and environmental protection policy? Are we running out of oil and natural gas? How has government regulated energy? What is the best way of curbing inflation? What purposes do patents serve? Should we protect the auto, steel, electronics, and apparel industries from foreign imports? What is the trend in radio and TV regulation? What will its impact be on the upcoming communications revolution?

Of course everything cannot be said all at once, so in these first four chapters comprising Part I we begin at the beginning. This chapter sets out some basic *definitions*, outlines the main *functions* that society calls upon business and government to perform, and surveys the *values* that society uses in evaluating both business and government. In brief, the purpose of this chapter is to specify our preferences as a society, to delineate what is good and bad. By inference, we also indicate what problems arise when either business or government fail to satisfy those preferences.

On the business side, our focus is actually on markets rather than on business as such, because markets are the institutions through which businesses serve society's interests. Accordingly, we shall apply this chapter's findings to Chapter 2, which explains what is good and bad about markets. On the good side, markets can effectively "regulate" businesses for society's great benefit, and the first object of Chapter 2 is to explain why such private free enterprise regulation is generally superior to government intervention. The second object there is to show why markets are occasionally deficient. In Chapter 3 we shift attention to the government, detailing government's good and bad aspects. Finally, to conclude Part I, Chapter 4 surveys the main ideologies that help determine the mix of private free enterprise and government intervention that we actually experience in the United States. It also sketches the history of government intervention from our country's birth to the present.

Stated differently the purpose of these first few chapters is threefold:

1. To explain broadly the *problems* needing attention, such as monopoly power and hazardous pollution.
2. To specify potential policy *solutions* (including do nothing) and establish criteria, such as benefit-cost analysis, for *choosing* among alternative solutions.
3. To survey the *feasibility* of implementing the various policy options by gaining an appreciation of *political ideologies and historical context.*

Lest you get irritated by all the theory you encounter at the outset, the importance of finding theoretical models that match problems with proper solutions can be illustrated by a poignant example of two competing theories. By far the most disturbing problem in seventeenth-century Monte Lupo, Italy was the plague. On the one side were public health officials who, although ignorant of the role of rats and fleas, correctly theorized from empirical study that the spread of the disease could be checked by enforcing a policy of quarantine and segregation on the populace. On the other side were the town's religious leaders, who believed that the plague was a scourge sent by God to punish the people. Following this theory they urged that everyone be brought together in massive religious processions and rituals to atone for their sins. Unfortunately, this last solution was implemented, partly because of political feasibilities. The people themselves preferred processions to quarantine regulations.[1]

[1] Carlo M. Cipolla, *Faith, Reason, and the Plague in Seventeenth Century Tuscany* (Ithaca, N.Y.: Cornell University Press, 1979).

I. Basic Definitions

Simply put, a **market** is an organized process by which buyers and sellers exchange goods and services for money, the medium of exchange. Notice that every market has two sides to it—a demand side (made up of buyers) and a supply side (made up of sellers). Notice also that markets can be local, regional, national, or international in scope. When the exchange alternatives of either buyers or sellers are geographically limited—as is true of barbering and cement manufacturing, for example—then exchange and competition are correspondingly limited in geographic scope. Strictly speaking, the word "industry" denotes a much broader concept than market because an industry can include numerous local or regional markets. When we speak of the construction industry we usually refer to something more than local business. In practice, however, "market" and "industry" are often used synonymously, without careful distinction, a practice we too will follow when precision is not required.

Most generally, **government** is the process within a group for making and enforcing decisions that affect human behavior. Public government can claim a monopoly of the legitimate use of physical force or coercion within a given territory. Indeed, some scholars place particular emphasis on this matter of force:

> Legitimate force is the thread that runs through the inputs and outputs of the political system, giving it its special quality and salience and its coherence as a system. The inputs into the political system are all in some way related to claims for the employment of legitimate compulsion, whether these are demands for war or for recreational facilities. The outputs of the political system are also all in some way related to legitimate physical compulsion, however remote the relationship may be.[2]

[2] Gabriel A. Almond and James S. Colman (eds.) *The Politics of the Developing Areas* (Princeton: Princeton University Press, 1960), p. 7.

The "market" and the "government" are institutions. An *institution* may be defined as selected elements of a scheme of values mobilized and coordinated to accomplish a particular purpose or function.[3] Accordingly, this definition implies that markets and government each have two principal aspects—a *value* aspect and a *functional* aspect.

II. The Functional Aspect

A. Markets

With respect to function, we rely on markets to cope with the fundamental problem of scarcity, which is what economics is all about. Scarcity would be no problem if wants were severely curtailed. Scarcity would be no problem if our productive capabilities knew no bounds. But, alas, neither of these conditions holds for our society. We have neither limited wants nor unlimited resources. Quite the contrary, Americans are by far the most prosperous people who have ever lived; yet we still want more goods and services—more than our limited resources of land, capital, labor, energy, and time can produce. Proof of this statement is easy: markets, prices, wages, and all the other trappings of our economy would not exist save for scarcity.

To be more specific about the function of markets, crucial decisions must be made and the preferences of society must be accounted for in making those decisions. The *input function* of markets is to account for those preferences and signal scarcity's constraints. That is to say, buyers' and sellers' preferences are articulated and communicated through myriad markets by actions of paying and receiving. The *output function* of markets is to provide answers to the four basic questions that scarcity rudely forces upon us:

[3] Talcott Parsons and Neil Smelser, *Economy and Society* (New York: Free Press, 1965), p. 102.

1. *What goods and services shall we produce and in what amounts?* At first glance the answer may seem simple and obvious. We need such basics as food, clothing, and shelter. But even in this context our limitations impose trade-offs. Shall it be more "Twinkies" and less "Granola"; more apartments and fewer single-family dwellings; more sweaters and fewer jackets? What combination of goods is most desirable?

2. *How are goods and services to be produced?* Many different methods of production are possible for most goods. Cigars, for instance, can be made by man as well as by machine. What mixture of the two will it be? Should coal be mined by strip or underground methods? In short, what combination of resource commitments is most efficient?

3. *Who shall get and consume the goods and services we produce?* There are two aspects to this question. One aspect relates to income distribution—what share of our total national income should each household receive? The other aspect relates to rationing of specific goods. Not enough gasoline can be produced for everyone to get as much as they would like. Hence some form of rationing is required.

4. *How shall we maintain flexibility for changes over time?* No condition of scarcity is static, ironclad, or unchanging. Advances in technology and better educational attainments continually expand our productive capabilities. Consumer tastes also alter. Thus we are confronted with questions of change. Shall we convert to nuclear power, steam autos, digital watches, electronic calculators, and nine-track tapes? Decisions of acceptance and rejection must continually be made. Flexibility allows us to probe such new opportunities as they arise.

By and large we entrust these decisions to the *market,* to millions of consumers, workers, employers, land owners, investors, and proprietors, each pursuing self-interest in the market place. *The function of markets is to coordinate and control this decentralized decision-making process, which answers these four crucial questions.*

B. The Government

Government, too, is an answer machine, one that dabbles, and in some countries even dominates, in deciding these economic questions of what, how, who, and what's new. Speaking more broadly to include the political system generally, the governmental process likewise has input functions and output functions.[4] The *input functions* include (1) preference articulation by means of citizens' letters, interest groups, referenda, and the like, (2) preference aggregation, mainly through party platforms, congressional compromises, coalitions, and broadly based interest groups like "agriculture," and (3) political communication through governmental and independent media, mainly the press, radio, and TV. The *output functions* are, most broadly, (1) rule making or legislating, (2) rule application or law enforcement, and

[4] Almond and Colman, *op. cit.,* pp. 17–58.

(3) rule adjudication in the judicial branch of government. Table 1–1 summarizes for both markets and government.

The main economic powers delegated to the U.S. federal government, as enumerated in Article I, Section 8 of the Constitution, are these:

- To lay and collect Taxes, Duties, Imposts and Excises, to pay the Debts and provide for the common Defence and the general Welfare. . . .
- To borrow Money. . . .
- To regulate Commerce with foreign Nations and among the several States. . . .
- To coin Money, regulate the value thereof . . . and fix the Standard of Weights and Measures. . . .
- To establish Post Offices and Post Roads;
- To promote the progress of Science and useful Arts, by securing for limited Times to Authors and Inventors the exclusive Right to their respective Writing and Discoveries. . . .

The most important of these clauses for our purpose is the so-called "commerce clause," which grants power "To regulate Commerce . . . among the several States. . . ." This plus the other clauses permits extensive govern-

---

Table 1–1. The Main Institutional Functions

Functions of the Market System	Functions of the Government System

Input Functions:
  1. Preference articulation
  2. Economic communication
	Input Functions:
	  1. Preference articulation
	  2. Preference aggregation
	  3. Political communication

Output Functions:
  1. Decide *what* to produce
  2. Decide *how* to produce
  3. Decide *who* gets the goodies
  4. Decide *what's new*
	Output Functions:
	  1. Rule making (legislative)
	  2. Rule application (exec.)
	  3. Rule adjudication (judic.)

ment participation in deciding the economic questions of what, how, who, and what's new, thereby nosing into the market's domain. Not mentioned among the four basic questions concerning scarcity is an economic area where the market formerly held free reign but now most definitely is the province of the federal government for good or ill—namely, maintenance of aggregate economic stability.

III. The Value Aspect[5]

As far as values are concerned, our society generally believes that, at their best, markets tend to perform their functions of coordination and control very nicely. That is to say, the market system accords well with many of our society's values by (1) typically providing fairly good answers to the four basic economic questions, and (2) arriving at these answers in an appealing way. Exactly what these answers are and exactly how the market system goes about arriving at them will be discussed in the next chapter. Right now we need to explain which values we refer to and thereby specify what is meant here by "good" and "appealing." We also need to note that such favorable assessments of the market system imply rather unfavorable scores for the government in these matters. Two chief reasons for looking warily upon the government system are apparent from our previous discussion: (1) Government decision making entails preference aggregation to arrive at generally applicable policies—such as all cars must have safety belts—something which may brutalize individual preferences. (2) Lurking beneath practically all government policy is that unsavory element of coercion.

In the present context, **values** are simply generalized concepts of the desirable. They are

objectives, ends, or aims that guide our attitudes and actions. Among the most generalized concepts of the desirable are such notions as "welfare and happiness," "freedom," "justice," and "equality." These may be called **ultimate** values because they reign supreme in the minds of most western men and women.

Although these are undeniably noble aims, they are also too vague and too ill-defined to provide a basis for specific institutional arrangements and policy decisions; so, for purposes of actual application, they can be translated into more specific concepts—like "full employment" and "allocation efficiency"—which may be called **proximate** values. Table 1–2 presents a summary list of proximate values that are relevant here, together with the ultimate values from which they are derived. Allocation efficiency, full employment, clean environment, and health and safety, for example, are several proximate values that convey the spirit of "welfare and happiness." The list is intended to be more illustrative than exhaustive, so only a brief discussion of it is warranted.

Freedom. Proximate values reflecting freedom include such notions as "free choice in consumption and occupation," and "free entry and investment." They imply active, unhampered participation in the economic decision-making process by all of us. The market furthers these objectives because the market affords free expression to individual choice in deciding answers to the key economic questions outlined earlier—what, how, who, and what's new? Unfettered individual choice is possible *only* under favorable circumstances, however. For if markets are burdened with barriers to entry, monopoly power, price fixing, or similar restraints of trade—imposed *either* by government *or* by private groups—then this freedom is sharply curtailed. Although the government has often imposed these and other restraints (usually under the influence and for the benefit of special interest groups), most people in our

---

[5] For a more extensive discussion of values see Donald S. Watson, *Economic Policy, Business and Government* (Boston: Houghton Mifflin, 1960), pp. 24–25.

Table 1–2. Some Proximate Values and the Ultimate Values from Which They Derive

Ultimate Values	Proximate Values
Freedom	Free choice in consumption and occupation Free entry and investment Limited government intervention Free political parties National security
Equality	Diffusion of economic and political power Equal bargaining power for buyers/sellers Equal opportunity Limited income inequality
Justice and fairness	Prohibition of unfair practices Fair labor standards Honesty Full disclosure Fair return on fair value
Welfare and happiness	Allocation and technical efficiency Full employment Price stability Health and safety Clean environment
Progress	Rising real income Technological advancement Productivity improvement

society favor "limited government intervention" and "free political parties," both of which tend to inhibit centralized command and coercion. Thus, to the extent government intervention is properly called for, most would probably agree that it should be for purposes of *preventing* private restraints of trade rather than for *imposing* official restraints.

Equality. When one person's freedom encroaches upon another person's freedom, some criterion is needed to resolve the conflict; in our society the ideal criterion is "equality" or "equity."[6] This usually means that everybody's preferences and aspirations are weighted equally, as in the political cliché: one man, one vote. In economics, the notion that each individual's dollar counts the same as anyone else's dollar reflects a similar sentiment. Among the more important proximate values stemming from equality are "a wide diffusion of economic and political power," "equal bargaining power on both sides of an exchange transaction," "equal opportunity, regardless of race, religion, sex, or national origin," and "*limited in*equality in the distribution of income." Under favorable conditions, the market system can further these objectives as well as those associated with freedom.

Justice and Fairness. The market is often given high marks for justice and fairness because, under ideal circumstances, it generates

[6] Robert A. Dahl and Charles E. Lindblom, *Politics, Economics, and Welfare* (New York: Harper & Row Publishers, 1963), p. 41.

answers to the key economic questions that are not arbitrary, despotic, or peremptory in nature. Adam Smith's metaphorical "invisible hand" eloquently illustrates this deduction. Unfortunately, real world circumstances often fall short of the ideal, so that free pursuit of profits in the market place may not always yield fair or just results. As Vernon Mund has written, "Profit can be made not only by producing more and better goods but also by using inferior materials, by artificially restricting supply to secure monopoly profits, by misleading and deceiving consumers, and by exploiting labor."[7] Thus, to account for these sad possibilities and to introduce several forms of market regulation that will be discussed in later chapters, we have listed "full-disclosure," "honesty," and "prohibition of unfair practices" among the proximate values of Table 1–2.

Welfare, Happiness, and Progress. The foregoing discussion of freedom, equality, justice, and fairness helps to explain our earlier statement that the market system arrives at answers to the key economic questions in a *particularly appealing way,* but it remains to be demonstrated that the answers themselves are *fairly good answers.* In other words, as far as markets are concerned, the foregoing values relate more to the decision-making process than to the decisions made—to *means* rather than to *ends.* So, what about ends? Fortunately for us, the answers provided by the market system (again under favorable circumstances) comport fairly well with our society's concepts of welfare, happiness, and progress. As already indicated, a thorough exploration of these answers is deferred until later chapters when we can elaborate on the meaning of the phrases "favorable circumstances" and "ideal conditions" that have echoed interchangeably across these pages. Nevertheless, for a prelude, we

can note briefly that the market system is generally efficient and flexible. Thus, markets answer the question "what will be produced" by allocating labor and material resources to the production of goods and services yielding the greatest social satisfaction. And, with respect to the question of how goods are produced, markets encourage the use of low-cost production techniques that consume the least amount of scarce resources possible for a given bundle of output. Finally, flexibility: the market is generally receptive to good new ideas and new resource capabilities so that, with each passing year, we can produce more and better goods with less and less time, effort, and waste; all of which implies progress. As regards "clean environment" and "health and safety," which are also mentioned as proximate values in Table 1–2, the market alone has not performed very well in the past. The reason for this failure will be discussed later.

Although these ultimate and proximate values are widely shared and vigorously advocated by most people in our society (why else would they pop up so conspicuously in most political speeches?), they are also sources of conflict, frustration, and disappointment simply because they are not always consistent with each other. Among the more obvious examples of inconsistency, consider the following:

1. "Health and safety" may be furthered by requiring seat belts and a collapsible steering wheel in every auto, but this requirement would inevitably interfere with "free choice in consumption."
2. Measures designed to procure a "clean environment," such as banning the use of sulfur laden coal (which is our most abundant energy resource), may seriously diminish what we can achieve in the way of "rising real income."
3. Enforcement of "honesty" and the "prohibition of unfair practices" in the marketing

---

[7] Vernon A. Mund, *Government and Business,* 4th ed. (New York: Harper & Row Publishers, 1965), p. 24.

of products may conflict with many people's concepts of "limited government intervention."

4. Patents may be deemed the best means of encouraging "technological progress," but each patent confers monopolistic privileges that run counter to both "free entry" and "diffusion of economic power."

Lest the picture painted by these examples look too bleak, we hasten to add that in many instances there may not be inconsistencies among values, and in other instances the inconsistencies may be so mild that they are readily amenable to resolution and compromise. Still, as just suggested, inconsistencies do exist and are often sharp, which helps to explain several important facts of political-economic life.

First, for various reasons (including material self-interest, educational background, emotional empathy, and social position) each individual gives differing *weights* and *definitions* to these values. It is the particular weight and definition that guides each person's judgment of conflicts among values, precluding the possibility of unanimous agreement on almost anything.

Second, several "economic philosophies" or "schools of thought" have evolved that differ primarily in terms of the weights they apply to these values and the definitions they give to them. Thus, for example, "conservatives" generally believe that "freedom" is superior to "equality" and "fairness." They prefer less government intervention—even at the expense of more private monopoly power, greater consumer deception, and aggravated income inequalities. In contrast, "liberals" often stress "equality" and "fairness" over "freedom," and their list of preferences is consequently quite different from that of "conservatives."

Third, people's definitions and weights are by no means static or immutable. They obviously change with time and events. Indeed,

economic policy formulation has been described as "a trial and error process of self-correcting value judgments."[8] Nothing is absolute or final, especially in this field. *Knowledge* and *policy* have within them and between them certain irreconcilable inconsistencies. They are both undergoing continuous review and revision, and opinions about both are strongly influenced by values.

IV. Ethics: Goals and Imperatives

Table 1–2 makes no distinction between moral and nonmoral values, such as "justice" and "progressiveness." Likewise it makes no distinction between ethical criteria based on achieving some ultimate goal, such as "efficiency," and ethical criteria based on moral imperatives, such as "honesty." Yet a full understanding of how policies can be judged "right" and "wrong" rests on just such distinctions.

Moral philosophers inform us that there are two ethical standards for evaluating policies as outlined in Table 1–3.[9] One type is teleological, from the Greek word *telos* or "end." A **teleological standard** judges the rightness or wrongness of acts, rules, and policies by the end results or ultimate nonmoral consequences they produce. Such ends might be the satisfaction of consumer preferences, the maximization of gross national product, or the speed of technological change.[10] Teleological standards are typically concerned with ends that are *continuously* variable, subject to *balancing*, and offer

---

[8] H. H. Liebhafsky's entire book *American Government and Business* (New York: Wiley and Sons, 1971) is devoted to this theme, but see especially Chapters 1, 2, 6 and 8.

[9] William K. Frankena, *Ethics* (Englewood Cliffs, N.J.: Prentice-Hall, 1963); Charles Fried, *Right and Wrong* (Cambridge: Harvard University Press, 1978).

[10] Such ends cannot be "morally" desirable in and of themselves because the teleological standard would then be circular.

Table 1–3.   A Comparison of Characteristics of Ethical Criteria

Teleological Ethics	Imperative Ethics
1. Some nonmoral end is served, e.g., satisfaction of consumer preferences	1. Rightness or wrongness intrinsic to the deed, e.g., honesty for its own sake
2. Continuous variables involved, e.g., dollar benefits and costs	2. Discrete prescriptions, e.g., do not kill
3. Balance or adding up involved	3. No balance, categorical imperative
4. Comparisons of policies to find which is "better"	4. Absolute, policies judged "right" or "wrong" independently

opportunities of *comparison.* An important example drawn from economics is "cost-benefit" analysis, which purports to satisfy society's preferences by (1) casting all the relevant effects of alternative policies into dollar terms, (2) comparing the costs and benefits, and (3) recommending the policy that, on balance, yields the greatest benefit less cost. A more general teleological rule is this: "An act *ought to be done* if and only if it or the rule under which it falls produces, will probably produce, or is intended to produce *a greater balance of good over evil* than any available alternative."[11]

In contrast, a nonteleological or **imperative standard** holds that actions or rules are morally right or wrong in and of themselves, regardless of their consequences or end effects. Thus a rule such as "Thou shalt not commit murder, no matter what," would be an imperative rule. "You should never lie," is another. Note that such rules have a flavor of finality, have discrete "yes-no" qualities that cannot be quantified, have no reference to balancing good and bad consequences, and have an air of absoluteness.

To illustrate the two views, suppose that the government has the resources to build one of two dams, Dam A or Dam B, but not both.

Suppose further that a benefit-cost analysis reveals net benefits of $3 billion for A and $2 billion for B. A teleological economist would say that A "ought to be built" because of the nice comparative consequences. Suppose, however, that either A or B would completely wipe out three species of mammals. An environmentalist adopting an imperative standard might say "we should build *neither* A or B" because it is "immoral" to commit "genocide" against other species. Our teleological economist might at this point try to meet the protest of our nonteleological environmentalist by first apologizing for leaving the endangered animals out of account and then reckoning the monetary value of the lost species at $2.5 billion, based on a survey of how much people would be willing to pay to protect these three classes of creatures from oblivion. Once the $2.5 billion is deducted from the $3 and $2 billion of net benefits in the original analysis, the teleological economist might now admit that Dam B was indeed damnable but still insist that A was desirable because of the remaining net positive benefit of $0.5 billion. Would this persuade the environmentalist? No, not if the "no genocide against species" is truly a moral imperative to the environmentalist, something warranting even the risk of jail, or worse, in its defense.

[11] Frankena, *op. cit.,* p. 13.

The reader must thus be put on notice that most economists and perhaps the bulk of businessmen as well tend to rely on teleological ethics. If a potent chemical quickens the maturity of chickens, increasing productivity and reducing the consumers' cost of broilers by $500 million per year, it does not much matter that, "statistically" or "randomly," ten people will die excruciating deaths from the chemical each year, given that those deaths can be "valued" at, say, $1 million each, for a total of $10 million, which cannot outweigh the $500 million. Or what about theft and fraud? According to prominent economist Roland McKean they are wrong not for any intrinsic reason but because of their teleologic cost savings: "honesty can save extra burglar alarms, time clocks, monitoring devices, legal actions, hours spent checking up on each other's statements, time wasted when appointments and promises are broken, energy and good humor squandered on bitterness and reprisal, and gains from trades that would otherwise not take place."[12] Or, further, what about punishment for criminal acts? Gary Becker, an equally prominent economist, argues that imprisonment not only reduces possible sources of crime, it also prevents inmates from producing and earning. Penalizing very productive people (those who earn high salaries) in this way thus detracts substantially from GNP. Becker therefore proposes fines and freedom instead of incarceration for such people because of society's alleged net benefit.[13] But of course this teleological view completely ignores any ethical standard that proper retribution is "right" regardless of the consequences.

Although the present writer is an economist, he is by no means a strict teleologist. He believes that a blend of teleological and imperative standards is both possible and desirable, especially when trying to comprehend and assess public policy. The fact that imperative standards tend to be *discrete* and teleological standards tend to be *continuous* offers an opportunity for such blending because these characteristics permit teleological optimization *subject* to imperative constraints.[14] Thus, for example, one could devise a system of electric power generation that maximized society's net benefit, subject to the constraint that no more nuclear plants be built if most everyone came to consider "nukes" morally odious. Or we might have a policy that businessmen could promote their products all they want to, so long as they did not engage in false advertising. Oddly enough, economists theorize constantly about optimizing various things (e.g., profits) subject to constraints (e.g., technology), yet many seem blind to the possibility and necessity of blending teleological and imperative ethics in this fashion.[15] In short, the end does *not* always justify the means, even though the end we shall generally propound is the laudable one of satisfying people's preferences. After all, those preferences appear to include many ethical notions of an imperative nature.

Summary

Markets and government are our nation's key institutions. Problems arise when either of these institutions fail to live up to what society

[12] Roland N. McKean, "Collective Choice," in James W. McKie (ed.) *Social Responsibility and the Business Predicament* (Washington, D.C.: Brookings Institution, 1974), p. 121.

[13] Gary S. Becker, "Crime and Punishment: An Economic Approach," *Journal of Political Economy* (March/April 1968), pp. 169–217.

[14] Duncan MacRae, Jr. and James A. Wilde, *Policy Analysis for Public Decisions* (North Scituate, Mass.: Duxbury Press, 1979), p. 54. This approach is also implied by G. Warren Nutter, "On Economism," *Journal of Law & Economics* (October 1979), pp. 263–268.

[15] Some economists are so rutted to teleological thinking that they fail to realize their ethical judgments. Can you find the contradiction in the following? "This book makes no moral assumptions and is strictly utilitarian in its approach to legal institutions." Gordon Tullock, *The Logic of the Law* (New York: Basic Books, 1971), p. vi.

expects of them. Excessively priced and unsafe products, for instance, would not satisfy the preferences of those in society, signaling a problem. Likewise, outrageously costly and coercive government intervention, even if aimed at remedying market deficiencies, would be less than desirable. Problems of both kinds are the concern of this book.

A few first steps in assessing government policies toward business have now been taken. Business markets, government, and society have been defined. The ways in which markets and government serve society have been outlined in Table 1–1. We find that the basic function of both is, in two words, *decision making*. Markets are called upon for private, decentralized, individualized, capitalistic decision making. Government is called upon for collective, official decision making. The input functions of both thus include preference articulation and communication, but the government side also includes preference aggregation because government decisions are collective. The output or substantive function of markets is to coordinate and control private decision making in finding answers to the basic questions scarcity imposes upon us—what, how, who, and what's new. The output functions of government are, most broadly, rule making, rule application, and rule adjudication. Less broadly and most importantly for our purposes, the government is authorized by the Constitution to "regulate commerce" and thereby to influence what, how, who, and what's new.

We shall be evaluating these institutions in two main ways: (1) *how* they go about making their decisions, a question of *means*, and (2) *how good* are the results, a question of *ends*. Such evaluation necessarily entails the application of ethical criteria or value judgments, some of which are *moral* value judgments. In this connection one must distinguish between *teleological standards*, which focus on the nonmoral outcomes or results of acts or rules, and *imperative standards*, which hold that certain acts or rules are right or wrong in themselves, regardless of the economic or other consequences. Both types of standards may be found in the government's formulation and execution of policy. Both types of standards are employed by scholars and other folks to evaluate those policies. Hence both will be encountered often on our journey.

Questions and Exercises for Chapter 1

1. "Government is to the market what an umpire is to a baseball game." In what ways is this true? In what ways false?
2. Although the market and government differ in definition and function, society tends to judge them by the same criteria, outlined in Table 1–2. Why? Could it be that, in the end, their functions are often quite similar?
3. For each question raised by scarcity, select one or two proximate values you think are particularly pertinent and then explain your choice.
4. Pick a distinctly different society than our own—e.g., a society of Buddhist monks or Iranians—and draw up a list of value judgments you think appropriate.
5. Would you consider the following to be governed by teleological or imperative standards? "Equal opportunity." "Clean environment." "Full employment." Explain your answer for each.
6. Explain why wanting "efficiency" is a value judgment.

Chapter 2

The Market:
Ideal and Real

Every man hath a good and bad angel attending on him in particular,
all his long life.
—Robert Burton

Having sketched the place markets occupy in our economy and having described the basic ideals that will be applied in our evaluation of markets, we are ready for a more detailed analysis. Our objectives now are (1) to explain *how* markets operate under various circumstances, a descriptive undertaking, and (2) to analyze *how well* markets satisfy society's economic preferences, a normative undertaking that will open the door to potential public policies.

First, this chapter develops a useful way of looking at markets. Second, perfect competition, which can serve as the theoretically ideal market, is described and analyzed. This ideal is especially useful in explaining one particular standard of economic goodness—efficiency or Pareto optimality. Third, this chapter itemizes the problems besetting real world markets, problems that might justify government intervention in search of solutions. Review of those government actions—both good and bad—is saved for the next chapter.

I. A Way of Looking at Markets

A systematic way of examining markets is necessary if any headway is to be made in analyzing market operations or evaluating how well various markets perform their function. In essence, all that is required is (1) a workable categorization of the principal attributes of markets and (2) a theoretical scheme tying these attributes together. The process is analogous to analyzing the operation of an automobile—the categorization of attributes (or parts) would distinguish between the electrical system, fuel supply system, drive train, and so on, and the theoretical scheme would relate each of these attributes to the others to explain how the machine worked.

The traditional model of markets is outlined in Figure 2–1.[1] As indicated there, the principal components of market analysis are the basic conditions, structure, conduct, and performance. The **basic conditions** may be thought of as characteristics that are either unalterably

[1] Basic Sources include Edward Mason, "Price and Production of Large-Scale Enterprise," *American Economic Review*, Supplement (March, 1939), pp. 61–74; Joe Bain, *Industrial Organization* (New York: Wiley & Sons, 1959); J. M. Clark, *Competition as a Dynamic Process* (Washington, D.C.: Brookings Institution, 1961); and F. M. Scherer, *Industrial Market Structure and Economic Performance* (Chicago: Rand McNally, 1970).

inherent to the product (as is largely true of price elasticity of demand, purchase method, and product durability) or relatively impervious to easy manipulation by policy (as is largely true of growth rate, technology, and historical background). The elements of market **structure** also tend to be stable over time, but they can be affected by either private or government policy. Among the more important variables of structure are the number of sellers and their size distribution (both of which can be altered by antitrust divestiture and dissolution), product differentiation (determined chiefly by pri-

Figure 2–1. A Model of Market Analysis

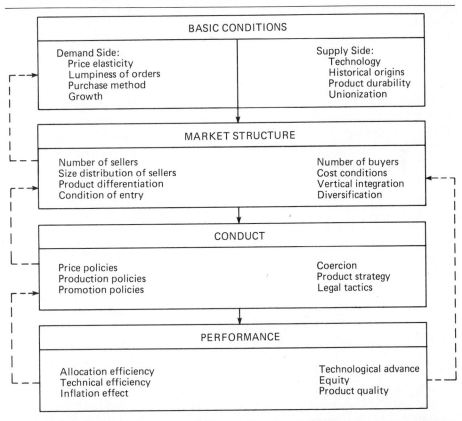

vate advertising and promotion), and the condition of entry (which is affected by patents, licensing, and product differentiation, among other things). The word **conduct** denotes behavior, policy, and strategy on the part of firms in the market, so the several items listed under conduct in Figure 2–1 reflect action, not static condition. Finally, **performance** relates to achievements or end results as determined by such variables as efficiency, technological advance, and product quality. In short, structure and conduct relate to *how* the market functions within the limits of its basic conditions, whereas performance relates to *how well* the market functions.

The arrows of Figure 2–1 indicate possible relationships among these attributes. In particular, traditional theory assumes a causal flow running from the basic conditions and structure to conduct and performance. Technology and growth, for instance, could greatly influence the number and size distribution of firms in the market. In turn, the structural characteristics of number and size distribution might determine price and production policies (conduct) that cause good or bad allocation and technical efficiency (performance). The broken lines of Figure 2–1 represent causal flows running in the opposite direction from those of the traditional model. They too will occasionally attract our attention.

Now, a first inkling of how one might evaluate markets can be gained by noting several crude correspondences between the values listed in Table 1–2 of the last chapter and the attributes outlined here in Figure 2–1. Excluding the basic conditions because they are for the most part predetermined, we may first notice that good market structure would reflect the kinds of proximate values listed earlier under "Freedom" and "Equality." Thus, a structure having numerous buyers and sellers, easy entry, and the like could be said to foster "Diffusion of economic power," "Equal bargaining power," "Free entry and investment," "Free

choice in consumption and occupation," and "Equal opportunity." By the same token, market conduct that included no collusion, no misrepresentation, no price discrimination, and no predatory coercion would be conduct that conformed fairly well to the notions of "Justice and fairness" mentioned in Table 1–2—e.g., "Honesty," "Full disclosure," and "Prohibition of unfair practices." Finally, a market whose performance glittered brightly with allocation efficiency, technological advance, high product quality, and similar prizes would have to be judged beneficial in terms of "Welfare and happiness" and "Progress."

II. The Perfectly Competitive Model

Economic theory's conventional ideal, the specific model that comes fairly close to filling these various requirements, is perfect competition. In this section we (1) specify the structural conditions that must be met to obtain perfect competition, (2) show how these structural conditions affect market conduct, and (3) elaborate on the performance produced by this combination of structure and conduct. Emerging from this exercise is an understanding of a market's two essences—demand and supply.[2]

A. Perfect Competition: Structure and Demand

Perfect competition is defined by four basic structural conditions. First, perfect competition requires a very large number of relatively small buyers and sellers. Indeed, each buyer and each seller must be so small relative to the total market that none of them *individually* can affect product price by altering their volume of pur-

---

[2] For a more complete discussion of perfect competition see E. Mansfield, *Microeconomics: Theory and Applications,* 2nd ed. (New York: W. W. Norton & Company, 1976), Chapter 7, or some other theory text.

chases, if they are buyers, or their level of output, if they are sellers.

Second, the product of any one seller must be a perfect substitute for the product of any other seller. In economists' jargon, the product is homogeneous or standardized.

Third, perfect competition requires that productive resources be freely mobile into and out of markets. Of course any such movement will take time, and in the short run some factors like land and capital are said to be "fixed" because of their short-run immobility once they are committed to production. However, in the long run, all factors are variable and perfectly mobile. This means an absence of barriers to new firm entry—that is, an absence of patents, economies of scale and the like.

Finally, perfect competition requires that all market participants have full knowledge of the economic and technical data relevant to their decision making. Buyers must be aware of the price and product offerings of sellers. Sellers must know product prices, wage rates, material costs, and interest rates.

Under these several conditions the demand curve facing each individual firm will be perfectly elastic with respect to price. This is a supremely important statement, yet its specific content is meaningless without an understanding of two of its key terms "demand" and "elasticity." Although the reader is probably familiar with each concept, a brief review is perhaps warranted. In the very broad sense, **demand** refers to the quantity of product that would be purchased at various possible prices during some given period of time, holding all determinants of demand other than product price constant. Specifically, demand can refer (1) to the demand *of an individual buyer,* (2) to the demand *of all buyers* in the market taken together, or (3) to the demand *facing an individual seller* in the market. Generally speaking, structural conditions do not influence demand in the first two respects. That is to say, the purchases of a single buyer are only a function of

product price, income, tastes, prices of substitute goods (for example, coffee for tea or vice versa), prices of complements (for example, coffee and donuts), and expectations. Individual demand, as your own experience should tell you, is *not* a function of the number of sellers in the market or the condition of new firm entry. Similarly, since total market demand is simply the summation of all the demands of the individual buyers in the market, total market demand is a function of the same variables that determine individual demand (price, incomes, tastes, prices of related goods, and expectations), plus one additional factor—the number of buyers in the market. Now the number of buyers was mentioned as a structural element. But the number is typically large, so in all but a few instances we are safe in saying that *market structure does not directly affect market-wide demand.*

Figure 2–2 illustrates several **marketwide** demand curves. According to the conventional "law" of demand each demand curve must

Figure 2–2.   Examples of Marketwide Product Demand

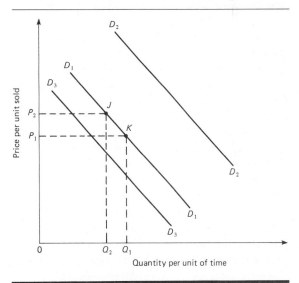

have a negative slope because price and quantity are inversely related. Thus, on curve D_1D_1, an increase in the price of the product from P_1 to P_2 causes quantity demanded to drop from Q_1 to Q_2, resulting in a movement along the demand curve from point K to J. Such movements along the demand curve, under the impetus of price changes, should not be confused with *shifts* of demand, which are caused by changes in variables *other* than the product's price. An increase in income, for instance, is likely to shift demand outward from D_1D_1 to D_2D_2. Conversely, a reduction of income is likely to shift demand down from D_1D_1 to D_3D_3, resulting in fewer purchases than before at each possible price.

Later, it will be important to know just *how responsive* demand is to variations in price. To measure such responsiveness, economists rely on the **elasticity** of demand in relation to price, which is defined as follows:

price elasticity of demand
$$= \frac{\text{percentage change in quantity demanded}}{\text{percentage change in price}}$$

Strictly speaking, the negative slope of demand always yields a negative elasticity, but the negative sign is usually suppressed for simplification. When the percentage change in quantity demanded exceeds the percentage change in price for some given price change, quantity demand is highly responsive to price and the elasticity ratio will be greater than 1, or "elastic." Conversely, if the percentage change in quantity demanded is less than the percentage change in price, demand is relatively *un*responsive to price variations and the elasticity will be less than 1, or "inelastic."

Although market-wide demand tends to be inversely related to price, this cannot be the same view of demand held by the typical *individual firm* selling in the market, unless, of course, there is only one firm in the market (a monopolist). In the case of perfect competi-

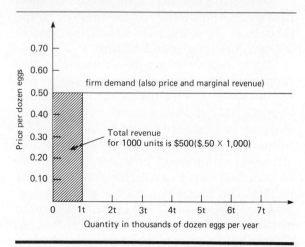

Figure 2–3.   **Demand of a Perfectly Competitive Seller**

tion, the product is standardized and each seller is so small relative to the total market that it views its demand as in Figure 2–3—a horizontal line running parallel to the quantity axis and intersecting the vertical axis at the going market price.

Thus, market structure is a *crucial determinant* of demand as viewed by the typical firm in the market, even though structure generally does *not* influence the market-wide demand curve. In and of itself this finding may seem meaningless, but it is precisely through this influence on the firm's view of demand that structure subsequently influences firm conduct and, thereby, market conduct as well. How does the firm's view of demand influence firm conduct? By influencing the way firms in the market go about maximizing their profits—assuming that firms want to maximize profits. In summary:

structure → firm's view of demand ↗ firm conduct

profit maximization

And the next step, before explicitly taking up conduct, is to extract the element of demand particularly relevant to the firm's profit maximizing calculation.

There are numerous profit maximizing rules of thumb (for example, "never give a sucker an even break"). The formal economic principle is, in essence, *equalize marginal revenue and marginal cost.* Because demand determines marginal revenue, we shall discuss the revenue portion of the formula first, postponing consideration of marginal cost until the next section. **Marginal revenue** *is the change in total revenue attributable to the sale of one more unit of output.* Indeed, "incremental revenue" might be a better name for it. As price and quantity are always the two basic components of demand, and as total revenue is always price *times* quantity sold, there is a very intimate relationship between demand and marginal revenue. In the purely competitive case, the firm's total revenue will rise directly with quantity sold at a constant rate of increase because, according to the firm's demand curve, price is constant over the firm's range of product sales. In other words, the additional sale of one unit of output always adds to total revenue an amount that *just equals the price.* Hence, price and marginal revenue are equal when, as shown in Figure 2–3, the demand curve of the firm is a perfectly elastic one. Using that figure's data, an additional sale of 1 dozen eggs adds 50 cents to the firm's total revenue regardless of whether it is the first dozen sold or the 3000th dozen sold. Hence, marginal revenue is 50 cents.

B. Perfect Competition: Supply and Conduct

Marginal cost, the second portion of the profit maximizing rule of thumb, may be defined as *the addition to total costs due to the additional production of one unit of output.* What are "total costs"? In the short run, total costs are made up of two components—total

fixed costs and total variable costs. The short run, as already mentioned, is a time period short enough for certain factors of production—such as land, buildings, and equipment—to be immobile. Those immobile factors generate **total fixed costs**—such as rent, debt repayments, and property taxes—that *in terms of total costs* do not vary with output. In terms of *cost per unit* of output or "average fixed cost," however, these costs actually decline with greater output because average fixed cost is the total fixed cost (a constant) divided by the number of units produced. Thus, as output rises these fixed costs are "spread" over a larger and larger number of units.

Total variable costs, on the other hand, are those costs associated with variable factors of production such as labor, raw materials, and purchased parts. In terms of *total* costs these costs *always* rise with greater amounts of output, but in terms of *per unit* or "average costs" these may fall, remain unchanged, or rise, depending on the prices and productivity of these variable factors as they are variously applied to the fixed factors. Average, or per-unit, variable cost is the total variable cost at some given level of output, divided by the number of units in that quantity of output. Thus, functionally speaking, if total variable cost rises less rapidly than quantity, per-unit variable cost will fall; if total variable cost rises one-for-one with quantity at a constant rate, per-unit variable cost will be constant; and, if the total rises more rapidly than the quantity, per-unit variable cost will rise.

Figure 2–4 depicts this family of cost curves on a per unit or average basis, according to conventional forms. ATC indicates short-run average total cost, and AVC indicates short-run average variable cost. Average fixed cost, AFC, constitutes the difference between ATC and AVC. When ATC is falling, marginal cost, MC, will be below ATC. Once ATC begins to rise, however, MC exceeds ATC. If the P = MR

Figure 2–4.   Shortrun Cost Curves of the Firm Together with Perfectly Competitive Demand

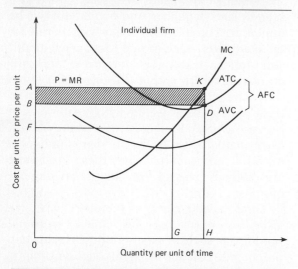

(price equals marginal revenue) line represents the individual firm's demand curve for a prevailing price of *OA*, profit maximization is achieved by producing *OH* units of output because, at that level of output, marginal cost just equals marginal revenue at point *K*. Bearing in mind that total profits are simply total revenue less total cost, the profit-maximizing firm will add to its output so long as the added revenue thereby obtained, MR, exceeds the added cost thereby incurred, MC. This is true of all output levels up to *OH*. However, once the added cost of added output, MC, exceeds the added revenue obtained, MR, total profits will begin to fall. Hence, the astute firm will not produce an output greater than *OH*. At output *OH* total economic profit is the shaded rectangle *BAKD*, which is the economic profit per unit, *KD*, times the number of units produced *AK*. This is called **economic profit** or **excess profit** because the average total cost *includes* a "normal" profit for the investors that is just sufficiently large, say 7% per year, to pay the

cost of capital. Provision of this normal profit rate discourages the investors from withdrawing their capital in the long run and investing it elsewhere.

At price *OF* there would be neither excess profit nor normal profit; there would be a loss. Still, in the short run, the firm would continue to produce an amount *OG*, which would again equate marginal revenue (now *OF*) with marginal cost. The firm will thus minimize its losses. Only if price were to drop so low that the firm could not recover its variable cost AVC on each unit would it minimize loss by closing down. The firm should *never* lose in total dollars more than its total fixed cost.

Two major conclusions emerge from this analysis. First, since price equals marginal revenue for the perfectly competitive firm, the MR = MC profit rule of thumb causes price to equal marginal cost and fulfills the optimal welfare requirement to be explained shortly. Second, the supply curve for the firm is identical to its marginal cost curve above the AVC curve. Over the range of possible prices, the quantity offered for sale by the firm may be read from the MC curve. It follows, then, that market-wide short-run supply is determined by simply adding up the short-run supplies of all individual firms in the market at each possible price, as is illustrated in Figure 2–5.

C. Demand, Supply, and Performance

When the downward sloping market-wide demand curve and the upward sloping market-wide supply curve are viewed together, the result is Figure 2–6. To complete the mechanics of *how* the market operates, we note that the intersection of demand and supply, *E*, is an equilibrium position because price at that point, P_1, will not be budged up or down by discrepancies between demand and supply. A price higher than P_1, such as P_2, could not last because a glut of quantity supplied (Q_2) over

Figure 2–5. Horizontal Summation of Firm Supply Curves for Industry Supply

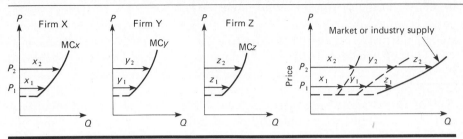

quantity demanded (Q_o), measured by distance *AB*, would with competition press price down until demand matched supply. Conversely, a price below P_1 would tend to rise as the excess of demand over supply bid price up until equilibrium was reached. That is, price is determined by the mating of demand and supply.

In the short run, price P_1 might mean excess profits for firms in the market, due, perhaps, to a recent boom in demand. Losses are also possible in the short run, due for instance to depressed demand. In the long run, however, entry would wipe out excess profits and exit

Figure 2–6. Demand, Supply, and Market Equilibrium

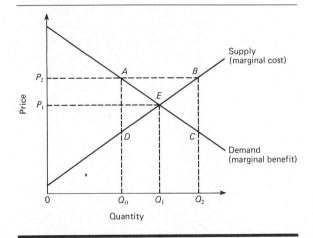

would tend to erase any losses. Entry implies expanding supply and downward price adjustment, while exit contracts supply and bolsters price. In the long run, after all adjustments are completed, equilibrium implies only "normal" profit, with average total costs and marginal costs equaling price. Thus entry and exit are essential to competitive control.

To assess *how well* this market performs we must evaluate its answers to the basic questions of what, how, who, and what's new. The questions of "what" and "how" receive answers in this case—allocation efficiency and technical efficiency—that economists rousingly applaud because society's preferences are remarkably well-satisfied in these respects, given nature's skimpiness.

Technological Efficiency. The nice answer to "How are goods produced?" is most easily seen because we know that firms in this kind of market will be forced by competition to adopt the most efficient, lowest cost technologies available, and firms will also be compelled to operate at the low point on their long-run average cost curves. Otherwise, their costs would exceed price and they could not long survive.

Allocation Efficiency. The nice answer to "What should be produced?" is grasped through an appreciation of the fact that Q_1 in Figure 2–6 is just the right amount. Any marginal unit of output associated with a lesser amount, such as Q_o, yields a social benefit, A, that exceeds the social cost of producing that unit, D. So long as a unit's benefits exceed its costs in this way, additional units of output should be produced, which holds true up to Q_1. Output should not exceed Q_1, however, because any marginal unit associated with a greater amount, such as Q_2, carries a social cost, B, that exceeds social benefit, C. Thus, if the ideal output is one that maximizes "total benefit − total cost," as guided by society's preferences, Q_1 is that output, where "marginal social benefit = marginal social cost," or MSB = MSC. Net *pluses* occur up to Q_1, as added benefits exceed added costs. Net *minuses* arise thereafter.

Another way of appreciating this result, one that stresses the problem of producing an optimal *mix* of goods when constrained by scarcity, focuses on the P = MC, or price equals marginal cost, condition. Price, as read off the demand curve, indicates the value of the output of productive resources when they are used *here* to provide this commodity, say eggs. Marginal cost, as read off the supply curve, indicates the value of the resources if they were used *elsewhere* to produce other things like wheat, books, records, whatever. After all, the producers of eggs must pay enough for labor, land, energy, and capital to attract them away from those alternative activities. In short, then:

price = value of resources here
marginal cost = value of resources elsewhere

Ideally, *value here should equal value elsewhere,* which is attained when P = MC.

Assume otherwise as a test. If value here exceeded value elsewhere, as A exceeds D in Figure 2–6 at Q_o, then resources are more valuable here and should therefore be transferred from elsewhere to here, expanding output to Q_1. Competitive markets spur such transfers as profits would be greater here than elsewhere. Conversely, if value elsewhere exceeded value here, as B exceeds C in Figure 2–6, then resources are worth more elsewhere than here, and output here should be reduced to Q_1 from Q_2, freeing resources for more worthy application elsewhere. Competitive markets foster such transfers by offering greater profit elsewhere than here in such cases. Table 2–1 puts all this in a nutshell.

Taken together, technical and allocative efficiency achieve what is called **Pareto optimality,** after its formulator Vilfredo Pareto. This ideal is *a situation where no one can be made better off without making someone else worse off.* Stated otherwise, we are *not* at Pareto optimality if Smith's lot can be improved at no loss to anyone else—Jones, Adams, whoever. This is the chief ethical criteria behind benefit-cost analysis, so we shall return to it frequently. Presently, we merely need to note that ideal markets move society toward Pareto optimality because they entail *exchange.* Whenever *free* and *voluntary* exchange occurs with no adverse third party effects, at least one person

Table 2–1. **Various Resource Allocation Conditions**

	Optimal allocation	*Under allocation*	*Over allocation*
Market result	P = MC	P > MC	P < MC
General requirement	MSB = MSC	MSB > MSC	MSB < MSC
English translation	value here = value elsewhere	value here > value elsewhere	value here < value elsewhere

is made better off and no one is made worse off (as each party to the exchange sees his own well-being). Notice that this is not the world of the Godfather, where people are given offers they "cannot refuse" (because the consequences of refusal are bloody). It is the world of free and voluntary exchange, and such exchange would simply not occur unless at least one person's lot were improved. Usually, of course, *both* parties to an exchange benefit. Your trade of $500 for a stereo set makes you *and* the retailer better off. Exchange or market processes can therefore move society from inefficiency toward efficiency.

Equity.   The foregoing achievements of the perfectly competitive model are indeed marvelous. Strictly speaking, however, the model cannot claim perfection on the ethical criteria of equity—i.e., the question of "who gets the goods and services?" The term "equity" does not have nearly the clarity of "efficiency," but it generally means some "equitable" distribution of income or "equal opportunity." Equity and efficiency *are separable* in the theoretical sense that efficiency can be achieved regardless of whether or not the income distribution is "equitable" or "just." Equity and efficiency *are related* in the sense that the prevailing distribution will substantially influence the kinds of goods included in an efficient mix. Thus a lopsided, unequal distribution of income could yield an efficient mix that includes more Rolls Royces and more caviar than a distribution that is relatively equal. Although theory cannot heighten the attraction of perfect competition by lights of equity, intuition tells us that its absence of excess long-run profits could further ideals of equity.

Innovation.   Similar agnosticism applies for the question of "What's new?" The perfectly competitive model is perfectly static, fixed in time, and by definition progressive performance in new products and new processes requires *dynamic* developments. Although it has been shown in both theory and evidence that

vigorous competition contributes to good performance in these respects, the model of *perfect* competition is not capable of any really solid conclusions on this score.

Summary

Under certain circumstances, then, the market system is a wonderful social machine. It is attractive in both means and ends. Its structure, conduct, and performance furthers most if not all of the value judgments outlined earlier. Unfortunately, the perfectly competitive model is quite unrealistic (e.g., countless sellers) and in some respects even undesirable (e.g., standardized products), so we cannot and should not slavishly pursue its formula. Still, it is attractive enough that it provides a touchstone for practically all derivative standards of evaluation, such as "benefit-cost analysis" and "workable competition," both of which we encounter later.

III. Problems with Real Markets

If you are one who believes that problems make life interesting, then you should find Table 2–2 and the ensuing discussion of it thoroughly engrossing. For outside the economic Camelot of perfect competition there is crowd of instances where real world free-enterprise markets do not live up to the expecta or preferences of society. Among the system's many past feats are the f Faulty baby cribs that killed over 1 per year; a forty per cent increase in of steel following the merger of 170 s panies; enough pollution to cause a catch fire; a concentration of wealth one-half of one per cent of the p owned thirty per cent; parts fraud for mated one out of every two TV set re

The importance of these shortcom

Table 2–2.   Problems with Private Free Enterprise Markets (MSB = Marginal Social Benefit, MSC = Marginal Social Cost)

A. Imperfections
  1. Monopoly power: MSB > MSC
    a. Artificially attained (e.g., mergers, cartels)
    b. Natural monopoly (e.g., public utilities)
  2. Information inadequacies
    a. Errors of commission MSB < MSC
    b. Errors of omission MSB > MSC
B. Market Failures
  1. Externalities
    a. External benefits MSB > MSC
    b. External costs MSB < MSC
  2. Public goods MSB > MSC
    a. People excludable, but zero marginal cost (highways)
    b. Nonexcludables (national defense, administration of laws)
  3. Common property resources MSB < MSC
C. Dynamic Incapacities
  1. Micro instability and transition immobilities
  2. Macro instability
  3. Growth: short-run protection and promotion for long-run gain
D. Ethical Criteria Other Than Efficiency
  1. Equity
    a. Income distribution
    b. Equal opportunity
    c. Resource conservation
  2. Merit goods: education, health, safety
  3. Demerit goods: liquor, tobacco, hazardous products
  4. Miscellaneous political and social goals

countless others is obvious. They may justify or explain government intervention.

Before probing Table 2–2's particulars, note that the first two broad categories, "Imperfections" and "Failures," assume acceptance of "efficiency" as the chief ethical criterion to be concerned about. The direction of deviation from "marginal-social-benefit-equals-marginal-social-cost" is indicated in each instance by MSB > MSC (for *under*allocations of resources to "here") and by MSB < MSC (for *over*allocations of resources to "here"). Such designations are not appropriate for the last two broad categories because they concern problems arising outside the efficiency context. Whereas the first categories refer to free market equilibri-

ums that are undesirable, the last two are not really concerned with static equilibriums at all. "Dynamic Incapacities" includes problems encounterd in moving from one equilibrium to another, such as the difficulties people may face in rapidly converting from a world of cheap energy to a world of expensive energy. "Ethical Criteria Other Than Efficiency" distinguishes itself by giving due recognition to the fact that free-market results may not conform to society's notions of "morality" or "fairness" or "equity." Thus, for instance, the free market may be super-efficient in providing liquor, sex, gambling, and marijuana, but such efficiency would be (and has been) rejected by moral outrage. The differences in these broad categories are clarified by filtration through more detailed discussion.

A. *Imperfections*

1. MONOPOLY POWER

Three assumptions of the perfectly competitive model precluded the possibility of monopoly power—a large number of relatively small sellers, easy entry, and standardized products. These gave firms perfectly elastic demand curves. They were "price takers," not "price makers." Though Farmer Brown may fit this mold, IBM, GM, Procter & Gamble, DuPont, and the other giant firms that account for the bulk of our industrial output do not. Most of these enterprises are "oligopolists," operating in industries dominated by just a "few" sellers, industries also protected by barriers to entry and providing differentiated, not standardized, products. These several characteristics bestow "monopoly power" of various degrees. And at the noncompetitive extreme, full-fledged monopoly prevails, with just one seller, blockaded entry, and a product that could be considered perfectly differentiated owing to an absence of close substitutes.

The conduct and performance implications of these structural imperfections are outlined in Table 2–3, where "Profits" are the index of allocation inefficiency. Four traditional market types are summarized there—*perfect competition, monopolistic competition, oligopoly,* and *monopoly.* Among the more obvious linkages between structure and conduct depicted is that between the number of firms and price policy. Purely competitive firms have no price policy because they take price as given and determine their production with an eye to maximizing profits, which on the whole end up normal. Under oligopoly, however, with just a few sellers, each firm knows that its price and output actions are likely to affect its rivals' behavior; hence "recognized interdependence" is said to

prevail in oligopoly. Only the monopolist enjoys full independence of *both* price and production policy because he is the sole supplier in his market.

Another simple example of causal flow concerns the relationship between product type and promotion policy. Intensive brand name advertising is likely to arise only for products that are differentiable; that is, products that people *believe* can have significant brand differences, whether or not the differences are real. Examples include cosmetics, soft drinks, and autos—each of which is vigorously advertised by brand. In contrast, standardized products—like wheat and potatoes—might be promoted on an industry-wide basis or by large segments of the industry, but the perfect substitutability of various suppliers' offerings of these products makes brand advertising and promotion by individual producers unprofitable. Table 2–3 also acknowledges the possibility of institutional or political advertising.

The relationship between condition of entry and profits also deserves mention. According to traditional theory, industry profits can be excessively high in the long run only if the entry of new firms into the industry is at least partially impeded. Otherwise, such high profits would attract newcomers, which would in turn expand production, lower prices, and reduce profits. Thus, Table 2–3 specifies a positive, direct relationship between the height of barriers to entry (structure) and the likely level of industry profits (performance).

Graphically, the impact of imperfect structures would be shown by *firm* demand curves whose downward slope gave some power over price. Pure monopoly is depicted in Figure 2–7, where firm and industry demand are identical. The inefficient misallocation, MSB > MSC, emerges from the divergence between price and marginal cost in the monopolist's profit maximizing solution. As before, the rule of thumb for maximizing profit is marginal cost

Table 2–3. Basic Market Types

Market Type	Structure			Conduct			Performance		
	Number of Firms	Entry Condition	Product Type	Price Policy	Production Policy	Promotion Policy*	Profits	Technical Efficiency	Progressiveness
Perfect Competition	Very large number	Easy	Standardized	None	Independent	b	Normal	Good	Poor perhaps
Monopolistic Competition	Large number	Easy	Differentiated	Unrecognized interdependence		a	Normal	Moderately good	Fair
Oligopoly	Few	Impeded	Standardized or differentiated	Recognized interdependence		a, b, c	Somewhat excessive	Poor perhaps	Good
Monopoly	One	Blocked	Perfectly differentiated	Independent		a ≡ b, c	Excessive	Poor perhaps	Poor perhaps

* Key: a = promotion of firm's brand product; b = industry or marketwide advertising and promotion; c = institutional or political advertising.

equals marginal revenue, which occurs at point E in Figure 2–7 with output OQ_1 and price OP_1. Although the MC = MR rule applies here as under perfect competition, the result is markedly different in this case because the downward sloping demand of the monopolist generates a downward sloping marginal revenue curve that lies below the demand curve. Stated differently, marginal revenue is below price at each output. This is because each unit sold *adds* to total revenue an amount equal to the price of that unit, but from this the monopolist must *subtract* the price reductions necessary to sustain the sale of all preceding units. Economic or excess profit per unit in Figure 2–7 is indicated by the distance DG. Total dollar excess profit is consequently the area $DGHP_1$, which is per unit profit times the number of units.

The misallocation of resources is indicated by the fact that MSB, at D, is greater than MSC,

at E. Resources should be transferred from elsewhere into here, expanding output above Q_1, but entry barriers prevent this.

Table 2–2 distinguishes between "artificially" attained monopoly power and "natural" monopoly. Sources of artificial monopoly power include merger, predatory practices, government licensing, and other factors of human creation. In contrast, natural monopoly stems from technical imperatives or basic conditions, such as economies of scale, which make a single firm the lowest-cost means of supply. Examples include local telephone service, water supply, and electricity.

The customary policy for dealing with artificial monopolies is antitrust aimed at attaining and maintaining competitive structure and conduct in the belief that good performance will then follow automatically. Prohibitions against monopolization, anticompetitive mergers, and restrictive conduct have this focus and aim. The typical policy approach to natural monopoly is quite different. Structural dominance by a single firm is endorsed and even encouraged in the belief that any attempt to enforce competition would be futile (because monopoly is inevitable) and even stupid (given that numerous firms would mean high-cost production or shoddy service). Good performance is then sought through direct regulation of performance by public utility commissions or, less frequently, by outright public ownership and operation.

2. INFORMATION INADEQUACIES

The second broad category of market imperfections itemized in Table 2–2—information inadequacies—honors the fact that real world buyers are often led astray by ignorance, misjudgment, and sundry other deviations from the perfection assumed in perfect competition. This is particularly true of household consumers as opposed to professional business and government buyers who tend to be experienced, well-

Figure 2–7. Monopoly Equilibrium Solution

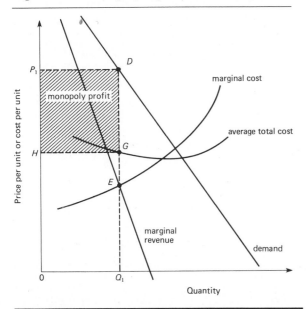

informed experts. Thus, for instance, consumer ineptitude emerges from studies of the correlation between price level and brand quality. For a given product, low quality should sell only at a low price and high quality should sell at a high price, yielding a correlation coefficient near +1 if consumers really know what they are doing. But observed correlations are on average always much closer to zero than to one, and the range across products includes a substantial number of goods with *negative* correlations.[3]

Of course we could not reasonably expect consumers to invest the necessary time, effort, and expense to become *perfectly* informed. Furthermore, private enterprise does supply some information by way of advertising and buyer's guides like *Consumer Reports.* But the very nature of the commodity in question—information—is such that imperfections prevent its optimal provision by free markets. One problem is that sellers of information may face the same problem as the little boy who climbs and shakes the apple tree but gets few of the fallen apples because his buddies on the ground run off with the loot before he can get down. This is "inappropriability," and it often applies to information because information may be spread by means outside the control of the information's original producer—for example, piracy by word of mouth. When a private producer of information is not rewarded in just proportion to the social value of his effort, he extends less effort than is socially optimal. A second and more striking problem arises because buyers of information cannot be truly

well informed about the information they want to buy. If they were, they would not then need to buy the information.[4] In other words, the seller of information cannot let potential buyers meticulously examine his product prior to sale lest he thereby give it away free. Buyers of information therefore do not know the value of the product they seek (information) until after they buy it.

Advertising is often informative, but the purpose of advertising is not to inform. Its purpose is to persuade, so it is informative only to the extent the informative approach persuades, which is true mainly of ads for producers' goods, not consumers' goods. Indeed, it can be shown that advertising is *least* informative where it is *most* intense, and these conditions correspond to products about which consumers are inherently *least* informed—drugs, beer, soft drinks, prepared foods, cosmetics, detergents, and the like.[5] Still worse, advertisers frequently have an incentive to mislead, misrepresent, and even lie, behaviors that cannot be said to contribute to consumer competence.

Later, two directions of consumer error will be detailed. *Errors of commission* occur when buyers make purchases on the basis of excessively favorable prepurchase assessments. The favoritism then leads to more spending than accuracy would entail and a consequent *over*allocation of resources to the favored brand or product. Conversely, *errors of omission* arise when buyers buy *less* than they would with full knowledge. The misallocation here would obviously be an *under*allocation.

B. Market Failures

Market failures occur when in one sense or another markets fail to exist. Free-enterprise

[3] Alfred R. Oxenfeldt, "Consumer Knowledge: Its Measurement and Extent," *Review of Economics and Statistics* (October 1950), pp. 300–315; R. T. Morris and C. S. Bronson, "The Chaos of Competition Indicated by Consumer Reports," *Journal of Marketing* (July 1969), pp. 26–34; Monroe P. Friedman, "Quality and Price Considerations in Rational Decision Making," *Journal of Consumer Affairs* (Summer 1967), pp. 13–23; Peter C. Riesz, "Price-Quality Correlations for Packaged Food Products," *Journal of Consumer Affairs* (Winter 1979), pp. 236–247.

[4] Kenneth Arrow, "Economic Welfare and the Allocation of Resources for Invention," in *The Rate and Direction of Inventive Activity: Economic and Social Factors* (New York: National Bureau of Economic Research, 1962).

[5] Douglas F. Greer, *Industrial Organization and Public Policy* (New York: Macmillan, 1980), pp. 62–80.

markets for clean air, clean water, national defense, criminal justice, and other highly desirable goods and services cannot be expected to flourish in the absence of some form of government intervention. Without viable markets, society's benefits and costs have no private decentralized place of registration and realization. Stated differently, a world of perfect competition all around would not be sufficient to attain Pareto optimality. Much more would be required—an absence of externalities, public goods, and common property resources.

1. EXTERNALITIES

When Jones and Smith engage in free and voluntary exchange, they weigh only the benefits and costs they themselves experience. They do not take into account any benefits bestowed or costs imposed on third parties, say, Wong and the rest of us. Yet such "external" benefits and costs often arise, and the market's failure to account for them leads to free-market misallocations of "not enough" in the case of external benefits and "too much" in the case of external costs.

External Benefits. Your planting of a flower garden in your front yard benefits your neighbors as well as yourself. An airline's installation of engine silencers for the benefit of its passengers also benefits groundlings near airports.

When benefits extend beyond buyers as in these instances, the price buyers are willing to pay is not a good index of the social value of the purchased good. Price is an underestimate of the value of resources used "here" as opposed to "elsewhere." Figure 2–8 indicates the implications by showing two demand curves, one reflecting only the benefits buyers alone perceive, D_1, the other, D_2, reflecting *all* of society's benefits, external benefits as well. More technically, D_1 includes only marginal *private* benefit, MPB, whereas D_2, represents marginal *social* benefit, MSB, the difference being external benefit. The free-market solution is output Q_1, which emerges from the intersec-

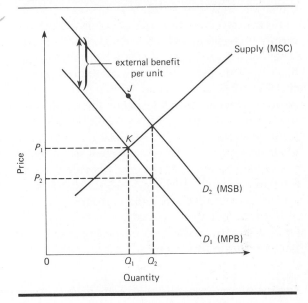

Figure 2–8. **External Benefit and Underallocation**

tion of D_1 (or MPB) and supply (MSC). The optimal solution, however, would be output Q_2, where D_2 and supply meet and where MSB = MSC. Most simply stated, the problem is one of "not enough" production in light of society's true preferences. There is no market registering these preferences and rewarding producers for greater deeds done, so with the free-market's Q_1, MSB at J exceeds MSC at K, or MSB > MSC. To hint at policy solutions, a subsidy equaling the external benefit would lower price to P_2 and thereby lead to optimal output Q_2.

External Costs. External costs are imposed on society and are *not* borne by producers or consumers in the course of production and consumption. Pollution provides the classic example of an external cost; pollution imposes costs of avoidance (air conditioning, moving out of town), of repair (painting, medical treatment), and of raw damage (death, ugly air) that are not paid for out of the pockets of polluters. Acting in their own best interests, market participants equate price with their own *private* marginal cost. But, when external costs are recognized and added to these private costs, the result is MSB < MSC.

Figure 2–9 illustrates this problem with two supply curves—S_1, which reflects only *private* costs (and is therefore also labeled MPC), and S_2, which includes both private and external costs for all costs to society (MSC). A free competitive market would produce Q_4, as that is the result associated with P = MC, or MSB = MPC. But this is "too much." At Q_4 the marginal social cost M exceeds marginal social benefit N, so value elsewhere exceeds value here. Resources should be shifted out of this market into others until Q_3 is achieved and MSB = MSC at G, but the free-market system fails to comply because these external costs are not imposed on producers here.

Whereas subsidies might be an appropriate policy to encourage added output in cases of external benefit, taxes might discourage the output of products laced with external costs. A per-unit tax matching external costs—the vertical difference between S_1 and S_2 in Figure 2–9—would raise costs of production to the point of reflecting all of society's costs, moving the market to output Q_3 and price P_3.

2. PUBLIC GOODS

There are various definitions of *public goods,* but there are three elements common to most definitions: (1) Their production and consumption usually coincide, so they cannot be inventoried. (2) One individual's consumption does not subtract from any other individual's consumption. And (3) additional consumers can partake

Figure 2–9.   External Cost and Overallocation

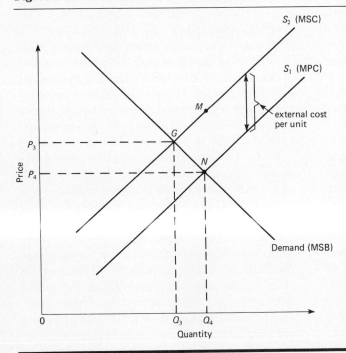

of these goods at no additional social cost or near zero cost.[6] With marginal social costs of consumption approaching zero, the nature of the free-market failure leaps to mind. *Any* positive price charged for these goods, as would be necessary to reward free-market suppliers, would exceed marginal cost. The resulting P > MC, or more generally MSB > MSC, would then lead to the free market's underallocation of resources to these goods.

Excludable Public Goods. Two subcategories of public goods may be usefully distinguished.[7] The first may be called *excludables*. These public goods are illustrated by highways and bridges as long as congestion is no problem. In the absence of congestion, these are public goods because, once the highway or bridge is available, it costs nothing to have an additional trip or crossing. People can, in principle, be excluded from the use of highways and bridges by the judicious construction of limited entry points, and fares can be collected with toll booths, thus the name *excludable* public goods. But such restrictions are usually not imposed because they are costly and lead to an underallocation of resources to highways and bridges.

Nonexcludable Public Goods. The second subcategory, the one of greatest interest to us, includes public goods like national defense, antitrust law enforcement, and clean air. Exclusion of individuals from their consumption is impossible even in principle, because we consume these goods *collectively*. If you wish, you may consume more apple cider, a private good, than I do. Indeed, the more for you the less for me once cider output is given for the season. But whatever the level of national defense—

say $197 billion worth in planes, tanks, ships, soldiers, etc.—we each and every one consume that amount precisely, as that is a pure *collective* good.

A main problem with free-market provision of these goods is the "free rider." Imagine, if you will, the invention of an auto pollution control device that would provide the collective good of clean air in your city if almost all auto owners paid the modest $150 necessary to get it. Would you and everyone else scurry to garages and gas stations for its installation? Probably not. In fact, such a pollution control package was offered some years ago and its sales fizzled. Two possibilities deflate your motivation: (1) the possibility that even though you do not buy the device almost everyone else does, in which case you are a "free rider," getting clean air without paying a dime, or (2) the possibility that you pay your $150 for clean air but hardly anyone else does, in which case you have lost $150.

This, then, is what distinguishes these nonexcludable public goods from ordinary goods in the free-market setting. With an ordinary good, you get it if you pay; you don't get it if you don't pay. Choice is individualized. Amounts may vary with taste and fortune among separate souls. Paying and receiving correspond closely. With a public good, however, you may get it even if you don't pay, and you may not get it even if you do pay. Free markets tend to be stunted under such conditions.

3. COMMON PROPERTY RESOURCES

Closely related to the foregoing are common property resources, such as fisheries, the radio spectrum, deep-ocean minerals, and at one time oil. These resources tend to be abused or used up too rapidly with competitive exploitation because the private costs of those using them fall short of the full social costs. With excessive haste in milking these resources, MSB is less than MSC.

[6] Paul A. Samuelson, "The Pure Theory of Public Expenditure," *Review of Economics and Statistics* (November 1954), pp. 386–389; James M. Buchanan, *The Demand and Supply of Public Goods* (Chicago: Rand McNally, 1968).

[7] For a good discussion see Duncan MacRae, Jr., and James A. Wilde, *Policy Analysis for Public Decisions* (North Scituate, Mass.: Duxbury Press, 1979), pp. 179–186.

A fisherman, for example, will face costs for fuel, labor, sea-worthy capital equipment, and so on. He will also impose costs on others, however, as additions to his catch reduce the plentitude of fish available to other fishermen, causing them to spend more time, effort, and energy for any given number of fish they may successfully net. The same of course applies to each fisherman. This communal working at cross-purposes is a form of external cost, which when not taken into account leads to an error in the direction of overallocation, or in this case overfishing.

One corrective in many such cases is government's improved definition of property rights. Other approaches include quota systems, severance taxes, and government stewardship through public ownership. For international problems, like the recovery of mineral-bearing nodules from the ocean floor, treaties are needed.

C. Dynamic Incapacities

To this point we have merely sorted out desirable and undesirable equilibrium solutions, using Pareto optimality as a sieve. But situations of disequilibrium are equally important. Indeed, disequilibrium is the normal state of the world, and some economists claim a greater concern for the attendant "dynamic" problems than for the "comparative static" problems of previous pages.

1. MICRO INSTABILITY AND TRANSITION IMMOBILITIES

Substantial shifts of a market's supply and demand curves—due to cyclical swings, the vagaries of the weather, and other contingencies—can cause rocky instability, especially when the shapes of those curves bear acute inelasticities. During the first decades of this century, for instance, prior to federal intervention in agriculture, farm incomes in some regions

varied *hundreds* of percentage points from one year to the next.[8] Serious instability has also plagued petroleum markets at various times, as nature has alternately hidden and disclosed her black gold, and as OPEC countries have occasionally withheld supplies. Such instabilities can lead to inefficiencies as producers and consumers try to hedge their bets in rather costly ways. Moreover, the instability itself may be judged rattling, injurious to national defense, and even downright painful for some in society, spawning government programs like "price supports," "commodity agreements," and "insurance reserves."

Disequilibrium in particular markets may also accompany marked changes from one equilibrium to another. An obvious problem in this connection might be the *delay* society experiences in realizing the added welfare a new equilibrium will bring. As Peter Steiner has written, "If resources respond to market signals surely but slowly, the market process may prove an expensive way to achieve resource shifts."[9] Likewise, the burdens of shifting may press particularly hard on certain members of society. The move from Q_4 to Q_3 in Figure 2-9, for instance, benefits society as a whole but may hurt the paper makers, steelworkers, and others whose relocation out of polluting industries is necessitated by the transition. Indeed, failure to meet this problem may create strong political opposition to solving the external cost problem. More generally, such transitional disruptions are referred to as "frictional unemployment," and government has sought to alleviate the welfare strain with unemployment compensation, job training, and pay-

---

[8] Dale E. Hathaway, *Government and Agriculture: Economic Policy in a Democratic Society* (New York: Macmillan, 1963), pp. 45–46.

[9] Peter O. Steiner, "The Public Sector and the Public Interest," in Haveman and Margolis (eds.) *Public Expenditures and Policy Analysis* (Chicago: Rand McNally, 1977), pp. 36–37.

ments to transform industries hard hit by import competition.

2. MACRO INSTABILITY

The Great Depression uncorked an era of fervent social concern for macroeconomic disequilibriums. Depression and recession are undesirable because they frustrate the employment and income aspirations of many people. Inflation has been an even more bruising bane of late. Rapid inflation drastically reshuffles people's real incomes, as some keep up and others, especially those on fixed incomes, fall behind. It also creates speculators who dabble in otherwise worthless games of buy and sell. It shrinks savings, disrupts corporate finance, and undermines long-term projects.

The total dollar losses society suffers from macro instabilities probably exceed its losses from market imperfections and failures. Thus policy efforts abound in this realm. And even though this book focuses most diligently on micro issues, we cannot afford to ignore these macro issues insofar as they have microeconomic connections.

3. GROWTH: SHORT-RUN PROTECTION AND PROMOTION FOR LONG-RUN GAIN

In the week these words were written Congress passed a $20 billion subsidy program to promote the development of synthetic fuels (oil distilled from tar sands, oil shale, and coal), the Supreme Court ruled that patents could apply to manmade organisms created from recombinant DNA technology, and *Business Week* published a special issue bemoaning the U.S. economy's languid growth and urging a massive effort by business, government, and labor to achieve the "Reindustrialization of America." Each of these developments illustrates society's deep-seated concern for long-run achievement, for growth, for research and development, and for freedom from foreign dependency. Moreover, these events illustrate society's doubt that the free-market system can always perform satisfactorily on these scores. Thus society willingly accepts some short-run sacrifices to offer inducements—such as the seventeen year grant of patent monopoly or the $20 billion synfuels outlay—in hopes of building brighter futures. The exchange may often look no better than the few beans Jack-in-the-Beanstalk got for his mother's cow, but then we all know what happened to lucky Jack in the end.

For energy especially, it may be argued that there are immense external benefits from technological progress, benefits such as strengthened national defense, general economic prosperity, and improved foreign trade balances. Because private firms are unable to appropriate such benefits, their bland free-market inducements may occasionally need to be sweetened with government honey.[10]

D. Ethical Criteria Other Than Efficiency

The last broad category of Table 2–2 acknowledges that free-market solutions may be rejected on value judgment grounds. The efficient satisfaction of given individual preferences is an attractive ethical criteria, but there are other ethical criteria that decisively influence policy. After all, it is not a "Statue of Efficiency" that graces New York harbor. And A. Lincoln, W. Shakespeare, F. Nightingale, and M. L. King are not revered for their furtherance of Pareto optimality. It will become apparent that many of these other criteria rest on nonteleological imperatives.

1. EQUITY

Two ethical criteria guide assessments of equity. *Horizontal equity* holds that equals should be treated equally. A main difficulty here of course lies in delineating and measur-

[10] John E. Tilton, *U.S. Energy R & D Policy* (Washington, D.C.: Resources for the Future, 1974), pp. 22–66.

ing the relevant characteristics that define "equals." Should two families with the same income be taxed equally even though the source of one family's income is inherited property and the other's is manual labor? Should the water pollution of two agricultural enterprises be reduced by equal percentages even though one is a small dairy farm and the other is a gigantic corporate chain of beef feed lots? Despite the difficulties, it should be clear that horizontal equity was the main force behind such legislation as the Equal Pay Act of 1963, the Civil Rights Act of 1964, and the Equal Employment Opportunity Act of 1972.

Vertical equity, the second standard, holds that unequals should be treated unequally. Once again problems of definition preclude perfectly clear applications, but this notion guides decisions concerning two particular unequals who have been with us since ancient times—the rich and the poor. Sympathy for the poor instructs that we should not reward the rich with pennies taken from the poor, that the chief cost burden of a government program should not fall on the poor, and that if price differentials are to be permitted they should favor the poor rather than the rich. We shall later encounter many specifics engendered by this sympathy, not all of them good.

Less ancient are questions of equity between generations. For most of history, living mankind seems to have been rather nonchalant about the plight of subsequent generations. The tacit assumption of each generation appears to have been that progress presides, that those who follow would certainly have fatter times. Lately, however, this assumption has been called into question. Future generations may not appreciate our shoddy storage of millions of tons of toxic wastes. They may not have the magic technology we assume they will have to get along comfortably without oil. In short, our market system has no way of registering the willingness of future generations to pay us for

the preservation of their options. And some present generation commentators argue that we should not blithely and selfishly eliminate those options. They call for intergenerational equity or fairness, which when translated into policy comes out looking a lot like conservation.[11]

2 & 3. MERIT AND DEMERIT GOODS

Several ethical criteria hostile to the ethic of consumer preference satisfaction can be captured in the concept of "merit goods" and its opposite, "demerit goods." As Duncan MacRae and James Wilde say, "These concepts refer to goods that are judged to be good or bad for consumers, *regardless* of the consumers' preferences."[12] Education, fuel efficient cars, motorcycle helmets, and retirement insurance are examples of merit goods. Government provision of such goods, or regulation or subsidy to encourage market provision, assumes that consumers may not freely or wisely buy goods or services whose main benefits are realized in the long run rather than the short run. Conversely, some goods and services may be judged particularly attractive in short-term seductiveness but harmful in their long-term consequences, warranting a bad reputation and the tag "demerit" good. Cigarettes, liquor, narcotics, gambling, snake-oil medicines, and easy-to-open poison containers might be among these. Official discouragement of these goods might be partly based on external costs, as is illustrated by the fact that liquor is a major cause of highway fatalities. But it is also based on paternalistic judgments that ignore some people's preferences.

Stated a bit more technically, intervention on grounds of merit and demerit goods tram-

---

[11] Talbot Page, *Conservation and Economic Efficiency* (Baltimore: Johns Hopkins University Press, 1977), especially chapters 8 and 9; Herman E. Daly, *Steady-State Economics* (San Francisco: W. H. Freeman and Co., 1977).

[12] MacRae and Wilde, *op. cit.,* p. 188.

ples on the ethic of consumer sovereignty, which is part of Pareto optimality. **Consumer sovereignty** asserts that people's preferences are somehow given and unchanging, that those preferences ought to be fully respected, and that the market is efficient because it forces producers to satisfy those sacred preferences as well as possible within the bounds of scarcity. Thus, support for merit and demerit measures is usually based on some theory that consumer's are not "really" sovereign, that their interests would be served better by nonmarket means. One of the most famous of these theories is propounded by John Kenneth Galbraith. He argues that consumers' tastes are *not* innately given. Rather, their tastes are manipulated by producers through advertising, style variation, and other means of persuasion.[13] Galbraith thus replaces consumer sovereignty with "producer sovereignty," which does not necessarily serve the consumer interest. Just how accurate Galbraith's theory is, is uncertain. When polled, a vast majority of people claim that advertising causes them to buy things they don't really need or can't afford.[14] The econometric evidence, however, is mixed.[15] In any event, dismissal of Galbraith would not dismiss the problem, because there are other, more sophisticated theories of similar thrust.[16] All this obvi-

ously overlaps with our previous discussion of information problems.

Closely related to merit and demerit goods are areas where policy is brought into play largely on *moral* grounds, where the consumer's or producer's material welfare is not so much at issue (as in the preceeding), but his or her behavior is, in itself, judged to be right or wrong. Gladiatorial contests, pronography, painful slaughter of animals, extermination of species like the bald eagle and great blue whale, abortion—each of these fires strong moral indignation among millions in our society. And each of these therefore provoke policies of discouragement. It might be possible to fit these offenses into some standard economic shortcoming. Pornography establishments, for instance, allegedly have adverse effects on surrounding areas or "external costs" —i.e., deteriorating property values, higher crime rates, and depressed neighborhood conditions.[17] But this is stretching economics a bit too far and needlessly so. Economics cannot explain everything.[18] Further, its teleological ethics must occasionally give way to imperative ethics, at least in this writer's opinion.[19]

4. MISCELLANEOUS POLITICAL AND SOCIAL GOALS

Finally, the goodness and badness of the free-market system is often judged by a variety of criteria that do not easily fit into any of the foregoing categories. Mention of a few of these miscellaneous goals to be cited later will give you the basic idea.

[13] John Kenneth Galbraith, *The New Industrial State* (Boston: Houghton Mifflin Co., 1967), pp. 198–210.

[14] R. A. Bauer and S. A. Greyser, *Advertising in America: The Consumer View* (Boston: Division of Research Graduate School of Business Administration, Harvard University, 1968), p. 71.

[15] William S. Comanor and Thomas A. Wilson, *Advertising and Market Power* (Cambridge: Harvard University Press, 1974), pp. 64–92; Ronald P. Wilder, "Advertising and Inter-Industry Competition: Testing a Galbraithian Hypothesis," *Journal of Industrial Economics* (March 1974), pp. 215–226; Henry G. Grabowski, "The Effects of Advertising on the Interindustry Distribution of Demand," *NBER Explorations in Economic Research* (Winter 1976), pp. 21–75.

[16] Herbert Gintis, "Consumer Behavior and the Concept of Sovereignty: Explanations of Social Decay," *American Economic Review* (May 1972), pp. 267–278; A. Dixit

and V. Norman, "Advertising and Welfare," *Bell Journal of Economics* (Spring 1978), pp. 1–17; Robert A. Pollak, "Endogenous Tastes in Demand and Welfare Analysis," *American Economic Review* (May 1978), pp. 374–379.

[17] William Toner, *Regulating Sex Businesses* (Chicago: American Society of Planning Officials, 1977).

[18] Tibor Scitovsky, "The Place of Economic Welfare in Human Welfare," *Quarterly Review of Economics and Business* (Autumn 1973), pp. 7–19.

[19] G. Warren Nutter, "On Economism," *Journal of Law and Economics* (October 1979), pp. 263–268.

Let's start with decentralization of economic power. To sing the praises of the market, perfect competition in particular, solely in the key of efficiency seriously limits one's repertoire. As will become apparent in Part II, a main purpose of the antitrust laws is not efficiency, but rather decentralization of power and the maintenance of competition.

> The greatest common denominator in antitrust decisions is a commitment to smallness and decentralization as ways of discouraging the concentration of discretionary authority.
>
> —*Donald Dewey*[20]

> The grounds for the policy include not only dislike of restriction of output and of one-sided bargaining power but also desire to prevent excessive concentration of wealth and power, desire to keep open the channels of opportunity, and concern lest monopolistic controls of business lead to political oligarchy.
>
> —*Corwin Edwards*[21]

By the same token, there appears to be a soft spot in the heart of many Americans for small business. In social character, in charitable contributions to community, and in furtherance of independence and self-reliance, small business is often thought to be worthy of society's special support and attention. Such sentiments have found policy expression in the Small Business Administration's assistance programs, in the Robinson-Patman Act's prohibition of price discrimination injurious to competitors, and in favorable treatment under federal environmental, safety, and health regulations.

Other miscellaneous ethical standards that will make appearances later are honesty and fairness. "False advertising," "unfair competition," and "payola" are the focus of policies, at least partly it seems, because they reflect behavior of scandalous repute.

Summary

Free markets are genuinely marvelous. Their attractions may be pinned on any or all of their three main attributes—structure, conduct, and performance. Under ideal conditions of perfect competition, structure reflects a very large number of well-informed participants, standardized products, and easy entry and exit. This structure may be applauded in and of itself, for it serves such values as freedom, decentralization, and equal opportunity. What is more, such a market automatically achieves results in conduct and performance that conform fairly well to other desirables—fairness, justice, and most particularly allocation and technical efficiency. At its best, the free market squeezes the last ounce of welfare possible out of scarcity, where welfare is measured by the satisfaction of individual preferences. As Michael Klass and Leonard Weiss put it:

> When markets are competitive and participants well informed, the firms that sell are generally forced to produce those goods for which consumers are willing to pay, and to do so at minimum cost to buyers. Products and services are offered in a range of varieties and qualities, as determined by consumer tastes and incomes, and by costs of production. Shortages are eliminated automatically either through rationing by price or incentives offered to expand production of scarce goods and services. The prospect of profits provides a strong inducement to find and exploit new prod-

---

[20] Donald Dewey, "The New Learning: One Man's View," in *Industrial Concentration: The New Learning,* edited by H. J. Goldschmid, H. M. Mann, and J. F. Weston (Boston: Little, Brown and Co., 1974) p. 13.

[21] Corwin Edwards, *Maintaining Competition* (New York: McGraw Hill, 1949), p. 9. See also Hans Thorelli, *The Federal Antitrust Policy* (Baltimore: Johns Hopkins University Press, 1955), pp. 570–571; Richard Hofstadter, "What Happened to the Antitrust Movement?" in Cheit (ed.) *The Business Establishment* (New York: John Wiley & Sons, 1964), pp. 113–151, and Robert Pitofsky, "The Political Content of Antitrust," *University of Pennsylvania Law Review* (April 1979), pp. 1051–1081.

ucts and techniques. More generally, decisions are made by those directly concerned, and by those with specific knowledge of the situation. The flexibility of the market system and its adaptability to change provides the most general case for private decision in free markets.[22]

The achievement of *efficiency* or *Pareto optimality* is summarized in the equation: marginal social benefit = marginal social cost, or MSB = MSC. The perfectly competitive market attains this standard by equating price and marginal cost, or P = MC, where price reflects *all* the social benefits and marginal cost represents *all* the social costs (i.e., externalities are absent).

Unfortunately, free markets frequently come up short. As outlined in Table 2–2, they may suffer imperfections, failures, dynamic incapacities, and ethical inadequacies unrelated to efficiency. Imperfections and failures produce equilibriums that deviate from *Pareto optimal* efficiency. A market's deviation in the direction of underallocation of resources, or "not enough," is symbolized by MSB > MSC. Deviation in the direction of overallocation, or "too much," is reflected by MSB < MSC. In either case, correction gives society benefits that exceed the costs of change.

Dynamic incapacities arise from jarring instabilities, painfully prolonged disequilibriums, transition traumas, and gaps between short-run forces and long-run fortunes. Macroeconomic problems of inflation and unemployment are particularly important because of the massive costs they impose on society. Microeconomic problems of this type fit the micro focus of this book a bit better, so they will receive greater attention.

Finally, government interference in the market place is often based on ethical criteria that cannot be calibrated in benefit-cost ac-

counting. "Equity," "fairness," "honesty," "morality," and "decentralization" are among these criteria. Your value judgments determine whether or not you agree that considerations of this kind should guide government policy. As for myself, you should be warned that I am an economist, one of a breed that tends to be uncomfortable analyzing virtues and vices other than those measured in dollar benefits and costs. Still, I shall try to overcome my discomfort because the world is not ruled by economists (luckily so, perhaps).

Questions and Exercises for Chapter 2

1. Why can it be said that "structure" and "conduct" relate to *how* a market works whereas "performance" reflects *how well* it works?
2. Explain in your own words why the purely competitive market is "efficient."
3. Two optimality conditions have been specified: (a) price = marginal cost and (b) marginal social benefit = marginal social cost. Draw a graph for each, then explain their *similarities* (e.g., Why are they optimals?) and *differences* (i.e., Are they general or particular, private or social optimals? When one holds does the other?).
4. Which of the problems mentioned in Table 2–2 pertain to the scarcity question "What should be produced in what amounts"? (Do the same for the other scarcity questions— How? Who? What's new?)
5. Why are market imperfections and failures alike? Why are they different? (Bring structure and performance into your answer.)
6. The text claims that most if not all problems in segment D of Table 2–2 are problems when judged by nonteleological imperatives. Explain.

[22] Michael Klass and Leonard Weiss, *Study on Federal Regulation*, Volume IV, "Framework for Regulation," U.S. Senate, Committee on Governmental Affairs, (December 1979), pp. xi–xii.

Chapter 3

Government Policy: Ideal and Real

People often appear to think of government as some sort of half-drugged servant: if one can only get him to act, he will of course do exactly what one has in mind. Without exception though . . . there are numerous inherent shortcomings.
—Roland McKean

We have seen that the wardrobe of the free-market system is generally a fine one for society to wear. But we have also found a long laundry list of stains that society might ask government to clean up, namely imperfections, failures, dynamic difficulties, and miscellaneous ethical blotches.

Our format for discussing the role of government in this chapter follows our earlier format for markets. In broad division, it first presents the good news, with a look at government under ideal circumstances. Next comes the bad news, with a catalogue of the government's real-word shortcomings. Our discussion of the ideal state is further divided into two parts—one for political *process,* the other for political *performance*—a division that corresponds to the two questions of *how* and *how well* the market works. Similarly, there is a convenient correspondence for our discussion of the government's real-world shortcomings because

those bedevilments may be labeled imperfections, failures, dynamic problems, and miscellaneous ethical stumbles. Without embroidery, we cover:

I. IDEAL GOVERNMENT
   A. Political processes or "How" (preference articulation, preference aggregation, etc.)
   B. Political performance or "How well"
      1. Allocation efficiency (benefit-cost)
      2. Dynamic welfare (stability, growth)
      3. Equity and other desirables (bliss)
II. REAL GOVERNMENT
   A. Imperfections (misallocation)
   B. Failures (misallocation)
   C. Dynamic difficulties (delays, etc.)
   D. Other ethical shortcomings (e.g., inequity)

The discussion presumes that the major ethical criteria previously applied to markets—allocation efficiency and economic equity in particular—are also the appropriate ethical criteria to apply to government. You should be warned that many would disagree with that presumption. Goodness and badness in markets are fairly widely agreed upon, thanks to the idea of Pareto optimality. But goodness and badness in government are nowhere nearly as well-defined. Even if we ignore the anarchists and the totalitarians, we confront a spectrum of alternative ethical criteria.[1] It could thus be argued that the government should not be gauged by Pareto efficiency or related yardsticks.

Our present course can be defended on several grounds, however. First, the application of economic criteria seems reasonable insofar as we are concerned with the government's intervention in economic matters. In such other matters as treason, kidnapping, and blackmail, we may readily grant that economic ethics have no place. But our primary concerns are instances where the government attempts to rescue us from the market's deficiencies. Second, the Pareto ethic generally offers a fairly clear, concise, and consistent criterion. Can the same qualities be attributed to such slippery notions as "justice" or "self-realization"? Probably not. Third, it must be stressed that we shall not follow the Pareto ethic with pathological rigidity. Our discussion gives equal time to dynamic considerations and other ethical convictions. Thus, for example, we acknowledge that society may wish to protect and promote small business even at some loss in allocation efficiency.

All of this is to say that, once again, the satisfaction of personal preferences will be taken as the chief barometer of achievement. Still, satisfaction of personal preferences does not always correspond to society's pursuit of the general welfare, so several qualifications are accepted.

I. Government at Its Best

A. Political Processes (How?)

The political methods and procedural steps taken to reach government policies can be as important as the policies themselves. An athlete can lose gracefully if the game is played fairly. So, too, a citizen who happens to come out on the short end of a government decision will tend to accept his lot more readily if he believes the political proceedings were on the level. In essence, the procedures should fit the many qualities connoting goodness in government—democracy, impartiality, clarity, consistency, and so on.

Table 3–1 partitions the procedural steps into four parts (with loose correspondence to the political functions outlined in Chapter 1). The steps are fairly self evident—problem recognition, policy formulation, policy application, and private sector compliance.

1. PROBLEM RECOGNITION AND PREFERENCE ARTICULATION

Accurate articulation of citizens' preferences is of course crucial. Aside from the obvious ideal of one-person-one-vote, there are several further conditions fostering accuracy. *Full participation* would require that all folks affected by any policy be heard from. In some cases this is obviously not possible or practical. We cannot reliably hear from future generations or the insane. We do not jump at the slightest suggestions of children or criminals. Yet the basic idea is unexceptionable. Nearly everyone should

---

[1] John H. Hallowell, *The Moral Foundation of Democracy* (Chicago: University of Chicago Press, 1954); John Rawls, *A Theory of Justice* (Cambridge: Harvard University Press, 1971); Robert Nozick, *Anarchy, State, and Utopia* (New York: Basic Books, 1974); Mark A. Lutz and Kenneth Lux, *The Challenge of Humanistic Economics* (Melo Park, CA: Benjamin/Cummings Publishing Co., 1979); H. H. Liebhafsky, *American Government and Business* (New York: John Wiley & Sons, 1971), pp. 18–39, 565–571.

Table 3–1. Ideal Governmental Procedures

---

1. Problem Recognition: Preference Articulation
   a. One-person—one-vote
   b. Full participation by society's members
   c. Full information on problem
   d. Full employment to ease burden of change
2. Policy Formulation (Aggregation and Legislation)
   a. Preference aggregation through ideal voting rules and representation
   b. Selection of proper focus for policy: structure, conduct, or performance
   c. Selection of proper instrument for policy, e.g., tax, subsidy, direct regulation, etc.
3. Policy Application (Executive Enforcement and Judicial Review)
   a. Impartial application, consistency
   b. Efficient and expedicious application
   c. Minimum interference with private decision making
   d. Penalty fits the crime
4. Private Sector Compliance
   a. Clear knowledge of behavior required
   b. Appropriate incentives to comply
   c. Dependable and automatic compliance
   d. Low cost means for private party compliance

---

have a vote and use it when his or her fate is affected.

Full information would require that all these participants be completely knowledgeable about the policy options—the benefits, the costs, the short-run implications, and the long-run consequences. This requirement too is difficult to meet, given the horrendous complexities and mountainous number of policies posed by our modern world. Indeed, even experts cannot tell us precisely where taxes will bite, nor the degree of calamity caused by cholesterol in our food.

Implicit in the market ideal of Pareto efficiency was an assumption of full employment. In an ideal political context, *full employment* would permit voters to judge policies solely on intrinsic merit, without worry or hope about

their jobs.[2] Thus, when voting for or against a 10¢ deposit on soda pop containers, each person should decide on the basis of allocative benefits (reduced litter, lower container costs) and allocative costs (inconvenience, higher costs of deposit procedures). If bottle plant workers vote against the measure solely from fright of job loss, the ideal calculation would be upset, at least as it relates to Pareto efficiency. In setting out the ideal of perfect competition, we did not allow suppliers of any product to influence the demand for that product (other than as mere consumers like the rest of us).

2. POLICY FORMULATION: AGGREGATION AND LEGISLATION

Voting Rules. Majority rule seems as sacred as mom and apple pie. Yet it cannot, in general, be accepted as the ideal voting rule because it gives the majority an opportunity to "tyrannize" the minority.

To illustrate, imagine a ballot proposition that if passed would provide 330 days of clean air per year instead of the present 300. Note the public good here: *everyone* would get 30 additional clean days regardless of their personal preferences. Assume further that this change would cost $15 per person per year, or $.50 for each additional day of clean air. Those voting in favor of the measure would think this a good deal. Indeed, many on the yes side would willingly pay for *more* additional clean days at $.50 each, or pay *more* than $15 for the 30 specified on the ballot. Conversely, those voting against the proposition would not value clean air as highly. They would feel that $15 was too high a price to pay for 30 additional clean days, or they would feel that they should get more than 30 days for that kind of money. The implication is, then, that majority rule will

[2] D. T. Savage, M. Burke, J. D. Coupe, T. D. Duchesneau, D. F. Wihry, and J. A. Wilson, *Economics of Environmental Improvement* (Boston: Houghton-Mifflin Co., 1974), pp. 130–132.

make one of these groups worse off. If the proposition passes the nay-sayers will sulk. If it fails, the yea-sayers suffer. Yet the Pareto ideal is to make some better off *without* making anyone worse off.

Another way of stating this is that, under majority rule, the median voter—i.e., the middle one that swings the outcome off 50–50 dead center—is the voter of greatest consequence, and, in a narrow race, the only voter whose preferences are most nearly satisfied. The power of the median voter is observed in the tendency of presidential candidates to snuggle close to the middle-of-the-road, to abandon extreme positions of either the left or right. Moreover, as Anthony Downs observes, competition over the median turf "forces both [political] parties to be much less than perfectly clear about what they stand for."[3]

The *ideal* for dealing with allocation improvements such as public goods or externalities is thus *unanimous rule* rather than majority rule. If in fact a Pareto improvement is possible from a change, then it should also be possible to specify that change in a ballot proposition that could gain unanimous consent. To continue our example of clean air, the 30 additional days of benefit could not be varied to suit individual preferences because they are a public good, but the cost of $15 per head might be individually variable. Those fervently desiring greater cleanliness would still support the proposition if their cost were raised to $40, say, or whatever would more closely approach their willingness to pay. Conversely, opponents could be converted into supporters by amendments *lowering* their cost burden to levels just less than their willingness to pay. With support all around, unanimity emerges.

This endorsement of unanimity is admittedly utopian. The problems of practicality are gar-

gantuan. How can we learn each individual's preference for a proposition when it is in his or her interest to "free ride," to keep that preference hidden or understated given the public good nature of the decision? How can we be sure that no egocentric nitwit will take the opportunity to play last hold-out just to gain notoriety? In reality, few if any decisions would ever be made under a rule of unanimity.[4]

Moreover, unanimity can claim perfection *only* when applied to policies improving *allocation efficiency*. Policies that deliberately redistribute income to achieve some greater degree of *equality* cannot be decided under unanimous procedures for the simple reason that they necessarily hurt some folks while helping others. A unanimous rule would be hopeless in such instances. Thus it has been argued that truly ideal procedures would require different voting rules for different types of policies: a unanimous rule for allocation improvements, and a majority rule for equity adjustments.[5] Theoretical problems remain, and this neat dichotomy certainly does not wash away the practical difficulties, but we shall momentarily postpone further allusions to reality.

The Focus of Policy. Given that markets have three different parts that are vulnerable to policy manipulation—structure, conduct, and performance—government has some range of choice when selecting its focus for policy. Moreover, the choice can be important. By analogy, if a car's sputter comes from a dirty fuel line, it does little good to focus our repairs on the tires or upholstery.

Table 3–2 illustrates the principle of proper focus by outlining the most fitting targets of policies designed to remedy the market imper-

---

[3] A. Downs, *An Economic Theory of Democracy* (New York: Harper & Row, 1957), p. 136.

[4] James M. Buchanan, *The Demand and Supply of Public Goods* (Chicago: Rand McNally & Co., 1968), pp. 94–95.

[5] Dennis C. Mueller, *Public Choice* (Cambridge University Press, 1979), pp. 223–225, 263–270.

Table 3–2. Basic Government Policies Concerning Markets

Policy Type	Structure	Conduct	Performance
Maintenance of competition with antitrust	1. Monopoly law 2. Merger laws	1. Price-fixing law 2. Price discrimination law 3. Exclusive dealing law 4. Tying law	
Public utility regulation of natural monopolies		1. Price regulation in telephone, electricity and gas 2. Abandonment of service and extension of service	1. Profit regulation 2. Service requirements 3. Safety 4. Innovation regulation
Information improvement	1. Disclosure of information, truth-in-lending 2. Grading and standardization, general weights and measures 3. Trademark and copyright protection	1. False advertising 2. Deceptive practices	

fections listed at the top of Table 2–2 in the last chapter. Policies countering "artificial" blemishes in competition would best be directed toward structure and conduct rather than performance, because good performance would tend to follow automatically if structure and conduct were made workably competitive. Antimonopoly law could deconcentrate monopolized markets and merger law could prevent anticompetitive combinations. Preservation of rivalrous conduct could be furthered by prohibitions on restrictive practices like price-fixing and tying. It is important to note that structure and conduct would also be the proper focus if the intent of policy were to maintain competition as an end in itself, regardless of the consequences for performance.

Where technological imperatives spawn "natural" monopolies, the best strategy would probably be acceptance of monopoly structure but regulation of conduct and performance— surveillance of price patterns, product quality, and profit level in particular. Such regulation is a difficult and distorting exercise, one that occasions much more intervention in the daily affairs of business than competition policy. At the same time, regulation may be judged superior to outright government ownership, a still more meddlesome policy option for handling the problem of monopoly. Thus, an array of the alternatives from least to most intrusive would read: competition, regulation, then government ownership.

Imperfections of ignorance and misinformation could also be treated with performance regulation, in which case the government would have to specify product standards, check assembly-line compliance, levy penalties for noncompliance, and in various other ways get quite nosey. As suggested in Table 3–2, however, the alternatives of disclosing information (a structural approach) and curbing misleading claims (a conduct approach) are generally superior in efficacy and efficiency. These approaches leave buyers greater leeway; they do not choke off the consumers' range of choice; and they entail scant bureaucracy.

Regarding other market problems, we shall postpone discussion of policy focus except for two especially significant cases. One concerns pollution. The best method of curing most pollution problems is to levy a "tax" or "emission fee" on the polluter. This could be considered a structural approach, as it alters the cost structure facing the polluter, thereby indirectly inducing improved performance. Present policy is different, however. It regulates performance directly, with consequences that we shall criticize later. The second broad case concerns instances of government protection and promotion of industry. In those instances it would be best if government paid profit subsidies—a performance measure—rather than tamper with structure (by barring entry, say) or change conduct (by enforcing price controls or encouraging cartels, for example).

Selection of Policy Instruments. A corollary to the foregoing is that excellence in government requires selection of the best instrument to do the job at hand. Appreciation of this platitude hinges on explanations of "best" and "instrument."

Policy **"instruments"** are means rather than ends. They are usually the guts of legislation. They are what government actually does on a daily basis. Instruments are also as varied as cooking utensils. The main ones are mentioned in Table 3–3 together with the problems they are best suited for, not necessarily those they are actually employed against. The table conceals the still greater variety that will be encountered throughout the book for two reasons. First, each instrument mentioned covers a vast territory. Take "subsidies" for instance. They can take the form of direct subsidies, such as grants of money and land, or indirect subsidies, such as tax exemptions, loan guarantees, or stockpile purchases. Likewise, insurance may

Table 3–3. Policy Instruments and Problems Addressed

Problem	Policy Instrument
Monopoly power & restraint of trade	Antitrust
Natural monopoly	Public utility regulation
Information inadequacies	Information disclosure
	Prohibitions on misrepresentation
	Trademark rights
External benefits	Subsidy
External costs	Regulatory prohibitions, taxes, fees
Public goods	Public provision or subsidy
Common property resources	Regulation, public ownership
Instabilities	Loans, insurance
Transition immobilities	Temporary payments, job retraining
Macroeconomic instability	Monetary and fiscal policies
Growth and promotion	Tax exemptions, public works, patents
Equity	Transfer payments
Merit goods	Subsidy, information provision
Demerit goods	Taxes, prohibitions
Safety	Regulation, information disclosure

come packaged as unemployment compensation, social security, or crop insurance. Second, many policy instruments are not mentioned in Table 3–3, because they are rarely appropriate for anything. These include (1) direct price controls outside the public utility context, (2) licensing and other forms of entry constraint, (3) tariffs and quotas, and (4) moral suasion.

As for what is **"best"** in an instrument, there are many criteria by which to judge. Among the most obvious are speed of effect, precision, and sufficiency.[6] In *speed,* which is the time passing from implementation to effect, brevity is usually best. Quickness is especially important in policies treating instability.

Precision refers to the exactness with which the desired end is achieved. And of course, ideal instruments are precise instruments. If one antitrust tool is nearly always procompetitive whereas an alternative tool is procompetitive two-thirds of the time and anticompetitive one-third of the time, then wisdom would dictate selection of the former over the latter. Unfortunately most instruments operate rather clumsily.

The *sufficiency,* or strength of an instrument, is best when neither too potent nor too weak to achieve the intended result. Thus, ideally, an effluent tax on a polluting industry should be just high enough to curtail pollution until marginal social benefit matches marginal social cost; not so high as to close the industry down completely, nor so low as to barely make a dent in the degree of environmental damage. In other aspects of policy, strength depends on breadth of coverage, intensity of surveillance, and severity of remedies. But mention of these elements moves us beyond issues of policy formulation into issues of policy application and compliance.

3 & 4. POLICY APPLICATION AND COMPLIANCE

With ample notice, the Food and Drug Administration banned DES, a synthetic hormone used to spur growth in cattle and a known carcinogen (cause of cancer), after November 1, 1979. Confident of quick compliance, the FDA shortly thereafter discontinued monitoring meat for DES contamination and turned its attention to other matters. But six months later

it was discovered that compliance was spotty, that as many as 10% of the country's cattlemen failed to heed the government's order.[7]

Ideally, policy application and compliance would conform to the features mentioned in the last half of Table 3–1 (see page 40). Those features are largely self-evident, fulfilling the spirit of such qualities as impartiality, consistency, efficiency, clarity, appropriateness, dependability, unobtrusiveness, and self-operation. It will be noted that achievement of these qualities depends on more than bureaucratic procedures, company compliance efforts, and the like. It also depends on achievements made earlier in the policy process, namely, good diagnosis of the nature of the problem, registration of society's preferences, skillful selection of policy focus, wise choice of policy instrument, and so on. In the absence of universal heroism, fantastic feats at the later stages cannot be expected without building on solid foundations.

B. Political Performance (How Well?)

Ideal processes are desirable in themselves. But the best proof of the pudding is, as they always say, in the eating. Thus we come to government performance as it is measured by (1) benefit-cost analysis, (2) dynamic welfare, and (3) miscellaneous ethical convictions.

1. BENEFIT-COST ANALYSIS (FOR OPTIMAL ALLOCATIONS)

From July 1979 to April 1980 federal regulations specified that, during the winter, temperatures in most commercial and industrial buildings could not be heated to more than 65 degrees and, during the summer, could not be cooled to less than 78 degrees. This was an energy conservation measure, the main benefit of which was the saving of about 40.5 million barrels of oil, or $810 million, assuming a price

[6] Donald Watson, *Economic Policy: Business and Government* (Boston: Houghton Mifflin, 1960), pp. 165–167.

[7] *Wall Street Journal,* July 15, 1980, p. 48.

of $20 per barrel. There were costs, however. In addition to the costs of keeping energy bureaucrats in bread and butter, there were substantial costs borne by businesses when the productivity of their workers fell. In the winter, typists complained that their cold fingers hit more wrong keys than usual, and telephone assembly-line workers said the cold robbed them of dexterity. In the summer, accounts receivable clerks were delayed when papers kept sticking to their elbows and reports of general sluggishness were heard throughout the land.[8] Whether the total monetary cost of these adversities exceeded the $810 million benefit is unknown, but if it did, the wisdom of the policy could be questioned.

To the extent allocation efficiency, i.e., Pareto optimality, is accepted as the standard by which to judge government performance, *excellence would require that policies be implemented or expanded only when the added social benefits of the change exceeded the added social costs, up to the point where costs equal benefits.* The similarity between this standard and that emerging from ideal markets, as pictured earlier in Figure 2–6, is no accident. The idea is that if government is going to pick up where markets leave off, then ideally it should simulate the ideal results of the market. Satisfaction of personal preferences is the target. Resources are the ammunition.

Stated succinctly, benefit is "value here" and cost is "value elsewhere." Stated technically, the **benefit** of a policy change is *the maximum amount people who gain would be willing to pay* to have resources used in the way the policy entails. The **cost** of a policy change is *the minimum amount people who make sacrifices must receive to be fully compensated* when the resources are not used in other ways.[9] This follows the logic of the ideal marketplace, where

[8] *Wall Street Journal*, March 11, 1980, p. 48.
[9] This so-called compensating variation is the most widely prescribed concept of benefit and cost. E. J. Mishan,

demand is "maximum willingness to pay" and supply is "minimum willingness to receive." Stated numerically, the government's grade rating of tires might cost $50 million per year (for tires destroyed in tests, test equipment, salaries of test personnel, tags reporting results, and for other resources). But if consumers of tires would be willing to pay $75 million per year for this information (as measured by their savings from better purchase accuracy and from lower tire prices due to greater competition), then the program would be a good one. Efficiency would improve.

Figure 3–1 loosely illustrates the benefits and costs from antitrust action that converts a monopoly industry into a competitive industry. Constant unit costs are assumed for simplicity. Under monopoly, price is P_1 and quantity is Q_1. Under competition, price is P_2 and quantity is Q_2. Thus the relevant benefits and costs derive from the increased output from Q_1 to Q_2 and the reduced price from P_1 to P_2. The total benefit from change matches the area under the demand curve, which is Q_1ABQ_2, because that is the amount folks are willing to pay for the added output. The total cost of producing the added output, or the minimum suppliers must receive, is the area under the "cost per unit" curve, Q_1CBQ_2, because that is the cost per unit times the number of additional units. Not pictured are the costs of lawyers' time in prosecuting the case, court costs, and the like, but let's momentarily assume that these legal costs are small enough to be ignored. Then the benefit less cost is the difference between these

Economics for Social Decisions: Elements of Cost-Benefit Analysis (New York: Praeger, 1973), pp. 14–15. But there are serious problems with this and substitute concepts on theoretical and practical levels. A good summary is by A. Myrick Freeman III, *The Benefits of Environmental Improvement* (Baltimore: Johns Hopkins University Press, 1979), pp. 33–61. In the end Freeman takes a leap of faith, believing it "better to use the data at hand . . . than to forego the opportunity to shed perhaps a little light on a policy issue because the data were not perfect." p. 59.

Figure 3–1.   Benefit-cost From Antitrust Action

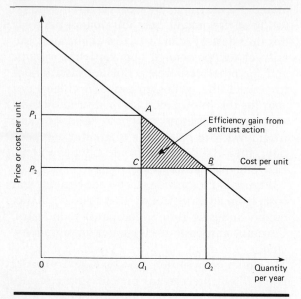

OP_1AQ_1, part of which, rectangle P_2P_1AC, is excess profit. The seller's revenue for this quantity after change is OP_2CQ_1. The difference, P_2P_1AC, is transfered from the producer's pocket to the consumer's. Indeed, as will be explained shortly, it would be best at this point if equity considerations were kept out of the story by assuming that the consumer-gainers actually paid producer-losers to compensate them for the loss of P_2P_1AC. Then there would be no redistribution effect at all. And triangle ABC still represents the resulting Pareto-efficiency improvement.

Figure 3–2 illustrates the benefits and costs associated with a tax on pollution, where the tax rate just equals the external costs of the pollution. In this case, the direction of reallocation is opposite to that just discussed, namely a decrease in output and increase in price rather than an increase in output and decrease in price. Thus the "benefits" in this case are

Figure 3–2.   Benefits and Costs From Pollution Tax

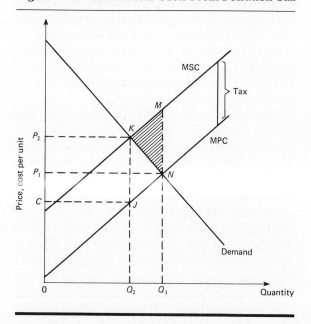

areas, that is, the shaded triangle ABC. In equation form, with Δ indicating "change in":

$$\Delta \text{ Net benefit} = \Delta \text{ Social benefit} - \Delta \text{ Social cost}$$

$$ABC \qquad = \quad Q_1ABQ_2 \quad - Q_1CBQ_2$$

If the legal expenses are factored in, and time frozen to one year, then the more precise net benefit would be ABC less those costs.

It must be stressed that this is only the *efficiency gain* associated with the *reallocation of resources* from elsewhere to here and the associated jump in quantity from Q_1 to Q_2. Consumers also gain from the reduced price on all the units purchased prior to the antitrust action, ranging over O to Q_1. This total savings is area P_2P_1AC, which is the price difference times quantity. But this is not counted in the above calculation because it represents a *transfer* of money from the sellers to the buyers, or a possible improvement in *equity* rather than an improvement in allocation *efficiency*. The seller's revenue before the action is best thought of as *cost reductions,* particularly a reduction in the external cost caused by pollution, and these benefits still reflect willingness to pay, particularly the willingness of those wanting to reduce the level of pollution. Similarly, the "costs" in this case are best thought of as *benefit reductions,* because reduced output and higher prices "here" mean that benefits are foregone here. Consumers, producers, and employees bear the cost.

The pretax, free-market result is an equilibrium at N, with price P_1 and quantity Q_1. After the tax, which corresponds to KJ per unit and MN per unit, the market moves to point K as the cost of the tax is added to the marginal private cost MPC. The total *benefit* from the change is the area Q_1MKQ_2, because that is the reduced social cost of moving from Q_1 to Q_2, counting both reduced private costs of Q_1NJQ_2 and reduced external costs of $NMKJ$. Conversely, the total *cost* (i.e., foregone benefit) associated with the change is the area under the demand curve over the Q_1–Q_2 range, or Q_1NKQ_2. Thus the net benefit from the tax is the shaded area KMN. Algebraically, this change reads:

$$\Delta \text{ Net benefit} = \Delta \text{ Social benefit} - \Delta \text{ Social cost}$$

$$KMN \quad = \quad Q_1MKQ_2 \quad - Q_1NKQ_2$$

Notice that reallocation beyond this point, to quantities less than Q_2, would not be optimal because the cost of further reductions in Q, as read off the demand curve, exceed the benefits, as read off the MSC curve. Notice, too, that efficient allocation does not necessarily imply elimination of the pollution, only its abatement.

By these lights, ideal performance in government requires more than mere adherence to the benefit-cost technique, it also requires perfection of the technique. To attain such perfection numerous conditions must be met, perfect knowledge and distributional neutrality being the most important.

Perfect knowledge requires that all the relevant benefits and costs must be identified and measured in dollar values. However simple this may sound, it is anything but simple. Almost every change in policy has myriad benefits and costs that ideally need identification and measurement. Where people's lives are at stake, as they are in safety and environmental issues, they must be counted and evaluated. Where species are threatened, they must be monetarily weighed. Where market prices are used to estimate wage costs, building materials expense, the value of crop outputs, and the many other tangible items entering the analysis, those market prices must accurately reflect marginal social benefits and marginal social costs. When benefits and costs included in the reckoning are spread over time, the true social rate of time preference (interest rate) must be known to convert all values into comparable present-value form through discounting. All externalities raised by policy action must also be accounted for, as when for instance government dams kill fish or add salinity to river water.

Distribution neutrality requires that no adverse changes in the distribution of well-being occur when the benefit-cost criteria is applied. This condition could easily be met (a) if those folks experiencing the benefits were exactly the same as those bearing the costs, or (b) if each dollar of benefit to gainers could always be given the same equity or distributional weight as a dollar of cost to losers. Inconveniently, however, those who gain and those who lose are usually *not* the same folks. And what is more, it is doubtful that we can justifiably give equal weight to all the dollars involved. Thus, blind pursuit of the benefit-cost criteria, with nothing more, might make the rich richer and the poor poorer if those who gain are typically rich and those who lose are typically poor.

The ideal of distribution neutrality therefore requires that the gainers of reallocation policies always compensate the losers, as suggested a moment ago in our example of monopoly. In all cases where benefits actually exceed costs, gainers *should be able* to pay losers and still come out ahead. The ideal of requiring that such payments *actually be made* assures that income *inequality will at least not grow worse.* It also corresponds to the market ethic of voluntary exchange, which implies no rip-offs. Finally, it dovetails with our earlier observation that unanimous blessing is best for allocation improvements.[10]

2. DYNAMIC WELFARE (STABILITY AND GROWTH)

Where issues of static resource allocation are at stake, Pareto optimality provides a standard of excellence by which to judge government performance because that is a widely accepted ideal in evaluating market performance. In other areas of economic concern, such as stability and growth, there is no clear consensus on what constitutes good market performance, so there is likewise no clear consensus on what constitutes good governmental performance. To be sure, there are some vague notions that gain wide enough acceptance to drive any Gallup Poll of popularity through the roof, notions like "full employment" and "price stability." But the closer one gets to concrete yardsticks, such as "3.5 per cent unemployment" and "5 per cent annual growth in real GNP per capita," the smaller the group one can find in support of those yardsticks.

Rather than waffle our way through every aspect of dynamic behavior with this message,

we can focus on growth to illustrate the point. In times past economic growth was universally applauded as glorious, so the ideal standard was something like: "the more, the better."[11] As the founder of economics, Adam Smith, wrote in 1776:

> it is in the progressive state, while the society is advancing to the further acquisition, rather than when it has acquired its full complement of riches, that the conditions of the labouring poor, of the great body of the people, seems to be the happiest and most comfortable. It is hard in the stationary, and miserable in the declining state.[12]

Even as late as 1960 a good text on government and business accurately celebrated the apparent unanimity of the day:

> Who would question the desirability of economic growth? . . . The goodness of economic growth follows from the basic attitudes and beliefs shared by all. On the desirability of this goal there is no partisan wrangling, no conflict of rival economic philosophies, no clash between business and labor ideologies.[13]

Conformity of convictions has now crumbled, however. A growing contingent of doubters is questioning the *possibility* and the *desirability* of vigorous economic growth. In questioning desirability, the issue of main inter-

---

[10] In practice, most economists follow the "Kaldor criteria," which says that a policy should be accepted if those who gain *could* fully compensate those who lose. It does not require *actual* payment. But of course this criterion is merely one of *potential* Pareto improvement, not actual. I think potentials are nice but not ideal. Nicholas Kaldor, "Welfare Propositions of Economics and Interpersonal Comparisons of Utility," *Economic Journal,* Vol. 49, pp. 549–552; Alan T. Peacock and Charles K. Rowley, *Welfare Economics: A Liberal Restatement* (London: M. Robertson, 1975).

[11] Technically, this is not quite right. A theoretically attractive limit to growth based on free-market operation can be derived by assuming that people prefer present consumption over future consumption as measured by the rate of interest they must be paid to forego present consumption in anticipation of greater future consumption. This interest rate may then guide both saving and investment activity, which investment then generates growth. But this classical formulation ignored many problems also affecting the question of optimal growth, such as the optimal rate of natural resource extraction, and the optimal rate of population change. So to this writer's knowledge no clear consensus on a precise optimum currently exists among economists.

[12] Adam Smith, *Wealth of Nations,* Book I, Chap. VIII, Cannan edition (Modern Library), p. 81.

[13] Donald S. Watson, *Economic Policy: Business and Government* (Boston: Houghton Mifflin Company, 1960), pp. 470–471.

est here, skeptics claim that growth does not really improve the subjective satisfaction of individuals,[14] that it produces bad by-products of air pollution, water degradation, toxic waste, and disruptive congestion, which will eventually make matters worse,[15] and that much growth has been based on a rate of resource extraction—especially of nonrenewables like oil and natural gas—too rapid to be either wise for ourselves or comforting to future generations.[16] Although these awesome considerations are probably not yet serious enough to warrant a complete halt to growth, some portion of potential growth might prudently be sacrificed to preserve the environment and nonrenewable resources. The criterion applicable to environmental protection has already been discussed. The criterion applicable to resource extraction is a rate that keeps the real price (nominal price divided by an overall price index) from rising over time.[17]

To the extent there are no precisely defined welfare criteria for evaluating solutions to dynamic problems, we are forced to rely on rather crude value judgments as to what is good and bad. Thus "more" stability may be "better" than "less," but freedom and flexibility in economic change require *some* instability. "Speedy" adoption of new technologies may

be "desirable," but "too much" speed would probably be disruptively costly. And so on. The role of rough value judgments is even more important in assessing government performance in the area of equity, our next topic.

3. EQUITY AND OTHER DESIRABLES

During the mid–1970s, the top twenty percent of American families enjoyed approximately 32.8% of the country's income while the lowest twenty percent accounted for about 11.7% (after adjustment for in-kind transfers to the poor, such as medical care, housing, and education).[18] Is this the "ideal" or "best" result the government should achieve in income distribution or equity? No one knows. Economists cannot demonstrate that one distribution is better than another. They offer no formulation of an ideal. Indeed, if anything, economists have demonstrated the *impossibility* of attaining a democratically determined consensus on what the ideal should be.[19] The puzzle remains a puzzle mainly because of the nature of the problem: changes in distribution create gainers and losers. In judging such changes, value judgments play a particularly dominant role.

A brief review of the debate between egalitarians and nonegalitarians will unearth the ethical judgments. Let's take *teleological* arguments first—that is, those favoring or opposing redistributions on grounds that the *end result* is good or bad. The classic teleological argument favoring redistribution is "utilitarianism." Comparing the mental and emotional states of the rich and the poor, a utilitarian would argue that $1,000 means less to a family with $100,000 annual income than it does to a family with

[14] Tibor Scitovsky, *The Joyless Economy* (New York: Oxford University Press, 1976), pp. 133–145; Staffan B. Linder, *The Harried Leisure Class* (New York: Columbia University Press, 1970); Fred Hirsch, *The Social Limits to Growth* (Cambridge, Mass.: Harvard University Press, 1978).

[15] E. J. Mishan, *The Economic Growth Debate* (London: Allen & Unwin, Ltd., 1977); Allen Schnaiberg, *The Environment from Surplus to Scarcity* (New York: Oxford University Press, 1980).

[16] Herman E. Daly, *Steady-State Economics: The Economics of Biophysical Equilibrium and Moral Growth* (San Francisco: W. H. Freeman & Co., 1977). See also the papers by P. R. Ehrlich, A. H. Ehrlich, J. P. Holdren, and Georgescu-Roegen in H. E. Daly (ed.), *Economics, Ecology, Ethics* (San Francisco: Freeman, 1980).

[17] Talbot Page, *Conservation and Economic Efficiency* (Baltimore: Johns Hopkins University Press, 1977), pp. 143–207.

[18] Edgar K. Browning and Jacquelene M. Browning, *Public Finance and the Price System* (New York: Macmillan Publishing Co., 1979), p. 202.

[19] The classic proof is that of Kenneth Arrow, *Social Choice and Individual Values* (New York: John Wiley & Sons, 1951). There have since been attempts to show possibility, but they suffer various deficiencies. For a review see Dennis C. Mueller, *op. cit.* pp. 184–206.

$5,000 annual income. Therefore, if government were to take $1,000 from the rich and give it to the poor, the relatively small loss of "utility" by the rich would be more than offset by the relatively large gain of "utility" by the poor.[20] The implication is one of greater good for a greater number. In contrast, a *non*egalitarian argument of the same teleological stripe would maintain that *in*equality has desirable consequences. Poverty builds character. Wealth encourages risk-taking and investment that bolsters economic growth, benefiting everyone. Moreover, it may be argued that the prospect of earning one's way up the ladder provides incentive to work hard, to use one's talents to the fullest, and so on.[21]

Nonteleological theories argue in favor of ethical convictions that are said to be good or bad in themselves. An egalitarian might argue, for instance, that people in an affluent society have a *right* to some minimum level of sustenance or, failing that, a *right* to minimum levels of certain goods and services like health care and education, provision of which should not hinge on income level alone.[22] While this line of argument stresses some equalization of *realized welfare*, related lines urge the attainment of equal *opportunity* as a basic right—equal opportunity in employment and education in particular. *Non*egalitarian theories of the non-teleological type are also possible and even pop-

ular in some circles. Rather than be concerned with the "rights" of the underprivileged, these theories, as you might well expect, are especially concerned about protecting or furthering the "rights" of the privileged. One of the most widely cited of these theories is that of Robert Nozick, who argues that *process* is all important, that so long as people attain their riches through "just" acquisition they have an absolute *right* to every penny so acquired, regardless of any consequences for the poor. Basically, you originally acquire something "justly" if you take something that belongs to nobody, without thereby lessening the lot of others. Subsequently, voluntary exchange, gifts, and inheritance are also "just."[23] The intriguing implications of this theory may be appreciated by imagining what the world would be like if Christopher Columbus and his heirs could have claimed America as their property for all time. A related argument, propounded by Irving Kristol, holds that compulsory redistributions seriously compromise "liberty," the greatest of all blessings.[24]

Given the circumstances, one might wonder whether there is widespread agreement about anything even remotely related to this issue. Yet the following standards seem acceptable to most folks:

1. Substantial protection of equal *opportunity* in employment seems desirable and defensible to prevent discrimination based on race, religion, and sex.
2. Compulsory redistribution of income can be justified for the aged, infirm, disabled, and truly destitute to assure their subsistence if not opulence.
3. To the extent the wealthy gain their riches by questionable means, such as fraud and

[20] Jeremy Bentham originated the argument more than a century ago. A modern, sophisticated version is that of J. C. Harsanyi, *Rational Behavior and Bargaining Equilibrium in Games and Social Situations* (Cambridge: Cambridge University Press, 1977).

[21] Irving Kristol, "Thoughts on Equality and Egalitarianism," in C. D. Campbell (ed.) *Income Redistribution* (Washington, D.C.: American Enterprise Institute, 1977), pp. 35–42. See also Richard Sennett, "Our Hearts Belong to Daddy" *New York Review of Books* (May 1, 1980), pp. 32–35.

[22] Arthur M. Okun, "Further Thoughts on Equality and Efficiency," in Campbell *op. cit.* p. 28. See also the papers by Lester Thurow and Charles Fried in *Markets and Morals,* edited by G. Dworkin, G. Berment, and P. G. Brown (Washington, D.C.: Hemisphere Publishing Co., 1977).

[23] Robert Nozick, *Anarchy, State, and Utopia* (New York: Basic Books, 1974).

[24] Irving Kristol, "What is Social Justice?" *Wall Street Journal,* August 12, 1976.

artificial monopolization, their rights to retention of the treasure may be questioned.
4. Taking from the needy to benefit the affluent is unambiguously frowned upon.

Performance standards are also nebulous in still other areas of ethical conviction—such as safety, health, competition for its own sake, preservation of small business, and so on. Some people, economists especially, like to think that most if not all these other goals should meet benefit-cost criteria. And this book, too, will occasionally speak of the benefits and costs of, say, safety regulation and environmental protection. However, benefit-cost cannot always carry this burden. As we shall see, it has serious weaknesses in practical application and ethical conviction, the last of which is explained by Steven Kelman:

> since the costs of injury are borne by its victims, while its benefits are reaped by its perpetrators, simple cost-benefit calculations may be less important than more abstract conceptions of justice, fairness and human dignity. We would not condone a rape even if it could be demonstrated that the rapist derived enormous pleasure from his actions, while the victim suffered in only small ways. Behind the conception of "rights" is the notion that some concept of justice, fairness, and human dignity demands that individuals ought to be able to perform certain acts, despite the harm to others, and ought to be protected against certain acts, despite the loss this causes to the would-be perpetrators. Thus we undertake no cost-benefit analysis of the effects of freedom of speech or trial by jury before allowing them to continue.[25]

To the extent this view is adopted, little of precision can be said of ideal goals. Goals must emerge from a social stew of various value judgments, stirred and blended by political processes. What *can* be said is that, *once a goal is set, it should be achieved efficiently.* Assume for instance, that society, without knowing the precise benefits, deems it desirable to have no more than 80 decibels of noise reaching the eardrums of manufacturing workers. Assume further that this objective could be achieved only one of two ways: (1) modifications to machinery, including extensive noise insulation, or (2) workers wearing hearing protectors that are inconvenient but not too uncomfortable. If the cost of method (1) is $3 billion annually and the cost of method (2) is $0.5 billion annually, then the latter method should be adopted.[26] It would be *cost effective.* It would be using the fewest resources to achieve the stated goal.

Readers not nodding off at this point will notice that cost-effectiveness is a first cousin of benefit-cost. Under benefit-cost, *both* the dollar benefits and the dollar costs are known and variable. Under cost-effectiveness, either the benefits are fixed in physical standards and the dollar costs are variable (as in the noise example), or the dollar costs are fixed and the hard-to-measure benefits are variable. It should be obvious that cost-effectiveness is a handy way of assesssing ideal performance in instances where ethics *other* than allocation efficiency are being served. Nonteleological ethics tend to set minimums, which in turn fix goals or budgets.[27]

Summary

The ideal of having consensus ideals for every governmental occasion eludes us. Everyone

[25] Steven Kelman, "Regulation that Works," *The New Republic* (November 25, 1978), p. 19. See also Kelman, "Cost-Benefit Analysis: An Ethical Critique," *Regulation* (Jan/Feb 1981), pp. 33–40.

[26] John F. Morrall III, "Exposure to Occupational Noise," in J. C. Miller III, and B. Yandle (eds.) *Benefit-Cost Analyses of Social Regulation* (Washington, D.C.: American Enterprise Institute, 1979), pp. 33–58.

[27] For still other methods see John A. Sinden and Albert C. Worrell, *Unpriced Values* (New York: John Wiley & Son, 1979), Chapter 11.

has his own notion of utopia, and the overlap among these notions is limited. Nevertheless, there is enough overlap to venture the assertion that, ideally, the governmental decision making *process* should be as democratic as possible, with fairly full participation, abundant knowledge, and minimum potential for minority injury. The focus of policies should be fitting. The choice of instruments should be adroit. And the steps of application and compliance should abide by the guidelines of Table 3–1. Overlapping ideals concerning government *performance* include the satisfaction of benefit-cost criteria where allocation efficiency is the objective, and cost-effectiveness where ethical convictions fix a beneficial nonmonetary goal or where budget constraints freeze the costs. Additional ideals also prevail, like equity and stability, but nothing that can claim precision. All in all, there may be enough in the way of ideals to recognize the government's shortcomings. And it is to those shortcomings that we now turn.

II. Real Government

As we have seen, one does not have to look far to find flaws in markets. Imagining ideal government remedies is equally easy. There is a temptation to conclude, then, that government *should* always intervene. But the temptation should be stoutly resisted. Government too is flawed, and its intervention may make a bad situation worse.

Before we explore those flaws, which are itemized in Table 3–4,[28] it must be stressed that

[28] This list draws mainly from George J. Stigler, "The Government of the Economy" in E. Mansfield (ed.) *Economics: Readings, Issues, and Cases*, 3rd edition (New York: W. W. Norton & Co., 1980), pp. 35–48; J. D. Gwartney and R. Stroup, *Microeconomics: Private and Public Choice*, 2nd edition (New York: Academic Press, 1979), pp. 439–451; and Charles Wolf, Jr., "A Theory of Nonmarket Failure: Framework for Implementation Analysis," *Journal of Law & Economics* (April 1979), pp. 107–139.

Table 3–4.   Government Shortcomings

A. Imperfections Like Those of Markets (Misallocation)
   1. Monopoly power (no competition or bankruptcy for government)
   2. Voter ignorance and nonparticipation
   3. Official ignorance
B. Failures (Misallocations from Gaps in Benefit-Cost)
   1. Special interest effects
   2. External costs in government
   3. Bundle purchases by electorate
   4. Uniform treatment of diverse situations
C. Dynamic Problems (Delay and Myopia)
   1. Delays and inaction
   2. Short-run cost, long-run benefit: inaction
   3. Short-run benefit, long-run cost: overaction
D. Other Ethical Criteria
   1. Distributional inequity
   2. National defense

---

jumping to conclusions by an opposite chain of reasoning must also be resisted. When government botches the job a bit, it does not necessarily follow that the market would do better. The market might do worse. Waste in the military, for instance, is a perennial problem, but turning national defense over to the free-market would prove disastrous. Thus the main implication of what follows is not that government ought to be pushed into the nearest abyss, but rather that society must choose between two faulty mechanisms—the market and the government. Care is required to choose the least imperfect in each instance of need. And, overall, some mix of the two seems best, depending on the situation.

A. Imperfections Mimicking Those of Markets

1. MONOPOLY POWER

First, and most obviously, government is by nature a monopolist. It is not goaded by competition to be lean, productive, or competent, although public spiritedness among government employees may provide some measure of these qualities. Moreover, government does not face bankruptcy, the means by which costly failure is ended in private enterprise. The government often never knows when to quit.

Take old Sanford, for example, a horse whose tale is told by Professor Almarin Phillips of the University of Pennsylvania:

> Not long ago, my wife and I had occasion to wander through New Market, a restored section of Philadelphia. There, harnessed to a renovated, four-wheeled Studebaker carriage, was a well-aged bay horse. Neatly lettered on the side of the carriage was "P.U.C. 3714." For a regulated price of $10, old Sanford, as the horse was called, takes passengers for a regulated ride of one-half hour.
>
> Shortly after our ride with old Sanford, I had occasion to talk with Commissioner Helen O'Bannon of the Pennsylvania Public Utility Commission. "Why," I asked, after explaining the delights of travel with old Sanford, "is that business regulated?" Commissioner O'Bannon, a reform-oriented member of the commission, replied, "You know as well as I do. It started before there were automobiles in the taxi service, and no one has seriously pressed for deregulation."[29]

2. VOTER IGNORANCE AND NONPARTICIPATION

There are public good aspects, i.e., free-rider problems, in the political process. Citizens tend to feel like grains of sand, believing that great efforts on their part to become informed and to participate actively will in the end make very little difference. They might "pay" and "not get" or "get" and "not pay." Indeed, we would surely go daft if each of us were to become intently concerned about all the problems that plague us—energy shortages, water pollution, inflation, auto safety, drug abuse, traffic congestion, abortion, trashy television programs, health care for the elderly, nuclear power, student cheating, excess population growth, Arab-Israeli conflicts, business fraud, tax reform, Cambodian relief . . . blah, blah, blah (the list alone would take at least a day to write).

This is not to say that people are generally apathetic. They are *selectively* apathetic. Each person seems to have a subjective list of priorities, with a few items at the top that get most of the worry and commitment. Of course people's lists differ, and most change with time. This explains why at any one moment excitement over any one issue varies across the populace, and why the aggregate rankings of concern vary from year to year. In 1912, monopoly was a very hot topic. In 1970, environmental protection reached a peak of popularity.

Knowledge and participation are thus less than perfect. And the consequences, like 50% of the electorate not voting, are sometimes astounding. The Survey Research Center once interviewed the same sample of Americans three times, with an interval of two years between each interview. These folks were asked whether they would "agree" or "disagree" with statements like "The government should leave things like electric power and housing for private businessmen to handle," and "If Negroes are not getting fair treatment in jobs and housing, the government should see to it that they do." Analysis of the responses reveal that "faced with typical items of this kind, only about thirteen people out of twenty manage to locate themselves even on the same *side* of the controversy in successive interrogations, when ten out of twenty could have done so by chance alone."[30]

[29] Almarin Phillips, "Regulation and Its Alternatives" in *Regulating Business: The Search for an Optimum* (San Francisco: Institute for Contemporary Studies, 1978), p. 159.

[30] Conclusion of P. E. Converse, quoted by Brian M. Barry, *Sociologists, Economists, and Democracy* (London: Collier-Macmillan, 1970), p. 127.

3. OFFICIAL IGNORANCE OR ERROR

Should the Civil Aeronautics Board impose elaborately expensive regulations on the airlines in order to assure that several dozen small towns get air service? Should the government try to regulate the manufacturing techniques of tens of thousands of plants in order to curb pollution when an effluent tax would do the job better?

These real-life queries illustrate government imperfections arising at least in part from official ignorance. They relate to ill-advised instrument selection and policy focus. The problem of official ignorance also prevents proper benefit-cost calculations. Comparing eight independent studies of what benefits would be derived from eliminating air pollution as of about 1970, we find a remarkable range of $2 billion to $35.4 billion, with most of the "best" estimates falling between $10 and $20 billion.[31] Safety is similar. The National Highway Traffic Safety Administration received five estimates of the lives that would be saved annually by passive restraints such as air bags in automobiles, all from supposed experts like General Motors and Economics and Science Planning, Inc. The estimates ranged from 2,700 lives saved to 19,000.[32] Converting numbers like these into dollar values compounds the variance because estimates of the value of human life also span an immense range—$260,000 to $1,000,000 by application of what is currently regarded as the best estimation technique.[33] "Unfortunately," as Joanne Linnerooth concludes, "it appears that there are limited possibilities to provide policy makers with meaningful data on personal willingness to pay for reduced mortality risk, regardless of whether these data are obtained from market behavior, from questionnaires or indirectly from personal lifetime earnings."[34]

Of course these failings are not necessarily the government's fault. The knowledge eludes even the best professors. The point is that limitations in ken must be appreciated.

B. Failures (*Gaps in Benefit-Cost*)

1. SPECIAL INTEREST EFFECTS

Preference articulation and aggregation in the real world are heavily influenced by a few thousand interest groups. These bands are typically formed by parties sharing some common, everyday economic interest—such as the Association of American Railroads, American Pharmaceutical Association, American Petroleum Institute, AFL-CIO, American Bar Association, United Auto Workers, and American Medical Association. But there are also "cause groups," which spring up around specific issues, such as the Environmental Defense Fund, Energy Action, Consumer Federation of America, and Action for Children's Television. It is in these interest groups, then, that we find most participation and knowledge.

Much public policy furthers *neither* economic efficiency *nor* greater equality, and a major explanation for this failure lies in special interest politics. When the benefits of a policy are concentrated among a relatively few, and the costs are diffusely spread by little bits throughout society, then the special interests who benefit will have the advantage of being able to muster particularly well-organized, vociferous support in favor of passage, while selective apathy will silence the many who bear the

---

[31] Council on Environmental Quality, *Environmental Quality-1975* (Washington D.C.: U.S.G.P.O., 1975), p. 517.

[32] U.S. Congress, House, Subcommittee on Oversight and Investigations of the Committee on Interstate and Foreign Commerce, *Federal Regulation and Regulatory Reform* (October 1976), pp. 507–508.

[33] Richard Thaler and Sherwin Rosen, "The Value of Saving a Life: Evidence from the Labor Market," in N. Terleckyz (ed.), *Household Production and Consumption* (New York: Columbia University Press for NBER, 1976), pp. 265–298; W. Kip Viscusi, "Labor Market Valuations of Life and Limb: Empirical Evidence and Policy Implications," *Public Policy* (Summer 1978), pp. 359–386.

[34] Joanne Linnerooth, "The Value of Human Life: A Review of the Models," *Economic Inquiry* (January 1979), p. 72.

cost. Thus, for years economists have pointed out that quota and tariff protection against steel and sugar imports is inefficient, that restrictive licensing of barbers, taxis, and countless other services is anticompetitive and costly to consumers, that cartelization of the milk industry is not in the public interest, and so on. Yet all of these policies and more like them abound because special interest groups exploit the mismatch between concentrated benefits and diffuse costs. Setting the message in concrete, a 1980 study of the Federal Trade Commission staff estimated that import restrictions on five products alone cost U.S. consumers $2 billion annually, while the benefits to the industries were at most $281 million. The products studied were color television sets, textiles, citizens' band radios, shoes, and sugar.[35]

When a policy change carries an opposite distribution of benefits and costs, with benefits diffused and costs concentrated, the problem is reversed. Then the cost side typically has the more powerful interest group representation, raising the hurdles against change. This seems to explain why *de*regulation is usually more difficult to attain than original regulation when that regulation serves narrow economic interests like trucking, agriculture, or banking. It also seems to explain why measures in the broad public interest—like safety, antitrust, environmental protection, and equal opportunity—are taken only as a result of severe crisis. Calamity tends to elevate issues to the top of people's selective apathy lists, thereby precipitating "cause" organizations, intensifying public outcries, and provoking political support. Thus action in cases of diffuse benefit and concentrated cost is by no means impossible, but it tends to be timorous and halting.[36] The his-

tory of environmental protection policy, for instance, dates from the last century. But nothing was "really" accomplished until a string of tragedies incited action in the early 1970s.[37]

2. EXTERNAL COSTS IN GOVERNMENT

When it comes to external costs, government is sometimes the problem, not the solution. Within the standard framework, government is often a major polluter. Aside from such obvious offenses as municipal government failure to treat raw sewage, the government defiles the environment with military bases, dams, irrigation projects, and canals. Indeed, the federal government has been accused of being the single greatest source of water pollution in the western United States.[38]

Another form of external cost occurs when one government agency pursues a policy that contradicts the policy of another agency. This might be called internal-external cost, or incoherent-inconsistency. Whatever it is called, it is less than ideal, shrinking the likelihood of optimal allocations. Table 3–5 outlines several examples.

3. BUNDLE PURCHASES BY THE ELECTORATE

Ideally, citizens should be able to express their opinions on each governmental decision separately, much the same way they are able to make marginal adjustments in the marketplace, spending a little more here and a little less there. But such is not the case. The political process works in bundles, which are imprecise. As James Gwartney and Richard Stroup ex-

[35] *Wall Street Journal*, July 25, 1980, p. 2.
[36] James Q. Wilson, "The Politics of Regulation," in J. W. McKie (ed.), *Social Responsibility and the Business Predicament* (Washington, D.C.: Brookings Institution, 1974), pp. 143–146; John E. Sinclair, *Interest Groups in America* (Morristown, N.J.: General Learning Press, 1976), pp. 46–47.

[37] John Esposito, *Vanishing Air: The Report on Air Pollution* (New York: Grossman Publishers, 1970); David Zwick and Mary Benstock, *Water Wasteland* (New York: Grossman Publishers, 1971); John C. Whitaker, *Striking a Balance: Environment and Natural Resources Policy in the Nixon-Ford Years* (Washington, D.C.: American Enterprise Institute, 1976).

[38] Richard L. Berkman and W. Kip Viscusi, *Damning the West* (New York: Grossman Publishers, 1973).

Table 3–5.   Examples of Government Externalities or Contradictory Policies, Circa 1980

On the one hand . . .	*. . . on the other*
The Environmental Protection Agency pushes hard for stringent air pollution controls.	The Energy Dept. pushes companies to switch from clean imported oil to dirtier coal.
The National Highway Traffic Safety Administration mandates weight-adding safety equipment for cars.	The Transportation Dept. insists on lighter vehicles to conserve gasoline.
The Justice Dept. offers guidance to companies on complying with the Foreign Corrupt Practices Act.	The Securities and Exchange Commission will not promise immunity from prosecution for practices Justice might permit.
The Environmental Protection Agency restricts use of pesticides.	The Agriculture Dept. promotes pesticides for agricultural and forestry uses.
The Energy Dept. tries to keep down rail rates for hauling coal, to encourage plant conversions.	The Transportation Dept. tries to keep coal rates high to bolster the ailing railroads.
The Occupational Health and Safety Administration wants guard rails along beef-killing operations to prevent worker falls.	The Agriculture Dept. says the guard rails are unsanitary because carcasses touch them.

plain, voters are usually forced to act through a legislator or president who represents a "bundle" of political goods and tax prices:

> The voter either gets the bundle of political goods offered by candidate A or the bundle offered by candidate B. Often, neither of these bundles of political goods represents what a specific consumer (voter) would like to have. The political consumer does not have the freedom to "shop around" buying some goods from any of several suppliers. He is forced to accept the bundle favored by the majority coalition.[39]

Moreover, most government services are financed from general funds, so citizens and their representatives are not presented proposals that directly link the government service with the tax to finance it. This use of general fund financing can create "fiscal illusions" on the part of voters that they are under- or over-taxed, leading to an over- or under-expansion of government operations.[40]

4. UNIFORM TREATMENT OF DIVERSE SITUATIONS

A corollary of the bundle problem is uniformity. The uniformity is partly due to a striving for equal treatment, but much more to the need for administrative simplicity. Thus the cars in tiny Paradise, California, must meet the same pollution standards as those in smoggy Los Angeles; wealthy people with salaries exceeding $100,000 must belong to Social Security just like low-paid toothpick packers; the 55 mph speed limit applies to the busy Washington, D.C. Beltway and to the desolate flatlands of west Texas; prohibitions against price

[39] Gwartney and Stroup, *op. cit.*, p. 445.

[40] Mueller, *op. cit.*, p. 90.

Figure 3–3.   Days Elapsed in Formal, on the Record Regulatory Proceedings (1975)

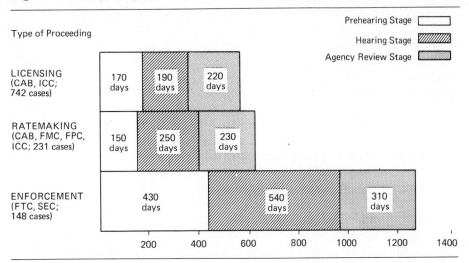

Source: U.S. Senate, Committee on Governmental Affairs, *Study on Federal Regulation,* Vol. IV, "Delay in the Regulatory Process," (July 1977), p. 6.

discrimination face Bruce's Juices with the same force as Campbell's Soup Company; the minimum wage law treats janitors and journeyman pipe-fitters alike; all wheat farmers get the same level of price support regardless of their size, cost per bushel, or location; no swimming pool slide may slip beneath the standards of the Consumer Product Safety Commission; and so on. As George Stigler quipped, "We ought to call him Uncle Same."[41]

C. Dynamic Problems (*Delay and Myopia*)

1. DELAYS AND INACTION

To some extent, delay is inevitable and even desirable in government actions. ("Haste makes . . .") There is a difference, however, between delay occasioned by prudent consideration and delay deriving from dalliance, inertia, confusion, inability, and laziness. There are no bene-

fits from such delay and the economic and human costs can be staggering.

Evidence of undue delay in the federal regulatory process is rampant.[42] A Senate committee's questionnaire survey of about a thousand lawyers who practice regularly before federal commissions revealed that, in their opinion, "undue delay" was by far the most important deficiency of federal regulation. Administrative law judges, who are key personnel inside regulatory agencies, were also surveyed by the committee. Sixty-seven per cent of the judges ranked "undue delay" as one of the top three problems of regulation. In still another survey, 96 per cent of the Federal Trade Commission's own attorneys admitted that cases were not "handled in a timely fashion."

What is the basis for these opinions? Figure 3–3 gives you some idea. The chart derives from

[41] Stigler, *op. cit.,* p. 38.

[42] The following samples come from U.S. Congress, Senate, Committee on Governmental Affairs, *Study on Federal Regulation,* Volume IV, "Delay in the Regulatory Process," (July 1977), pp. 1–25.

data on six regulatory agencies collected by the Administrative Conference of the United States. The data concerned cases that were actually referred to an administrative law judge for a hearing and that were concluded in 1975. Cases successfully terminated without hearing were thus excluded. As indicated, the regulatory process is less than swift. From beginning to end, licensing proceedings averaged more than 19 months duration, ratemaking cases typically took 21 months, and enforcement actions were strung out over three years.

It should be recognized that these statistics concern fairly *routine* matters. When new regulations pass Congress, implementation must start afresh, with calendar consumption indicated by the fact that it took six years—from initial legislation to ultimate specification—to get safety regulations for mechanical hazards like sharp edges and sharp points in children's toys. Indeed, it took a citizens' lawsuit against the government to pry the regulations loose.[43]

Inadequate agency resources, "due process" requirements, outside (industry) obstruction, personnel slowness, and designed-in checks and balances are among the major causes of delays. Moreover, many agencies suffer cumbersome organization structures and maze-like procedural sequences, as illustrated in Figure 3–4, which shows the organizational structure of how matters are handled in the Federal Trade Commission. In practice, most of the levels of FTC review pictured are not actually touched, or several are consolidated. Still, the chart gives the general idea.

Although there are no precise estimates of the costs of undue delay, they probably run into the billions. If, on the government's side, one assumed that one-twelfth of the regulatory time spent was wasted, the cost in 1976 dollars would be about $240 million annually. On the business side, the total cost of coping with regulation is estimated to range between $16 and $130 billion. Thus, if even a small fraction of this private cost is occasioned by undue delay, it alone would easily surpass the billion mark. All without redeeming benefits.

2. SHORT-RUN COST, LONG-RUN BENEFIT: INACTION

Voters and their political representatives tend to be shortsighted. The priorities on voters' selective apathy lists seem heavily influenced by immediacy. And elected officials seem to have time horizons limited to the next election. Therefore, government policies with high *short-run cost* as compared to amply off-setting *future benefits* tend to be unduly slighted, leading to inaction. The instincts of the political process are, in short, not generally geared to squirrelling away nuts against hard winters.

Gwartney and Stroup point out that this helps to explain why public action in areas like safety, energy, trade balance, environmental protection, and inflation is crisis-oriented—with little more than lip service being paid to problems until eleventh-hour efforts are spent. "Given the public sector bias against proposals with current costs but future benefits that are difficult to identify, the crisis phenomenon is understandable."[44]

3. SHORT-RUN BENEFIT, LONG-RUN COST: ACTION

When benefits are concentrated in the near-term and costs are concentrated in the distant-term, shortsightedness has the opposite effect—namely, hasty or excessive action. This deficiency is especially evident in the area of macroeconomic stability. The benefits of reduced unemployment and spritely prosperity can be obtained in the short run by expansive government policies like deficit spending and rapid money supply growth. But the long-run cost of these policies is inflation. Another example is direct wage-price control to check inflation.

[43] Ibid., pp. 17–19.

[44] Gwartney and Stroup, *op. cit.*, p. 447.

Figure 3-4. Flow Diagram—"How the FTC Operates"

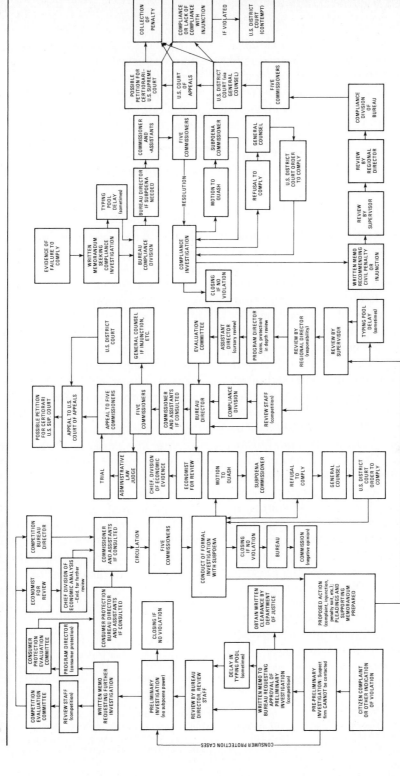

Source: U.S. Senate, Committee on Governmental Affairs, *Study of Federal Regulation*, Volume IV, "Delay in the Regulatory Process," 95th Congress, 1st session (1977), p. 3.

59

The short-run benefit of quick price stability is bought at the long-run cost of massive inefficiencies in product markets, dementing inequities in labor markets, and eventually, because of cheating, widespread disrespect for the law. In fact, "stabilization" policies that were not really stabilizing in the long run preceded the presidential elections of 1964, 1968, 1972, and 1976.

D. Other Ethical Criteria

It should by now be apparent that, in practice, government rarely bases its actions on careful benefit-cost analysis, that distribution neutrality in allocation decisions is never honored, that unanimity is never the voting rule, and that most of the other ideals based on economic criteria are rarely pursued. Apparently, real politics and sound economics seldom seem to match. To some unknown extent this is perhaps as it should be, for simple benefit-cost criteria must sometimes give way to other ethical considerations. As noted earlier, "rights" alone may often justify government regulation.

A related but different tack is that of Duncan MacRae, who argues that the economic ethic of preference satisfaction is often at odds with human welfare. To the extent this is true, and to the extent welfare is really what counts, it is wrong to criticize government for departing from the ethic of benefit-cost preference satisfaction. In defending his position MacRae points out that policies not conforming to existing preferences may in the end *change* those preferences for the better. Moreover, the general welfare might well be served if government considers the interests of persons affected but *not* represented in official chambers—i.e., children, future generations, disfranchised minorities, resident aliens, and foreigners.[45]

By these lights it may be comforting to know that empirical analyses of congressional voting behavior find ideology and noneconomic ethics playing a major role.[46] Economic interests alone are by no means the guide. Yet, we must of course be wary in condoning departures from preference satisfaction. Enlarging one's "rights" often shrinks another's. And not every regulation can be justified by rights. As for laws altering preferences, laws often fail to change society for the better, as Prohibition dramatically demonstrated. And some laws may even change society for the worse, as illustrated by the Jim Crow laws enforcing racial segregation.[47]

When it comes to business regulation, most of the government's deficiencies in this realm of ethics arise from conflicts and inconsistencies when one ethic is served at the inadvertent cost of another. For example, the Robinson-Patman Act serves a notion of "fairness" to small business but probably at the expense of "maintaining competition." For another example, environmental regulations further the amenity rights of people, but, as Table 3–6 shows, they do so at the expense of distributional equity. Through higher commodity prices, higher taxes, and other such effects, people in low income classes pay a substantially higher portion of their income for environmental improvement than those in high income brackets, a distribution of burden that runs contrary to estimates of who gains greatest benefit.

Government disregard for cost-effectiveness creates yet another brand of deficiency. Taking certain goals as given by noneconomic impera-

---

[45] Duncan MacRae, Jr., *The Social Function of Social Science* (New Haven, Conn.: Yale University Press, 1976), pp. 186–202.

[46] James B. Kau and Paul H. Rubin, "Self-Interest, Ideology and Logrolling in Congressional Voting," *Journal of Law & Economics* (October 1979), pp. 365–384. On the other hand see A. L. Danielsen and P. H. Rubin, "An Empirical Investigation of Voting on Energy Issues" *Public Choice* (Fall 1977), pp. 121–128; and Sharon M. Oster, "An Analysis of Some Causes of Interstate Differences in Consumer Regulations," *Economic Inquiry* (January 1980), pp. 39–54.

[47] C. Van Woodward, *The Strange Career of Jim Crow*, 2nd ed. (Oxford University Press, 1966).

Table 3–6.   Per Family Pollution Control Costs as a Percentage of Income (Average by Income Class)

| Income Class | Grand Total | Air Pollution | | Water Pollution* |
		Industry & Govt.	Automobile	
Less than $3,000	12.4%	3.4%	4.8%	4.2%
$ 3,000– 3,999	9.1	2.4	3.6	3.1
$ 4,000– 5,999	7.9	2.1	3.0	2.8
$ 6,000– 7,999	6.9	1.9	2.5	2.5
$ 8,000– 9,999	6.2	1.7	2.2	2.3
$10,000–11,999	5.8	1.6	2.0	2.2
$12,000–14,999	5.4	1.6	1.8	2.0
$15,000–19,999	5.0	1.4	1.6	2.0
$20,000–24,999	4.6	1.4	1.3	1.9
$25,000–plus	3.4	1.1	0.7	1.6

* Best practical technology standard excluding runoff.

Source: Leonard P. Gianessi and Henry M. Peskin, "The Distribution of the Costs of Federal Water Pollution Control Policy," *Land Economics* (February 1980), pp. 99–100.

tives, analysts have unearthed many instances where targets could be hit at substantially less cost—e.g., 40 to 50 per cent savings in pollution abatement on the Delaware River,[48] 25 to 40 per cent savings in meeting atmospheric sulfur-emission standards in St. Louis and Cleveland,[49] and 25 per cent savings in the costs of procuring weapon systems for the Department of Defense.[50] The upshot is that, even when judged by ethical criteria that may put government in a most favorable light, deficiencies can be discovered.

A Qualifying Reminder.   It may be argued that in some respects and in some instances,

the government's flaws may be a source of strength instead of weakness. If the state always moved swiftly and reflected every personal whim precisely, our society, as George Stigler says, "would become the victim of every fad in morals and every popular fallacy in philosophy."[51] If the state could overcome its proclivity toward uniformity of treatment, adapting all laws to minute individual circumstances, the result might well be capricious control, immense uncertainty, and inequitable favoritism. If the government always gave up easily, shedding its often annoying persistence, it might never have won World War II nor put a man on the moon. But of course these reflections merely underscore a point made earlier. Wisdom would have us relying on markets in some respects and government in others. Paradise is not to be found in either alone. Thus in the chapters remaining we shall explore blends and mixes, old ones actually observed and new ones wishfully sought.

[48] A. V. Kneese, S. E. Rolfe, and J. W. Harned, eds., *Managing the Environment: International Economic Cooperation for Pollution Control* (New York: Praeger Publishers, 1971), p. 272.

[49] T. H. Bingham and A. K. Miedema, Final Report, *Allocative and Distributive Effects of Alternative Air Quality Attainment Policies* (Research Triangle Park, N.C.: Research Triangle Institute, October 1974), pp. 54, 93.

[50] U.S. Senate, Committee on the Judiciary, Subcommittee on Antitrust and Monopoly, Hearings, *Competition in Defense Procurement* (1968), pp. 53–55.

[51] Stigler, *op. cit.,* p. 38.

Summary

This chapter ticks off characteristics of government in the ideal and real, using individual preferences as the main measuring rod. The political *process* requires (1) problem recognition through preference articulation, (2) policy formulation, entailing preference aggregation and legislation, (3) policy application, and (4) private sector compliance. Model attributes for each of these steps are outlined in Table 3–1. Among the most important are full participation, full information, and full employment in the first stage, plus proper selections of voting rules, policy focuses, and policy instruments in the second stage. The last stages are deftly handled if qualities like impartiality, consistency, efficiency, unobtrusiveness, clarity, and dependability are achieved.

As for results, ideal performance in allocation efficiency would square with benefit-cost: policies committing resources only when the added social benefits exceed the added social costs up to the point where costs equal benefits. Such, theoretically, is the golden rule of remedies for market "imperfections" and "failures." Widely accepted performance ideals for other policy objectives simply do not exist. Indeed, it has been argued that democratic determination of a clear, concise ideal criterion for equity is impossible. Thus we are left with such vague guides as "minimum sustenance" for the poor, "maintenance of competition" for its own sake, and "product safety" where hazards are particularly sneaky and dangerous.

When actual government is examined under the admittedly dim light of these ideals, we find blemishes abounding. As suggested in Table 3–4, government perpetuates misallocations of "too much" and "too little" owing to imperfections and failures. Monopoly and freedom from bankruptcy foster misguided persistence and inefficiency. Ignorance among voters and officials invites dead-end journeys. Special interest effects tip the balance of power in favor of those experiencing concentrated benefits or costs. Externalities of various kinds produce benefit-cost mismatches. And lumpiness in the electoral process and in the treatment of diverse individual circumstances often leads to crude, sometimes heavy-handed outcomes.

Delay and myopia create dynamic problems. Although some delay is good, undue delay is not. Lacking in benefits, its costs are huge. Myopia gives disproportionate weight to current as compared to future costs and benefits. When the costs are immediate and the benefits far off (as when we try to stop smoking), there is a tendency to postpone or even abandon action. A reverse sequence stimulates the opposite tendency of inducing action when abstinence is best (much as the costs of late night revelry appear only the next morning).

Finally, despite the ill-defined nature of ethical criteria other than allocation efficiency, deficiencies are discernible by such lights. Inconsistencies crop up when progress in one direction, like safety, entails regress in another, like equity. Furthermore, government fails tests of cost-effectiveness rather regularly.

Taking this and the last chapter together, we find defects in both markets and government. Society has no perfect servant. But tasks must nevertheless be assigned. The trick is to find what's right for the lazy butler and what's right for the awkward maid.

Questions and Exercises for Chapter 3

1. Compare and contrast the following particular match-ups of "ideal" and "real" government:
   a. Full participation in procedure (ideal) *versus* voter ignorance and selective apathy (real).

b. Efficient and expeditious instrument application (ideal) *versus* delays and inaction (real).

c. Cost-benefit performance (ideal) *versus* special interest effects and official ignorance (real).

d. Cost-benefit performance (ideal) *versus* short-run/long-run benefit-cost (real)

e. Minimum interference with private decision making (ideal) *versus* government as a monopolist (real).

f. Equity performance (ideal) *versus* special interest effects and distributional inequity in Table 3–6 (real).

2. Use your knowledge of benefit-cost as illustrated in Figure 3–2 (which cured the problem of Figure 2–9) to do a similar analysis curing the "external benefit" problem of Figure 2–8 with a subsidy.

3. Some pundits say that government performance should not be governed by Pareto (efficiency) criterion. Argue for and against this in light of this chapter's findings.

Chapter 4

Philosophical and Historical Background

History is philosophy learned from examples.
—Dionysius of Halicarnassus

Ponder the public debate on some current economic policy. What arguments bestir Congress and the press? Are words like "freedom," "fairness", and "justice" bandied about? Are historical lessons cited and precedents invoked? More than likely they are. Hence the purpose of this chapter is to provide this background.

We begin with economic philosophies. The full ideological spectrum ranges from right to left with positions that can be labeled Libertarian, Conservative, Moderate, Liberal, and Socialist. Libertarians advocate completely free markets, with virtually no government intervention whatever. Socialists advocate the extreme opposite—pervasive government intervention even to the point of doing away with private property. Neither of these extremes has much of a following in the United States, so we may ignore them. Most of the interesting action occurs on the Conservative-Moderate-Liberal portion of the spectrum. Here we find our leading politicians, economists, journalists, and businesspeople. For convenience and clarity we shall focus solely on Conservatives and Liberals. Moderates span the range in between,

so it will be easy for the reader to fill in the center by imagining blends of these two schools of thought.

These philosophies—Conservative and Liberal—differ in their value judgments, their views of capitalism, their assessments of government, and their mental outlooks. In turn, these differences decisively influence judgments on economic policy. So after surveying philosophical positions, we shall indicate where people of each persuasion stand on several major policy issues like antitrust and product safety. One sweeping generalization that emerges is easy to state at the outset: Conservatives typically place tremendous faith in free market capitalism, stressing its good points and down-playing its bad points. Their view of government runs in reverse. That is, government's flaws get close attention while its virtues tend to be neglected. Liberals hold contrary views. On the whole they tend to be more skeptical of markets and more favorable toward government intervention than Conservatives.

The last half of this chapter recounts historical foundations built over the past century. Two sweeping conclusions emerge from this backward glance. First, there is a general trend toward ever greater government intervention in the United States economy. Whereas laissez-faire (from the French "allow to do") characterized the economy ten decades ago, government regulation, supervision, subsidization, taxation, and intercession tatoo today's economy. Second, this tide toward greater government involvement did not swell steadily with time. Rather, it grew with alternating periods of spurt and pause, vacillating between eras of Liberalism and Conservatism, the first of which often floated on slogans like New Freedom, New Deal, and The Great Society.

I. Major Economic Philosophies

English economist Joan Robinson once said that an ideology is like an elephant—you cannot precisely define an elephant, but you know one when you see one. Thus Conservative and Liberal positions cannot be delineated with perfect clarity. Moreover, summarization imparts to each a misleading stiffness. Many Conservatives would disagree with any statement purporting to describe the representative "Conservative" position on a particular issue. The same could be said of Liberals. Even the use of these labels meets criticism. Many Conservatives prefer to be called "Liberals" because this designation stems from the Latin word meaning "free," and Conservatives elevate "freedom" to the very highest priority among value judgments. Conservatives also claim classical liberalism of the 18th and 19th centuries as their chief ideological heritage, so they lament "the corruption of the term liberalism" and register their "reluctance to surrender the term to proponents of measures that would destroy liberty."[1] Liberals counter by contending that modern Conservatives cannot commandeer the vocabulary of liberalism without committing the "Great Train Robbery of American intellectual history."[2]

Risky as the attempt may be, a summary of these philosophies is nevertheless quite pertinent.[3]

A. Conservative Beliefs

The Nature of Mankind. Anchoring the Conservative economic philosophy is a particular view of human nature, concisely captured in the name *Homo economicus,* or economic man. All men (and women) are believed to be (1) inherently materialistic, that is, filled with substantial "wants," "desires," and "preferences" for goods and services, and (2) completely rational in pursuing their own self-interest. The main implication of these notions is individualism. Satisfaction of individual wants is or should be the main objective of any social order, and individuals themselves are the best judges of the worth of those wants and the means of fulfilling them.

Value Judgments. As measured by their own words, Conservatives stress "freedom." Any conflict with other value judgments such as equality, security, or fairness is usually resolved in favor of freedom. Its prominence is conveyed by Milton Friedman, a leading spokesman for Conservatives and a Nobel laureate in economics, who writes, "As [Conserva-

---

[1] Milton Friedman, *Capitalism and Freedom* (Chicago: University of Chicago Press, 1962), p. 6.

[2] Clinton Rossiter, *Conservatism in America* (New York: Vintage Books, 1962), pp. 128–131; Mark A. Lutz and Kenneth Lux, *The Challenge of Humanistic Economics* (Menlo Park, Calif.: Benjamin/Cummings Publishing Co., 1979), pp. 27–29.

[3] For other surveys see Robert B. Carson, *Microeconomic Issues Today, Alternative Approaches* (New York: St. Martin's Press, 1980); Benjamin Ward, *The Ideal Worlds of Economics* (New York: Basic Books, 1979); Donald S. Watson, *Economic Policy: Business and Government* (Boston: Houghton Mifflin Co., 1960), Chapters 2, 3, and 4; Rossiter, *op. cit.,* Chapter 1.

tives], we take freedom of the individual, or perhaps the family, as our ultimate goal in judging social arrangements."[4]

When it comes to defining freedom, Conservatives usually mean freedom from government. Friedrich A. Hayek's book *Road to Serfdom* indicates this by its title and by its main theses: (1) that government intervention in the economy heralds socialism, (2) that freedom and democracy cannot exist under socialism, and (3) that therefore the trend toward government intervention should be abruptly reversed.[5]

The Conservative's precepts on "equality" follow from his views on freedom and human nature. The significant equality is equality of opportunity or equality of economic liberty, not equality of income or wealth or any other economic result. Men should be equal in their *right* to hold property and their *right* to enter contracts. But pressing equality much beyond this tramples freedom. Each individual must experience the consequences of his own behavior. As Clinton Rossiter puts it, "The drunkard belonged in the ditch, the lazy man in the poorhouse, the dullard in the shack, the hard-working man in the cottage, the hard-working and talented man in the mansion."[6]

Accordingly, the Conservative ideal of "justice" is *commutative* justice, which is income distribution according to an individual's effort, skill, property holdings, and work performance. This may be contrasted with *distributive* justice, which is distribution of income based on some notion of "need." Conservatives would care for crippled, insane, and otherwise helpless souls, but they would reject more generous notions of distributive justice.

Regard for Markets. Conservatives have great faith in the beneficence of free markets. How can the individualistic and materialistic instincts of man be controlled and coordinated to avoid chaos, to serve the maximum satisfaction of society? "The market or price system," they answer. According to a currently best-selling Conservative book:

> Adam Smith's flash of genius was his recognition that the prices that emerged from voluntary transactions between buyers and sellers—for short, the free market—could coordinate the activity of millions of people each seeking his own interest, in such a way as to make everyone better off. It was a startling idea then, and it remains one today, that economic order can emerge as the unintended consequence of the actions of many people, each seeking his own interest.
>
> The price system works so well, so efficiently, that we are not aware of it most of the time.[7]

Most conservatives are careful to qualify their faith by specifying that *competitive* markets, not just any markets, are the ones required, because competition provides *alternatives* for consumers and employees (and for merchants and employers as well). There is, then, freedom to choose. No one is pushed into deals. Competition protects consumers and employees from coercion. Henry Simons may have said it best over thirty years ago: "*the great enemy of democracy is monopoly, in all its forms.*"[8]

None of the free market's trappings cause Conservatives to flinch in their faith. Advertising, for instance, is praised by many Conserva-

[4] Friedman, *op. cit.*, p. 12.

[5] Friedrich A. Hayek, *The Road to Serfdom*, (Chicago: University of Chicago Press, 1944). Alternatively, freedom is defined as the availability of choice, and conservatives assume that individuals always prefer a choice to a lack of choice. Gordon Tullock, *The Logic of the Law* (New York: Basic Books, 1971). The problem with this is that people often prefer a lack of choice and call upon the government to implement restrictions of such "freedom." Would you favor giving people the choice of driving on the left or right hand side of the street, whichever they fancy, whenever they travel?

[6] Rossiter, *op. cit.*, p. 132.

[7] Milton Friedman and Rose Friedman, *Free to Choose* (New York: Harcourt Brace Jovanovich, 1980), pp. 13–14.

[8] Henry C. Simons, *Economic Policy for a Free Society* (Chicago: University of Chicago Press, 1948), p. 43 (emphasis in original).

tives as an unmitigated blessing, informing consumers rather than persuading them, gently guiding consumers to their best buys rather than manipulating them.[9] Thus, consumer sovereignty and rationality reign supreme. The free market is said to register consumer preferences with commendable accuracy.

Regard for Government. If the free market is the Conservative's delight, government is his despair. His mention of government is often coupled with allusions to despotism or tyranny. To quote Friedman again:

> Fundamentally, there are only two ways of coordinating the economic activities of millions. One is central direction involving the use of coercion—the technique of the army and of the modern totalitarian state. The other is voluntary cooperation of individuals—the technique of the market place.[10]

Government not only endangers individual freedom, its efforts rarely improve economic conditions. Rather, its efforts, however well-intended, usually make matters worse. Minimum wage laws throw people out of work. Monetary policy destabilizes the economy. Drug regulation on the whole creates more costs than benefits. And so on. Thus, the Conservative's distaste for government rests on more than moral or ethical sensitivities. It rests on perceived impracticalities.

Accordingly, the Conservative's ideal constitution for government action is short. "That government is best which governs least," could be their motto. Even so, they are not anarchists. They prescribe government action for:[11]

1. Prevention of coercion or violence by individuals.

2. Provision for defense from foreign attack.
3. Enforcement of property rights and legal contracts.
4. Regulation of the monetary system in a conservative manner.
5. Provision of certain public goods like highways, sewers, and city parks.
6. Assurance of some minimal degree of security and care for cripples, the mentally retarded, orphans, and old folks.

Beyond these matters, Conservatives are divided. Some condone government intervention to assuage external costs like pollution (as long as the "benefits" exceed the "costs"), while others seem to believe that the free market is so efficient that external costs do not distort market results very seriously at all.[12] Some endorse and others oppose safety regulation. Perhaps the most curious area of disagreement concerns antitrust and public utility regulation. Conservatives of yesteryear, sticking to the logic that only competitive markets produce the glories of freedom, efficiency, fairness, and so forth, argued for (1) vigorous antitrust policies to combat private restraints of trade and artificial monopoly, plus (2) government regulation or ownership of natural monopoly.[13] More recently, however, Conservatives have become anti-anti-

---

[9] Dean A. Worcester, Jr., *Welfare Gains from Advertising: The Problem of Regulation* (Washington, D.C.: American Enterprise Institute, 1978).

[10] *Capitalism and Freedom*, Milton Friedman, p. 13.

[11] Ibid., pp. 22–36; Friedman and Friedman, *op. cit.*, pp. 27–33; Simons, *op. cit.*, pp. 40–77.

[12] Ronald Coase, "The Problem of Social Cost," *Journal of Law and Economics* (October 1969), pp. 1–44. This position has since come under withering attack from nonconservatives. See, e.g., H. H. Liebhafsky, "The Problem of Social Cost—An Alternative Approach," *Natural Resources Journal* (1973), pp. 615–76; S. Todd Lowry, "Bargain and Contract Theory in Law and Economics," in W. J. Samuels (ed.) *The Chicago School of Political Economy* (East Lansing: Michigan State University Graduate School of Business Administration, Division of Research, 1976), pp. 215–36; Mark Kelman, "Consumption Theory, Production Theory, and Ideology in the Coase Theorem," *Southern California Law Review* (March 1979), pp. 669–98.

[13] Simons, *op. cit.*, pp. 40–62, 81–83, 107–120; George J. Stigler, "The Case Against Big Business," *Fortune* (May 1952), pp. 123–127; Stigler, "Mergers and Preventive Antitrust Policy," *University of Pennsylvania Law Review* (November 1955), pp. 176–184.

trust,[14] and they tend to doubt that public utility regulation or state ownership of natural monopolies is either necessary or wise.[15]

Explaining this switch to accommodation and approval of big business is not easy, but there seem to be three main reasons.[16] First, Conservatives now make the empirical judgment that monopoly power is rare or nonexistent, so there is in their view no "real" problem at all. Despite oligopolistic and monopolistic dominance of many major U.S. industries (telephones, autos, drugs, petroleum, soft drinks, detergents, and so forth), Conservatives find competition everywhere—in interindustry rivalry, in dynamic change over time, in the fragility of cartels, in low barriers to entry, in countervailing power, and in international trade. Second, for instances where monopoly power cannot be dismissed as illusory, modern Conservatives claim to find a great deal of goodness in big business—efficiency and progressiveness, in particular. Indeed, many Conservatives set freedom, decentralization, and other individualistic goals aside at this point to argue that the main aim of antitrust should be "economic efficiency." This leads to the result that nonconservatives are now the main defenders of antitrust on grounds of liberty.[17] Finally, to the extent Conservatives admit that monopoly *does* exist and *is* undesirable, many still do not brook. Here they face a choice between two evils—government and big business—and many of them choose big business as the lesser of the two. This choice is not surprising, given the Conservatives' strong skepticism of officialdom.

Frame of Mind. Among many Conservatives, defense of laissez-faire capitalism and steadfast opposition to government intervention border on the dogmatic. Conservatives of the past have contended that their's is the only philosophy conforming to the "laws" of nature, religion, economics, sociology, and morality.[18] Social Darwinism was one such Conservative doctrine (advocating "survival of the fittest," economically and socially, as absolutely essential).[19] Most modern Conservatives have dropped references to religion, natural science, and Truth with a capital "T", but they often argue that their position is free of value judgments. Some strain to bolster their authority with favorable interpretations of anthropological evidence, and still others seek to explain every aspect of life in terms of economic rationality.[20] In these several ways and others, Conservatives, especially those on the extreme right, evince doctrinaire inclinations.

[14] For recent Stigler see *Report of Nixon's Task Force on Productivity and Competition* (February 18, 1969), reprinted in *The Journal of Reprints for Antitrust Law and Economics* (Winter 1969), pp. 827–881. Robert H. Bork, *The Antitrust Paradox: A Policy at War with Itself* (New York: Basic Books, 1978).

[15] Friedman, *op. cit.*, p. 28; Harold Demsetz, "Why Regulate Utilities?" *Journal of Law and Economics* (April 1968), pp. 55–66.

[16] Friedman, *op. cit.*, pp. 119–32; John S. McGee, *In Defense of Industrial Concentration* (New York: Praeger Publishers, 1971); Yale Brozen (ed.), *The Competitive Economy* (Morristown, N.J.: General Learning Press, 1975); Robert H. Bork and Ward S. Bowman, Jr., "The Crisis in Antitrust," *Columbia Law Review* (March 1965), pp. 363–375.

[17] Harlan M. Blake and William K. Jones, "In Defense of Antitrust," *Columbia Law Review* (March 1965), pp. 377–399; Robert Pitofsky, "The Political Content of Antitrust," *University of Pennsylvania Law Review* (April 1979), pp. 1051–1081.

[18] Eric F. Goldman, *Rendevous with Destiny* (New York: Vintage Books, 1956) Chapter 5.

[19] Richard Hofstadter, *Social Darwinism in American Thought* (Boston: Beacon Press, 1955).

[20] Eirik Furubotn and Svetozar Pejovich (eds.) *The Economics of Property Rights* (Cambridge, Mass.: Ballinger Publishing Co., 1974); Gary Becker, Elizabeth Landes, and Robert Michael, "An Economic Analysis of Marital Instability," *Journal of Political Economy* (December 1977), pp. 1141–87; William M. Landes, "An Economic Study of U.S. Aircraft Hijacking, 1961–1976," *Journal of Law and Economics* (April 1978), pp. 1–31; Richard A. Posner, "A Theory of Primitive Society, With Special Reference to Law," *Journal of Law and Economics* (April 1980), pp. 1–53. For a critical analysis of the first of these see A. A. Schmid in *The Chicago School of Political Economy, op. cit.*, and for an interesting contrast to the last item read Calvin Martin, *Keepers of the Game* (Berkeley: University of California Press, 1978).

Extent of Popularity. Though apparently a minority, Conservatives constitute a *very* strong and influential minority in our society. The affinity of businessmen for the Conservative position is widely known and readily understandable, an affinity which is affirmed through advertising campaigns touting the benefits of free-enterprise capitalism, through substantial financial support for Conservative political candidates, and through extensive lobbying to erode government controls. In politics, there are numerous prominent and potent standard bearers for the Conservative cause—Barry Goldwater, Orrin Hatch, Jack Kemp, Robert Dole, Strom Thurmond, and Ronald Reagan, to name just a few. Among academics, Milton Friedman is undoubtedly the most widely known Conservative, what with his best-selling books, his *Newsweek* column, and his frequent appearances on T.V. In addition, the departments of economics and business at several major universities could be considered bastions of Conservative thought—the University of Chicago, UCLA, and Virginia Polytechnic and State University, in particular. Conservatism, in short, is quite popular.

B. Liberal Philosophy

Frame of Mind. The Liberal's philosophy cannot be characterized as clearly as the Conservative's, in part because Liberals seem to be less philosophical. In general, however, Liberalism stands for positive and active government intervention in economic affairs, but not to the extent advocated by Socialists (or Communists). Words often associated with the Liberal stance are welfare state, mixed capitalism, progressivism, regulated capitalism, and reformism.

One particularly distinguishing characteristic of a Liberal is his pragmatism. Whereas many Conservatives often follow their ideologies dogmatically, Liberals display flexibility.

That is to say, Liberals usually measure ideas and policies by the cogency with which they address problems and by the results obtained. Their thinking is *ad hoc;* their method, trial-and-error. During the Great Depression, for instance, Franklin D. Roosevelt was willing to try *anything that might work* to lift the country out of its misery. "Above all," he snorted, "try something." In the early days of the New Deal this included a suspension of the antitrust laws and sweeping cartelization of industry under the National Recovery Administration. Later, after failure with that tack, he tried the opposite by reinstating the antitrust laws and pressing their enforcement with greater vigor than America has seen before or since.[21] More recent times have witnessed extensive *de*regulation in energy, finance, transportation, and communication, all spearheaded by such Liberals as Jimmy Carter and Ted Kennedy, despite the Liberal origins of those regulations in the first place. In legal circles, pragmatism also goes by names like "instrumentalism" and "sociological jurisprudence."

The Nature of Mankind. Liberals reject *Homo economicus* for his unrealistically cold and calculating manner. Their view of man makes room for "needs," for "cooperation," and for "fallibility." To quote John Maynard Keynes:

The world is *not* so governed from above that private and social interest always coincide. It is *not* a correct deduction from the Principles of Economics that enlightened self-interest always operates in the public interest. Nor is it true that self-interest generally *is* enlightened; more often individuals acting separately to promote their own ends are too ignorant or too weak to attain even these. Experience does *not* show that individuals, when they make up a social unit, are al-

[21] E. W. Hawley, *The New Deal and the Problem of Monopoly* (Princeton, N.J.: Princeton University Press, 1966).

ways less clear-sighted than when they act separately.[22]

Moreover, Liberals are less eager than most Conservatives to use materialistic human pleasure as the measure of all things. Liberals therefore seem more willing to grant rights of painless slaughter to animals even though such may be "uneconomic," and to extend rights of preservation to trees even though the "benefits" to a human minority may not exceed the "costs" to the majority.

Value Judgments. Liberals ardently defend freedom, even the freedom to do foolish things. But they define freedom as Nobel laureate Paul Samuelson does, to permit substantial government intervention:

> I must raise some questions about the notion that absence of government means increase in "freedom". Is freedom simply a quantifiable magnitude, as much [Conservative] discussion seems to presume? Traffic lights coerce me and limit my freedom. Yet in the midst of a traffic jam on the unopen road, was I really "free" before there were lights? And has the algebraic total of freedom, for me or the representative motorist or the group as a whole, been increased or decreased by the introduction of well-engineered stop lights? Stop lights, you know, are also go lights.[23]

To Liberals, freedom thus includes freedom from oppressively long work hours, stock fraud, stiffling pollution, and seriously hazardous products. Similarly, Liberals more readily accept government intervention to further equality than do Conservatives.

Regard for Market. Like Conservatives, Liberals hold the free-market (and private property) in high regard. They admire its potentials for efficiency, fairness, flexibility, prosperity, and progress. Even so, Liberals readily find market flaws—the imperfections, failures, and ethical deficiencies outlined two chapters ago. Liberal politicians recognize these flaws not so much from the theories of economists or the polemics of leftist ideologues, but from real world observation and historical experience as illuminated by their value judgments. Thus, if the market system generates unemployment of 25%, something is wrong. If it produces cars that unnecessarily kill and maim, something is wrong. If it fosters false advertising, something is wrong. And since the market system is neither sacred nor shielded by categorical rights, Liberals are quite willing to tinker with possible governmental remedies.

Regard for Government. As Liberals see it, government can *strengthen* the operation of market forces where they produce desirable results. Antitrust and consumer information policies, both of which improve market structures, illustrate this approach. In addition, government can *modify* market forces or *overturn* them where the results are deemed undesirable. Direct regulation of auto safety and provision of sewage treatment exemplify this approach. Underlying either approach are two Liberal tenets regarding government:[24]

> The first is that in a capitalist democracy it is possible to separate political affairs from the dominance of economic power, and that the actions of the government can thus be made to reflect the interest of the people.
>
> The second is that the government has expanded its role in the economy in the last few decades in order to fulfill those needs of society that the private sector could not or would not.

---

[22] John M. Keynes, "The End of Laissez Faire," in *Essays in Persuasion* (New York: Norton, 1963), p. 312. (emphasis in original)

[23] Paul Samuelson, "Personal Freedoms and Economic Freedoms in the Mixed Economy," in E. F. Cheit (ed.), *The Business Establishment* (New York: John Wiley & Sons, 1964), pp. 218–219. For elaboration see Karl Polanyi, *The Great Transformation* (Boston: Beacon Press, 1957), pp. 249–258.

[24] Richard Romano and Melvin Leiman, *Views on Capitalism*, 2nd Edition (Beverly Hills: Glencoe Press, 1975), p. 142.

The thrust for growth in the public sector thus emanates from the demands of a general population living in a changing social and economic climate.

Many Liberals seem to think the government can do anything. Still, most Liberals have developed, especially in recent years, an appreciation for government's blemishes. Their attitude is reflected in Winston Churchill's remark that democracy appears to be the worst form of government until one considers the alternatives. Balance is best; experimentation, permissible. "Dogmatic absolutes being thus ruled out," Paul Samuelson explains, "democratic society is left in the position of pragmatically attempting to choose among partial evils so as to preserve as much as possible of human liberties and freedoms."[25]

Extent of Popularity. Given current tendencies of many people to drift to the right, statements concerning Liberalism's popularity may be imminently perishable. Assuming a broad definition, however, this camp has a wide following, or at least it did in the recent past. Even the Conservative business community often displays more than a tincture of Liberalism. A 1980 Conference Board survey found that the three hundred executives it polled accepted the underlying need for "virtually every" federal regulatory program then on the books. Their complaints did not attack principle, but rather castigated execution: "the regulatory system as a whole is poorly managed and marred by jurisdictional overlaps and conflicts, duplicative or overly detailed reporting requirements, and lengthy delays in setting standards and issuing rules and permits."[26]

[25] Samuelson, *op. cit.*, p. 224.
[26] *Business Week,* June 30, 1980, p. 67. Accepting this criticism the Liberal Carter administration established a Regulatory Council to improve the management of 18 federal agencies, requiring them, among other things, to make economic analyses or major regulations. Results were mixed.

II. Specific Policy Positions

What emerges from the foregoing may seem paradoxical. In ultimate *objective,* both philosophies profess a deep concern for the interests and welfare of the people. Neither philosophy, except perhaps in its most extreme variations, openly advocates harsh treatment of some folks to pry loose benefits for others. What, then, separates them? Mainly two things it seems. The first is different *definitions* of what comprises "interests" and "welfare." In the Conservative's ideal world, for instance, the "freedom" of the disadvantaged outweighs their poverty, or loss to fraud, or other injury. The second is different institutional *mechanics.* To Conservatives, only capitalist, free-enterprise markets register people's preferences accurately, and any argument to the contrary must bear a heavy burden of proof that the market blunders. To Liberals, capitalistic markets are usually the best template for reflecting people's preferences, but democratic government can likewise be responsive, so there is ample room for tampering to improve or supplant the market.

When these differences in the abstract are reduced to differences in the concrete, we find an array of varied positions on specific policies. Table 4–1 puts these in a nutshell at some risk of misrepresentation by oversimplification. Once again it must be stressed that a continuum bridges these schools of thought. Clustering tends to draw caricatures. Still, as items 1 and 4 of Table 4–1 suggest, modern Conservatives take the monopoly problem lightly (for reasons mentioned earlier), while Liberals staunchly support antitrust enforcement where competition is deemed possible and advocate public utility regulation where natural monopoly prevails.

Multinational corporations (or MNCs) like IBM, Exxon, GE, and Coca Cola, span the globe, dominating foreign markets to a degree that

Table 4–1. Some Comparisons Between Economic Philosophies on Major Policy Issues

Issues	Conservative	Liberal
1. Monopoly and Restraint of Trade	1. No serious problem—should relax antitrust laws	1. Serious problem; enforce and maybe strengthen antitrust laws
2. Multinational Corporations	2. MNCs beneficial; no policy	2. Surveillance and moderate control justified
3. Consumer Fraud, Misrepresentation	3. Competition protects consumers; little need for policy	3. Information disclosure plus ban on fraud
4. Public Utility Regulation	4. Remove or reduce all such regulation	4. Appropriate for natural monopoly situations
5. Energy Shortage	5. Abandon all government intervention	5. Tax excess profits and subsidize new resource development
6. Inflation	6. Fixed and limited rate of money supply expansion	6. Money restraint plus limited wage–price control or procompetition policy
7. Product Safety	7. Information disclosure alone	7. Product regulation and information disclosure
8. Labor Safety	8. Liability law and competition protect workers	8. Some regulation needed, especially for health, workmen's compensation, and child labor
9. Environmental Protection	9. Limited tax inducements at most	9. Tax inducements plus regulation and subsidy
10. Agriculture	10. Free market	10. Some say free market; others, price or income supports

often matches or exceeds their dominance at home. They therefore occupy a branch of the monopoly problem, and generate divergent reactions among philosophical schools. Conservatives look favorably upon MNCs, arguing that they promote efficient allocations of the world's resources; benefit poor nations with transfers of technology and capital; stimulate U.S. exports; and develop the export potentials of backward areas. Liberals appreciate these pluses to some degree, but they are also skeptical. They argue that MNCs can use their power and international flexibility to undermine the national interests of the U.S. and other countries, especially others of weak and less-developed stature. Among the tricks MNCs have up their sleeves, "transfer" pricing, cartelization, bribery, and extraction of "unfair" terms in technology agreements are the most frequently denounced. Accordingly, Liberals tend to support a "code of ethics" for MNCs, with surveillance and some degree of enforcement.

As for protecting consumers from unsafe products, Conservatives argue that the free market shields consumers by keeping hazardous mistakes "on a small scale" and by allowing consumers to "experiment for themselves, decide what features they like and what features they do not like."[27] Government should keep out of the marketplace because, "If it is appropriate for the government to protect us from using dangerous bicycles and cap guns, the logic calls for prohibiting still more dangerous activities such as hang-gliding, motorcycling, and skiing."[28] Information disclosures are tolerated to a limited degree: "Insofar as the government has information not generally available about the merits or demerits of the items we ingest or activities we engage in, let it give us the information. But let it leave us free to choose what chances we want to take with our own lives."[29] The Conservative's faith in the market extends to working conditions, where the "most reliable and effective protection for most workers is provided by the existence of many employers" competing for the employee's services.[30] Even policies that Conservatives admit may "have had a favorable effect on conditions of work . . . like workmen's compensation and child labor laws," are needless policies because their achievements would have been attained by the market anyway, given that they "simply embodied in law practices that had already become common in the private market,

perhaps extending them somewhat to fringe areas."[31] To stem pollution, some Conservatives concede a need for emission taxes, but only cautiously and reluctantly, urging that the "imperfect market may, after all, do as well or better than the imperfect government."[32]

Liberals disagree. They sanction direct regulation, taxation, information disclosure, and related policies to correct the market's imperfections and failures. Moreover, they applaud most of the results:

Many of the protections instituted by these programs have been so successful that the security they provide is taken for granted: pasteurization, meat and poultry inspection, control of patent medicines are among the classical examples of success. Also, we rarely acknowledge the excellent Federal performance in such areas as aviation safety or drug testing requirements or highway safety. CPSC Commissioner Pittle has recently outlined some of the benefits from those and similar programs which include: a 40-per cent reduction in ingestions of poisons by children over a 4-year period, due to safety packaging requirements; a decrease of 45 per cent in the number of crib deaths, since the safety standards for cribs became effective in 1974; the saving of some 28,000 lives between 1966 and 1974 as well as a substantial reduction in serious injuries, because of Federal motor vehicle safety regulations; and what appears to be a complete elimination of flame-burn injuries involved in children's sleepwear, as a result of Government standards for that clothing.[33]

Liberals admit that the government can occasionally go too far in these areas, but trust the democratic process to correct large errors, as happened when Congress and the FDA bowed to public demands that saccharin, a pop-

[27] Milton Friedman and Rose Friedman, *op. cit.*, p. 212.
[28] Ibid., p. 227.
[29] Ibid., p. 227.
[30] Ibid., p. 246.

[31] Ibid., p. 243.
[32] Ibid., p. 218.
[33] Michael W. Klass and Leonard W. Weiss, *Study on Federal Regulation* Vol. VI, *Framework for Regulation*, U.S. Senate, Committee on Governmental Affairs, (1978), p. 34.

ular but carcinogenic artificial sweetener, not be banned.

On the energy front, Conservatives blame past problems on erroneous, ill-conceived, and unjustified government policy, price controls in particular. The Conservatives' favored approach is, in this light, no mystery. Liberals, on the other hand, point an accusing finger at OPEC and other lumps of monopoly power. Moreover, their concern for equity leads them to decry the massive shift of riches from energy consumers to energy producers that would result from a complete conversion to laissez-faire in this area. They therefore support the excess profits tax that now accompanies decontrol of petroleum prices, and they urge that the proceeds be funneled into the development of new energy resources as well as into relief for impoverished energy consumers.[34]

On inflation, Conservatives call for strict money supply constraint and balanced federal budgets. Liberals likewise recognize the importance of monetary and fiscal stringency, but their knees tend to weaken when given the opportunity to put their monetary-fiscal policies where their collective mouth is because they fear that stringency alone would produce terrible side effects on employment. Many Liberals thus advocate a multipronged attack in which the monetary-fiscal prong is flanked by one or more complementary policies—such as temporary wage-price control, a tax-based income policy, or sweeping procompetition policies for labor and business—in order to achieve less inflation without markedly augmenting unemployment.

Finally, among politicians, different positions in farm policy arise mainly from geography not philosophy, with many Conservative southerners and midwesterners betraying their ideology by backing government aid to agriculture.

Speaking very generally, however, Liberals have been the chief architects of crop insurance, price supports, income subsidies, and related farm supports, whereas Conservatives have criticized such policies.

III. Historical Roots

A. The Sweeping View

However tantalizing or compelling philosophical arguments may be, they serve mainly as stage props, adding color to the unfolding drama of economic, political, and social history. Contributing to policies more greatly than ideological tracts are wars, depressions, financial panics, technological revolutions, and sundry other events. What makes no sense philosophically or economically often makes good sense historically.

A two word summary of the steps government intervention has taken would be simply "ever more." In *level of authority* the march of policy in any area usually began at the local or state level and then proceeded to the national and occasionally even the international level. Public utility regulation, for instance, started in Colonial times with local controls over inns, ferries, roads, and bridges; advanced during the late eighteen and early nineteen hundreds to surveillance of railroads, grain elevators, and other businesses "affected with a public interest;" only to wind up with federal public utility regulation of interstate dealings in transportation, communications, and energy. Environmental protection policy followed a similar course. Local ordinances concerning sewage treatment, garbage disposal and trash burning came first. State authorities eventually added their clout, as most notably illustrated by California's early steps during the 1950s and 1960s to limit automobile pollution. Finally, federal environmental intervention blossomed prodigiously in the early 1970s.

---

[34] Robert Stobaugh and Daniel Yergin (eds.), *Energy Future* (New York: Random House, 1979).

History's expanding government interference is also indicated by *scope of industrial coverage*. Starting in the republic's earliest times with controls or franchises for harbors, ports, canals, highways, and bridges, the government's attention thereafter broadened to encompass railroading, drug manufacturing, food processing, banking, agriculture, barbering, undertaking, physician's services, plumbing, and telecommunications. Controls over electric utilities, radio broadcasters, truckers, oil producers, oystermen, retailers, wholesalers, jobbers, distillers, insurers, stock brokers, and chiropractors followed. Spread has progressed within old agencies, such as the Texas Railroad Commission's branching out to regulate oil and gas production. Further, the spread for any one problem, such as product safety, often ripples outward from a few items to so many that new government agencies have to be created to police them all. Federal product safety regulation began with foods, drugs, and cosmetics (FDA, 1906, 1938); stretched to flammable fabrics and toxic substances (FTC, 1954, and FDA, 1960, but since shifted to CPSC); then reached autos, motorcycles, and related equipment (NHTSA, 1966); swamped boats (Coast Guard, 1971); and finally culminated with coverage of virtually every other consumer product on the market (CPSC, 1972). Indeed, an important hallmark of much recent regulation—environmental protection, equal employment opportunity, and job safety as well as product safety—has been its ubiquitous compass.

As for *types or tools of intervention*, U.S. history begins with (1) protective measures, such as tariffs, patents, and exclusive franchises; progresses to (2) subsidies and land grants to encourage agricultural settlement, railroad expansion, agricultural education, and other pioneering endeavors; introduces (3) public utility regulation during the last century; moves shortly thereafter into (4) antitrust policy with the Sherman Act of 1890; branches into (5) conservation under the prodding of Theodore Roosevelt; takes up (6) product safety and job safety, beginning in limited areas like food and drugs for consumers and mining for workers; unveils (7) prohibitions against unfair practices and misrepresentation with the FTC Act of 1914 and Wheeler-Lea Act of 1938; presses (8) bank and finance supervision beginning with the Federal Reserve Act of 1913, the Federal Home Loan Bank Act of 1932, and the Securities Act of 1933; undertakes (9) product labeling and information disclosure; covers (10) oil production control; introduces (11) equal opportunity in employment, housing, and consumer credit; steps into (12) regulation for environmental protection; and so on.

This sweep toward "ever more" might be best appreciated when quantified. Figure 4–1

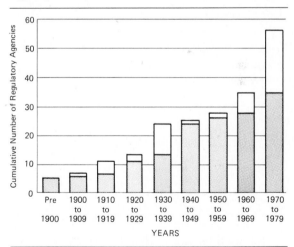

Figure 4–1. A Historical Perspective to Federal Agency Growth

Source: Center for the Study of American Business, *Directory of Federal Regulatory Agencies* (St. Louis: Washington University, 1980 edition), p. 2.

Note: Agencies do not total 57 functions between two or more spin-off agencies. The date that the parent organization was established was used to create the chart.

depicts the expansion in raw numbers of federal regulatory agencies. At the outset, in 1900, only six regulatory agencies graced the federal bureaucracy. By the end of 1979, nearly sixty agencies could be counted, a ten-fold increase. Decades of particularly rapid multiplication, as indicated by the white segments showing agency additions, were 1910 to 1919, 1930 to 1939, 1960 to 1969, and 1970 to 1979. Other decades were sleepy by comparison.

Alternatively, Figure 4–2 depicts the mush-rooming growth of federal intervention by showing the number of major regulatory laws passed by Congress during each decade of this century. Of the two subcategories of legislation specified, "economic legislation" refers to laws governing price policies, mergers, monopolization, imports, finance, agriculture, transportation, and the like. "Social legislation," on the other hand, refers to forms of business regulation that are designed to improve social conditions, such as to gain clean air and water, safety

Figure 4–2.   A Decade by Decade Comparison of Major Regulatory Legislation

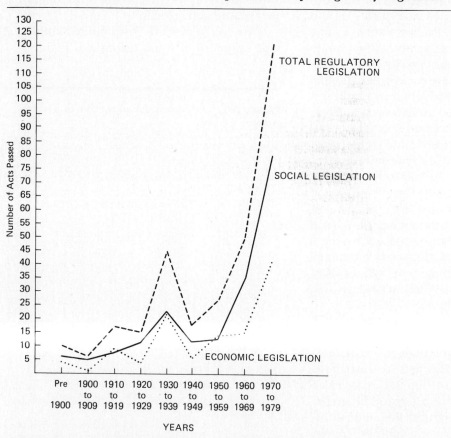

Source: Center for the Study of American Business, *Directory of Federal Regulatory Agencies* (St. Louis: Washington University, 1980 edition), p. 5.

of consumers and workers, equal employment opportunity, and highway beautification. Looking first at the combined total, we once again see a ten-fold multiplication—from ten items of legislation to well over a hundred—punctuated by the same decades of especially feverish activity: the 1910s, 1930s, 1960s, and 1970s. Looking next at each subcategory, we see that during most of this century the total was divided fairly evenly between economic and social legislation. But during the last two decades social legislation has outstripped economic legislation by a mile.

Lest it appear that these statistics give an exaggerated impression of government's burgeoning growth, alternate yardsticks could be wielded. Taking all levels of government together—federal, state, and local—expenditures for activities other than national defense, poverty relief, and social security rose from 6.7 per cent of the gross national product in 1902 to 16.6 per cent in 1940. After holding fairly steady at 16% until the early 1960s, these expenditures then leaped to more than 20 per cent of GNP by the late 1970s. This three-fold awakening is matched by trends in federal government nonmilitary employment as a percentage of the civilian labor force, which moved upward from 0.8% in 1901 to 1.7% in 1939, to 2.7% in 1979.

The foregoing measures relate only to the government's side of the ledger. They do not reflect the cost burdens shouldered by businesses attempting to comply with all the rules and regulations. Unfortunately, data on compliance costs are not available for the distant past, and recent data are at best sketchy. We therefore have no solid information on trends or present weight of private burdens. Still, Murray Weidenbaum has estimated that, in general, private sector compliance costs tend to be about 20 times the amount spent by the federal government to operate its regulatory agencies. Applying his multiplier of 20 to projected government expenditures for fiscal 1979, Weiden-

baum calculated that "the aggregate cost of government regulation may come to $102.7 billion, consisting of $4.8 billion of direct expenses by the Federal regulatory agencies and $97.9 billion of costs of compliance on the part of the private sector."[35] Less comprehensively but more carefully, the accounting firm of Arthur Anderson & Company studied the costs incurred by 48 major companies to comply with the regulations of six federal agencies in 1977. Largely because of environmental protection, the costs came to $2.6 billion, a tidy sum compared to the companies' net income after taxes of $16.6 billion, or their total capital expenditures of $25.8 billion.[36] Addressing the issue from yet a different angle, Robert Crandall has estimated that the consumer price index would have been roughly one per cent lower in 1977 if government regulatory intervention had not been as prevalent as it was.[37]

B. 1877–1920: Concentration and Progressivism

It all started, at least its modern headwaters started, just about one hundred years ago. Depression haunted the 1870s. The 1880s then brought prosperity, but they also brought giantism to commerce:

> During the Eighties huge corporations kept rising like so many portents of a Europeanized future. In the decade after the depression more than five thousand firms were wrought into giant combines, virtually all of which were pushing to-

[35] Murray Weidenbaum, *The Costs of Government Regulation of Business,* Study for the Subcommittee on Economic Growth and Stabilization of the Joint Economic Committee, U.S. Congress (1978), p. 4.

[36] Arthur Anderson & Co., *Cost of Government Regulation Study* (Washington, D.C.: The Business Roundtable, 1979), p. 14.

[37] Robert W. Crandall, "Federal Government Initiatives to Reduce the Price Level," *Brookings Papers on Economic Activity* (No. 2, 1978), pp. 401–440.

ward monopolies in their fields. At the end of the decade United States Senator John Sherman, whose basic friendliness to business could not be questioned, spoke the worry of a good many of his countrymen. "If we are unable or unwilling [to take action against the trusts]," Sherman told the Senate, "there will soon be a trust for every production and a master to fix the price of every necessity of life."[38]

Action was taken, timorous and ineffectual action at first, but action that set the pattern for government control up to this day. In 1877 the U.S. Supreme Court ruled in *Munn* v. *Illinois* that the Illinois legislature legally could fix the maximum price charged for warehousing grain. "When private property is devoted to a public use, it is subject to public regulation," concluded the Court. Before *Munn,* state regulatory power was limited to cases of franchise or pure monopoly. *Munn* introduced the public's right to regulate private business that is merely "affected with a public interest."[39]

Moreover, *Munn* served as precedent when Congress established the Interstate Commerce Commission (ICC) in 1887 to regulate the railroads. And the immensity and importance of the railroads to the economy of that time cannot be grasped today without imagining some kind of momentous collective movement among our modern airline, truck, bus, and railroad enterprises. Although some historians and economists have argued that the railroads themselves were the main impetus behind the ICC's establishment, urging regulation in hopes that it would officially enforce protective cartelization in railroading, such does not seem to have been the case. Agitation for regulation came mainly from disgruntled shippers—farmers in the south and midwest who had successfully pressed for such regulation at the state level prior to 1887, and east coast merchants

and manufacturers who felt that railroad rates were structured to their disadvantage, fostering the low-cost penetration of competing products from inland rivals. In particular, "reform agitation in New York during the 1870s was the most important factor leading to the Act of 1887."[40] The fact that long-haul rates were frequently lower than short-haul rates was especially irritating to many shippers, so the Act of 1887 declared that rates must be "reasonable." More sweeping federal action came three years later in 1890 with the Sherman Antitrust Act, which outlawed restraints of trade and monopolization.

These several events turned out to be no more than a few rays of light in the dawning of a new age, the full blaze of sun being much delayed. First, the Supreme Court thereafter retreated from the *Munn* doctrine to strike down abundant regulatory legislation by evoking notions of "due process" and "freedom of contract."[41] The most famous (or infamous) of these cases was *Lochner* v. *New York* (1905), which killed a New York law limiting bakery workers to a ten-hour work day and a sixty-hour work week.[42] The law had been based on extensive research disclosing that many bakers sweated through "more than one hundred hours per week" in hot bakeshops that were "damp, fetid, and devoid of proper ventilation and light," some with ceilings so low the bakers were forced to "work in a stooped position."[43] Second, the Interstate Commerce Commission wallowed in failure for at least twenty years. The reasons for this failure are now no mystery:

[38] Eric F. Goldman, *Rendezvous with Destiny* (New York: Vintage Books, 1956) p. 28.

[39] *Munn* v. *Illinois,* 94 U.S. 113 (1877).

[40] Albro Martin, "The Troubled Subject of Railroad Regulation in the Gilded Age—A Reappraisal," *Journal of American History* (September 1974), pp. 339–371.

[41] Arthur S. Miller, *The Supreme Court and American Capitalism* (New York: The Free Press, 1968), pp. 50–62.

[42] *Lochner* v. *New York,* 198 U.S. 45 (1905).

[43] Quoted by Lawrence M. Friedman, "Freedom of Contract and Occupational Licensing 1890–1910: A Legal and Social Study," *California Law Review* (May 1965), p. 490.

Federal regulation on such a large scale was new to the country; procedures had to be worked out and legal precedents developed. . . . More important was the strong opposition after 1890 of the railroads and the attitude of the courts, which appeared to have little sympathy with the purpose of the act. Of sixteen decisions on rate cases appealed to the Supreme Court for enforcement between 1887 and 1905, fifteen were decided in favor of the carriers and but one sustained in part for the commission.[44]

Finally and similarly, early enforcement of the Sherman Act was handicapped by a lack of adequate administrative funding and by a Supreme Court wedded to the belief that "manufacturing is not commerce." Thus in *United States* v. *E.C. Knight Company* (1895), the Court ruled that the Sherman Act could not be used against the American Sugar Refining Company, which through merger had garnered control of about 90 per cent of the U.S. sugar industry.[45]

The ambivalence of government policy toward business in those days is underscored by the fact that government, especially state government, not only failed to control and constrain monopolistic combinations, it actually took steps that encouraged combinations. These developments were part of the far-reaching social changes occurring in what has been dubbed the "associational movement" of the late nineteenth century. An economic and social order made up of many contending interest groups or collectives was at that time rapidly replacing the relatively atomistic, independent, individualistic, and pioneering disorder that prevailed in pre-Civil War America. Lawrence Friedman delineates four broad classes of economic associations—one each for industrial enterprises, labor, professionals or small businessmen, and farmers—as follows: "first, 'trusts' and other associations of industrial firms, loosely or tightly organized, including trade associations; second, labor unions; third, associations of occupations and small businesses (for example, retail druggists' associations, the master barbers, bar associations); fourth, farmers' organizations, including the state granges, the American Society of Equity, and farmers' cooperatives."[46] Economically and politically, labor unions and farm organizations were then the weakest of the lot. They languished under financial privation, unwieldy numbers of potential members, and government hostility. Illustrative of the hostility, early application of the Sherman Act was aimed mainly at crushing labor unions instead of business monopolies, and in 1887 President Cleveland blocked a congressional appropriation of $10,000 to aid drought-stricken farmers in buying new grain seed with a declaration that "though the people support the Government, the Government should not support the people."[47]

In contrast, changes in the law were assisting the associative movement among industrial enterprises and professional groups. Throughout most of the 1800s, corporate forms of business were severely curtailed by the states, which then, as now, held the power to grant certificates of incorporation. Corporations were typically limited by their certificates to very narrowly defined activities, such as providing railroad transportation between two points. Their capitalization was often tightly capped. Their life spans were relatively brief. And they could not own stock in other corporations. These shackles stunted corporate size and frustrated combinations except insofar as businessmen could devise evasions, one such evasion being the "trust." The first trust was the Stan-

[44] Harold U. Faulkner, *The Decline of Laissez Faire, 1897–1917* (New York: Harper Torchbooks, 1968), pp. 187–188.

[45] *United States* v. *E.C. Knight Company* 156 U.S. 1 (1895).

[46] Lawrence Friedman, *op. cit.*, pp. 503–504.

[47] Eric Goldman, *op. cit.*, p. 33.

dard Oil Trust, founded in 1882 when share-holders of fifty oil refineries surrendered their stock for trust certificates. (Hence the word "trust" came to mean monopoly.) Despite evasions, perpetuation of certificate restrictions would certainly have crimped today's *Fortune 500*. "But," as Roger Sherman writes, "states abandoned many of these restrictions when they began to compete with each other to raise revenue by granting [lax] corporate charters in the 1890s. . . . The modern business corporation with its wide range of rights and powers was born during this period."[48] We might amend this to read *big* corporation, for it was this newly granted leniency that facilitated a massive merger movement from 1897 to 1903, a movement that converted approximately 71 important oligopolistic or near-competitive industries into near monopolies dominated by such firms as U.S. Steel, U.S. Gypsum, Du Pont, American Tobacco, International Paper, International Harvester, American Can, and National Biscuit.

State legal developments of the day were equally friendly to occupational licensure, which ostensibly protects the public from unscrupulous, incompetent, and dangerous professionals, but which also entails some degree of officially sanctioned cartelization. Licensing usually grants economic control to a governing board made up of the occupation's practitioners. This board determines or heavily influences the criteria for licensing candidates (exams, apprenticeships, and such) to the exclusion of all unlicensed practitioners. And the board also promulgates codes of "proper" pricing, advertising, and professional conduct, all with at least one eye fixed on economic self-interest. The associational movement provided the seed bed, and occupational licensing won many successes that still linger in state laws:

By 1910 in Wisconsin, for example, doctors, veterinaries, pharmacists, midwives, nurses, embalmers, and barbers had all achieved some form of licensing. Wisconsin had experimented, too, with plumbers' licensing; many states regulated this occupation. Other "professions" were licensed in scattered jurisdictions. Some of these trades were soon to extend their licensing statutes throughout the land.[49]

Thus it was that, up until about 1910, the philosophical temperment of government was, on balance, decidedly Conservative—largely laissez-faire with probusiness leanings. But "reform" was afoot. Among the first reformers were the Populists, whose party platform of 1892 emphasized that "the powers of government should be expanded . . . to the end that oppression, injustice, and poverty shall eventually cease in the land." Aside from farm relief, rights for women, an income tax, an expanded currency, and various election reform measures, the Populists wanted to strengthen the moribund Interstate Commerce Act of 1887 and the Sherman Antitrust Act of 1890 to the point of effectively regulating or dissolving monopolies. Though influential to the point of seeing many of their proposals eventually adopted, the Populists never gained federal power. Led by eccentrics like "Sockless" Jerry Simpson, who "easily left the impression of a howl from the backwoods," and supported mainly by ignorant farmers and beggarly paupers, the Populist Party never won wide acceptance among the middle classes. It was, in short, a party of irresponsible and rabid failures.

Beginning in about 1900, however, reform began to acquire respectability. It was boosted (1) by the inadvertent presidency of Theodore Roosevelt, who was openly curt toward big-business men, (2) by the insolent attitude and crude conduct of enterprising "robber barons," who could be so insensitive as to say things like,

---

[48] Roger Sherman, *Antitrust Policies and Issues* (Reading, Mass.: Addison-Wesley, 1978), p. 3.

[49] Lawrence Friedman, *op. cit.*, p. 510.

"The public be damned" (W. H. Vanderbilt), and (3) by the sensational revelations of the "muckrakers," whose popular investigative journalism for respectable magazines and newspapers exposed many sordid business (and government) practices from food adulteration to oil monopolization to union corruption. The "Progressives" spearheading the movement represented mainly *middle-class* views. "On one side they feared the power of the plutocracy, on the other the poverty and restlessness of the masses."[50] Their remedies to calm the needy on the bottom came mainly from state legislatures:

> In the years following 1900 an impressive body of legislation was passed dealing with workmen's compensation, the labor of women and children, hours of work, minimum wages for women, and old-age pensions. Even when much allowance is made for spottiness in administration and enforcement, and for the toll that judicial decisions took of them, the net effect of these laws in remedying the crassest abuses of industrialism was very considerable.[51]

Their solutions for the plutocratic topside were sharply debated during the presidential election of 1912 when two Progressive candidates dominated the scene. On the one hand, Theodore Roosevelt, running for a third term after a four year vacation from the presidency, propounded a policy of New Nationalism. "Combinations in industry," Roosevelt declared, "are the result of an imperative economic law." Accordingly, he would allow concentration and monopolization to proceed unchecked *but closely regulate* the resulting behemouths in the "public interest," presumably much as the ICC regulated the railroads following the improvements brought by the Hepburn Act of 1906. On the other hand, Woodrow Wilson advocated New Freedom, in-

sisting that widespread monopoly was not inevitable, that competition could be and should be restored by deconcentration plus tariff cuts, that moreover *competition should be continuously maintained by revitalized antitrust policy.* Of the two methods of controlling monopoly power, Wilson's was actually the more conservative because it entailed much less government intervention.

Wilson won. The Federal Reserve Act followed in 1913 to staunch the "money trust." Tariffs were cut substantially in the same year. Shortly thereafter in 1914 the Federal Trade Commission was established to "prevent . . . unfair methods of competition in commerce." And one month later Congress passed the Clayton Antitrust Act, which among other things (1) strengthened the remedies open to private parties under the Sherman Act, (2) prohibited certain anticompetitive business practices like predatory pricing, and (3) outlawed anticompetitive mergers achieved by stock acquisition. These several measures emerged despite the fact that in 1911, just prior to their passage, enforcement of the Sherman Act had reached a pinnacle of sorts with the Supreme Court's dissolution of two of the most notorious trusts of the day—the Standard Oil Company and the American Tobacco Company.

While at the national level the regulatory approach was rejected in favor of the competitive approach, state governments were busy establishing commission regulation over such public utilities as gas, light, power, and telephone companies. Led by the actions of New York and Wisconsin in 1907, more than two-thirds of the states had regulatory commissions by 1920.

C. 1921–1959: Crash, Collectivization, and Security

The Roaring 20s were actually very quiet from the perspective of this chronicle. The con-

[50] Richard Hofstadter, *The Age of Reform* (New York: Vintage Books, 1955), p. 238.
[51] Ibid., p. 242.

servative administrations of Harding, Coolidge, and Hoover presided over a temporary prosperity with a friendly, accommodating attitude toward business. Then between 1929 and 1933 the economy fell apart. GNP plunged from $104 billion to $56 billion. Wholesale and consumer prices tumbled by one-third and one-fourth, respectively. Industrial production sank by one-half. And unemployment soared to nearly 25% of the workforce.

The disaster pulled Franklin Roosevelt into office and sparked a massive explosion of government activity symbolized by a startling accumulation of official acronyms—RFC, NIRA, AAA, WPA, CCC, FDIC, SEC, TVA, FCC, NLRB, and others. The intent was security and recovery.[52]

Four major forms of intervention emerged, setting enduring precedents. The first may be called *passive cartelization*, under which the government suspended the antitrust laws and to various degrees encouraged economic groups to cooperate, coordinate, and rationalize their behavior. Under the National Recovery Administration (NRA), for instance, industries were urged to draft "codes of fair competition" that set minimum prices, prescribed terms of sale, controlled output, regulated working conditions, and the like. By June 7, 1934, some 459 codes covering over 90% of the eligible industries had been approved. But the biggest firms in each industry dominated the game, oligopolistic industries took advantage of consumers, and competitive industries remained competitive, spreading disillusion. NRA was finally throttled by the Supreme Court for being unconstitutional, and after March 1938 antitrust was revived for most industries with intense vigor under Assistant Attorney General Thurman Arnold. Still, ves-

tages of passive cartelization survived for groups that were considered disadvantaged or weak as compared to their economic counterparts, the idea being one of protection through counterorganization. Thus, for example, labor unions were promoted by the National Labor Relations Act of 1935, which gave unions the right to organize free from employer pressures. Similarly, the Agricultural Marketing Agreement Act of 1938 permitted collective conduct in milk and fruit production. Small wholesale and retail traders were granted different but related exemptions from competition with passage of the Robinson-Patman Act (1938) and the Miller-Tydings Act (1937).

Second, *active cartelization* also blossomed. Whereas, passive cartelization entailed little more than government approval, active cartelization entailed extensive government participation, enforcement, and regulation—setting prices, curtailing outputs, restricting entry, allocating territories, and the like. The alleged intent in most cases was once again to prevent "destructive competition" or to gain a "fair balance of power" between buyers and sellers. These regulations were therefore often welcomed by those affected. Examples include (1) trucking regulation under an expanded ICC, (2) agriculture price supports under the Agricultural Adjustment Act and subsequent farm legislation, (3) airline regulation under the Civil Aeronautics Board, (4) radio spectrum management under the Federal Communications Commission, (5) shipping protection and subsidization under the Federal Maritime Commission, and (6) coal cartelization under the National Bituminous Coal Commission.[53] It is interesting to note that the New Deal's cartelization efforts, both active and passive, de-

---

[52] For a brief account see Jonathan Hughes, "Roots of Regulation: The New Deal," in G. M. Walton (ed.) *Regulatory Change in an Atmosphere of Crisis* (New York: Academic Press, 1979), pp. 31–55.

[53] For a detailed treatment on all these efforts see E. W. Hawley, *The New Deal and the Problem of Monopoly* (Princeton: Princeton University Press, 1966), Chaps. 10–14.

scended from Teddy Roosevelt's rejected New Nationalism.

Government *insurance* provided a third major avenue toward security. The term "insurance" is used loosely here to indicate no more than the presence of contributory payments of some kind, as opposed to pure hand-outs, plus protection against losses. Still with us from the New Deal is insurance against the loss of income from unemployment (state unemployment compensation systems), against depositor losses in bank failures (FDIC), against dependency from disability and old age (Social Security), and against crop loss (Federal Crop Insurance Corporation).

Finally, *subsidies* flowed. Though certainly not new, government subsidies took several novel twists during the Depression and they climbed to new heights. Among indirect aids to business, Roosevelt increased public works spending to an annual rate 100% above Hoover's level. TVA became the most famous New Deal project. More directly, the Reconstruction Finance Corporation (RFC) was established in 1932. Offering direct loans to such diverse businesses as railroads, banks, and insurance companies, it kept many from going under. The Rural Electrification Administration (REA) made low-cost loans to cooperative associations to build and operate electric facilities in the hinter lands. And through other agencies direct subsidies supported everything from leaf raking to the arts to the airlines.

However much these various New Deal dealings may have contributed to the security of their beneficiaries, they did not bring economic recovery. World War II can be credited with that feat. After recovery, government intervention entered a period of consolidation and conservative calm, as indicated earlier in Figures 4–1 and 4–2. The Employment Act of 1946 created the Council of Economic Advisors and endorsed federal activism in aggregate economic affairs. The Celler-Kefauver Act (1950) bolstered antitrust in the area of mergers. And the Small Business Administration was established in 1953. But little more that is worthy of note transpired in the way of policy innovation.

What is worthy of note is that most of the New Deal's innovations endured in one shape or another well into the 1950's and beyond. Now, long after the fearsome shadow of the Great Depression has passed, the government's telephone directory still lists the CCC, TVA, CAB, SEC, REA, OASI, and many others. The Reconstruction Finance Corporation died in 1953, but largely for reasons of scandalous mismanagement rather than obsolescence. And, indeed, as this is written, pressure is building to reinstate the RFC or something like it to lend businesses massive transfusions of capital for the "reindustrialization" of America.

D. 1960–1978: The Era of "Social" Regulation

In *economic* regulation, the sixties and seventies brought no abrupt departures from the heritage of earlier years, just a new spurt. Table 4–2 gives a chronology of the period's major economic regulatory legislation, which amounted to little more than a broadening, deepening, and refining of old policies and agencies.

Take mergers for example. The basic policy had been set in 1914 and 1950. The Bank Merger Act of 1960 modified its application to banks, and the Antitrust Improvement Act of 1976 introduced merger notification procedures. Simultaneously, the courts were busy building a body of case law interpreting the old acts.

The only areas of significant change came about in (1) consumer information improvement, such as the Fair Packaging and Labeling Act and the Truth-in-Lending Act; (2) matters arising from technological change, such as the

Table 4–2. Chronology of Major Economic Regulatory Legislation 1960–1978

Year	Legislation	Agency to Which Law Applies
General Business		
1962	Trade Expansion Act	International Trade Commission
1966	Fair Packaging and Labeling Act	Federal Trade Commission
1974	Council on Wage and Price Stability Act	Council on Wage and Price Stability
1975	Magnuson-Moss Federal Trade Commission Improvement Act	Federal Trade Commission
1976	Antitrust Improvement Act	Federal Trade Commission
Finance and Banking		
1960	Bank Merger Act	Federal Reserve System
1968	Truth-in-Lending Act	Federal Reserve System
		Federal Trade Commission
		Comptroller of the Currency
		Federal Home Loan Bank Board
1970	Fair Credit Reporting Act	Comptroller of the Currency
		Federal Reserve System
1973	NOW Accounts Act	Federal Home Loan Bank Board
		Comptroller of the Currency
		Federal Reserve System
1974	Equal Credit Opportunity Act	(same as above)
Industry-Specific Agencies		
1962	Communications Satellite Act	Federal Communications Commission
1969	Natural Gas Pipeline Safety Act	Federal Energy Regulatory Commission
1973	Emergency Petroleum Allocation Act	Federal Energy Regulatory Commission
1973	Regional Rail Reorganization Act	Interstate Commerce Commission
1974	Commodity Exchange Act Amendments	Commodity Futures Trading Commission
1976	Railroad Revitalization and Regulatory Reform Act	Interstate Commerce Commission
1978	Airline Deregulation Act	Civil Aeronautics Board

Source: Ronald J. Penoyer, *Directory of Federal Regulatory Agencies* (St. Louis: Center for the Study of American Business, Washington University, 1980), pp. 99–108.

Communications Satellite Act; (3) a spell of peacetime wage and price control; and (4) efforts to revitalize rather than merely regulate America's railroads. Few new agencies in the old commission mold were established, the Commodities Futures Trading Commission being the most notable.

The period's brightest fireworks were provided by burgeoning *social* regulation (albeit having an economic impact). Table 4–3 outlines this chronology, dividing the legislation three ways—consumer health and safety, job safety and work conditions, and environment *cum* energy. Many factors prompted this striking expansion. Sobering crises erupted—contaminating the air, burning ghettos, crippling babies, and killing motorists. Popular books, such as Rachel Carson's *Silent Spring* and Ralph Nader's *Unsafe at Any Speed*, broadcast the sad news. Well organized interest groups sprang up and perked up, representing consumers, workers, environmentalists, and disadvantaged minorities. All was not well.

From this atmosphere, policies and agencies

Table 4–3. Chronology of Major Social Regulatory Legislation, 1960–1978

Year	Legislation	Agency to which Law Applies
Consumer Safety and Health		
1962	Drug Amendments of 1962	Food and Drug Administration
1966	Highway Safety Act	National Highway Traffic Safety Administration
1966	Federal Hazardous Substances Act	Food and Drug Administration
1970	Poison Prevention Packaging Act	Consumer Product Safety Commission
1972	Consumer Product Safety Act	Consumer Product Safety Commission
1974	Mobile Home Construction and Safety Standards Act	Housing and Urban Development
1974	Hazardous Material Transportation Act	Federal Highway Administration Materials Transportation Bureau
1976	Medical Devices Amendments	Food and Drug Administration
Job Safety and Work Conditions		
1963	Equal Pay Act	Equal Employment Opportunity Commission
1964	Civil Rights Act	Equal Employment Opportunity Commission
1969	Coal Mine Health and Safety Act	Mine Safety and Health Administration
1970	Occupation Safety and Health Act	Occupational Safety and Health Administration
1972	Equal Employment Opportunity Act	Equal Employment Opportunity Commission
1977	Mine Safety and Health Amendments	Mine Safety and Health Administration
1978	Pregnancy Discrimination Act	Equal Employment Opportunity Commission
Environment and Energy		
1970	National Environmental Improvement Act	Council on Environmental Quality
1970	Clean Air Act Amendments	Environmental Protection Agency
1972	Water Pollution Control Act Amendments	Environmental Protection Agency
1973	Endangered Species Act	Fish and Wildlife Service
1974	Federal Energy Act	Economic Regulatory Administration
1976	Toxic Substances Control Act	Environmental Protection Agency
1977	Dept. of Energy Reorganization Act	Economic Regulatory Administration
1977	Clean Air Act Amendments	Environmental Protection Agency
1977	Surface Mining Control and Reclamation Act	Department of Interior

Source: Ronald J. Penoyer, *Directory of Federal Regulatory Agencies* (St. Louis: Center for the Study of American Business, Washington University, 1980), pp. 83–98.

multiplied apace. Their novelty lay not so much in their essentials as in their emphasis and profusion. First, the new agencies were given especially wide scopes of industrial coverage. Whereas oldsters like the ICC, FDA, and FCC attended to at most a few industries, the Environmental Protection Agency (EPA), Equal Employment Opportunity Commission (EEOC), Consumer Product Safety Commis-

sion (CPSC), and Occupational Safety and Health Administration (OSHA) were given jurisdictions spanning nearly the entire length and width of the private sector. An important consequence of this far-ranging characteristic is that it lessens the degree to which the regulated industries can extract favoritism from the agencies. The older agencies have often been accused of being "captured" by their wards.

Second, this broader coverage has typically been accompanied by a narrower material focus as compared to older agencies. That is to say, the veteran agencies have often been concerned with the totality of business operations of their charges—pricing, product quality, entry, plant location, service offerings, and so on. In contrast, the newcomers restrict their attention to, say, employment practices (EEOC), or design safety (CPSC), or polluting practices (EPA). As Murry Weidenbaum observes, "This restriction prevents the agency from developing too close a concern with the overall well-being of any company or industry. Rather, it can result in a total lack of concern over the effects of its specific actions on a company or industry."[54]

There is, finally, a trend toward increased regulation by line operating departments and bureaus in the executive branch of the government as well as by independent commissions patterned after the ICC, CAB, and FTC. Examples include the Occupational Safety and Health Administration, housed in the Department of Labor; the Materials Transportation Bureau, which strives to assure the safe transportation of hazardous substances (their containers, mode of shipment, etc.) and which is located in the Department of Transportation.[55] Of course this recognition of line offices is not meant to slight the new independent agencies—EPA, CPSC, EEOC, CFTC, and NCUA.

E. 1979–Present: Deregulation, Retrenchment?

History is supposed to repeat itself, and it appears to be complying in the case at hand. So far, the 1980s seem to be following the example of the 1890s, 1920s, and 1950s. That is, the

most recent explosion of government tinkering seems to be waning. Beginning with the deregulation of the airlines in 1978, first by the prodding of CAB Chairman Alfred Kahn and then by liberating legislation, retrenchment then spread to railroads, trucking, energy, banking, and communications. It should be noted that relaxation has been largely confined to areas in which there was little economic justification for regulation in the first place, areas that would be governed by competition in the absence of intervention. In telephone communications, for instance, deregulation has hit equipment manufacturing, long-distance transmission, and computor interconnection, but not basic, local phone service.

More broadly, all small businesses have been winning exemptions from broad classes of social regulation because compliance costs have in the past been particularly damaging to tiny enterprises. Several other broad-based measures have seen minor breakthroughs and may someday soon see the full light of day. One is the "sunset" restriction, which sets an automatic limit to a program's existence or requires explicit justification for a program's renewal. Such applies to CPSC now, and once won Senate support for most federal programs. Another is the "legislative veto," which allows the House or the Senate or both to vote down regulatory rulings within, say, ninety days. Such now applies to many Federal Trade Commission regulations.

Among the factors contributing to this deregulation trend, the most interesting is a reversal of the historic pattern: private-crisis-government-response. The government has, in the eyes of many, created some crises of its own, thereby becoming the problem, not the solution. Energy shortages provoked by low price ceilings and environmental regulations, and costly transportation inefficiencies due to regulatory entry barriers and route restrictions—these and other difficulties have attracted atten-

---

[54] Murray Weidenbaum, *op. cit.*, p. 10.
[55] For a nice run down on all agencies see *Federal Regulatory Directory 1979–1980* (Washington, D.C.: Congressional Quarterly Inc., 1979).

tion to the government's failings. Aiding the cause are "muckraking" books, some even from Ralph Nader's shop, like *Interstate Commerce Omission*[56] and *The Monopoly Makers.*[57] Moreover, Conservatives gained power, led by President Reagan.

This reform movement has been building for quite some time, and much credit for recent changes should go to some parts of government itself. Major studies critical of various aspects of regulation have repeatedly been sponsored or conducted by government (in 1937, 1949, 1955, 1960, 1968, 1972, 1976, and 1978). The Antitrust Division of the Department of Justice has argued the case for freer market competition before many regulatory agencies. And the Council on Wage and Price Stability has questioned on cost-benefit grounds the wisdom of many regulations. It will be interesting to see just how far deregulation goes.

Summary

It should now be clear that current public policies toward business are woven from philosophical and historical threads as well as the previous chapters' largely theoretical fibers. Oversimplifying the rich range of economic philosophies, we have fabricated Conservative and Liberal flags.

Conservatives have the greatest faith in capitalist, free-enterprise markets and the least regard for government intervention. This combination of positions derives largely from the Conservative's beliefs that (1) human nature corresponds closely to that of *Homo economicus,* an acquisitive, rational, knowledgeable creature who almost always acts wisely in his own self interest; (2) freedom should reign su-

preme, without more than minor compromise for such other ends as equity, fairness, safety, and security; and (3) government ineptitude transforms even the best of intentions into bad results.

In contrast, Liberals have greater faith in government than Conservatives, advocating "mixed capitalism" or the "welfare state." To Liberals, (1) humans display vulnerabilities and needs uncharacteristic of *Homo economicus;* (2) freedom should be honored, but defined in a way to include freedom from the market's worst offenses and tempered to allow much equality; and (3) market imperfections and failures should be taken very seriously, to the point of attempting pragmatic policy remedies.

The history of government intervention in many ways traces a see-saw battle between Liberals and Conservatives, with Liberals winning more often than not over the long pull. Periods of particularly rapid growth in officialdom—the 1910s, 1930s, 1960s, and 1970s—were fertilized by the appearance of what many folks believed were awesome developments, namely, the combination movement at the turn of the century, the Great Depression, the outbreak of racial strife, and so on. Periods of relatively Conservative consolidation or retrenchment followed these spurts, but never to the extent of large-scale dismantlement (at least not until recently). The overall result is that government has become mountainous by any measure—number of agencies, size of regulatory budgets, proportion of people employed in government, private cost of compliance, and so on.

The 1980s should provide an especially interesting chapter for future chronicles. A consensus seems to be building that government has in many areas overstepped its proper bounds. But opinion is divided as to remedy. Liberals have proposed and in some cases won passage of new legislative or constitutional devices that would allow continued government activism, subject, however, to a shorter leash. "Sunset"

[56] Robert Fellmeth, *The Interstate Commerce Omission* (New York: Grossman Publishers, 1970).

[57] Mark J. Green (ed.), *The Monopoly Makers* (New York: Grossman Publishers, 1973).

laws, "legislative veto," and "cost-benefit re-view" are examples. Conservatives, on the other hand, would prefer that the government simply do less, thereby leaving the market freer. Whichever approach predominates, one thing seems certain: history's inertia will prevent a return to the days when government was content to deliver the mail, set a tariff, issue currency, distribute public lands, and fight the Indians.

Questions and Exercises for Chapter 4

1. Is it possible to be Conservative on some issues but Liberal on others? Explain your yes or no.

2. To what extent do philosophies shape history? To what extent does history influence the popularity of philosophies? (The 1930s and 1980s might be of particular relevance for these questions.)

3. The election of 1912 chose between New Nationalism and New Freedom (both "Liberal" or "Progressive"). What elements of each can you find in FDR's New Deal?

4. Outline the spread of government along dimensions of level, scope, and instrument.

5. Distinguish "economic" and "social" regulation in focus, scope, and history.

6. On the basis of this chapter's information, both philosophical and empirical, why do you think Richard Nixon, president during 1969–1974, could be called a "moderate"? (Use Eisenhower, 1953–60 as an alternative.)

Part II

Antitrust Policy

"It so happens, Gregory, that your Grandfather Sloan was detained by an agency of our government over an honest misunderstanding concerning certain antitrust matters! He was not 'busted by the Feds'!"

Source: Drawing by W. Miller; © 1971 The New Yorker Magazine, Inc.

Chapter 5

Introduction to Antitrust Policy

the public interest is best protected from the evils of monopoly and price control by the maintenance of competition.
—Chief Justice Stone

The antitrust laws of the United States are in many ways unique. No other country can boast of a bigger body of law for monopolies and restrictive business practices. No other area of U.S. policy toward business can be considered more basic. As James McKie once remarked, "Perhaps the simplest kind of government intervention in the economic system is to ensure that the private system itself will work satisfactorily, by preserving effectively competitive markets. It is a Deistic kind of intervention: it sets the rules and conditions for the game, and then lets the system run itself."[1]

The purpose of this chapter is, first, to specify the problems addressed by antitrust policy. Second, the aims of antitrust policy receive attention. Third, an outline of the statutory laws is given, followed by a description of the agencies that enforce them. Finally, exceptions are ex-

plored. Ensuing chapters review specific antitrust policies in detail.

I. The Problems

Previous chapters explained why competition was desirable. But those explanations were sketchy. Elaboration and empiricism are now in order, organized around the three main elements of any market—structure, conduct, and performance. Reduced to barest essentials, the problem is one of market power—its mere attainment or possession (as reflected in structure), its exercise (as revealed in anticompetitive conduct), and its consequences (as measured by performance).

A. Structure

The ill effects of monopoly power, or more generally, market power, have long been recognized. Aristotle tells of a Sicilian who monop-

---

[1] James W. McKie, "Government Intervention in the Economy of the United States," in Peter Maunder (ed.), *Government Intervention in the Developed Economy* (New York: Praeger Publishers, 1979), p. 74.

Table 5–1. Selected Major Mergers Causing High Concentration 1895–1904

Company (or Combine)	Number of Firms Disappearing	Rough Estimate of Market Controlled (%)
U.S. Steel	170	65
U.S. Gypsum	29	80
American Tobacco	162	90
American Smelting & Refining	12	85
DuPont de Nemours	65	85
Diamond Match	38	85
American Can	64	65–75
International Harvester	4	70
National Biscuit (Nabisco)	27	70
Otis Elevator	6	65

Source: Ralph L. Nelson, *Merger Movements in American Industry 1895–1956* (Princeton, N.J.: Princeton University Press, 1959), pp. 161–62.

olized the iron trade, thereby profiting 100%.[2] Grassroots sentiment against monopoly power is based on more, however. It is based on a distrust of *power itself,* power that can be measured by such structural conditions as market concentration, barriers to entry, product differentiation, and firm diversification.

1. MARKET CONCENTRATION

The president of Western Auto Supply Company, Joseph Grissom, recently acknowledged the power bestowed by large market share when he said, "I would rather have 50% of one market than 10% of five markets. That way we can influence the market rather than react to it."[3]

Percentages above 50 would presumably look even better to Mr. Grissom. They certainly

were attractive to the organizers and promoters of some of America's largest firms. Table 5–1 gives examples by reporting basic data on the merger history of ten major U.S. companies that ascended to dominance during the years 1895–1904, a period of feverish merger activity. These ten firms accounted for the disappearance of 577 formerly independent companies, thereby gaining single firm market shares ranging from 65% in the case of U.S. Steel and Otis Elevator to 90% in the case of American Tobacco. The *market share of the leading firm* is thus one method of measuring market concentration, a method occasionally disclosing dominance.

Aside from public utilities and merchants in one-horse towns, leading firm market shares of the size observed in Table 5–1 are now relatively rare, thanks in part to antitrust policy. Many of our most familiar leading firms presently hold market shares well below those of Table 5–1: General Motors in autos, 47%

[2] Ernest Barker (ed.), *The Politics of Aristotle* (New York: Oxford University Press, 1962), p. 31.
[3] *Business Week,* October 9, 1978, p. 143.

(counting imports); Anheuser-Busch in beer, 30%; Kellogg in cereals, 45%; Xerox in copying equipment, 54%; Coca-Cola in soft drinks, 34%; Alcoa in aluminum, 32%; Procter & Gamble in detergents, 50%. Still, market power prevails in these markets and others like them because of the collective power of just a few firms. This power may be measured by the market share held by several leading firms taken together, or the **concentration ratio.** The *four-firm* concentration ratio is the one most widely cited because that is the form used by the U.S. Census Bureau when reporting concentration. Table 5–2 gives a sample of concentration ratios for retailing, banking, mining and manufacturing. Those numbers roughly indicate the pattern of concentration generally. That is, four-firm concentration above 80 or below 20 is relatively rare. The vast bulk of markets could be called oligopolies, with four-firm ratios ranging from 80 on the "tight" end to 20 on the "loose" end. The average concentration ratio in manufacturing, for instance, is somewhere between 40 and 60 per cent, depending on how broadly or narrowly manufacturing markets are defined.

This last sentence waves a caution flag—that is, market definition matters. Given the combined dollar sales of four top firms, say $10 billion, conversion of this number into a percentage of total market sales can yield various results depending on the volume of sales included in the marketwide total. A broad definition of the market would tend to raise marketwide sales and thereby lower the concentration ratio. Conversely, a narrow definition of the market would tend to lower marketwide sales and thereby raise the concentration ratio. Pharmaceuticals provide an example both ways. Broadly defined, "pharmaceutical preparations" has a four-firm ratio of about 26 per cent. Narrowly defined, however, by individual therapeutic groups, the ratios are much higher—e.g., anesthetics, 69; antiarthritics, 95; and sul-

fonamides, 79.[4] This discrepancy between broad and narrow definitions in drugs arises because a few firms tend to dominate each therapeutic group but the same firms do not dominate *all* therapeutic groups. When all therapeutic groups are lumped together, the fraction of the "total" business accounted for by any one firm then shrinks.

Properly defined, the "market" *includes* all firms actually competing with each other and *excludes* noncompeting firms. Such inclusion-exclusion applies to *product* delineation, as illustrated by the drug example, and to *geographic* scope, which is illustrated in Table 5–2 by the distinction between nationally and locally distributed manufactured goods (and also by the narrowly drawn local markets for grocery retailing and commercial banking).

The causes of high as opposed to low concentration vary greatly, but for present purposes only two broad categories of causes need to be acknowledged—those which are "natural" or economically "warranted," and those which are "artificial" or deliberately "contrived." Among *natural* causes we find (1) large economies of scale relative to the extent of the market, (2) unusually scarce resource inputs, and (3) early or late stages in the industry's life cycle. Antitrust policy cannot be very concerned with high concentration produced and perpetuated by these factors because the concentration would be thrust upon the leading firms, it would be necessary to achieving efficiency, or it would be difficult if not impossible to dissolve. Among *artificial* causes of concentration we find (1) mergers of otherwise competing firms, as illustrated by the examples of Table 5–1, (2) restrictive business practices like predatory pricing, and (3) product differentiation. It is of course these kinds of causes that antitrust policy might counter. Indeed, these possibilities explain a

[4] John Vernon, "Concentration, Promotion, and Market Share Stability in the Pharmaceutical Industry," *Journal of Industrial Economics* (July 1971), pp. 246–266.

Table 5–2. Selected Concentration Ratios in Manufacturing, Mining, Grocery Retailing, and Banking, Circa Early 1970s

Industry	Four-firm Concentration Ratio
Manufacturing: National Market Products	
Cereal breakfast foods	99
Glass containers	55
Primary aluminum	79
Aircraft engines	74
Paperboard mills	29
Soap and detergents	62
Blast furnaces and steel mills	45
Manufacturing: Local Market Products[1]	
Ice cream	70
Fluid milk	57
Brick and structural tile	87
Concrete	52
Mining	
Copper	75
Sulfur	72
Iron ore	64
Coal	31
Grocery Retailing	
Atlanta, Georgia	55
Cincinnati, Ohio	49
Washington, D.C.	76
San Diego, California	55
Commercial Banking[2]	
Baltimore, Maryland	64
Chicago, Illinois	43
Des Moines, Iowa	71
Pittsburgh, Pennsylvania	80
San Francisco, California	78

Notes: [1] These represent averages of the many local concentration ratios computed.
[2] These are actually three-firm ratios, instead of four-firm ratios, as the banking authorities publish their data on that basis.
   Sources: For the several sources see Douglas F. Greer, *Industrial Organization and Public Policy* (New York: Macmillan Publishing Company, 1980), pp. 119–126; and *Grocery Retailing Concentration in Metropolitan Areas, Economic Census Years 1954–72,* Bureau of Economics, Federal Trade Commission, 1979.

crucial assumption underlying any antitrust policy aimed at maintaining competitively structured markets, namely, the assumption that, for most markets, a monopolistically high level of concentration is not technically inevitable, not economically justifiable, and not indelible.

This distinction between concentration that is natural and artificial, warranted and unwarranted, is very important. Many critics of antitrust defend large aggregations of power by contending that *all* concentration derives from efficiency or some related blessing.[5] Whether or not this is true, however, depends on the empirical evidence. And the best evidence available discloses that, indeed, *some* instances of high concentration *are* warranted by economies of scale, *but only some*. Efficiency in automobile production, for example, apparently requires that a firm's output reach at least one million cars per year or there-abouts.[6] This amounts to roughly 10 per cent of annual U.S. auto sales, implying that the industry would have room for no more than about ten efficient oligopolistic firms. Other highly concentrated industries evincing substantial economies of scale relative to total sales are turbogenerators and refrigerators. The question has been studied intensely for many more industries than these, however, and the appropriate generalization to be drawn is that these are not typical of industry as a whole. To quote the conclusion of a leading study in this regard: "national market seller concentration appears in most industries to be much higher than it needs to be for leading firms to take advantage of all but slight residual multiplant scale economies."[7]

A similar conclusion holds for other natural factors that may warrant high concentration, like scarce inputs and industry life cycles. Scarce inputs favor fewness only in rare instances, such as molybdenum mining (with its unique ore deposits), or genetic engineering (with its scarce technical personnel). Life-cycle effects, which are more frequent, may occur in industries that follow a history of distinct phases—that is, birth, growth, maturity, and decline. At birth, an entire industry may well be made up of a sole innovator, one protected from rivals by secret knowhow or key patents (which grant monopoly rights for seventeen years). Xerox was such an innovator. With growth and maturity, imitators may then successfully invade the new field, reducing concentration with their competition. Finally, in the event obsolescence and decline set in with old age, high concentration may return as survivors dwindle. The accuracy of this scenario varies from industry to industry, however. Many industries, like autos, defy the pattern with competitive births and oligopolistic adolescences.[8] All in all, then, *some* instances of especially lofty concentration are warranted on these natural grounds, but like economies of scale they too fall short of giving a generalized accounting.

2. BARRIERS TO ENTRY

Any factor that inhibits new entry into an unusually profitable market may be called a *barrier to entry*. Like high concentration, high barriers to entry may be either "naturally" or "artificially" elevated, bestowing power on established firms in either case.

As with concentration, economies of scale may pose a *natural barrier*. Figure 5–1 illustrates this possibility. Long-run cost per unit, *LRUC*, falls with ever greater scales of opera-

---

[5] John S. McGee, *In Defense of Industrial Concentration* (New York: Praeger Publishers, 1971); Sam Peltzman, "The Gains and Losses from Industrial Concentration," *Journal of Law & Economics* (October 1977), pp. 229–263.

[6] Lawrence White, *The Automobile Industry Since 1945* (Cambridge: Harvard University Press, 1971), Chap. 4.

[7] F. M. Scherer, A. Beckenstein, E. Kaufer, and R. D. Murphy, *The Economics of Multi-Plant Operation* (Cambridge: Harvard University Press, 1975), p. 339. See also Joe Bain, *Barriers to New Competition* (Cambridge: Harvard University Press, 1965), Leonard W. Weiss, "Optimal Plant Size and the Extent of Suboptimal Capacity," in Masson and Qualls (eds.) *Essays on Industrial Organization* (Cambridge: Ballinger Publishing Co., 1976), pp. 123–141, F. M. Scherer, "The Causes and Consequences of Rising Industrial Concentration," *Journal of Law & Economics* (April 1979), pp. 191–208; and H. P. Marvel, "Foreign Trade and Domestic Competition," *Economic Inquiry* (January 1980), pp. 114–115.

[8] William G. Shepherd, *The Treatment of Market Power* (New York: Columbia University Press, 1975), pp. 51–53.

Figure 5–1. Economies of Scale Acting as a Barrier to the Entry of a Third Firm

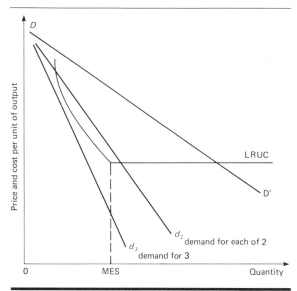

result: no third firm entry because existing firms will have already built efficient plants, and the added output of an entrant's efficient plant would be so large relative to industry demand that, after entry, product price would fall below the entrant's cost per unit.

If the capital costs of building a minimum efficient scale of operations are substantial, $2 billion, say, those costs could likewise pose a natural barrier to all but the very wealthiest potential entrants. Another possibility is that the unit-cost curve of potential entrants lies above the unit-cost curve of established firms at all possible levels of output, thereby likewise impeding entry.

Many of the most potent *artificial, or man-made, barriers* are erected by government policy. Patents, for instance, grant exclusive rights lasting seventeen years, rights which may or may not be important depending on the significance of the inventions concerned. Though artificial barriers, patents are beneficial to the extent they stimulate technological progress. They therefore may be warranted barriers. Unfortunately, patents may also be used to build unwarranted barriers. Exclusive cross licensing, aggressive acquisition, blocking out, and fraudulent attainment are a few of the anticompetitive manipulations associated with patents. Occupational licensing is another official barrier that may be abused, however beneficial the intent of such licensing may be. More directly within the reach of businessmen, vertical integration may pose a barrier.

This does not exhaust the list of artificial barriers. But most of those remaining will be discussed as matters of conduct rather than of structure.

3. PRODUCT DIFFERENTIATION

Product differentiation is a source of market power when it gives sellers power over price. That power may stem from many genuine, objective nonprice elements—such as flavor, dur-

tion up to an output level *MES*, which indicates minimum efficient scale. Assume that this long-run unit cost curve confronts established firms and would-be entrants alike. Assume further that *DD'* is industry demand. Then if two existing firms share industry demand equally, each firm would view its demand as d_2, which is half of *DD'* at each possible price. Since d_2 lies above *LRUC* over a considerable range, each of the two firms could produce and sell at a profit. However, a potential entrant would not have such a favorable view of the situation. If it is assumed that demand would be split evenly three ways in the event of a third firm's entry (a very optimistic assumption for a new entrant to make), each firm's demand would then become d_3, which is one third of *DD'* at each possible price. But given d_3, there is *no* plant scale that yields a profit to the entrant. There is no point at which *LRUC* falls below d_3. The

Table 5–3. Some of the Largest U.S. Industrial Corporations, 1979

Company (chief product)	Sales ($ billions)	Rank in Sales	Assets ($ billions)	Rank in Assets
Exxon (oil)	$79.1	1	$49.5	1
General Motors (motor vehicles)	66.3	2	32.2	2
Mobil (oil)	44.7	3	27.5	3
Ford Motors (motor vehicles)	43.5	4	23.5	5
Texaco (oil)	38.4	5	23.0	6
Standard Oil of California (oil)	29.9	6	18.1	7
Gulf Oil (oil)	23.9	7	17.3	8
IBM (office equipment)	22.9	8	24.5	4
General Electric (electronics)	22.4	9	16.6	10
Standard Oil, Indiana (oil)	18.6	10	17.1	9
ITT (electronics)	17.2	11	15.1	12
U.S. Steel (metals)	12.9	14	11.0	15
Du Pont (chemicals)	12.6	16	8.9	19
Sun (oil)	10.7	20	7.5	23
Procter & Gamble (detergents)	9.3	23	5.6	34
Goodyear (tires, rubber)	8.2	28	5.3	38
Eastman Kodak (photography)	8.0	31	3.9	56
Beatrice Foods (foods)	7.5	35	3.7	60
Xerox (office equipment)	7.0	40	6.6	27

Source: Fortune, May 5, 1980, pp. 276–77.

ability, and convenience of location in retailing. A Mercedes-Benz is thus really worth more than a Chevy Citation. On the other hand, that power may be grounded on spurious, subjective influences—such as exhortative advertising or frivolous "designer labels." Thus all brands of liquid chlorine bleach are essentially identical (5.25% sodium hypochlorite plus 94.75% water), as are all brands of aspirin (5 grains of $C_9H_8O_4$), yet the heavily advertised brands of these products sell at premium prices and account for more sales volume than unadvertised, private label brands.

ReaLemon brand reconstituted lemon juice, for example, captured 90 per cent of its market during the 1950s and 1960s by virtue of strong brand allegiance. A measure of that trademark's power was disclosed in 1962 when Borden paid $12.4 million to acquire ReaLemon,

an amount four-times greater than the book value of the company's assets at the time.[9]

4. DIVERSIFICATION

Most of the largest corporations span many markets, (1) diversifying backward or forward into different stages of their production process to become *vertically integrated,* (2) diversifying into widely differing fields—such as meat packing, aerospace, and steel—to become *conglomerates,* and (3) spreading operations and subsidiaries hither and yon internationally to become *mutinationals.* Take the prominent corporations listed in Table 5–3 for instance. Each is associated in the popular mind with

[9] For details see Richard Schmalensee, "On the Use of Economic Models in Antitrust: The *ReaLemon* Case," *University of Pennsylvania Law Review* (April, 1979), pp. 994–1050.

some relatively narrow activity, such as photographic equipment (Kodak), oil (Mobil), or computers (IBM). Yet, in fact, each engages in a vast array of enterprises scattered over the globe. Lodged at the top and typical of the big oil companies is Exxon, with vertically integrated operations in petroleum mining, transportation, refining, and marketing; with 73% of its total revenues coming from foreign sources; and with conglomerated activities in uranium, chemicals, and office equipment. Then there is General Motors, with numerous auto parts subsidiaries; with large plants in Europe and Latin America; plus substantial activities in locomotives, trucks, buses, consumer finance, and electric appliances. Mobil owns Montgomery Ward; General Electric controls Utah International Mining. More than half of IBM's revenues originate overseas. ITT is into practically everything from bread to hotels to cables to insurance, owning over 200 installations in over 25 countries. And so on.

The powers conferred by diversification are difficult to measure and subject to dispute. But one thing is almost certain: Diversification boosts absolute firm size and this size in turn contributes to *aggregate concentration*, which is the total economic activity, very broadly defined, accounted for by the leading firms. It is estimated, for instance, that in 1976 the 200 largest manufacturing corporations accounted for 61.4% of all manufacturing assets, up from 47.7% in 1950.[10] The asset holdings of the largest 200 corporations in other broad fields in 1974 were as follows: finance, insurance, and real estate, 47.8%; services, 33.5%; wholesale and retail trade, 30.9%; and transportation, communication, and public utilities, 86.8%.[11]

Figure 5–2 gives a historical profile of aggregate concentration, one primarily concerned with manufacturing. Different measures of size, different definitions of scope, and different notions of how many firms constitute a "few" obviously affect the picture. But, generally speaking, aggregate concentration has risen.[12]

5. OTHER STRUCTURAL FEATURES

Instances where one or more of the foregoing variables reaches lofty heights may indeed portend ominous results for competition. But the ultimate consequences for competitive conduct and performance often depend heavily on other, more subtle structural conditions. An industry having, say, only three large firms may nevertheless be quite competitive (or rivalrous) if sales go in very large and infrequently negotiated lots, if technological change moves briskly, and if price elasticity of demand is quite high. Lumpy sales and high price elasticity raise the pay-offs gained from price shading. Rapid technological change adds turmoil to any market by upsetting collusive understandings, by aggravating uncertainty, and by stimulating competition in innovation and invention. Accordingly, an important qualification is in order. High concentration (or high entry barriers, and so forth) may or may not pose a problem worthy of antitrust attention depending on the circumstances.

B. Conduct

Anticompetitive conduct falls into two broad classes: (1) *collusive actions*, wherein rivals act jointly to achieve monopolistic aims, and (2) *individual exclusionary policies* that bolster a

[10] Willard F. Mueller, *The Celler-Kefauver Act: The First 27 Years*, U.S. House of Representatives, Committee on the Judiciary, Subcommittee on Monopolies and Commercial Law (1980), p. 116.

[11] U.S. Senate, Committee on the Judiciary, Subcommittee on Antitrust, Monopoly and Business Rights, *Mergers and Economic Concentration*, Hearings, Part 1 (1979), pp. 89–92.

[12] For contrary views see statements by Weston and Schwartzman, ibid, pp. 536–614. Notice that series #8 in Figure 5–2 is compatible with series #6 and #7 because manufacturing is declining and services expanding as portions of GNP. Since services are unconcentrated, their expanding share lowers aggregate concentration as measured broadly by nonfinancial corporate assets.

Figure 5–2.   The Long-Term Trend of Aggregate Concentration: Eight Individual Series

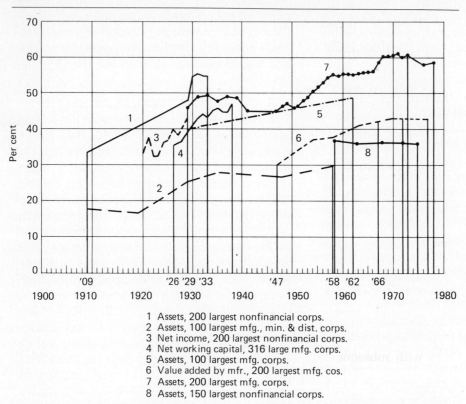

1 Assets, 200 largest nonfinancial corps.
2 Assets, 100 largest mfg., min. & dist. corps.
3 Net income, 200 largest nonfinancial corps.
4 Net working capital, 316 large mfg. corps.
5 Assets, 100 largest mfg. corps.
6 Value added by mfr., 200 largest mfg. cos.
7 Assets, 200 largest mfg. corps.
8 Assets, 150 largest nonfinancial corps.

Source: John M. Blair, *Economic Concentration* (New York: Harcourt Brace Jovanovich, 1972), p. 63; Lawrence White, "Mergers and Aggregate Concentration," in Keenan and White (eds.) *Mergers and Acquisitions* (Lexington, Mass.: Lexington Books, 1982), pp. 97–111.

firm's power vis-a-vis existing or potential rivals. The first is generally inclusive; the second exclusive.

1. COLLUSIVE ACTIONS

Collusion may be *implicit*, in which case rivals act uniformly through tacit "understanding" and "conscious parallelism," usually aided by price leadership. It may also be *explicit*, in which case rivals enter into an express cartel agreement to fix prices, to allocate sales territories, or to curb competition in some other way. Implicit collusion is possible only when structural conditions are especially accommodating, that is, when concentration is quite high, entry is at least partially impeded, sales are not particularly lumpy, and the like. Explicit collusion has a much broader range of habitat. It may serve as a substitute for implicit collusion when structural conditions are tightly oligopolistic but not quite right for tacit agreement. On the other hand, explicit cartelization may also arise under structural conditions that would ordinarily produce quite vigorous competition. Most commonly, though, cartel conduct appears to occur somewhere between these two extremes in moderately to tightly knit oligopolistic markets. For example, a sample of thirty-five explicit price-fixing agreements came from markets with an average four-firm concentration ratio of 77 per cent, which is well above the all manufacturing average but nowhere near 100 per cent.[13] In a different sample of 606 cases of price fixing, the median number of firms actively involved was 8, which gives a rough idea of the median number of firms in cartelized markets. By contrast, the median number of firms in manufacturing markets generally is about 18.[14]

When effective, implicit and explicit collusion leads to higher prices. Certainly the most dramatic demonstration of this result is provided by the Organization of Petroleum Exporting Countries (OPEC), which is a cartel comprised of 13 of the world's leading oil producers. Beginning with a quadrupling of price in late 1973 and continuing with subsequent price hikes ranging from 5 to 60 per cent, OPEC has had a colossal impact on the world economy. More generally, nearly twenty statistical studies have shown that market concentration and price level are positively associated. A study of grocery retailing, for instance, indicated that the price of a "standard" grocery basket of goods was 5.3 per cent higher where local four-firm concentration was 70 as compared to 40.[15] Other products and services

yielding similar evidence include gasoline retailing, life insurance, business loans, newspaper advertising space, bond underwriting, and drug retailing.[16]

2. EXCLUSIONARY PRACTICES

Exclusionary practices may be collusively contrived, as is true of collective boycotts and exclusive cross licensing of patents. More commonly, though, individual firms wield exclusionary weapons. *Predatory pricing* is one such weapon. Here, a relatively large, "deep pocketed" firm aggressively cuts price below cost for purposes of imposing losses on smaller existing rivals, or threatening financial injury to potential rivals, thereby driving them from the market or softening them up for eventual merger. After so garnering market power, the predator can raise price in hopes of recovering battle losses. Two of the most notorious monopolies built in the days of the robber barons—Standard Oil of New Jersey and American Tobacco—were found guilty of such predatory behavior.[17]

Price discrimination occurs when the seller sets different prices relative to costs to different buyers. Such discrimination can be anticompetitive when used systematically by a powerful firm. But it can also be procompetitive, as when a small firm shades prices, catch-as-catch-can, to stimulate sales during a slump.

Under *tying arrangements*, a seller gives buyers access to one line of the seller's goods only if the buyer purchases others as well. A tying arrangement exists, for instance, when

[13] George A. Hay and Daniel Kelley, "An Empirical Survey of Price-Fixing Conspiracies," *Journal of Law and Economics* (April 1974), pp. 13–38.

[14] A. G. Fraas and D. F. Greer, "Market Structure and Price Collusion: An Empirical Analysis," *Journal of Industrial Economics* (September 1977), pp. 21–44.

[15] B. W. Marion, W. F. Mueller, R. W. Cotteril, F. E. Geithman, and J. R. Schmelzer, *The Profit and Price Performance of Leading Food Chains 1970–74*, Joint Economic Committee, U.S. Congress, 95th Congress, 1st Session (1977), p. 66.

[16] Reuben Kessel, "A Study of the Effects of Competition in the Tax-Exempt Bond Market," *Journal of Political Economy* (July, 1971), pp. 706–738; Howard P. Marvel, "Competition and Price Levels in the Retail Gasoline Market," *Review of Economics and Statistics* (May 1978), pp. 252–258. Other studies are cited in D. Greer, *Industrial Organization and Public Policy* (New York: Macmillan, 1980), p. 320.

[17] *United States* v. *Standard Oil Company of New Jersey*, 221 U.S. 1 (1911); *United States* v. *American Tobacco Company*, 221 U.S. 106 (1911).

a manufacturer of canning machines requires that his canning-machine customers also buy their cans from him. If the seller has monopoly power over the tying good, machines in this example, he might with this method extract greater monopoly profits than otherwise, and he may lessen competition in the tied-good market.

A practice related to tying is *exclusive dealing*, whereby a seller prohibits his buyers from buying goods from the seller's rivals. For instance, an auto manufacturer might require that its franchised dealers carry only its line of products, shunning rivals' offerings. When used by a relatively small or fledgling manufacturer, exclusive dealing can be procompetitive to the extent it fires the interests and efforts of the manufacturer's retailers or protects the manufacturer's good will. In the hands of a dominant manufacturer with strong brand image, however, the practice can heighten entry barriers.[18]

C. Performance

1. PROFIT

As suggested earlier, structure and conduct may affect many different aspects of performance—that is, profit level, technical efficiency, technological progress, inflation, and unemployment. Of these, none has been more thoroughly studied than *profit level*, which when excessively high tends to reflect poor performance in allocation efficiency (because, as shown earlier in Figure 2–7, price is then above marginal cost) and poor performance in income equity (to the extent relatively rich owners collect the excess profits at the expense of relatively poor consumers). More than 80 statistical studies have tested the relationship between profit level and various measures of market power, and all but a few have found a positive

relationship, suggesting that monopolistic and oligopolistic structures generally do have adverse consequences for performance in this respect.[19]

Figures 5–3(a) and 5–3(b) illustrate these results for *concentration*. Such positive associations as these have been found for several different measures of profit, for many different measures of concentration, and for substantially different time periods. Moreover, the positive relationship holds for broad interindustry samples (including all manufacturing industries), narrow interindustry samples (limited to producer goods, for instance), and *intra*industry samples across diverse geographic markets (such as those in banking and grocery retailing). The positive relationship also emerges from data gathered from every corner of the world.

It is now fairly well established that the *market share* of a firm also carries a positive impact on profit, and substantially so. By one estimate, pretax return on investment rises about 5 percentage points for every 10 percentage point increase in market share.[20] Many factors contribute to this relationship—among them, the market power and/or efficiency associated with greater market share.[21]

Interindustry variances in *entry barriers* have been estimated by variances in economies of scale, capital requirements, advertising in-

[18] Richard Caves, *American Industry: Structure, Conduct, Performance* (Englewood Cliffs, N.J.: Prentice-Hall, 1977), 4th ed., p. 96.

[19] For surveys see Leonard W. Weiss, "The Concentration-Profits Relationship," in *Industrial Concentration: The New Learning*, edited by H. Goldschmid, M. Mann, and F. Weston (Boston: Little, Brown, 1974), pp. 196–200); Stephen A. Rhoades, "Structure-Performance Studies in Banking: A Summary and Evaluation," Staff Economic Studies, No. 92 (Board of Governors of the Federal Reserve System, 1977); F. M. Scherer, *Industrial Market Structure and Economic Performance*, 2nd ed. (Chicago: Rand McNally, 1980), pp. 267–295.

[20] R. D. Buzzell, B. T. Gale, and R. G. M. Sultan, "Market Share—A Key to Profitability," *Harvard Business Review* (January/February 1975), pp. 97–106.

[21] R. E. Caves and T. A. Pugel, *Intraindustry Differences in Conduct and Performance* (New York University, Graduate School of Business Monograph Series in Financial Economics, 1980); D. J. Ravenscraft, "Structure-Profit Relationships at Line of Business and Industry Level," FTC Paper (1981).

Figure 5–3. Positive Relationships Between Profit and Concentration

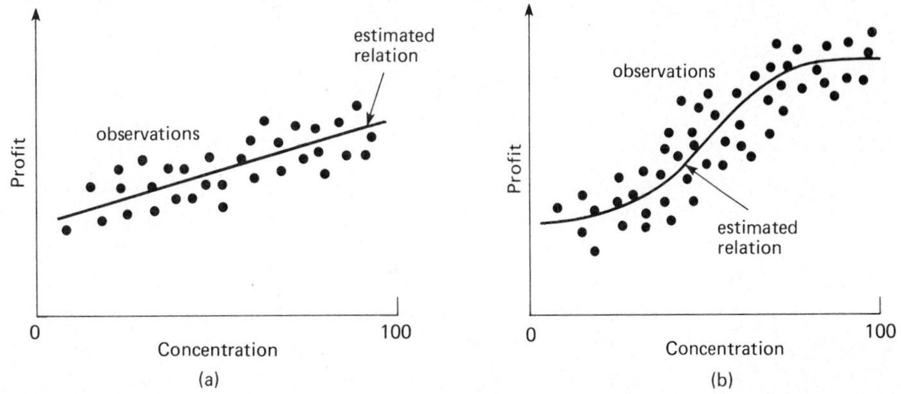

tensity, and the risk faced by small firms occupying market fringes.[22] When tested, these measures tend to reveal a positive association between the height of entry barriers and profit. Table 5–4 gives numerical values for advertising (which doubles as a measure of product differentiation) from a study of food manufacturing firms, a study that also found an effect from concentration similar to that depicted in Figure 5–3(b). For any given level of concentration, profit is 4.4 percentage points higher when advertising as a percentage of sales is 5% as compared to 1% (e.g., $10.7 - 6.3 = 4.4$ from the top line). Such a strong positive effect is limited to products for which advertising is particularly potent in image-building, namely, relatively low-priced convenience goods with "hidden"

Table 5–4. Profit Rates of Food Manufacturing Firms Associated with Levels of Industry Concentration and Advertising to Sales Ratios

Four-Firm Concentration	Advertising to Sales Ratio (%)				
	1.0	2.0	3.0	4.0	5.0
40	6.3	7.4	8.5	9.6	10.7
50	9.3	10.4	11.5	12.6	13.7
60	11.0	12.1	13.2	14.3	15.4
70	11.5	12.6	13.7	14.8	15.9

Source: William H. Kelly, On the Influence of Market Structure on the Profit Performance of Food Manufacturing Companies (Federal Trade Commission, 1969), p. 7.

[22] R. E. Caves, J. Khalilzadeh-Shirazi, and M. E. Porter, "Scale Economies in Statistical Analyses of Market Power," Review of Economics and Statistics (May 1975), pp. 133–140; William S. Comanor and Thomas A. Wilson, "Advertising, Market Structure, and Performance," Review of Economics and Statistics (November 1967), pp. 423–40; Dale Orr, "An Index of Entry Barriers and its Application to the Structure Performance Relationship," Journal of Industrial Economics (September 1974), pp. 39–49; and Robert J. Stonebraker, "Corporate Profits and the Risk of Entry," Review of Economics and Statistics (February 1976), pp. 33–39.

qualities—e.g., prepared foods, soda pop, detergent, beer, cigarettes, and drugs. For other products (and services) advertising can even be procompetitive.[23]

2. TECHNICAL EFFICIENCY

On the face of it, one might expect to find a positive association between technical effi-

[23] D. F. Greer, Industrial Organization and Public Policy (New York: Macmillan, 1980), pp. 386–393.

ciency (i.e., productivity) and market power because market power is often grounded on genuine economies of scale. To some extent this is probably true. But there are also reasons to expect that a lack of competition leads to lassitude, inertia, delay, and other adverse effects on productivity that have come to be called *X-inefficiency*.[24] Several examples of competitive impact come from cartel case studies. In a study of price fixing in the gymnasium seating, rock salt, and structural steel industries, Bruce Erickson found cost increases of 10–23% due to competition's strangulation.[25] After a massive study of cartel records, Corwin Edwards concluded that available evidence "indicates that the characteristic purposes of cartels point away from efficiency and that their activities tend to diminish efficiency."[26]

Intermarket statistical assessments of X-inefficiency are difficult to devise. But the few so far completed indicate that X-inefficiency is positively associated with market power. In one of the most interesting of these, Walter Primeaux carefully compared costs of electricity production in two separate sets of cities—those with electric utility *monopolies* and those with direct competition between *two firms* (of which there were 49 cities). He found "that average cost is reduced, at the mean, by 10.75 per cent because of competition. This reflects a quantitative value of the presence of X-efficiency gained through competition."[27]

3. PROGRESSIVENESS

Technological progress entails three steps—invention, innovation, and diffusion. Invention is the first realization and crude proof that something will work. Innovation is the first commercial application of the invention. And diffusion is the spread of its adoption. Performance at each step has been measured various ways, permitting tests of the influence of *firm size* generally and *market concentration* in particular. In both respects there appear to be *some* benefits to bigness but those benefits are usually exhausted well before reaching the aggregate sizes of the top 100 or market concentration ratios in the 70s.[28]

Early theorizing on the relation between progress and *firm size* stressed the virtues of bigness. But two decades of subsequent study have shown that emphasis to be misplaced. In the aggregate, R & D effort is concentrated in the hands of the top 600 firms, but *inventive* output is not commensurate with the input of these firms. Within specific industries there is *no* evidence indicating that R & D intensity, relative to firm size, increases beyond medium sized firms. Indeed, the largest firms are much less spirited than medium sized firms in many industries. Moreover, within most industries, inventive output does not match measured input, apparently because diseconomies of scale occur beyond moderate size levels.

The record regarding *innovation* and firm size is much the same. The largest firms cannot claim credit for a disproportionate share of the innovations. Except in chemicals, firms of less than ponderous proportions are the best. The largest firms in some industries lead in diffusion.

[24] W. S. Comanor and H. Leibenstein, "Allocative Efficiency, X-Efficiency and the Measurement of Welfare Losses," *Economica* (August 1969), p. 304.

[25] W. Bruce Erickson, "Price Fixing Conspiracies: Their Long-term Impact," *Journal of Industrial Economics* (March 1976), pp. 189–202.

[26] Corwin D. Edwards, *Economic and Political Aspects of International Cartels*, U.S. Senate, Subcommittee on War Mobilization of the Committee on Military Affairs, 78th Congress, Second Session (1944), p. 40.

[27] Walter J. Primeaux, "An Assessment of X-Efficiency Gained Through Competition," *Review of Economics and Statistics* (February 1977), pp. 105–08.

[28] For surveys see Scherer, *op. cit.*, pp. 407–438; M. I. Kamien and N. L. Schwartz, "Market Structure and Innovation: A Survey," *Journal of Economic Literature* (March 1975), pp. 1–37; E. Mansfield, J. Rapoport, A. Romeo, E. Villani, S. Wagner, and F. Husic, *The Production and Application of New Industrial Technology* (New York: W. W. Norton, 1977), pp. 1–20.

But their showing in that respect is tarnished by several qualifications.

The influence of market *concentration* is still somewhat uncertain because test results conflict. Nevertheless, several faint outlines seem discernable. First, it is perhaps most plausible to suppose that neither monopoly nor pure competition are very good for vigorous advance. Incentive and ability blend in the middle ranges of structure, as evidence on R & D effort seems to bear out. Second, the facts concerning innovation indicate that the relative performance of leading firms diminishes as concentration increases. Finally, several studies of diffusion testify to the benefits of competitive structures. Other things being equal, high concentration and lofty entry barriers hinder the spread of technological breakthroughs.

4. INFLATION AND UNEMPLOYMENT

Economists typically consider inflation and unemployment to be the responsibility of macroeconomic fiscal and monetary policy rather than antitrust policy because these problems usually have macroeconomic origins unrelated to market structure. Indeed, some economists believe that market structure has nothing whatever to do with these problems. Still, among economists who appreciate the macroeconomic characteristics of these problems, there are many who maintain that market power may well have an adverse influence. This influence is neither simple nor obvious. Inflation cannot, for instance, be due to monopolistic prices that forever rise relative to competitive prices. Simple theory and observation tell us that a monopolist's price *level* will tend to be *relatively* high. But that's all. Rate of change in price level, which is what inflation is all about, is something altogether different. And industry concentration is generally unrelated to individual industries' rates of price change over the long run.

The adverse influence, then, appears in two forms. The *first*, and most widely supported by available evidence, is that oligopolistic market power tends to make prices relatively sticky or inflexible on the down side. That is, when confronted with slack demand such as that produced by a recession, oligopolists tend to cut their output instead of their prices. Indeed, oligopolists occasionally raise their prices in the face of flagging demand (as compared to more competitive firms). In turn, this behavior seriously frustrates macroeconomic policy makers because their chief weapon against inflation is the deliberate curtailment of aggregate demand (recession) by means of stringent monetary and fiscal policy. Price rigidity on the downside thus fosters higher and longer unemployment than otherwise for each patch of ground gained in the battle against inflation. With sacrifices in unemployment accentuated in this way, appropriate macro policies will be unduly delayed, or timorously applied, or more costly than necessary when vigorously applied.[29]

The *second* adverse influence that market power may impose is more pervasive and persistent yet more difficult to detect and verify—namely, an inflationary bias over the entire business cycle. The most likely source of this bias is a combination of labor market power, in the form of unionization, and product market power. And unionization and concentration tend to be highly correlated. Briefly stated, the confluence of these powers *enables* labor to

[29] See for examples P. Cagan, "Changes in the Recession Behavior of Wholesale Prices in the 1920's and Post-World War II," *Explorations in Economic Research NBER* (Winter 1975), pp. 54–104; A. E. Kahn, "Market Power Inflation: A Conceptual Overview," in *The Roots of Inflation* (New York: Burt Franklin & Co., 1975); and "Interview with Friedrich von Hayek," *Business Week* (December 15, 1980), pp. 110, 114. A corollary to oligopolistic price rigidity is oligopolistic employment instability; see Robert M. Feinberg, "Market Structure and Employment Instability," *Review of Economics and Statistics* (November 1979), pp. 497–505.

make a short-run reach for greater real-income share even in the absence of the structural alterations that would in fact permit the long-run realization of this goal, and this press for added income causes wage and price inflation.

The role of product market power in this wage-push inflation could be substantial because union motives are likely to be most effectively expressed in highly concentrated industries with barriers to new (nonunion) firm entry. The higher profits of such industries provide a "target" for unions to "shoot at." Moreover, firms in these industries may be less resistant than competitive firms to union demands because (1) they can more easily raise prices, (2) they may want to maintain labor queues in anticipation of fluctuations in production, and (3) they may gain some prestige from paying premium wages. Under these circumstances, product market power would have an indirect inflationary effect through wages.[30]

It must be stressed that, as above, this cost-push inflationary force could be prevented by an appropriately stringent monetary-fiscal policy. But once again this check could be achieved only at the expense of substantially greater unemployment than otherwise. In other words, these two forms of inflationary influence tend to deprive the macro authorities of simultaneous control over *both* aggregate price level and employment level. Laudable official achievements in one respect therefore inflict losses in the other.

Summary

The path leading to antitrust policy is thus lit by a vast array of candles from economic theory and evidence. To be sure, some parts of the path are better illuminated than others,

but the general direction is fairly clear. It may be assumed, then, that antitrust policy is desirable, possible, and necessary. Such policy is *desirable* because competition is usually desirable. Competitive structure, conduct, and performance typically serve the public interest by gratifying many, if not most, of the value judgments specified in Chapter 1. Antitrust policy is *possible* because it is not hopelessly at odds with economies of scale or with technological progress or with business initiative. Finally, antitrust policy is *necessary* because the desired degree of competition is not self-sustaining, not automatically forthcoming. In the absence of antitrust policy, mergers among competitors would be much more common, cartels would flourish, and the use of various exclusionary and otherwise anticompetitive practices would abound simply because businesses stand to profit by them.

If one or more of these three assumptions is rejected for all or part of antitrust policy, then all or part of such policy may be discarded. Thus some critics claim that antitrust is neither desirable nor possible because bigness is best and monopolistic control is inevitable in most industries. These critics typically look upon utility type regulation and government ownership as the preferred courses of action.[31] Still other critics argue that antitrust is unnecessary because competition is everywhere, is self-maintaining, and is too intense to be stifled by greedy businessmen.[32] Partial acceptance of these critical views is reflected in the fact that we have a *mix* of policies, a mix that includes utility regulation, government ownership, and outright antitrust exemptions. But acceptance to the point of abandoning all or a major portion of our antitrust policy must be regarded as a remote and unwise possibility.

[31] John Kenneth Galbraith, *The New Industrial State* (Boston: Houghton Mifflin, 1967).

[32] Robert Bork, *The Antitrust Paradox* (New York: Basic Books, 1978).

[30] D. Greer, *op. cit.*, pp. 508–539.

II. The Aims of Antitrust Policy

Antitrust policy may serve a variety of ends, enough of a variety to spark controversy over what ends should be chosen.[33] For our purposes, four possible aims may be considered—(a) the maintenance of competition as an end in itself, (b) the prohibition of unfair business conduct, (c) the achievement of desirable economic performance, efficiency in particular, and (d) the containment of absolute business size.[34]

(a) The Maintenance of Competition. As Carl Kaysen and Donald Turner remark, "Competition as an end in itself draws its justification from the desirability of limiting business power."[35] This, then, is largely a structural goal, whose earmarks would include such features as (1) fairly free entry and investment, (2) an ample number of alternative sellers and buyers in markets, and (3) no more than moderate concentration. Conduct could also be covered, with hard prohibitions against cartelization. It is important to note that these are standards for *workable competition,* not perfect competition. The requirements for perfect competition are so extremely unrealistic, given the natural deviations mentioned previously, as to be poor guides to policy. Thus workable competition is a less precise but more realistic derivative.

While business power is thus most typically reckoned in economic features, it may also carry political and social implications because political and social power are often grounded on economic power. Senator Kefauver gave expression to this view when in defense of his antimerger act he argued: "Through monopolistic mergers the people are losing power to direct their own economic welfare. When they lose the power to direct their economic welfare they also lose the means to direct their political future."[36]

(b) Fair Conduct. The foregoing relates primarily to the *mere possession* of market power, not to its *exercise.* In contrast, aims of fair conduct relate more to the way business power is used rather than its mere presence. Should sellers be allowed to engage in tying and exclusive dealing? Should large buyers get their supplies more cheaply than small buyers merely because of bargaining power? Also, what about group boycotts and aggregated rebates? Antitrust could attempt to lay down certain standards of fair business conduct that would curtail these kinds of practices without necessarily attacking the economic power that makes them onerous.

(c) Desirable Economic Performance. Because market structure and conduct greatly affect economic performance, antitrust policy could be concerned with structure and conduct *only* in so far as they clearly produce poor performance, while overlooking any concentrations of power or unfair practices that had no discernable effect on performance or promised potential improvements therein. Advocates of this aim typically ignore performance as it relates to progressiveness, macrostability, or income equity. Rather they advocate allocative and technical efficiency as the sole aims for antitrust.[37]

(d) Limiting Big Business. Given the substantial contributions that product and geographic diversification can make to business size, antitrust could serve a goal of limiting absolute firm size (apart from any aim of limiting

---

[33] See e.g., R. H. Bork, W. S. Bowman, Jr., H. M. Blake, and W. K. Jones, "The Goals of Antitrust: A Dialogue on Policy," *Columbia Law Review* (March 1965), pp. 363–443.

[34] Carl Kaysen and Donald F. Turner, *Antitrust Policy* (Cambridge: Harvard University Press, 1959), pp. 11–22.

[35] Ibid., p. 14.

[36] Quoted by Robert Pitofsky, "The Political Content of Antitrust," *University of Pennsylvania Law Review* (April 1979), p. 1063.

[37] Robert Bork, "Legislative Intent and the Policy of the Sherman Act," *Journal of Law and Economics* (October 1966), pp. 7–48.

power in particular markets). For political and social reasons many Americans, Thomas Jefferson among them, have seen danger in gargantuan aggregations of power. An outsized conglomerate may, for instance, "gain favors regarding taxes, import competition, government contracts, and other amenities which will give it an advantage over its rivals."[38] Conversely, small independent businesses may be encouraged and protected under this aim if we consider them to be the sentinels of democracy, the benefactors of local communities, and the exemplars of good citizenship.

These four objectives being the main possibilities, what are the actualities? Which of these aims is the target of U.S. antitrust policy as revealed in the pronouncements and actions of our legislatures, enforcement agencies, and courts? In fact, there is no clearcut answer. All four have apparently played a part, depending on time, circumstance, and source. But, at least until recently, maintenance of competition and fair conduct seem to have dominated. To cite some authorities:

· If there has been any persistent policy and approach, it has been that of protecting competitive opportunities and competitive processes by preventing unfair, unreasonable, or coercive conduct . . .[39]
· The rationale of antitrust is essentially a desire to provide legal checks to restrain economic power and is not a pursuit of efficiency as such.[40]
· Taken as a whole the legislative history [of the Celler-Kefauver Act] illuminates congressional concern with the protection of *competition* . . .[41]

Of late, many conservative commentators and several court opinions have argued that, to the contrary, the sole aim of antitrust was originally and now should be economic efficiency.[42] This position has been challenged on several grounds, however. First, the historical record does not support the notion that economic efficiency riled the original legislators. Indeed, the Sherman Act was passed well before economists had developed the meaning of allocative efficiency as we know it today. Efficiencies from scale economies were appreciated at the time, but antitrust certainly cannot provide these efficiencies.[43] Second, and aside from original intent, one may question whether economic efficiency *should* be the sole aim of antitrust. Skeptics question the practicality, clarity, accuracy, and general wisdom of such an approach.[44]

The alert reader might wonder whether this dispute poses any hopeless dilemmas. As we have seen, empirical evidence demonstrates that success at maintaining competition will quite likely bear fruits of efficiency, not to men-

[38] Kenneth G. Elzinga, "The Goals of Antitrust: Other Than Competition and Efficiency, What Else Counts," *University of Pennsylvania Law Review* (June 1977), p. 1198.
[39] Kaysen and Turner, *op. cit.*, p. 18.
[40] A. D. Neale, *The Antitrust Laws of the U.S.A.,* (Cambridge: Cambridge University Press, 1962), p. 487.
[41] The Supreme Court in *Brown Shoe Co.* v. *U.S.*, 370 U.S. 294 (1962).

[42] Bork, *op. cit.;* Richard A. Posner, *Antitrust Law: An Economic Perspective* (Chicago: University of Chicago Press, 1976).
[43] In fact, the Sherman Act was passed over the strenuous objections of prominent economists who thought that all big businesses were forged from such efficiencies. F. M. Scherer, "The Posnerian Harvest: Separating Wheat from Chaff," *Yale Law Review* (April 1977), pp. 974–984; William L. Baldwin, *Antitrust and the Changing Corporation* (Durham, N.C.: Duke University Press, 1961), pp. 3–39; Richard Hofstadter, "What Happened to the Antitrust Movement" in E. F. Cheit (ed.), *The Business Establishment* (New York: John Wiley & Sons; 1964), pp. 113–151; Hans B. Thorelli, *The Federal Antitrust Policy* (Stockholm, 1954).
[44] Scherer, ibid; Lawrence A. Sullivan, *Handbook of the Law of Antitrust* (St. Paul, Minn.: West Publishing, 1977), pp. 2–8; Roger Sherman, *Antitrust Policies and Issues* (Reading, Mass.: Addison-Wesley, 1978), pp. 25–26; Walter Adams, "The Case for Structural Tests," in Weston and Peltzman (eds.) *Public Policy Toward Mergers* (Pacific Palisades: Goodyear, 1969), pp. 13–26; and Lawrence A. Sullivan, "Antitrust Microeconomics and Politics: Reflections on Some Recent Relationships," *California Law Review* (January 1980), pp. 1–12.

tion such other fruits of good performance as spirited progressiveness, equitable income distribution, and economic stability. Yet there is some substance to the debate because those advocating the efficiency approach question the evidence linking competition with good results. They favor giving greater latitude to big business. And the rising frequency of court judgments adopting the efficiency approach has led to decisions with distinctive earmarks.

Another recent debate on aims has been stirred by liberals, like Senator Edward Kennedy, who advocate a larger role for absolute limits on corporate size. Such advocacy is grounded mainly on political and social considerations,[45] but to date it has made little headway.

III. Outline of the Antitrust Laws

A. Statutes

The objective of maintaining free and fair competition may be found in the language of the antitrust statutes themselves. Very briefly, the laws have five main divisions.

1. *Collusion.* Under Section 1 of the Sherman Act, it is illegal to enter into a contract, combination, or conspiracy in restraint of trade. This forbids cartelization to fix prices or allocate territories and bans collective boycotts.
2. *Monopolization.* Under Section 2 of the Sherman Act, it is illegal to monopolize, to attempt to monopolize, or to combine or conspire to monopolize trade. (Despite the word "monopolize," market shares of less than 100% may be in violation.)
3. *Exclusionary Practices.* The Clayton Act, in Section 2 (as amended by the Robinson-Pat-

man Act) and Section 3, prohibits price discrimination, exclusive dealing, tying, and related practices where the effect may substantially lessen competition.
4. *Mergers.* Section 7 of the Clayton Act (as amended by the Celler-Kefauver Act) bans mergers that may substantially lessen competition.
5. *Unfair or deceptive practices.* The Federal Trade Commission Act makes it illegal to use unfair or deceptive practices (regardless of their impact on competition).

Because anticompetitive effects need not be shown to establish the illegality of deceptive practices, our discussion of those practices will be postponed until Part III of the book. As for the rest, it will be noted that maintenance of competition is the thrust of the law. Cartel participants cannot defend themselves by claiming that their conspiracy boosts employment. Anticompetitive mergers are not excused in the event they produce efficiencies.

B. Remedies

Violations of the Sherman Act may be greeted by either criminal or civil proceedings. If **criminal** the proceedings may establish guilt by jury trial, wherein the violation must be shown by proof beyond a reasonable doubt, or by the defendant's plea of guilty. The remedies in such cases may be *fines,* or *imprisonment,* or both. Criminal proceedings may be settled without trial, however, in which case the out-of-court settlement is called a *nolo contendere* plea (I do not wish to content). Although technically speaking nolo contendere pleas are not admissions of guilt, they too can result in rather severe penalties. Given the severity of the consequences of criminal proceedings, and given the stiff standards of proof they require, such proceedings are usually confined to violations of Section 1 of the Sherman Act. Section

[45] U.S. Senate, Subcommittee on Antitrust, Monopoly and Business Rights of the Committee on the Judiciary, *Mergers and Economic Concentration, Hearings,* Part 1, 96th Congress, 1st Session (Washington, D.C., 1979).

2 typically prompts civil actions, as is always true of the other statutes.

Civil proceedings may be awakened by any of the offenses mentioned. They may likewise result in trials, but the vast majority of civil proceedings are terminated by *consent decrees*—that is, negotiated settlements subject to court approval. The remedies accompanying civil offenses are supposed to be corrective, not punitive as in criminal proceedings. Civil remedies are therefore less dramatic than fines and imprisonment, but they are often no less serious to guilty parties. These remedies include injunction, divestiture, and treble damages. An *injunction,* or cease-and-desist order, typically prohibits an antitrust violator from some specified future conduct. For instance, mergers may be banned for ten years or tying may be proscribed indefinitely. If *divestiture* is ordered (or agreed to under a consent decree), the defendant must sell off a part of its business, or dissolve into a number of separate independent entities. Such structural surgery is, for obvious reasons, limited to violations of the monopolization and merger statutes. Lastly, *treble damages* may be extracted from violators by *private* parties who feel injured by the violators' antitrust offenses, provided those private parties can successfully sue for such damages. These treble damage actions are almost wholly confined to transgressions involving cartelization and exclusionary practices. Though essentially private (as opposed to public) actions, state attorneys general may sue on behalf of their residents under the *parens patriae* provision of the Antitrust Improvements Act of 1976. It should be noted that private plaintiffs have the dual burden of proving *both* violations and damages. If a violation has been previously proven by trial verdict or guilty plea in a government case, the first half of a private plaintiff's burden is generally satisfied. That is, *prima facie* proof of wrongdoing has been established. But if the government settles its case with a consent decree or nolo contendere, the private plaintiff's burden remains whole and heavy. Thus, for purposes of evading private treble damage suits, defendants in government suits often like to settle those suits without trial. Of course private plaintiffs may still file suit in any event, and may sue even when there is no official action at all.

IV. Enforcement

A. Introduction

Federal government enforcement is shared by the Antitrust Division of the Department of Justice and the Federal Trade Commission. (A large number of states also have their own antitrust laws, which are enforced by state attorneys general.) Private enforcement, instigated by offended enterprises or consumers, is generally conducted by private lawyers in the "antitrust bar," now numbering 10,000 or so in membership. These folks also spend a great deal of their very valuable time and talent (often billed at well over $100 per hour) *defending* those on the receiving end of government and private actions.

Table 5–5 gives some rough, historical idea of the extent and focus of official enforcement activity by reporting the number of antitrust cases and number of specific allegations in those cases from the origins of the Antitrust Division and the FTC up through 1969. The operations of the two agencies overlap substantially. The main reason for this overlap is that the Antitrust Division and the FTC have concurrent jurisdiction to enforce the Clayton Act and its amendments. The Sherman Act is, technically speaking, the sole province of the Antitrust Division while the Federal Trade Commission Act is enforceable only by the FTC. Overlap occurs in these areas also, however, because the FTC can reach violations of the Sherman Act through

Table 5–5. Number of Antitrust Violations Alleged up to 1970, Antitrust Division of Department of Justice and Federal Trade Commission

Violation Charged	Antitrust Division (1890–1969)	Federal Trade Commission (1915–1969)
Horizontal Price-Fixing	989	291
Boycott	245	125
Monopolization	370	60
Merger	194	187
Tying	65	89
Exclusive Dealing	140	152
Price Discrimination	123	144*
Violence	47	18
Labor	125	11
Patents	165	7
Other	261	221
Total Cases	1551**	1305

* Excludes Robinson-Patman cases except those charging predatory price discrimination.
** Total allegations exceed total cases because of multiple allegations per case.

Source: Richard A. Posner, "A Statistical Study of Antitrust Enforcement," *Journal of Law & Economics* (October 1970), pp. 398, 408.

actions brought under the broad language of the FTC Act. That is to say, the "unfair methods of competition" condemned by the FTC Act have been interpreted by the courts to include those things running afoul of the Sherman Act. The result is that, in practice, overlap prevails except in two main respects. For one, only the Antitrust Division can press criminal charges. For another, only the FTC enforces the FTC Act and the Robinson-Patman amendment to the Clayton Act. Faced with concurrent jurisdiction in other antitrust areas, the Department of Justice and the FTC exchange notifications and clearances to assure that they do not duplicate their efforts on specific cases. This exchange seems to have worked fairly well.

Of course there are no such clearances be-tween private plaintiffs and the official agencies, but private actions by nature tend to march to the beat of different drummers. When it comes to proving violations, aggrieved private parties readily allow and even encourage the government to bear the expense. Private plaintiffs can then concentrate their resources on treble damage suits, riding the wakes of government victories. When the government does not act, private parties are entirely on their own. Budget boundaries and bureaucratic judgments keep the government from bearing the expense in many instances, leaving ample room for private action. All told, over the past thirty years, private suits have outnumbered government suits substantially. The 1950s witnessed about 300 private suits per year. The pace then quickened to reach about 1,500 such suits per year in the late 1970s. In 1978, for instance, 1,435, or 95%, of all 1,507 antitrust cases commencing in U.S. Federal District Courts were private cases.[46] Public and private divergence extends to subject matter too. The vast majority of these private cases are not concerned with structural matters such as monopolization and merger, but rather with conduct abuses like price discrimination and exclusive dealing.

Subsequent chapters will reveal that relatively few of the thousands of cases ever brought, public or private, are real block-busters. Relatively few set legal precedence. Relatively few send businessmen to jail. Relatively few result in the wholesale restructuring of industries.

B. The Antitrust Division of the Department of Justice

Where do the Antitrust Division's cases begin? Usually with staff lawyers, somewhere in the bottom half of the organization structure

[46] *Annual Report of the Director of the Administrative Office of the U.S. Courts, 1978,* Table 28, p. 78.

Thumbnail Sketch 1:   Antitrust Division, U.S. Department of Justice

---

Established: 1903

Purpose: To administer and enforce antitrust and related laws.

Legislative Authority: Sherman Act of 1890; Clayton Act of 1914; Celler-Kefauver Act of 1950; Hart-Scott-Rodino Antitrust Improvement Act of 1976; various statutory provisions which require government regulatory agencies to consider preservation of competition.

Regulatory Activity: Investigates possible violations, conducts grand jury proceedings for criminal cases, prepares and argues cases in federal courts, pursues appeals, and negotiates and enforces final judgments.

Organization: The agency is a part of the Department of Justice and is headed by an Assistant Attorney General. Major subdivisions include General Litigation Section, Foreign Commerce Section, Regulated Industries Section, and Consumer Affairs Section.

Budget: 1982 Estimate, $44 million.

Staff: 1982 Estimate, 829.

---

given in Figure 5–4. The lawyers supervising the division are political appointees rather than career bureaucrats, and although they have final approval on which cases will be brought, they rarely initiate cases.

An investigation usually springs from the complaints of citizens, of businessmen, of other government agencies, or from reports in the business press. From there, the investigation may progress to rather formal stages, including the use of a grand jury in criminal proceedings. Most investigations never go beyond preliminary probings, but for those that do, a draft complaint will be drawn up, a supporting report will be written, and numerous consultations will be held among division personnel. Upon approval of the Assistant Attorney General for Antitrust, the case is then filed in one of our ninety Federal District Courts for trial or settlement sanction. From there on, the federal courts become the instrument through which the Department of Justice must work,

as traced in Figure 5–5. The decision of the District Court may be appealed by either plaintiff or defendant to the appropriate Circuit Court of Appeals (there are eleven of them). Eventually, the case may be appealed to a third and final level, the Supreme Court, which may or may not grant a hearing depending on whether at least four of the nine members of that august body want to review the case. (Acceptance is called granting *certiorari.*)

The ultimate test of a division lawyer's work-product is how well it stands up in court. In this context, a "star" government lawyer *prosecutes* adroitly:

> He is proud of having been trained to be an aggressive, bright but nonintellectual, technically competent, two-fisted prosecutor. He conceives of himself as an adversary, and he wants to win; but more than that, he wants to win by virtue of his character—his persuasiveness, hard work, canniness, and charm—as much as by force of intellect. He conceives of his practice of law as

Figure 5–4. Structure of the Antitrust Division

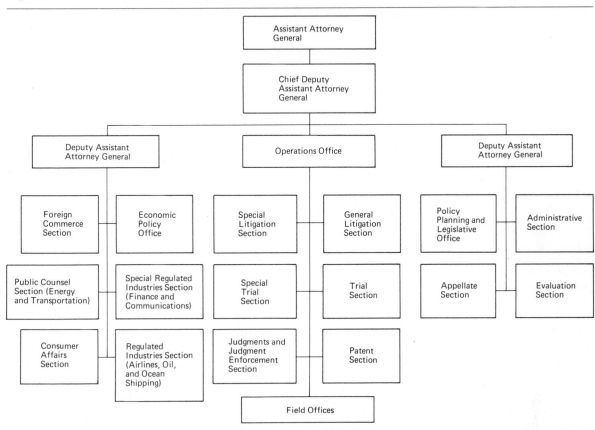

an active and combative occupation rather than as a calling that at times resembles academic scholarship in the thoroughness of its research and its concern with clarity and distinctions. And antitrust law attracts him not because of its close connection with economic theory but because its cases are exciting cases, with important consequences and with powerful men for opponents.[47]

To some extent, this picture of legal professionalism is tainted by occasional accusations

of impropriety, or worse, corruption at high levels. Whether there is a large or small number of such accusations is of course a judgment call. According to one authority on the division's operations, Suzanne Weaver, the number is so small as to cause her to wonder why the division has been corrupted so little. "Part of the answer," she says, "seems to be found in the nature of antitrust work: division personnel rarely work alone on a matter of any size, and they must frequently provide extensive written justification of their actions. Part probably comes from the fact of competition: for every business-

[47] Suzanne Weaver, *Decision to Prosecute: Organization and Public Policy in the Antitrust Division* (Cambridge: MIT Press, 1977), p. 52.

Figure 5–5. The Process of Antitrust Decisions and Litigation

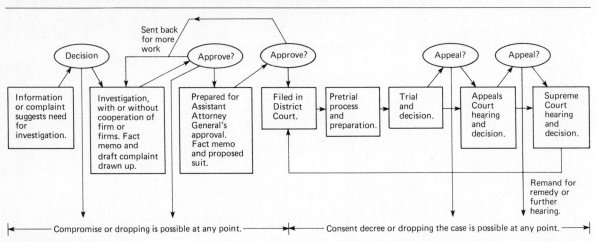

Source: William G. Shepherd and Clair Wilcox, *Public Policies Toward Business* (Homewood, Ill.: Richard Irwin, Inc., 1979), p. 103, reprinted with permission.

man who is enraged by having to defend himself against an antitrust prosecution, there is another who is absolutely delighted to see him suffering."[48]

Although good market performance is not the express aim of antitrust policy, such performance is by no means irrelevant. We therefore should heed Leonard Weiss's benefit-cost analysis of the Antitrust Division's work. Drawing upon empirical evidence of the extent to which prices are elevated by various anticompetitive practices, and making certain assumptions about the probabilities of successfully prosecuting cases against those practices, Weiss estimated the equity and efficiency gains bestowed upon consumers from the division's enforcement efforts during 1968–1970. Table 5–6 presents the monetary values of these estimates. The equity or distribution gains substantially

outshine the allocation efficiency gains in each instance by the very nature of the arithmetic. As pictured earlier in Figure 3–1 (on page 46), the income distribution gains represent the value of consumer price reductions, area P_1ACP_2, whereas the value of improved allocation efficiency is limited to the area ABC. Note also that these benefits in Table 5–6 are expressed in terms of thousands of dollars per lawyer-year. To compare these benefits with costs, Weiss estimates the government's cost of a lawyer year to have been $32 thousand, a cost well below all but one of the benefit figures. Furthermore, if estimated private defense costs are added to the government's costs, $192 thousand becomes the figure for comparison. And this cost also amounts to no more than a mere fraction of the estimated benefit in all but two instances—allocation efficiency in criminal collusion and exclusionary practices. Thus it appears that, for the most part, antitrust policy gives good value for the money when measured

[48] Suzanne Weaver, "Antitrust Division of the Department of Justice," in J. Q. Wilson (ed.), *The Politics of Regulation* (New York: Basic Books, 1980), p. 149.

Table 5–6.   Estimated Benefits Per Lawyer Year of Antitrust Division Cases 1968–1970

Type of Case	Distribution Gain Per Lawyer-Year ($ thousands)	Allocation Efficiency Gain Per Lawyer-Year ($ thousands)
Criminal Collusion	900	46
Civil Collusion	46,700	1,398
Monopolization	13,700	958
Horizontal Merger	17,600	355
Exclusionary Practices	2,800	14
Regulation-Practices*	52,800	2,640

* Cases in which the division argues for competition before regulatory agencies.
   Source: Leonard W. Weiss "An Analysis of the Allocation of Antitrust Division Resources," in J. A. Dalton and S. Levin (eds.), *The Antitrust Dilemma* (Lexington, Mass.: Lexington Books, 1974), pp. 50, 53.

solely (and perhaps inappropriately) by economic criteria.[49]

C. The Federal Trade Commission

Housed in a quaint triangular building on Pennsylvania Avenue in Washington, D.C., the Federal Trade Commission is headed by a panel of five commissioners each appointed to seven-year terms by the President and approved by the Senate. A supporting staff includes nearly 1400 others—administrative law judges, lawyers, economists, and so on—scattered about in the groups outlined in Figure 5–6 (and in regional offices throughout the U.S.). The Commission's work is divided into two main areas under the Bureau of Competition and the Bureau of Consumer Protection. The first is of interest here because it is responsible for antitrust

[49] This is not to say, however, that the division's cases are selected so as to maximize the extent to which the benefits exceed the costs. Extensive study of this question led John Siegfried to conclude that "economic variables have little influence on the Antitrust Division." Siegfried, "The Determinants of Antitrust Activity," *Journal of Law & Economics* (October 1975), p. 573.

matters. The second is responsible for deceptive advertising and related matters that will be taken up later. Lawyers dominate both these branches, so economic input is supplied by the Bureau of Economics, a separate but coequal branch staffed with economists.

Unlike the Justice Department, which files its cases in Federal District Courts, almost all formal FTC proceedings are initiated by an administrative complaint issued to one or more "respondents," who are then tried before an "administrative law judge." Though an integral part of the Commission, these administrative law judges maintain an appropriate degree of independence so they can serve as impartial triers of facts, following procedures and setting standards of proof very similar to those found in District Court civil trials. As Figure 5–7 suggests, either the respondents or the FTC staff attorneys may seek alteration of the administrative law judge's opinion by appeal to the Commission itself. The FTC then reviews the case, scrutinizing the issues, exhibits, and trial record. If the FTC's decision satisfies the respondent, it then becomes final. But disgruntled respondents may appeal FTC decisions to federal

Figure 5–6. Federal Trade Commission

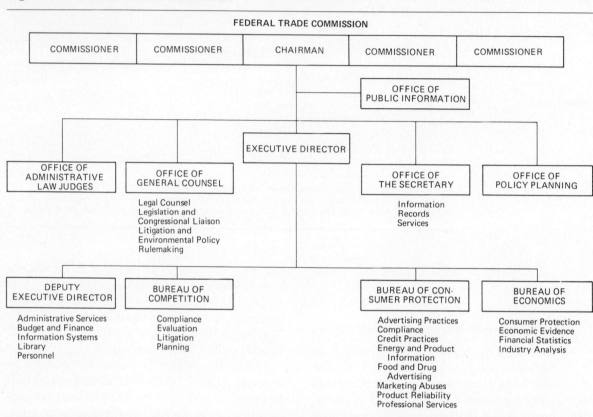

FEDERAL TRADE COMMISSION

| COMMISSIONER | COMMISSIONER | CHAIRMAN | COMMISSIONER | COMMISSIONER |

OFFICE OF PUBLIC INFORMATION

EXECUTIVE DIRECTOR

| OFFICE OF ADMINISTRATIVE LAW JUDGES | OFFICE OF GENERAL COUNSEL | OFFICE OF THE SECRETARY | OFFICE OF POLICY PLANNING |

OFFICE OF GENERAL COUNSEL
Legal Counsel
Legislation and Congressional Liaison
Litigation and Environmental Policy
Rulemaking

OFFICE OF THE SECRETARY
Information
Records
Services

| DEPUTY EXECUTIVE DIRECTOR | BUREAU OF COMPETITION | BUREAU OF CONSUMER PROTECTION | BUREAU OF ECONOMICS |

DEPUTY EXECUTIVE DIRECTOR
Administrative Services
Budget and Finance
Information Systems
Library
Personnel

BUREAU OF COMPETITION
Compliance
Evaluation
Litigation
Planning

BUREAU OF CONSUMER PROTECTION
Advertising Practices
Compliance
Credit Practices
Energy and Product Information
Food and Drug Advertising
Marketing Abuses
Product Reliability
Professional Services

BUREAU OF ECONOMICS
Consumer Protection
Economic Evidence
Financial Statistics
Industry Analysis

appellate courts including (eventually or directly depending on the circumstances) the Supreme Court.

FTC procedures differ from Antitrust Division procedures in other ways as well. The FTC's inability to bring criminal actions accounts for many of these further differences. The chief remedy relied upon by the FTC, for instance, is simply a "cease-and-desist" order, which if disobeyed can elicit daily fines of up to $10,000. This is supplemented by an occasional divestiture order in structural cases. Another major difference, is that, under the Mag-nuson-Moss Act of 1975 the Commission may bring federal or state civil actions to obtain redress for consumers or businesses injured by certain violations of the FTC Act. The Magnuson-Moss Act also provides the FTC with authority to formulate "trade regulation rules," which can be very much like legislation, carrying the force of law and setting standards for entire industries. These trade regulation rules are employed primarily to combat deceptive practices rather than antitrust trespasses, however, so our treatment of them is postponed.

Space limitations parch these procedural de-

Figure 5–7. Steps in FTC Actions

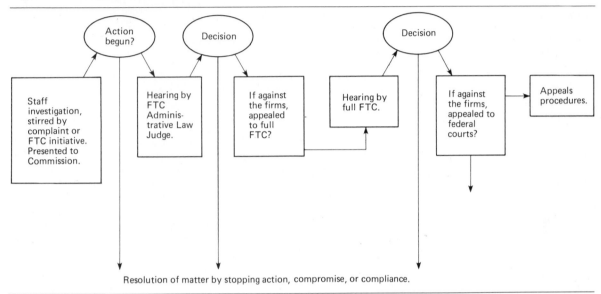

Resolution of matter by stopping action, compromise, or compliance.

Source: Shepherd and Wilcox, *op. cit.,* p. 113.

scriptions, rendering them dry. So a bit of moisture may be added by mentioning the recent history of dissension between the Bureau of Competition and Bureau of Economics over which cases the FTC should bring. The differences of opinion on how best to allocate the agency's scarce resources boils down to this. The Bureau of Competition, with its prosecution-minded lawyers, has favored conduct cases that are fairly clear-cut, easily manageable, and largely noninnovative. The Bureau of Economics, on the other hand, has urged that greater attention be paid to structural cases, which tend to be complex, protracted, and trailblazing, but which at the same time may in the end yield greater consumer benefits per dollar of enforcement expenditure. Resolution of the dispute as it affects specific cases rests with the Commission, which must approve the issuance

of all complaints. And during the 1970s the Commission did allocate more of its resources to structural cases than in earlier times.

A major constraint on the extent to which the FTC can shift in the structural direction lies in the inability of the Commission to attract competent, permanent lawyers interested in prosecuting such cases. The turnover of FTC staff attorneys is almost shocking. During the 1970s, between 13 and 25 per cent of the FTC's attorneys left *each year.* Of those leaving, 90 per cent had fewer than four years tenure with the FTC. And only a small fraction, about 10 per cent, of each year's recruits joins with expectations of staying on more than four years. For most, the FTC is thus no more than a springboard to a lucrative career in private practice, a springboard that offers novices greater opportunity for valuable trial experi-

---

Thumbnail Sketch 2:   Federal Trade Commission

Established: 1914

Purpose: To maintain vigorous, free, fair and nondeceptive competition in the market place.

Legislative Authority: Federal Trade Commission Act of 1914; Clayton Act of 1914; Export Trade Act of 1918; Robinson-Patman Act of 1936; Product Labeling Acts of 1940, 1951, 1958, and 1966; Truth-in-Lending Act of 1969; Fair Credit Acts of 1970 and 1974; Magnuson-Moss Warranty—FTC Improvement Act of 1975.

Regulatory Activity: The FTC has authority to "prevent" through cease-and-desist orders and other means: (1) general trade restraints such as price-fixing; (2) activities that tend to lessen competition such as mergers, tying, price discrimination; (3) false or deceptive advertising; (4) untruthful labeling of textile and fur products; (5) other unfair or deceptive practices.

Organization: A five member, independent commission with quasi-judicial, quasi-executive, and quasi-legislative power, supported by bureaus for competition, consumer protection, and economics.

Budget: 1982 Estimate, $69 million.

Staff: 1982 Estimate, 1380.

---

ence than is offered by private law firms or corporations.

The *Exxon* case, a large structural effort, illustrates the consequences. It "was filed in July 1973; by 1976, some forty attorneys had been assigned to work part- or full-time on the case. Of the original staff, only one lawyer remained on the case in 1976, and only four others were still working in the Bureau of Competition."[50] Adding to the problem, the FTC's scanty stock of experienced senior attorneys includes very few who like structural cases.

Another factor dampening the FTC's ardor for large structural cases is the political opposition such cases can provoke. Although an "independent" agency, the Commission's independence is compromised by the President's power of appointment and by Congress's power over

the purse strings. In making Commission appointments, for instance

the White House takes into account a number of factors: the candidate's political background, the sources of his support, his policy preferences, and the likely reaction of the Senate to this nomination. Often, the candidate is unfamiliar with the commission's work; in such cases, the backing of an influential politician or group may weigh more heavily than the nominee's fitness for a commissionership.[51]

The tethering effect of tight purse strings was spectacularly displayed in the spring of 1980 when Congress's esteem for the FTC sank so low that the agency's funding was temporarily cut off completely (a rare humiliation among bureaucracies). The irony in this is that the agency's activism during the 1970s triggered

[50] Robert A. Katzmann, "Federal Trade Commission," in J. Q. Wilson, *op. cit.*, pp. 154, 175.

[51] Ibid., p. 182.

the rebuke, but the activism had developed as a constructive response to mountains of criticism during the late 1960s that the FTC was too timid, too inept, and too inactive.[52]

D. Private Suits

Table 5–7 offers a statistical summary of the primary violations alleged in a sample of 281 private antitrust cases filed in Federal Court for the Southern District of New York during the period 1973–1978 (a sample fairly representative of all private suits at the time). The striking thing about this table is its sharp tilt toward what may be called conduct abuses, in contrast to the ample attention paid to structural matters by the government agencies, as shown earlier in Table 5–5. Whereas mergers and monopolization account for about 25% of all government allegations, they account for no more than about 8% of private allegations. Conversely, allegations of wrongful dealer termination, manufacturer's refusal to sell, vertical price-fixing, exclusive dealing, and tying show up much more prominently in private as compared to government cases.

There are many reasons for this difference. First, the time and expense of structural cases loom very large, leaving few outside the government to pick up the tab as a plaintiff. Second, damages are especially difficult to prove in instances of merger and monopolization. Third, many private plaintiffs use the antitrust laws merely as a handy weapon to gain leverage in business disputes, and claims of conduct abuse seem to serve this purpose best (especially when the defendant lacks the market

[52] See, e.g., E. F. Cox, R. C. Fellmeth, J. E. Schulz, *The Consumer and the Federal Trade Commission* (New York: Richard W. Baron Publishing Co., 1969) and *Report of the ABA Commission to Study the Federal Trade Commission,* September 15, 1969, reprinted in *The Journal of Reprints for Antitrust Law and Economics* (Winter 1969), pp. 883–1009.

Table 5–7. Primary Violations Alleged in a Sample of Private Antitrust Suits Filed in the Southern District of New York 1973–1978

Violation Alleged	Number of Cases	Per Cent of Cases
Dealer Termination and Boycotts	73	26%
Vertical Price-Fixing and Market Allocation	56	20
Exclusive Dealing and Tying	48	17
Price Discrimination	20	7
Patent or Copyright Abuse	19	7
Merger and Joint Venture	19	7
Predatory Pricing	11	4
Horizontal Price-Fixing	7	2
Monopolization	4	1
Other	24	9
Total Cases	281	100%

Source: National Economic Research Associates, *A Statistical Analysis of Private Antitrust Litigation: Final Report Prepared for the American Bar Association Section of Antitrust Law* (October 1979), p. 29 and Table B6.

power to raise even slight structural suspicions). Finally, the possibilities of collecting treble damages probably give hungry private plaintiffs particularly enticing incentive. Damage claims of $100 million after trebling seem common.

Given the many private suits filed each year, it is fortunate for the courts that very few mature into trial combat. Indeed, if the sample referred to in Table 5–7 is representative, well over 60 per cent of all private cases end in simple voluntary dismissal. Nearly 20 per cent more are otherwise settled prior to trial. Whether most of these many abandonments are due to the plaintiffs' lack of resources or to a lack of merit in their allegations is unknown, but probably a mix of both. The typical plaintiff is financially small, both absolutely and relative to the defendant. Moreover, suits actually ending in trial are usually decided in favor of the defendants (most winning by summary judgment).[53]

To the extent private cases are meritorious, they contribute *positively* to the overall enforcement effort. Suits under well-established parts of the law stimulate compliance. Private suits may also lead to new and much needed law, thereby complementing official efforts. On the other hand, private cases can contribute *negatively*. Those built on skimpy factual foundations merely congest the courts. Those that are poorly argued, or framed in such a way as to distort the issues, may end up setting undesirable precedents. Whether the pluses of private cases exceed the minuses is of course a matter of judgment. In any event, the official agencies still spearhead the formulation and refinement of mainstream policy.

V. Exemptions from Antitrust

Since passage of the Sherman Act in 1890 exemptions from antitrust have accumulated like attic junk. Some of the most important guard export cartels, labor unions, agricultural cooperatives, and regulated industries from the reaches of the law.

The first of these was the 1918 Webb-Pomerene Act exemption of export cartels. Export associations organized under the Act can fix prices on their foreign sales, allocate foreign territories, operate a single sales agency, and act in other ways that would clearly violate Section 1 of the Sherman Act. Only a few constraints apply: (1) Webb cartels must register with the Federal Trade Commission, supplying such information as the FTC may require. (2) They cannot restrain trade within the United

States or artificially influence domestic prices. (3) They cannot coerce domestic competitors who wish to export independently. The intent of the exemption was to assist American exporters, especially small enterprises, by allowing coordinated marketing efforts, larger and more efficient scales of merchandising, volume buying of transportation services, and the like. Yet, despite the apparent advantages the loophole allows, few exporters have exploited it. In 1965, for instance, only 29 active export cartels were registered with the FTC, and these accounted for a piddling 4.2 per cent of total U.S. exports. What is more, large firms from concentrated markets dominate the registration roles, not the dwarfs Congress expected. Of the total value of 1962 Webb-assisted exports, 77 per cent was shipped by firms located in industries where 50 per cent or more of domestic production was accounted for by the leading eight firms.[54] Although the record of the Webb Act is thus mixed, industry spokesmen intermittently urge an expansion of the exemption to include services as well as commodities and to permit collaborations on transfers of technology.[55]

Exemptions for agricultural organizations are granted by a number of federal statutes. The Capper-Volstead Act of 1922, for instance, allows farmers, ranchers, and dairymen to collectively process and market their products (subject to certain conditions) so long as they do not "unduly" enhance the prices of those products. The theory here is that, independently, farmers cannot market their yields efficiently or match the bargaining power of buyers, but collectively they can achieve these aims without attaining the power to restrain trade.

---

[53] National Economic Research Associates, *A Statistical Analysis of Private Antitrust Litigation* (October 1979), p. 44.

[54] Federal Trade Commission, *Economic Report on Webb-Pomerene Associations: A 50 Year Review* (Washington, D.C., 1967), pp. 23, 45. See also David A. Larson, "An Economic Analysis of the Webb-Pomerene Act," *Journal of Law & Economics* (October 1970), pp. 461–500.

[55] U.S. Senate, Subcommittee on Foreign Commerce and Tourism, *Export Expansion Act of 1971, Hearings*, 92nd Cong., 2nd Sess. (1972).

(Actually many do restrain trade; milk coops especially.)

The rationale of equal bargaining power also motivated labor union immunity. Attempts by workers to secure higher wages and better working conditions were especially encouraged by the National Labor Relations Act of 1935. Unions forfeit their exemption, however, when they conspire with businesses to bolster a price fixing agreement or drive nonunion enterprises from the field.[56] Likewise, an association of business proprietors cannot assume the disguise of a labor union in hopes of escaping the Sherman Act by subterfuge.[57]

Certainly the most pervasive exemptions relate to regulated industries. No one-sentence summary can capture the scope of these exemptions, for they are as various as the regulated industries themselves—banking, insurance, electric power, ocean shipping, communications, and so on. One way or another, however, permissiveness more or less prevails, resulting in price-fixing rings, anticompetitive mergers, entry restrictions, and other restraints. Regulation of economic results may check the otherwise bad implications. Moreover, in recent years the deregulation movement has stripped some industries of their most comfortable immunities, exposing them to the cold winds of competition. Details on these developments will occupy us in subsequent chapters.[58] Other areas where exemptions have recently been relaxed or abandoned include business practices in learned professions like architecture, in professional team sports, and resale price maintenance.[59]

[56] *Allen Bradley Co.* v. *Local 3, IBEW*, 325 U.S. 797 (1945); *UMW* v. *Pennington*, 381 U.S. 657 (1965).

[57] *Los Angeles Meat & Provision Drivers Union* v. *U.S.*, 371 U.S. 94 (1962).

[58] Almarin Phillips (ed.), *Promoting Competition in Regulated Markets* (Washington, D.C.: Brookings Institution, 1975).

[59] Roger G. Noll, "Major League Team Sports," in Walter Adams (ed.), *The Structure of American Industry* (New York: Macmillan Publishing Co., 1977), pp. 365–400.

Summary

The central problem addressed by antitrust policy is market power. Our review of economic evidence—as manifested in market structure, conduct, and performance—reveals the desirability, possibility, and necessity of such a policy. As regards *desirability,* competitive market structure, conduct, and performance typically serve society's interests. They imply decentralized decision making, fair dealing, efficiency, equity, progress, and general prosperity. The *possibility* of antitrust policy is assured by the fact that many if not most deviations from workable competition are achieved by artificial as opposed to natural means. In other words, attempts to maintain competition are not hopelessly at odds with massive economies of scale; they do not undermine technological progress; and they do not in other ways raise prohibitive costs. Lastly, antitrust appears to be *necessary* in light of the fact that competition can be suppressed or crippled; competition is not, in other words, automatic or inevitable, at least not to the degree that seems desirable. In the absence of antitrust, businesses usually have the incentive and often have the ability to monopolize, cartelize, or otherwise restrain trade.

The specific aims any antitrust policy might adopt include four main options: (1) maintenance of competition as an end in itself (or as a means to political-social decentralization), (2) prescription of fair conduct, (3) good market preformance, and (4) absolute limitations on corporate size. Legislative, judicial, and scholarly tradition support selection of the first two options for U.S. policy, although traces of support may be found for all four. Greater use of goals (3) and (4) have been urged of late by two very diverse schools of critical thought. Conservatives, who have recently risen to power and who would like to see the relaxation of much antitrust law, argue for the exclusive acceptance of goal (3) in a narrow form, namely, economic efficiency. Liberals, who find appeal in an expansion of antitrust, unsuccessfully argue that goal (4) should be added to the first two, especially for purposes of curbing large conglomerate mergers.

In essence, the antitrust laws prohibit restraints of trade, monopolization, and unfair methods of competition plus mergers and various restrictive practices when they may lessen competition. Structure and conduct share the focus. Performance may indirectly benefit, but only presumptively. The remedies backing up these provisions fall into five main classes: fines and imprisonment for criminal violations, plus injunctions, divestitures, and treble damages under civil actions. These remedies may be reached either by trial or negotiated settlements. The latter are more common in practice than the former, and in government suits go by the names nolo contendere and consent decree.

Enforcement suits may be initiated by the Antitrust Division of the Department of Justice, the Federal Trade Commission, or private plaintiffs, only the first of which can press criminal proceedings. The official agencies enjoy concurrent jurisdiction, but continuing coordination between them eliminates duplication on specific cases. Case selection entails much sorting, sifting, and deliberation. As intended, most cases emerging from the agencies stand up well under trial test. The cases remaining tend to be innovative probes searching the boundaries of law and economics. Private suits cannot, on the whole, qualify for such flattery. But they offer occasional surprises, and certainly amount to more than just trash.

Where the underlying assumptions of antitrust do not hold, where ambivalence in our commitment to competition leads to permissiveness, and where "interest" groups succeed in securing escape, exemptions prevail. Of late, many immunities have been removed, but they remain largely in place for export cartels, agricultural cooperatives, labor unions, and regulated industries.

Questions and Exercises for Chapter 5

1. What kinds of empirical evidence or theoretical reasoning would call into question the need for antitrust policy?
2. Why is structure the focus of much antitrust policy (i.e., that concerning monopolization and merger)?
3. What do you think should be the goal(s) of antitrust policy and why?
4. How do the Department of Justice and the Federal Trade Commission differ in their powers, procedures, and remedies?
5. It might be said that, in the courtroom, factual evidence is more important than economic theory. Why?
6. Quantity but not quality characterize private suits. True or False? Why?
7. Discuss exemptions in light of (a) the assumptions underlying antitrust, (b) the goals of antitrust, and (c) special interest politics.

Chapter 6

Antitrust Policy: Collusive Restraints of Trade

Between 1969 and 1973 I saw the retail price of a loaf of bread in Phoenix go from 35¢ to 69¢. At least 15% of that increase could be traced to our conspiracy. There's no question that price-fixing is a cost factor for the consumer.
—Confession of Donald Phillips
Former vice-president of Baird's Bread Company

The most venerable words in antitrust law make up Section 1 of the Sherman Act (1890), which states that:

> Every contract, combination . . . or conspiracy, in restraint of trade or commerce among the several States, or with foreign nations, is hereby declared to be illegal.

The problem with this is that it cannot mean what it says. If *every* agreement that restrained trade in some way were illegal, then commerce would shrivel to death. Long-term supply contracts, for instance, impose restraints on buyer's and sellers. Another problem with Section 1 is its brevity. Its disarmingly simple language hides potent barbs. As with all antitrust laws, extensive judicial interpretation must therefore be made. The statute's words resemble land mines set to explode when tripped by specific cases.

This chapter surveys the battle field of Section 1 cases in three steps. First, we must distinguish between several possible rules of legal analysis, per se rules and rules of reason in particular. Second, clear-cut cases like direct price-fixing receive attention. Consideration of gray areas like "conscious parallelism" and trade association "information activities" comes next. One class of Section 1 cases we cannot cover concerns collective boycotts, which are essentially per se illegal.

I. Rules and Remedies

A. Rules of Analysis

Many business agreements whose purpose is not to restrain trade may nevertheless include some incidental or ancillary restraints.

Sam's Bakery, for instance, may be sold to Joe under a contract that prohibits Sam from starting a new bakery within two miles of the old one for five years. Such a "covenant not to compete" enables Joe to get what he is paying for—a bakery with established goodwill. Early judicial interpretations of the Sherman Act held that such minor incidental restraints escaped condemnation. The courts recognized that Congress was after bigger game, namely, "all concerted arrangements which are adopted for the purpose of reducing competition, or which, regardless of purpose, have a significant tendency to reduce competition."[1] The key question, then, is whether an arrangement has the *purpose* or *effect* of seriously damaging competition. In turn, this question may be answered through application of one of two subsidiary rules, a *per se rule* or *rule of reason.*

If conduct is governed by a *per se rule,* prosecuting authorities need do no more to establish violation than prove that the offending conduct actually occurred. Direct price-fixing qualifies for this kind of treatment, so proof by such evidence as minutes of competitors' meetings or exchange of letters would be enough. No inquiry into the rationale of the conspirators, or the economic condition of the industry, or the impact on price level, or other considerations need be made. By contrast, a *rule of reason* would entail a more open-ended analysis, one where circumstances, consequences, and motives played a big part. As the Supreme Court puts it:

> There are, thus, two complementary categories of antitrust analysis. In the first category are agreements whose nature and effect are so plainly anticompetitive that no elaborate study of the industry is needed to establish their illegality—they are "illegal per se"—in the second category are agreements whose competitive effect can only be

evaluated by analyzing the facts peculiar to the business, the history of the restraint, and the reasons why it was imposed.[2]

Aside from direct price-fixing, conduct subject to per se analysis includes collusion to restrain output, to divide market territories, or to allocate customers. Monopolizing, merging, tying, and exclusive dealing are, on the other hand, governed by the rule of reason.

It is important to note that the rule of reason is usually applied under U.S. law only to determine whether, on balance, *competition is lessened,* not whether, on balance, some act is *generally good or bad.* Continuing the above quote on the Supreme Court's comparison of per se and rule of reason analysis,

> In either event, the purpose of the analysis is to form a judgment about the competitive significance of the restraint; it is not to decide whether a policy favoring competition is in the public interest, or in the interest of the members of an industry. Subject to exceptions defined by statute, that policy decision has been made by the Congress.[3]

Of course U.S. antitrust policy could be broadened. Reasonableness could be determined by comparing the costs of lessened competition with *any* alleged social benefits, in which case we would then have what F. M. Scherer calls an *expanded rule of reason.*[4] Such an approach is used by the British, whose law bans price-fixing agreements unless participants can prove that such an agreement is necessary to the provision of some specific social benefit, which benefit outweighs the detriments of restriction. Eight such potential benefits, or "gateways" to cartelization, are

[1] Lawrence A. Sullivan, *Handbook of the Law of Antitrust* (St. Paul: West Publishing Co., 1977), p. 166.

[2] *National Society of Professional Engineers* v. *U.S.* 434 U.S. 679, at 692 (1978).

[3] Ibid.

[4] F. M. Scherer, *Industrial Market Structure and Economic Performance,* 2nd Ed. (Chicago: Rand McNally, 1980), p. 502.

mentioned in English law, including (a) the protection of customers or their property against physical injury, (b) the prevention of serious and persistent adverse effects on employment in an industrialized area, and (c) the prevention of stunted export sales.[5] Such an approach is also used in the United States for a few regulated industries like banking and railroading. But such expanded rules of reason are explicitly provided by Congress in statute law, and the courts have not adopted an expanded rule of reason except insofar as Congress mandates such an approach.

Supreme Court rejection of a rule of reason approach for price-fixing most recently and resoundingly occurred in its judgment of *National Society of Professional Engineers* v. *U.S.* (1978).[6] The Society's Code of Ethics prohibited construction engineers from bidding competitively when offering their services, such as designing bridges and office buildings. This restrained engineers from submitting "any form of price information to a prospective customer which would enable that customer to make a price comparison on engineering services." The Society readily admitted the restraint, but defended it by arguing that competitive bidding would lead to shoddy engineering workmanship, endangering "public health, safety, and welfare." Rejecting the opportunity to weigh the detriments of the restraint against its alleged advantages, the Supreme Court wrote that:

> The Sherman Act reflects a legislative judgment that ultimately competition will not only produce lower prices, but also better goods and services. . . . Even assuming occasional exceptions to the presumed consequences of competition, the statutory policy precludes inquiry into

the question of whether competition is good or bad.[7]

The reasons the Court prefers a per se approach when dealing with blatant restraints of trade can be briefly appreciated: the benefits of such a rule in reduced legal expenses, reduced business uncertainty, and reduced court confusion exceed the costs of an occasional error in enforcement. As Justice Black explained it over twenty years ago, "The principle of *per se* unreasonableness . . . avoids the necessity for an incredibly complicated and prolonged economic investigation into the entire history of the industry involved, as well as related industries, in an effort to determine at large whether a particular restraint has been unreasonable—an inquiry so often wholly fruitless when undertaken."[8]

The Court's most explicit early expression of the *per se* doctrine is found in its 1927 opinion *U.S.* v. *Trenton Potteries.* Twenty-three corporations producing 82% of the vitreous pottery fixtures (bathroom bowls, tubs, and so on) in the United States were accused of conspiring to fix prices and limit production. The Court rejected their argument that the "reasonableness" of their prices should be considered, saying that:

> The aim and result of every price-fixing agreement, if effective, is the elimination of one form of competition. The power to fix prices, whether reasonably exercised or not, involves power to control the market and to fix arbitrary and unreasonable prices. The reasonable price fixed today may through economic and business changes become the unreasonable price of tomorrow. Once established, it may be maintained unchanged because of the absence of competition secured by

---

[5] Corwin D. Edwards, *Cartelization in Western Europe* (Washington, D.C.: U.S. Department of State, 1964), pp. 37–38.

[6] 434 U.S. 679 (1978).

[7] Ibid., p. 695. On the other hand, the Court softened its line a bit in a recent, rather unique private case involving the collective representation of copyright holders in what is called "blanket licensing." *Broadcast Music, Inc.* v. *Columbia Broadcasting System, Inc.,* 441 U.S. 1 (1979).

[8] *Northern Pacific Railway* v. *U.S.,* 356 U.S. 1, 5 (1958).

the agreement for a price reasonable when fixed. Agreements which create such potential power may well be held to be *in themselves* unreasonable or unlawful restraints . . .[9]

B. Remedies

This rigorous, per se standard of illegality might lead you to think that businessmen strenuously shun complicity in conspiracies for fear of being caught. Alas, life is not so simple. Well over a thousand civil and criminal prosecutions have been brought under Section 1 and many more will surely follow. During the 1970s the Justice Department launched about twenty criminal cases a year, some of them against the nation's most prominent business enterprises. In 1980, *Fortune* magazine canvassed the 1,043 companies that appeared at some point on its lists of the 800 largest corporations during the 1970s in order to compile a catalog of instances in which those corporations were successfully prosecuted for serious violations of federal law during that decade. There were five improprieties surveyed—bribery, criminal fraud, illegal political contributions, tax evasion, and criminal antitrust violations (essentially price-fixing). The startling results disclosed that, 117, or 11% of these corporations proved to be seriously delinquent at least once during the 1970s, and many of them were multiple offenders. In all, 163 separate offenses were tabulated, and the lion's share of these, 98, were antitrust violations.[10] Table 6–1 gives a glimpse of some of the guilty.

What is more, some industries distinguish themselves with near chronic delinquency.

Since the *Trenton Potteries* case of 1927, for instance, members of the vitreous plumbing fixture industry have twice been caught and found guilty of further price-fixing (a rather unsanitary record). The latest conspiracy, in the 1960s, came to light when Internal Revenue Service agents stumbled onto three tape recordings of price-fixing meetings stashed in the abandoned desk of a man they were investigating for income tax evasion. Estimates of impact indicate that prices were lifted roughly 7% on $1 billion worth of business. "Price-fixing rather than competition has been a way of life in the industry," commented an industry official who testified as a key government witness.[11]

A major contributor to the problem of widespread and repeated offenses has been the prevalence of kid glove penalties. Until recently, criminal violations were merely misdemeanors; fines could be measured in peanuts ($50,000 at most); suspended sentences were fashionable; jailings were extremely rare and brief; and many civil cases were brought. In short, crime paid. Donald Phillips, the confessed price-fixer we quoted at the outset, put it this way: "When you're doing $30 million a year and stand to gain $3 million by fixing prices, a $30,000 fine doesn't mean much."[12]

Some trend toward stiffer penalties has developed, however. The Sherman Act was amended, effective January 1, 1975, to make criminal violation a potential *felony*, punishable by as many as three years in prison, with fines as high as $100,000 for individuals and $1 million for corporations. Thus, for stark comparison, we may observe that from 1890 to 1970 only 19 people actually went to jail for pure antitrust violations for a total of 28 months. Yet during 1977 alone, and not counting misdemeanors, three and a half times that amount of jail time befell offenders. Maximums are still

---

[9] *U.S* v. *Trenton Potteries*, 273 U.S. 392, 397 (1927), (Emphasis added).
[10] Others of note: 28 cases of kickbacks, bribery, or illegal rebates, 21 instances of illegal political contributions, and 11 cases of fraud. Only domestic cases were included; "the list would have been longer had it included foreign bribes and kickbacks." *Fortune* (December 1, 1980), p. 57.

[11] See *Washington Post*, June 6, 1971; and *Fortune*, December 1969.
[12] *Business Week*, June 2, 1975, p. 48.

Table 6–1.   Major Companies Running Afoul of Sherman Act, Section 1, During the 1970s

Company	Offense and Date of Settlement
Allied Chemical	*1974*—Fixing prices of dyes. Pleaded nolo contendere.
Bethlehem Steel	*1973–74*—Two cases of fixing prices of steel reinforcing bars. Company and one employee pleaded nolo; another convicted after trial.
Combustion Engineering	*1973*—Fixing prices of chromite sand. Company and executive pleaded nolo.
Dean Foods	*1977*—Price fixing of dairy products. Nolo pleas by company and executive.
Du Pont	*1974*—Fixing prices of dyes. Nolo plea.
FMC	*1976*—Fixing prices of persulfates. Company and executive pleaded nolo.
Flintkote	*1973*—Fixing prices of gypsum board. Company, chairman, and president pleaded nolo.
Gulf Oil	*1978*—Fixing uranium prices. Pleaded guilty.
ITT	*1972*—ITT Continental Baking Subsidiary charged with fixing prices of bread. Nolo plea.
International Paper	*1974*—Fixing prices of paper labels. Company and two executives pleaded nolo. *1976*—Fixing prices of folding cartons. Company and four executives pleaded nolo. *1978*—Fixing prices of corrugated containers. Nolo plea. Fined $617,000.
Purolator	*1978*—Bid rigging and allocation of markets for security services. Nolo plea.
R. J. Reynolds Ind.	*1979*—Fixing prices of ocean shipping. Nolo plea. Fined $1 million.
Rockwell International	*1978*—Fixing prices of gas meters. Pleaded guilty.

Source: Irwin Ross, "How Lawless Are Big Companies?," *Fortune* (December 1, 1980), pp. 59–61.

rarely imposed. But the law may no longer be taken lightly.

Liability for treble damages adds still further punch. Fines in the plumbing fixture case mentioned above totaled only $752,500. The treble damages, however, were reckoned at $210 million, of which $28 million was actually paid as a result of out-of-court settlements with victimized plaintiffs.[13]

[13] For more on penalties see K. G. Elzinga and W. Breit, *The Antitrust Penalties: A Study in Law and Economics* (New Haven, Conn.: Yale University Press, 1976).

II. Varieties of Violation: Direct Agreements

A. Introduction

Given a punitive per se rule, the key remaining question is *what* constitutes "price-fixing" or "collusive restraint." Businessmen have demonstrated skill when it comes to colluding. Their artistry may be divided into two categories—(1) cases with clear evidence of anticompetitive collusion, and (2) cases offering no more than circumstantial evidence. This section covers the first category. Section III handles the second.

For sheer simplicity of obvious evidence, no collusive technique tops the *single sales agency*, whereby producers refuse to sell directly to their customers and instead sell through a common central agency that sets price for all participants. Equally obvious would be a short, written *contract* specifying minimum prices. Only a bit more complicated, is the *market allocation* approach, whereby each cartel member is assigned exclusive access to certain geographic areas or customers. The classic *Addyston Pipe & Steel* case of 1899 provides a good example of this last tactic. Six manufacturers of cast iron pipe, including Addyston, entered into agreement that, among other things, assigned certain southern and central United States cities to individual members of the cartel. These "reserved cities" were the exclusive province of the designated member. The price at which pipe was sold in each reserved city was determined jointly by the cartel, the member to whom the business was assigned paying a fixed bonus into the cartel's profit sharing pool. In order to give appearances of continued competition other members submitted fictitious bids to customers in reserved cities, "fictitious" because these bids were always at prices higher than those charged by the designated member.[14]

More modern, more complicated, and more sensational cases of express collusion come from the oil, electrical equipment, paper, and uranium industries.

B. Dancing Partners in Oil

One of the Justice Department's most celebrated victories was *U.S.* v. *Socony-Vacuum* (now called Mobil) in 1940. The defendants were major integrated oil companies accounting for 83% of all gasoline sales in the Midwestern states. They instituted a "dancing partner" program in the Midwest, under which each major agreed to buy the "surplus" gasoline of some particular independent refinery. "Surplus" was gasoline that could not be disposed of except at "distressed" prices. The independents were small and lacked spacious storage facilities. They consequently sold their "surpluses" at whatever discounted price they could get.

The defendant majors were not accused of direct price-fixing. The essence of the accusation was that removal of excess supply from the market *indirectly* propped up the price. To be sure, the defendants argued that their activities did not constitute price-fixing. They were even so bold as to argue before the Supreme Court that their innocence was confirmed by their buying most heavily when prices were *falling* and lightly when prices were *rising*. But of course this is exactly the way an indirect method of price support should work. And the Court was not fooled:

> That price-fixing includes more than the mere establishment of uniform prices is clearly evident from the Trenton Potteries case itself . . . purchases at or under the market are one species of price-fixing. In this [oil] case, the result was

---

[14] *Addyston Pipe and Steel Company* v. *U.S.*, 175 U.S. 211 (1899).

to place a floor under the market—a floor which served the function of increasing the stability and firmness of market prices. . . . Under the Sherman Act a combination formed for the purpose and with the effect of raising, depressing, fixing, pegging, or stabilizing the price of a commodity in interstate or foreign commerce is illegal *per se*.[15]

C. The Electrical Equipment Cases[16]

The electric equipment cases are to American price-fixing what Watergate is to American political corruption. The collusive activity began some time in the 1920s or 1930s. At first it was a rather casual adjunct to the industry's trade association activities, involving just a few products. By the 1950s, however, conspiracy had spread to every corner of the trade. Table 6–2 gives some idea of the vast scope of the price-fixing and of the structure of the markets involved. Roughly $7 billion of business was involved. The products ranged from $2 insulators to multimillion dollar turbine generators. The average number of firms participating in each market was 6.6. Several of the larger participants—such as General Electric and Westinghouse—operated and conspired in many of the markets. Smaller firms—like Moloney Electric and Wagner—were more specialized. In all, 29 firms and 44 individuals were indicted during 1960 for criminal conspiracies in 20 separate product lines.

Table 6–2 gives the impression that high concentration and a paucity of firms might have permitted tacit collusion in four or five of these markets. But conditions not revealed in the table provided substantial competitive pull,

thereby inducing explicit collusion. First, many of these products were not standardized but custom made and differentiable. Various collusive steps were taken to standardize product quality, especially in the early years. Second, many items of equipment were sold in big chunks, which amplified the incentive to cut prices to gain business. Even within given product lines, large orders received larger discounts off "book" price than small orders. A third factor was the volatility of the business cycle in the electrical apparatus field. These goods are durable capital equipment and experience fluctuations in demand far beyond those encountered by most other industries. Slack demand seems to have caused much price-cutting, even when the conspiracies were in high gear. Finally, technological change was fairly brisk during the decades involved.

Collusive procedures and experiences varied from product to product, from sealed-bid sales to off-the-shelf transactions, and from higher to lower levels of management. One common thread, however, was the atmosphere of skullduggery surrounding all the conspiracies. Code names, pay-phone communications, plain envelope mailings, destruction of evidence, clandestine meetings in out-of-the-way places, faked expense account records, and secret market allocations all entered the plot. Perhaps the most sensational technique devised was the "phases of the moon" system developed for sealed-bid switchgear sales:

> This system was intended to fix automatically the price each conspirator would quote, with a rotation of the low price among competitors to create the illusion of random competition. The contemplated range of bid prices was modest. According to the "moon sheet," which was in effect from December 5, 1958 through April 10, 1959, position would be rotated among the five major competitors every two weeks.[17]

---

[15] *U.S.* v. *Socony-Vacuum Oil Co.,* 310 U.S. 150 (1940).

[16] This section draws from R. G. M. Sultan, *Pricing in the Electrical Oligopoly, Vol. 1* (Cambridge, Mass.: Harvard University Press, 1974); C. C. Walton and F. W. Cleveland, Jr., *Corporations on Trial: The Electrical Cases* (Belmont, Calif.: Wadsworth, 1964); and R. A. Smith, *Corporations in Crisis* (Garden City, N.Y.: Anchor Books, 1966), Chapters 5 and 6.

[17] Sultan, *op. cit.,* p. 39.

**Table 6–2. Extent and Coverage of the Electrical Equipment
Price-Fixing Conspiracies**

Product	Annual (1959) Dollar Sales ($ millions)	Number of Firms Indicted	Share of Market (%)
Turbine generators	$400*	3 (6)*	95 (100)
Industrial control equipment	262*	9*	75*
Power transformers	210	6	100
Power switchgear assemblies	125	5 (8)*	100
Circuit breakers	75	5	100
Power switching equipment	35*	8 (15)*	90–95*
Condensers	32	7	75–85
Distribution transformers	220	8	96
Low-voltage distribution equip.	200*	6 (10)*	95*
Meters	71	3	100
Insulators	28	8	100
Power capacitors	24	6	100
Instrumental transformers	16*	3 (4)*	95*
Network transformers	15	6	90
Low-voltage power circuit breakers	9	3 (5)*	100
Isolated phase bus	7.6	4	100
Navy and marine switchgear	7	3	80
Open-fuse cutouts	6	8	75
Bushings	6	4	100
Lightning arresters	16	7	100

* Includes companies named as co-conspirators but not indicted.

Source: Adapted from *Corporations on Trial: The Electrical Cases* by Clarence C. Walton and Frederick W. Cleveland, Jr., © 1964 by Wadsworth Publishing Company, Inc., Belmont, California 94002. Reprinted by permission of the publisher.

Despite all the shenanigans, it is not clear that the conspirators were able to raise or stabilize prices appreciably in all product lines. Double-crossing was fairly commonplace. A "white sale" drove prices down to 60% of book in 1955. Many participants have made self-serving claims that their efforts failed, and it can be argued that supply and demand remained prime determinants of price level.[18] On the other hand, a federal trial judge was persuaded by the evidence that prices of turbine genera-tors would have been 21% lower were it not for the conspiracy. In addition, much evidence indicates a substantial price impact in the sealed-bid sector of the trade plus some indirect overall effect via stabilization of market shares.[19] In any event, economic consequences were relevant only to the treble damage suits, which yielded $400 million, or thereabouts. The government's criminal suits were settled under the per se rule, with seven executives

[18] Sultan is the industry's best defender, ibid.

[19] Sultan, *op. cit.*, p. 85, 210, 273; J. D. Ogur, "Competition and Market Share Instability," Staff Report to the Federal Trade Commission (August 1976), pp. 30–47.

serving brief stints in the slammer and with fines totaling $1,954,000, the bulk of which was paid by the companies.

D. The Paper Products Cases[20]

During the mid-1970s, two paper product workers, disgruntled by job loss and paultry severance pay, spilled the beans on their former employers. They gave the Justice Department evidence of price-fixing in paper labels (the kind that go on food cans) and consumer bags (like those for cookies). One thing led to another and further investigation revealed conspiracies in three other paper product fields—folding cartons (such as those for breakfast cereal and cake mix), corrugated containers and sheets (large cardboard boxes), and fine paper (like these pages). In fact, the folding carton case began unfolding when a witness in the paper label case testified: "Hell, I used to work for the folding carton division and they do the same thing over there." The overall result was a series of criminal, civil, and treble damage cases during the late 1970s that rivaled the electrical equipment cases in scope, scale, and sensationalism.

In one segment of the industry, competing manufacturers actually met to set prices. But the most common mode of operation in these cases took a rough form of customer allocation. When a paper products customer sought offers from the colluding suppliers, each potential supplier telephoned the company that previously held the business to find out how much that company was bidding. Knowing that bid price, these other potential suppliers would come in with *higher* bids. Thus, in effect, paper product customers were unwittingly wedded to their traditional suppliers, and no supplier

could increase its market share at a rival's expense through price-cutting.

Taking all these cases together, fines and damages exceeded $500 million. The vast bulk of this money came from the folding carton and corrugated container segments, enveloping the biggest cases of the lot. In folding cartons, for instance, twenty-three companies and fifty individuals were indicted. All but one of the defendant companies and two of the accused individuals elected to plead *nolo contendere*. As it turned out, the timing of these pleas could not have been worse, for they occurred shortly after Congress had stiffened the penalties for antitrust violations. Donald Baker, then head of the Justice Department's Antitrust Division, took the opportunity to argue before the judge that an example should be set, that pocket-change fines would not be enough under the new law. Although the judge shied away from imposing maximum penalties, he nevertheless responded to the situation by sentencing fourteen people to jail terms ranging from five days to sixty days, most of which were later reduced with agreements to work on worthy projects. One of the highest ranking business executives ever to serve time was caught up in this group—R. Harper Brown, then president of Container Corporation, who ended up with fifteen days in prison plus nine months' probation and twelve hours per week in penitent good works.

E. The Uranium Cartel or "Club"[21]

In the fall of 1975, Westinghouse Corporation, one of the largest suppliers of nuclear reac-

---

[20] For an interesting account of the folding carton offenses see J. Sonnenfeld and P. L. Lawrence, *Harvard Business Review* (July–Aug. 1978), pp. 145–157. See also *Forbes* (June 25, 1979), pp. 33–36.

[21] For details see June H. Taylor and Michael D. Yokell, *Yellowcake: The International Uranium Cartel* (New York: Pergamon Press, 1979), Geoffrey Rothwell, "Market Coordination by the Uranium Oxide Industry," *Antitrust Bulletin* (Spring 1980), pp. 233–268, and U.S. Congress, House, Subcommittee on Oversight and Investigations of the Committee on Interstate and Foreign Commerce, *International Uranium Cartel*, Hearings Vols. 1 and 2, 95th Congress, 1st Sess. (1977).

tors for generating electricity, stunned the business world by defaulting on commitments to deliver approximately eighty million pounds of uranium "yellowcake," the raw material of nuclear fuel fabrication. The reason for defaulting was simple: Westinghouse would have lost roughly $2 billion if it had honored its contracts, a loss caused by an enormous increase in the price of yellowcake. Westinghouse was merely a middleman in this market, buying yellowcake from mining and milling companies, then selling it to electric utilities. When the miners' price for yellowcake was $6 to $10 a pound during 1971–1974, Westinghouse committed itself to supplying twenty-seven electric utilities at prices averaging $10 a pound. But the supply was for *future* delivery, and Westinghouse unwisely did not buy for the future while it sold. When the future arrived, Westinghouse's buying price was skyrocketing—first to $14 in late 1974, then to $26 in August 1975 just before the default. Shortly thereafter in 1976 price escalated further to $41 a pound for a 600% increase in just 30 months.

In August 1976, the drama heightened. Secret memos and letters were stolen from the files of Mary Kathleen Uranium Company in Australia and made public through a bit of trickery. They revealed incriminating details of an international uranium producers' cartel, or "Club" as members called it. Starting in 1972, the Club included every major yellowcake producer in the free world outside the United States and was surreptitiously aided by the governments of the principal producing countries—Canada, South Africa, France, and Australia. The United States market was excluded at the time because U.S. policy prevented the importation of yellowcake. U.S. prices nevertheless followed world prices fairly closely because of certain links between the domestic and world markets. The link receiving greatest U.S. attention was the cartel participation of Gulf Minerals Limited, a Canadian sub-

sidiary of the Gulf Oil Corporation. Moreover, circumstantial evidence indicates the existence of some collusion among U.S. producers in the U.S. market.

The Club divided the international uranium market, established minimum prices, set terms and conditions, rigged bidding procedures, and laid plans to eliminate middlemen like Westinghouse. Details were worked out in a series of meetings in Paris, Cannes, Sydney, and elsewhere. Market quotas, such as those illustrated in Table 6–3 were modified from time to time to reflect changes in each participant's productive capacity, especially that of Australia.

The cartel probably cannot be blamed for all of the mid–70's leap in yellowcake price because other factors also contributed. Still, precise estimates of the cartel's influence are hampered by the fact that the most revealing evidence of the cartel's activities remains hidden outside the U.S. International collusive acts adversely affecting U.S. trade and commerce are subject to prosecution under the Sherman Act, but only insofar as these acts are perpetrated by private parties rather than foreign governments, and only insofar as U.S. enforcement officials and courts can gain access to evidence that all too often is sequestered abroad (sometimes at the insistence of foreign governments).[22] Foreign cartel activities in quinine, radios, watches, and other products have thus been attacked under Section 1 along with uranium. But much information on the Club remains abroad.

The Justice Department filed misdemeanor charges against Gulf Oil, to which Gulf pleaded *nolo contendere.*[23] In more rousing action,

[22] Leading cases in this regard include *American Banana Co.* v. *United Fruit Co.*, 213 U.S. 347 (1909); *U.S.* v. *Pacific & Arctic Ry. & Nav. Co.*, 228 U.S. 87 (1913); and *U.S.* v. *Sisal Sales Corp.*, 274 U.S. 268 (1927).

[23] *Wall Street Journal*, June 5, 1978, p. 2. Gulf has insisted that the Canadian government forced its cartel participation, an excuse that prompted a witty Congressman to call Gulf a "corporate Patty Hearst."

Table 6–3. The Uranium Club's Market Quotas in Percentages as Decided March, 1974, for Deliveries Through 1983

Cartel Participants	Period of Reference		
	1972–1977	1978–1980	1981–1983
Canadian producers	37.30%	21.86%	26.87%
South African producers	26.40	18.30	14.77
French producers	24.20	18.38	22.39
Australian producers	7.60	27.81	24.57
Rio Tinto Zinc	4.50	13.65	11.40

Note: Except for Rio Tinto Zinc, with subsidiaries, affiliates, or joint ventures in every one of the participating countries, the quotas were set by country. Allocations within individual countries were achieved by subcartels, such as NUFCOR of South Africa.

Source: J. H. Taylor and M. D. Yokell, *Yellowcake: The International Uranium Cartel* (New York: Pergamon Press, 1979), p. 81.

Westinghouse sued Gulf and twenty-eight other foreign and domestic yellowcake suppliers for billions of dollars in damages. In turn, Gulf countersued, accusing Westinghouse of conspiring to monopolize the nuclear reactor market and thereby whacking Gulf with billions of dollars in damages. Legally and economically the cases were very complex. About forty law firms, including a nice sample of the nation's most prestigious, entered the arena (so many that presiding trial judge Prentice Marshall called this "The Lawyers' Full-Employment Case"). A full-scale battle was avoided however when in 1981 out-of-court settlements gave Westinghouse hundreds of millions in damages.

F. Damages and Illinois Brick

Left unmentioned in the foregoing tally of whopping damages is a question that has recently sparked burning controversy: *Who may sue for damages?* Is it only those who purchase *directly* from colluders, such as the cereal manufacturers who bought folding cartons to package cornflakes? What if those direct purchasers merely "pass on" the higher prices they pay with higher prices charged to their buyers, such as grocery retailers? And what if, in turn, some or all of those higher costs are passed further on to ultimate cornflake consumers like you and me? Can we as downstream buyers sue for damages too?

In 1977 the Supreme Court handed down a key opinion on this issue—*Illinois Brick Co. v. Illinois*,[24] which involved downstream plaintiffs suing members of a cartel. The Court held that *only direct purchasers* can sue to collect illegal overcharges, even when those overcharges have been passed on to subsequent downstream buyers. The Court reached this conclusion for essentially three reasons. *First, unfair multiplication.* In an earlier case, *Hanover Shoe, Inc. v. United Shoe Machinery Corp.*,[25] the Court ruled that an antitrust violator may not defend itself from the damage

---

[24] *Illinois Brick Co. v. Illinois* 431 U.S. 720 (1977).
[25] *Hanover Shoe, Inc. v. United Shoe Machinery Corp.*, 382 U.S. 481 (1968).

claims of direct buyers by arguing that those buyers had passed on the overcharges. Having thus given direct buyers a crack at the treble damages, even when the single damages had been passed on, the Court in *Illinois Brick* said that downstream buyers could not also sue because such suits would subject violators to unfair risks of multiple treble damage liability. *Second, simplicity.* The Court stressed the complexity of attempting to deal with passing-on issues, so to keep things simple it would ignore the claims of downstream buyers. *Finally, deterrence.* The Court felt that the deterrent effect of treble damage liability would be maximized by giving rights of action to direct purchasers only, whether or not those direct purchasers were in fact injured.

The immense debate touched off by *Illinois Brick* spilled into Congress, where legislation overturning the decision has been repeatedly introduced but to date never passed. A feeling for the difficulties in reaching a satisfactory resolution may be gained by asking yourself where you would stand on the ticklish issues. You probably agree that violators should not be subject to multiple liability, not in light of the ruinous damages that might result, but should direct purchasers who pass on overcharges be given great windfalls while those truly damaged cannot recoup? Simplicity in court proceedings also has its attractions, but why can't that be compromised out of fairness to final consumers? Can we count on direct purchasers to pursue aggressively their damage opportunities, thereby providing deterrence, when those purchasers may be vulnerably dependent on their offending and perhaps revengeful suppliers for continued prosperity? Why not simply overturn *Hanover* and allow pass-through as a defense?[26]

[26] For the answers of others see Robert G. Harris and Lawrence A. Sullivan, "Passing on the Monopoly Overcharge: A Comprehensive Policy Analysis," *Univ. of Pennsylvania Law Review* (December 1979), pp. 269–360 and

III. Gray Areas and Circumstantial Evidence

A. Introduction

Express agreements are without doubt per se illegal. But what if firms behave uniformly, like a well-rehearsed chorus line, without generating evidence of meetings, phone calls, or other concrete communications? What if rivals do no more than *tacitly* agree, perhaps through price leadership?

Such "conscious parallelism" frequently occurs where market conditions are particularly conducive to a meeting of minds—that is, very few firms, very high concentration, standardized product, inelastic demand, slow growth, and smoothly flowing small-lot sales. Under these conditions, each firm can readily appreciate that price competition will lessen profit rather than increase it. (An Appendix to this chapter gives the reasons for this.) All firms may therefore avoid price competition, all acting uniformly yet independently. Legal treatment of such conduct is ticklish but important.

A related problem arises when firms exchange information on prices, costs, or other factors. The anticompetitive results just hypothesized were largely based on each firm's *certainty* about the acts of rivals and an inability to discount secretly. Stated conversely, *un*certainty can often contribute to competition. Thus interfirm exchanges of information may heighten knowledge, lessen uncertainty, and thereby facilitate collusion even in the absence of any express agreement about how to act upon the knowledge. Trade associations pose particular problems in this connection.

Our heightened knowledge of the law in these areas is best gained by discussing trade associations first and conscious parallelism sec-

the references therein, plus U.S. Senate, Committee on the Judiciary, *Antitrust Enforcement Act of 1979, S. 300,* Hearings, 96th Congress, 1st Sess. (1979).

ond, followed by two related topics—basing-point pricing and professional associations.

B. Trade Associations

Competitors are free to form, and to take active part in, trade associations. Because "education" is a prime purpose of trade associations, it is quite common for them to collect and disseminate information on a wide variety of subjects, prices included. Moreover, trade association meetings are conducive to talk of prices. As a former assistant manager for a textile firm once said: "I don't know what people would do at a trade association meeting if not discuss prices. They aren't going to talk just about labor contracts and new technology."[27] Fortunately for the consumer, trade association cover cannot immunize outright conspiracies from prosecution. In truth, approximately 30% of all cases brought by the government involve trade associations.

Still, the "information" activities of trade associations do pose problems for drawing the legal line between what does and what does not constitute price fixing. On the one hand, it can be argued that enhanced knowledge on the part of industry members lessens market imperfections, thereby fostering more effective competition. On the other hand, too much knowledge may inhibit price competition, as indicated above.

Illegal information activities are illustrated by the *American Column and Lumber* case of 1921.[28] The hardwood flooring trade association involved required each of 365 participants to submit six reports to its secretary; (1) a daily report of all actual sales; (2) a daily shipping report, with exact copies of the invoices; (3) a monthly production report; (4) a monthly stock report; (5) current price lists; and (6) inspection

reports. In turn, the trade association secretary supplied detailed reports to the firms from this information. The exchange was supplemented by monthly meetings where, among other things, speakers urged cartel-like cooperation with exhortations such as, "If there is *no increase in production,* particularly in oak, there is going to be good business," and *"No man is safe in increasing production."* The Supreme Court decided this was "not the conduct of competitors."

In subsequent cases the Court had frowned upon trade association programs involving elaborate standardization of the conditions surrounding sales, reports of future prices, and requirements that members must adhere to their reported prices. An especially important case concerning exchanges of information was *U.S. v. Container Corp. of America* (1969).[29] Although not exactly a trade association case, this case broke new ground because its analysis looked at conduct *and* structure together, rather than conduct alone, to determine the legality of an information exchange program. Moreover, this combination analysis took the Court about as far as it could go in condemning such exchanges.

The conduct at issue in *Container,* whose defendants were eighteen of fifty-one manufacturers of corrugated containers in the Southeast, was on its face seemingly innocuous:

> all that was present was a request by each defendant of its competitor for information as to the most recent price charged or quoted, whenever it needed such information and whenever it was not available from another source. Each defendant on receiving that request usually furnished the data with the expectation that it would be furnished reciprocal information when it wanted it.

---

[27] *Business Week,* June 2, 1975, p. 48.

[28] *American Column and Lumber Co. et. al.* v. *United States,* 257 U.S. 377 (1921).

[29] *United States* v. *Container Corp. of America, et al.,* 393 U.S. 333 (1969). For a more recent and related case see *United States* v. *United States Gypsum Co., et al.,* 438 U.S. 422 (1978).

These exchanges were apparently infrequent and irregular. Moreover, sellers were free to deviate from their quotes, and those receiving quotes often undercut the informant's prices. Nevertheless, the Court's majority found a violation here, stressing the oligopolistic market *structure*, which apparently solidified this conduct into noticeable if minor adverse *effects*:

> the corrugated container industry is dominated by relatively few sellers. The product is fungible and the competition for sales is price. The demand is inelastic, as buyers place orders only for immediate, short-run needs. The exchange of price data tends toward price uniformity. For a lower price does not mean a larger share of the available business but a sharing of existing business at a lower return. Stabilizing prices as well as raising them is within the ban of Section 1 of the Sherman Act . . .

Three dissenters to the *Container* opinion voiced opposite structural views. They emphasized the large number of sellers (fifty-one in total) and the ease of entry (possible with an investment of only $50,000 to $75,000). The structural analysis of the majority may therefore be questioned. Still, it is significant that the Court was of one mind on the importance of using structural conditions to gauge the competitive consequences of information exchange, a development we may applaud.

From this and earlier cases it may be concluded that price information exchanges appear to be lawful only when the industry's structure is rather competitive and "when they limit price reports to past transactions, preserve the anonymity of individual traders, make data available to buyers as well as sellers, and permit departure from prices that are filed."[30]

---

[30] Clair Wilcox, *Public Policies Toward Business*, 3rd ed. (Homewood, Ill.: Richard Irwin, 1966), p. 129.

C. Conscious Parallelism

How have the courts handled this problem? Does mere conscious parallelism fall within the meaning of "contract, combination, or conspiracy," as specified by the Sherman Act? The simplified answer that we must limit ourselves to here comes in two installments. First, *in and of itself*, conscious parallelism is not illegal. It does not provide conclusive circumstantial evidence of conspiracy. (No more than everyone's living is proof of a conspiracy to breathe, as Lawrence Sullivan says.[31]) The Supreme Court's clearest statement to this effect is found in the *Theatre Enterprises* case of 1954:

> this Court has never held that proof of parallel business behavior conclusively establishes agreement or, phrased differently, that such behavior itself constitutes a Sherman Act offense . . . "conscious parallelism" has not yet read conspiracy out of the Sherman Act entirely.[32]

Second, and on the other hand, consciously parallel behavior may well indicate an unlawful conspiracy or agreement *when viewed in conjunction with additional facts*. These additional facts, or "plus factors," may be subdivided into two categories:

1. Additional independent evidence of a more formal agreement, as illustrated by the following:[33]
   a. Elaborate exchanges of information, such as those encountered in trade association cases.
   b. Simultaneous and substantial price increases (coupled with output reductions) unexplained by any increase in cost.

---

[31] Sullivan, *op. cit.*, p. 315.

[32] *Theatre Enterprises, Inc.* v. *Paramount Film Distributing Corp.*, 346 U.S. 537 (1954).

[33] D. F. Turner, "The Definition of Agreement Under the Sherman Act: Conscious Parallelism and Refusals to Deal," *Harvard Law Review* (February 1962), pp. 655–706, and R. A. Posner, *Antitrust Law, An Economic Perspective* (Chicago: University of Chicago Press, 1976), pp. 62–70.

c. Unnatural product standardization or false denials of interfirm quality differences.

d. Identical sealed bidding on nonstandard items (for example, large turbine generators).

e. Basing-point pricing systems, whereby all sellers quote identical delivered prices to any given buyer despite substantial transportation costs and widely differing delivery distances.

2. Additional independent evidence that the conduct is restrictive or *exclusionary*, such as

a. Parallel buying up of scarce raw materials that are not, in fact, used.

b. Parallel and predatory price-cutting.

c. Cross-licensing of patents.

The *American Tobacco* Case of 1946 is illustrative of the plus factors.[34] Unlawful conspiracy was found in that case even though there was no evidence of meetings in smoke-filled rooms or other rendezvous. Parallel pricing behavior (based on Reynold's leadership) was placed in the context of additional facts, as follows. During the early decades of this century, the cigarette industry came to be divided primarily between Reynolds, American, and Liggett & Myers. The popularity of "Camels" gave Reynolds a 40% share of the market by 1920, top spot, and rights to leadership. Between 1923 and 1941, American and Liggett & Myers stuck to Reynolds' prices like a Marlboro tattoo. There were eight list price changes during the period. Reynolds led six of them, with the others following usually not more than a day behind. The two Reynolds did *not* lead were price *cuts* initiated by American in 1933 under remarkable circumstances.

The circumstances were these: as the nation slid into the Great Depression and the prices

of leaf tobacco and other cigarette materials were falling along with commodity prices in general, R. J. Reynolds led two bold increases in the wholesale price of cigarettes—7% in October 1929 and another 7% in June 1931. Consequently, retail prices of popular brands wound up at 15 cents. Now this may not seem like much by today's inflated standards, but it was enough to give the three companies profits that exceeded 30% of net sales less tax. At the time of the last of these 7% increases the so-called "10-cent" brands accounted for less than 1% of the total market. For obvious reasons, however, their sales thereafter skyrocketed to account eventually for more than 20% of the market in the final two months of 1932. Upon feeling this slap, the three large companies retaliated. American led a 12% wholesale price cut on January 3, 1933, then initiated a second cut of 8% one month later, bringing the retail prices of the three companies down to 10 and 11 cents. This knocked the 10-cent brands' market share back to 7% almost immediately. Further pressure was applied when the three majors bought up cheap tobacco they did not use but the 10-cent brands would have used. After about a year the three large companies slowly began to raise their prices again. The renewed escalation enabled the 10-cent brands to regain a bit of their lost ground but never to recoup it completely. Thus, in sum, (1) prices were raised despite cost reductions and a massive depression; (2) the three largest companies bought up cheap tobacco they did not use; and (3) the three largest companies cut prices only after the 10-cent brands won a healthy market share. The Court declared that "No formal agreement is necessary to constitute an unlawful conspiracy." In this case, conspiracy was proved "from the evidence of the action taken in concert" and from "other circumstances."

Further appreciation of the "parallelism plus" doctrine may be gained by contrasting two cases—*U.S.* v. *C-O Two Fire Equipment*

[34] *American Tobacco Co.* v. *United States*, 328 U.S. 781 (1946).

$Co.$[35] and *U.S.* v. *Pevely Dairy Co.*[36] Violation was found in the first but not the second:

> In the *C-O Two* case, four competing manufacturers of fire extinguishers had regularly communicated with each other, had engaged in a meticulous program of product standardization, raised prices at a time of industry surplus, made identical bids on public contracts, used substantially identical licensing agreements with distributors . . . and carefully policed these agreements. On this evidence a finding of conspiracy was warranted. . . . In *Pevely,* the product [milk] was identical due to natural causes and health requirements applicable to processing. Defendants also had substantially identical cost structures because each paid the same government-controlled price for raw milk and the same wages which resulted from bargaining with the same union. In this context, the court concluded, identity of prices was wellnigh inevitable, and as consistent with the assumption that defendants had not reached a consensual accord as with the conclusion that they had.[37]

These clouded references to product standardization should not be taken to indicate that such agreements are always illegal. As we shall see later, some standardization, such as uniform bed sizes, is procompetitive and efficient. It is merely the case that standardization can under certain circumstances also aid price collusion.

D. Basing Point Pricing as Conscious Parallelism

One item on the list of "plus" factors deserves special elaboration because of its complexity and its propagation of a whole family of cases—namely, basing-point pricing. A simple example of this is the old "Pittsburgh Plus"

---

[35] *C-O Two Fire Equip. Co.* v. *United States,* 197 F. 2d 489 (9th Cir.) cert. denied 344 U.S. 892 (1952).

[36] *Pevely Dairy Co.* v. *United States,* 178 F. 2d 363 (8th Cir.), cert. denied 339 U.S. 942 (1950).

[37] Lawrence Sullivan, *op. cit.,* p. 318.

single basing-point system of the steel industry. Until 1924 all steel producers, regardless of their mill locations, quoted prices as if they were shipping from Pittsburgh. A steel company located in Gary, Indiana, when quoting a price to a buyer located in nearby Chicago, would add to the factory price the railroad freight cost from Pittsburgh to Chicago, rather than the slight freight cost from Gary to Chicago. The excess transportation charge pinned on the buyer was called "phantom freight."

Conversely, if the Gary plant was quoting a price to a buyer in New York, it would add to the factory price the freight cost from Pittsburgh to New York, rather than the larger and truer freight cost from Gary to New York. This undercharging of New York buyers meant that the seller had to "absorb freight." The mills located at the "base," in Pittsburgh, neither charged phantom freight nor absorbed freight on *any sale.* Their transport charges matched their transport costs. But sellers at all other locations dealt shamelessly in fictitious transport figures. When they were located closer to the buyer than the Pittsburgh mills, they quoted phantom freight. When they were located farther from the buyer than the Pittsburgh mills, they absorbed freight.

The system is illustrated in Figure 6-1, where horizontal distance represents geographic distance (with Chicago, Pittsburgh, and New York located west to east) and vertical distance represents seller's cost—manufacturing cost first (which does not differ with location) and transportation cost second (which goes up with distance travelled). Thus the transportation cost of mill M_1 shipping to buyer B_1 is zero, but to buyer B_2 it is yx and to buyer B_3 it is vz. Under "Pittsburgh Plus," the double shafted line emanating from Pittsburgh would be the delivered price line for *all* sellers. Price x would be quoted to buyer B_2 by M_2 and M_3 as well as M_1, even though the transport costs of M_2 and M_3 would be quite different, as indi-

Figure 6–1.   The Pittsburgh Plus Basing-point System

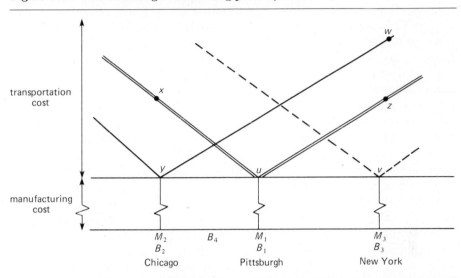

cated by the single solid and broken lines, respectively. Delivered price to buyer B_1 would be u. To buyer B_3 it would be z. When M_2 charges buyer B_2 price x, it is charging phantom freight equal to xy. When M_2 charges buyer B_3 price z, it must absorb the wz portion of total freight cost wv.

The Pittsburgh Plus system achieved one particularly important result. As a given *buyer* saw it, *all sellers* were quoting exactly the same price to him. This did not mean that all buyers were quoted the same price, as buyers close to the base saw low identical quotes and buyers distant from the base saw high identical quotes. Yet each buyer saw but one price. The single base system of Pittsburgh Plus was abandoned under pressure from the FTC in 1924. Yet this uniform result still held after the steel industry converted to a *multiple* basing-point system by introducing Gary and Birmingham as additional bases. The base closest to the buyer then provided the key to all quotes.

Why would the sellers want to quote identi-cal prices to each buyer? To facilitate collusion and effective price leadership. These systems simplify the pricing of colluding firms. They nullify any interfirm cost advantages attributable to geographic location. They enable the leader to lead with ease from the base. They permit price discrimination as when in Figure 6–1 seller M_2 charges a high price x to low cost buyer B_2 while charging a low price of u to high cost buyer B_1. They have also been attacked on these grounds as indicative or supportive of restrictive agreements.

Attacks against basing-point pricing in steel, cement, and corn oil were carried out in the late 1940s with the aid of evidence indicating artificially contrived support.[38] The circulation

---

[38] *Corn Products Refining Company* v. *Federal Trade Commission*, 324 U.S. 726 (1945); *FTC* v. *Cement Institute*, 333 U.S. 683 (1948); *Triangle Conduit and Cable Co.* v. *FTC*, 168 F. 2d 175 (7th Cir. 1948). In *Cement* price uniformity was strikingly illustrated when each of eleven companies, bidding for a 6,000 barrel government order in 1936, submitted sealed bids of $3.286854 per barrel.

of uniform railroad rate books, the policing of shipments to prevent destination diversion or truck hauling, the creation of fictitious railrates to places not served by railroads, the complete absence of f.o.b. pricing—all these and other facets of the systems revealed that they were not innocently natural competitive developments but rather conspiracies. Moreover, the products involved—steel, cement, and corn syrup—indicated that such systems are especially pertinent to homogenous, bulky commodities with relatively high transportation costs. In steel, for instance, transportation averages 10% of buyers' total cost.

Official attention to basing-point pricing rekindled during the late 1970s when the plywood industry was caught in a scheme that was simultaneously simple and complex.[39] Prior to 1963 all construction plywood was produced from Douglas fir in the Pacific Northwest. The South had abundant yellow pine timber, but the peculiar resins and pitch of yellow pine prevented its bonding into a durable sandwich board. Development of a new glue solved this problem, giving birth to a Southern pine plywood industry. This Southern branch grew prodigiously from one producer in 1963 to twenty-five in 1973, nurtured in part by freight cost advantages vis-a-vis the Northwest industry. Southern plywood could be delivered in Chicago, for example, at half the transport cost of Northwestern plywood, a potential saving of 10% to plywood purchasers off their total delivered price. Yet the full potential of this saving was not realized by buyers because the Southern mills priced their plywood as if it had been shipped from a fictitious base mill in Portland, Oregon, discounting slightly so as to make Southern pine plywood a bit more attractive

price-wise. Georgia-Pacific initiated the system when it expanded beyond the Northwest into the South but declined to offer f.o.b. mill prices at its Southern mills for buyers desirous of providing their own transportation (although G-P did offer f.o.b. prices from its Northwest mills). Subsequent Southern producers, even those without Northwest mills, followed Georgia-Pacific's lead, to the financial disappointment of Southern and Eastern plywood purchasers. Complexities arose, however, because the system was not, strictly speaking, a Portland-base-price-plus-freight system. Moreover, plywood prices vary sharply with variations in construction demand and vary somewhat between producers, giving appearances of some competition. Nevertheless, upon trial and deliberation, the Federal Trade Commission concluded that the industry's pricing system illegally restrained price competition and maintained an undue amount of phantom freight for Southern producers.[40] This opinion may be reversed on appeal, but the case illustrates that basing-point pricing is more than just a fossil of ancient enforcement.

E. The Professions

The late 1970s witnessed a flurry of activity in applying Section 1 of the Sherman Act to professional societies—producing cases bearing a hybrid relationship to those concerning trade associations, concious parallelism, and direct price-fixing. The story best begins with one Lewis H. Goldfarb, a government attorney, and his wife Ruth. While arranging to buy a home in Virginia, this young couple discovered that all lawyers charged no less than 1% of the price of the home for a routine title search, the fee being derived from a "recommended" mini-

[39] For details see Samuel M. Loescher, "Economic Collusion, Civil Conspiracy, and Treble Damage Deterrents: The Sherman Act Breakthrough with Southern Plywood," *The Quarterly Review of Economics and Business* (Winter 1980), pp. 6–35.

[40] *In the Matter of Boise Cascade Corp. et al.,* 91 FTC 1 (1978).

mum fee schedule promulgated by the Fairfax County Bar Association and enforced by the Virginia State Bar. The Goldfarbs sued under Section 1. The defendant bar associations argued that, among other things, lawyers were different from other folks, that they were members of a "learned profession" dedicated to the public's service rather than to profit's call, not in "trade or commerce" at all, and therefore exempt from the Sherman Act. Unconvinced, the trial court decided against the bar associations.

At this point we are treated to an intriguing spectacle. Defense counsel advised the bars not to appeal, urging them to cut their losses and settle quietly. But the lawyers being sued by a lawyer did not take their lawyer's advice and appealed anyway. When the case reached the lawyers on the Supreme Court, they found for lawyer Goldfarb. They found the fee schedule to be "a fixed, rigid price floor" rather than an advisory aid to attorneys. Furthermore, as for the "learned profession" exemption, they could not "find support for the proposition that Congress intended any such sweeping exclusion." In a bit of obvious understatement, Chief Justice Burger noted that the practice of law had a "business aspect" and "plays an important part in commercial intercourse."[41]

The Goldfarbs apparently inspired the FTC and Justice Department to act against "learned professions" generally even before the Supreme Court ruled on *Goldfarb*. During the summer of 1972, for instance, the American Institute of Certified Public Accountants, American Institute of Architects, American Society of Civil Engineers, and American Society of Mechanical Engineers all agreed under Justice Department prodding to abandon their antibidding strictures. Subsequently, the Federal Trade Commission obtained consent decrees from a number of medical groups prohibiting practices construed as price-fixing. These include the American College of Radiology, the American Academy of Orthopedic Surgeons, and the American College of Obstetricians and Gynecologists.[42] When challenged by recalcitrant "learned professions," the authorities did not cave in and won, as illustrated by *U.S.* v. *National Society of Professional Engineers*,[43] which carried the high court in 1978 (and which we mentioned earlier when discussing per se rules).

Further, professional society restraints other than price fixing have come under official and private party attack. An especially common restraint on competition has been the prohibition of price advertising or *all* advertising. Lee Benham demonstrated the anticompetitive effect of such restrictions when in the early 1960s he compared the retail prices of eyeglasses in states that legally restricted optometrist's advertising and retail prices in states that had few or no restrictions on advertising. Comparing the most and least restrictive states, he found average prices of $37.48 and $17.98, respectively, a 100% difference.[44] Similarly, John Cady analyzed state restrictions on pharmacists' price advertising. Comparing the retail prices of ten representative prescription drugs across states, he found that prohibitions of price advertising *raised* prices an average of 4.3%.[45]

---

[41] *Lewis H. Goldfarb* v. *Virginia State Bar et al.*, 421 U.S. 773 (1975).

[42] The groups did not set prices directly but used an indirect formula called a "relative value scale." The scale specified comparative values in nonmonetary units, such as operation X was 2.5 times operation Y. These values, however, were convertible into dollar amounts by application of a "dollar conversion factor."

[43] *National Society of Professional Engineers* v. *U.S.* 435 U.S. 679 (1978).

[44] Lee Benham, "The Effect of Advertising on the Price of Eyeglasses," *Journal of Law & Economics* (October 1972), pp. 337–352.

[45] John F. Cady, "An Estimate of the Price Effects of Restrictions on Drug Price Advertising," *Economic Inquiry* (December 1976), pp. 493–510.

The FTC has moved against such restrictions by optometrists, pharmacists, doctors, dentists, and lawyers, but not always with complete success. There are intervening complexities, such as the fact that many such restrictions are *expressly* imposed by state laws rather than merely suggested or permitted, immunizing them to some degree from federal attack.[46] In *Bates* v. *State Bar of Arizona* (1977)[47] for instance, the U.S. Supreme Court held that the Sherman Act could not nullify a ban on advertising by lawyers because that ban had been expressly commanded by state authorities. Even so, such restraints may be shattered by other means, and the *Bates* majority broke the advertising ban for violating the Constitution's first amendment. "Free speech" includes "commercial speech" apparently. And we now see lawyers pitching on TV right along with the brewers and soapers. More substantive results have come in dramatic reductions in legal fees for many routine services. In Phoenix, for instance, where *Bates* originated, the going rate for an uncontested divorce went from $350 before *Bates* to between $150 and $200 after *Bates*. And legal name changes in Manhattan dropped from $150 to $75.[48]

---

[46] The key case here is *Parker* v. *Brown*, 317 U.S. 341 (1943). For discussion see S. Paul Posner, "The Proper Relationship Between State Regulation and the Federal Antitrust Laws," 49 *New York University Law Review* (1974), pp. 693–739; J. H. Young and A. F. Troy, "Federal Trade Commission Preemption of State Regulation: A Reevaluation," 12 *Suffolk University Law Review* (1978), pp. 1248–1281.

[47] *Bates* v. *State Bar of Arizona*, 433 U.S. 350 (1977). But see also *Cantor* v. *Detroit Edison Co.*, 428 U.S. 579 (1976).

[48] *Wall Street Journal* (October 18, 1978), p. 1. See also *Wall Street Journal* (July 31, 1980), pp. 1, 9. The ambivalence of government policy should be obvious here. On the one hand we have the FTC and Justice Department attempting to instill the healthy upheavals of competition, while on the other hand we have states curbing competition through their "regulation" of professions. Over 1500 state licensing boards provide more or less protective umbrellas for dog trainers, landscapers, doctors, funeral directors, and so on indefinitely.

Summary

All court trials and government hearings are stenographically recorded and transcribed. In 1980 it was revealed that five companies performing these services had been rigging bids for government contracts for nearly twenty years, covering more than $30 million worth in business. Guilty pleas and fines were extracted from the conspirators.[49]

Thus price-fixing goes on almost daily, even under the government's nose by businesses that could not be better informed about the law. The heart of the law in this context is Section 1 of the Sherman Act which prohibits "contract combination, or conspiracy in restraint of trade." This language gains potency through application of a *per se* rule, wherein motives, economic conditions, and the like are of no account. Violation is established merely by proof that the offending conduct actually occurred, in particular, explicit price-fixing, market allocation, bid rigging, or collective boycott. Clearcut offenses may now be punished by harsh criminal remedies. In addition, civil proceedings raise liability for single damages to government and treble damages to private parties. Though more ominous penalties now threaten the guilty than before, the population of offenders has apparently not diminished much.

Despite the per se rule, there are some gray areas where shadows of uncertainty complicate matters. As regards price-fixing, trade association information exchange programs pose particular problems. Information exchanges can invigorate or deflate competition depending on their characteristics and surrounding circumstances. Those with restrictive elements, such as prenotification of price changes, or those housed in tight-knit oligopolistic structures stand exposed to official attack. Conscious parallelism creates related difficulties because be-

---

[49] *Wall Street Journal*, June 9, 1980, p. 16.

havioral uniformity may or may not indicate illegal conspiracy. A rule has emerged, however. Conscious parallelism *alone* escapes. Conscious parallelism that is coupled with *additional evidence* of collusion does not escape. The plus factors include elaborate basing-point pricing, exchanges of information, artificial standardization of product, and predatory pricing.

An area that represents a hybrid of those above is restraints in professional societies. Protected for many years by appearances of state sanction and questions of commercial definition, the learned professions have recently experienced an upheaval from application of the Sherman Act. Strictures on pricing conduct and advertising in particular have been loosened or destroyed, bringing greater competition into the lives of doctors, dentists, pharmacists, lawyers, optometrists, engineers, and accountants.

Questions and Exercises for Chapter 6

1. It can be argued that explicit price-fixing arises most commonly where structural conditions are neither so uncompetitive as to allow tacit collusion nor so intensely competitive as to preclude collusion altogether. Why? (Hint: focus on the *need* to collude to achieve joint profit maximization and the *ability* to collude at all.)
2. In which case—the electrical equipment case of 1959 or the tobacco case of 1946— do you think application of the law was most effective in restoring competition? Why?
3. What evidence would you need to prosecute a case of illegal collusion? What evidence would you *not* need?
4. Are criminal penalties appropriate to per se offenses? Would they be appropriate to rule of reason offenses?

5. Would identical bids verify collusion? Would nonidentical bids disprove collusion?
6. How would you resolve the "passed through" damages problem?
7. Why can basing-point pricing be considered a "plus factor" in moving parallelism across the line of illegality?
8. What was the importance of *Goldfarb?*

Appendix to Chapter 6: Oligopolistic Interdependence

The incentive (and ability) to collude instead of compete is most easily seen as it relates to one structural variable—market share (and its corollary, concentration). Whereas a purely competitive firm and monopolist each face one demand curve (shown earlier in Figures 2–3 and 2–7, respectively), an oligopolist may see two demand curves as shown in Figure 6–2. The oligopolist firm might perceive either one or portions of both of these demand curves, depending on what assumptions it makes concerning its rivals' behavior. If the firm assumes that its rivals will follow any price change it makes up or down from P_o, which is the going price, then it will consider the "followship demand," FF', the applicable demand curve. In contrast, the "nonfollowship demand" curve, NN', is based on the assumption that rivals in the market do *not* follow the price changes of the firm depicted but instead leave their prices unchanged at P_o. The elasticity of FF' is much lower than the elasticity of NN' at point S because the followship in FF' leaves market share for this firm unchanged. The added sales from a price cut or lost sales from a price increase along FF' derive solely from sale variations at marketwide level. In contrast, price changes that are *not* followed cause *shifts* of customers among firms as well as marketwide sales variations—a shift away from rivals toward this firm if price is cut below P_o or a shift toward

Figure 6–2.   Oligopolistic Interdependence and the Incentive to Collude

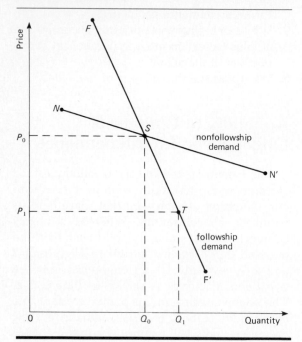

them diverges substantially from FF' and is highly elastic. Regarding point (2), visibility, large firms tend to see FF' more clearly than NN', while small firms see NN' more clearly than large firms. A price cut by a large firm is, for example, more noticeable among its rivals and more likely to be actually followed than a price cut by a small firm.

In short, firms with large market shares tend to see inelastic demand curves (like FF'), whereas firms with small shares tend to see elastic demand curves (like NN'). A middle-sized firm might see a mix—SN for price increases and SF' for price decreases thereby producing a kinked demand curve. Because elasticities are crucial to what happens to total revenue (and therefore profit) in the event of a price change, these diverse views will influence price behavior. A price *decrease* increases total revenue if elasticity is high (greater than 1) but decreases total revenue if elasticity is low (less than 1). Visually compare total revenue OP_0SQ_0 with total revenue OP_1TQ_1 on the inelastic followship demand of Figure 6–2 to fully appreciate this. Conversely, a price *increase* decreases total revenue if elasticity is high but increases total revenue if elasticity is low. Thus a market comprised only of large firms, tight oligopoly, will have members who shun price decreases and who appreciate the profitability of collusive price increases because they tend to see demand curves like FF'. Each firm foresees the probability that if it cuts price, its rivals will also cut prices to preserve market shares. Each firm then foresees that price cuts will not yield greater profits through relatively greater quantity sales. Rather, each anticipates lower profits from the lower revenues associated with lower prices on fairly constant sales.

On the other hand, a market comprised entirely of relatively small firms will have members who are enticed to cut price and who are hesitant to raise price. Markets of mixed, small–large composition may include those who are

rivals away from this firm if price is raised above P_0. Hence NN' is more elastic than FF'.

Structure, as measured primarily by market share, enters the story by affecting two things—(1) the extent to which these two demand curves diverge, and (2) the assumption the firm actually makes about followship and nonfollowship (that is, the "visibility" of the curves). Regarding point (1) a firm with a very large market share confronts curves that are fairly close. For example, an unfollowed price cut by a firm already having 90% of the market would gain very little added sales from rivals (reflected in S toward N') as compared to the marketwide added sales (reflected in S toward F'). Small firms, in contrast, can experience wide swings in sales due to share shifts as compared to marketwide developments, so NN' for

trying to collude plus a lot of "cheaters" who try to probe their elastic nonfollowship demand curves with price cuts below cartel imposed levels. Secrecy may encourage price cutting because it curbs followship.

The influence of other structural features may be analyzed in similar fashion. If, for instance, sales are lumpy, as they are for airplanes and pipeline steel, price shading is encouraged because a small cut can create enormous sales. If overall market demand is highly elastic, the *FF'* curve will likewise be elastic and collusion will be difficult as even large firms will be drawn into price competition.

Chapter 7

Monopolization: Power and Intent

Every day in our lives monopoly takes its toll.
—Senator Estes Kefauver

Practically everything about monopolization is big. The companies are big. The cases are big. The stakes are big. And chapters written about it are big.

We begin by exploring the wording of the Sherman Act and its rule of reason interpretation. Next we trace the history of monopolization law through three eras—(1) 1890–1940, the era of dastardly deeds, (2) 1945–1970, the era of *Alcoa,* and (3) 1970–present, an era of refinement and retreat.

I. The Sherman Act: Section 2

A. *The Rule of Reason*

Section 2 of the Sherman Act declares that:

Every person who shall monopolize, or attempt to monopolize, or combine or conspire with any other person or persons, to monopolize any part of the trade or commerce among the several States, or with foreign nations, shall be deemed guilty of a felony . . .

Although Section 2 covers those who "combine or conspire" to monopolize, it is primarily concerned with single firm activities and structural conditions. Having said that, we have not—unlike Budweiser—said it all. Why the word "monopolize"? Why not "monopoly"? What is the test of monopolization? How large a market share is required? What is meant by a "part of trade or commerce"?

A simple, definitive summary of answers to these questions might seem feasible. The Sherman Act is, after all, approaching its hundredth anniversary, and several hundred cases have been brought by the Justice Department under Section 2. Most issues, it would seem, should be settled now. Unfortunately, they are not. Judicial personnel, economic knowledge, political philosophies, and business practices change over time, much as fashion changes. Even more significant, the wording of the statute was left vague enough to invoke extensive judgment, opinion, estimation, and even hunch.

A Sherman Act Section 2 violation is not as clear cut as shoplifting or murder. Price-fixing is similar to these crimes in that, under Section 1, it is a per se offense. Just as one can be caught in the act of shoplifting, so a group of competitors can be caught in a smoke-filled room conspiring to raise their prices. But monopolizers cannot be caught in the act. They are never really caught at all. They are accused and judged by a "rule of reason." The result is drawn-out deliberations. Trials of three years are not unheard of, and in one case more than 1200 witnesses testified.

The crime of monopolization is not established without proof of two factors: (1) substantial market power, and (2) intent. As Justice William Douglas wrote in the *Grinnell* case, the offense of monopoly "has two elements: (1) the possession of monopoly power in the relevant market and (2) willful acquisition or maintenance of that power . . ."[1] Reason is exercised to establish both elements. In appraising monopoly **power,** the courts have considered barriers to entry of various kinds—including patents, pecuniary and real economies of scale, product differentiation, absolute capital costs, and several conduct-related barriers. Profits, too, have come under review. The one index of monopoly power consistently receiving greatest attention, however, is the market share of the accused. Indeed, although the Supreme Court has defined monopoly power as "the power to control prices or exclude competition," it has acted as if the "existence of such power ordinarily may be inferred from the predominant share of the market." (*Grinnell* again.) In this interpretation, reason must be called upon to answer two key questions: What is the relevant market? What market share is sufficient to establish unlawful power?

B. Market Definition: Power Question 1

Section 2 refers to "any part of trade or commerce," a phrase now taken to mean "relevant market." Unfortunately, markets do not have bright-line boundaries as do nations or continents. Their borders are often more like rubber, susceptible to compression or expansion by the forces of argument and evidence. This sponginess is perhaps best appreciated by considering some of the many factors that influence market determination:[2]

1. Product Market
The product itself is one issue.

a. *The physical characteristics of products:* Blade razors and electric razors may constitute different markets despite their similar end uses.

b. *Distinct customers or end uses of products:* Money is money, but commercial banks and finance companies may occupy different loan markets because finance company loans, in contrast to bank loans, tend to go to relatively high-risk borrowers for such purposes as debt consolidation.

c. *Cross-elasticity of demand:* If price changes for books have no impact on the demand for phonograph records, and vice versa, books and records could not be considered close substitutes in the eyes of consumers.

d. *The absolute level of product prices, apart from consideration of cross-elasticities:* First-run motion picture theaters might comprise a separate market because they command a substantial price premium relative to subsequent-run theaters.

e. *Unique production facilities or supply elasticities:* Aluminum ingots made from scrap might be excluded from the market for aluminum ingots made from bauxite, because scrap has a low price elasticity of supply.

f. *Industry recognition or firm behavior:* The scope of trade association membership, the

---

[1] *U.S.* v. *Grinnell Corporation,* 384 U.S. 563 (1966).

[2] For an overview see Alvin M. Stein and Barry J. Brett, "Market Definition and Market Power In Antitrust Cases— An Empirical Primer on When, Why and How," *New York Law School Law Review* 24 (1979), pp. 639–676.

nature of a firm's internal organization, the rivalries revealed in competitors' advertising, and the classifications used to record and report economic data may be helpful in delineating market boundaries.

2. GEOGRAPHIC MARKET

Some of the foregoing may guide delineation of geographic markets (as when price levels vary markedly from spot to spot), but the following more typically signal regional range.

a. *Transportation costs:* If high relative to product value, transportation costs will tend to limit geographic scope.
b. *Legal barriers:* Tariffs and quotas may exclude foreign competition. Likewise states may impose legal restrictions inhibiting full-fledged interstate competition.
c. *Product differentiation:* Localized product differentiation may cause a narrower geographic scope than otherwise.

The diversity of judgments the relevant market has provoked may be illustrated by two contrasting cases.

In *Du Pont* (1956) a majority of the Supreme Court defined the market broadly to include *all* flexible packaging materials (cellophane, foil, pliofilm, polyethylene, and so on) instead of merely cellophane, which Du Pont dominated.[3] The decisive argument for the Court's majority was cross-elasticity of demand, as may be seen from the opinion:

> If a slight decrease in the price of cellophane causes a considerable number of customers of other flexible wrappings to switch to cellophane, it would be an indication that a high cross-elasticity of demand exists between them; that the products compete in the same market. The court below held that the "great sensitivity of customers

in the flexible packaging markets to price or quality changes" prevented DuPont from possessing monopoly control over price. . . . We conclude that cellophane's interchangeability with other materials mentioned suffices to make it a part of this flexible packaging material market.

Although Du Pont produced 75% of all cellophane sold in the United States, this amounted to only 14% of all "flexible packaging." Hence the broad definition made a big difference, and Du Pont won acquittal.

Three dissenting justices had doubts. They felt that cellophane was virtually unique. Cellophane's price, in particular, had been two to seven times higher than that of many comparable materials between 1924 and 1950. Yet during this period "cellophane enjoyed phenomenal growth," *more* growth than could be expected "if close substitutes were available at from one seventh to one half cellophane's price." Furthermore, they thought cross elasticity was low, not high. The price of cellophane fell substantially while other prices remained unchanged. Indeed, "during the period 1933–1946 the prices for glassine and waxed paper actually increased in the face of a 21% decline in the price of cellophane." If substantial "shifts of business" due to "price sensitivity" had in fact occurred, producers of these rival materials would have had to follow cellophane's price down lest they lose sales.[4]

Ten years later, in the *Grinnell* case (1966) a majority of the Court spoke as the minority did in *Du Pont.* They defined the market narrowly to include only "accredited central station protective services" (whereby a client's property is wired for burglaries and fires, signals of which are then sent electronically to a continuously manned central station accredited by insurance underwriters). Other means of

---

[3] *U.S.* v. *E.I. duPont de Nemours Company,* 351 U.S. 377 (1956).

[4] For an economic critique see, G. W. Stocking and W. F. Mueller, "The Cellophane Case and the New Competition," *American Economic Review* (March 1955), pp. 29–63.

property protection were excluded from the relevant market for various reasons:[5]

> Watchmen service is far more costly and less reliable. Systems that set off an audible alarm at the site of a fire or burglary are cheaper but often less reliable. They may be inoperable without anyone's knowing it . . . Proprietary systems that a customer purchases and operates are available, but they can be used only by a very large business or by government. . . . And, as noted, insurance companies generally allow a greater reduction in premiums for accredited central station service than for other types of protection.

Because Grinnell had 87% of the market as defined, the Court could not let it off the hook like an undersized trout. Grinnell suffered some dismemberment.

C. Market Share: Power Question 2

The cases cited indicate that a market share of 14% does not amount to illegal monopoly but 87% does. What about the area in between? What market share makes an illegal "monopoly"? In two major cases the Supreme Court ruled that 64% of the farm machinery industry and 50% of the steel industry did not amount to monopoly. An influential appeals court judge, Learned Hand, once expressed the opinion that, while any percentage over 90 "is enough to constitute a monopoly; it is doubtful whether sixty or sixty-four per cent would be enough; and certainly thirty-three per cent is not."[6] For these several reasons the consensus seems to hold that market shares below 60% lie snugly beneath the Court's reach. And even 70 or 75% may manage to escape its grasp.

D. Intent

Actually, there is even more uncertainty than the above figures suggest. The issue of intent is also important. Generally speaking, there is a trade off between the market share and the degree of intent the prosecuting attorneys must prove to win a guilty verdict. A clear-cut case of 95% market share would now probably run afoul of the law with very little proof of intent. Conversely, intent would gain importance when a market share of less than 60% was involved.

Indeed, it will be recalled that Section 2 forbids mere *attempts* to monopolize as well as monopolization itself. Although the scope of this offense is much disputed and unclear, it seems safe to say that the requirements for proving a charge of "attempt" are now much more rigorous with respect to intent than they are in cases of pure monopolization. Traditionally, proof of an attempt to monopolize requires two elements: (1) a *specific intent* to monopolize and (2) a *dangerous probability of success*.[7] The requirement of specific intent—such as would be shown by clearly anticompetitive acts like blatant predatory pricing, coercive refusals to deal, sabotage, and gross misrepresentation—arises because in this context the monopolization is not actually achieved. Without indications of specific intent, a court could not be sure that monopolization was what the defendant had in mind. Moving beyond attempts to situations where monopoly has been achieved, only "general" intent need be proved because any specific intent is then largely manifest in the end result.[8]

Use of the word "monopolize" in the Sherman Act (rather than "monopoly") implies that simple possession of a large market share is not

---

[5] *U.S.* v. *Grinnell Corporation et al.,* 384 U.S. 563 (1966).

[6] *U.S.* v. *Aluminum Company of America,* 148 F. 2d 416 (1945), 424.

[7] Lawrence Sullivan, *Handbook of the Law of Antitrust* (St. Paul, Minn.: West Publishing Co., 1977), pp. 134–140.

[8] The "dangerous probability" requirement has stirred controversy of late because some lower courts have recently held that near monopoly or a high probability of actual monopolization are necessary to a finding of dangerous probability. See especially *U.S.* v. *Empire Gas Co.* 537 F.2d 296 (8th Cir. 1976), *cert. denied,* 429 U.S. 1122 (1977).

itself frowned upon, at least not enough to earn a conviction. An illegality requires more: some positive drive, some purposeful behavior, some "intent" to seize and exert power in the market. Only a moment's reflection reveals the wisdom of this policy. What of the innovator whose creativity establishes a whole new industry, occupied at first by just his firm? What of the last surviving firm in a dying industry? What of the superefficient firm that underprices everyone else through genuine economies of scale or some natural advantages of location? What of a large market share gained purely by competitive skill? To pounce on these monopolies would have to be regarded as cruel (since they are actually "innocent"), stupid (since it would be punishing good performance), and irrational (since no efficient structural remedy, such as dissolution, could ensue). Thus a finding of intent to monopolize is essential, even though it may not be easy.

In Section 2 cases a monopolist's intent is not determined by subjecting its owners and officers to lie detector tests or psychoanalysis. Intent emerges from the firm's particular acts or its general course of action. With this statement we come to the point where, for pedagogical purposes, three more or less distinct eras of Section 2 interpretation may be distinguished depending on what the courts have required of plaintiffs to prove intent.

- *1890–1940:* In the early days, the Supreme Court usually held that an offensive degree of intent could be established only with evidence of abusive acts. This could be called the era of leniency because "well-behaved" monopolists with as much as 90% of the market were welcomed if not cherished.
- *1945–1970:* The *Alcoa* case of 1945 set a very stringent standard, excusing monopolists only when power was "thrust upon" them, as if by accident. Little was needed to show offensive intent because "no monop-

olist monopolizes unconcious of what he is doing."[9]
- *1970–Present:* Most recently the pendulum has swung back toward leniency. A string of lower court decisions gives monopolists spacious room for aggressive, if not abusive, conduct. Still, this era's record is mixed because the Supreme Court has not spoken and Congress has toyed with the idea of abandoning intent altogether.

We shall take up each era successively.

II. The Early Days: 1890–1940

A. An Overview

Before *Alcoa*, the Supreme Court usually held that an offensive degree of intent could be established only with evidence of abusive, predatory, or criminal acts. The types of conduct that qualified included the following: (1) predatory pricing, that is, cutting prices below costs on certain products or in certain regions and subsidizing the resulting losses with profits made elsewhere; (2) predatory promotional spending or predatory pricing on "fighting brands" or "bogus independent" firms or upon new facilities or new products; (3) physical violence to competitors, their customers, or their products; (4) exaction of special advantages from suppliers, such as "railroad rebates"; (5) misuse of patents, copyrights, or trademarks; and (6) preclusion of competitive opportunities by refusals to sell, exclusive dealing arrangements, or anticompetitive tie-in sales.

For the most part, this list of "predatory tactics" is derived from the major early cases listed in Table 7–1. The first five cases mentioned there ended in convictions. The last five men-

[9] *U.S.* v. *Aluminum Company of America*, 148 F. 2d 416 (1945).

Table 7–1. Major Section 2 Cases, 1911 to 1927

	Industry	Percentage of the industry (%)	Predatory Tactics Present?	Date of Final Judgment
I. Unlawful monopolies				
Standard Oil of N.J.	Petroleum	85–90	Yes	1911
American Tobacco Co.	Tobacco products	76–97	Yes	1911
E. I. Du Pont	Explosives	64–100	Yes	1911
Eastman Kodak Co.	Photo equipment	75–80	Yes	1915
Corn Products Refining Co.	Glucose	53	Yes	1916
II. Cases of acquittal				
United Shoe Machinery Co.	Shoe machinery	90	No	1917
American Can Co.	Packers' cans	50	Yes	1916
Quaker Oats Co.	Rolled oats cereal	75	No	1916
U.S. Steel Corp.	Steel	50	No	1920
International Harvester Co.	Harvesters	64	No	1927

Source: Milton Handler, *Trade Regulation*, 3rd ed. (New York: Foundation Press, 1960), pp. 378–79.

tioned ended in acquittals. Notice from the center column that the market shares of the convicted monopolizers are not markedly greater than those of the acquitted firms, although in the latter group there are two with only 50% of industry sales. The big difference lies in the next column, where a "Yes" indicates that obviously predatory tactics were used by the defendant and a "No" indicates a fairly clean slate in this regard. With but one exception, those guilty of dirty tricks were also found guilty of monopolizing. Conversely, the "good" trusts managed to get off. The obvious implication must be qualified by the possibility that changes in court personnel could have made some difference, as suggested perhaps by the dates of the decisions in the last column. Another qualification that lessens the strength of the argument is the exclusion of several railroad cases from consideration. Between 1904 and 1922, the Supreme Court decided against three railroad combinations that did not employ predatory practices to gain substantial market shares.[10] Even so, we can buttress the message of Table 7–1 by consulting the Court's opinions.

B. Standard Oil of New Jersey (1911)

Standard Oil (now Exxon) was the most notorious monopoly of its time. First organized in Ohio in 1870, by 1872 it had acquired all but a few of the three dozen refineries in Cleveland. Additionally, it had garnered complete control of the pipe lines running from oil fields to refineries in Cleveland, Pittsburgh, Philadelphia, New York, and New Jersey. Further transportation advantages were gained from the railroads through preferential rates and large rebates. From this strategic footing Standard Oil was able to force competitors to join the combination or be driven out of business.

[10] Northern Securities Co. (1904), Union Pacific (1912), and Southern Pacific (1922).

As a result, the combine grew to control 90 per cent of the petroleum industry, a dominance that produced enormous profits. Under legal attack from authorities in Ohio, the company was reorganized in 1899 as Standard Oil of New Jersey, a holding company. The new combine continued to exact preferential treatment from railroads and to cut crude oil supplies to competing refiners. Business espionage, local price warfare, and the operation of bogus independents were also Standard tactics. As the Supreme Court said, "The pathway of the combination . . . is strewn with the wrecks resulting from crushing out, without regard to law, the individual rights of others."[11]

In writing the Supreme Court's opinion, Chief Justice White emphasized intent, contrasting the tainted history of Standard Oil with what he called "normal methods of industrial development." Thus, by implication, the Court acknowledged that power alone was not enough, that monopoly in the concrete was condoned absent the willful drive. In applying this interpretation of Section 2 to the facts of Standard Oil, White said that the combine's merging and acquiring alone gave rise to a "prima-facie presumption of intent." He went on, however, to state that this prima-facie presumption was "made conclusive" by considering the rapacious conduct of the New Jersey corporation.

In sum, White gave birth to an infantile form of the rule of reason as we know it today. He found himself "irresistibly driven to the conclusion that the very genius for commercial development and organization which it would seem was manifested from the beginning soon begot

an intent and purpose to exclude others . . . by acts and dealings wholly inconsistent with . . . normal methods." Given its context, White's "rule of reason" came to mean that a monopolist would not be forced to walk the plank unless he had *behaved unreasonably*.

Dissolution of the combine followed, yielding thirty-four separate companies. Historically, these offspring tended to be regionally and vertically specialized—e.g., Standard Oil of California (now Chevron), Standard Oil of Ohio (Sohio), Standard Oil of New York (Mobil), Standard Oil of Indiana (American), and Standard Oil of New Jersey (Exxon).[12] With time, they spread into each other's territory to compete.

C. American Tobacco (1911)

The story in tobacco is similar to that in oil except that advertising and promotion were big weapons.[13] The story centers on James Duke, whose power play started in cigarettes, then spread to other branches of the trade. By 1885 Duke had secured 11–18% of total cigarette sales for his company through an arduous promotional effort. He then escalated ad and promotional outlays to nearly 20% of sales, thereby forcing a five-firm merger in 1889 and acquiring 80% control of all cigarette sales. His American Tobacco Company grew still further until he held 93% of the market in 1899. Coincident with this final gathering of power, cigarette ad expense as a per cent of sales fell to 11% in 1894, then to 0.5% in 1899. And cigarette profits swelled to 56% of sales in 1899.

With these stupendous profits Duke was able to launch massive predatory campaigns to capture other tobacco markets, which were at the time bigger than cigarettes. One measure of

[11] *Standard Oil Company of New Jersey* v. *U.S.*, 221 U.S. 1 (1911). John McGee has argued that Standard's predatory pricing was less than alleged, even nonexistent, "Predatory Price Cutting: The Standard Oil (N.J.) Case," *Journal of Law & Economics* (October 1958), pp. 137–169. But his account has been questioned by F. M. Scherer, *Industrial Market Structure and Economic Performance* (Chicago: Rand McNally, 1970), pp. 274–276.

[12] Others included Atlantic Refining, Conoco, Marathon, Std. of Kentucky, Std. of Louisiana, and Std. of Nebraska.
[13] For a summary see D. F. Greer, "Some Case History Evidence on the Advertising-Concentration Relationship," *Antitrust Bulletin* (Summer 1975), pp. 311–315.

this effort is the American Tobacco Company's annual advertising and selling cost as a percentage of sales at crest levels in the target markets—28.9% for plug and twist, 24.4% for smoking tobacco, 31.7% for fine-cut chewing, and 49.9% for cigars. Duke even went so far as to introduce deliberately unprofitable "fighting brands," one of which was appropriately called "Battle Ax." Losses ensued; mergers followed; and after the entire industry (except for cigars) was under American's thumb, advertising receded substantially to such relatively peaceful neighborhoods as 4 and 10% of sales.

Just before the Supreme Court's ruling against American in 1911 the combine controlled the following shares: smoking tobacco, 76.2%; chewing tobacco, 84.4%; cigarettes 86.1%; snuff, 96.5%; cigars 14.4%. Stressing the crude behavior of the combine, the Court found American's acts unreasonable. Dissolution ensued, creating oligopoly in place of monopoly.[14] Competition improved, but not markedly.

D. United States Steel (1920)

A chain of mergers occured around the turn of the century, eliminating the independence of 170 steel companies and culminating in the formation of U.S. Steel Corporation in 1901. When formed, this behemoth accounted for 66 per cent of all American steel production. Its market power is evident in the fact that U.S. Steel's capitalization was double the market value of the stock of its constituent companies. Still, the Corporation's market share dwindled a bit by 1911, when, flush with success in *Standard Oil* and *American Tobacco,* the Justice Department filed suit. Its share fell further, and in 1920 U.S. Steel won acquittal.

In acquitting United States Steel the Court held that the corporation's 50% market share (at the time of the case) did not amount to ex-

cessive power, and, even if it had amounted to excessive power, the corporation had not abused it: "It resorted to none of the brutalities or tyrannies that the cases illustrate of other combinations." The corporation "did not oppress or coerce its competitors . . . it did not undersell its competitors in some localities by reducing its prices there below those maintained elsewhere, or require its customers to enter into contracts limiting their purchases or restricting them in resale prices; it did not obtain customers by secret rebates . . . there was no evidence that it attempted to crush its competitors or drive them out of the market . . ." In short: "The corporation is undoubtedly of impressive size. . . . But the law does not make mere size an offense, or the existence of unexerted power an offense. It, we repeat, requires overt acts . . ."[15] U. S. Steel was indeed a combination formed by *merger.* But merger was not then considered evidence of intent even though it is obviously an "overt act."

Allowing monopoly by merger was no mere oversight, for in a stinging dissent Justice Day reminds the majority that the Sherman Act expressly bans "combinations" and goes on to argue that the "contention must be rejected that the [U.S. Steel] combination was an inevitable evolution of industrial tendencies compelling union of endeavor." Nevertheless, the view that abusive "overt acts" were required to prove intent prevailed in this and other opinions of the day.

III. The *ALCOA* Era: 1945–1970

A. An Overview

Although the *U.S. Steel* interpretation may not have gutted Section 2, it certainly bloodied it a bit. Section 2 lay incapacitated until 1945, when the *Alcoa* decision brought recupera-

---

[14] *U.S.* v. *American Tobacco Co.,* 221 U.S. 106 (1911).

[15] *U.S.* v. *United States Steel Corporation,* 251 U.S. 417 (1920).

tion.[16] In essence, *Alcoa* lengthened the list of intent indications beyond predatory and abusive tactics. According to *Alcoa*, unlawful intent can almost be assumed unless the defendant is a "passive beneficiary" of monopoly power or has had monopoly power "thrust upon" him. To *any* extent the monopolist reaches out to grasp or strives actively to hold his dominant position, he is denied the right to claim that he has no unlawful intent. This hard line is softened by other language in the opinion that exempts monopoly gained by "superior skill, foresight and industry." Subsequent cases changed the wording to permit monopoly grounded on "a superior product, business acumen or historic accident."[17] But the *Alcoa* interpretation remained fairly well intact for nearly three decades.

B. Alcoa (1945)[18]

The Aluminum Company of America provides many interesting economic lessons as well as legal lessons. For more than half a century it dominated all four stages of the United States aluminum industry: (1) bauxite ore mining, (2) conversion of bauxite into aluminum oxide or alumina, (3) electrolytic reduction of alumina into aluminum ingots, and (4) fabrication of aluminum products, such as cable, foil, pots and pans, sheets, and extrusions. Alcoa's dominance derived mainly from various barriers to entry:

Patents. Until 1886, the processes for extracting pure aluminum were so difficult and costly that it was a precious metal like gold or platinum. In that year, just after graduating

[16] *U.S.* v. *Aluminum Company of America*, 148 F. 2d 416 (2d Cir. 1945).

[17] *U.S.* v. *Grinnell Corp.*, 384 U.S. 563 (1966).

[18] Primary sources for this section are L. W. Weiss, *Economics and American Industry* (New York: John Wiley & Sons, 1961), Chapter 5; Merton J. Peck, *Competition in the Aluminum Industry: 1945–1958* (Cambridge, Mass.: Harvard University Press, 1961).

from Oberlin College, Charles Hall discovered electrolytic reduction of alumina into aluminum. His discovery was later duplicated by C. S. Bradley. Alcoa acquired the rights to both their patents, and thereby excluded potential entrants legally until 1909.

Resources Controlled. Resource limitations also barred entry. Alcoa integrated backwards into bauxite mining and electric power, the two key resources for producing aluminum. Although these resources were too plentiful to be fully preempted by a single firm, Alcoa vigorously acquired, developed, and built the lowest cost sources of each.

Economies of Scale. As if all that were not enough, economies of scale constituted an additional barrier. Of the several stages of the production process, the second stage—conversion of bauxite into alumina—yielded the greatest efficiencies from increased size. Until 1938 there was only *one* alumina plant in the entire United States. The unit costs of a 500,000-ton per year plant embodying 1940 technology were 10–20% below the unit costs of a 100,000-ton plant. And it was not until 1942 that United States consumption of alumina topped 500,000 tons. The dire implications for entry into alumina production during that era should be obvious. Economies were not nearly so pronounced for reduction and fabrication (there being four smelting plants in the United States during the 1930s and a goodly number of fabricators).

Nonetheless the barriers associated with alumina spilled over into these other stages because Alcoa was *vertically integrated*. However efficient a producer of ingot or fabricated products might be, he was ultimately dependent on Alcoa for his raw materials and simultaneously competing with Alcoa as a seller. This put independents in a precarious position. Alcoa could control the independents' costs *and* selling price. Were Alcoa unkind enough to raise its price of ingot and lower its price of foil, say, the foil fabricators would be in a bind. The "price squeeze" would pinch the margin between their costs and selling price. Just such a squeeze was alleged in 1926 and 1927, when Alcoa reduced the margin between ingot and certain types of aluminum sheet from 16 cents a pound to 7 cents a pound and then kept it there until 1932. Two independent rollers of sheet initiated an antitrust suit that was settled out of court.

The Antitrust Suit. The government lost its antitrust suit at the district court level in 1941 after a three-year trial. The district judge relied heavily on the *U.S. Steel* case of 1920. He felt that mere size, unaccompanied by dastardly deeds, did not violate Section 2. The Supreme Court could not hear the Justice Department's appeal because four Court Justices disqualified themselves on grounds of prior participation in the case, leaving less than a quorum. However, the New York Circuit Court of Appeals was designated court of last resort for the case. That three-judge panel, acting under the leadership of Judge Learned Hand, decided against Alcoa, thereby reversing the lower court and boldly overturning precedent.[19]

On the question of market power, the Circuit Court determined that Alcoa controlled over 90% of primary aluminum sales in the United States, the other 10% being accounted for by imports. "That percentage," Hand said, "is enough to constitute a monopoly." On the issue of intent, the Court *rejected* the notion that evil acts must be in evidence. Lacking substantial judicial precedent for this position, the Court looked to congressional intent:

> [Congress] did not condone "good trusts" and condemn "bad" ones; it forbade all. Moreover, in so doing it was not necessarily actuated by economic motives alone. It is possible, because of

its indirect social or moral effect, to prefer a system of small producers . . . to one in which the great mass of those engaged must accept the direction of a few.

By this interpretation a monopolist could escape only if its monopoly had been "thrust upon it," only if "superior skill, foresight and industry" were the basis for its success. Was this true of Alcoa? The Court thought not, emphasizing conditions of entry:

> It would completely misconstrue "Alcoa's" position in 1940 to hold that it was the passive beneficiary of a monopoly. . . . This increase and this continued undisturbed control did not fall undesigned into "Alcoa's" lap. . . . There were at least one or two abortive attempts to enter the industry, but "Alcoa" effectively anticipated and forestalled all competition . . . It was not inevitable that it should always anticipate increases in the demand for ingot and be prepared to supply them. Nothing compelled it to keep doubling and redoubling its capacity before others entered the field.

Assistance to Entrants. Today, partly as a result of this decision, Alcoa accounts for less than one third of all United States aluminum ingot capacity. The government did not bring this about by breaking Alcoa into fragments. Instead, it encouraged and subsidized new entry into the industry. Shortly after World War II, the government's war plants were sold at bargain-basement prices to Reynolds and Kaiser (two former fabricators). This move alone reduced Alcoa's market share to 50%. Later, during the Cold and Korean Wars of the 1950s, the government aided the entry of Anaconda, Harvey (now owned by Martin Marietta), and Ormet. These firms were the beneficiaries of rapid amortization certificates, government-guaranteed construction loans, long-term contracts to supply the government's stockpile of aluminum, and cut-rate government electricity. Changing economic conditions also helped. The demand for aluminum in the United States

[19] *U.S.* v. *Aluminum Company of America,* 148 F.2d 416 (1945).

has increased 3000% since 1940 and 1000% since 1950. Simultaneously, costs as a function of plant size have not altered appreciably. As a consequence, economies of scale have shrunk to the point at which a minimum efficient scale alumina plant would account for only about 8% of total United States capacity, and a minimum efficient scale ingot plant would account for only about 3%. These developments enabled still further entry during the 1960s and 1970s.

C. United Shoe Machinery (1953)

U.S. v. *United Shoe Machinery* was tried in 1953, was decided against United Shoe, and was affirmed per curiam by the Supreme Court in 1954.[20] United was found to supply somewhere between 75 and 85% of the machines used in boot and shoe manufacturing. Moreover, it was the only machinery producer offering a full line of equipment. United had many sources of market power, but the following are especially noteworthy:

1. Like Alcoa, United held patents covering the fundamentals of shoe machinery manufacture at the turn of the century. These basic patents were long expired by the 1950s, and with some effort competitors could "invent around" United's later patents. Still, at the time of the suit, United held 2675 patents, some of which it acquired and some of which impeded entry.
2. A logical strategy for a new entrant would have been to start with one or two machine types and then branch out into a more complete line. Indeed, this was the approach of United's major rival, Compo, which specialized in "cementing" machines. United's answer to the challenge, however, was a dis-

---

[20] *U.S.* v. *United Shoe Machinery Corp.*, 110 F. Supp. 295 (D. Mass. 1953), aff'd per curiam, 347 U.S. 521 (1954). See also Carl Kaysen, *United States* v. *United Shoe Machinery Corporation* (Cambridge, Mass.: Harvard University Press, 1956).

criminatory price policy that fixed a lower rate of return where competition was of major significance and a higher rate of return where competition was weak or nonexistent.
3. There was some weak evidence of economies of scale. Economies were suggested by the fact that United had only one manufacturing plant. The evidence is weak, however, because the plant was essentially a large "job shop" with a wide variety of products and small orders. Mass production techniques were not involved.
4. Finally, United never sold its machines; it only leased them. This policy precluded competition from a second-hand market. Furthermore, the terms of the leases restricted entry into new machinery production. Ten years was the standard lease duration. If a lessee wished to return a machine before the end of his ten-year term, he paid a penalty that tapered down from a substantial amount in the early years to a small amount in the later years. If he was returning the machine for replacement, he paid a lower penalty if he took another United machine than if he switched to a rival manufacturer's machine. Moreover, service was tied in. No separate charges were made for repairs and maintenance, with the result that a newly entering firm had to build a service organization as well as manufacturing and marketing capabilities.

On the basis of these facts, the court ruled against United, saying that the "defendant has, and exercises, such overwhelming strength in the shoe machinery market that it controls that market." What is more, "this strength excludes some potential, and limits some actual, competition." Regarding intent, the court conceded that "United's power does not rest on predatory practices." However, United's lease-only system, its restrictive lease clauses, its price discrimination, and its acquisition of patents are not practices which can be properly described as the inevitable consequences of ability, natural forces, or law. They represent something more. . . . They are contracts, arrangements, and policies which, instead of encouraging competition based on pure merit, further the dominance of a particular firm. In this sense they are *unnatural* barriers . . . [italics added]

The court ordered United to sell as well as lease its machines, to modify the terms of its leases, and to divest itself of some assets.

Among other cases of the *Alcoa* era, *Grinnell* (1966) is notable for saying that monopolization based on "superior product, business acumen, or historic accident" would not be illegal. Grinnell Corp. did not pass the test.[21]

IV. 1970-Present: Refinement and Retreat

The ground work for a hard-line against dominant firms was laid with the *Alcoa* era, but there was little follow-through. United Shoe and a few others suffered some dismemberment then. But the government seemed to be ignoring real giants like GM and IBM. At least two factors could explain the timidity of officialdom—(1) inadequate resources and (2) inadequate legal clout.

The *first* is easiest to explain because it is easy to imagine the immense resources consumed by a "big case." Dozens of years, scores of lawyers, millions of dollars, thousands of documents, hundreds of witnesses, hordes of motions, and countless other items drain plaintiffs and defendants in these cases. To bring a decent case against a genuine giant the Antitrust Division would have to be revamped, reorganized, and refinanced. Estimates of the social benefit/cost ratios of big cases are generally favorable—for instance, Standard Oil, 67; American Tobacco, 21; Alcoa 19; and United Shoe Machinery 5.[22] But inertia curbs commitment.

The *second* problem, inadequate legal clout, arose from gaps in the law. Up to this point we have seen the law's firm grasp of two rather polar conditions, outright cartelization and obvious monopolization. There is a space between, however, one that eludes antitrust treatment. That space is occupied by tight-knit oligopolies. If four fairly equal-sized firms control an industry, for example, they may skirt Section 1 with tacit collusion while at the same time ducking Section 2 because none of them individually has more than 30% of the business. Many of the nation's behemoth's fall into this category—very big absolutely but not really big relative to a relevant market. This could be called the **structural gap**.

An additional gap in the law applied even for firms with very large market shares, namely, uncertainty as to what kinds of conduct would indicate intent. What, specifically, could pass innocently for "a superior product, business acumen, or historic accident"? It was clear that blatantly predatory practices, major mergers, and restrictive licensing would not pass. It was equally clear that dominance built on significant innovation or economies of scale would pass. But what of the middle ground? What about aggressive expansion of capacity, voluminous advertising, trivial new product proliferation, and deep but above cost price cutting? Their uncertain implications for intent opened a **conduct gap**. The uncertainty stemmed from the difficulty of trying to curb monopoly without squashing business incentive. *Alcoa* was not much help on this score, as seen by the inconsis-

[21] *U.S.* v. *Grinnell Corporation,* 384 U.S. 563 (1966). The case apparently stimulated competition substantially. See Don E. Waldman, *Antitrust Action and Market Structure* (Lexington, Mass.: Lexington Books, 1978), pp. 49–57.

[22] William G. Shepherd, *The Treatment of Market Power* (New York: Columbia University Press, 1975), Chap. 7 and Appendix 3.

tency in two of Judge Hand's statements—(1) Congress "did not condone 'good trusts' and condemn 'bad' ones; it forbad all;" and yet (2) "The successful competitor, having been urged to compete, must not be turned upon when he wins." This tension, a circuit court has recently complained, "makes the cryptic *Alcoa* opinion a litigant's wishing well, into which, it sometimes seems, one may peer and find nearly anything he wishes."[23]

Against this background, the 1970s opened auspiciously for proponents of vigorous antitrust policy. The authorities launched several "big" cases against IBM, Xerox, and AT&T. Enforcement resources grew rapidly. And attempts to close the structural and conduct gaps in stringent fashion were embodied in new legislative proposals for industrial deconcentration and in innovative cases against "shared monopolies." The temper of the times was captured in a lengthy *Business Week* special report on the "mounting political pressure to toughen antitrust enforcement." The report concluded that "Business almost certainly faces even tougher antitrust enforcement and possibly even a new antitrust law aimed at breaking up the corporate giants in the country's basic industries."[24]

The ominous storm blew over by the early 1980s, however, producing little more than light rain. The light rain came in the form of consent settlements in the *Xerox* and *AT&T* cases, settlements that were momentous to Xerox and AT&T but not really important to resolution of either the structural gap or the conduct gap (as these were rather special cases). The structural gap cleanly escaped closure when the proposed legislation died in Congress and the "shared" monopoly cases died in the

FTC. The conduct gap narrowed in the direction of greater, not lesser, *leniency* for dominant firms when the case against IBM was dropped by the Justice Department in January 1982, the groundwork for the abandonment being laid by a string of circuit court decisions favorable to aggressive dominant firms—in particular, *Berkey Photo,* v. *Eastman Kodak Company* (1979), and *California Computer Products* v. *IBM* (1979)—and by the installment of a conservative, William Baxter, in the office of Assistant Attorney General for Antitrust. To outline our coverage of these developments:

A. Shades of a Tougher Stance; *Xerox* and *AT&T*
B. Continuation of a Structural Gap
  1. Unpassed Legislation
  2. "Shared" Monopoly Dies on the Vine
C. Closing the Conduct Gap
  1. *Berkey* v. *Kodak* (1979)
  2. *Calcomp* v. *IBM* (1979)
  3. *U.S.* v. *IBM* (dismissed 1982)

A. Shades of a Tougher Stance: Xerox and AT&T

Xerox. Two "big" government cases provide the most dramatic signs of a stimulated Section 2 during this current era. In 1973 the FTC charged Xerox with monopolizing the copier industry, alleging that Xerox controlled 95% of the plain-paper copier business and 86% of the total office-copier market. The allegations of offensive conduct paralleled those of *United Shoe Machinery.* That is, Xerox's licensing, pricing, and patent policies were said to exclude competition artificially. Xerox responded by negotiating a settlement in 1975, one that provided for (1) licensing patents on reasonable royalties, (2) supplying "knowhow" to competitors, (3) modifying price policies, and (4) selling as well as leasing copy machines. The consent decree has been denounced for being

---

[23] *Berkey Photo* v. *Eastman Kodak Co.,* 603 F2d 263 (2d Cir. 1979).

[24] "Is John Sherman's Antitrust Obsolete?" *Business Week,* March 23, 1974, pp. 47–56. See also *Business Week,* December 13, 1976, pp. 52–59.

ineffectual, but it may have helped the entry of Savin, IBM, and others—entries that jolted the industry with new competition.[25]

AT&T. The American Telephone & Telegraph case was launched by the Justice Department in 1974. Admitting that AT&T's monopoly of most telephone service could be justified by "natural" economies of scale, the Justice Department claimed that AT&T should not be allowed to extend that monopoly power into contiguous fields where economies were significantly less consequential—equipment manufacturing in particular. Thus the government sought to split AT&T into portions representing regulated "natural" monopoly activities and *non*regulated, potentially competitive activities. Such a split would prevent AT&T from using its monopoly power in regulated markets to subsidize its operation in unregulated markets, hurting competition in the latter. The suit was settled in early 1982 by a consent decree that will cause AT&T to shed its regulated regional phone service utility companies, leaving a unit comprised of AT&T Long Lines, Bell Laboratories, and Western Electric. Complete review of the case is reserved for Chapter 16, which covers communications. Suffice it to say here that this case is unique; it portends little for firms untouched by public utility regulation.[26]

B. Continuation of the Structural Gap

1. CONGRESSIONAL ACTION (OR INACTION)
The problems of (1) immune oligopolies, (2) conduct uncertainties, and (3) mammouth cases might all be alleviated if the law shifted toward a more purely structural orientation, one essentially eliminating the intent requirement. A number of such proposals have been made, each presenting essentially the same thrust— namely, dissolution of an industry's leading firms should follow almost automatically once it is found that some high concentration threshold has been crossed for a substantial duration. Defenses against dismemberment are usually allowed by such proposals, but they are limited to proofs that the concentration was grounded on either economies of scale in production or valid patents.[27]

The Industrial Reorganization Act proposed by the late Senator Philip Hart in 1973 provides an example. Under this scheme, the rule of reason would be curtailed. There would be a *presumption* of monopoly power whenever one or more of the following criteria were met:[28]

1. Four or fewer firms accounted for half or more of an industry's sales in a single year.
2. There has been no substantial price competition for three consecutive years among two or more firms within the industry.
3. A company's average rate of return (after taxes) exceeds 15% of its net worth for each of five consecutive years.

However, a company running afoul of one of these criteria would not face automatic fragmentation. A special commission would review the case, at which time the company could defend itself by showing that its power was due "solely to the ownership of valid patents, lawfully acquired and lawfully used," *or* that its divestiture would "result in a loss of substantial economies." Predictably, this proposed legislation touched off bitter controversy, and it is

---

[25] Don E. Waldman, "Economic Benefits in the *IBM*, *AT&T*, and *Xerox* cases: Government Antitrust in the 70's," *Antitrust Law and Economics Review* (No. 2, 1980), pp. 75–92.

[26] *Wall Street Journal*, January 11, 1982, pp. 1, 4; January 12, 1982, p. 3; January 21, 1982, pp. 1, 21.

[27] See, e.g., *The Report of the Task Force on Antitrust Policy* (for President Johnson), reprinted in *The Journal of Reprints for Antitrust Law & Economics* (Winter 1969), Part 1, pp. 633–826.

[28] *The Industrial Reorganization Act, Hearings* before the U.S. Senate Subcommittee on Antitrust and Monopoly of the Committee on the Judiciary, Part I (1973).

doubtful whether such a stringent measure can ever pass. Its benefits are too vague to many observers, and its business opponents are too powerful in the halls of Congress.

More recently a blue ribbon panel called the National Commission for the Review of Antitrust Laws and Procedures urged congressional consideration of a "no fault" monopoly law. In this approach, government prosecutors would *never need to prove intent*, only "persistent monopoly power."

> the Commission believes that persistent monopoly power, in all but the most exceptional instance, can only result from culpable conduct. Thus, the Commission concludes that, as a practical matter, liability can safely be presumed without an affirmative showing of culpable conduct.[29]

The Commissioners could not agree, however, on the means of implementing this "no fault" philosophy, so they just mentioned three possible avenues and urged congressional study. (Although this recommendation fell on deaf ears, several other Commission recommendations to speed up big cases were passed in 1980.)

2. "SHARED MONOPOLY"

Not waiting for Congress to plug the structural gap, the FTC filed suit in 1972 charging three large breakfast cereal producers with "shared monopoly."[30] Kellogg, General Mills, and General Foods collectively account for 81% of the ready-to-eat cereal market. But individually, the largest (Kellogg) controls no more than 45%. The accusations bringing these firms together under one suit were legal novelties:

1. *Brand proliferation.* The companies introduced 150 brands between 1950 and 1970, advertising them heavily and artificially differentiating them, thereby feigning competition and discouraging new entry.
2. *Control shelf space.* They crowded competitors off grocers' shelves with their countless brands and marketing clout.
3. *Forbearance.* They minimized price competition by tacit mutual agreement not to challenge each other's price increases and by limiting coupons, premiums, and cents-off deals.

The remedies sought involved more than dissolution. They included the forced licensing to other companies of any new brands developed by Kellogg, General Mills, and General Foods.

The companies won, though. In January 1982 the FTC decided to let stand the trial judge's ruling that the case should be dismissed. As one commissioner put it, the FTC should not restructure oligopolies "without a clear supportive signal from the Congress."[31] Thus it may be doubted that the structural gap will ever be closed by innovative judicial interpretations of existing statutes.

C. Narrowing the Conduct Gap with Leniency

If anything, judicial interpretation has recently turned in a lenient, rather than a stringent, direction. While the National Commission for the Review of Antitrust Laws and Procedures was arguing that, in all but the "most exceptional instance," monopoly power could not persist without "culpable conduct," the lower courts were busy exonerating Kodak and IBM of monopolization in major private suits. These courts found that many allegedly exclusionary practices merely reflected these firms' "superior product, business acumen," or "skill, foresight, and industry"—not the willful main-

---

[29] National Commission for the Review of the Antitrust Laws and Procedures, *Report to the President and the Attorney General* (Washington D.C., January 1979), p. 156.
[30] *In the Matter of Kellogg Co., et al.,* Docket #8883, Complaint, April 26, 1972.

[31] *Wall Street Journal,* January 18, 1982, p. 6.

tenance of monopoly power. As one commentator put it, these cases give a monopolist "greater freedom to fight off its competitors." And in so doing, "they invite comparison with the earliest Section 2 cases," which required "overt acts" for proof of intent.[32]

1. KODAK (1979)[33]

Kodak lords over the photography industry, dominating the manufacture of still cameras, film, and paper used to print color pictures. During the late 60s and early 70s its shares of these markets ranged from 64 to 94 per cent. In photofinishing, however, it held about 10%.

Berkey is primarily a photofinisher, but between 1966 and 1978 it competed with Kodak in still cameras. Disappointed with its lack of success in still cameras, Berkey sued Kodak for monopolizing the camera and film markets. A jury favored Berkey, but the circuit court of appeals reversed, and the Supreme Court let the reversal stand.

Berkey's claims concerning Kodak's massive dominance were never questioned. As the court put it, "If a finding of monopoly power were all that were necessary to complete a violation of Section 2, our task in this case would be considerably lightened." Berkey's claims concerning intent were severely questioned, however. These claims centered on Kodak's introduction in 1972 of its 110 compact camera *system*. The word "system" needs stress because it was more than just a new camera, it included entirely new film (Kodacolor II), film format, and photofinishing. Kodak decided upon its package approach rather haltingly, in large part because of uncertainties as to the adequacy of its old film and the performance

capabilities of its new film. Berkey challenged the introduction of the 110 system using essentially three arguments:

> *first,* that because Kodak set *de facto* standards for the photography industry, it had a special duty to refrain from surprise innovations and was required to make adequate predisclosure to enable rivals to stay competitive with it; *second,* that the introduction of Kodacolor II as part of the 110 system was not technically necessary for the new camera and was instead a use of Kodak's monopoly power in film to gain a competitive advantage in cameras; and *finally,* that limiting Kodacolor II to the 110 format unlawfully foreclosed competition by other manufacturers in existing formats.[34]

While rejecting Berkey's arguments the circuit court explicitly rejected *Alcoa's* "thrust upon" standard. Kodak, the court said, may "compete aggressively," even to the point of using its *combined* film and camera capabilities to bolster its faltering camera sales. An integrated business does not "offend the Sherman Act whenever one of its departments benefits from association with a division possessing a monopoly in its own market."

2. CALCOMP (1979)[35]

In 1969 and 1970 IBM began to suffer substantial competition from "plug compatible" peripherals manufacturers, or PCMs. By May 1971 the PCMs had 14.5% of IBM's disk-drive market and 13.7% of its tape-drive market. Moreover, these shares would have been about 20% by 1976 had IBM not done something. But IBM did do something. On May 27, 1971, it introduced long-term leases coupled with price reductions of 20–35% on equipment vulnerable to such competition.

Within 48 hours PCM company stock-prices

---

[32] John A. Maher, "Draining the *ALCOA* 'Wishing Well'. The Section 2 Conduct Requirement after *Kodak* and *Calcomp*," *Fordham Law Review* (December 1979), pp. 294–295.

[33] *Berkey Photo, Inc.* v. *Eastman Kodak Company* 603 F.2d 263 (2d Cir. 1979), cert. denied 444 U.S. 1093 (1980).

[34] Maher, *op. cit.,* pp. 312–313 (emphasis added).

[35] *California Computer Products, Inc., et al.* v. *International Business Machines,* 613 F.2d 727 (9th Cir. 1979).

began a nose dive (Telex down 14%, Memorex down 15%, Marshall Laboratories down 18%), and within the year following, PCM equipment orders were off 44% from the previous year, despite deep defensive price cuts by the PCM companies. They lost money for the next 2 years. For its part, IBM made up its lost revenues by increasing prices in other product lines—central processing units, card equipment, and maintenance services—just two months after the May reductions. These increases varied from 4 to 8% on equipment, and some maintenance charges rose 25%.

This and related episodes sparked a rash of PCM suits charging IBM with monopolization of peripherals markets.[36] CalComp's suit was typical, and all of CalComp's allegations of IBM wrongdoing were rejected by the circuit court. *First,* IBM's price cuts on peripherals were allegedly predatory. But this claim was rejected because CalComp failed to prove that IBM's prices were below cost. *Second,* CalComp argued that IBM's recoupment with price increases on other products was an unlawful use of IMB's power in the main frame market. This claim also lost its wheels, however, because *complete* recoupment had not been shown and because rising costs may have justified those price increases (suspicious timing notwithstanding). *Third,* CalComp contended that IMB had coupled its price reductions with unnecessary and artificial changes in its peripheral equipment design, which changes were specifically aimed at crippling the PMCs. Rejecting this contention, the court noted that the new models were not completely lacking in advantages over the old, so they offered similar performance at reduced prices. In language reminiscent of *U.S. Steel,* the court concluded that IBM's conduct was not "*unreasonably* restrictive of competition."

[36] *Telex Corp.* v. *IBM.,* 510 F.2d 894 (10 Cir. 1975), *Memorex Corp.* v. *IBM,* 636 F.2d 1188 (9th Cir. 1980), *Transamerica Computer Co.* v. *IBM,* 481 F. Supp. 965 (1979).

SUMMARY

Kodak and *CalComp* thus closed a good deal of the conduct gap by providing cover for a monopolist's "hard competition." Berkey's instructions seem especially solid. Monopolists may innovate significantly improved products without disclosure of trade secrets or provision of other aids to rivals. Monopolists need not restrain their research and development efforts. Furthermore, diversified monopolists may exploit benefits of association among their various divisions insofar as those benefits are based on "more efficient production, greater ability to develop complementary products, reduced transaction costs," and so forth: (*not* including coercive acts like tying).

The clear teaching from *CalComp* is that a monopolist may fend off rivals with price cuts so long as its prices remain profitable—that is, remain above average total cost. Beyond this, *CalComp's* lessons become muddled and even questionable. In particular, the Ninth Circuit Court gave its opinion on a very important issue that was not presented in the facts of *CalComp* when it said that *even deeper* price reductions "down to the point of marginal cost [or average variable cost] are consistent with competition on the merits." This is a reiteration of what the same circuit said in an earlier case,[37] but this position has been rejected by other courts[38] and the Supreme Court has yet to lend its official approval. Thus the question of just how deep a monopolist may innocently reduce its prices remains open. This question is extremely important, much debated, and therefore deserving of an Appendix to this chapter.

In any event, *Berkey* and *CalComp* paved

[37] *Janich Brothers* v. *American Distilling Co.,* 570 F. 2d 848 (9th Cir. 1978) *cert. denied* 439 U.S. 829 (1978).
[38] *Transamerica Computer Co.* v. *IBM Corp.,* CCH, para. 62,989 (D.C. N.Ca., October 1979), and *O. Hommel Company* v. *Ferro Corp.,* CCH, para. 62,720 (D.C. W.Pa., June 1979). Indeed, the 9th Circuit itself recently backed off: *William Inglis & Sons Baking Co.* v. *ITT Continental,* —— F.2d —— (9th Cir. 1981).

the way for Reagan's Assistant Attorney General Baxter, who withdrew the government's big case against IBM even though it had been prosecuted for thirteen years under four presidents previous to Reagan and was just months away from a district court opinion. This withdrawal was historic.

3. IBM (DISMISSED 1982)[39]

As shown in Figure 7–1, a computer system has numerous components, much as a stereo system has. IBM, Sperry Rand, and the other big companies are called **systems suppliers,** for they produce and market a full line of "hardware" equipment together with "software" programs and services to run their systems. A second sector is made up of **plug-compatible** or **peripherals** manufacturers. They produce printers, tape drives, disc drives and other individual items of peripheral equipment that can be plugged into the central system. Third, there are a host of service bureaus, consulting groups, programmers, and leasing firms that deal primarily in services rather than manufacturing. They are often lumped together as **software houses.** Finally, the newest segment of the industry sells **minicomputers.** These are small, relatively low-cost computers. Responsibility for development of these devices rests not with the huge systems suppliers but with smaller firms like Data General, Hewlett-Packard, and Varian.

IBM's Market Share.[40]   Before Baxter, the Justice Department contended that the market should be defined narrowly to include "general purpose" computers and peripheral products compatible with IBM equipment—systems suppliers, essentially. Moreover, the Department

---

³⁹ *U.S.* v. *International Business Machines Corp.,* 69 CIV 200, So. Dist. of N.Y.
⁴⁰ For brief discussion see Leonard W. Weiss, "The Structure-Conduct-Performance Paradigm and Antitrust," *Univ. of Pennsylvania Law Review* (April 1979), pp. 1124–1130.

Figure 7–1.   Overview of a Computer System

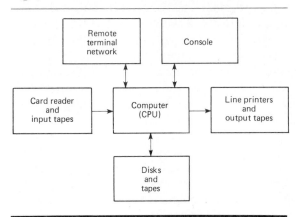

measured market shares in terms of the lease value of computers *installed*—that is, the rental value of all general purpose systems in use whether leased or purchased. By this reckoning, IBM's annual market share ranged between 68 and 75 per cent over the period 1964–1972.

In contrast, IBM argued the market should include practically everything having to do with computers. Inclusion of all electronic data processing businesses reduced IBM's market share to 33 per cent. Moreover, this 33 per cent figure threw together all annual revenues from sales and rentals. It was not based on installed equipment.

IBM's Intent.   IBM contended that, even if the 68 to 75 per cent figures were accurate, its power derived from superior skill, foresight, and industry. But the historical record is far from clear on this point.

From 1924 IBM has supplied a broad line of business machines. Its early forte was punch card tabulating equipment. In 1935, IBM had under lease 85.7% of all tabulating machines, 86.1% of all sorting machines, and 82% of all punch card installations then used in the United

States. IBM did not fully appreciate the computer's potential until 1951, when one of IBM's best customers, the U.S. Census Bureau, accepted delivery of the world's first commercial computer from Univac, a division of Remington Rand (now Sperry Rand). At the time, IBM held 90% of the punch card tabulating machine market, and Remington Rand accounted for the remaining 10%. Hence, IBM rightly viewed Univac I as a threat to its existence.

Shortly after IBM entered the computer field (delivering its first machine in 1953), two other business machine manufacturers joined IBM and Sperry Rand—National Cash Register (NCR) and Burroughs. As it turned out, prior business-machine experience was a crucial determinant of success in computers. IBM's big advantage lay in its accumulation of tabulating machine customers who had vast amounts of data already coded on punch cards, plus a natural interest in any means of rapidly processing them. IBM catered to this group by designing its computers to read their cards. IBM had more than just good contacts, it had a good reputation; and during 1956, "IBM shipped 85.2% of the value of new systems, and Remington Rand only 9.7%—approximately the same relative shares as then existing in the tabulating machine market."[41]

IBM's "lag-behind-then-recover-quickly" pattern of behavior became almost commonplace thereafter. Remington Rand and RCA were the first to introduce transistorized computers. Philco introduced the first large-scale solid state system. Data General was the first with medium-scale integration and complete semiconductor memories. Honeywell and Burroughs were the most innovative with operating systems and compilers. General Electric developed time sharing. And so on. Attempted entry often motivated these efforts. What is more, these efforts nibbled away much of IBM's early market share, but IBM always managed a rebound by duplication. By contrast, many of these innovators are no longer producing computers.

Several barriers to entry into the general purpose field protected IBM from those innovative would-be competitors. In economies of scale, a 10% share of the market or thereabouts seems to have been necessary to achieve full production efficiency. In product differentiation, two interrelated factors fostered fairly intense brand loyalty when it came to complete systems—(1) buyer ignorance, and (2) a lack of standardization.[42] Finally, capital requirements for new entry amounted to about $1 billion, a princely sum.

Specific Charges.   On intent, the Justice Department levied a number of specific charges. It alleged that IBM tried to maintain control and to inhibit entry deliberately through a wide variety of questionable marketing, financial, and technical maneuvers. These included:

"Bundling," whereby IBM quoted a *single* price for hardware, software, and related support. (IBM unbundled in 1970, after the suit.)

"Fighting machines," whereby IBM introduced selected computers with inordinately low prices in those sectors of the industry where its competitors appeared to be on the verge of success.

"Paper machines," whereby IBM tried to dissuade computer users from acquiring or leasing Control Data's 6600 (an advanced, truly remarkable machine) by announcing that IBM would soon have a comparable and perhaps even superior product, when in fact IBM had no such thing.

After reviewing the evidence amassed against IBM, Assistant Attorney General Baxter was not convinced, so he withdrew the suit in January 1982. He said that several of the acts

[41] Gerald Brock, *The U.S. Computer Industry: A Study of Market Power* (Cambridge, Mass.: Ballinger Publishing Co., 1975), p. 13.

[42] Ibid., p. 47, 51.

attributed to IBM "may have occurred." But he said the most persuasive instances took place outside the market covered by the lawsuit. He did not think IBM had committed any "serious business improprieties," so the case was "without merit" and the government's chances of winning were "only one in ten thousand."[43]

Several days later Judge Edelstein, who had presided over six years of trial only to be denied the chance to decide the case, was quoted as saying that Mr. Baxter suffered from "myopia and misunderstanding of the antitrust laws and this case specifically." "Even one with a prodigious intellect," Edelstein said, "couldn't be expected to come up with a reasoned evaluation" of the case in the four or five months Mr. Baxter spent studying it.[44]

An interesting irony is that IBM's dismissal and AT&T's consent decree were announced on the same day, January 8, 1982. Thus although IBM may have been let off the hook, AT&T was unleashed into unregulated markets at the same time. AT&T may one day become IBM's most vigorous foe.

In short, the structural approach grounded on *Alcoa* and shaped into proposals for "no fault" legislation thus seems forsaken if not forgotten. Illegal monopoly will apparently not be found without proof of *palpably anticompetitive conduct,* a conduct approach reminiscent of *U.S. Steel.* The structural approach could be faulted for possibly punishing some meritorious winners of the competitive battle, thereby casting a wet blanket on incentives.[45] On the other hand, the conduct approach of *Berkey, Cal-Comp,* and Mr. Baxter might yield more artificial monopoly power than is desirable.

During the *Alcoa* era a large dominant firm could not do the same things as a smaller rival— e.g., vary price sharply depending on competitive conditions, aggressively build plants to meet anticipated demand, license instead of sell goods, or accumulate acquired patents. Though "normal" or "reasonable" for a small firm, such tactics could not be used by a dominant firm to maintain dominance—i.e., drive smaller rivals from the field. Now there is apparently greater freedom for a "monopoly" to defend its position.

Summary

The Sherman Act outlaws monopolization. Establishing a violation requires proof of two elements: (1) substantial market power, and (2) intent. Reason, estimation, and hunch make appraisal of these elements uncertain. Hence we find very big cases in this area. Just about everything is considered except the rainfall in Indianapolis.

When attempting to examine market power, the courts consider barriers to entry of various kinds and profits. The item receiving greatest attention, however, is market share. Broad definitions of the market tend to favor defendants; narrow definitions favor the prosecutors. Which way the court will turn in any particular case is often unpredictable. Once a market definition is established, percentage points become all important. The consensus is that a market share well below 60% lies beneath the reach of the law (unless abusive practices are present), whereas shares above 80% make Justice Department attorneys look good in court.

On the issue of intent, interpretations may be divided into three periods. (1) Before *Alcoa* in 1945, intent could be demonstrated only by evidence of predatory, exclusionary, or unfair acts. The rule of reason essentially meant condemnation of unreasonable behavior. (2) After *Alcoa* and until recently, intent could be dem-

---

[43] *Wall Street Journal,* January 11, 1982, pp. 1, 6; January 26, 1982, p. 10.

[44] *Wall Street Journal,* January 26, 1982, p. 10.

[45] Defenders of the structural approach point out, however, that power meritoriously gained cannot justify an award of perpetual power. Patents, for instance, last only 17 years.

onstrated by evidence that a dominant firm's actions were not "honestly industrial," not "passive," not reflective of "superior skill," "superior product," "business acumen," or "historic accident." This reading of Section 2 left monopolists room to maneuver, but not much. (3) The period since about 1970 reveals conflicting strains and ambiguity, mainly because of a *structural gap*, which left tight-knit oligopoly or "shared monopoly" largely untouched, and a *conduct gap*, which left unclear the status of conduct that was neither so bad as to be clearly abusive nor so good as to be plainly passive. Contributing to the muddle is a basic tension in the law as inherited from *Alcoa,* a tension created by a willingness to condone monopoly (pure and simple) and a simultaneous desire to condemn monopolization (tainted and crude).

Thus the early portion of the current period witnessed efforts to confirm and even extend *Alcoa.* Big cases were brought against Xerox, AT&T, and IBM. The FTC instituted shared monopoly proceedings against the cereal oligopolists. In addition, "presumptive rules," or "no-fault" structural tests were proposed, whereby defendants would have to prove their innocence if they transgressed some previously specified criteria, such as having more than 40% of the market for three years running. Such legislation would have closed the structural gap by reaching oligopolists and closed the conduct gap by limiting what dominant firms could do without demonstrating intent.

Most recently, however, these rumblings have been silenced. *Xerox* and *AT&T* were settled by stringent consent decrees. But the shared monopoly proceedings and legislative proposals came to naught, leaving the structural gap untouched. Moreover, the conduct gap has been largely closed in the lenient direction with substantial movement away from *Alcoa* toward *U.S. Steel. Kodak* and *CalComp* led the way. Baxter's withdrawal of *IBM* capped

the trend. Whether these developments take us too far in condoning monopolization is a much debated question.

Questions and Exercises for Chapter 7

1. Why is it necessary to define the relevant market in a monopolization case? What factors are considered for a definition?
2. Why is intent necessary for a Section 2 violation? What is the economic rationale for requiring evidence of intent?
3. Why do *Standard Oil* and *U.S. Steel,* taken together seem to define an "era of dastardly deeds"?
4. Compare and contrast the facts of *Alcoa* and *IBM.* Which of the following would be easiest to argue: (1) both guilty, (2) both innocent, (3) Alcoa guilty/IBM innocent, or (4) Alcoa innocent/IBM guilty? Explain your choice.
5. Do the exercise called for in (4) above comparing *United Shoe* and *CalComp.*
6. What is the economic rationale for allowing defenses like economies of scale in Senator Hart's proposed structural legislation? How does this question relate to question (2) above?
7. Why is it appropriate to discuss "no fault" monopoly proposals within the context of a broader discussion of intent?
8. Why are *Du Pont* and *Grinnell* contrasting cases on market definition?
9. Compare and contrast the AVC and ATC rules of the Appendix.

Appendix to Chapter 7: An AVC Rule versus an ATC Rule

In stating that a monopolist's price may fall to marginal or average variable cost, the Ninth

Figure 7–2. Cost Curves for Comparison of AVC and ATC Rules

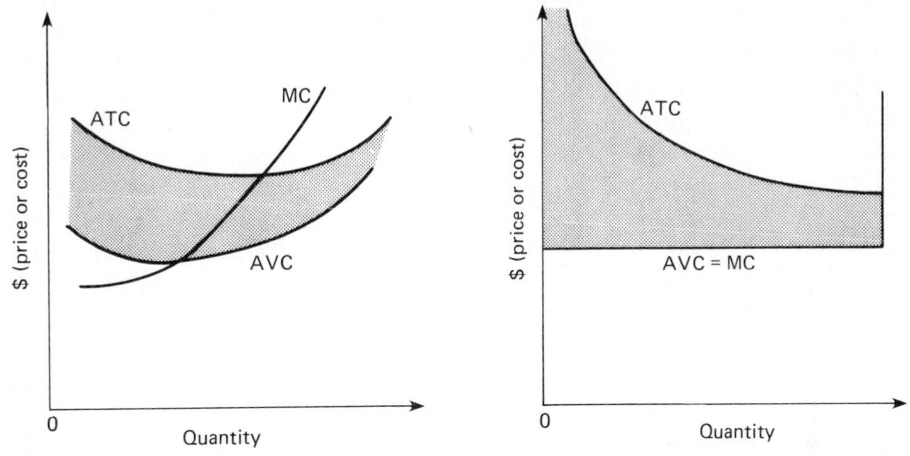

Circuit in *CalComp* is adopting what has come to be called the Areeda-Turner Rule, after its main advocates, Professors Areeda and Turner.[1] We shall call it the AVC rule, as it is most pertinent in its average variable cost form. Succinctly stated, the AVC rule would permit monopolists to cut price down to average variable costs but no further. As shown in Figure 7–2, which shows two cost configurations depending on technology, the AVC curves mark the threshold. Price-quantity combinations below the AVC lines (below the gray areas) would be illegal; price-quantity combinations anywhere above the AVC lines would be legal. The main justification for such a standard is short-run allocative efficiency. That is to say, AVC approximates marginal cost, MC, and static welfare economics theorizes that prices equal to marginal cost are allocatively efficient. Proponents

of the AVC rule also claim it is simple and practical to employ.

Criticisms of the AVC rule have been diverse and numerous.[2] Its service to allocative efficiency and its alleged ease of application have both been questioned. Moreover, the use of short-run data to detect long-run strategic behavior has been challenged as illogical. Of greatest interest to us here, however, is a criticism that is easily appreciated: namely, the AVC rule produces a defendant's paradise, a monopolist's heaven. Notice from Figure 7–2 that *any* price below average *total* cost, ATC, is one that generates losses. If price falls below ATC *and* AVC, then the losses are so great

[1] Phillip Areeda and Donald F. Turner, "Predatory Pricing and Related Practices under Section 2 of the Sherman Act," 88 *Harvard Law Review* (1975), pp. 697–733. See also Areeda and Turner, *Antitrust Law* (Boston: Little, Brown and Co., 1978), Vol. III, pp. 148–194.

[2] F. M. Scherer, "Predatory Pricing and the Sherman Act: A Comment," 89 *Harvard Law Review* 869 (1976); Oliver Williamson, "Predatory Pricing: A Strategic and Welfare Analysis," 87 *Yale Law Journal* 284 (1977); William J. Baumol, "Quasi-Permanence of Price Reductions: A Policy for Prevention of Predatory Pricing," 89 *Yale Law Journal* 1 (1979); Paul L. Joskow and Alvin K. Klevorick, "A Framework for Analyzing Predatory Pricing Policy," 89 *Yale Law Journal* 213 (1979); and Roland H. Koller II, "When Is Pricing Predatory?" *Antitrust Bulletin* (Summer 1979), pp. 283–306.

that in the short run the firm would normally shut down to minimize its losses.[3] If price falls below ATC but is above AVC so as to be in the gray area, the firm will not shut down immediately, but eventually it will. Thus a monopolist with abundant financial reserves could, under the AVC rule, drive less financially secure but equally efficient rivals from the market without fear of prosecution merely by pricing *below ATC* and *above AVC.* The requirement of a "deep financial pocket" does not detract from the point. Monopolists are often if not usually well-heeled. The point is that the AVC rule is inaccurate. Under it, wolves are mistaken for sheep. Given this bias, the AVC rule fails to maintain competition (whatever its merits in short-run allocative efficiency). Its full-fledged adoption could well push us back to pre-*Standard Oil*, not to mention pre-*Alcoa.*

What is a better rule? Together with numerous others, the present author advocates a two-part standard keyed to average *total* cost, or ATC rule.[4] That is, culpable monopolistic con-

duct would be shown by (1) pricing below average total cost, plus (2) substantial evidence of predatory intent. The call for explicit evidence of intent is necessary because prices fall below ATC all the time for wholly innocent reasons (i.e., drastically flagging sales, short-term promotions, spoiling perishables, and so forth). Pricing below AVC as well as ATC would be one possible indicator of intent because such very deep pricing cannot be loss minimizing. Other indicators include (a) documents revealing long-term business plans of injurious price cutting activity, (b) bribing distributors to refuse service to victims, (c) building immense new capacity in a market which is clearly not large enough to utilize fully that capacity at a profitable price, and (d) extremely sharp escalation of advertising outlays for a prolonged period of time.

In terms of Figure 7–2, pricing in the gray area may or may not be predatory, so indicators of intent are needed to sort out the wolves from the sheep, the anticompetitive from the procompetitive. Really deep price-cutting, below AVC, is itself indicative of intent.[5]

---

[3] The most a firm should ever lose (if it is loss minimizing) is its total fixed cost. Prices not covering average variable cost by, say, one dollar per unit lead to loss equal to all fixed cost *plus* $1 for every unit produced and sold.

[4] D. F. Greer "A Critique of Areeda and Turner's Standard for Predatory Practices," *Antitrust Bulletin* (Summer 1979), pp. 233–261; Richard A. Posner, *Antitrust Law: An Economic Perspective* (Chicago: University of Chicago Press, 1976), pp. 184–195; National Commission to Review

Antitrust Laws and Procedures, *op. cit.*, 149–151; Maher, *op. cit.*

[5] It should be noted that "predatory pricing" can be used for purposes other than driving out rivals or curbing new entry. In particular it can be used to discipline cartel "cheaters" or enforce price leadership. See, e.g., *U.S.* v. *Empire Gas Corp.*, 537 F. 2d 296 (1976).

Chapter 8

Merger Policy

The game of picking up companies is open to everybody. All you have to do is have indefatigable drive, a desire to perpetuate yourself or your family in control of an industry, or an unabsorbed appetite for corporate power.
—Meshulam Riklis
(*who parlayed $25,000 into a $755 million empire fittingly called Rapid-American, Inc.*)

Just over three decades have passed since President Truman signed into law the Celler-Kefauver Act of 1950, the most important piece of antitrust legislation of the last half-century. Vigorous enforcement during the Act's first twenty-seven years resulted in 437 merger complaints, challenging 1,406 acquisitions with combined assets exceeding $40 billion.[1]

Yet there is a paradox here. Merger activity has recently reached historic heights. 1929's long-standing record was broken in 1967, when mergers in manufacturing and mining numbered 1496, thereby exceeding the previous high of 1245 established in 1929. That previous high was then nearly doubled the very next year, 1968, when 2407 mergers were recorded. More recently, in the early 1980s, individual acquisitions of billions of dollars have become common.

[1] Willard F. Mueller, *The Celler-Kefauver Act: The First 27 Years*, U.S. House of Representatives, Committee on the Judiciary, Subcommittee on Monopolies and Commercial Law (Nov. 7, 1979), pp. 7–8.

This chapter explores this paradox and related matters. We begin with a brief description of various types of mergers and proceed to a historical review of merger activity. An outline of the causes of mergers comes next, followed by a rundown of policy developments under the Celler-Kefauver Act.

I. Background

A. Merger Types

The union of two or more direct competitors is called a **horizontal** merger. The combining companies operate in the same market, as is illustrated in Figure 8–1. Bethlehem Steel's acquisition of the Youngstown Sheet and Tube Company in 1957 is an example. A **vertical** merger links companies that operate at different stages of the production-distribution process. This too is illustrated in Figure 8–1, and Bethlehem would provide an example of this type were it to acquire Ford Motors, a big buyer

Figure 8–1. Types of Mergers

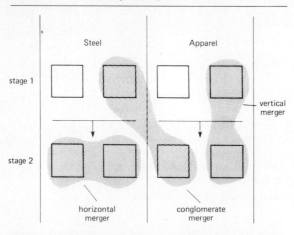

of steel. Broadly speaking, **conglomerate** mergers are all those that are neither horizontal nor vertical. This conglomerate definition covers a lot of ground, however, so the category may be subdivided into three classes: (1) **product extension,** involving producers of two different but related products, such as bleach and detergent; (2) **market extension,** involving firms producing the same product but occupying different geographic markets, for example, dairies in two distant towns; and (3) **pure conglomerate,** involving firms with nothing at all in common, as would be true of a retail grocer and a furniture manufacturer.

B. Some History

A glance at Figure 8–2 reveals why it is customary to speak of three major merger movements in American history. The first movement occurred around the turn of the century. Over the seven-year period 1897–1903, 2864 mergers were recorded in mining and manufacturing. Measured against our current and more recently set records, this record may not seem like much. However, measured against the economy of 1900 and the resulting market concentration, this first great wave was awesome. Horizontal mergers dominated the scene. Moreover, simultaneous *multiple* mergers, which are now very rare, were an everyday affair. Ralph Nelson found that mergers involving at least five firms accounted for 75% of firm disappearances during this period.[2] This turn-of-the-century merger boom produced such giant companies as U.S. Steel, U.S. Gypsum, International Harvester, Du Pont, American Tobacco, International Paper, American Sugar Refining, American Can, U.S. Rubber, Pittsburgh Plate Glass, and National Biscuit. Jesse Markham summarized the overall movement neatly when he wrote, "The conversion of approximately 71 important oligopolistic or near-competitive industries into near monopolies by merger between 1890 and 1904 left an imprint on the structure of the American economy that fifty years have not yet erased."[3]

The second major merger wave arose during the Roaring Twenties. From 1925 through 1930, 5382 mergers were recorded for manufacturing and mining. During the peak year of 1929, ownership shares moved at the feverish pace of more than four mergers per business day. This second movement exceeded the first not only in numbers tallied but also in variety of merger types. Horizontal mergers were again very popular, but vertical, market-extension, and product-extension mergers were also in vogue. It was during this second period that General Foods Corporation put together a string of product-extension acquisitions to become the first big food conglomerate. Its acquisitions included Maxwell House Coffee, Jello,

[2] Ralph L. Nelson, *Merger Movements in American Industry, 1895–1956* (Princeton, N.J.: Princeton University Press, 1959) p. 29.

[3] Jesse W. Markham, "Survey of the Evidence and Findings on Mergers," in *Business Concentration and Price Policy* (Princeton, N.J.: Princeton University Press, 1955), p. 180.

Figure 8–2. Number of Manufacturing and Mining Firms Acquired, 1895–1975

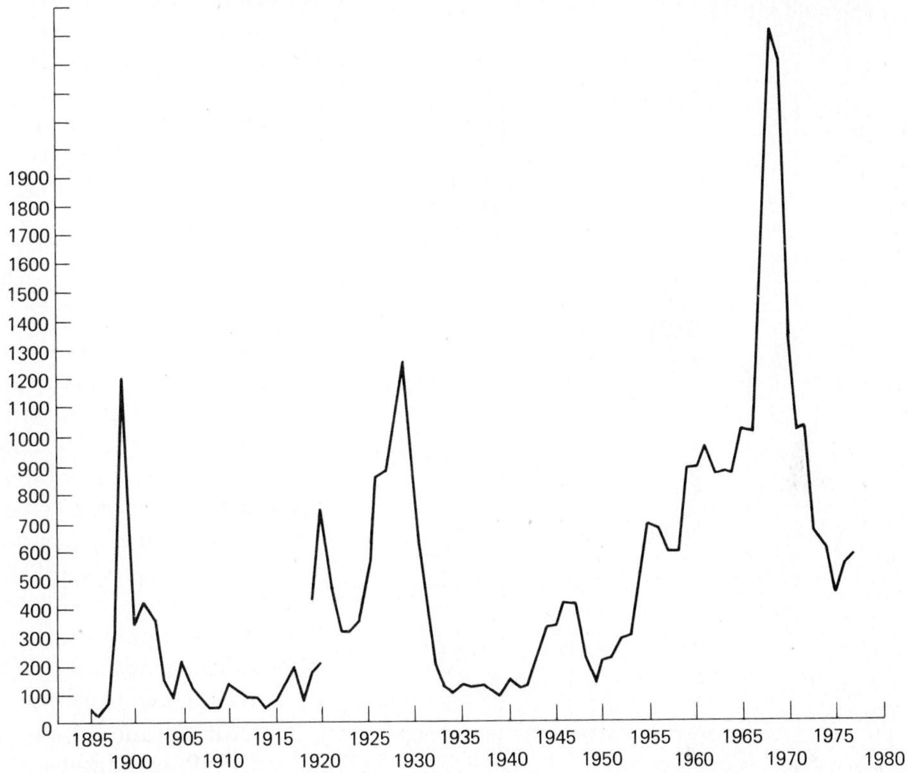

Source: Ralph L. Nelson, *Merger Movements in American Industry,* 1895–1956 (1959), p. 37; Temporary National Economic Committee, *The Structure of American Industry,* Monograph 27 (1941), p. 233; Federal Trade Commission, Bureau of Economics.

Baker's Chocolate, Sanka, Birds Eye, and Swans Down Cake Flour. Unlike the first merger movement, these years also witnessed countless mergers in sectors other than manufacturing and mining. According to Markham, at least 2750 utilities, 1060 banks, and 10,520 retail stores were swallowed up by acquisition during the twenties.[4]

After two decades of nothing more than a

rather meager ripple in the late 1940s, momentum began to build once again in the mid-1950s. Thereafter, the movement swelled incredibly. From 1960 through 1970 the Federal Trade Commission recorded 25,598 mergers. Slightly more than half of these were in manufacturing and mining. The total value of manufacturing and mining assets acquired over this period exceeded $65 billion. This sector's peak year was 1968, when 2407 firms amounting to more than $13.3 billion were acquired. Putting

[4] Ibid., pp. 168–69.

Figure 8–3. Distribution of Total Acquired Assets in Large Manufacturing and Mining Mergers, by Type, 1948–1978

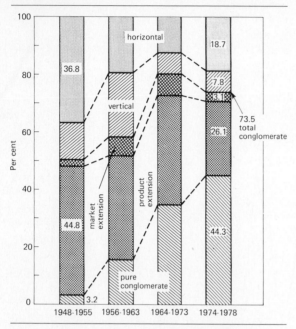

Source: Federal Trade Commission, Bureau of Economics.

3 shows the trend of the last three decades in percentage of *assets* acquired by merger type. As we shall see shortly, much of this trend away from horizontal couplings and toward conglomerate couplings, especially toward pure conglomerates, was due to public policy. The enforcement agencies cracked down rather hard on horizontal mergers whereas they generally ignored conglomerates.

II. Reasons for Merger

When counting the *reasons* for merger, one can get by with only the fingers on one hand, but just barely. In simplest terms, corporate marriage is merely a matter of finding a price that buyers are willing to pay and sellers are willing to accept. Going beyond this truism, however, we encounter complexities. Some motives are constant in the sense that they explain a fairly steady stream of mergers year in and year out. Other motives are more cyclical, a characteristic that helps explain why merger activity heats up and cools down over time. In other words, there are two interrelated issues—underlying cause and timing.

A. Timing of Mergers

Let us consider timing first. Several researchers have found a high positive correlation between the number of mergers per year and the general business cycle.[6] Merger frequency tends to rise and fall as the average level of stock market prices rises and falls.

Exactly why this correlation exists is not entirely clear. Experts speculate that owners of firms expecting eventually to sell out may feel they can get the best deal when stock prices

the matter in relative terms and using an averaging process, we can deduce that, over the period 1953–1968, approximately 21% of all manufacturing and mining assets were acquired.[5]

After a lull in the mid-1970s, the pace quickened again, as shown in Figure 8–2. Many of the most spectacular recent acquisitions have been made by oil companies, whose financial coffers have grown fat off the leaness of energy supplies.

As for merger types, these latest waves have been quite different from those of yesteryear. Horizontal mergers have become much less numerous than conglomerate mergers. Figure 8–

[5] Federal Trade Commission, *Economic Report on Corporate Mergers* (Washington, D.C., 1969), p. 666.

[6] Nelson, *op. cit.,* pp. 106–26; Markham, *op. cit.,* pp. 146–54; and Willard Mueller, testimony in *Economic Concentration,* Hearings before the Senate Subcommittee on Antitrust and Monopoly, Part 2 (1965), p. 506.

are generally high. Conversely, from the buyers point of view, the basic problem is raising enough cash and securities to make an attractive offer. Hence, acquiring firms may find funds for acquisitions easier and cheaper to come by when stock prices are high.

B. Underlying Causes of Mergers

Underlying causes involve as much intuitive understanding as timing does. They are, however, less mysterious. Sellers and buyers may see things differently while benefiting mutually.[7] *Sellers* appear to have two major reasons for wanting to seek out a buyer. First, and most obvious, is the "failing firm" problem. As every used car owner knows, poor performance may prompt a sale. In the case of business enterprises, failure is measured in terms of declining revenues, disappointing profits, recurring losses, and even bankruptcy. Although any such aspect of failure may be an important motive for the sale of a small firm, it could be no more than a very minor motive for most sales of large firms. It has been estimated, for example, that only about 4.8% of all "large" firms bought between 1948 and 1968 were suffering losses before their acquisition, where "large" was defined as having at least $10 million in assets.[8]

A second class of seller's motives relates to individually or family owned firms that are typically small. Merger may be the easiest means for an aging owner-manager to "cash-in" on his lifetime effort and perpetuate the business after his retirement. Some income and estate tax considerations also favor the sale of such firms. Again, however, these seem to be minor factors, mere droplets in the tidal waves of time past.

Of greater importance and keener interest are the *buyers'* motives. After all, the prices buyers pay to former owners typically exceed the book value of the purchased firms' assets and the market value of the former owners' stock holdings. This excess, or "premium," usually varies between 10 and 30%, but may go as high as 50% or more.[9] In early 1977, for example, prospective acquirers of Milgo Electronics were offering to pay $36 a share, whereas the former selling price was only $20 a share. Indeed, buyers may be so aggressive that they occasionally pull a "raid" or "takeover," in which case they succeed in buying a firm whose management opposes the acquisition. Stock owners who sell out against the management's wishes in these instances may not dislike their reluctant managers (although they frequently do); they may merely feel they have received an "offer they cannot refuse." Lest this give the impression that all merger motives are one-sided, we hasten to add that the following list of buyer's motives includes items that could very well be considered "mutual" motives. Buyers and sellers may both benefit if the whole is worth more than the sum of its parts.

1. MONOPOLY POWER

U.S. Steel was apparently worth more than the sum of its 170 parts. Prior to merger in 1901, the total value of the tangible property of the separate firms stood at roughly $700 million. After merger, U.S. Steel estimated its value at close to $1400 million. Why the enormous difference? Market power. After merger, U.S.

---

[7] For an excellent discussion of causes see Peter O. Steiner, *Mergers: Motives, Effects, Policies* (Ann Arbor, Mich.: University of Michigan Press, 1975), especially Chapter 2.

[8] Stanley E. Boyle, "Pre-Merger Growth and Profit Characteristics of Large Conglomerate Mergers in the United States: 1948–1968," *St. Johns Law Review* (Spring 1970, Special Edition), pp. 160–161. See also Robert L. Conn, "The Failing Firm/Industry Doctrines in Conglomerate Mergers," *Journal of Industrial Economics* (March 1976), pp. 181–187.

[9] Steiner, *op. cit.*, p. 179; J. Fred Weston, "Determination of Share Exchange Ratios in Mergers," in *The Corporate Merger*, edited by W. Alberts and J. Segal (Chicago: University of Chicago Press, 1974), pp. 131–138.

Steel produced two thirds of all United States semifinished steel and similar percentages of all rails, tin plate, rods, and other products. The consequences for the price of pig iron are pictured in Figure 8–4, which shows two price trend lines, one deflated by the wholesale price index, the other not. The discontinuous price jump of about 50% in 1901 coincides with the formation of U.S. Steel. This may lead the astute reader to suspect a substantial rise in annual profit rates also, and you would be correct.

U.S. Steel provides just one example. As we have already seen, there were many other huge horizontal mergers at the turn of the century that were probably motivated by the rewards of monopoly. The 70–90% market shares of those days speak fairly plainly for themselves. But a more explicit statement was made by Thomas Edison when he explained the formation of the General Electric Company in this way: "The consolidation of the companies . . . will do away with a competition which has become so sharp that the product of the factories

has been worth little more than ordinary hardware."[10]

Whether market power could motivate vertical and conglomerate mergers as well as horizontal mergers is a much debated question. These other forms of merger produce no immediate or obvious increases in market share for the consolidated firm. Nor do they promise added *market* concentration. Hence, theories and empirical tests of possible adverse competitive effects of these mergers must attack the question indirectly.

The major potentially anticompetitive effects of vertical mergers are (1) *foreclosure,* wherein nonintegrated businesses at one level of the production-distribution chain are foreclosed from dealing with suppliers or buyers at other levels because those other suppliers or buyers are owned by vertically integrated rivals, and (2) strengthened *barriers to entry,* which may arise from the foreclosure of potential entrants and the enlarged capital cost requirements associated with multilevel entry.[11] U.S. Steel provides an example of the barrier effect because the main source of its market power was its aggressive vertical acquisition of most iron ore supplies in North America. Charles Schwab, a prominent steel executive of the day, explained the consequences of U.S. Steel's 75% ore control while testifying in 1911:

> *Mr. Schwab.* I do not believe there will be any great development in iron and steel by new companies, but rather development by the companies now in business.
> *Mr. Chairman.* Now, explain that to us.
> *Mr. Schwab.* For the reason that the possibility of a new company getting at a sufficiently large

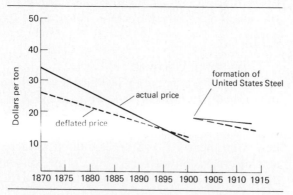

Figure 8–4. Pig Iron Price Trend, Before and After U.S. Steel

Source: Parsons and Ray, "The United States Steel Consolidation: The Creation of Market Control." *Journal of Law and Economics* (April 1975), p. 186.

[10] H. C. Passer, *The Electrical Manufacturers: 1875–1900* (Cambridge, Mass.: Harvard University Press, 1953), p. 326.
[11] Willard F. Mueller, "Public Policy Toward Vertical Mergers," in *Public Policy Toward Mergers,* edited by F. Weston and S. Peltzman (Pacific Palisades, Calif.: Goodyear, 1969), pp. 150–166.

supply of raw materials would make it exceedingly difficult if not impossible.[12]

As for conglomerate mergers, we can note that the greater size and diversity they gain improves the possibility of *reciprocity*. This is a policy of "I buy from you if you buy from me," and it may tend to foreclose rivals from affected markets. Conglomerate mergers may also eliminate *potential* competitors. In either event, profits might follow from the added power implied. Substantiation or refutation of these and other possible effects is difficult in particular cases and in general. However, several researchers have found that the market shares of firms acquired by conglomerates do not usually grow inordinately after acquisition. They say this shows an absence of adverse competitive effect,[13] implying that most conglomerate mergers could not be motivated by quests for market power.

2. RISK SPREADING THROUGH DIVERSIFICATION

Suppose you want to get two dozen eggs delivered to your grandmother. Suppose further that she lives in the woods, and the only available delivery service relies on brave but clumsy six-year-old girls attired in red. Experience shows that stumbles over roots and stones make successful egg delivery by any one girl a 50:50 proposition (even apart from the danger of wolves). Your problem then is this: If you want at least *some* of your two dozen eggs to get through, what delivery arrangements should you make? Placing the entire shipment in the hands of one girl means a 0.5 probability that *none* will arrive. However, if you give one dozen to one girl and one dozen to another,

there is only one chance in four that no eggs will be delivered because that is the probability of both girls falling down. Similarly, the split shipment offers one chance in four that all eggs will arrive safely. Two times in every four, one dozen will be broken and one dozen will get through. This example was developed by Roger Sherman to demonstrate the power of diversification in reducing risks.[14] He also demonstrates that still further diversification yields further risk reduction: "The best thing to do is to send 24 girls, each with one egg. The chance that no egg will arrive is then infinitesimally small, and it becomes very probable that about 12 eggs will arrive safely." The obvious moral (don't put all your eggs in one basket) may motivate many vertical and conglomerate mergers.

Diversification, however, is not always favorable; nor is merger the only means of achieving diversification. The conditions required for a positive effect for an acquiring firm are more limited than this simple example suggests.[15] In particular, the variances of the components of a combination must be essentially independent of each other. (The independence of several delivery girls would be severely compromised if they all held hands and thereby tripped over each other.) Failure to meet the conditions necessary for risk reduction may explain why researchers have been unable to find any risk reduction among conglomerate mergers generally.[16] Indeed, the gyrations of some conglomerates, such as LTV and Litton, offer evidence that mergers often augment risk rather than reduce it.

---

[12] Parsons and Ray, *op. cit.*, p. 198.

[13] L. G. Goldberg, "Conglomerate Mergers and Concentration Ratios," *Review of Economics and Statistics* (August 1974), pp. 303–309; S. E. Boyle and P. W. Jaynes, *Economic Report on Conglomerate Merger Performance* (Washington, D.C.: Federal Trade Commission, 1972), pp. 82–83.

[14] Roger Sherman, *The Economics of Industry* (Boston: Little, Brown and Co., 1974), p. 105.

[15] H. Bierman, Jr. and J. L. Thomas, "A Note on Mergers and Risk," *Antitrust Bulletin* (Fall 1974), pp. 523–529.

[16] B. Lev and G. Mandelker, "The Microeconomic Consequences of Corporate Mergers," *Journal of Business* (January 1972), pp. 85–104; Samuel R. Reid, *The New Industrial Order* (New York: McGraw-Hill, 1976), pp. 94–98; R. W. Melicher and D. F. Rush, "The Performance of Conglomerate Firms: Recent Risk and Return Experience," *Journal of Finance* (May 1973), pp. 381–388.

3. ECONOMIC EFFICIENCY

The larger size that mergers bring to combinations may yield lower costs of various kinds. These efficiencies may be divided into two broad groups—pecuniary economies and technical economies. **Pecuniary economies** are monetary savings derived from buying inputs more cheaply. Pecuniary gains thus include such things as larger "volume discounts" for the bulk purchase of raw materials or advertising space, lower interest rates on borrowed capital, and greater negotiating strength vis-a-vis labor, tax assessors, and others. In contrast, **technical economies** of scale are "genuine" cost savings. They imply fewer real inputs for a given level of output. Their primary sources are (1) greater specialization of equipment and operators, (2) high speed automation, (3) scaled-up equipment, and (4), in the case of vertical mergers, a refined coordination of effort between several stages of the production process.

Well then, do mergers really produce such economies? Briefly, the general answer is "yes" and "no." It is "yes" if we look only at the justifications businessmen most frequently offer the public for their mergers. It is "no" if we look at the evidence assembled and assessed by most economists studying the question. As Dennis Mueller puts it, the empirical literature draws a surprisingly consistent picture: "Whatever the stated or unstated goals of managers are, the mergers they have consummated have on average not generated extra profits for the acquiring firms, have not resulted in increased economic efficiency."[17] Thus, although *some* mergers may yield economies, they usually do not.

4. SPECULATIVE AND FINANCIAL MOTIVES

Several influences may raise the price of an acquiring company's stock after a merger or series of mergers, even *without* any increment in market power, or economies of scale, or reduced risk, or enhanced real profit flows, or changes of the real assets under the combined control of the merging companies. Such stock price increases stem from speculation and often feed further speculation. They may stem from the mere *expectation* of real changes, as would be the case if investors expected a merger to capture as much market power as U.S. Steel acquired. Indeed, around the turn of the century many merger "promoters" exploited the expectations of investors by arranging mergers that had little chance of achieving real monopoly power while exaggerating monopoly power's prospects, planting rumors, and pointing to U.S. Steel's success. Once expectations were running wild and the deal was closed, promoters would hasten to sell the stock they obtained as a promotion fee to unsuspecting investor-speculators. These unfortunate folks often "took a bath." Shaw Livermore estimated that 141 of a sample of 328 mergers consumated between 1888 and 1905 were financial failures.[18]

Disclosure regulations have long since discouraged this unscrupulous practice. More recently (and more significantly for our own pocket books) we have the use of what Wall Streeters call "Confederate money" or "P/E

---

[17] Dennis C. Mueller, "The Effects of Conglomerate Mergers," *Journal of Banking and Finance,* 1 (December 1977), pp. 315–344. In addition to Mueller's citations see G. Meeks, *Disappointing Marriage: A Study of the Gains from Mergers* (Cambridge, U.K.; Cambridge University Press, 1977); and D. W. Colenutt and P. P. O'Donnell, "The Consistency of Monopolies and Mergers Commission Merger Reports," *Antitrust Bulletin* (Spring 1978), pp. 51–82. Indeed, it is interesting that during 1979–1980 many conglomerates developed a "divestiture trend" in hopes of improving their efficiency and profitability. In these two

years, for instance, ITT shed 33 companies with combined annual sales exceeding $1 billion. Others unloading baggage included Bendix, GAF, Esmark, and Gulf & Western. For a dissenting view on efficiency, see J. Fred Weston, "Industrial Concentration, Mergers, and Growth: A Summary" in *Mergers and Economic Efficiency*, Vol. 1. (U.S. Department of Commerce, 1980), pp. 38–44.

[18] Shaw Livermore, "The Success of Industrial Mergers," *Quarterly Journal of Economics* (November 1935), pp. 68–96.

magic." This can occur when a conglomerate issues new stock to acquire a firm with a lower price/earnings ratio than its own. When the conglomerate's new stock is exchanged for the stock of the acquired firm, earnings per share of the conglomerate jump, leading investors to buoy the conglomerate's price/earnings ratio, thereby supporting still further acquisitions. Evidence indicates that such price/earnings manipulation played a major role in the merger movement of the sixties.[19] Exactly how major is a matter of opinion. Some experts estimate that its role was the principal reason behind at least 20% of all mergers occurring in 1967.[20]

5. GROWTH AND PERSONAL AGGRANDIZEMENT

This survey would not be complete without mention of sheer growth and personal aggrandizement as motives. Just how important they are it is impossible to say. The Napoleonic aspirations of acquisitive business leaders cannot be captured by statistics, except insofar as statistics may disprove the importance of other, more publicly professed and more socially acceptable motives, such as economies of scale. You, the reader, are free to judge for yourself. You may draw upon your knowledge of human nature and your reading of whatever biographical material you may wish to look into. Two typical examples you will find are:

- Harold Geneen led ITT in the acquisition of more than 250 companies. A close colleague of his once said, "Three things should be written on Hal Geneen's tombstone— earnings per share, 15% growth per year, and size."[21]

- Charles G. Bluhdorn, who guided Gulf & Western Industries through more than 80 acquisitions in 11 years, had this to say about his company and himself: "No mountain is high enough for us, nothing is impossible. The sky is the limit. . . . I came to this country without a penny, and built a company with 100,000 employees. This is what America is all about . . . to be able to do what I've done is a matter of pride to me and to the country."[22]

To summarize, the motives for merger are many and varied. No one explanation clearly surpasses all others. At any one time, there is a diversity of inducements; over time, trends of intention shift.

III. Merger Policy

There are two keys to understanding United States government policy toward mergers. First, the private interests and motives of business managers and stockholders are *not* accorded any weight in such policy. Why? As far as a merger may be socially beneficial, the benefits are usually attainable by means *other* than merger. Economies of scale and diversification, for example, can be achieved by internal expansion as successfully as by merger. In the case of the failing firm or the aging owner-manager in search of a friendly savior, a strict rule denying anticompetitive mergers would probably exclude no more than a few prospective buyers, leaving open the possibility of sale to any number of other possible—and more suitable—acquirers. Conversely, for motives that are grounded on purely private gains or socially detrimental pursuits, a strict policy will either

[19] Steiner, *op. cit.*, pp. 203–204; Walter J. Mead, "Instantaneous Merger Profit as a Conglomerate Merger Motive," *Western Economic Journal* (December 1969), pp. 295–306.
[20] *Business Week*, March 2, 1968, p. 42.
[21] Spoken by Richard H. Griebel, a former ITT executive and president of Lehigh Valley Industries, *Business Week*, May 9, 1970, p. 61. For more on Geneen see Anthony Sampson, *The Sovereign State of ITT* (Fawcett Crest Paperback, 1974).

[22] *Business Week*, July 5, 1969, p. 34. For more solid evidence favoring growth see Alan R. Beckenstein, "Merger Activity and Merger Theories: An Empirical Investigation," *Antitrust Bulletin* (Spring 1979), pp. 105–128.

be neutral or favorable to the public interest.[23]

The second key was introduced in Chapter 2. Maintenance of competition by structural dispersal of power is a policy objective in and of itself. Many if not most congressmen and judges believe that the growth of large economic groups "could lead only to increasing government control; freedom would corrode and the nation would drift into some form of totalitarianism"[24]

For these several reasons, the law governing most mergers has a structural focus and is designed to curb market power in the early stages (to "nip it in the bud" before it fully blossoms). Indeed, as stated in the preamble to the original Clayton Bill, the purpose of the Clayton Act of 1914 was "to arrest the creation of trusts, conspiracies and monopolies *in their incipiency and before consummation.*" Section 7 of the Clayton Act prohibited potentially anticompetitive mergers—but it had enormous loopholes. These were not plugged until 1950, with passage of the Celler-Kefauver Amendment. The amended statute outlaws mergers

> where in any line of commerce in any section of the country, the effect of such acquisition may be substantially to lessen competition, or tend to create a monopoly.

The Act is enforced by the Justice Department and the Federal Trade Commission. Although hundreds of cases have been decided under the Act, we shall review only a few of the more important ones. Before we do, a brief outline of what to look for may be helpful:

1. The phrase "in any line of commerce" refers to product markets. Major factors affecting the courts' definition of relevant product markets include (a) the product's physical characteristics and uses, (b) unique produc-

tion facilities, (c) distinct customers, (d) cross-elasticity of demand with substitutes, and (e) the absolute price level of possible substitutes.

2. The phrase "in any section of the country" refers to particular geographic markets. Major factors affecting the courts' definition of relevant geographic markets include (a) the costs of transportation, (b) legal restrictions on geographic scope, (c) the extent to which local demand is met by outside supply—for example, little in from outside, and (d) the extent to which local production is shipped to other areas—for example, little out from inside.[25]

3. The phrase "may be . . . to lessen competition" reflects the importance of *probable* adverse effect. In this regard the major factors considered by the courts differ somewhat depending on whether the merger at issue is horizontal, vertical, or conglomerate. Factors for (a) *horizontal mergers* include the market shares and ranks of the merging firms; concentration in the market; *trends* in market shares and concentration; merger history in the market; declines in the absolute number of firms; and the elimination of a strong, competitively vigorous independent firm. Factors considered for (b) *vertical mergers,* where foreclosure and entry barriers are the potentially adverse effects, include the market shares of the merging firms (each at their respective levels in the production-distribution process); and the trend toward vertical integration in the industry. Factors considered for (c) *conglomerate mergers* include the elimination of a prime potential entrant; the danger of reciprocal

---

[23] Derek C. Bok, "Section 7 of the Clayton Act and the Merging of Law and Economics," *Harvard Law Review* (1960), p. 308.

[24] Ibid., p. 235.

[25] K. G. Elzinga and T. F. Hogarty, "The Problem of Geographic Market Delineation in Antimerger Suits," *Antitrust Bulletin* (Spring 1973), pp. 45–81. See also Ira Horowitz, "Market Definition in Antitrust Analysis: A Regression Based Approach," *Southern Economic Journal* (July 1981), pp. 1–16.

buying; and any severe disparity of size between the acquired firm and its competitors.

IV. Horizontal Mergers

THE BETHLEHEM-YOUNGSTOWN CASE (1958)[26]

Bethlehem Steel's acquisition of Youngstown Sheet & Tube in 1957 was the first large merger challenged under the Celler-Kefauver Act. The firms ranked second and sixth nationally among steel producers. Their combined ingot capacity amounted to 21% of total industry capacity. The number one firm, U.S. Steel, had a 30% share at the time, so this merger would have boosted the share of U.S. Steel and Bethlehem taken together from 45 to 50%. In the court's opinion, "This would add substantially to concentration in an already highly concentrated industry and reduce unduly the already limited number of integrated steel companies." The court was also impressed by the fact that, historically, mergers accounted "for the existing high degree of concentration in the industry." Aside from U.S. Steel's origins, "Bethlehem's growth in substantial measure is the result of mergers."

Bethlehem's defense for acquiring Youngstown Sheet & Tube was that the national market was not the relevant geographic market for steel products. It's attorneys urged acceptance of three separate markets within the United States—eastern, midcontinental, and western. Since all of Youngstown's plants were located in the midcontinent area whereas all of Bethlehem's plants were either eastern or western, the defense went on to argue that the high costs of steel transportation prevented head-on competition between the merging firms. Moreover, they claimed that the acquisition would bring Bethlehem into the Chicago area, where it could then compete more effectively with U.S. Steel, the dominant force in that area.

The court rejected these arguments. It said that, even though Bethlehem did not have ingot capacity in the midcontinent area, Bethlehem's annual shipments of more than 2 million tons into the area indicated direct competition with Youngstown. Direct rivalry prevailed in other sections of the country as well. Furthermore, the court recognized that market delineation "must be made on the basis of where *potentially* they could make sales." In other words, Bethlehem was surely capable of entering the Chicago market by internal expansion instead of by acquisition. As for the argument that the combined companies could better compete with U.S. Steel, the same faulty logic could justify successive mergers until just two or three firms were left in the industry, a situation that could hardly be considered competitive. Thus the merger was enjoined. The benefits of the court's denial were realized for all to see when a few years later Bethlehem *did* build a massive steel plant thirty miles east of Chicago.

THE BROWN SHOE CASE (1962)[27]

Failure to appeal the *Bethlehem* case enabled *Brown Shoe* to achieve the distinction of being the first case to reach the Supreme Court under the Celler-Kefauver Act. In 1955, the date of this merger, Brown was the fourth largest manufacturer of shoes in the United States, accounting for about 4% of total shoe production. Brown was also a big shoe retailer, owning or controlling over 1230 retail shops. The mate in Brown's merger was Kinney, which likewise engaged in shoe manufacturing and retailing. Retailing was Kinney's *forte*, however, as it was at the time the nation's larg-

---

[26] *United States* v. *Bethlehem Steel Corp.,* 168 F. Supp. 576 (1958).

[27] *Brown Shoe Company* v. *United States,* 370 U.S. 294 (1962).

est "independent" retail shoe chain, with over 400 stores in more than 270 cities and about 1.2% of all retail shoe sales by dollar volume. The case thus had vertical as well as horizontal aspects. Here we take up the horizontal aspects at retail level, saving the vertical aspects for later.

The Supreme Court decided that relevant product lines could be drawn to distinguish men's, women's, and children's shoes. Defendant Brown wanted still narrower delineations such as "medium-priced" and "low-priced" shoes, but the Court did not agree. As for geographic markets at retail level, the Court decided upon "cities with a population exceeding 10,000 and their environs in which both Brown and Kinney retailed shoes." By this definition, the market shares of the merging companies were enough to arouse the Court's disapproval. For example, the combined share of Brown and Kinney sales of women's shoes exceeded 20% in 32 cities. And in children's shoes, their combined share exceeded 20% in 31 cities. In addition to raw shares, *trends* caught the Court's attention: "We cannot avoid the mandate of Congress that tendencies toward concentration in industry are to be curbed in their incipiency, particularly when those tendencies are being accelerated through giant steps striding across a hundred cities at a time. In the light of the trends in this industry we agree with the Government and the court below that this is an appropriate place at which to call a halt."

THE CONTINENTAL CAN CASE (1964)[28]

In this case the Supreme Court held illegal a merger between Continental Can, the nation's second largest manufacturer of metal containers, and Hazel-Atlas Glass Company, the nation's third largest producer of glass containers. It was generally agreed that the entire

[28] *United States* v. *Continental Can Co.*, 378 U.S. 441 (1964).

country constituted the geographic market. Thus product market delineation became the critical issue. Table 8–1 shows the shares of these companies under alternative product market definitions. Continental produced no glass containers, and Hazel-Atlas produced no metal cans. A narrow definition that kept the two products separate would therefore mean no change in market shares as a result of the merger. Conversely, a broad definition combining metal and glass would imply direct competition between the companies and a jump in market share for Continental from 21.9 to 25%. Note that a still broader definition, one including paper and plastic as well as metal and glass, would also place these firms in the same market, but it would give them much lower market shares.

A majority of the Court thought that metal and glass containers combined could be considered a proper "line of commerce" for purposes of Section 7:

> Metal has replaced glass and glass has replaced metal as the leading container for some important uses; both are used for other purposes; each is trying to expand its share of the market at the expense of the other; and each is attempting to preempt for itself every use for which its product is physically suitable, even though some such uses have traditionally been regarded as the exclusive domain of the competing industry.

Up to that time this interproduct competition had been especially sharp for packaging beer, soft drinks, and baby food. To a lesser degree it extended to household chemicals and other areas. From recognition of these aspects of competition, it was a small step to a conclusion of merger illegality. The firms were large and highly ranked. Moreover, "the product market embracing the combined metal and glass container industries was dominated by six firms having a total of 70.1% of the business." The Court felt that where "concentration is al-

Table 8–1.   Percentage of Metal and Glass Container Shipments Accounted for by Continental Can and Hazel-Atlas, 1955

Product Market	Continental Can	Hazel-Atlas	Continental and Hazel-Atlas Combined
Metal containers	33.0	None	33.0
Glass containers	None	9.6	9.6
Metal and glass containers	21.9	3.1	25.0

Source: U.S. v. Continental Can Co. 378 U.S. 441 (1964).

ready great, the importance of preventing even slight increases in concentration . . . is correspondingly great."

THE VON'S CASE (1966)[29]

This case is to horizontal mergers what the sixth commandment is to homicide. The acquisition was denied, although neither firm involved was really very big and, by usual standards, the market was not highly concentrated. Von's ranked third among retail grocery store chains in the Los Angeles area when in 1960 it acquired Shopping Bag Food Stores, which ranked sixth. Their market shares were, respectively, 4.3 and 3.2%. Hence, their combined sales amounted to 7.5%. This would have boosted the four-firm concentration ratio in the Los Angeles market from 24.4% before merger to 28.8% after. Moreover, 8-firm and 12-firm concentration had been on the rise prior to merger.

These facts might have been moderately damning. But Justice Black chose to neglect them when writing the Supreme Court's majority opinion. He stressed other factors:

the number of owners operating a single store in the Los Angeles retail grocery market de-

[29] United States v. Von's Grocery Co., 384 U.S. 270 (1966).

creased from 5,365 in 1950 to 3,818 in 1961. By 1963, three years after merger, the number of single store owners had dropped still further to 3,590. During roughly the same period from 1953 to 1962 the number of chains with two or more grocery stores increased from 96 to 150. While the grocery business was being concentrated into the hands of fewer and fewer owners, the small companies were continually being absorbed by the larger firms through mergers.

Indeed, Black defines concentration in terms of the *number* of independent firms. He goes on to state that "the basic purpose of the 1950 Celler-Kefauver Bill was to prevent economic concentration in the American economy by keeping a large number of small competitors in business." By this reasoning, a divestiture order was unavoidable.

However laudable these sentiments might be, we may question as a matter of economics whether the massive demise of mom-and-pop grocery stores in Los Angeles was due to mergers like the one denied. Divestiture of Shopping Bag did not resurrect them. They fell by the wayside for reasons of economies of scale, cheap automobile transportation to shopping centers, easy parking in the shopping centers, and the like. Thus the Court seems to have set a stringent legal standard while deferring to a moderate standard of economic proficiency.

THE PABST CASE (1966)[30]

Both standards carried over into the Pabst case, another denial decided just after the Von's case. In 1958 Pabst was the nation's tenth largest brewer. It acquired Blatz, the eighteenth largest. This merger made Pabst the nation's fifth largest brewer with 4.49% of nationwide sales volume. Thus, in terms of a broad national definition of the market, the ranks and shares involved here were rather low, even lower than those in Von's. Government prosecutors therefore argued acceptance of Wisconsin and a three-state area made up of Wisconsin, Illinois, and Michigan as relevant geographic markets. In Wisconsin, for instance, Blatz had been the largest seller and Pabst had been fourth; after the merger Pabst was first with 23.95% of state sales. The Supreme Court bought the idea of limited state markets without any economic justification:

> The language of [the Act] requires merely that the Government prove the merger has a substantial anticompetitive effect somewhere in the United States—"in *any* section" of the United States. This phrase does not call for the delineation of a "section of the country" by metes and bounds as a surveyor would lay off a plot of ground.

The Court's cavalier treatment of the market definition problem has been strongly criticized.

Recent Developments

In 1968, the Justice Department promulgated a set of "merger guidelines," which specified market share combinations that would "ordinarily" be challenged by the government. Based on cases like *Von's* and *Pabst*, these guidelines were quite strict. For example, a merger of two firms having market shares as low as 10% and 2% in a market where the four-firm concentration ratio exceeded 74% would have violated the 1968 guidelines. This stern stand led some commentators to conclude that horizontal mergers were almost per se illegal.

However, the 1970s and 1980s proved that the law is not that stringent. For example, in grocery retailing the enforcement agencies gave the green light during 1975–76 to three substantial horizontal mergers by large companies—Lucky, Allied, and A & P.[31] Moreover, the government has lost a number of recent cases. Among these, *Pillsbury* (1979) is one of the most interesting. In this case, FTC attorneys challenged a 1976 merger between Pillsbury and Fox Deluxe Foods, both of which produced frozen pizza. Before merger, Pillsbury held 15.4% of the market and Fox accounted for 2.4%. Moreover, there was some trend toward concentration in the market. Nevertheless, the Commission decided *not* to ban the merger on grounds that (1) the merger was not substantially anticompetitive, and (2) Fox owners were exiting from the market and there was a need to preserve exit opportunities for small firms.[32] Explaining the importance of exit opportunities, the FTC argued that the *entry* of new, small firms into the industry would be discouraged if their opportunities to sell out were restricted by law. Thus, maintenance of exit opportunity would, according to the FTC, rebound to make entry easier.

Finally, and most recently, Reagan's Assistant Attorney General William Baxter rewrote the merger guidelines in 1982 to better reflect the relaxed attitude of the courts. While loosening the merger rules, the new guidelines incorporated two new twists. *First,* they measure structural impact by *Herfindahl indexes,* which are simply transformations of market share

---

[30] *United States* v. *Pabst Brewing Co.,* 384 U.S. 540 (1966).

[31] Willard F. Mueller, *The Celler-Kefauver Act . . . op. cit.,* p. 47.

[32] *In the Matter of the Pillsbury Co.,* CCH Para. 21,586 (June 1979), FTC Dkt. 9091.

data—transformations that many economists, besides Orris Herfindahl, their inventor, find useful. Market shares are squared, so that, for example, a share of 10% becomes 100, a share of 2% becomes 4, and their combination of 12% becomes 144. Moreover, instead of measuring market concentration by the sum of the shares of the four leading firms, the Herfindahl index of concentration *squares* the shares of *all* firms and then adds them up. For example, the Herfindahl index for a market of five firms with shares of 35%, 25%, 20%, 15%, and 5%, would be

$$35^2 + 25^2 + 20^2 + 15^2 + 5^2 = 1225 + 625 + 400$$
$$+ 225 + 25 = 2500$$

This squaring of market shares gives especially large weight to especially large market shares, so it may be a better reflection of anticompetitive impact than market shares plain and simple. The new guidelines permit horizontal mergers in markets having a post-merger Herfindahl of 1000 or less, pose a warning in the 1000–1800 range, and threaten serious trouble for any substantial merger in markets with Herfindahls greater than 1800.

The *second* new twist in the guidelines is that they incorporate consideration of factors other than market shares and concentration when deciding whether to challenge particular mergers. That is to say, competition may be either less or more intense than is suggested by a given level of concentration. It may be *less* intense if, for example, barriers to entry are particularly high or if extensive joint venture activity inhibits competitive independence. Conversely, competition may be *more* intense if (1) there is *rapid technological change* to stifle collusive understandings and disrupt stodgy strategies, or (2) there is *rapid industry growth*, which creates market turbulence and reduces incentives to collude, or (3) especially *easy entry* to provide potential competition, or (4) substantial *instability of market*

shares, something which can signal vigorous competition despite high concentration. Stressing these factors that intensify competition, the new guidelines will permit horizontal mergers that would probably have been challenged under the old guidelines, but they might still maintain a moderately firm stance against horizontal mergers.[33]

Treatment of vertical and conglomerate mergers seems to be easing as well.

V. Vertical Mergers

Short of monopoly, the critical issue in nearly all vertical merger cases is "foreclosure." Before merger, numerous suppliers can compete for each independent user's purchases. After merger, supplier and user are linked by common ownership. Products then typically flow between the merged firms as far as is practicable, and the sales opportunities of other suppliers diminish. If the vertical linkage is trivial, as would be true of a farmer owning a roadside vegetable stand, competition is not affected. If, on the other hand, the foreclosure covers a wide portion of the total market, there may be anticompetitive consequences.

THE BROWN SHOE CASE (1962): VERTICAL ASPECTS[34]

Prior to Brown Shoe's acquisition of Kinney in 1955, Brown had acquired a very large number of retail shops. Thus, Kinney was just one

---

[33] *Wall Street Journal,* November 16, 1981, p. 2. Statement of Assistant Attorney General Baxter before the Subcommittee on Monopolies and Commercial Law of the Committee on the Judiciary, U.S. Senate, August 26, 1981; David Ranii, "The Antitrust Revolution," *National Law Journal* (Nov. 9, 1981), pp. 1, 18–19. A few cases support Baxter in this. See *U.S.* v. *General Dynamics,* 415 U.S. 486 (1974); *Kaiser Aluminum & Chemical Corp.* v. *FTC,* 1981–2 Trade Cases, para. 64,149 (7th Cir. 1981).

[34] *Brown Shoe Company* v. *United States,* 370 U.S. 294 (1962).

in a series of vertical mergers by Brown. In effect, then, Brown was attempting to accumulate captive retail distributors who would buy heavily from Brown's manufacturing arm.

On these vertical aspects the Supreme Court stressed several points. First, since Kinney was the largest independent retail chain, the Court felt that, in this industry, "no merger between a manufacturer and an independent retailer could involve a larger potential market foreclosure." Second, the evidence showed that Brown would use the acquisition "to force Brown shoes into Kinney stores." Third, there was a *trend* toward vertical integration in the industry, a trend in which the acquiring manufacturers had "become increasingly important sources of supply for their acquired outlets," and the "necessary corollary of these trends is the foreclosure of independent manufacturers from markets otherwise open to them." Although Brown's attorneys argued that the shoe industry was composed of a large number of manufacturers and retailers, the Court rejected their arguments on grounds that "remaining vigor cannot immunize a merger if the trend in that industry is toward oligopoly." The Court thus ordered divestiture.

THE CEMENT CASES (1961–1967)

Approximately three fourths of all cement is used to produce ready-mixed concrete (cement premixed with sand or other aggregate). Prior to 1960 there was virtually no integration between the cement and ready-mixed concrete industries. By 1966, however, after an outbreak of merger activity, at least 40 ready-mix concrete companies had been acquired by leading cement companies, and several large producers of ready-mixed concrete had begun to make cement. The Federal Trade Commission issued a series of complaints, directed its staff to make an industry-wide investigation, and in January 1967 issued a policy statement challenging

vertical mergers in the industry, all of which seems to have reduced acquisition activity appreciably.[35]

In the eyes of the FTC, the relevant geographic markets were regional because 90% of all cement is shipped no more than 160 miles. Within the regional markets four-firm concentration typically exceeded 50%, in part because of economies of scale. Thus it was felt that the vertical merger movement threatened foreclosure in at least some regional markets. Areas particularly affected were Kansas City, Richmond, and Memphis, where more than 30% of all cement produced was consumed by "captive" ready-mix concrete companies. According to the Commission:

> When one or more major ready-mixed concrete firms are tied through ownership to particular cement suppliers, the resulting foreclosure not only may be significant in the short run, but may impose heavy long-run burdens on the disadvantaged cement suppliers who continue selling in markets affected by integration. Acquisitions of leading cement consumers in markets containing comparatively few volume buyers may have the effect of substantially disrupting the competitive situation at the cement level. . . .

In sum, vertical mergers are not likely to be challenged unless there is some *horizontal* problem at one or both of the market levels involved. If the markets are concentrated and the merging firms have substantial shares at their respective levels, the merger's anticompetitive potential could be serious because possible foreclosure is then serious.

---

[35] Federal Trade Commission, *Economic Report on Mergers and Vertical Integration in the Cement Industry* (Washington, D.C. 1966); Enforcement Policy with Respect to Vertical Mergers in the Cement Industry, January 1967, in Commerce Clearing House, 1971 *Trade Regulation Reports*, #4520.

VI. Conglomerate Mergers

The record-breaking merger statistics of the sixties show that the law has been almost inconsequential when it comes to conglomerate acquisitions. If a big conglomerate merger can be twisted into a horizontal or vertical configuration (as happened in the *Continental Can/ Hazel-Atlas Glass* case), its chances of legal survival shrink considerably. If, however, it can withstand twisting, its chances of challenge must be somewhere below one in a thousand. In other words, officials are reluctant to apply curbs except where mergers clearly affect *particular markets*.

Thus challenges to **product-extension** and **market-extension** mergers are frequently based on arguments of *potential competition*. Absent its acquisition of the leading bleach company, for instance, a major detergent manufacturer might have entered the bleach market by itself through internal expansion (*de novo*), or by "toehold" acquisition of a small bleach producer, thereby increasing the number of competitors in the bleach market or lessening concentration. Even in the absence of any intended *de novo* entry or toehold acquisition, potential competition might still be worth preserving. If, for example, a western brewer remains at the edge of the eastern market, its presence might constrain the activities of the eastern brewers. They would be less likely to charge excessive prices for their beer. The *Procter & Gamble* and *Falstaff* cases reviewed below flesh out these examples, and the former illustrates an additional hook on which to hang a challenge—namely, the "entrenchment" or "deep pocket" effect.

Pure conglomerates are less likely to affect specific markets. If *reciprocity* can be shown, as it was in *Consolidated Foods*, the merger may be vulnerable. If the merging parties are truly dominant firms (IBM and GM, say), that too might be vulnerable. But these instances are so rare as to leave pure conglomerates essentially untouchable.

THE PROCTER & GAMBLE CASE (1967)[36]

Procter & Gamble's 1958 acquisition of Clorox Chemical Co. could be considered a product extension merger. Among other things, Procter was the dominant producer of soaps and detergents, accounting for 54.4% of all packaged detergent sales. Clorox, on the other hand, was the nation's leading manufacturer of household liquid bleach, with approximately 48.8% of total sales at the time. As these statistics suggest, the markets for detergents and bleach were both highly concentrated. The Supreme Court decided that the merger was illegal, but not wholly or even mainly because of these market shares.

Anticompetitive effects were found in several respects. First, and most obviously, Procter was a prime prospective entrant into the bleach industry. Thus, "the merger would seriously diminish potential competition by eliminating Procter as a potential entrant." Indeed, prior to the acquisition, "Procter was in the course of diversifying into product lines related to its basic detergent-soap-cleanser business," and liquid bleach was a distinct possibility because it is used with detergent.

Second, the Court expressed concern that the merger would confer anticompetitive advantages in the realm of marketing. Although all liquid bleach is chemically identical (5.25% sodium hypochlorite and 94.75% water), it is nevertheless highly differentiated. Clorox spent more than 12% of its sales revenues on advertising, and priced its bleach at a premium relative to unadvertised brands. For its part, Procter was the nation's leading advertiser (and still is).

The Court therefore felt that Procter would

---

[36] *Federal Trade Commission* v. *Procter & Gamble Co.*, 386 U.S. 568 (1967).

unduly strengthen Clorox against other firms in the bleach market by extending to Clorox the same volume discounts on advertising that it received from the advertising media. Moreover, "retailers might be induced to give Clorox preferred shelf space since it would be manufactured by Procter, which also produced a number of other products marketed by retailers." In sum, "the substitution of the powerful acquiring firm for the smaller, but already dominant, firm may substantially reduce the competitive structure of the industry by raising entry barriers and dissuading the smaller firms from aggressively competing."

THE FALSTAFF CASE (1973)[37]

In 1965, Falstaff Brewing Corp. acquired the Narragansett Brewing Company of New England. Although at the time Falstaff was the fourth largest brewer in the United States, it covered only three-fifths of the nation and sold no beer in New England. Thus, Falstaff was extending its market by grabbing Narragansett, which at the time was the largest selling beer in the Northeastern area, holding 20% of the market. The market itself was moderately concentrated, with four firms accounting for 61% of sales in 1965.

The District Court found in favor of Falstaff mainly because Falstaff executives had testified that their company was not a potential competitor in New England. They said they definitely would not enter *de novo*. A majority of the Supreme Court, however, held that this was not enough. They directed the District Court to assess the possibility that Falstaff was *perceived* as a potential entrant *by the brewers already in New England*. With this case, then, the Court accepted a broad interpretation of the potential competition doctrine:

> In developing and applying the doctrine, the Court has recognized that a market extension merger may be unlawful if the target market is substantially concentrated, if the acquiring firm has the characteristics, capabilities, and economic incentive to render it a perceived potential *de novo* entrant, and if the acquiring firm's premerger presence on the fringe of the target market in fact tempered oligopolistic behavior on the part of existing participants in that market. In other words the Court has interpreted Sec. 7 as encompassing what is commonly known as the "wings effect" . . .[38]

On reconsideration the District Court again found Falstaff innocent, ruling that Falstaff was *not* a perceived potential entrant in the New England beer market. It should be noted that similar fates awaited subsequent cases of this type. In banking especially, the government has had little success in arguing the doctrine of perceived potential entry. Thus, the evidence must be pretty solid that the firm at bar is perceived to be a potential entrant for this doctrine to sway the courts toward guilty verdicts.

THE CONSOLIDATED FOODS CASE (1965)[39]

The Federal Trade Commission found that Consolidated, a large wholesaler and retailer of food products, had violated the law by its purchase of Gentry, Inc., a manufacturer of dehydrated onion and garlic. Reciprocity proved to be the key. Gentry sold its onion and garlic to pickle packers, canners, and other food processors. In turn, many of these processors sold to distributor Consolidated. Once Consolidated acquired Gentry, it asked these processors to buy their needed onion and garlic from Gentry, in light of the fact that Consolidated was buying from them. During the first seven years after merger, Gentry's share of the combined onion and garlic business rose from 32% to 35%.

---

[37] *United States* v. *Falstaff Brewing Corp.*, 410 U.S. 526 (1973).

[38] *United States* v. *Marine Bancorporation, Inc.*, 418 U.S. 602 (1974).

[39] *FTC* v. *Consolidated Foods Corporation*, 380 U.S. 592 (1965).

On appeal, the Supreme Court sided with the FTC against Consolidated, saying,

> We do not go so far as to say any acquisition, no matter how small, violates Section 7 if there is a probability of reciprocal buying . . . But where, as here, the acquisition is of a company that commands a substantial share of the market, a finding of probability of reciprocal buying by the Commission . . . should be honored, if there is substantial evidence to support it.

THE ITT-GRINNEL CASE (1970)[40]

This case is of interest because the Justice Department tried to argue that a finding of specific anticompetitive effect in specific product and geographic markets was *not* required for illegality. It argued instead that, in the wake of a "trend among large diversified industrial firms to acquire other large corporations," it could be concluded that "anticompetitive consequences will appear in numerous though *undesignated* individual 'lines of commerce.'"

The merger at issue was ITT's acquisition of Grinnell, a very large manufacturer of automatic sprinkler devices and related products. Since ITT had been a major participant in the conglomerate merger mania, and since Grinnell was big, this was as good a case as any to test the theory that adding to *aggregate concentration* alone was offensive under the law. But the District Court did not agree, and the Justice Department lost:

> The Court's short answer to this claim . . . is that the legislative history, the statute itself and the controlling decisional law all make it clear beyond a peradventure of a doubt that in a Section 7 case the alleged anticompetitive effects of a merger must be examined in the context of *specific product and geographic markets;* and the determination of such markets is a necessary predicate to a determination of whether there has been a substantial lessening of competition within an area of effective competition. To ask the Court to rule with respect to alleged anticompetitive consequences in *undesignated lines of commerce* is tantamount to asking the Court to engage in judicial legislation. This the Court most emphatically refuses to do.

The District Court opinion was not reviewed by the Supreme Court because the case was settled by consent decree prior to appeal.[41] Thus, the law is still in flux. For the present, though, we have finally bumped into the outer limit of the law. As this limit is limited, conglomerate mergers proceed apace.

The new guidelines for conglomerates reflect this. They merely suggest possible challenges where main potential entrants are eliminated.

VII. Remedies and Notification

Judicial statements of legality tell only part of the story. *Remedies* are equally important. For if illegal mergers are allowed to stand, they might just as well be declared legal. The record on this score is blemished because total divestiture to achieve premerger status is by no means always achieved. The data for 1951–1977 prove the point:

> Total divestiture was accomplished in 53 per cent of the completed cases brought by the antitrust agencies. The assets divested represented only 44 per cent of the total assets challenged in all complaints. On the other hand, no divestiture was achieved in 7 per cent of the completed cases. . . . The remaining cases either were dismissed (13 per cent) or achieved only partial divestiture (27 per cent).[42]

Even when divestiture is achieved there may be little remedial improvement if, as is all too common, the divested assets create a nonviable

---

[40] *United States* v. *International Telephone and Telegraph Corp.,* 324 F. Supp. 19 (D. Conn. 1970).

[41] For a similar district court opinion see *United States* v. *Northwest Industries,* 301 F. Supp. 1066 (N.D.Ill. 1969) at 1096.

[42] Willard Mueller, *The Celler-Kefauver Act . . . , op. cit.,* p. 89. This excludes banking cases.

firm or are absorbed by a rival. The latter form of phoney relief is illustrated by the *Continental Can* case discussed earlier. Continental had to sell the Hazel-Atlas Glass company. But it sold Hazel to the Brockway Glass Company, which was the fourth largest producer of *glass* products in the country. Had Brockway bought Hazel-Atlas in the first place, it would most likely have perpetrated an illegal horizontal merger.[43]

One of the main reasons divestiture is reluctantly and imperfectly imposed is that it is difficult to unscramble the eggs once they are scrambled. Less scrambling occurs when the antitrust agencies are given advance notice of mergers, for then preliminary injunctions can often be obtained preventing the merger's consummation until after completion of legal review. This, in fact, was the purpose of the premerger notification provisions of the Hart-Scott-Rodino Act of 1976. Specifically, the Antitrust Division of the Department of Justice and the Federal Trade Commission must receive thirty day notice of acquisitions where one of the parties to the transaction has sales or assets of $100 million or more and the other party has sales or assets of $10 million or more.[44]

VIII. Proposed Changes in the Law

Table 8–2 confirms the impression conveyed by the previous pages, namely, big horizontal and vertical mergers may be pretty well policed, but big conglomerate mergers, especially the "pure" variety, face no more than token control. Approximately 27.6% of all big horizontal mergers occurring between 1951–1977 were challenged, enough to account for over 62% of all challenges to big mergers. In contrast, only 2.3% of the big conglomerate mergers were challenged, and all but four of these were product or market extension mergers. Only 4 of the 575 pure conglomerates tallied, or 0.7%, sparked formal official reaction.

Some observers have argued that such leniency toward large conglomerates is unwise, that the law should be changed to impede ponderous pure conglomerate acquisitions. Those offering new proposals generally recognize that, in strictly *economic* terms, large conglomeracy is neither clearly good nor uniformly bad. Accordingly, they urge that checks be imposed to preserve "political democracy" and "decentralized decision making."

One such proposal by Senator Edward Kennedy in 1979 would have banned the acquisition of any firm with sales or assets of $2 billion or more by another firm in this size class. For acquisitions above $350 million but below $2 billion this legislation would presume illegality but permit *either* an efficiencies defense *or* a divestiture of old assets equal to those of the new acquisition. In effect, acquisitions *of* Fortune 500 firms *by* Fortune 500 firms would have been greatly discouraged. An alternative proposal by the staff of the Federal Trade Commission at about the same time would permit mergers among the largest firms as long as the acquiring firm divests or "spins off" another viable firm of about the same size as the acquired firm within a reasonable time period, say three years.[45]

As long as Reagan is President no such mea-

---

[43] For further discussion see Kenneth G. Elzinga, "The Antimerger Law: Pyrrhic Victories?" *Journal of Law and Economics* (April 1969), pp. 43–78.

[44] CCH Trade Reg. Rep. No. 344, Pt. II (July 1978). Actually, the rules are much more complex than this. See the lament of Hugh Latimer, "Premerger Notification," *Regulation* (June 1979), pp. 46–52.

[45] For debate of these and other proposals see *Mergers and Economic Concentration*, Hearings, Subcommittee on Antitrust, Monopoly and Business Rights of the Committee on the Judiciary, U.S. Senate, 96th Cong., 1st Sess. (1979).

Table 8–2.   Challenges to Large* Acquisitions in Manufacturing and Mining as Compared to Total Acquisitions, by Type, 1951–1977

Type of Merger	Total Number of Large* Acquisitions	Number of Acquisitions Challenged	Challenged as Per Cent of Total	Per Cent Distribution of Challenges
Horizontal	427	118	27.6%	62.1%
Vertical	236	34	14.4	17.9
Conglomerate	1,669	38	2.3	20.0
Market extension	97	11	11.3	5.8
Product extension	997	23	2.3	12.1
Pure	575	4	.7	2.1
Totals	2,332	190	8.1	100.0

* Large acquisitions are those where the acquired firm had assets of $10 million or more.
Source: Willard F. Mueller, *The Celler-Kefauver Act: The First 27 Years,* U.S. House of Representatives, Committee on the Judiciary, Subcommittee on Monopolies and Commercial Law (Nov. 7, 1979), p. 13.

sure could conceivably become law. Perhaps a better approach, one that might stand a better chance gaining the support of conservatives and liberals alike, would be to change the *tax* system, which encourages corporate growth by acquisition (and monopolization as well). This encouragement comes in two related ways. First, corporate earnings that are paid out as dividends are taxed twice, once as corporate profits and once as individual income. This encourages the retention of corporate earnings, which can then be used for acquisitions. Second, reinvested retained earnings are eventually taxed because they lead to capital gains when owners sell their stock, but individual capital gains are taxed at a lower rate than dividend income. This likewise encourages earnings retention and growth by acquisition.

Tax reform could take any one of a number of routes, some of which have wide support among economists: (1) tax dividend income and capital gains at the same rate; (2) place an especially high tax on retained corporate earnings;

or (3) move to a progressive value added tax.[46] These tax approaches have the advantage of being "self-administering." Messy problems with imposed spin offs and efficiency defenses would be avoided. Moreover, they would encourage greater use of the external capital market and thereby possibly improve capital market efficiency. Still, the political obstacles to such reforms are very large indeed.

Summary

History reveals an annual stream of mergers that occasionally swells to a flood. Around the

[46] Milton Friedman, *Capitalism and Freedom* (Chicago: University of Chicago Press, 1962), pp. 130–133; Samuel Loescher, "Limiting Corporate Power," *Journal of Economic Issues* (June 1979), pp. 557–571; Dennis Mueller, "Do We Want a New, Tough Antimerger Law?", *Antitrust Bulletin* (Winter 1979), pp. 807–836. On the practical problems see Charles E. McLure, Jr., *Must Corporate Income be Taxed Twice?* (Washington, D.C.: Brookings Institution, 1979).

turn of the century thousands of multifirm horizontal mergers transformed many manufacturing and mining industries into tight-knit oligopolies and near monopolies. A second major movement during the late 1920s brought further horizontal couplings and introduced extensive vertical and conglomerate activity as well. Most recently, the 1950s and 1960s witnessed the largest merger movement of all. During the 1960s 25,598 mergers were recorded, involving scores of billions of dollars in assets. Most acquisitions were conglomerate in nature, and the most active acquirers were conglomerates.

Generally speaking, merger frequency tends to rise and fall as the average level of stock market prices rises and falls. Thus, the timing of mergers is influenced by financial considerations. In addition, there are several basic underlying stimulants to merger, all of which have played some role in the past, none of which has clearly dominated the scene: (1) The pursuit of market power is most clearly associated with horizontal mergers. The first merger movement provides the best examples of this—including the U.S. Steel merger of 1901. (2) A desire to diversify, and thereby reduce risk, motivates many conglomerate mergers. Although some mergers may further this goal, most apparently do not. (3) Businessmen like to justify their mergers with claims of efficiency or economies of scale. Such claims may occasionally be valid, but the available evidence indicates that these claims are overly optimistic (if that is the right word). (4) Speculation contributed substantially to the merger movement of the sixties. (5) We cannot rule out growth and personal aggrandizement, although these factors are difficult to quantify.

As for policy, most law makers seem to favor structural standards that ignore motives. To the extent that a merger may be socially beneficial, the benefits are usually attainable by other means, such as internal expansion or mutual fund organizations for investments. Errors of denial can thus be fairly easily rectified. However, structural stringency has been achieved only in the case of horizontal mergers and, to a lesser extent, vertical mergers. Conglomerate mergers are largely untouchable under current law, unless they can be pushed or pulled into vertical or horizontal shape by manipulations of "the market's" definition.

The main reason for this disparity is that illegality hinges on a showing of potentially adverse competitive effect in some specific market or markets. This burden of proof is most easily carried in horizontal mergers, where market shares, concentration ratios, and related structural measures readily provide the needed indications. The indicia of potential competitive effect for vertical mergers are similarly structural and only slightly less convenient. However, the harbingers of impact for conglomerates tend to be conduct oriented, thereby defying easy measurement. Substantial absolute size is not itself now subject to serious constraint.

Questions and Exercises for Chapter 8

1. Why is it customary to speak of three major merger waves in American history? Were they all alike? Explain.
2. Why have conglomerate mergers become the main type observed?
3. Compare and contrast "monopoly power" and "risk spreading" as possible merger motives. Which is most likely for horizontal mergers? For conglomerates? Why?
4. What were the main indicators of "may be . . . to lessen competition" used by the Court in horizontal cases *Brown Shoe* and *Von's?* Is the Court consistent?
5. Does the law handle claims like Bethlehem's claim of more vigorous competition

against U.S. Steel differently than claims of improved efficiency? Explain. Is there any wisdom in this stance?

6. How do Baxter's new horizontal guidelines temper or qualify the traditional indicators of probable competitive effect? Explain.
7. Use the cement cases to explain what is meant by "foreclosure."
8. Are conglomerate mergers completely free from challenge? If not, which ones are most vulnerable? Which ones are least vulnerable?
9. Compare and contrast *Continental Can* and *Procter & Gamble* in (a) product market definition and (b) indicators of competitive effect. Can you imagine CC being tried like P&G, or vice versa? Why? Why not?
10. What changes in the law would you make? Defend your proposals.

Chapter 9

Price Discrimination: The Robinson-Patman Act

That the Robinson-Patman Act . . . is the most controversial of our antitrust laws may be the understatement of the century.
—Frederick Rowe

There are many things in life that can be either good or bad or both simultaneously, depending on the circumstances—wealth and wine to name just two. The same applies to price discrimination. Under some circumstances, it may increase competition. At times it may lessen competition. This good/bad dichotomy makes public policy in this area a delicate exercise. Indeed, public policy itself can be procompetitive or anticompetitive. That is to say, policy cannot easily extract pure essence of good when treating acts of uncertain and variable virtue.

The purpose of this chapter is to review and assess price discrimination policy. The statute law in this area began in 1914 with Section 2 of the Clayton Act. This was greatly altered by the Robinson-Patman Amendment of 1936. Now, more than a thousand enforcement actions later, we confront a large body of case law that requires summary consideration. The controversy sparked by this policy also receives attention. Before considering legal matters,

however, we should explore a simple economic definition of price discrimination.

I. Economic Definition

Price discrimination occurs whenever a seller sells the same commodity or service at more than one price. Moreover, even if the sale items are not exactly the same, economic theory says that price discrimination occurs if the seller sells very similar products at different price/cost ratios. IBM, for instance, used to rent two disk-drive systems that differed only slightly in cost and model number (the 2314 and 2319) but immensely in price ($1455 a month versus $1000). The broad definition includes cases in which costs differ and identical prices are charged, and cases involving high prices on low-cost sales coupled with low prices on high-cost sales.

Three conditions are essential for price discrimination: (1) The seller must have some *mar-*

ket power. A purely competitive firm does not have sufficient control over price to engage in discrimination. (2) The seller must confront buyers who have *differing price elasticities of demand.* These elasticity differences among classes of buyers may be due to differences in income level, differences in "needs," differences in the availability of substitutes, differences in use of the product, and so on. Without different elasticities, buyers would not willingly pay different prices. (3) These various buyer elements must be kept *separate.* Without separation, low-price customers could resell their purchases to the high-price customers, subverting the seller's ability to identify and segregate the different demands.

Figure 9–1 illustrates these points with a conventional economic model of price discrimination. The negatively sloped demand curves indicate monopoly power. Differences in their angles of descent and intercepts indicate differing elasticities of demand at each possible price, with the result that buyers in market X have the relatively more elastic demand. Total unit cost (TUC) is the same in both markets because the product is basically the same. Moreover, TUC is assumed to be constant. This means that TUC and marginal cost (MC) are identical. Following the conventional profit maximizing formula of MR = MC, we find that P_x and Q_x are the optimal combination in market X, whereas P_y and Q_y are the optimal combination in market Y. Shading indicates excess profits. Notice that price in the relatively elastic market, P_x, is substantially below price in the relatively inelastic market, P_y. Indeed, nothing would be sold in market X at price P_y. Notice also that if these markets could not be kept separate, their demands, their elasticities, and of course their buyers, too, would blend, leaving only one market for the seller instead of two.

Moving from this general economic model to legal matters requires that three observations be borne in mind. First, the law covers price discrimination that occurs within a given market as well as that which occurs across markets. Indeed, intramarket discrimination between buyers may be said to be its primary concern. Second, the law is concerned with discrimination only insofar as it may injure compe-

Figure 9–1. Price Discrimination in Theory

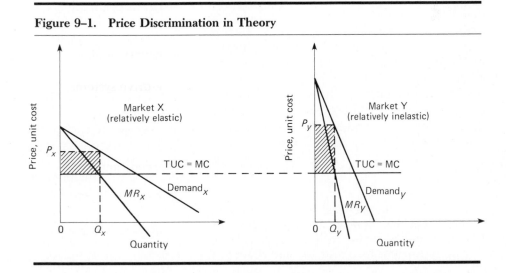

tition or competitors. Price discrimination itself is not condemned, so *countless* instances of price discrimination go untouched by the law (as when you get a better deal on a new car than your neighbor). Third, the law addresses mere price differences rather than price/cost differences. The one exception to this legal quirk is the "cost justification" defense, something that will be explained shortly.

II. Price Discrimination Law

The Clayton Act's original Section 2 outlawed only flagrantly predatory price discrimination. Its limited scope, plus several loopholes, yielded few prosecutions. While this law lay idle, chain stores revolutionized grocery, drug, and department store merchandising. Small, single-shop, "mom-and-pop" stores suffered and, during the Great Depression, began dropping like blighted apples. The outcries of their owners caused the Federal Trade Commission to study and report. Although the FTC's report found much virtue in chain stores, it also found that "a most substantial part of the chains' ability to undersell independents" could be attributed to the chains' ability to buy goods from manufacturers more cheaply than independents could. The chains' **oligopsony** buying power "forced" manufacturers to discriminate in favor of chains. Moreover, their large size enabled chains to buy directly from manufacturers, thereby sidestepping independent brokers, wholesalers, jobbers, and other middlemen as well as underselling independent retailers. So Congress went to bat for small business. In the words of Congressman Patman, mid-1935:

> The day of the independent merchant is gone unless something is done and done quickly. He cannot possibly survive under that system. So we have reached the cross road; we must either turn

the food . . . business of this country . . . over to a few corporate chains, or we have got to pass laws that will give the people, who built this country in time of peace and who saved it in time of war, an opportunity to exist. . . .[1]

In short, the purpose of the Robinson-Patman Act of 1936 went well beyond the traditional antitrust purpose of maintaining competition. It injected two new objectives: *protection* of small business and maintenance of *fair* or "equitable" price relationships between buyers who compete with each other as sellers.

A. Subsection 1(a) of Robinson-Patman

The aims of protection and equity lurk beneath the tortured language of all six main subsections in the Act, especially 2(a). Subsection 2(a) prohibits a seller from charging *different prices to different purchasers* of "goods of like grade and quality" where the effect "may be substantially"

1. "to lessen competition or tend to create a monopoly in any line of commerce," or
2. "to injure, destroy, or prevent competition with any person" (or company)
   (a) "who either grants or"
   (b) "knowingly receives" the benefit of the discrimination, or
   (c) "with customers of either of them."

Thus, there are two definitions of **illegal competitive effect**: (1) a *broad* definition that refers to substantial lessening of competition in the *market as a whole,* and (2) a *narrow* definition that refers to injury to *particular competitors.* The broad definition reflects the traditional antitrust aim of maintaining competition, and its language matches that applying to mergers. In

[1] Hearings Before the House Committee on the Judiciary on *Bills to Amend the Clayton Act*, 74th Congress First Session (1935), pp. 5–6.

contrast, it is the narrow definition that reflects the aims of protection, equity, and fairness.

Either of these two forms of competitive damage may occur in

(a) the seller's market, which is called **primary level injury**
(b) the buyers' market, which is called **secondary level injury**
(c) the market containing customers of the buyers, which is called **tertiary level injury.**

If, for example, a manufacturer cuts price to one wholesaler but not to others, it might damage competition among manufacturers (primary level), or among wholesalers (secondary level), or among retailers who buy from the wholesalers (tertiary level). If it were a matter of direct sales to retailers, then retailers would be the buyers of the discriminating seller, and they would then be considered "secondary" level. If this sounds confusing, take heart. You are not alone, as indicated by itemization of the first common criticism of the Act.

Common Criticism 1: The Act is "a roughly hewn, unfinished block of legislative phraseology," a "masterpiece of obscurity," a source of "crystal clear confusion."[2]

Compounding the confusion, several types of price discrimination have been found injurious to competition. They are (1) volume or quantity discounts, (2) territorial price discrimination, (3) functional discounts, and (4) catch-as-catch-can price discrimination. These are outlined in Table 9–1, together with indications of the level at which they are said to damage competition and the specified breadths of injury typically used in the past by the FTC and appellate courts when enforcing the statute. The dashes in the table identify combinations of level and type that are rarely attacked under

the law. These blank combinations are eligible for illegality, but the authorities tend to ignore them. The bottom row of Table 9–1 shows the defenses discriminators of each type occasionally use to fend off FTC attorneys. These defenses—"cost" and "good faith"—are explicitly recognized by the Robinson-Patman Act:

- *Cost defense:* "nothing herein . . . shall prevent differentials which make only due allowance for differences in the cost of manufacture, sale, or delivery resulting from [differing methods of sale or delivery]."
- *Good faith defense,* Subsection 2(b): "nothing herein . . . shall prevent a seller rebutting the prima-facie case . . . by showing that his lower price . . . was made in good faith to meet an equally low price of a competitor . . ."

Unfortunately, these defenses do not offer much protection in practice. The cost defense has fallen into disuse because the FTC and appellate courts have been rather stingy in allowing its application. They require elaborate proofs and reject justifications based on reallocations of overhead costs. The meeting competition in good faith defense is disallowed if the price reduction is excessively aggressive (gaining business rather than merely keeping it), or if it continues after lower prices of competitors are known to have been raised. Moreover, the firm may not meet competition if it has reason to believe that the price being met is itself unlawful.

For a time the good faith meeting-competition defense was also disallowed if the discriminating seller lacked precise knowledge of his competitors' prices, but in two major recent cases the Supreme Court changed that interpretation. In the first, *U.S.* v. *United States Gypsum Co.* (1978),[3] defendants were accused of

---

[2] "Eine Kleine Juristische Schlummergeschichte," *Harvard Law Review* (March 1966), p. 922.

[3] *United States* v. *United States Gypsum Co.,* 438 U.S. 422 (1978).

Table 9–1.   Summary Outline of Injury Definition Applied, Given the Basic Types of Discrimination Found to be Illegal and Market Level of Reference

Level of Injury	Type of Price Discrimination			
	Volume or Quantity Discounts	Territorial Price Discrimination	Functional Discounts	Catch-as-Catch-Can Pricing
Primary level	Broad or narrow	Broad or narrow	—	Narrow
Secondary level	Narrow	Narrow	Narrow	Narrow
Tertiary level	—	—	Narrow	—
Main line of possible defense	Cost	Good faith	Cost or good faith	Good faith

price fixing through an exchange of information about current bid prices. Claiming that price verification through information exchange was necessary to comply with the Robinson-Patman's meeting-competition defense, the defendants argued that their behavior should be excused. The Supreme Court, however, rejected the argument, saying that absolute certainty about lower competitor prices (as might be obtained through an exchange of price information) was not necessary to invoke the meeting-competition defense. A simple good faith belief was good enough. In the second case, *A&P* v. *Federal Trade Commission* (1979)[4] the A&P grocery chain had levered a very low price for private label milk out of Borden by telling Borden that its initial bid for the business was so high that it was "not even in the ball park." Borden asked A&P how far down it would have to go to be competitive, but A&P refused to say. Whereupon Borden cut its bid substantially and won the contract without knowing that its bid was $83,000 lower than the nearest competitor. The FTC found this in violation, but on appeal the Supreme Court reversed. The Court's reasoning in this case was similar to that in *Gypsum*, namely, a requirement of precise knowledge would produce price uniformity and rigidity. Precise knowledge would, in other words, reduce uncertainty and thereby "lead to price matching and anticompetitive cooperation among sellers."

Despite this greater latitude recently granted the good faith meeting-competition defense, neither it nor the cost justification defense are interpreted as liberally as many critics of the law would like. Thus another point of controversy may be noted.

Common Criticism 2: By amendment or reinterpretation, the defenses open to discriminators ought to be liberalized.

Before delving further into the case law concerning the Act, we may note in its language two major anomalies. First, despite its origins, the statute's fire is focused not on the power or conduct of oligopsonistic *buyers* but rather on the conduct of *sellers*. As Corwin Edwards observes:

> The avowed purpose of the Congress was to use the law of price discrimination to curb the buying power of chain stores and other large buyers.

---

[4] *Great Atlantic & Pacific Tea Co.* v. *Federal Trade Commission*, 440 U.S. 69 (1979).

However, the means to be employed consisted primarily in forbidding sellers, the presumed victims of that buying power, from granting the concessions that were exacted from them. . . . If the statute was an effort to protect competition from the pressure of powerful buyers on weak sellers, it was anomalous to provide that protection primarily by action against weak sellers who succumbed to the pressure. Such a process bears some resemblance to an effort to stamp out mugging by making it an offense to permit oneself to be mugged.[5]

A second notable quirk concerns the statute's definition of price discrimination. Price differences unjustified by cost differences are "discriminatory," but cost differences unaccompanied by price differences are not. In other words, the economic definition of discrimination—differing price/cost ratios, even if prices are identical—is rejected by the statute in favor of a definition that hinges almost entirely on price differences alone. The consequences of this approach are illustrated by the *Binney & Smith* case. Binney & Smith, Co., was found by the FTC to have sold school supplies at a uniform price to both jobbers, who are middlemen, and large retail chains. This price uniformity, though obviously injurious to jobbers, was not questioned by the FTC.[6]

Common Criticism 3: Even accepting the Act's purposes as proper, the statute is ill-conceived. Indeed, many proponents of protection and fairness are disappointed with it.

Before discussing the types of discrimination listed in Table 9–1, we should first specify the kinds of evidence that indicate "broad" or "narrow" injury, the two designations comprising the body of Table 9–1. **Broad (or market-wide) injury** to competition is indicated by substantial reductions in the number of competitors in the market, elevated barriers to entry, a lack of competitive behavior in pricing, or foreclosure of substantial parts of the market to existing competitors. **Narrow (or competitor) injury** is indicated by simple price differences among customers, or a price difference coupled with diversion of business from the disadvantaged buyer toward the favored buyer, or diversions away from a nondiscriminating seller toward a discriminating seller. Injuries embraced by this narrow definition are clearly more personal than those embraced by the broad definition. That is, the discrimination appears to cripple a *single* firm or particular *class* of firms. Obviously, the broad definition coincides more nearly with a purely economic definition of competition, while the narrow definition coincides with some notions of fairness.

A quick glance at Table 9–1 reveals that narrow evidence of injury has been more commonly used by the FTC, especially when judging injury at secondary and tertiary levels. At primary level, broad injury has been found only in cases concerning volume or quantity discounts and territorial price discrimination.[7]

Volume and Quantity Discounts. Quantity discounts are based on the amount purchased in a *single* transaction, with large quantities lowering price. Volume discounts are based on *cumulative* purchases, involving numerous transactions, during some stated period of time, such as one year. Of the two, volume discounts are least likely to be cost-justifiable and more anticompetitive in the broad sense. For these reasons the FTC has attacked volume discounts much more vigorously than it has quantity discounts. At primary level, volume discounts can

---

[5] Corwin D. Edwards, *The Price Discrimination Law* (Washington, D.C.: Brookings Institution, 1959), p. 63.

[6] Edwards, *op. cit.*, p. 311. See also *In the Matter of Bird and Son*, 25 FTC 548 (1937).

[7] R. C. Brooks, Jr., Testimony, *Small Business and the Robinson-Patman Act*, Hearings before the Special Subcommittee on Small Business and the Robinson-Patman Act of the Select Committee on Small Business, U.S. Congress, House, 91st Congress, Second Session (1970), Vol. 2, p. 657.

heighten barriers to entry or foreclose small sellers from substantial segments of the market.[8] An Appendix to this chapter illustrates this.

Although such discounts may have genuine anticompetitive effects at primary (sellers') level, very few cases have actually been argued on these grounds. The rarity may be due to a dearth of situations causing broad injury at primary level. Then again, it may also be a consequence of the fact that, under the Act, volume and quantity discounts are more easily prosecuted on grounds of narrow injury at the secondary or buyer level. Recall that a major purpose of the Act was to make such prosecutions as these easier.

The classic case here is *Morton Salt,* decided by the Supreme Court in 1948. Morton sold its table salt at $1.60 a case in less-than-carload lots, at $1.50 a case for carload lots, and at still lower prices of $1.40 and $1.35 for annual volumes exceeding 5000 and 50,000 cases, respectively. In defense of these prices, Morton claimed that they were equally available to all, that salt was just one tiny item in grocers' inventories, and that therefore competitive injury could not arise. Rejecting these arguments the Court concluded as follows:

> The legislative history of the Robinson-Patman Act makes it abundantly clear that Congress considered it to be an evil that a large buyer could secure a competitive advantage over a small buyer solely because of the large buyer's quantity purchasing ability. . . . Here the Commission found what would appear to be obvious, that the competitive opportunities of certain merchants were injured when they had to pay [Morton] substantially more for their goods than their competitors had to pay. . . . That [Morton's] quantity discounts did result in price differentials between competing purchasers sufficient to influence their

resale price of salt was shown by the evidence. . . . Congress intended to protect a merchant from competitive injury attributable to discriminatory prices on any or all goods sold in interstate commerce, whether the particular goods constituted a major or minor portion of his stock. . . . [In] enacting the Robinson-Patman Act Congress was especially concerned with protecting small business. . . .[9]

This narrow, numerical interpretation of injury was later carried to such extremes that during the 1950s the FTC inferred injury despite evidence that "the beneficiaries of the discrimination were small and weak," and despite "unanimous statements by the disfavored customers that they were not injured."[10] Since then, this hard line has softened somewhat, but a fairly stringent interpretation of secondary line injury still prevails.

Critics of this policy argue that although individual *competitors* may suffer, *competition,* may not. Such discrimination in favor of large buyers is said to "introduce flexibility into the distributive system, helping to compress traditional markups, and prevent or disrupt a rigid stratification of functions." Moreover, a large buyer "which does indeed make possible cost savings on the part of its suppliers may yet, in facing impure markets, have to coerce suppliers into giving it the concessions which its greater efficiency justifies."[11] In short, price discrimination may increase price flexibility and rivalry at primary and secondary levels; it may also contribute to efficiency. Even so, enhanced competition is not automatic. Price concessions are not always passed on to consumers or spread throughout the market. Moreover, loss of even

---

[8] R. C. Brooks, Jr., "Volume Discounts as Barriers to Entry and Access," *Journal of Political Economy* (February 1961), p. 65.

[9] *Federal Trade Commission* v. *Morton Salt Co.,* 334 U.S. 37 (1948).

[10] Edwards, *op. cit.,* p. 533, referring to Standard Motor Products (Docket No. 5721), and Moog Industries (Docket No. 5723).

[11] J. B. Dirlam and A. E. Kahn, *Fair Competition* (Ithaca, N.Y.: Cornell University Press, 1954), pp. 204–205.

a few competitors diminishes competition where there are only a few to begin with. The ultimate effect depends heavily on the circumstances. Hence controversy will continue.[12]

Territorial Price Discrimination. This type of discrimination takes two forms: (1) selective geographic price cutting and (2) fictional freight charges imposed under basing-point pricing systems. The former has produced many illegal primary line injuries, whereas the later has been charged with injuring competition at secondary level. As indicated in Table 9–1, neither can be defended by cost justifications. Because geographic price cutting includes "predatory pricing," several primary line cases of this sort cast a good light on the Robinson-Patman Act. In fact, they give the FTC its finest hours of enforcement.[13] These cases contain poignant examples of genuine broad injury to competition; they also contain striking evidence of predatory intent. Some excerpts from business correspondence follow:

> "So by continuing our efforts and putting a crimp into him wherever possible, we may ultimately curb this competition if we should not succeed in eliminating it entirely."
>
> "Don't try to follow me. If you do, we will put you out of business."

The latter message was no idle threat; ensuing below-cost prices ultimately throttled the smaller competitor.[14]

Still, geographic price discrimination may also be procompetitive. It may be used for promotional purposes; for entering new geographic markets; or for further penetrating established markets to spread overhead costs. When used for these laudable purposes, it is usually less systematic than the "sharp-shooting" associated with predation. Nevertheless, procompetitive territorial pricing has occasionally been attacked by the FTC. In the *Page Dairy* case, for instance, the FTC myopically went after a firm whose unsystematic price discrimination was actually undermining its competitors' efforts at cartelization.[15]

The line between geographic price cutting that is predatory or destructive of competition and that which promotes or expands competition is difficult to draw. "But," according to the critics, "one thing is certain: it cannot be drawn merely at the point where a price reduction diverts trade from a competitor."[16]

Common Criticism 4: As interpreted, the law stifles genuine price competition, thereby raising and stiffening price levels.

Returning to the bright side of the coin, the FTC put the Robinson-Patman Act to good use in attacking collusive basing-point price systems in the *Corn Products Refining* case of 1945 and others.[17] As we have seen, basing-point systems are price-fixing mechanisms, but the FTC's initial assault was based on narrow secondary line injury under Subsection 2(a). (Later, in *Cement Institute*,[18] a restraint of trade approach was applied.) The defendant in *Corn Products* produced glucose in Chicago

[12] For a good discussion of the circumstances see ibid, Chapters 7 and 8. See also L. S. Keyes, "Price Discrimination in Law and Economics," *Southern Economic Journal* (April 1961), pp. 320–328.

[13] *E. B. Muller & Co.* v. *FTC*, 142 F. 2d 511 (6th Cir. 1944); *Maryland Baking Co.* v. *FTC*, 243 F. 2d 716 (4th Cir. 1957); *Forster Mfg. Co.* v. *FTC*, 335 F. 2d 47 (1st Cir. 1964). Among private cases see *Volasco Prods. Co.* v. *Lloyd A. Fry Roofing Co.*, 346 F. 2d 661 (6th Cir. 1965); *Moore* v. *Mead's Fine Bread Co.*, 348 U.S. 115 (1954); and *Continental Baking Co.* v. *Old Homestead Bread Co.*, 476 F. 2d 97 (10th Cir. 1973).

[14] *Forster Manufacturing Co.*, *op. cit.*

[15] Edwards, *op. cit.*, pp. 443–444. For a related example see William K. Jones, Testimony, *Small Business and the Robinson-Patman Act*, Hearings before Special Subcommittee on Small Business of the Select Committee on Small Business, House, 91st Congress, First Session (1969), Vol. 1, p. 109.

[16] Philip Elman, "The Robinson-Patman Act and Antitrust Policy: A Time for Reappraisal," *Washington Law Review*, Vol. 42 (1966), p. 13.

[17] *Corn Products Refining Company* v. *FTC*, 324 U.S. 726 (1945).

[18] *FTC* v. *Cement Institute*, 333 U.S. 683 (1948).

and Kansas City plants, but maintained Chicago as a single basing point. Thus, both plants sold only at delivered prices computed as if all shipments originated in Chicago. Kansas City candy manufacturers who bought glucose from the Kansas City plant were charged phantom freight, as if the sweetening had come all the way from Chicago. After hearing the case on appeal, the Supreme Court accepted the FTC's finding that the candy manufacturers located in Kansas City competed with those in Chicago. The Court also bought the idea that, though small, the price differentials on glucose would affect the candy makers' costs and final prices. The cost differences were said to be "enough to divert business from one manufacturer to another." Consequently, narrow competitive injury was adjudged at the secondary or buyer level (between candy manufacturers), and the price system was banned.

Functional Discounts.   As indicated by Table 9–1, primary level injury is not usually associated with functional discounts, but findings of narrow injury at secondary and tertiary levels have been frequent. By definition, functional discounts are determined not by amounts purchased or buyer location but rather by the functional characteristics of buyers. Functions in the "traditional" distribution network are well known: Producers sell to wholesalers, who sell at a higher price to jobbers, who in turn sell at a higher price to retailers, who finally sell at a still higher price to consumers. Other functional differences may be based on other buyer classifications, such as government versus private.

The problem of illegal price discrimination arises when folks of different functions compete. Most commonly, "traditional" channels get jumbled, as when resale competition crops up between resellers in different classifications, or when a producer sells at various levels in the distribution network to someone's disadvantage. In other words, discrimination between buyers who are *not* in competition with each other is *not* a violation. The FTC has never ruled against a functional discount per se; somebody down the line must be disadvantaged relative to his competitors.

For example, if a producer charges a lower price to its direct-buying retailers than to its independent wholesalers, competition may be injured at the *retail* level between its direct buyers and the *customers* of the independent wholesalers. In *Tri-Valley Packing Association v. FTC*, a processor of canned fruits and vegetables sold its canned goods at lower prices to certain retail chains with buying agencies in San Francisco than it charged retailers and wholesalers who did not have buying agencies in San Francisco. The FTC and appellate court found violation of Subsection 2(a) because the direct buying retailers had an advantage over their competitors who had to buy from the higher paying wholesalers.[19]

A different problem arises when a buyer performs a dual role, say wholesaling *and* retailing, in which case he may get a large wholesaler's discount that gives him a competitive advantage when reselling as a retailer but not when reselling as a wholesaler.[20] Critics point out that compliance with the Robinson-Patman Act in these instances often raises a serious inconsistency. Compliance implies that the producer must control the prices at which his independent middlemen resell. But such control involves the producer in "resale price maintenance," or vertical price fixing, which is generally illegal under Section 1 of the Sherman Act.[21]

Common Criticism 5: Compliance with the price discrimination law in this and other re-

---

[19] *Tri-Valley Packing Ass'n* v. FTC, 329 F. 2d 694 (9th Cir. 1964).

[20] *FTC v. Standard Oil Co.*, 355 U.S. 396 (1958) and 340 U.S. 231 (1951); *Mueller Company v. FTC*, 323 F. 2d 44 (7th Cir., 1963).

[21] Edwards, *op. cit.*, p. 312.

spects is inconsistent with other antitrust policies.

Catch-as-Catch-Can-Discrimination.   This is a miscellaneous category, best explained by illustration. In four cases, brought during the 1940s, the FTC found that competition among manufacturers of rubber stamps had been injured by price discrimination. This was a highly competitive market, with 70 manufacturers in New York City alone. The companies chastised were very small, 10–20 employees being typical. Moreover, they charged whatever prices were necessary "to get the business." That is, concessions varied from one customer to another in catch-as-catch-can fashion: "Moss's price for a one-line stamp, two inches long, varied from 4 cents to 15 cents, and for a one-line stamp three inches long, from 4 cents to 30 cents . . . [and so on]."[22] The FTC found primary line injury on grounds that this diverted trade *to* the discriminator *from* his competitors. Since price concessions typically have the effect of diverting business, "the principle adopted in these cases means that *any* discrimination large enough to serve as an effective inducement to buy is unlawful in the absence of one of the statutory justifications [cost or good faith]."[23]

Need we say this policy was injurious to competition? The effects of this brand of policy emerged from an extensive study conducted by Corwin Edwards on the effects of decisions in 83 pre-1957 cases of all kinds (so far as these effects could be ascertained by interviews with the businessmen involved): "There is a consensus of opinion among both buyers and sellers that the result has been to diminish the flexibility of prices."[24] Edwards found no clear tendency for prices to rise or fall as a result of early Robinson-Patman enforcement. Adjust-

ments in all directions were observed. However, the interviews "strongly" indicated stickier and less flexible prices. Fortunately, the FTC seems to have responded to this criticism, for it has not prosecuted any cases like those in rubber stamps since the mid-1960s.

Another form of miscellaneous price discrimination that may be procompetitive is "under-the-table" discounting by oligopolists:

> Oligopolists may be unwilling to chance price reduction unless . . . they can make them secretly and selectively; they may similarly be unwilling to attempt promotional pricing except in a selective fashion. To require open, nondiscriminatory pricing may therefore deprive oligopoly markets of their only sources of price flexibility and rivalry.[25]

Although critics of the law have accused the FTC of discouraging such under-the-table discrimination, the charge cannot be verified by specific cases of the last 20 years.

An Overview.   Critical analyses of the Robinson-Patman Act suggest that procompetitive discriminations may be distinguished from anticompetitive discriminations by whether they are unsystematic or systematic and whether they are perpetrated by firms with small or large market shares. *Systematic, large-firm discriminations tend to be anticompetitive, whereas unsystematic, small-firm discriminations tend to be competitive.* But there are exceptions.

The criticism may give the added impression that enforcement zealous enough to crush many small-firm discriminations must have also stamped out large-firm discriminations altogether. But this inference would be fallacious. Discrimination can take many forms not reached by the law. A powerful seller may favor particular buyers by making uniform price reductions upon that part of his product line most important to those particular buyers. Moreover,

---

[22] Ibid., p. 479.
[23] Ibid., p. 482 (emphasis added).
[24] Ibid., p. 630.

[25] Dirlam and Kahn, *op. cit.*, p. 204.

a powerful seller can sometimes refuse to sell to those he disfavors. Similarly, a powerful buyer, deprived of discriminatory price concessions, can nevertheless obtain substantial advantages in acquiring goods:

It can (a) take a seller's entire output at a low price; (b) obtain low prices from sellers who are meeting some other seller's lawful competition; (c) buy goods cheaply abroad; (d) obtain low prices upon goods so differentiated from what bears higher prices that the prohibition of the law is inapplicable; (e) obtain goods of premium quality without paying a premium price; (f) buy large amounts under long-term contract when prices are unusually low; or (g) produce goods for itself.[26]

For these many reasons, chain stores have thrived despite the law. The shrewd reader may think up other avenues of evasion. Brokerage payments and preferential promotional services or allowances cannot be among them, however. Discrimination via these routes is foreclosed by Subsections 2(c), (d), and (e) of the Robinson-Patman Act, each of which warrants a few words.

B. Subsections 2(c), (d), and (e)

As may be seen from Table 9–2, these portions of the Robinson-Patman Act are *not* simple extensions of Subsection 2(a) governing seller's price differences. Whereas some kind of probable competitive injury must be shown under 2(a), such is not the case for (c), (d), and (e). Furthermore, whereas 2(a) discriminators may defend themselves by cost justifications or demonstrations of meeting competition in good faith, those running afoul of Subsections 2(c), (d), and (e) may not, except for (d) and (e) with respect to good faith. In other words, these additional provisions of the Act specify what could be considered *per se* violations.

Subsection 2(c), the **brokerage provision**, outlaws payment or receipt of brokerage fees that cross the sales transaction from seller to buyer. It also prohibits any compensation *in lieu* of brokerage. Brokers (whose job it is to match up buyers and sellers without ever taking title to the goods) are quite active in the grocery game plus a few other distributive trades. Subsection 2(c) was aimed primarily at a practice in the food industry by which chain stores large enough to buy direct, without benefit of brokers, got price reductions equivalent to the brokerage fees that sellers would have otherwise paid. In practice, however, this provision outlawed *all* brokerage commissions, large or small, except those paid to a truly independent broker. At times, 2(c)'s rigorous application has harpooned marketing arrangements that helped small concerns. In the *Biddle* case, for instance, Biddle sold market-information services to 2400 grocery buyers—placing their orders with sellers, collecting brokerage from sellers, and then passing some brokerage on to the buyers in the form of reduced information fees.[27] This practice was declared illegal, however, as were others equally beneficial to small independents.[28] The courts held that "The seller may not pay the buyer brokerage on the latter's purchases for his own account" (period). The Supreme Court's *Broch* opinion of 1960[29] has since introduced a modicum of flexibility into brokerage cases, but a modicum is not a magnum.

Subsection 2(d) makes it unlawful for a seller to make any **payment to a buyer** in consideration of the buyer's promotion of the seller's goods, unless similar payments are made available on "proportionately equal terms" to *all* competing buyers. Subsection 2(e) makes it unlawful for the seller himself to **provide promo-**

---

[26] Corwin D. Edwards, "Control of the Single Firm: Its Place in Antitrust Policy," *Law & Contemporary Problems* (Summer 1965), p. 477.

[27] *Biddle Purchasing Co., v. FTC*, 96 F. 2d 687 (1938).
[28] See, e.g., *Quality Bakers* v. *FTC*, 114 F. 2d 393 (1940); and *Southgate Brokerage Co.* v. *FTC* 150 F. 2d 607 (1945).
[29] *FTC* v. *Henry Broch & Co.*, 363 U.S. 166 (1960).

Table 9–2.   Comparative Outline of Subsections 2(a), (c), (d), (e), and (f), of the Robinson-Patman Act

Subsection	*(1)* Competitive Injury Required?	*(2)* Cost Defense Available?	*(3)* Good Faith Defense Available?	*(4)* Violator is Buyer or Seller?
2(a) General	Yes	Yes	Yes	Seller
2(c) Brokerage	No	No	No	Both
2(d) Promotional pay	No	No	Yes	Seller
2(e) Services	No	No	Yes	Seller
2(f) Buyer inducement	Buyer liability for knowingly inducing violation of one of the above			

tional services to or through a buyer unless he provides opportunity for such services on "proportionally equal terms" to *all* other competing buyers.

For example, if Revlon were to provide Macy's, Bullock's, and Sears, with in-store demonstrators of Revlon cosmetics, or if they *paid* these large retailers to conduct these demonstrations, then Revlon would have to make equal-proportionate opportunities of some kind open to all retailers who compete with Macy's, Bullock's, and Sears in cosmetics. You may ask proportionate to what? And in what way? Does that mean that Revlon must circulate a midget giving one-shot 15-minute demonstrations amongst independent corner drug stores for every fully developed model it sets up in Macy's for a weekend visit?

The FTC and the courts have chopped through a thick jungle of questions such as these during the past 40 years. And, in order to guide the ordinary, time-pressed businessman through the treacherous path so cleared, the FTC has kindly drawn up a long "Guide for Advertising Allowances and other Merchandising Payments and Services" that attempts to clarify the case law for laymen. Among other

things, it states that a seller's burden under the law is heavier than mere selection of the appropriate allowances or services. He must (1) know which customers compete with each other, (2) notify each competing buyer that these aids are available, and (3) police the destination of any payments to make sure they are properly spent.[30] Although the general economic effect of these regulations is unclear, a multitude of small merchants seems to support them on grounds of fairness and equity. Interviews with apparel merchants, after intensive FTC activity concerning 2(d), turned up the following typical response: "It cleaned up the problem of individually negotiated advertising allowances which was inherently unfair to the small guy."[31] Although most economists do not ridicule such sentiments, they tend to be skeptical, even cynical.

[30] P. Areeda, *Antitrust Analysis* (Boston: Little, Brown and Co., 1974), p. 951–960.

[31] *Recent Efforts to Amend or Repeal the Robinson-Patman Act,* Part 1, Hearings before the Ad Hoc Subcommittee on Antitrust . . . and Related Matters of the Committee on Small Business, U.S. Congress, House, 94th Congress, First Session (1975), pp. 282–312.

Common Criticism 6: Subsections 2(c), (d) and (e) should not pose per se violations. Discriminations of any kind should be subjected to tests of competitive injury and be allowed liberal cost and good faith defenses.

C. Subsection 2(f), Buyer Inducement

Subsection 2(f) makes it unlawful for any buyer "knowingly to induce or receive a discrimination in price which is prohibited by this Section." Here Congress finally addressed the problem it was really most worked up about—the big buyer who pressures his suppliers for discriminatory concessions. However, this subsection has been used more sparingly than a spare tire because the Supreme Court has made it difficult for the FTC to apply. The FTC's attorneys have the burden of proving (1) that an illegally injurious discrimination occurred, (2) that it was not cost justified, and (3) that the buyer *knew* it was not cost justified.

Ordinary 2(a) cases require no more of the FTC's attorneys than item (1). In 2(a) cases the burden of proof regarding costs naturally rests with the discriminator who wants to defend himself, and buyer knowledge is irrelevant. This absence of items (2) and (3) makes "kid stuff" of typical 2(a) prosecutions. But according to the Supreme Court's view of 2(f), a buyer cannot be expected to know the details of his supplier's cost, and a buyer may therefore be unaware that the bargain prices he pays are illegal.[32] Off hand, this ruling might make any such prosecutions seem impossible, since wiley buyers might evade offenses by maintaining a state of carefully contrived ignorance. But prosecution is merely difficult. The Court has said that buyer knowledge of unjustified discounts may be inferred "where his experience in the trade should make it clear that a difference in price exceeds a difference in cost."[33]

D. Declining Robinson-Patman Enforcement

On the one side we have seen corrective action appropriate to antitrust policy. On the other side we have seen official applications of dubious merit—attacks on harmless trade practices, protective interventions where injury was slight, and even anticompetitive proceedings. The controversy between those seeing Dr. Jekyll and those seeing Mr. Hyde reached a particularly high pitch during the late 1960s and early 1970s. Two task forces on antitrust policy appointed by two successive presidents (Johnson and Nixon), plus a blue-ribbon committee appointed by the American Bar Association, severely criticized the Act and the FTC's enforcement of it. Later, President Ford's people in the Justice Department proposed radical modifications in the statute. Central to this and similar proposals is abolition of the narrow-injury test, but some critics have urged *complete abolition* of the Robinson-Patman Act. In response to these developments, Congress held three sets of hearings,[34] but no new legislation came of them, primarily because small-business trade associations mobilized to thwart reform. Small business merchants seem to revere the current law with religious fervor, despite the fact that it has often been used to their disadvantage. "Please don't let the Robinson-Patman Act die," they plead. "All small businesses need it to survive."[35] Admittedly, the Act's principal achievements lie in the realms of protection and fairness (though not necessarily fairness to consumers).

For its part, the FTC seems to have responded to the criticism by drastically altering its enforcement policies. In 1963 the FTC is-

---

[32] *Automatic Canteen Co.*, v. *FTC*, 346 U.S. 61.
[33] C. Wilcox and W. G. Shepherd, *Public Policies Toward Business* (Homewood, Ill.: R. D. Irwin, 1975), pp. 183–184.

[34] *Recent Efforts to Amend or Repeal . . . , op. cit.*, Parts 1, 2, and 3; *Small Business and the Robinson-Patman Act, op. cit.*, 3 volumes; *Price Discrimination Legislation—1969*, Hearings before the Subcommittee on Antitrust and Monopoly of the Committee on the Judiciary, U.S. Senate, 91st Congress First Session (1969).
[35] *Recent Efforts to Amend or Repeal . . . , op cit.*, Part 3, p. 207.

sued 219 complaints and 250 orders under the Act; in 1969 it issued just 8 complaints plus 9 orders; and, for the year ending June 30, 1975, the FTC issued only 2 complaints and 3 orders. As one Commissioner recently put it, "Robinson-Patman is being slowly anesthetized."[36] Although the FTC's formal proceedings have diminished to token proportions, its informal efforts have apparently not flagged as much.

The FTC's nonlitigative procedures include Industry Guides and Trade Regulation Rules, each of which gives the FTC a "guiding presence" of varying compulsion in targeted industries. Even more informally, the Commission's attorneys may issue "warnings" to possible violators and may accept "assurances of voluntary compliance." Aside from official enforcement, private suits are also possible and quite common. In truth, a private treble damage suit, *Utah Pie Co* v. *Continental Baking Co.*,[37] was the fuse that ignited much of the recent debate. The Utah Pie Company, a small Salt Lake City purveyor of frozen pies, sued three formidable pie opponents—Continental, Carnation, and Pet—for injuriously cutting prices below cost in Salt Lake City while maintaining prices elsewhere. In 1967, the Supreme Court held that the three national firms had violated Subsection 2(a) despite the fact that Utah Pie had enjoyed the largest share of the local market and had maintained profits throughout the price war. According to one critic, the Supreme Court used subsection 2(a) "to strike directly at price competition itself."[38]

Summary

The Robinson-Patman Act has been called the "Magna Carta" of small business. Others

[36] "Robinson-Patman is not Dead—Merely Dormant," address by Paul Rand Dixon, May 21, 1975 (mimeo).

[37] *Utah Pie Co.* v. *Continental Baking Co.*, 386 U.S. 685 (1967).

[38] W. S. Bowman, "Restraint of Trade by the Supreme Court: The Utah Pie Case," *Yale Law Journal* (November 1967), p. 70.

have named it "Typhoid Mary." Ever since it amended Section 2 of the Clayton Act in 1936, it has stirred controversy. Perhaps *any* law governing price discrimination would be controversial. Price discrimination always entails a high price somewhere and a low price somewhere else. Those who see evil in price discrimination tend to see the high price more readily than the low price. Those who see goodness in price discrimination seem to have reverse viewing capabilities. In addition to viewer attitudes, circumstances make a difference.

In any event, the Robinson-Patman Act outlaws price differences where the effect may be broad or narrow competitive injury at any one of three levels—primary, secondary, or tertiary—unless the difference can be defended on grounds of "cost justification" or "good faith" price mimicry. Four major classes of price discrimination have been found to violate these standards at least occasionally: (1) volume or quantity discounts, (2) territorial discrimination, (3) functional discounts, and (4) catch-as-catch-can pricing. The first two are particularly prone to true anticompetitive effects, and a number of these cases cast the FTC in good light. On the other hand, attacks against all four have produced instances of ill-advised enforcement.

Subsections 2(c), (d), and (e) prohibit any discrimination that takes the form of brokerage payments, discounts in lieu of brokerage, payments for promotion or other services, and direct provision of promotion or other service. These are generally *per se* prohibitions because potential competitive injury need not be shown and, for the most part, these practices cannot be defended on grounds of cost or good faith. Finally, Subsection 2(f) addresses the problem that Congress was most concerned about, for it bans knowing inducement or receipt of an unlawfully discriminatory price. Despite the efforts of Congress and the FTC, the Act has apparently not stemmed the advance of chain stores. Chains have found ways around the law.

In addition, the FTC has recently eased up on the Act's enforcement, at least in terms of formal proceedings and orders.

Questions and Exercises for Chapter 9

1. Why was the Robinson-Patman Act passed? How does it differ from other antitrust legislation?
2. Compare and contrast narrow and broad injury? Which corresponds most closely with traditional antitrust?
3. How are the economic and R-P Act definitions of price discrimination alike? How do they differ?
4. Has the growth of chain stores been stifled by the law? Explain.
5. Why is it easier to prosecute quantity discount violations at secondary level than primary level?
6. Compare and contrast territorial and functional discounts in (a) definition, (b) level of likely anticompetitive effect, and (c) lines of defense.
7. Why has the FTC stopped attacking catch-as-catch-can discrimination? Is this good or bad?

Appendix to Chapter 9: Volume Discounts as Barriers to Entry

Figure 9–2 illustrates a volume discount structure. Buyers purchasing 1 to 200 units per month pay $8 per unit. Buyers purchasing 201 to 400 units per month pay $7 per unit on *all* units (even units 1–200). Volumes in the 401–600 range yield per unit price of $6. And volumes in excess of 600 lower price to $5 per unit.

If this were the price structure of a dominant

established supplier, it could pose a barrier to entry to smaller but equally efficient potential suppliers. Suppose, for example, that a small potential supplier does not have the capacity to supply a big buyer with all his requirements of 500 units per month. Indeed, because of uncertainty, this big buyer may not want to buy all his 500 units per month from the newcomer even if the newcomer has the capacity. The buyer might prefer instead to purchase small trial quantities or to build ties with two suppliers, the old and the new. What price would the potential supplier have to charge in order to get this big buyer to buy 200 units from him? Would it be the going price the buyer pays to the established supplier, namely, $6 per unit as shown in Figure 9–2? No. It would have to be a substantially lower price than $6. Why? Because the buyer's purchase of 200 units from the potential supplier would drop the buyer's purchases from the established supplier below 400 units to 300 (500 − 200 = 300), thereby causing the buyer to lose part of his discount from the established supplier. Price on the 300 units from the established supplier jumps from $6 to $7, costing the buyer $300. Hence, the price the potential supplier charges must be low enough to compensate the buyer for this loss. Otherwise he won't make the sale. The potential supplier's price must be $4.50 per unit. This is derived by noting that, at a price of $6, the 200 units would cost the buyer $1,200. From this, the potential supplier must subtract the $300 the buyer loses in dollar discounts, leaving the potential supplier with $900 revenue on 200 units, which amounts to $4.50 per unit (900/200). The shaded areas in Figure 9–2 indicate the buyer's lost discount and the potential supplier's price reduction below $6 per unit.

Of course the potential seller could charge $6 if he sold no more than 100 units to the buyer, because such lesser volumes would not cause the buyer to lose his $6 price from the

Figure 9–2.   Volume Discount Structure

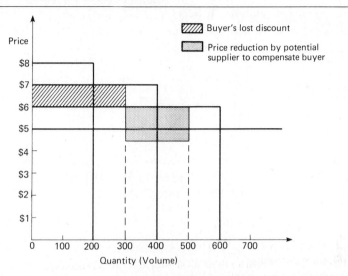

established seller. Small buyers may also be available. But the competitive implications of these possibilities are limited:

> Foreclosed from selling to the larger customers, the smaller supplier may be prevented from ever growing to a size sufficient to enable him to com-

pete for this business. Potential competition may thus be suppressed by the volume-discount structure.[39]

[39] Robert C. Brooks, Jr., "Volume Discounts as Barriers to Entry and Access," *Journal of Political Economy* (February 1961), p. 65.

Chapter 10

Vertical Market Restrictions

The sensitive focal points of the competitive general market system
are, as the name implies, in marketing by individual enterprises and
in the buying choices of their customers.
—E. T. Grether

As we have seen, the lion's share of antitrust law addresses horizontal restraints and monopolization. Now we explore the lamb's share—antitrust concerning vertical restraints. Tying, exclusive dealing, resale price maintenance, and territorial restrictions fit this description because they operate between sellers and buyers. In order of their treatment in this chapter:

1. *Tying* occurs when the seller allows the buyer to buy one line of the seller's goods *only* if the buyer also buys other goods too, as would be true if IBM "tied" punch cards to its computers.

2. *Exclusive dealing* binds a buyer (usually a retailer) to make *all* his purchases of a given line of goods from a particular seller (usually a manufacturer). This differs from tying in that it may cover a considerable range of goods and it limits buyers to a single source of supply. This would be true for instance if an appliance store agreed with General Electric to carry only G.E. appliances.

3. *Resale price maintenance* occurs when manufacturers or other suppliers set the prices that their distributors may charge. Were Pontiac to insist that its auto dealers stick to the suggested retail prices given on window stickers, it would be practicing resale price maintenance.

4. *Territorial restrictions* give distributors exclusive territories or assigned locations. Thus Coca-Cola might assign Boston to one bottler, Providence to another bottler, and still other areas to other bottlers, prohibiting each bottler from raiding the territories of others.

Businessmen offer various justifications for these practices, and some justifications are good enough that public interests are served as well as private business interests. Such goodness depends on the structural circumstances, however. When *small firms* in highly *competitive markets* engage in these practices, the results may tilt toward *goodness*. On the other hand, when used by *large firms* in *oligopolistic settings* these vertical restraints tend to be *anticompetitive*.

Table 10–1 summarizes these potential competitive problems with simple labels. Tying and exclusive dealing tend to be *exclusionary* because they discourage new entry or handicap small rivals. Resale price maintenance and ter-

Table 10–1. Outline of Vertical Restraints

Restrictive Practice	Potential Anticompetitive Effect	Main Statute Law	Judicial Rule Applied
1. Tying	Exclusionary	Clayton, Sec. 3 and Sherman, Sec. 1	Mixed: per se, rule of reason
2. Exclusive dealing	Exclusionary	Clayton, Sec. 3	Rule of reason
3. Resale price maintenance	Collusive	Sherman, Sec. 1	Per se rule
4. Territorial restrictions	Collusive	Sherman, Sec. 1	Rule of reason

ritorial restraints are said to be *collusive* because they may have cartel-like consequences. They may promote oligopolistic interdependence, thereby aiding tacit or explicit price collusion. Table 10–1 also indicates the main statutory laws and judicial rules governing these practices. Thus Table 10–1 outlines this chapter.

Esoteric though these restraints and policies may seem, their importance has grown immensely with the explosive growth of franchising. Beginning with auto dealerships, soft drink bottlers, and gasoline service stations many decades ago, franchising has now spread to fast food, real estate, hotels, convenience stores, rental services, and even suntan parlors. Total franchise sales were a whopping $337 billion in 1980, nearly three times greater than ten years earlier. And franchise establishments numbered nearly 500,000 in 1980.[1] Surveys of franchise companies reveal their heavy use of various forms of exclusive dealing, tying, and territorial allocation.[2] Moreover, the case law in these areas carries many familiar names from

franchising—Chicken Delight, Dunkin Donuts, Standard Oil of California, and Coca-Cola to name just a few. Still, more than just franchising is involved. Nearly all forms of distribution are affected by policies in these areas, even direct sales to some extent.

I. Tying

A. Business Justifications for Tying

The sale of one item is often tied to the sale of another with innocuous purpose and effect—multigame season tickets for instance. An understanding of policy is therefore best grounded on an understanding of some of the main purposes served by tying.

Economies and Conveniences. Shirts sold with buttons, autos with tires, and pencils with erasers illustrate combinations more efficiently manufactured and distributed together than apart. These ties are so close that we think of each as being one product, the parts of which come in fixed proportions, such as seven buttons to a shirt. Since consumers would probably have to pay more for the privilege of buying separate parts, these ties are economically "natural."

Goodwill. A franchisor of fast food might

[1] U.S. Department of Commerce, *Franchising in the Economy 1978–1980* (Washington, D.C.: 1980), pp. 71–74.

[2] Donald N. Thompson, *Franchise Operations and Antitrust* (Lexington, Mass.: Heath Lexington Books, 1971), pp. 45–52.

require that his franchisees purchase their chickens, cooking equipment, and packaging materials from the franchisor, thereby tying these materials to use of a trade name. In this way the franchisor could assure standardization of quality (not necessarily high quality) among his many franchisees. Without such assurance, one fast-food outlet might exploit the general reputation of the trade name by offering poor quality while charging rich prices.

Price Discrimination.[3] A machine's consumption of materials, such as paper, ink, staples, or film, may, like a meter, measure intensity of use. Thus, when meters are impractical, easily tampered with, or prohibitively expensive, manufacturers of machines may try to sell or lease their machines at a low rate and tie-in the sale of materials priced well above cost. In this way, customers with intense demands would pay more than marginal users. Moreover, profits would be greater than those obtained without such price discrimination, especially if the producer has monopoly power in the machine's market. Notice that this tie-in may merely *exploit* more fully some already existing monopoly power. It does not necessarily entail an *extension* of market power into the tied-good's market. For example, even in the absence of antitrust policy, Xerox could not monopolize the paper industry if it tied copy paper to its machines because very little paper is used for that specific purpose.

However laudable these several justifications may be, they do not necessarily justify a lenient policy on tying. Where economies are present, the lower costs could be reflected in a lower price for the combination product as compared to the constituent parts. Where goodwill is an issue, quality specifications and surveillance may substitute for forced ties. And where price

discrimination is at stake, untying would reduce monopoly profits, but buyers would not feel hurt by this.[4]

B. Adverse Competitive Effects

To some, a major problem with tying is that it can be anticompetitive. It can raise barriers to entry in the market of the tied good or seriously disadvantage smaller tied-good competitors. Both effects are exclusionary, but neither effect necessarily occurs. It depends on the circumstances. If a firm has a monopoly in the tying good, and the tying and tied goods are complements used in varying proportions, such as bread and butter, the problem is particularly pernicious. William Baldwin and David McFarland explain:

> Assume that a seller with a complete monopoly on bread ties sales of his brand of butter to the bread, where butter was formerly sold in a perfectly competitive market. If there is no use for butter except to spread on bread, the tie-in will lead to a complete monopoly in the butter market. In any event, the bread monopolist will achieve some degree of monopoly power in the butter market.[5]

A different but more concrete example is offered by Kodak, which a while back tied film processing (developing) to its sale of film. When tied, Kodak enjoyed a 90 per cent share of the amateur film and film processing industry. As a result of a 1954 antitrust consent decree, however, Kodak severed the tie, licensed its processing technology to new entrants, and agreed to substantial divestiture of its processing facilities. A flood of new entry followed, which combined with the divestiture to cause Kodak's pro-

---

[3] M. L. Burstein, "A Theory of Full-Line Forcing," *Northwestern University Law Review* (March-April 1960), pp. 62–95.

[4] James M. Ferguson, "Tying Arrangements and Reciprocity: An Economic Analysis," *Law and Contemporary Problems* (Summer 1965), pp. 553–565.

[5] W. L. Baldwin and David McFarland, "Tying Arrangements in Law and Economics," *Antitrust Bulletin* (September-October 1963), p. 769.

cessing market share to tumble 55 percentage points in just five years. With entry, prices of film processing fell substantially. Although Kodak retained its near monopoly on film, and even raised prices on film, it appears that the new-found competition in processing benefitted shutterbugs.[6]

C. The Law on Tying

Section 1 of the Sherman Act covers tying, but the most explicit prohibition is found in Section 3 of the Clayton Act, which bans tie-in sales "where the effect . . . may be to substantially lessen competition or tend to create a monopoly." Judicial interpretation of these Acts approaches a per se rule. Ties are, in the Supreme Court's opinion, *"unreasonable in and of themselves* whenever a party has sufficient economic power with respect to the tying product to appreciably restrain free competition in the market for the tied product and a 'not insubstantial' amount of interstate commerce is affected."[7] This statement discloses, however, certain *rule-of-reason* elements, particularly for judgments about "sufficient economic power." Thus it is best to summarize by saying that violations will be found when the answers to *all* the following questions are "yes":

1. Are two products (or services) involved?
2. Does the seller possess sufficient economic power in the market of the tying product?
3. Is there substantial commerce in the tied goods?
4. Are defenses of "reasonableness" absent?

[6] Don E. Waldman, *Antitrust Action and Market Structure* (Lexington, Mass.: Lexington Books, 1978), pp. 143–150. It should be noted that tying's anticompetitive effect need not be limited to exclusion. It may, for instance, aid cartel discipline. See F. J. Cummins and W. E. Ruhter, "The *Northern Pacific* Case," *Journal of Law and Economics* (October 1979), pp. 329–350.

[7] *Northern Pacific Railroad Co.* v. *United States,* 356 U.S. 1 (1958). Emphasis added.

Of these questions, the first and third rarely raise thorny problems. The first is needed merely to prevent single products, like shirts with buttons, from being considered two products. The third is easily answered because "substantial commerce" seems to mean to the Court anything over a million dollars worth of business.

As regards "sufficient economic power" in the tying good, question (2), the Supreme Court has found a variety of conditions providing yes answers: (a) a large market share or "market dominance" in the tying good, (b) patents, copyrights, or trademarks for the tying good, (c) high barriers to entry in the tying-good market, and (4) uniqueness or "special desirability" of the tying good.

For example, a landmark case in patents is *International Salt* of 1947.[8] International had a "limited" patent monopoly over salt dispensing machines used in food processing. Users of the machines had to buy their salt from International or find other machines. International argued that preservation of goodwill required the tie-in, that only its own salt was of sufficient purity to provide top-quality dispensing. The Supreme Court rejected this assertion, observing that no evidence had been presented to show "that the machine is allergic to salt of equal quality produced by anyone except International." Moreover, the presence of the patents caused the Court to dispense some salty per se references, such as, "it is unreasonable, per se, to foreclose competitors from any substantial market."

Requisite power based on copyrights and uniqueness is illustrated by *U.S.* v. *Loew's, Inc.* (1962), which involved "block-booking." When selling motion pictures to television stations, Loew's had "conditioned the license or sale of one or more feature films upon the acceptance by the station of a package or block containing

[8] *International Salt Co.* v. *U.S.,* 332 U.S. 392 (1947).

one or more unwanted or inferior films." Put bluntly, the practice could tie *Gone With the Wind* and *Getting Gertie's Garter*. On the question of economic power, the Supreme Court decided that each film "was in itself a unique product"; that feature films "were not fungible"; that "since each defendant by reason of its copyright had a 'monopolistic' position as to each tying product, 'sufficient economic power' to impose an appreciable restraint on free competition in the tied product was present."[9] On this precedent the distributors of *Star Wars* had to back down when caught tying a mediocre film to that biggest money-maker of all time.

When potent patents, copyrights, or trademarks do not conveniently show tying-good power, the courts can get bogged down in matters that plague monopolization cases. What is the relevant market? What market share constitutes market power? In *Times-Picayune* the Court defined the relevant tying-good market as all newspaper advertising in New Orleans, a definition that let the defendant off the hook.[10] In *Fortner Enterprises* the Court found the defendant lacking sufficient market power in the credit market and lacking any special "uniqueness" such as would "force" the tied product on buyers.[11]

Finally, the fourth question concerning reasonable defenses has on rare occasions been answered in favor of defendants. The defendant in *U.S.* v. *Jerrold Electronics,* for instance, was an early 1950s pioneer in the development of community television antenna systems. Rather than sell separately its bits and pieces of equip-ment and technical services, Jerrold sold only on a full systems basis, including services for layout, installation, and maintenance as well as equipment. There was no question that Jerrold had hefty market power in the tying good—equipment—given its 75% market share. Nor was there any question of substantial business in the tied services. Nevertheless, Jerrold successfully defended its tying with proof that the industry was at the time very young, that these antenna systems were extremely delicate, and that full control through tying was required in order to build customer confidence in the industry and preserve Jerrold's reputation. In short, this was a goodwill defense in an infant-industry context. The court agreed, but granted only a *temporary* waiver, as these special conditions would evaporate with the passage of time—the industry maturing and the equipment toughening.[12]

Even where goodwill *can* be protected by a tie, the tie will not be approved if less restrictive alternatives are available. Chicken Delight, for instance, pleaded goodwill in defense of its tying.[13] To use the trade name, franchisees had to buy chickens and cookware from the franchisor. Yet the court found that these things could be readily obtained from other sources and quality could be maintained by setting specifications.[14]

In sum, tying is virtually a per se violation when there is power in the tying good. Still, in the absence of patents or such, rule-of-reason judgment enters the determination of power. Also, certain rule-of-reason defenses are possible but rarely acceptable.

[9] *U.S.* v. *Loew's Inc.*, 371 U.S. 38 (1962).

[10] *Times-Picayune Publishing Co.* v. *U.S.*, 354 U.S. 594 (1953). This definition was erroneous, however. See J. Dirlam and A. E. Kahn, *Fair Competition: The Law and Economics of Antitrust Policy* (Ithaca, N.Y.: Cornell University Press, 1954), pp. 106–108.

[11] *Fortner Enterprises Inc.* v. *United States Steel Corp.*, 429 U.S. 610 (1977), preceded by 394 U.S. 495 (1969).

[12] *U.S.* v. *Jerrold Electronics,* 187 F. Supp. 545 (E.D.Pa. 1960), affirmed per curiam 365 U.S. 567 (1961). For another successful use of the goodwill defense, see *Dehydrating Process Co.* v. *A. O. Smith Corp.*, 292 F. 2d 653 (1st Cir. 1961).

[13] *Siegel* v. *Chicken Delight, Inc.*, 448 F. 2d 43 (1971).

[14] See also *In re Data General Corp. Antitrust Litigation*, 490 F. Supp. 1089 (1980) at pp. 1120–1124.

II. Exclusive Dealing

Under an exclusive dealing agreement, the buyer obtains the seller's product on condition that he will not deal in the products of the seller's rivals. The buyer, say a sugar wholesaler, agrees to secure his total requirements of sugar from one supplier, say Amstar.

A. Business Justifications for Exclusive Dealing

From the supplier's point of view, exclusive dealing assures that distributors will devote their undivided energy to the supplier's products, something particularly important where personal sales, repair service, and promotion are required. Moreover, exclusive dealers often represent the manufacturer's interests more religiously. In 1974, for instance, Amstar stopped selling its sugar through general sugar brokers who served as agents for more than one sugar refiner. The stated reason for this action was that these general brokers acted with such "customer orientation" toward *their* buyers that "they at times acted more nearly as purchasing agents" for their buyers than sales agents for Amstar, causing Amstar lost profits. Thereafter Amstar sold only through exclusive dealing "direct brokers," who carried only Amstar sugar, and through its own sales force.[15]

From the buyer's or distributor's point of view, there are a number of reasons for accepting exclusive dealing:

- Supplies may be more certain and steady, especially in times of shortage.
- Specialization entails lower inventories than would be required with several brands of the same product.
- If exclusive dealing is rejected, the buyer may no longer be a buyer (that is, the seller forces acceptance).

[15] *Fuchs Sugar and Syrups, Inc. et al.* v. *Amstar Corp.*, CCH para 62,700 (CA–2, June 1979).

- Acceptance may be conceded in exchange for a commitment from the seller that protects the buyer-dealer from the competition of other buyer-dealers handling the same brand (for example, territorial assignments or limits on the number of dealerships in an area).

Recognizing that exclusive dealing offers advantages for buyers as well as sellers the Supreme Court has been a bit more lenient toward exclusive dealing as compared to tying, which the Court views as being a boon only to sellers.

B. Adverse Competitive Effects

Exclusive dealing may foreclose new entrants or small suppliers from main distribution channels, especially when used singly or collectively by dominant manufacturers or franchisors. Anticompetitive effects may ensue:

> Once a large or dominant supplier in a market obtains for his exclusive use a correspondingly large share of available outlets on a lower level of distribution, he has probably imposed prohibitive cost disadvantages on existing or potential rivals, since they are likely to have to create new outlets in order to participate in the market. The same is true where a group of suppliers collectively (if not collusively) obtain exclusive obligations from dealers—and thus produce an aggregate foreclosure.[16]

In essence, then, exclusive dealing is a form of contractual vertical integration.

C. The Law on Exclusive Dealing

Section 3 of the Clayton Act covers exclusive dealing as well as tying, for it bans sales or leases conditioned on an "agreement or understand-

[16] D. N. Thompson, *op. cit.*, p. 59. See also Oliver Williamson, "Assessing Vertical Market Restrictions" *University of Pennsylvania Law Review* (April 1979), pp. 960–966.

ing that the lessee or purchaser . . . shall not use or deal in the [goods or wares] of a competitor" of the seller or lessor, where the effect "may be to substantially lessen competition." According to the Supreme Court's interpretation of Section 3, exclusive dealing is not per se illegal. Hence the Court considers economic conditions and purposes when determining illegalities. Two main factors are the seller's market share and the prevalence of the practice among all sellers.

Two milestones in the evolution of this rule of reason policy are the Supreme Court's decisions in *Standard Stations* (1948) and *Tampa Electric* (1961). At issue in the former case were contracts obligating 5937 Standard service stations to take their full gasoline requirements and in some instances tires, batteries, and accessories as well, from Standard Oil Company of California. In addition, all other major suppliers used similar contracts. The Supreme Court *refused* to consider economic justification for the contracts and chose a test centering on the "quantitative substantiality" of the restraint. Stressing the fact that Standard's contracts covered 6.7% of the market and the fact that sales of $58 million were involved, the Court found a violation of Section 3 because the contracts "foreclosed competition in a substantial share of the line of commerce affected."[17] District and circuit courts thereafter applied the quantitative substantiality test until 1961.

In the *Tampa Electric* opinion of 1961, the Supreme Court said it *would* consider economic justifications for exclusive dealing. However, it is still uncertain just how important economic justifications will eventually become because the contract at issue in *Tampa* involved only 1% of the market, and, according to the Court, it would probably have gotten by the substantiality test anyway:

There is here neither a seller with a dominant position in the market . . . nor myriad outlets with substantial sales volume, coupled with an industry-wide practice of relying upon exclusive contracts . . . nor a plainly restrictive tying arrangement. . . . On the contrary, we seem to have only that type of contract which may well be of economic advantage to buyers as well as to sellers.[18]

Thus relatively small market shares and service to the buyers' interests will usually be enough to excuse exclusive dealing.[19] Moreover, much exclusive dealing escapes even when anticompetitive because it is hard to detect and prosecute. It need not be written into contracts. Manufacturers can reach *tacit* understandings with their distributors, understandings enforced by the manufacturers' refusals to deal. Although *collective* refusals to deal (boycotts) are essentially per se illegal, the courts have a long-standing tradition of recognizing the right of a manufacturer or other supplier to choose his distributors. This principle is most fully developed in the context of resale price maintenance, to which we turn next. Suffice it to say here that even dominant firms have been able to impose exclusive dealing using refusal to sell as their cat's paw.[20]

III. Resale Price Maintenance

Resale price maintenance, in pure form, is *vertical* price-fixing. A manufacturer specifies to its downstream wholesalers or retailers the minimum prices they may charge when reselling to their customers. A toaster manufacturer,

---

[17] *Standard Oil of California and Standard Stations, Inc.* v. *U.S.* 337 U.S. 293 (1949).

[18] *Tampa Electric Co.* v. *Nashville Coal Co., et al.,* 365 U.S. 320 (1961).

[19] Not always though, especially not if attacked under Section 5 of the FTC Act. See, e.g., *Federal Trade Commission* v. *Brown Shoe Company,* 384 U.S. 316 (1966).

[20] *Fuchs Sugar, op. cit.;* Thompson, *op. cit.,* Chap. 4; A. R. Oxenfelt, *Marketing Practices in the TV Set Industry* (New York: Columbia University Press, 1964), p. 123.

for instance, might require its retailers to price its toasters at $35 or more. To assure adherence to such resale prices, manufacturers typically must discipline mavericks by cutting off their supplies, delaying their shipments, or threatening some similar penalty.

A. Business Rationale for Resale Price Maintenance and Anticompetitive Effects

Although many manufacturers apparently like to engage in resale price maintenance, even though now largely illegal, it is not altogether clear why they like it. Casual reasoning would lead us to expect that once a manufacturer has set his own price, his interests would best be served by having the lowest price possible charged to final consumers, as that would maximize sales given the manufacturer's price. An efficient, competitive distribution system, earning the minimum distribution markup possible, would then seem most desirable. And resale price maintenance would not encourage distributor competition, efficiency, or markup minimization. Still, there are a few explanations deserving mention, because they help us assess whether a per se rule is justifiable.

First, it may be that the manufacturer is responding to the blandishments of his retailers, who use the manufacturer's resale price maintenance as a means of maintaining a retailer cartel. Here the manufacturer is not initiating the program, and the program is actually *horizontal* price-fixing at retail level enforced by the manufacturer, not vertical price-fixing. A rule preventing this seems quite acceptable. While passing this judgment, we should acknowledge that retailers need not engage in full-fledged cartelization to find comfort in resale price maintenance. In particular, it tends to shield small retailers from the price competition of larger, more efficient merchants. Numerous empirical studies have shown that

prices of many commodities tend to be higher with RPM than without; that these elevated prices preserve *in*efficiency; and that discount retailing is hampered.[21] Thus if society wished to nurture small businesses for the sake of furthering some populist value judgments, resale price maintenance might win acceptance. But such value judgments seem to be losing favor of late.

Second, resale price maintenance may be used to facilitate a cartel at manufacturers' level. The practice cements vertical relationships and aids cartel discipline by readily disclosing "cheaters" and "double-crossers." This too would actually be horizontal price-fixing, unworthy of saving from prohibition.

Third, it is often argued that some manufacturers want the retail price of their wares to be kept high because consumers equate a high price with high quality. In the absence of the support resale price maintenance offers, prices would fall, pulling down with them the brand's quality image. This justification is weak, however, because there is another way the same result could be attained. If a manufacturer wants a high retail price for his product he can simply jack up his own price. When downstream distributers pay the manufacturer more, they will in turn charge more.

Finally, the most appealing justification for resale price maintenance is this: Some products, like appliances, may be most effectively promoted through the provision of retailer services—such as demonstrations, fittings, bridal registers for wedding gifts, and repairs. Resale price maintenance may thus operate to protect retailers who offer these services from the

---

[21] See S. C. Hollander's summary in B. S. Yamey (ed.), *Resale Price Maintenance* (Chicago: Aldine, 1966), pp. 67–100; Leonard Weiss, *Case Studies in American Industry,* 3rd Ed. (New York: Wiley, 1980), pp. 282–288; J. F. Pickering, "The Abolition of Resale Price Maintenance in Great Britian," *Oxford Economic Papers* (March 1975), pp. 120–146.

poaching of discounters who do not offer these services. Full-Service-Sam would not last long if the customers he convinces to buy go down the street to consumate their purchases with Cut-Rate-Carl. So, the argument goes, Sam and his ilk must be protected.

B. The Law on Resale Price Maintenance

Under Section 1 of the Sherman Act, resale price maintenance is now regarded illegal per se. In light of the full-service dealer rationale just noted, however, a per se rule may seem too crude and too destructive of a laudable business practice (as compared with a rule of reason). Still, it can be argued in defense of the per se rule that these laudable ends can be reached by other, less restrictive means. A manufacturer, for instance, can require his retailers to provide certain services as a condition for continuing as his retailers. Even where such alternatives are limited, the present per se rule offers manufacturers much room to maneuver, enough room to achieve some degree of resale price maintenance.[22] In other words, there is a rather large loophole in the law, a hole punched by what may be called legal rights of unilateral refusal to sell.

To the extent resale price maintenance is *totally and completely* a *unilateral* undertaking on the part of an *individual manufacturer*, it is *not* considered a restraint of trade. Such legality is clearest in two situations: *First,* if the wholesalers and retailers down the line are wholly owned and operated by the manufacturer, as are some tire retailers, then resale price maintenance is internal to the firm and therefore perfectly permissible. Indeed, *re*sale, as such, doesn't even occur. This exemption can

be broadened a bit into a gray area, where distributors are not owned by the manufacturer, through the legal device of consignment sales. Here the manufacturer *retains title* to the goods and thereby bears certain risks. Resale is again avoided, the only sale being the final sale to consumers.

Second, resale price maintenance meets the legally unilateral standard if the manufacturer does *nothing more* than announce his desire that resale prices be maintained at or above some specified level and then refuses to sell to those who defy that desire. Anything beyond this unilateral program invites prosecution. Anything that smacks of multilateral agreement stands exposed. Retailers cannot agree to adhere to the suggested prices. Retailers cannot police each other's resale prices, squealing to the manufacturer on those scratching their itch to discount. Rebellious retailers cut off from supplies cannot be reinstated through an understanding with the manufacturer that they will not shade price again. Indeed, manufacturers best comply with unilateralism if, when they sever ties with a discounter, they do not mention the grounds for the divorce. Still, the manufacturer can engage in resale price maintenance through unilateral refusal to deal.

Each of these two avenues to unilateral legality has its own justification. The first is a technicality—i.e., resale price maintenance cannot occur if there is no resale. The second stems from a tradition of business practice—i.e., enterprises have a wide ranging right to choose those with whom they will do business, including the right of refusal to sell (even if they are choosy in the process).

Beyond these limits of unilateralism, however, resale price maintenance is per se illegal. Indeed, it can be criminally illegal, punishable as a felony, just like horizontal price-fixing. In 1980, for instance, Cuisinarts, Inc., was indicted for attempting to maintain and enforce minimum prices for its food processors. Pleading

[22] See for instance, Victor Goldberg, "Enforcing Resale Price Maintenance: The FTC Investigation of Lenox," *American Business Law Journal* (Summer 1980), pp. 225–256.

nolo contendere, the company was fined $250,000.[23] Such criminal action is very rare, and under the Reagan administration very doubtful. More common are civil suits, which in recent years have confronted such firms as Pendleton Woolen Mills, Lenox Company (producers of fine china), and Levi Strauss, the last of which ended up paying more than $12 million in civil damages.

The saga of per se illegality begins with *Dr. Miles Medical Co.* v. *John D. Park and Sons Co.* in 1911.[24] The Dr. Miles company manufactured proprietary medicines, and sought to prescribe the resale prices of both its wholesalers and retailers. Wholesaler Park and Sons refused to enter a resale contract with Dr. Miles, and undermined the program by cutting prices on Dr. Miles drugs it obtained from other wholesalers. Dr. Miles sued, but without success, because the Supreme Court decided that a manufacturer parts with control once he parts with the goods. "Where commodities have passed into the channels of trade and have been sold by complainant to dealers at prices satisfactory to complainant, the public is entitled to whatever advantage may be derived from competition in the subsequent traffic."

A lengthy interlude of legality occured when, during the Great Depression, many states responded to the urgings of retailers by enacting so-called "fair trade laws," which made resale price maintenance permissible. Notice it was *retailers,* not manufacturers, who lobbied most vehemently here, suggesting that retailers are shielded from competition when resale price maintenance is effective. Federal enabling legislation was needed to iron out the conflict between these fair trade laws and the Sherman Act, so Congress complied with the Miller-Tydings Act of 1937. This Act missed a stitch by failing to grant specific clearance to "nonsigner clauses," without which resale price maintenance was ineffectual. Nonsigner clauses bound *all* retailers in a state to maintain prices, those who signed contracts with manufacturers *and* those who did not sign (hence "non-signers"). Miller-Tydings was therefore patched up with the McGuire Act of 1952, which approved nonsigner clauses. This interlude ended, however, in 1975 with passage of the Consumer Goods Pricing Act of 1975. This Act removed these enabling exemptions, thereby locking legal fair trade pricing into the small cage of unilateral action outlined above.

As regards the first unilateral boundary— vertical ownership of the goods—the main early precedent is the *General Electric* case of 1926.[25] G.E. escaped the *Dr. Miles* rule by retaining title to its light bulbs, selling on consignment to independent dealers who agreed to resell at G.E.'s specified prices. Later, this consignment escape hatch was partially closed by the Court in *Simpson* v. *Union Oil Co.* (1964). Union Oil tried to maintain resale prices by selling on consignment to dealers like Simpson. But the Court found the consignment program to be a sham. "The risk of loss," it said, is on the dealers. "Their return is affected by the rise and fall in the market price." Hence the Court ruled that a "clever manipulation of words" could not camouflage a per se violation. A "consignment device" used to cover a vast "distribution system, fixing prices through many retail outlets" is illegal.[26] A gap thus opened between the "yes" of *G.E.* and the "no" of *Simpson.* We have neither the space nor patience to explore this gap here, but readers interested in contorted legal topography may look up *Alfred H. Hardwick* v. *Nu-Way Oil Co.* (1979).[27]

---

[23] *Wall Street Journal,* December 22, 1980, p. 28.

[24] *Dr. Miles Medical Co.* v. *John D. Park & Sons Co.,* 220 U.S. 373 (1911).

[25] *United States* v. *General Electric Co.,* 272 U.S. 476 (1926).

[26] *Simpson* v. *Union Oil Co.,* 377 U.S. 13 (1964).

[27] *Alfred H. Hardwick* v. *Nu-Way Oil Company,* 589 F.2d 806 (1979), cert. denied 444 U.S. 836 (1979).

As regards the second boundary of unilateralism—simple announcement plus cut offs—the leading precedent is *U.S.* v. *Colgate*,[28] decided only eight years after *Dr. Miles*. Colgate practiced resale price maintenance, disciplining maverick dealers with refusals to sell. But the Court was favorably impressed by Colgate's circumspection: "In the absence of any purpose to create or maintain a monopoly" a firm is free "to exercise his own independent discretion as to parties with whom he will deal; and of course, he may announce in advance the circumstances under which he will refuse to sell." Among the companies subsequently transgressing the Colgate line of leniency were Beech-Nut (gum and candies) and Parke-Davis (drugs and vitamins). In *Beech-Nut*[29] the Court found the accused enlisting the aid of special agents and compliant dealers for surveillances and enforcement. Further, Beech-Nut readmitted dismissed dealers into its fold after extracting from them assurances that their wayward ways were over. In *Parke-Davis*[30] the accused likewise took actions that led to "agreements: with its wholesalers and retailers." In particular, Parke-Davis had to deal with its retailers through its wholesalers, which proved awkward. As a result, Parke-Davis notified wholesalers of which retailers should be dropped, and coerced wholesalers into doing the dropping by threatening them with supply suspensions. Parke-Davis also wrested a promise to "abide" from at least one troublesome retailer. In short, "Parke-Davis did not content itself with announcing its policy regarding retail prices and following this with a simple refusal to have business relations with any retailers who disregarded that policy." Accordingly, the Court had to scold.

[28] *United States* v. *Colgate & Co.*, 250 U.S. 300 (1919).
[29] *Federal Trade Commission* v. *Beech-Nut Packing Co.*, 257 U.S. 441 (1922).
[30] *United States* v. *Parke-Davis and Co.*, 362 U.S. 29 (1960).

IV. Territorial Restrictions

Vertical territorial restrictions come in many forms—exclusive territories, areas of "prime responsibility," exclusive franchising, and limited outlet franchising among them. The basic result of all such restraints is the same, however,—more or less restrictive allocations of territories to the distributors or franchisees of a given brand, limiting intrabrand competition. If such restrictions were devised *horizontally* among distributors and franchisees they would obviously be per se violations of Sherman Section 1. If *vertically* imposed by manufacturers and franchisors, Sherman Section 1 is still the only applicable statute, but these restraints are not so obviously dangerous as to warrant per se treatment.

A. Business Justifications for Territorial Restrictions

Broadly stated, the main business justification for territorial restrictions is that they promote *inter*brand competition even though they may stifle *intra*brand competition. If, for example, the makers of Sylvania TV sets allocated territories among its distributors, these distributors could not compete against each other but they could channel their competitive efforts toward outselling RCA, Zenith, and Sony. There are a number of reasons why this might be so:

1. Distributors or franchisees may have to make considerable investments in their enterprise for facilities, advertising, inventory and so on. If the brand promoted is weak, the high risks facing distributors can be lessened by territorial protection. This would then aid in attracting new outlets.
2. For products needing full service retailing, such as demonstration, service, and credit, territorial isolation protects distributors who provide these costly services from the raids

of price discounters who do not provide such services.

3. Territorial isolation may aid quality maintenance if it facilitates the tracing and recall of faulty products and removes incentives one outlet may have for exploiting through adulteration the good reputation built up by other outlets of the same brand.

It should be noted that these justifications are most valid in instances where the manufacturer or franchisor is in a weak position vis-a-vis his rival manufacturers or franchisors. Moreover, these justifications are enfeebled by the fact that in many instances less restrictive means of attaining the same ends are available.[31] Still, these rationales cannot be dismissed lightly.

B. Adverse Competitive Effects

The potentially adverse competitive consequences of territorial restrictions are essentially the same as those associated with resale price maintenance, namely, cartel-like restraint, especially at distributor level where intrabrand competition is shackled. The greater the concentration at manufacturer or franchisor level, the more serious the problem. If for instance Chevrolet happened to capture 90 per cent of all U.S. auto sales, intrabrand competition among Chevy dealers would be the main form of competition remaining in the industry. And restraints on this competition could prove costly to consumers.

Even where concentration is relatively low, interbrand competition might be muted by strong product differentiation. Consumers loyally attached to their preferred brand would then probably benefit substantially by vigorous intrabrand competition. Intrabrand competition in soft drinks has been curbed as Coke, Pepsi, and the other major syrup manufacturers

allocated exclusive territories among their bottlers. And in 1973 FTC economists estimated that removal of these territorial restrictions would save soda pop drinkers approximately $250 million a year.[32] (Congress prevented removal, however, when it later passed legislation specifically exempting the soda pop industry. Intense industry lobbying paid off.)

The problem for wise policy in this area now becomes clear. Territorial restrictions blunt *intrabrand* competition, but they may foster *interbrand* competition.

C. The Law on Territorial Restrictions

Given the ambiguous character of this practice it is not surprising that a rule of reason now applies in assessing its legality. What is a bit surprising is that such a rule emerged under Section 1 of the Sherman Act, a section notorious for its per se interpretations.

The Supreme Court first fully confronted vertical territorial restraints in *United States* v. *White Motors* (1963).[33] White was a relatively small manufacturer of trucks who had assigned territories to its distributors and dealers. Recognizing that White might thereby be better able to compete with such giants of the industry as GMC and International Harvester, the Supreme Court held that a rule of reason should apply and remanded the case for lower court trial. Four years later in *Schwinn* the Supreme Court waffled a bit by judging a portion of Schwinn's plan under a per se rule and the rest under a rule of reason.[34] The ensuing confusion was cleared up in 1977 with *Continental TV* v. *GTE Sylvania*, which confirmed the rule of reason approach.[35]

---

[31] Thompson, *op. cit.*, Chap. 7.

[32] Cited by Barbara Katz, "Competition in the Soft Drink Industry," *Antitrust Bulletin* (Summer 1979), p. 280.
[33] *U.S.* v. *White Motor Co.*, 372 U.S. 253 (1963).
[34] *U.S.* v. *Arnold Schwinn & Co.*, 388 U.S. 365 (1967).
[35] *Continental TV, Inc., et al.* v. *GTE Sylvania Inc.*, 433 U.S. 36 (1977).

The facts of *Sylvania* were simple: Suffering from lagging TV set sales, Sylvania shifted its marketing strategy in the early 1960s to a program that included greater selectivity in choosing retailers. These franchised retailers were bound by contract not to sell except from locations approved by Sylvania. The strategy encouraged retailers to promote Sylvania sets more aggressively than before, thereby boosting Sylvania's market share from about 2% in 1962 to 5% in 1965. A fracas erupted, however, between Sylvania and one of its main San Francisco retailers, Continental TV, who fought Sylvania with a treble damage suit claiming the restrictions on dealer locations were illegal under the *Schwinn* decision.

Upon hearing the case the Supreme Court abandoned the per se portion of *Schwinn*, sided with Sylvania, and came out four-square for a rule of reason. Such was necessary, the Court held, to balance the harm of lessened intrabrand competition with the benefits of heightened interbrand competition:

> Vertical restrictions reduce intrabrand competition by limiting the number of sellers of a particular product competing for the business of a given group of buyers . . . [But . . .]
> Vertical restrictions promote interbrand competition by allowing the manufacturer to achieve certain efficiencies in the distribution of his products. These 'redeeming virtues' are implicit in every decision sustaining vertical restrictions under the rule of reason.

Although the Court felt the facts favored Sylvania, the Court offered little guidance on how the rule of reason should be applied in subsequent cases. Nevertheless, in light of what was said previously, we can conclude that the harm of lessened intrabrand competition is more likely to outweigh the benefit of heightened interbrand competition (1) the greater the market power of the manufacturer, (2) the greater the overall market concentration, (3) the stronger the tethers of product differentiation, (4) the older and richer the manufacturer in question, and (5) the more tightly drawn the constraint. So should the rule of reason develop.[36]

Summary

Tying, exclusive dealing, resale price maintenance, and territorial restrictions constitute vertical restrictions. Tying is the sale of two or more products contractually bound. Exclusive dealing prevents a buyer-distributor from dealing in more than one brand of a given line of wares. Resale price maintenance is vertical price-fixing. And territorial restrictions insulate distributors from intrabrand competition. Policies concerning these practices have gained importance with the remarkable growth of franchising.

Tying may gain efficiencies, preserve business good will through the preservation of quality, or aid price discrimination. Tying may also be used to leverage monopoly power from the tying-good's market into the tied-good's market, and therein lies the rub. It can be exclusionary. Under Section 1 of the Sherman Act and Section 3 of the Clayton Act, tying is judged illegal if (1) there really are two products involved; (2) the seller possesses sufficient economic power in the tying good; (3) there is substantial commerce in the tied good; and (4) no defenses of reasonableness afford themselves. Though laced with rule of reason potential,

[36] E. F. Zelek, Jr., L. W. Stern, and T. W. Dunfee, "A Rule of Reason Model After *Sylvania*," *California Law Review* (January 1980), pp. 13–47. For an early case along these lines see *Horst A. Eiberger et al.* v. *Sony Corporation of America*, CCH 62,336 (D.C.S.N.Y., October 1979). Sony was not only especially healthy, with 12% of a market in which five firms held 95% of the business, it used the restrictions for resale price maintenance. It should also be noted that whenever vertical restraints are in fact horizontal, as would be true if distributors *owned* the manufacturer or franchisor imposing the restraints, they would of course encounter the per se rule. *U.S.* v. *Sealy*, 388 U.S. 350 (1967).

these criteria boil down to a per se rule in many instances, such as tie-ins to patented products.

Exclusive dealing is also potentially exclusionary and also covered by Clayton Section 3. Nevertheless, given the possible benefits of this practice for distributors and ultimate consumers as well as instigating manufacturers, it is appropriate that a rule of reason prevail. The two main factors determining its legality are the seller's market share and the prevalence of the practice. If either or both are quite large, the exclusionary effect will be magnified and, with it, the likelihood of illegality.

Resale price maintenance and territorial restraints curb intrabrand competition among distributors, thereby inviting scrutiny under Section 1 of the Sherman Act. Of the two practices, the latter is the less restrictive, which may explain why it wins rule of reason status whereas the former is considered a per se offense. A main business justification for both is that they nourish incentives for vigorous, "full service" retailing and wholesaling. In the case of territorial allocations, such incentives may actually foster interbrand competition if used by the weak against the strong, something which further explains why the rule of reason prevails for such cases.

Regardless of the law, many vertical restraints escape through the use of tacit arrangements that are cemented by an ample freedom of choice in the selection of distributors and franchisees.

Questions and Exercises for Chapter 10

1. After specifying the several reasons why tying may be in the interests of businesses using it, explain which of these are in the social interest and which are not.
2. Why can it be said that tying is neither per se illegal nor rule of reason but "mixed"?
3. Is policy toward tying so tight that socially laudable uses of it are prevented? Explain.
4. Why are exclusive dealing and tying alike? Why are they different?
5. Given the similarities between tying and exclusive dealing, are policies toward them consistent? Explain.
6. When is resale price maintenance in the public interest and when is it not?
7. Resale price maintenance is said to be per se illegal but in the real world it is commonplace. Why?
8. Does the ruling in *Continental TV* v. *GTE Sylvania* make economic sense? Explain your yes or no.

Chapter 11

Multinational Corporations

The multinational corporate enterprise represents the contemporary
stage of development of the national corporate enterprise, which in
its turn developed from the local corporate enterprise, which in its
turn evolved from the noncorporate local enterprise.
—Harry G. Johnson

Mammoth oil companies are famous for their
international expanse. Their production facilities and marketing outlets blanket the globe.
The same could be said of almost all major U.S.
companies. Westinghouse's foreign operations
accounted for 25 per cent of its sales and profits
in 1978. Coca-Cola's foreign figures were even
higher at 45% of sales and 65% of profits in
1980.

Dating back centuries, multinationalism is
by no means new, but it has grown at a fantastic
rate of late. U.S. direct investment abroad burgeoned from $12 billion in 1950 to $193 billion
in 1979.[1] By the early 1970s, U.S. multinationals
conducted one-quarter of the world's merchandise export trade. And while U.S. companies
have flowered in foreign lands, foreign companies have scampered into the U.S. Big business
has, in short, outgrown national boundaries.

This spread of multinationalism has created
dozens of new policy issues. Many of these issues relate to antitrust because power is a basic

problem with multinationalism—power tran-
scending and evading the legal reach of individual nations. Before we take up specific policies,
however, we must find answers to several important preliminary questions. Hence this
chapter's outline:

  I. Who are the multinationals?
 II. How strong are they abroad?
III. Why have they become multinational?
IV. What is *good* about them?
 V. What is *bad* about them?
VI. What policies govern them?

I. Who Are the Multinationals?

A. *U.S. Multinationals*

Multinational corporations distinguish themselves most prominently with wholly owned
foreign subsidiaries, partially owned foreign
joint ventures, or patent and trademark licensing agreements abroad. If cosmopolitan
enough, these corporations have far-flung research and development activities, multina-

---

[1] O. G. Whichard, "Trends in the U.S. Direct Investment
Position Abroad, 1950–79," *Survey of Current Business*
(February 1981), pp. 39–56.

tional management organizations, and even global business strategies.

Those calling the United States home are also at home on lists of our leading corporations, such as the list in Table 5–3 on page 96 of Chapter 5. Indeed, as of 1978, General Motors and Exxon were far and away the two largest industrial companies in the world, each with over $60 billion in global sales, an amount exceeding the gross national product of most countries. Ford Motors, Mobil, Texaco, Standard Oil of California (Chevron), IBM, and GE also rank highly among multinational corporations. And in 1978, eleven of the world's fifteen leading multinationals were based in the U.S., these among them.

B. Non-U.S. Multinationals

Whereas several hundred multinationals originate from the U.S., several hundred more

spring from other lands. The largest of these are listed in Table 11–1, where it may be seen that European enterprises are especially well represented. Most of these firms, like their American bretheren, produce automotive and petroleum products. The sheer size of their home countries and prime industries help elevate these firms to the top of such lists, but we should not overlook several dozen rapidly rising Japanese multinationals—like Mitsubishi, Hitachi, and Matsushita—nor the many relatively small firms whose famous brand names speak of great popularity—Nestlé, Michelin, and Olivetti for instance.

II. How Strong Are the Multinationals?

In aggregate terms, roughly four hundred multinational enterprises produce perhaps as

Table 11–1. Twelve Giants of Industry Outside the U.S., 1980

Company	Home Country	Industry	Sales 1980 ($ billions)
1. Royal-Dutch Shell	Netherlands-Britain	Petroleum	$77.1
2. British Petroleum	Britain	Petroleum	48.0
3. ENI*	Italy	Petroleum	27.2
4. Fiat	Italy	Motor vehicles	25.2
5. Francaise des Petroles	France	Petroleum	23.9
6. Unilever	Britain-Netherlands	Food, soaps, cosmetics	23.6
7. Renault*	France	Motor vehicles	19.0
8. Petróleos de Venezuela*	Venezuela	Petroleum	18.8
9. Elf Aquitaine*	France	Petroleum	18.4
10. Philips	Netherlands	Electronics	18.4
11. Volkswagenwerk	Germany	Motor vehicles	18.3
12. Siemens	Germany	Electronics	18.0

* Government owned.
   Source: Fortune, August 10, 1981, p. 207.

much as one-third of the free-world's industrial output. Further indication of the awesome importance of multinationalism is given by the immense size of the Eurocurrency market, which is made up mainly of dollar deposits in banks outside the U.S. but includes other "stateless money" as well. The multinationals invest in and borrow from this capital market along with the world's governments. As of June 1979, the Eurocurrency market stood at $520 billion, up from $65 billion in 1970. This $520 billion was nearly twice the size of total government international reserve assets. Operated mainly by multinational banks, the Eurocurrency market lies outside the close control of any official central bank.[2]

On a less aggregated basis the eminence of multinationals is quite variable, but rough patterns are discernable. Variations along two dimensions seem particularly revealing. One dimension is the state of economic development of the host country. That is, the share of industrial activity in the hands of multinational firms appears to be greater in poor countries than in rich countries. The other dimension is the level of technology involved in the product or production process: the share of industrial activity accounted for by multinationals appears to be greatest where relatively sophisticated technology is involved and least where the technology is relatively rudimentary. Data for U.S. multinationals in 1970 illustrate these two dimensions taken together. At the high end, these firms could be credited with approximately 40% of the sales of such high technology wares as chemicals, electrical machinery, and transportation equipment in Brazil and Mexico. At the low end these firms accounted for only about 3 per cent of the combined sales of simple technology items like food, paper, textiles, and

wood products in the advanced countries of France and West Germany. In between these extremes, U.S. multinationals garnered about 12 per cent of simple technology sales in Brazil and Mexico, and 12 per cent of complex technology sales in France and West Germany.[3] There are of course exceptions to this pattern, but these exceptions often have obvious explanations. Over 50 per cent of Canada's heavy industry and mining is owned by non-Canadian corporations, an unusually high proportion due largely to Canada's close proximity to the United States.[4] But exceptions haunt all generalizations.

A survey of 180 U.S. multinationals in Mexico during the mid-1970s revealed that 44 per cent of them ranked first in their product line in Mexico and another 20 per cent ranked second. Similar results came from U.S. multinationals in Brazil, where 42 per cent ranked first and 26 per cent ranked second in their respective industries. Very large market shares went with these lofty positions. Twenty-five per cent of the surveyed multinationals in Mexico and Brazil had market shares exceeding 50 per cent. Another twenty-five per cent of these firms enjoyed market shares in the 25 to 50 per cent range.[5] In other words, multinationals are not merely big in *absolute* terms, they also tend to be big in *relative* terms, frequently dominating the markets in which they operate abroad, especially in less developed countries.

To say that multinational corporations typically capture hefty market shares in the less developed countries in which they operate is

---

[2] U.S. Congress, House Committee on Banking, Finance and Urban Affairs, *The Operation of U.S. Banks in the International Capital Markets* (Washington, D.C., 1979); and *Business Week*, August, 21, 1978, pp. 76–80.

[3] U.S. Senate, Committee on Finance, *Implications of Multinational Firms for World Trade and Investment and for U.S. Trade and Labor* (Washington D.C., 1973), pp. 735–746.

[4] *Wall Street Journal*, February 18, 1981, p. 1.

[5] Richard S. Newfarmer and Willard F. Mueller, *Multinational Corporations in Brazil and Mexico: Structural Sources of Economic and Noneconomic Power*, U.S. Senate, Subcommittee on Multinational Corporations, Committee on Foreign Relations (1975), pp. 83, 86, 132, 136.

not the same as saying that multinationals devote most of their attentions to the less developed countries. The vast bulk of multinational activity occurs within a circle made up of the developed countries of North America, Europe, and Japan. Thus in 1979, 72 per cent of U.S. direct foreign investment was located in what could be called developed countries. Less developed countries accounted for only 25 per cent of these investments, an amount just slightly above the share accounted for by Canada alone (21%). Conversely, most subsidiaries of foreign multinationals in the U.S. are of European parentage, and those European parents favor affiliations in prosperous countries just as much as their U.S. brethren.

III. Why Do Firms Become Multinationals?

The obvious motive for foreign investment is, in a word, profit. But such could be said of practically everything businesses do, so the question of motive deserves a more enlightening answer. That answer comes in several parts because there is no single explanation for all multinationalism, no solitary theory that can fit all the facts. Here we shall survey four of the main explanations—(1) resource extraction, (2) monopolistic advantages, (3) tariff jumping, and (4) comparative advantage.

A. Resource Extraction

Many multinational endeavors originate in efforts to secure raw materials that nature has placed in remote spots. Such was true for petroleum, many metal ores, and bananas, as is suggested by the very names of some of the oldest and largest multinational corporations—Standard Oil of New Jersey (Exxon), Rio Tinto Zinc, International Minerals & Chemical, and United

Fruit. Petroleum alone accounted for 36 per cent of all U.S. direct foreign investment in 1957, a share that has since fallen to 22 per cent.

A large chunk of Japan's rapidly growing direct foreign investment is also grounded on this motive. As Terutomo Ozawa explains:

> This pattern of behavior could be expected of a country that lacked natural resources yet emphasized the development of resource-consuming heavy and chemical industries. Here the economics is not a cost-pinching, short-term calculation but a security-primacy, long-term calculation. Japan's demand for and dependence on overseas resources have increased enormously . . .[6]

Much the same could be said, though perhaps less stridently, about Britain and the Netherlands, whose Royal-Dutch Shell, British Petroleum, and Unilever faced foreign resource dependency from their first stirrings.

B. Monopolistic Advantages

Foreign expansion for resource purposes tends to be "vertical" in the sense of backward integration toward raw materials. But much if not most present foreign expansion is actually "horizontal," in the sense of, say, an auto firm producing autos abroad. A major explanation for this horizontal multinationalism draws upon industrial organization theory for its insights.[7] In particular, it is observed that direct foreign investment frequently occurs in industries where monopolistic advantages prevail both at home and abroad. These advantages may be grounded in advanced technology (chemicals

[6] Terutomo Ozawa, *Multinationalism, Japanese Style* (Princeton, N.J.: Princeton University Press, 1979), pp. 22–24.

[7] Stephen Hymer, *The International Operations of National Firms* (Cambridge, Mass.: M.I.T. 1976); Richard Caves, "International Corporations: The Industrial Economics of Foreign Investment," *Economica* (February 1971), pp. 1–27.

and computers for example), potent product differentiation (as in the case of soft drinks and drugs), and economies of scale (as in autos). Note that many of these advantages are protected by "industrial property" rights at home and abroad—that is, patents, proprietary know-how, and trademarks. The basic idea is that these monopolistic advantages give the multinational enterprise an advantage over host country rivals, or at least give the multinational's foreign subsidiaries an equal chance in host country markets. Without such special advantages the foreigner would be at a *dis*advantage because local firms would naturally tend to be more familiar with local market conditions, local laws, local customs, and other local mysteries important to business success. A nice illustration of this is provided by Tandy Corporation, whose Radio Shack store in Holland geared its first Christmas promotion to December 25, unaware that the Dutch customarily exchange holiday gifts on December 6, St. Nicholas Day. They badly missed the market.[8]

Numerous statistical studies support this theory of direct foreign investment by finding high correlations between direct foreign investment on the one hand and four-firm concentration or advertising intensity or R & D expenditure on the other. In Mexico, for instance, foreign firms accounted for 100% of 1970 industry sales in transportation equipment, rubber, electrical equipment, and office equipment—all of which evince special advantages for member firms. In contrast, 1970 sales of foreign firms accounted for very small percentages in leather, textiles, and apparel—4.6%, 7.1%, and 4.0%, respectively.[9] Canadian experience further illustrates the importance of monopolistic advan-

tages. To quote the conclusion of one recent Canadian study:

> Where the advantages are potent (heavy advertising and research and development, heavy use of sophisticated managerial personnel and nonproduction workers generally) domestic-controlled establishments shrink to a competitive fringe. Conversely, the multinational presence shrinks where these assets are unimportant or where being small, local, and flexible affords a positive advantage.[10]

C. Tariff Jumping

National tariff barriers have in the past promoted much direct foreign investment. For example, formation of the European Economic Community (EEC) in the late 1950s led to low tariffs on *intra*-European trade but to high tariffs against *non*-European suppliers. U.S. exporters to Europe were thereby handicapped. So, instead of building plants in the U.S. and exporting to Europe, these firms leaped the EEC's tariff wall during the 1960s by building plants inside the EEC. They then could supply the EEC market duty free. High tariffs in less developed countries have had a similar effect.

The importance of tariff jumping in the past is revealed in a questionnaire survey of 76 U.S. multinationals in 1971. When asked why they had invested directly in foreign markets, 25 of these firms, or roughly one-third, mentioned among their answers, "Unable to reach market from U.S. because of tariffs, transportation costs, or nationalistic purchasing policies." The only reason given more frequent mention than this was "Maintain or increase market share locally," which likewise suggests a concern with

---

[8] "Radio Shack's Rough Trip," *Business Week*, May 30, 1977, p. 55.

[9] John M. Conner and Willard F. Mueller, "Manufacturing, Denationalization and Market Structure: Brazil, Mexico, and the United States," *Industrial Organization Review* (No. 2, 1978), pp. 86–105.

[10] R. E. Caves, M. E. Porter, A. M. Spence, and J. T. Scott, *Competition in The Open Economy* (Cambridge: Harvard University Press, 1980), pp. 91–92. See also R. E. Caves, "Causes of Direct Foreign Investment," *Review of Economics and Statistics* (August 1974), pp. 279–293.

overcoming the economic disadvantages of tariff and transportation costs that might inhibit the export of home productions.[11] If a similar survey were conducted today these factors would probably receive much less emphasis because tariff barriers and transportation costs have fallen, at least among advanced countries and for most industries. The motive is still important though, as newer barriers like "voluntary quotas" have replaced the old. (See Chapter 26.)

D. Comparative Advantage

When semiconductor companies like Texas Instruments and National Semiconductor build factories in Asia or Mexico for the "off-shore" assembly of electrical products, or when Japanese textile manufacturers establish mills in Taiwan or South Korea, their motivation springs from factors not easily incorporated into the foregoing considerations. Host country resources are not uprooted. Monopolistic advantages are not being exploited to penetrate host country markets. Indeed, host country markets are not even the destination of the products produced, so tariff jumping is likewise not involved. The ultimate destination is either the multinational's home market or international trade generally.

What appears to propel many of these direct investments is comparative advantages in host countries, a notion derived from classical trade theory. A U.S. firm may decide to supply the European market by locating a plant in Singapore. A Japanese firm in the same industry may supply the U.S. from a plant in Hong Kong. In this way capital, technology, and managerial talent can be moved across national boundaries to exploit the comparative advantages the host countries have in cheap, semiskilled labor or

in other immobile inputs. The more this brand of multinationalism grows, the more truly international the multinational corporations become. The simple home-host axis of attention breaks down as, for instance, capital from the Eurocurrency market is used by a U.S. multinational to build an operation in India that will use raw materials from Africa and ship final goods all over the globe. Curiously, many corporations enter this particular mode of international dependency and mobility not because of any monopolistic *strengths* at home or abroad, but rather because of *weaknesses* in competitive position. Their struggle for survival forces them to seek out and utilize comparative advantages wherever they might be.[12]

To summarize, several inducements encourage multinationalism. Backward integration into resource extraction, horizontal expansion to cash-in on monopolistic advantages, tariff jumping to maintain or expand local market positions, and geographic diversification in pursuit of comparative-competitive advantages are apparently the main motives. There are others—such as the achievement of earnings stability through international diversification—but these need not detain us.

One further observation is worthy of pause, however, the observation that motives frequently work in combination, spurring multinational undertakings through multiforces.

IV. What Is *Good* About Multinationals?

Multinationalism is obviously good for the multinationals themselves, for otherwise they would stay at home. But the question of their benefits and costs to the world in general and to home and host countries in particular remains open. In fact, this broader question has

---

[11] J. Frank Gaston, "Why Industry Invests Abroad," in *The Multinational Corporation*, Vol. 2 (U.S. Department of Commerce, 1973), pp. 6–10.

[12] Ozawa, *op. cit.,* pp. 54–75.

ignited tremendous controversy, with arguments for and against multinationals multiplying with each passing year.[13] Given the immensity of this subject we can do little more than outline the economic pros and cons as viewed by home and host countries, beginning first with the favorable prospects for home countires.

A. Arguments in Favor of MNCs: Home Country Perspective

1. BALANCE OF PAYMENTS

At first glance it might appear that a home country's balance of payments would suffer from multinationalism among its corporations because direct foreign investment implies a transfer of capital abroad. But the balance of payments effects may nevertheless be favorable to the home country because such investment eventually reaps returns in the form of interest, dividends, patent royalties, and other fees. Moreover, the capital for foreign expansion need not always come from home, given the alternative sources of Eurocurrency credit and offshore retained earnings. Finally, multinationals frequently export components for assembly abroad, which exports would help home country balance of payments. Thus, many contend a plus here.

2. SECURE RAW MATERIALS

As suggested earlier, multinationalism may help a home country secure lines of raw material supplies.

3. PROMOTE TRADE AND MONETARY STABILITY

A recent study of U.S. multinationals concludes that they "contribute significantly to the

effectiveness of international monetary arrangements, to the maintenance of liberal U.S. trade policies, and thus to these important national interests of the United States."[14]

B. Arguments Favoring Multinationals: Host Country Perspective

1. MOBILIZE HOME COUNTRY RESOURCES

A multinational's infusion of capital and managerial skill can mobilize host country resources, thereby boosting output and efficiency, expanding export sales, and improving the *host* country's balance of payments position. In other words, multinationals can provide the wherewithall to promote economic development and prosperity.

2. TRANSFER OF TECHNOLOGY

For less developed host countries the multinationals represent a major source of new technology. Over ninety per cent of the world's most advanced technology is in the hands of multinationals who may transfer it to less developed countries by direct foreign investment or licensing, thereby saving these countries the tremendous costs of developing that technology from scratch for themselves. Even developed host countries benefit, as the international diffusion of new knowledge would similarly add to their productive capabilities and product modernity.

3. INCREASED COMPETITION

Competition in a host country would be stimulated by the new entry of a multinational. Local firm market power would lessen, and overall concentration in the host country market could fall.

---

[13] For sweeping reviews, one pro and one con, see Raymon Vernon, *Storm Over The Multinationals* (Cambridge: Harvard University Press, 1977), and R. J. Barnet and R. E. Müller, *Global Reach* (New York: Simon and Schuster, 1974).

[14] C. F. Bergsten, T. Horst, and T. H. Moran, *American Multinationals and American Interests* (Washington, D.C.: Brookings Institution, 1978), pp. 303–304.

It must be stressed that empirical testing of these potential benefits for home and host countries is very difficult because most claimed benefits rest on an assumption that there are no good alternative sources of these benefits except multinationals. If, for example, their capital were not made available, it is assumed that host country capital sources or foreign aid could not easily fill the gap. This presents a research problem in the sense that nobody really knows what might have been, given that it hasn't been. Still, some evidence solidly favors multinationalism.

V. What Is *Bad* About Multinationals?

The arguments against multinationals also divide along home and host country lines. It will be obvious that several such arguments directly contradict favorable ones given above, in which cases both cannot be right, at least not as they apply to any one particular multinational project.

A. Arguments Against Multinationals: Home Perspective

1. WORSEN BALANCE OF PAYMENTS

Because multinationals often substitute capital outflows from home countries for exports it has been argued that they worsen the home country's balance of payments.

2. EXPORTING JOBS

To the extent multinationals build factories abroad rather than at home they give appearances of fostering employment abroad at the expense of employment at home. Moreover, it is argued that multinationalism weakens the bargaining power of labor as it gives corporations the option of moving production abroad if they do not wish to meet labor demands at

home. As in other cases, the validity of these contentions varies from industry to industry, obscuring any general conclusion. Still, some jobs apparently are exported and some labor unions are weakened, although the numbers and degrees involved do not seem particularly large.[15]

3. MARKET POWER IN HOME MARKET

As we have seen, multinationalism is often grounded on monopolistic advantages in home countries. A reverse casuality is also possible. That is, multinationalism itself may give a corporation certain advantages in its home market that purely domestic rivals cannot match. In particular, these advantages may stem from international vertical integration, the spreading of joint costs over many geographic markets, and cross-subsidization (which entails drawing on profits abroad to boost one's market position at home). Statistical search for the presence of such power-enhancement at home has converted the possibility into probability.[16]

B. Arguments Against Multinationals: Hosts' Perspective

1. NET CAPITAL OUTFLOW

Rather than provide net capital inflows that finance industrial expansion in host countries, multinationals may contribute to a net capital outflow from host countries, or so it is sometimes argued. Indeed, much financing for multinational enterprises abroad is obtained locally through retained earnings and host country credit.[17] When coupled with claims that multinationals remit "excess" profits and royalties to home, the contention gains plausibility. And when coupled with certain assumptions it is not

---

[15] Ibid, pp. 99–120.
[16] Ibid, pp. 230–248.
[17] Ronald Müller, "(More) on Multinationals: Poverty is the Product," *Foreign Policy* 13 (1973–74), pp. 85–88.

without empirical support in at least some cases.[18]

2. TRANSFER PRICING

Aggravating the possibility of net capital outflows is the problem of transfer pricing. When a subsidiary abroad buys raw materials, technology, or services from its parent multinational company, it is charged an arbitrary intracompany price that might well be exorbitant. For example, the multinational oil companies apparently overcharged their Canadian subsidiaries $3.2 billion on crude oil imported into Canada over the years 1958–1970.[19] Investigations in Colombia for the late 1960s disclosed that drug giant Hoffman-LaRoche was overcharging its subsidiary (as a percentage of world market prices) by 94% for Atelor, by 96% for Trimatoprium, by over 5,000% for Chlordiazepoxide, and by over 6,000% for Diazepam.[20] A major motive for this kind of behavior is taxes. By manipulating intracompany prices, multinationals can cause profits to show up in nations whose tax bite is least burdensome. Moreover, they can take profits out of a host country in a way that evades regulation.

3. INAPPROPRIATE TECHNOLOGY

Indonesia's importation of modern farm equipment, ranging from mechanical rice hullers to tillers and tractors, eliminated several hundred thousand jobs during the 1970s. Moreover, it has been estimated that Indonesia's exports supported 60,000 fewer jobs in 1979 than in 1971 despite the fact that exports expanded eightfold with the aid of multinational oil and mineral companies.[21] These experiences and many like them nurture arguments that, however attractive a multinationals' new technology might appear at superficial first sight, it is in the end often damaging to the interests of less developed countries. In particular, the technology too often tends to be labor-saving and capital-intensive—characteristics befitting the needs of the *advanced* countries where the technology originated, but *contrary* to the requirements of most *less developed* countries (which are so laden with labor as to have 680 million people needing work).[22]

4. DISTORTIONS OF DEMAND

Multinationalism grounded on monopolistic advantages in advertising, trademarks, and related product differentiation, like that of Coca-Cola, is often criticized for creating inappropriate tastes, especially in less developed countries.[23] A notorious example stems from the attempts of food manufacturers to expand their sales of infant formula at the expense of mother's milk in less developed countries. Whereas breast-feeding is cheap and nutritious, bottle feeding strains small budgets and often threatens babies' health. Among the many illiterate mothers in less developed countries who are persuaded to use infant formula but find it difficult to follow detailed instructions, bottles go unsterilized and formula gets overdiluted or contaminated.[24]

---

[18] Thomas J. Biersteker, *Distortion or Development?* (Cambridge: M.I.T. Press, 1978), pp. 85–102; S. Lall and P. Streeten, *Foreign Investment, Transnationals and Developing Countries* (Boulder, Colorado: Westview Press, 1977).

[19] Director of Investigation and Research, Combines Investigation Act, *The State of Competition in The Canadian Petroleum Industry* Vol. I (Ottawa, 1981), pp. 18–19, 61–70.

[20] S. Lall, "The International Pharmacentrical Industry and Less-Developed Countries," *Oxford Bulletin of Economics and Statistics* (August 1974), p. 161.

[21] *Wall Street Journal*, September 25, 1979, p. 1.

[22] L. T. Wells, "Economic Man and Engineering Man: Choice of Technology in a Low Wage Country," *Public Policy* (Summer 1973), pp. 39–42; L. J. White, "Appropriate Technology, X-Inefficiency and a Competitive Environment," *Quarterly Journal of Economics* (November 1976), pp. 575–589; Frances Stewart, "Technology and Employment in LDCs," *World Development* (March 1974), pp. 17–46.

[23] G. K. Helleiner, "The Role of Multinational Corporations in the Less Developed Countries' Trade in Technology," *World Development* (April 1975), pp. 161–189.

[24] For examples of misrepresention in drug promotion see Milton Silverman, *The Drugging of the Americas* (Berkeley: University of California Press, 1976).

5. QUESTIONABLE PAYMENTS

During the late 1970s over four hundred companies admitted that they had recently made over $700 million in economic and political payoffs to foreign heads of state, cabinet ministers, and other government officials in order to influence purchasing decisions, tax policies, and elections. Gulf Oil, for example, confessed to making secret payments of $4 million to the ruling party in South Korea. Exxon paid $59 million to Italian politicians over eight years to advance its "business objectives." And United Brands was found to have bribed Honduran officials $2.5 million to win tax breaks.[25] Despite explanations that in many cases this is "customary" in foreign countries, critics accuse multinationals of improperly, immorally, and illegally interfering in the official affairs of foreign host countries.

6. RESTRICTIVE BUSINESS TRADE PRACTICES

The massive size and economic power of major multinationals raises suspicions that they are all too frequently engaged in restrictive practices adversely affecting host countries—weak hosts in particular. Both horizontal and vertical restrictions have been found. Among "horizontal" offenses, monopolization is by no means unknown, but cartelization is surely the most commonly encountered.[26] The recently documented activities of the International Electrical Association (I.E.A.), an international cartel in heavy electrical equipment, illustrates the problem:

The cartel comprises over 50 European and Japanese producers and covers sales in most of the markets of the non-Communist world outside the United States, Western Europe, and Japan (amounting to almost $2 billion annually). . . . These cartel arrangements directly harm importing countries because of the onerous mark-up on cartelized sales as well as common policies among members restricting technology transfers to nonproducing countries. On the basis of data from one product section, it is estimated that successful collusive agreements may raise prices 15 to 25 percent above the competitive rate.[27]

"Vertical" restrictions arise in the distribution or licensing process. These include exclusive dealing, tying, and territorial allocations among foreign distributors. Evidence concerning restraints such as these comes from studies of contracts transferring technology from multinational corporations to producers in less developed countries. Table 11–2 summarizes the results of several such studies by the United Nations Conference on Trade and Development covering license agreements in India, the Philippines, and Spain. It may be seen that restrictions limiting the exports of licensees have been quite common. Tying provisions requiring licensees to purchase specified materials from the licensor or from other designated suppliers have been less frequent but common nevertheless. Still other restraints, such as minimum royalty payments, posttermination limitations, and restrictions on production methods appear very infrequently, but in certain individual instances they can be important.

In sum, multinationals cannot clearly qualify for supercitizenship awards. Abundant evidence of assorted evils is available to incite critics in home and host countries. Still, much of the adverse evidence is blunted by the same problem that affects favorable evidence and ar-

[25] T. N. Gladwin and Ingo Walter, "The Shadowy Underside of International Trade," *Saturday Review*, July 9, 1977, pp. 16–22; N. Jacoby, P. Nehemkis, and R. Eells, *Bribery and Extortion In World Business: A Study of Corporate Political Payments Abroad* (New York: Macmillan, 1977).

[26] *Restrictive Business Practices*, U. N. doc. TD/B/C.2/104/Rev. 1 (1971); *Restrictive Business Practices*, U. N. doc. TD/B/390 (1973); Robert E. Smith, "Cartels and The Shield of Ignorance," *Journal of International Law and Economics* (June 1973), pp. 53–83; and *Restrictive Business Practices of Multinational Enterprises* (Paris: OECD, 1977).

[27] Barbara Epstein and Richard S. Newfarmer, *International Electrical Association: A Continuing Cartel*, Report for the Committee on Interstate and Foreign Commerce, U.S. House of Representatives (June 1980), p. 12.

Table 11–2. Percentage of Contracts Studied Imposing Restrictions on Licensees, India, Philippines, and Spain

Type of Restriction	India (pre-1964)	India (1964–69)	Philippines (1970)	Spain (1950–73)
Global ban on exports	3.4%	0.9%	19.3%	44.4%
Partial ban on exports	40.0	46.2	13.0	25.9
Tied purchases	14.6	4.7	26.4	30.6
Minimum royalty restriction	5.2	1.2	5.1	N.A.*

* N.A. = not available

Source: United Nations, Conference on Trade and Development, *Restrictive Business Practices* U.N. doc. TD/B/C.2/104/Rev. 1 (1971); *Major Issues Arising from the Transfer of Technology: A Case Study of Spain,* U.N. doc. TD/B/AC.11/17 (1974).

gument—namely, no one really knows what might have been. Moreover, the evils cannot obliterate the considerable benefits of much multinationalism. It appears, then, that we have a mixed bag—some good and some bad—with the mix depending on the individual circumstances and particular issues.[28]

VI. What Policies Govern Multinationals?

Given that multinationals can neither be praised nor pilloried unconditionally, they have provoked ambiguous policy responses. On the one hand, home and host governments have often tried to encourage them with tax inducements, loan quarantees, and insurance protection. On the other hand, multinationals have

[28] For similar conclusions see Bergsten, Horst, and Moran, *op. cit.;* Biersteker, *op. cit.;* Benjamin I. Cohen, *Multinational Firms and Asian Exports* (New Haven: Yale University Press, 1975); I. A. Litvak and C. J. Maule, "Foreign Firms: Social Costs and Benefits in Developing Countries," *Public Policy* (Spring 1975), pp. 167–187.

posed enough of a problem from time to time and place to place that home and host country policies of various sorts have been implemented to control or discourage them. Space limitations force us to focus on this latter type, a focus that is best divided into three categories (a) home country policies, (b) host country policies, and (c) international policies.

A. *Home Country Control Policies*

1. U.S. ANTITRUST
Restrictive business practices and monopolization by U.S. multinationals are to some extent checked by Sections 1 and 2 of the Sherman Act because that Act applies to "commerce . . . with foreign nations" as well as to "commerce among the several states." The same *per se* and *rule of reason* approaches are involved as discussed earlier in Chapters 6 and 7. However, the anticompetitive acts of multinationals can be checked only insofar as they may affect U.S. commerce, where "commerce" is interpreted to include (1) protection of the

American consuming public, and (2) protection of *American* export and investment opportunities. Note: This does *not* mean that the reach of the Sherman Act is limited to conduct that takes place within our borders. When foreign acts have a substantial and foreseeable effect on U.S. commerce, they are subject to U.S. antitrust law regardless of where they occur.[29] Even the acts of foreign firms are covered.

The foreign reach of the Sherman Act is thus not purely elastic. If, for example, a cartel of multinationals has no direct or intended effect on U.S. consumers or U.S. export opportunities, then that cartel would be operating outside the scope of U.S. interests and law. Moreover, the jurisdictional reach of U.S. law has occasionally been abbreviated (a) by successfully argued defenses that the prohibited acts were *compelled* by foreign government laws or pressure,[30] and (b) by the limits of what is called "personal" jurisdiction, which refers to the fact that foreign firms who become defendants can often dodge court appearances, document disclosures, and enforcement penalities because they have nothing solid in the U.S. that authorities can get hold of, no assets in the United States to levy penalties or damages against.

One further gap in the law is the explicit legal exemption provided by the Webb-Pomerene Act (1918) for *export cartels* made up of domestic U.S. firms. This Act permits U.S. producers who properly register their "association" with the FTC to fix prices on their exports, allocate world markets among their members, and collude in other ways that without this exemption would violate the Sherman Act. The Webb-Pomerene exemption does not go so far as to allow export associations (a) to restrain domestic U.S. trade, or (b) to restrain the export trade of any U.S. competitor of the association, or (c) enter into cartel arrangements with foreign producers. But it goes far enough that about 4 per cent of U.S. export trade is in the hands of Webb associations.[31]

Apart from cartelization and monopolization, U.S. law may prohibit an international merger if the circumstances are right. In particular, both parties to the merger must be, according to the Clayton Act, "engaged in commerce," which by interpretation covers less ground than the "affects commerce" standard applied under the Sherman Act.[32] Moreover, there is the additional geographic limitation under Section 7 of the Clayton Act that the illegal merger must lessen competition in a *"section of the country,"* implying a relatively narrow scope for offensive competitive injury.

The foregoing outline of U.S. law in this area may be illuminated by brief reference to a few cases. In *U.S.* v. *Timken Roller Bearing* (1951), for instance, the government successfully prosecuted a Sherman Act Section 1 case against the famous American bearings manufacturer and two foreign co-conspirators.[33] The Court found that this international threesome maintained tight exclusive territories, fixed prices, colluded to exclude outside competition from their respective territories, and entered into still further cartel activities to curb the exports of independent U.S. competitors. One complicating catch to this case was the fact that American Timken had part ownership of the foreign co-conspirators involved. Indeed, the two foreigners—British and French—even shared the Timken name. The cartel agreements were

---

[29] *U.S.* v. *Aluminum Company of America,* 148 F. 2d 416 (2d Cir. 1945); *Steele* v. *Bulova Watch Co.,* 344 U.S. 280 (1952); *Continental Ore Co.* v. *Union Carbide,* 370 U.S. 690 (1962).

[30] *American Banana* v. *United Fruit Company,* 213 U.S. 347 (1909); *Continental Ore* v. *Union Carbide,* 370 U.S. 690 (1962).

[31] Federal Trade Commission, *Webb-Pomerene Associations: A 50-Year Review* (Washington, D.C., 1967), p. 35.

[32] *U.S.* v. *American Building Maintenance Industries,* 422 U.S. 271 (1975).

[33] *Timken Roller Bearing Co.* v. *U.S.,* 341 U.S. 593 (1951).

thus defended as being *intra*company policy rather than *inter*company conspiracy. But the Supreme Court rebuffed this argument saying that "common ownership or control of the contracting corporations does not liberate them from the impact of the antitrust laws."

A monopolization case brought against *United Fruit* (UF, now United Brands) during the 1950s illustrates application of Section 2 of the Sherman Act.[34] UF was first organized by merger back in the days of massive horizontal combinations and William McKinley. Thereafter it accounted for 60–80% of all United States and Canadian banana imports until 1954, when charges of monopolization were filed against it. While in North America UF cultivated the image of "Chiquita," in Central America it became known as "el pulpo" (the octopus). Among other things, it controlled 81% of the combined banana exports of Colombia, Costa Rica, Guatemala, Honduras, and Panama during the early 1950s. At the same time UF owned or controlled 56% of the mature banana acreage in these countries. All told, it controlled 2.7 million acres.

Against this background the Justice Department's accusation of 1954 seems plausible. The charges covered three broad areas: (1) general monopolization, (2) dominant control of land and transportation facilities, and (3) exclusionary and predatory practices. This last category obviously reflects intent, and if the case had gone to trial this accusation would have been more fully documented or disproved. As it stands, the complaint merely alleges in rather broad terms such tactics as engrossing, refusal to sell, and flooding local markets. These charges must have had some foundation, however, for UF agreed in 1958 to a consent decree that, by usual standards, was rather strict. Besides prohibiting UF from engaging further in exclusionary or predatory practices, the decree required UF to create out of its own assets a new competitor capable of importing into the United States a million banana "stems" per year—the rough equivalent of 35% of UF's imports in 1957. A plan for the divestiture was to be submitted by 1966, a plan that later brought the entry of Del Monte.

United States v. *Joseph Schlitz Brewing Company* (1966) illustrates application of Section 7 of the Clayton Act.[35] In 1964, when it was the second-largest brewer in the U.S., Schlitz acquired a controlling interest in Labatt, a large Canadian brewer that in turn owned a U.S. subsidiary, General Brewing Corporation, whose beer sold well in western states. Thus Schlitz gained control of its competitor General through its purchase of foreigner Labatt. Moreover, the merger ended some direct competition between Schlitz and Labatt because Labatt was beginning to market its premium Labatt beer through the General Brewing sales organization. The court found that Labatt "had the desire, the intention and the resourcefulness to enter the United States markets and to make General Brewing a stronger competitor in those markets." Hence, Schlitz's foreign acquisition lessened actual and potential competition in the U.S. in violation of Section 7.[36]

2. U.S. FOREIGN CORRUPT PRACTICES ACT

To meet the problem of questionable payments abroad, Congress passed the Foreign Corrupt Practices Act in 1977. Enforced by the Securities and Exchange Commission, this law threatens jolting fines and prison sentences for corporate officials caught paying bribes abroad. It also regulates corporate accounting practices to dry up secret slush funds because these funds were a major means of bribery in the past.

---

[34] There were section 1 elements as well. *U.S.* v. *United Fruit Company*, CCH Trade Cases para. 68, 941 (1958). For details see U.N. doc TD/B/390, *op cit.*, pp. 47–50.

[35] *U.S.* v. *Jos. Schlitz*, 253 F. Supp. 129 (N.D. Cal. 1966); 385 U.S. 37 (1966).

[36] For a lengthier summary of U.S. foreign antitrust, see Antitrust Division, Department of Justice, *Antitrust Guide for International Operations* (1977).

The law apparently had its intended effect. A General Accounting Office survey of major corporations revealed that officials of 76% of the responding companies thought the law had deterred bribery significantly. Nevertheless, the law may be repealed or greatly relaxed by the time you read this because many in Congress and the Reagan administration are sympathetic to the views of major U.S. companies presently calling for its abolition.[37]

3. U.S. CONTROLS ON TECHNOLOGY TRANSFERS

As in the case of international investments generally, the basic orientation of U.S. policy toward transfers of technology by its multinationals is one of neutrality, neither promoting nor discouraging such transfers. A major exception concerns technology of potential military significance. In cooperation with the Department of Defense, the Department of Commerce regulates the transfer of technology to preserve national security. All forms of transfer are covered, not just the export of machinery or equipment.

4. FOREIGN ANTITRUST POLICY

The home countries of major multinationals outside the U.S.—mainly in Europe and Japan—have antitrust policies that are generally much weaker than those of the U.S. "In any country," Corwin Edwards once wrote, "the relation of business to government is deeply rooted in political, constitutional, and legal traditions, in traditions as to the structure and relation of economic classes, and in traditions of social and religious ethics."[38] As it turns out,

the cultural heritage of no foreign country is equal to that of the U.S. when it comes to honoring competition. As a result, foreign multinationals confront no serious checks to their power or activities in their homelands. Whereas the U.S. has a per se rule banning cartels, foreign authorities tend to take a rule of reason approach, approving cartel activities that can be excused for promoting some perceived benefit such as boosting employment or exports. Whereas the U.S. will attack single-firm dominance because that dominance is in itself considered undesirable, foreign laws permit dominance and attack only serious "abuses" of that dominance.[39] (Although the Reagan administration may change this.)

Where U.S. and foreign laws tend toward equality, they tend toward equal leniency. For example, export cartels win as much approval in Europe as they win in the U.S. under the Webb-Pomerene Act. Moreover, multinationals seem to be more active in those European export cartels than U.S. export cartels. Data from West Germany, for instance, reveal that multinationals participate in 70 per cent of all German export cartels.[40] Because multinationals can belong to such cartels in more than one country they may even be able to influence competition among such export groups.

B. Host Country Control Policies

1. NATIONALIZATION AND DOMESTICATION

As noted above, many foreign countries have antitrust policies. These apply to multinationals operating in those countries as foreigners, but they are not as important as other policies affecting multinationals. One such policy is *nationalization*, in which case the host country's government buys or otherwise captures

[37] The main argument for relaxation is that inability to bribe has caused U.S. companies to loose exports. But as pointed out by N. C. Miller, many past bribes involved no exports whatever or involved U.S. companies competing against each other not against foreign competitors. "In fact," he reports, "there is no documentary evidence that U.S. companies have lost exports as a result of the 1977 law." *Wall Street Journal,* April 30, 1981, p. 22.
[38] Corwin D. Edwards, *Trade Regulations Overseas* (Dobbs Ferry, N.Y.: Oceana Publications, 1966), p. iii.

[39] For a survey see *Comparative Summary of Legislations on Restrictive Business Practices* (Paris: Organization for Economic Co-Operation and Development, 1978).
[40] Committee of Experts on Restrictive Business Practices, *Restrictive Business Practices of Multinational Enterprises* (Paris: OECD, 1977), p. 20.

the multinational's local assets and operations. Such nationalization recently occurred on a very grand scale in the OPEC countries, who used their fantastic oil earnings to buy (through compensated seizure) those parts of Exxon, Mobil, Shell, and their fellow oil giants that were located within their borders. Dozens of billions of dollars in assets changed hands in the process. No less ambitious but much less massive is Malaysia's 20-year plan, begun in 1970, to reduce foreign control of its industry from 60% to 30% by 1990. The government's Pernas agency has been busy buying into or acquiring subsidiaries of multinationals in such key industries as steel, tin, rubber, and palm oil. More examples abound.

Domestication also refers to local ownership policies, but private not government ownership. For many years after World War II, for instance, Japan strictly limited all direct investments, joint ventures, and licensing agreements to the point of denying foreign companies any more than a 49% equity interest in Japanese enterprises and insisting that at least half of any venture's directors and auditors be Japanese nationals. More recently many less developed countries have accepted foreign enterprises on their soil on condition that domestic ownership and management be phased-in over time. And in 1981 Canada ruffled many a multinational's feathers by embarking on a program of domestication and nationalization. Among other things, the government's Foreign Investment Review Agency will help Canadian companies purchase foreign-owned assets in Canada by guaranteeing private loans made for this purpose. The Agency will also conduct "performance evaluations" of foreign-owned companies, threatening those who flunk with the prospect of forced sale to domestic buyers.[41]

---

[41] Herbert Meyer, "Trudeau's War on U.S. Business," *Fortune*, April 6, 1981. For a survey of domestication policies see *National Treatment for Foreign-Controlled Enterprises Established in OECD Countries* (Paris: OECD, 1978).

2. REGULATION OF TRANSFER PRICING

Numerous host countries, including the United States, have attempted to curb abuses of transfer pricing by applying a variety of customs, tax, and restrictive practices laws. The main problem in all these efforts is, of course, to determine how close a multinational's arbitrary intracompany price comes to an appropriate "arm's length" price, when in practice such arm's length prices are often, if not usually, unavailable.[42]

3. REGULATION OF VERTICAL RESTRAINTS

Many governments, those in less developed countries especially, have tried to regulate vertical restraints by screening investment projects and licensing agreements to detect and root out offensive conduct. Mexico's law of 1972 covering technology agreements is typical of this approach, as indicated in the following official summary:

Contracts shall not be approved when they refer to technology freely available in the country; when the price or counterservice is out of proportion to the technology acquired . . . ; when they restrict the research or technological development of the purchaser; when they permit the technology supplier to interfere in the management of the purchaser company or oblige it to use, on a permanent basis, the personnel appointed by the supplier; when they establish the obligation to purchase inputs from the supplier only or to sell the goods produced by the technology imported exclusively to the supplier company; when they prohibit or restrict the export of goods in a way contrary to the country's interest; when they limit the size of production or impose prices on domestic production or on exports of the purchaser; when they prohibit the use of complementary technology; when they oblige the importer to sign exclusive sales or representation

---

[42] For a summary of policies see United Nations Conference on Trade and Development, *Dominant Positions of Market Power of Transnational Corporations: Use of The Transfer Pricing Mechanism*, U.N. doc TD/B/C.2/167 (1978), pp. 28–36.

contracts with the supplier company covering the national territory; when they establish excessively long terms of enforcement, which in no case may exceed a 10-year obligation on the importer company, or when they provide that claims arising from the interpretation or fulfilment of such contracts are to be submitted to the jurisdiction of foreign courts."[43]

An interesting variation on this theme is a code of similar rules established jointly in 1970 by members of the Andean Group (Bolivia, Chile, Colombia, Ecuador, Peru, and Venezuela). Although this code is common to these countries, it is administered by the individual nations separately.

C. International Policies

There are many problems associated with the home and host country policies outlined above.[44] None is more obvious than the problem of mismatched geographic scope. National laws are only national, whereas multinational corporations are multinational or, as some like to say, transnational. National governments, operating individually, have found it difficult to get good information out of multinationals let alone good behavior. Aside from the limits that local jurisdiction imposes, small countries are often limited by their fear that hard-line policies would simply cause multinationals to shift their business to more receptive or more timid countries. Stated differently, countries cannot be very bold if, in pursuit of the benefits multinationals offer, they compete against each other to attract multinationals to their shores.

For these and other reasons, recent years have seen efforts to establish *international*

measures for the control of multinational enterprises. In 1976 a set of "Guidelines for Multinational Enterprises" was negotiated by the Organization of Economic Co-operation and Development, or OECD, which is a loose-knit international organization of two-dozen industrialized countries from North America and Europe plus some others like Japan. In 1980 a branch of the UN, the United Nations Conference on Trade and Development (UNCTAD), completed a ten year effort to devise a code of conduct controlling restrictive business practices in international trade. And as these words are written, UNCTAD is putting the finishing touches on a code of conduct for the transfer of technology. These latter two efforts will probably have been endorsed by the full United Nations by the time you read this.

Although such codes and guidelines have enjoyed widespread official support in *principle*, the actual drafting of them has been a terribly complex process. The members of these international organizations bring widely divergent existing laws, economic interests, political ideologies, and regulatory outlooks to the negotiating table. It is not surprising, then, that the codes these organizations have so far produced tend to be softened with vague terminology and qualifying loopholes. Moreover, compliance with these codes is entirely voluntary.[45] The OECD's guidelines, for instance, cover such topics as information disclosure, competition, transfer pricing, employee relations, and technology transfer. On competition the guidelines state that:

Enterprises should. . . .
1. refrain from actions which would adversely affect competition in the relevant market by

[43] Government of Mexico, *Law on Transfer of Technology and The Use and Exploitation of Patents and Trademarks,* 1972, forward, p. 4.

[44] See, e.g., D. F. Greer, "Control of Terms and Conditions for International Transfers of Technology to Developing Countries," in *Competition in International Business: Law and Policy on Restrictive Practices* (New York: Columbia University Press, 1981), pp. 41–83.

[45] For discussions see Joel Davidow, "Multinationals, Host Governments and Regulation of Restrictive Business Practices," *Columbia Journal of World Business* (Summer 1980), pp. 14–19; L. R. Primoff, "International Regulation of Multinational Corporations and Business—The United Nations Takes Aim," 11, *Journal of International Law and Economics* (1977), pp. 287–324.

abusing a dominant position of market power, by means of, for example,

    a. anti-competitive acquisitions,

    b. predatory behavior toward competitors,

    c. unreasonable refusals to deal,

    d. anti-competitive abuse of [patents],

    e. discriminatory (i.e., unreasonably differentiated) pricing . . .

2. allow purchasers, distributors and licensees freedom to resell, export, purchase and develop their operations consistent with law, trade conditions, the need for specialization and sound commerical practice;

3. refrain from participating in or otherwise purposely strengthening the restrictive effects of international or domestic cartels or restrictive agreements which adversely affect or eliminate competition and which are not generally or specifically accepted under applicable national or international legislation . . .[46]

Understandably, the multinationals probably do not take these international efforts very seriously. The multinationals should nevertheless heed the words of Oscar Schachter who likened these efforts to the efforts of a cross-eyed javelin thrower: "They hold only slight promise and they may even be laughable, but they bear close watching."[47]

Summary

Multinational corporations have been around a long time, but in the past three decades they have sprouted and spread more quickly and widely than ever before. Collectively they now account for very big chunks of the free-world's economic activity, and individually the largest among them—like Exxon and GM—are bigger even than most of the world's countries. From the viewpoint of the multinationals themselves, North America, Europe, and Japan constitute their prime markets, mainly because of the healthy economic prosperity of those lands. From the viewpoint of host countries, however, the multinationals appear most awesome to the less developed countries, because their economies tend to be much more dominated by multinationals than those of advanced countries.

Although the immense size of the multinationals stems partly from their transnational diversification, it also derives from their prominence in specific national markets. The large market shares of U.S. multinationals in Latin America speak tellingly to this effect, not to mention the supremacy of companies like IBM in Europe and elsewhere.

Four explanations for multinationalism are particularly pertinent to our inquiry. (1) Backward integration to extract distant resources motivated many of the older multinationals, particularly the oil companies. (2) Firms possessing monopolistic advantages at home often deploy those same advantages abroad to their good profit. These advantages include technological wizardry, marketing prowess, and economies of scale. (3) Foreign investment may substitute for exports when foreign tariffs inhibit those exports. (4) Comparative advantage also helps to explain some multinationalism.

Although multinationals frequently bring benefits to home and host countries alike, they also raise serious problems. Given our interest in policy, we have focused most intently on the negative side of the ledger, which lists such items as monopoly power, transfer pricing, restrictive business practices (both horizontal and vertical), inappropriate technology, and "questionable" payments.

Policies governing these problems may be pigeonholed by source. Among home countries, the U.S. is most important. Its limited international application of a relatively strict antitrust policy—covering cartels (other than export car-

[46] *International Investment and Multinational Enterprises* (Paris: OECD, 1979 revised edition), p. 18–19.

[47] Address to Columbia Conference on Competition in International Business, Nov. 9, 1979.

tels), monopolization, and mergers among other things—is alone quite notable. Add to this the government's attempt to squash bribery and you have a peerless record. Among host countries, policies of nationalization and domestication are most notorious because they strike at the roots of multinationalism. Less widely publicized but often no less significant are host country attempts at conduct control—that is, regulations enforced through registration and review of agreements with foreign firms.

Finally, our review of international policies reveals a fledgling effort to curb the abuses of multinationals through moral suasion. Voluntary codes of conduct have emerged from diplomatic circles, codes formally endorsed by several international agencies—OECD, UNCTAD, and UN. Thus far these efforts have delivered nary a jolt to the multinationals, but they bear watching.

Questions and Exercises for Chapter 11

1. As measured by share of national markets, multinationals thrive best under what conditions? When are they less prominent?

2. Among the several economic motives for multinationalism, which seem most anticompetitive for host country industry or worldwide industry and which seem most procompetitive? Explain.

3. Why, in light of the motives for multinationalism, are most of the biggest multinationals based in North America and Europe?

4. Refute the assertion that, from a social point of view, multinationals are economically undesirable, both at home and abroad.

5. Why might host countries be less than delighted hosts for multinationals?

6. What are the strengths and the weaknesses of U.S. antitrust policy in dealing with multinationals (from the U.S. viewpoint)?

7. What is the most potent policy weapon of host countries and why? Does use of this weapon incur any economic costs in the way of lost benefits?

8. Identify and explain the Foreign Corrupt Practices Act.

9. What international policy steps have been taken? What are their strengths and weaknesses?

Part III

Information Policy

"Remember—we make no claims for Quill's pills, so if they do anything for you, think of what a pleasant surprise it will be."

Source: The Wall Street Journal. Used by permission of Cartoon Features Syndicate.

Chapter 12

Product Standardization and Information Disclosure

Informed consumers are essential to the fair and efficient functioning of a free-market economy.
—Congress of the United States
(Fair Packaging and Labeling Act)

During half-time of the 1981 Super Bowl game, Schlitz beer conducted a live TV "taste test." One hundred confirmed Michelob drinkers quaffed Schlitz and Michelob from unlabeled ceramic mugs. When dramatically asked to choose which beer they liked best, 50% of these "blinded" tasters pulled the switch for Schlitz and 50% picked Michelob. During playoff games a few weeks earlier, similar live taste tests of two hundred loyal Budweiser drinkers showed 48% choosing Schlitz over Bud. Claiming triumph, Schlitz later took out full-page ads in college newspapers to spread the news that half these loyal Bud and Michelob drinkers "preferred Schlitz over their own beer."

These tests were legitimate. But their true meaning was a bit different than the impression left by Schlitz. That is to say, most all American beers taste alike, a fact confirmed by numerous blind taste tests more carefully controlled than the Schlitz tests.[1] Given two beers that taste

alike, and given the law of averages, folks forced to decide between the two will normally choose 50–50. Its like a coin toss. Note, for instance, that no loyal Schlitz drinkers were included in the half-time TV tests because a Schlitz spokesman would have had to explain why roughly half of those Schlitz drinkers "preferred" Michelob or Bud.

Although most beers taste alike, people eagerly pay more for some brands than others. They are swayed by brand image; they express strong loyalties based on little more than labels and advertising. In short, buyers in this market apparently lack full knowledge, a problem that afflicts many other markets as well. The several consequences of such ignorance can often be serious economically. First, and most obviously, *inefficiency* in buying can be costly to consumers. Second, buyer ignorance can *stifle price*

---

[1] See, e.g., R. I. Allison and K. P. Uhl, "Influence of Beer Brand Identification on Taste Perception," *Journal of Marketing Research* (August 1964), pp. 36–39; S. H. Rewoldt, J. D. Scott, and M. R. Warshaw, *Introduction to Marketing Management* (Homewood, Ill.: Richard D. Irwin, Inc., 1973), pp. 177–190.

and quality competition among sellers. Third, this ignorance may encourage *wasteful forms of competition* such as noninformative, excess advertising.

The purpose of this chapter is (1) to examine this problem and its several consequences, and (2) to review two broad classes of policy solutions that can be called *standardization* and *information disclosure.* These policies operate on the principle of revelation. They are supposed to *educate* consumers, to *aid* them in making comparisons, and to *reveal* relevant product characteristics.

Other policies besides standardization and disclosure relate to the problem of buyer knowledge. We should therefore distinguish between the policies of immediate concern and two other broad groups of policies by listing all three together:

A. Forced *standardization* and *disclosure* of information (for example, contents labeling and grade rating).
B. *Prohibitions* against unfair and deceptive practices (such as bans on misleading advertising).
C. Direct regulation of *product features* and *production processes* (such as safety).

Whereas (A) the disclosure policies of the present chapter are generally *pre*scriptive and positive, policies (B) governing deceptive practices, which are discussed in the next chapter, are generally *pro*scriptive and negative. They prohibit misleading conduct but they do not usually require sellers to reveal information or aid consumers. Policies (C) that directly regulate product quality, efficacy, and safety are covered in Chapters 20 and 21. Under them, businessmen seem to be confronted with as many "thou shalts" as "thou shalt nots." In these cases the government attempts to protect consumers from unsafe, impure, and ineffective products not by informing consumers of these dangers (although that is part of the policy) but by di-rectly regulating product features and production processes. The consumer is, in other words, denied a free choice in these instances. This last approach is obviously the most severe of the policy options, and it is, accordingly, based on justifications that go well beyond buyer ignorance. The issue of safety, for instance, raises problems of external costs—thus its postponement to later chapters.

A policy that defies classification in any of the above categories is the issuance and enforcement of trademarks. In some ways, though, trademarks are a part of the problem, not the solution, and so they are taken up in this chapter.

I. The Problem

A. Buyer Knowledge

Under the ideal circumstances of perfect competition, reviewed in Chapter 2, it was assumed that all buyers pursued their goal of welfare optimum with the aid of perfect knowledge. This implies that each buyer:

1. Is an expert buyer, readily able to appraise product quality objectively.
2. Has a well-defined set of stable taste preferences or purchase requirements.
3. Is aware of all purchase alternatives and the terms offered by sellers.
4. Is able to calculate accurately the marginal gains and losses of choosing one combination of commodities over another to obtain the highest possible benefit for any given expenditure.

If all buyers met this description, it would be very difficult for sellers to sell them goods they did not really want, to exaggerate the quality of one brand over another, or to charge outrageous prices for goods more cheaply available elsewhere.

The key question is, then, *what determines buyer knowledge or the lack thereof?* The answer comes in two parts—**buyer character** and **product type.** For convenience we can divide all buyers into two broad groups: (1) professional business buyers and (2) household consumers. Products and services, on the other hand, may be divided into (1) search goods, (2) experience goods, and (3) credence goods.

Among buyers, business buyers come about as close to being highly knowledgeable and fully informed as one could normally expect. Indeed, professional purchasing agents of large firms specialize in buying such broad categories of goods and services as raw materials, transportation, insurance, heavy machinery, and office supplies. Moreover, they often have the assistance of engineers, scientists, financial wizards, and other experts who conduct tests, arrange favorable credit terms, guide negotiations, and the like—all with an eye to maximizing profits. Perhaps the most important reason for this highly developed expertise is the ability of professional buyers to spread the costs of obtaining this expertise over a large volume of purchases. Thus, their absolute total dollar costs of purchasing may be huge, but on a per-unit basis these costs will be small.

On the other hand, we have the typical American householder, who, by comparison, is a 91 pound weakling. Although not a moron, he or she runs a very small-scale operation. Of course, assistance from the spouse or helpmate may be offered, but it probably hinders as often as it helps in deciding which breakfast cereal is the most nutritious per dollar cost, which TV set is the most dependable, which laundry detergent gives the "whitest white," which bank offers the best loan terms, and so on.

Lest we overstate the ignorance and gullibility of the typical household consumer, we hasten to add that product type will also determine the degree to which the purchase decision is well informed. In the case of *search goods*—

like fresh fruits and vegetables, raw meat, apparel, shoes, jewelry, and maybe furniture as well—the consumer can judge on the basis of fairly simple inspection *prior* to actual purchase whether a given article is wholesome, handsomely styled, properly fitting, and reasonably priced for the level of quality it represents. At least in these instances, the consumer typically acts in a relatively well-informed manner, being much less sensitive to the blandishments of exhortative advertising, the attractiveness of package coloring, or the image conveyed by brand name.

In contrast, *experience goods* are those whose utility can be fully assessed only *after* purchase. To evaluate brands of bottled beer accurately, for example, consumers obviously have to buy alternative brands in order to experience their taste. And even after purchase, this experience with beer may not, as we have seen, be so scientifically expressed as to be very informative. The same holds for detergents, automobiles, appliances, cake mixes, and related products. It is largely the presence of hidden qualities and inadequate experience that makes these goods more unfathomable than search goods.

Finally, *credence goods* are those that cannot be fully evaluated through inspection, or normal use, or even simple study of general information. One's assessment of their value is either impossible or especially costly in relation to any additional information obtained. These goods include various drugs, cosmetics, medical devices, vitamin supplements, and oil additives whose performance is by nature rather "iffy." They may or may not work depending on the circumstances, so you can never be certain if they really do work. Inevitably, consumers are particularly error prone when it comes to credence goods.

Of course it is an oversimplification to categorize goods and services in this way. Goods and services most commonly comprise various blends of search, experience, and credence *qualities.* That is, search qualities are known before purchase, experience qualities become known costlessly after purchase, and credence qualities are expensive or impossible for individual consumers to judge even after purchase.[2]

From the foregoing we may derive a sneak preview of the purpose of standardization and disclosure policies: They should (1) make consumers more like professional buyers and (2) convert experience and credence qualities into search qualities. The freshness of milk, for example, is an experience quality unless plainly disclosed on the carton, in which case it then becomes a search quality. Educating consumers on the proper use of such disclosures gives them the powers of a professional.

Before delving into policy more deeply, however, we must first acknowledge more explicitly the adverse effects of buyer ignorance—(1) inefficiency, (2) imperfect competition, and (3) promotional waste. For this purpose simplification has great pedagogical value, so in the following we shall often speak of search and experience *goods* rather than qualities. Moreover, we shall forgo further discussion of credence qualities.

B. Consequence 1: Consumer Inefficiency

Aside from the high frequency of consumer complaints, there are several empirical measures revealing substantial inefficiency due to inaccuracies in consumer buying behavior. Self-admission is one. When asked whether "advertising leads people to buy things they don't

need or can't afford," 80% of all consumers surveyed say "yes."[3] Another measure is the degree to which price correlates with quality across brands within a given product class. If consumers were knowledgeable, low quality could sell only at low prices whereas high quality could justifiably command high prices. Thus a high positive correlation (maximum possible being +1.0) between price and quality for a given product would indicate efficient buying behavior, whereas a low correlation (approaching zero or even turning negative) would signal that something is seriously amiss.

Every study yet done of this type has found surprisingly low correlations, with many products producing negative coefficients. P. Riesz found an average correlation of only +.092 for forty packaged food products.[4] M. Friedman corroborates this result with an average correlation of +.09 for nine packaged food products.[5] R. T. Morris and C. S. Bronson's study of forty-eight diverse products (electric appliances, detergents, and tires included) produced a mean correlation of +.29.[6] Alfred Oxenfeldt's computation of correlations for thirty-five products in 1949 is particularly instructive because his sample included numerous search goods while the other studies were essentially confined to experience goods. Oxenfeldt's results for the eight products with highest correlation and the eight products with lowest correlation are presented in Table 12–1. Notice that those with highest

[2] For further discussion of these qualities see R. H. Holton, "Consumer Behavior, Market Imperfections and Public Policy," in *Industrial Organization and Development*, edited by Markham and Papanek (Boston: Houghton Mifflin, 1970), pp. 102–115; Phillip Nelson "Information and Consumer Behavior," *Journal of Political Economy* (March/April 1970), 311–319; M. R. Darby and E. Karni, "Free Competition and the Optimal Amount of Fraud," *Journal of Law and Economics* (April 1973), pp. 67–88.

[3] R. A. Bauer and Stephen A. Greyser, *Advertising in America: The Consumer View* (Boston: Division of Research, Graduate School of Business Administration, Harvard University, 1968), p. 71. See also *Advertising Age* (26 July 1976), p. 20.

[4] Peter C. Riesz, "Price-Quality Correlations for Packaged Food Products," *Journal of Consumer Affairs* (Winter 1979), pp. 236–247.

[5] Monroe Friedman, "Quality and Price Considerations in Rational Decision Making," *Journal of Consumer Affairs* (Summer 1967), pp. 13–23.

[6] R. T. Morris and C. S. Bronson, "The Chaos of Competition Indicated by Consumer Reports," *Journal of Marketing* (July 1969), pp. 26–34.

Table 12–1. Coefficients of Rank Correlation Between Brand Quality
Score and Brand Price

Product	Number of Brands Tested	Coefficient of Rank Correlation
Top eight products		
Boys' blouses (shirt type)	8	0.82
Men's hats	30	0.76
Women's slips (knitted)	28	0.75
Mechanical pencils	26	0.71
Women's slips (other than knit)	67	0.70
Men's shoes	52	0.70
Diapers, gauze	11	0.57
Children's shoes	8	0.55
Bottom eight products		
Yellow, white, and spice mixes	9	−0.11
Mayonnaise	25	−0.13
Men's hosiery (wool)	9	−0.20
Vacuum cleaners	17	−0.26
Biscuit mixes	10	−0.46
Hot roll mixes	3	−0.50
Waffle mixes	3	−0.50
Gingerbread mixes	6	−0.81

Source: Alfred R. Oxenfeldt, "Consumer Knowledge: Its Measurement and Extent," *Review of Economics and Statistics* (October 1950), p. 310.

correlations are all search goods, whereas seven of the eight lowest could be considered experience goods (the possible exception being men's hosiery). This suggests that consumers are more adept at buying search goods than experience goods (something that correlates well with common sense).

A clearer notion of the monetary costs of consumer errors—and the monetary benefits achieved by their elimination—can be gained through brief theoretical consideration of demand curves. In essence, benefits arise from *error avoidance*—errors of commission and omission.[7]

[7] The following draws heavily from S. Peltzman, "An Evaluation of Consumer Protection Legislation: The 1962 Drug Amendments," *Journal of Political Economy* (Sept./ Oct. 1973) pp. 1049–1091; T. McGuire, R. Nelson, and T.

An **error of commission** occurs when the buyer makes a purchase on the basis of an excessively favorable prepurchase assessment of the acquired good. In other words, the buyer gets not what he thinks he is getting but something less. The monetary loss of making such an error (or the gain from avoiding same) is illustrated in Figure 12–1 as the shaded area *ABC*. The demand curve *DACD* refers to what demand

Spavins, "Comment on the Peltzman Paper," *Journal of Political Economy* (June 1975), pp. 655–661; M. R. Darby and E. Karni, "Free Competition and the Optimal Amount of Fraud," *Journal of Law and Economics* (April 1973), pp. 67–88; George Akerlof, "The Market for 'Lemons': Quality Uncertainty and the Market Mechanism," *Quarterly Journal of Economics* (August 1970), pp. 488–500; and R. H. Nelson, "The Economics of Honest Trade Practices," *Journal of Industrial Economics* (June 1976), pp. 281–293.

Figure 12–1. The Monetary Loss from an Error of Commission

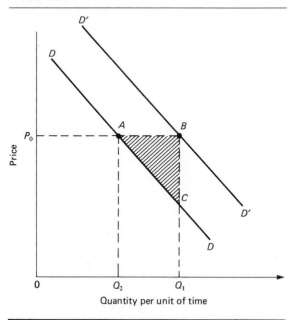

with full knowledge. The monetary loss from making such an error is illustrated in Figure 12–2 by the area GHE. In this case the demand curve $D'GED'$ depicts what the demand would be like if the commodity were correctly evaluated, whereas DHD represents the erroneously pessimistic demand of buyers who underestimate the value of the product. Given a constant price P_0, a corrective movement from the poorly chosen amount Q_1 to the proper amount Q_2 requires an additional cash outlay equal to area Q_1HEQ_2. But the move yields a greater addition to total benefit, indicated by Q_1GEQ_2. Subtracting the added cost from this added benefit yields a *net* benefit of HGE, which in technical jargon is the amount of "consumer's surplus" the consumer misses out on when he errs in the direction of omission. It may now be seen that errors of omission lead to *under*al-

would be like if the good were correctly evaluated, whereas $D'BD'$ depicts an erroneously optimistic level of demand. The latter lies to the right of the former since the uninformed buyer wants to buy more at each possible price than he would if he were fully informed. Thus, given a fixed price equal to OP_0 (or constant marginal costs of supply indicated by P_0AB), the consumer buys an excess equal to the difference between Q_1 and Q_2, that is, $Q_1 - Q_2$. The amount he pays for this excess is the area Q_2ABQ_1, price times the excess quantity. However, the *true value* of the extra units amounts only to Q_2ACQ_1, or the trapezoid below A and C. Thus, the difference between dollar outlay Q_2ABQ_1 and true value Q_2ACQ_1 is ABC, the net loss.

Errors of omission are the opposite. They occur when the buyer buys *less* than he would

Figure 12–2. The Monetary Loss from an Error of Omission

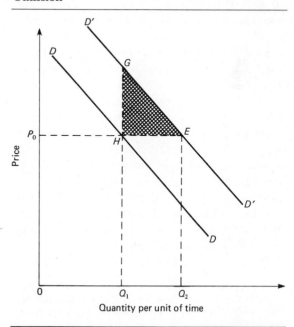

locations of resources to the particular products or brands, whereas errors of commission lead to *over*allocations to the chosen products or brands. Needless to say, both forms of error are *mis*allocations, and they often represent opposite sides of the same coin.

C. Consequence 2: Imperfect Competition

In the above analysis it was assumed that buyer knowledge would not affect overall price level. But the eradication of errors may enhance competition among sellers because they then find that their competitive efforts to reduce price or improve quality are rewarded by knowledgeably favorable consumer responses. That is to say, buyer ignorance reduces the ability of consumers to identify the best buy, and competition to provide best buys is therefore stifled.

As regards knowledge of price, for instance, A. Maurizi and T. Kelly found that posting gasoline prices on signs big enough to be visible to passing motorists has a significant tendency to reduce gasoline prices below what they would otherwise be. Their 1970 comparison of New York City, where there was no price posting, and Los Angeles, where price posting was very widespread, illustrates the point. Prices in New York would have been .73 cents per gallon lower for regular gas and 1.50 cents per gallon lower for premium gas (yielding a total saving of $25.4 million) if price posting in New York had been as extensive as it was in Los Angeles.[8] Moreover, Maurizi and Kelly estimate that posting by all gasoline stations on a nationwide basis would have saved consumers at least $525 million overall in 1975.

One obvious policy implication from this study of gasoline prices is that government should *not prohibit* private, voluntary dissemination of price information. The reason New York City experienced no gas price posting was because of just such a local prohibition. John Cady's analysis of prescription retail drug prices for the effect of state restrictions on retail drug price advertising confirms the point. Comparing retail prices of ten representative prescription drugs across states, he found that legal restrictions on price advertising *raised* prices an average of 4.3%, with the highest differential being 9.1% for one sampled product.[9]

More generally, casual observation tells us that competition to produce low tar and nicotine cigarettes has been especially vigorous since consumer information on these factors has burgeoned through ad disclosure. Similarly, the drive to improve gasoline mileage in cars cannot be totally unrelated to the public's recently improved information on mileage. Consumer knowledge also seems to reduce the adverse competitive impact of exhortative advertising. For *experience* goods like detergent, beer, soda pop, breakfast cereals, and the like, there is a very strong positive correlation between monopoly profits and the intensity of advertising outlay. On the other hand, for *search* goods and services, such a positive relationship is either slight or nonexistent. Indeed, there is some evidence indicating that to the extent search qualities prevail, advertising tends to be *pro*competitive because of price advertising rather than *anti*competitive.[10]

D. Consequence 3: Waste and Misdirection

When buyers are *well informed*—because of either individual knowledge or search quali-

---

[8] Alex Maurizi and Thom Kelly, *Prices and Consumer Information* (Washington, D.C.: American Enterprise Institute, 1978), p. 40.

[9] John F. Cady, "An Estimate of the Price Effects of Restrictions on Drug Price Advertising," *Economic Inquiry* (December 1976), pp. 493–510.

[10] See Douglas F. Greer, *Industrial Organization and Public Policy* (New York: Macmillan, 1980), pp. 389–392.

ties in the products they buy—advertising tends to be more informative and less wastefully intensive than when buyers are poorly informed. As regards information content, for instance, anyone who has leafed through *Mining Magazine* or *Electrical Review* will conclude that advertising directed toward professional buyers is largely informative, revealing performance specifications, prices, guarantees, and the like. "Because the audience for such advertising is expert," Corwin Edwards explains, "the characteristic advertisement in such publications is of a kind that might persuade an expert: it provides information, avoids garbled treatment of facts, and addresses itself to the reader's intelligence."[11]

This obviously does not hold for most consumer-aimed advertising, which is replete with fear appeals, sexual enticements, worthless endorsements, meaningless jingles (like "Coke is the real thing"), puffery, and other blatant trappings of exhortation and persuasion. But your own experience probably indicates there is a substantial variance across products and services in this respect. Where more search qualities are present, the advertising tends to be more informative. Grocery retailing, for instance, could be considered more of a search service than auto transmission repair, and the advertising of the former is much more informative. Confirming such casual observations from your own experience, scholarly studies indicate that advertisements for most apparel, footwear, household furnishings, and retailing are much more informative than advertisements for soft drinks, beer, cigarettes, detergents, prepared foods, and toiletries.[12]

A plausible explanation for this difference between search good and experience good advertising rests on the prepurchase evaluation that can be made of search goods. If the advertised properties of search goods stray too far from their actual properties, consumers are readily able to detect the discrepancies and penalize the promoters with refusals to buy. Advertisers of these products therefore feel constrained to use an informative approach.

As regards advertising intensity, producer search goods (bought by professional buyers) seem to have the lowest advertising to sales ratios of all products, averaging about 0.3 per cent of sales. Consumer experience goods rest at the other end of the spectrum, with advertising intensities high enough—often 4% to 15%—to arouse suspicions that resources are sometimes wasted on the promotion of such products. Between these two extremes we find producer experience goods and consumer search goods with advertising-to-sales ratios averaging approximately 1 per cent.[13]

We thus arrive at a rather interesting paradox: advertising intensity and information content are *inversely* related. Generally speaking, the greater the dollar outlay relative to product sales, the lower is the information content of the advertising messages. Furthermore, in terms of adequate amounts and efficient applications of buyer knowledge, it seems that advertising is *least* informative where the need for information is greatest (consumer experience goods), whereas it is most informative where the need for information is least (producer search goods). This paradox makes it clear that the purpose of advertising is *not* to inform buyers; it is to gain sales by influencing buyers. It also points out the potential need for public information policies (insofar as their benefits exceed their costs, neither of which, unfortunately, are easily quantified).

[11] C. D. Edwards, "Advertising and Competition," *Business Horizons* (February 1968), p. 60.

[12] Bauer and Greyser, *op. cit.,* pp. 296–297.

[13] There are, of course, many other variables affecting interindustry differences in advertising intensity. See, e.g., M. M. Metwally, "Product Categories that Advertise Most," *Journal of Advertising Research* (February 1980), pp. 25–31.

II. Trademarks

The next question is: what policies can boost buyer knowledge and thereby curb the adverse consequences of ignorance? Incredible though it may seem in light of what has been said thus far, one such policy is the issuance and enforcement of **trademarks.** To see this more clearly, the reader might try imagining what the world would be like without trademarks. Without them how could *Consumer Reports* tell us in March 1981 that Panasonic microwave ovens were better than the Sunbeam brand? Or how could a friend advise us that Levi's trousers are a good buy? How could we be sure that, having been wholly satisfied with an Arrow shirt, we could ever get another one from the same manufacturer? How could we sue the Coca-Cola Company for damages if we found a dead mouse in one of its soda bottles? In other words, it can be argued that, to the extent consumers do learn from experience and to the extent they do learn to buy what they like (rather than merely like what they buy), trademarks can minimize *repeated* errors merely by identifying the producers of good, bad, or mediocre goods and services. Similarly, trademarks are necessary to spreading an individual's or a testing agency's specific knowledge to others. And, finally, in extreme cases of error, individual producers may be held legally as well as economically accountable for their share in any disaster. As Richard Caves and William Murphy have so aptly put it, "By offering the seller's good name as hostage, the trademark provides the buyer with cheap information and assurance about product quality."[14]

Despite these considerable social benefits, the trademark laws as they stand also involve specific *social costs.* Trademark policies are based on the assumption that trademarks serve primarily to identify the *origin* of goods, and that the purposes of such identification are twofold:[15]

1. Protection is furnished the seller from "unfair" competition through the infringement of his mark by an imitator or poacher.
2. Protection is furnished buyers who might be deceived into purchasing the goods of one seller in the belief that the goods are another's.

Unfortunately, this emphasis on origin adds substantially to the social costs of the trademark system without contributing to its social benefits. Benefits derive from the *identification of a given level of quality,* not from the identification of a given origin. Identification of origin on an exclusive, perpetual, and carefully protected basis, as is now practiced, may serve *indirectly* to identify a given level of quality. But it also often facilitates the creation of substantial market power, power that translates into social costs, power achieved by exhortative advertising and other means of questionable social worth. As suggested earlier, the available evidence indicates that, when quality guarantees or quality identifications are established independently of trademarks (by professional buyers themselves, by government grade rating and standardization, by consumers search shopping for easily analyzable goods, and so on), monopoly power cannot be based on trademark differentiation and advertising, and burden-

---

[14] R. E. Caves and W. F. Murphy II, "Franchising: Firms, Markets, and Intangible Assets," *Southern Economic Journal* (April 1976), pp. 572–586. It may be worth noting that even the Russians use trademarks: "This makes it easy to establish the actual producer of the product in case it is necessary to call him to account for the poor quality of his goods. For this reason it is one of the most effective weapons in the battle for the quality of products . . ."

M. I. Goldman, "Product Differentiation and Advertising: Some Lessons From Soviet Experience," *Journal of Political Economy* (August 1960), pp. 346–357. Note too, however, that communists are not always "called to account" in the same manner as capitalists.

[15] E. W. Kintner and J. L. Lahr, *An Intellectual Property Law Primer* (New York: Macmillan Publishing Co., 1975) p. 250.

some social costs are avoided. The effects of the trademark system are therefore negative when (1) trademarks (and the persuasive advertising promoting them) provide the sole or major source of quality identification for the product *and* (2) grants of exclusive trademark use protect the goodwill (or monopoly) profits that attach to trademarks under such circumstances. Corrective policies could therefore be focused on one or both of the following objectives:

1. Permit trademarks to identify or guarantee quality but remove the rights of exclusivity and perpetuity currently awarded them.
2. Establish quality identifications and guarantees that are *independent* of the trademark system.

With respect to the first, nonexclusive trademark use, Edward Chamberlin once suggested a policy that would permit brand imitation as long as quality was maintained.[16] Such a policy would, of course, focus the law on identifying quality instead of origin. But this policy is rather radical, and its adoption is unlikely. Still, in some ways it would be only a small step beyond the rapidly spreading practice of franchising, whereby many producers are licensed to use the same trademark. Indeed, franchising has grown to such a point in the United States that it is no longer accurate to say that trademarks always identify origin. Among the many trademarks that do not identify origin are McDonald's, Mister Donut, Abbey Rents, Avis, Fruit of the Loom, BVD, Serta, and Arnold Palmer Dry Cleaning Centers.[17] In such instances a given level of quality (not necessarily high qual-

ity) is assured, since under United States law the owner of a trademark may license others to use the mark only as long as the licensor controls the "nature and quality" of the goods or services offered by the licensee-franchisee. If the owner of the mark does not exercise "control," the mark may be freely imitated by competitors.

With respect to the second possible focus of policy, quality identifications and guarantees that are independent of the trademark system, regulations abound. They merit the entire section that follows.

III. Standardization and Disclosure

As suggested by the heading "Standardization and Disclosure," information or identification policies other than trademarks may be divided into two categories.[18] And, as suggested by the items listed for each category, the ultimate purpose of these policies is to assist buyers—particularly consumers—in avoiding errors:

A. Standardization for easier price comparisons.
   1. Simplified quantity labeling.
   2. Uniform sizes.
   3. Price standardization, e.g., "unit" pricing.
   4. Warranty standards.
B. Quality disclosures.
   1. Ingredient disclosure.
   2. Open dating of perishables.
   3. Specific performance disclosures.
   4. Grade rating.

[16] Edward H. Chamberlin, *The Theory of Monopolistic Competition*, 8th ed. (Harvard University Press, 1962), p. 273; see also M. L. Greenhut, "Free Entry and the Trade Mark-Trade Name Product," *Southern Economic Journal* (October 1957), pp. 170–181.

[17] Standards of scholarship require that I identify the origin of these examples: Donald N. Thompson, *Franchise Operations and Antitrust* (Lexington, Mass.: Heath Lexington Books, 1971) pp. 5–27.

[18] This division and much else in this section owe their origin to David Hemenway, *Industrywide Voluntary Product Standards* (Cambridge, Mass.: Ballinger Publishing Co., 1975).

Standardization policies typically promote simplification or uniformity or both. The distinction between simplification and uniformity may be seen by an easy example. Suppose ten brick manufacturers were each making the same 50 kinds of brick. Since each producer offered a full range of 50 kinds, each firm's bricks would match those of the others and there would be perfect **uniformity** among sellers. With 50 varieties, however, the situation would not be simple. **Simplification** could be achieved if these firms agreed to cut down the number of their offerings to, say, 12 common types. This would yield a combination of simplification and uniformity—ten firms, each producing the same 12 kinds of brick. Alternatively, simplification could be achieved at the expense of uniformity. If each of the ten brick makers cut back their offerings to four *unique* items, with no one producing the same item, uniformity would disappear. The total, industry-wide variety, however, would have been simplified from 50 down to 40. As far as buyer errors are concerned, uniformity facilitates the comparison of different seller's offerings, whereas simplification may help to keep buyers' minds from boggling.

Quality disclosures are quite different. They sharpen the buyer's awareness of "better" or "worse." For example, all mattress manufacturers may uniformly adhere to a few simple sizes—twin, double, queen, and king. But this says nothing about the range of quality (and some mattresses may feel as if they were made from 50 kinds of brick). Disclosure of ingredients might be helpful in this case, and grade rating would be even more helpful. Policies revealing ingredients and grades may thus be considered quality disclosures.

Before we take a detailed look at specific policies, one more preliminary point needs attention: why must we rely on the government to elevate consumer knowledge in these ways? What is wrong with relying on free *private* enterprise? If information is a desirable "good," ought not profit opportunities abound for anyone supplying information? The answer to all these questions is, in a word, *imperfections*. The nature of the commodity in question—information—is such that imperfections prevent its optimal provision by private enterprise.

One imperfection is particularly interesting. Buyers of information cannot be truly *well informed* about the information they want to buy. If they were, they would not then need to buy the information.[19] In other words, the seller of information cannot let potential buyers meticulously examine his product prior to sale lest he thereby give it away free. Buyers of information therefore do not know the value of the product they seek (information) until after they buy it. They are consequently vulnerable to errors of commission and omission. Only with objective, outside, nonmarket assistance can they overcome this handicap.

A. Standardization for Easy Price Comparisons

1. SIMPLIFIED QUANTITY LABELING

Try this little test on yourself. Which box of detergent is the best buy—25 "jumbo" ounces for 53¢; 1½ pounds for 49¢; or 27½ "full" ounces for 55¢? Prior to the Fair Packaging and Labeling Act of 1966 (FPLA) grocery shoppers took, and failed, real-life tests like this more often than they probably care to remember. In 1965, for instance, a selected sample of 33 married women who were students or wives of students at Eastern Michigan University were asked to pick the most economical package for each of 20 supermarket products. Despite their above-average intelligence and their stimulated attention, these women typically

[19] Kenneth Arrow, "Economic Welfare and the Allocation of Resources to Invention," in *The Rate and Direction of Inventive Activity: Economic and Social Factors* (New York: National Bureau of Economic Research, 1962).

spent 9.14% more on these groceries than they should have.[20] Small wonder they erred, what with the commingling of weight and fluid volumes for the same products; the use of meaningless adjectives, such as "jumbo" and "full"; the frequent appearance of fractional quantity units; and the designation of servings as "small," "medium," and "large," without any common standard of reference.

The Fair Packaging and Labeling Act tidied things up a bit by providing:

1. The net quantity be stated in a uniform and prominent location on the package.
2. The net quantity be clearly expressed in a unit of measure appropriate to the product.
3. The net quantity of a "serving" must be stated if servings are mentioned.

This may not seem like much, but early and final versions of FPLA were vigorously opposed by business interests. It took five years of congressional hearings and a persistent effort on the part of the late Senator Hart of Michigan to get FPLA passed. Some opponents claimed that it was "a power grab based on the fallacious concepts that the consumer is Casper Milquetoast, business is Al Capone, and government is Superman."[21] Their opposition was based on what they apparently thought was a more accurate concept—the housewife as Superwoman. "We suggest," argued the editor of *Food Field Reporter*, "that the housewife . . . should be expected to take the time to divide fractionalized weights into fractionalized prices in order to determine the 'best buy.' "[22] Still others worried about what would happen to the Barbie doll: "Will the package have to say, in compliance with the act's rules, 'One doll, net,' on quantity, and then, on size, '34–21–34'?"[23] Despite such criticism, the FPLA seems to have worked fairly well. The Federal Trade Commission and Food and Drug Administration have encountered problems while enforcing the Act, but nothing insuperable. The problem of what to do with Barbie, for instance, was solved when the Federal Trade Commission declared that she was among the many commodities that were not covered by the Act—toys, chinaware, books, souvenirs, and mouse traps, to name only a few.

2. UNIFORM PACKAGE SIZES

As already suggested, it would be easier for consumers to compare the price per unit of various brands and volumes if sellers adhered to a few common sizes of packaging. Senator Hart tried to have some compulsory rules for packaging uniformity or "standardization" written into FPLA, but they were defeated by the opposition. Several *nonmandatory* standards have emerged from under the voluntary sections of the Act. Dry cereals, for example, are supposed to be packaged in whole ounces only. Jellies and preserves are now supposed to come in sizes of 10, 12, 16, 18, 20, 24, 28, 32, 48, or 64 ounces. However, these voluntary standards do not seem to be very helpful. For more stringent action we must look to state and foreign laws. In the United States, several states have standardized the packaging of bread, butter, margarine, flour, corn meal, and milk. Among foreign countries, Germany, France, England, and Canada have rather extensive mandatory standardization.[24] A few ex-

[20] M. P. Friedman, "Consumer Confusion in the Selection of Supermarket Products," *Journal of Applied Psychology* (December 1966), pp. 529–534.

[21] Michigan Chamber of Commerce, as quoted by R. L. Birmingham, "The Consumer as King: The Economics of Precarious Sovereignty," in *Consumerism*, edited by D. A. Aaker and G. S. Day (New York: Free Press, 1974), p. 186.

[22] A. Q. Mowbray, *The Thumb on the Scale* (New York: J. B. Lippincott Co., 1967), p. 72.

[23] *New York Times*, June 8, 1969.

[24] Committee on Consumer Policy, *Package Standardization, Unit Pricing, Deceptive Packaging* (Paris: Organization for Economic Co-operation and Development, 1975).

Table 12–2. Selected Canadian Standardization Regulations

Product	Prescribed Weight or Volume
Jellies and jams	$2\frac{1}{2}$, 6, 9, 12, 24, or 48 ounces
Eggs	Multiples of 12
Frozen peas, corn, liver beans, and spinach	12 ounces or 2 pounds
Fruit and vegetable juices	$5\frac{1}{2}$, 6, 10, 14, 19, 28, 48, or 100 fluid ounces
Single-ply paper napkins	Multiples of 30 napkins
Liquid/lotion shampoos	Multiples of 25 milliliters between 25 and 250 milliliters;
	Multiples of 50 milliliters over 250 milliliters

Source: Package Standardization, Unit Pricing, Deceptive Packaging (Paris: Organization for Economic Co-operation and Development, 1975), pp. 31–35.

amples of Canadian policy are shown in Table 12–2.

3. PRICE STANDARDIZATION

Price standardization is an approach still more helpful to consumers than package uniformity and simplification. It may be found in two major forms—unit pricing and truth-in-lending. **Unit pricing** translates all package prices into a price per standard weight or measure, such as 25.3 cents per pound, or 71.4 cents per hundred count. Representing price in this way helps consumers compare prices without superhuman computations. Numerous studies have shown that unit pricing greatly reduces price comparison errors. One such study found that with unit pricing people could pick the least cost item 25% more often than without, and at the same time cut down their shopping time considerably.[25] Extensive national regulations of this type exist only in Germany and

Switzerland. In the United States, eleven states have adopted unit-pricing regulations, led by Massachusetts in 1971.[26] Although United States laws thus have restricted application, many grocery stores have voluntarily adopted unit pricing. As a result, it appears that roughly half of all chain-operated supermarkets in the United States and one fourth of all independent supermarkets use unit pricing of some kind.

Of course, retailer adoption and actual consumer use of unit pricing are two different things. Surveys of consumers' use of unit pricing, where it is available, have shown a wide variation of shoppers claiming usage—from 9 to 68%—with an average of only 34%. In accord with the view that the typical shopper is not Superperson, it appears that one reason for this limited reliance on unit pricing is a complete lack of awareness. One study showed that 28% of those not using unit pricing simply didn't know about it. Obviously, limited use also limits the benefits that can be attributed to unit

[25] For a summary of this and other studies see General Accounting Office, *Report to the Congress on Food Labeling: Goals, Shortcomings, and Proposed Changes* (# MWD–75–19) January 1975. This is the main source for this section.

[26] *State Consumer Action: Summary '74,* Office of Consumer Affairs, Department of Health, Education, and Welfare [Pub. No. (OS) 75–116], pp. ix–x.

pricing. Thus, one survey estimated that only about 8.8% of observed purchases probably involved the use of unit pricing, and another study concluded that active use saves consumers only about 3% on their grocery bill. Multiplying these two estimates yields an estimated saving of no more than 0.264% on the cost of all purchases. Although this estimate is indeed small, it nevertheless appears to be greater than the costs borne by those retailers who have adopted unit pricing. Many consumer advocates therefore urge that federal legislation require nationwide unit pricing. They also urge that consumers be more thoroughly educated about its use.

Truth-in-lending (TIL) is one form of price standardization that since 1969 has been provided by United States government regulations.[27] However, the scope of these regulations is limited to consumer credit. Before adoption of TIL, numerous studies indicated that only a few people knew how much they actually paid for credit. Two such studies in the 1950s, for instance, indicated that 66–70% of consumers did not have even a vague idea of the annual *percentage rate*, let alone the dollar value, of interest they were paying on their *recent* installment purchases. They almost certainly did not know the interest rates charged by other credit suppliers, information that is, of course, necessary to comparative shopping. Why this vast ignorance? To make a long story short, there was no price standardization in the credit industry. One lender would use the "add-on" method; others would use a "discount rate," or an "annual percentage rate," or "monthly rate," or some combination of all three. Depending on the method, the price for

the same amount of credit might be quoted as being 1%, 7%, 12.83%, or 16%. Indeed, some lenders would not quote *any* rate of charge. They would merely state the number and amount of the monthly payments required.

The purpose of the Truth-in-Lending Law is to let consumers know exactly what the price of credit is and to let them compare the prices of various lenders. Moreover, as argued by the late Senator Paul Douglas (an early sponsor of the legislation and also a prominent economist): "The benefits of effective competition cannot be realized if the buyers (borrowers) do not have adequate knowledge of the alternatives which are available to them." To achieve these ends the law requires disclosure of two fundamental aspects of credit prices:

1. The *finance charge*, which is the amount of money paid to obtain the credit.
2. The *annual percentage rate*, or APR, which provides a simple way of comparing credit prices regardless of the dollar amount charged or the length of time over which payments are made.

This summary makes enforcement of the law by the Federal Reserve Board of Governors and the Federal Trade Commission sound easy, but it's not. The former's Regulation "Z" runs to nearly one hundred fine-printed pages. Still, this summary is not misleading, and from the consumer's viewpoint things are indeed simpler. Several studies of credit-cost awareness subsequent to TIL have discovered significant improvement in debtor knowledge.

4. WARRANTY STANDARDIZATION

The 1975 Magnuson-Moss Warranty-FTC Improvement Act contains a number of requirements for manufacturers regarding standards for written product warranties. For products priced above $15 manufacturers must now specify whether their warranty is "full" or "limited," where:

[27] Material for this topic may be found in *Consumer Credit in the United States,* Report of the National Commission on Consumer Finance (Washington D.C.: U.S. Government Printing Office, 1972) Chapter 10; and *Technical Studies, Vol. I,* of the same Commission, which includes papers by R. P. Shay, M. W. Schober, G. S. Day, and W. K. Brandt.

1. A *full warranty* means that charges for repair or replacement during the warranty period are either minimal or nil.
2. A *limited warranty* limits the seller's obligations, placing more financial responsibility on the consumer.

Moreover, the law holds that the terms and conditions of a written warranty must be stated "in simple and readily understood language." This was in response to consumer complaints that only sober Philadelphia lawyers could understand the language of most product warranties.

Early studies of the impact of this law indicate that its benefits may be rather limited. It appears to be the case, for instance, that only about 28% of all consumers actually read warranties before making their purchases, so warranty standardization would assist only a minority of consumers in comparative shopping.[28] Moreover, warranties are still very difficult to understand despite the law. Measuring language lucidity by the education level necessary to achieve understanding, one recent study of 125 warranties found that 34% of them were at "college graduate" level and 44% more were at "some college" level. Automobile warranties were found to be especially difficult, generating an average grade level score of 20.2.[29]

It should be noted, however, that the purposes of the Magnuson-Moss Act go well beyond warranty simplification. And in these other respects the Act seems to have been more successful. For instance, there appears to have been some shift from "limited" to "full" warranties, and warranty coverage in terms of duration, scope, and remedies seems to have

improved.[30] Moreover, the Act substantially increased the potency of the Federal Trade Commission in the area of consumer protection by assuring it the power to issue Trade Regulation Rules. These rules and the procedures necessary for their adoption will be discussed in the next chapter.

B. Quality Disclosures[31]

Critics of the policies ticked off heretofore correctly point out that they simply make price comparisons easier; they do not take into account differences in the *quality* of competing brands or products. Furthermore, some critics assert that these policies cause consumers to *overemphasize* price per unit and *overlook* quality per dollar spent. The latter argument is probably questionable. In any event, the general purpose of the following policies is to help buyers identify quality.

1. SIMPLE DISCLOSURE OF INGREDIENTS

The Wool Products Labeling Act of 1939, the Fur Products Labeling Act of 1951, and the Textile Fiber Products Identification Act of 1958 call for the disclosure of ingredients in fur and fiber products. All are enforced by the Federal Trade Commission. Under the first of these, almost all wool products must bear labels showing the percentage of the total fiber weight of "virgin" wool, reprocessed wool, and reused wool. Inclusion of any other fiber must also be identified by generic name (as opposed to trade name) if it exceeds 5% of the total. Similarly, the Fur Act requires fur product labels that disclose the true English name of the animal that grew the fur; the animal's home

---

[28] Federal Trade Commission, *Warranties Rules Consumer Baseline Study* (March 2, 1979), p. 129.

[29] F. Kelly Shuptrine and Ellen M. Moore, "Even After the Magnuson-Moss Act of 1975, Warranties Are Not Easy to Understand," *Journal of Consumer Affairs* (Winter 1980), pp. 394–404.

[30] T. Schmitt, L. Kauter, and R. Miller, *Impact Report on the Magnuson-Moss Warranty Act* (Washington, D.C.: Federal Trade Commission, 1980).

[31] For another survey see John A. Miller, "Product Labeling and Government Regulation," *Journal of Contemporary Business* (Vol. 7, No. 4, 1979), pp. 105–121.

country if the fur is imported; whether the fur is bleached, dyed, or otherwise artificially colored; and whether it is composed of paws, bellies, scraps, or waste fur. Thus, rabbit cannot be passed off as "Baltic Lion," and sheared muskrat cannot be called "Hudson Seal"—not as long as the FTC's agents stay awake on the job.

Finally, the main purpose of the Textile Act is to reduce confusion that might be caused by the proliferation of manmade chemical fibers and their many trade names. The law requires labels revealing the *generic* names and percentages of all fibers that go into a fabric, except those that constitute less than 5% of the fabric. Thus Dacron, which is a trade name, must be identified as "polyester," its generic name. Over seven hundred other trade names must be identified as belonging to one of seventeen generic families specified by the FTC. To the extent consumers know the properties of these generic fibers in terms of washing, pressing, dying, and wearing them, the law helps. To the extent consumers do not know, it does not help.

Ingredient labeling regulations for food products has a shorter but more complicated history.[32] Since about 1972 the Food and Drug Administration (FDA) has vigorously expanded its activity in labeling so that detailed disclosures of composition are now required on the labels of most processed food products. The disclosures include:

1. Nutrition information, such as vitamins, minerals, caloric content, carbohydrate content, and protein.
2. Information on cholesterol, fat, and fatty acid composition.
3. Special information on foods intended for infants, nursing mothers, diabetics, the allergic, and the obese.
4. Defining natural and artificial flavors, spices, and colorings.

2. OPEN DATING

Freshness is obviously an important aspect of the quality of perishable food products. For many years food manufacturers dated their products for inventory control and retailer rotation. Until recently, however, these dates were disguised by codes not known to the public (and often not even known to grocery store managers or clerks). Thus open dating is simply uncoded dating. As of 1979, federal law did not require open dating, but twenty-one states had some form of mandatory open dating with dairy products being the prime target.[33] In addition, many grocery chains have voluntarily adopted it. One problem that remains to be resolved is standardization. "Sell-by" dating is customary, but a confusing variety of other dating methods are also used—"packing date," "expiration date," and so on.

Another form of open dating relates to autos. As of 1975, thirty-seven states had entered the snake pit of used car sales by prohibiting odometer tampering. Thereafter, the federal government also stepped in with passage of the Motor Vehicle Information and Cost Savings Act. This law requires a written, true-mileage disclosure statement at the time of sale for all self-propelled vehicles except those that are over 24 years old or exceed 16,000 pounds. Moreover, the law prohibits disconnecting or resetting the odometer with intent to change the mileage reading or knowingly falsifying the written odometer statement.

[32] L. E. Hicks, *Product Labeling and the Law* (New York, AMACOM Division of American Management Associations, 1974).

[33] Congress of the United States, Office of Technology Assessment, *Open Shelf-Life Dating of Food* (Washington, D.C.: August 1979). A study prompting Minnesota's law found that 44 per cent of the baby formula being sold was overage and that since 64% of the store managers could not read a coded date, they could not rotate the stock.

3. SPECIFIC PERFORMANCE DISCLOSURES

Beginning with the 1977 models, all new cars sold in the United States have had labels disclosing the estimated number of miles they get per gallon of gas and an estimate of what yearly fuel cost would be if 15,000 miles were traveled per year. Thus, for example, the 1977 Volkswagen Rabbit Diesel, with a 90-cubic-inch engine, was reported to travel 44 miles per gallon and costs $188 in annual fuel expense. By contrast, the 1977 Dodge Royal Monaco with a 440-cubic-inch engine brandished a sticker saying that a standard year's travel in one of them would cost $886, since it averaged only 11 miles per gallon. The Federal Energy Act of 1975 requires these disclosures on the theory that they assist efficiency comparisons and in the hope that car buyers will react to these revelations by shying away from gas guzzlers.

The Federal Energy Act also requires that efficiency ratings appear on major home appliances like refrigerators, freezers, and dishwashers. Administered by the Federal Trade Commission through its rule-making procedures, this program is much more complex than is suggested by the simple energy labels adopted (see Figure 12–3 for a sample).[34] One particularly helpful feature of the label is that it places the appliance on a relative scale, so the shopper need not strain much in making comparisons of energy efficiency. Preliminary study of consumer response to this program indicates its favorable promise.[35]

Another illustration of specific performance disclosure is gasoline octane posting, which has been with us in one form or another since 1973, but only haphazardly enforced. The Federal Trade Commission, which has been the most

[34] Federal Trade Commission, *Labeling and Advertising of Consumer Appliances* (February 1979).
[35] D. L. McNeill and W. L. Wilkie, "Public Policy and Consumer Information: Impact of the New Energy Labels," *Journal of Consumer Research* (June 1979), pp. 1–11.

Figure 12–3.   Appliance Energy Disclosure

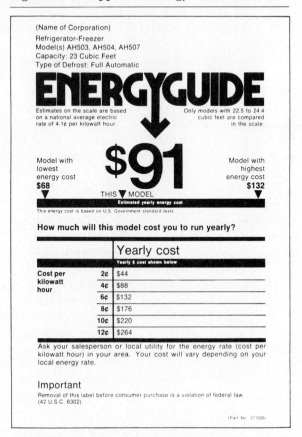

vigorous advocate of octane-posting; has argued that in the absence of octane-posting, motorists would waste more than $300 million a year by purchasing gasoline with higher octane than they really need. Most people seem to think that higher octane produces greater power. But this is not true. Octane indicates only the anti-knock properties of gasoline. The major brand petroleum companies have persistently opposed octane-posting for fear that it would lead people to recognize that all brands of gasoline of a given octane rating were pretty much alike (which they are).[36]

4. GRADE RATING

Disclosures of ingredients, freshness, dimensions, specific performance and the like may guide buyers toward ideal purchasing patterns. But how close to the ideal can these raw data take them? Several recent studies have demonstrated formally what most students already know from informal experience—namely, the information processing capabilities of the human mind are quite limited. Indeed, some evidence even suggests that beyond a certain point additional information merely confuses and frustrates consumers. Thereafter they no longer move toward their ideal decision, but rather *away* from it.[37] Thus grade rating is often recommended as a means of simplifying complex quality information into an ABC format.[38]

The most active federal agency in this respect is the U.S. Department of Agriculture, whose agents grade meat, eggs, butter, poultry, grain, fruits, and vegetables. Beef, for example, is graded "prime," "choice," and "good." This grading is not compulsory. Hence, large brand-name meat packers like Armour, Swift, Morrell,

and Wilson are given some elbow room to resist it. They prefer to promote the sale of beef under their own brand names whenever and wherever possible. Among the statistics that reflect resistance to grading, we find that during the 1950s only 27% of national packer beef was USDA graded, and all but one of the national brand-name packers advocated an end to federal grading. In contrast, the main supporters of the system are independent packers, retail food chains, independent retailers, and consumers. During 1955, for instance, 94% of all beef sold by retail food chains was USDA graded, and 85% of all chains surveyed said they favored compulsory grading or continuation of the present system. These and related data led W. F. Williams, E. K. Bowen, and F. C. Genovese to conclude that:

1. Grade standards have tended to intensify competition.
2. Unbranded packers and wholesalers increased in numbers and volume of meat processed, whereas branded packers declined greatly in number.
3. The system has tended to increase the accuracy, ease, and effectiveness of prices in reflecting value differences at each stage in the marketing system for beef by assisting consumers in the expression of their preferences.[39]

The biggest problem with USDA grade rating is its lack of standardization across products. Top rated apples, peaches, chickens, and some other foods are variously awarded grades of No. 1, Extra No. 1, Fancy, and Grade A. For still other products these grades would indicate second best. In 1980 the U.S. Department of Agriculture proposed changes that would standardize their grade designations, so by the time you

---

[36] See *Business Week* (May 31, 1976), p. 21 and F. C. Allvine and J. M. Patterson, *Competition Limited: The Marketing of Gasoline* (Bloomington, Ind.: Indiana University Press, 1972) pp. 24–25. It may be worth noting that the petroleum industry itself imposes extensive standards on its suppliers. According to the American Petroleum Institute: "All of our standards are written from the point of view of a consuming industry. . . . Our motive simply is to provide uniform performance requirements to the widest possible range of suppliers." Hemenway, *op. cit.*, p. 66.

[37] J. Jacoby, D. E. Speller, and Carol A. Kohn, "Brand Choice Behavior as a Function of Information Load," *Journal of Marketing Research* (February 1974), pp. 63–69; and J. Jacoby, D. E. Speller, and C. K. Berning, "Brand Choice Behavior as a Function of Information Load: Replication and Extention," *Journal of Consumer Research* (June 1974), pp. 33–42.

[38] J. R. Bettman, "Issues in Designing Consumer Information Environments," *Journal of Consumer Research* (December 1975), pp. 169–177.

[39] Willard F. Williams, E. K. Bowen, and F. C. Genovese, *Economic Effects of U.S. Grades for Beef,* U.S. Department of Agriculture Marketing Research Report No. 298 (Washington D.C., 1959) pp. vii, 158–180.

Table 12–3. Summary of United States Standardization and Disclosure Policies

Policy	Enforcement Agencies*	Products Covered
A. Standardization		
1. Fair Packaging and Labeling Act (1966)	FTC, FDA	Grocery store items, e.g., foods and detergents
2. Size uniformity and simplification	Various state authorities	Bread, margarine, flour, dairy products
3. Unit pricing	Various state authorities	Grocery store items
4. Truth in Lending Act (1969)	FTC, FRB	Consumer credit
5. Warranty standards	FTC	Durables over $15 with written warranty
B. Quality Disclosures		
1. Ingredient labeling:		
Wool Products Labeling Act (1939)	FTC	Wool products
Fur Product Labeling Act (1951)	FTC	Furs
Textile Fiber Identification Act (1958)	FTC	Textiles, apparel, etc.
Food, Drug and Cosmetic Act	FDA	Food products
2. Open dating of perishables	Various state authorities	Grocery perishables
3. Antitampering Odometer Law (1972)	NHTSA	Cars and trucks
4. Performance disclosures:		
Fuel efficiency	FEA, FTC	Autos, appliances
Octane rating	FTC, FEA	Gasoline
Tar and nicotine	FTC	Cigarettes
On time performance	ICC	Moving van services
5. Grade rating	USDA	Meat, eggs, butter, etc.
	NHTSA	Tires

* Key: FTC—Federal Trade Commission; FDA—Food and Drug Administration; FRB—Federal Reserve Board of Governors; NHTSA—National Highway Traffic Safety Administration; FEA—Federal Energy Administration; ICC—Interstate Commerce Commission; USDA—U.S. Department of Agriculture.

read this USDA may have clarified matters considerably.

Auto tires were the subject of an early demonstration of how grading could reduce buyers' erroneous reliance on brand names. Louis Bucklin found that, without grading, consumers tended to overestimate the value of heavily advertised national brands of tires as compared to mildy promoted distributor and local brands, but that with grade rating this bias tended to disappear.[40] Subsequent to that study, and despite sharp objections by major tire manufacturers, a grade rating system was put into effect by the Department of Transportation in 1979 and 1980. Tires are now rated on three characteristics:

[40] Louis P. Bucklin, "The Uniform Grading System for Tires: Its Effect upon Consumers and Industry Competition," *Antitrust Bulletin* (Winter 1974), pp. 783–801.

1. *Treadwear*, indicated by a numeral such as 90 or 120, with higher numerals indicating higher mileage.
2. *Traction*, where A, B, and C indicate good, fair, and poor traction on wet roads, respectively.
3. *Temperature*, where A indicates the coolest running tire, and B and C rank less well.

Tire manufacturers do their own testing and interpretation under the program, which has led to problems. Although the tests are uniform, they yield a range of results. And some companies interpret their results more conservatively than other companies, leading to different grades for very similar test results and different grades for very similarly priced tires.[41] Even so, the system is probably a step in the right direction.

Summary

An economy without well-informed buyers would be like a university without students. Fortunately, buyers are not *always* ignorant. But they frequently are, depending on their expertise and the product in question. Experience and credence goods are especially troublesome, for they cannot be easily and fully assessed prior to purchase, as can search goods. Where lapses occur a number of adverse consequences may follow: (1) errors of commission and omission, (2) imperfect competition, and (3) wasteful and misdirected promotion arising from sellers' attempts to exploit this ignorance. Consumers often rely heavily on trademarks to guide their purchasing decisions, since in a roundabout way trademarks often help to identify product quality. Even so, too heavy a reliance on trademarks and the advertising promoting them may contribute to erroneous purchasing behavior, in which case the owners of prominent trademarks gain at the expense of buyers.

[41] *Wall Street Journal*, December 31, 1980, p. 5.

Corrective policies have to focus on one or both of the following objectives: (1) Permit trademarks to identify quality, but remove the rights of ownership exclusivity and perpetuity that presently prevail. (2) Establish quality identifications independent of the trademark system. The first objective lies outside the realm of political possibility. The second has been furthered by two broad classes of policies—standardization (which includes simplified quantity labeling, uniform sizes, and unit pricing) and quality disclosures (which include ingredient labeling, open dating, performance disclosure, and grade rating). These are outlined in Table 12–3.

Questions and Exercises for Chapter 12

1. Why are professional buyers more knowledgeable than consumers generally?
2. With the aid of a diagram, explain why errors of commission result in allocation inefficiency. (Hint: Is there any divergence between marginal social benefit and marginal social cost with such errors?)
3. With the aid of a diagram, explain why errors of omission result in allocation inefficiency.
4. Distinguish between search and experience goods in (a) their characteristics, (b) their implications for competition, and (c) nature and intensity of advertising.
5. What is the basic rationale behind standardization and disclosure policies?
6. Compare and contrast standardization versus quality disclosure.
7. After identifying "unit pricing" and "truth-in-lending," explain why they are versions of "price standardization."
8. What is the connection between "search qualities" and (a) open dating and (b) performance disclosure?
9. What has been the economic impact of grade rating in meat packing?

Chapter 13

Unfair and Deceptive Practices

If there is a dividing line between liberty and license, it is where freedom
of speech is no longer respected as a procedure of truth and becomes
the unrestricted right to exploit ignorance and to incite the passions
of people.
—Walter Lippmann

It is a king-sized cancer on the economy. . . . I think repealing the
FTC would be a good idea.
—Representative Bill Frenzel
Republican—Minnesota

The next twenty pages are stunning, dazzling,
thrilling, blazing, chilling, tremulous with pas-
sion, and even haunting. The chapter is, in
short, a blockbuster.

These are lies, of course. But can you think
of a better way to herald a discussion of deceptive practices? The statute under review here
is Section 5 of the Federal Trade Commission
Act (as amended by the Wheeler-Lea Act of
1938), which states that *"Unfair methods of
competition in commerce, and unfair or deceptive acts or practices in commerce, are declared
unlawful."* Since passage of the FTC Act in
1914, more than 3300 cases of deception have
been prosecuted by the FTC.

Before delving into the details of what is prohibited by Section 5 of the FTC Act, it would

be wise to note briefly what is *not* prohibited
or controlled. The law does not protect the public from inane, absurd, tasteless, and boringly
repetitious advertising. Likewise, United States
policy places no limits on levels of dollar outlay.
Outlay limits have occasionally been imposed
in Europe, but not in the United States. Finally,
"puffing" is permitted, even though, strictly
speaking, much of it is mendacious.[1] Thus, our
senses are pelted by such exaggerations as

Budweiser is the King of beers

Zenith Chromacolor is the biggest breakthrough
in color TV

[1] I. L. Preston, *The Great American Blow-Up* (Madison,
Wis.: University of Wisconsin Press, 1975).

State Farm is all you need to know about insurance

Our survey of what is illegal comes in five parts and focuses primarily on advertising: (1) the criteria applied to determine deception; (2) specific examples of advertising that have collided with the criteria; (3) FTC procedures; (4) remedies applied to clean-up; and (5) miscellaneous unfair practices.

I. What Is "Deceptive"?

A. Truth, Falsity, and Deception

Innocent souls tend to think in simple terms: truth should be legal, falsity illegal. But this rule would be impractical, the controversies over truth being what they are. A better rule, the one actually applied by law, centers on the *deception* of potential buyers: "that which is not deceptive is legal, and that which is deceptive is illegal." This rule is different because falsity and deception are *not* necessarily the same. Although most false claims are deceptive, a claim may be false but not deceptive. Conversely, although most true claims are not deceptive, some true claims may be deceptive. These divergences arise because of the gap between any message's sender and receiver. Whereas truth and falsity hinge upon the literal content of the message sent, deception depends upon what goes on in the minds of folks receiving the message—that is, the potential buyers.

Take for example Exxon's promise to put a tiger in your tank. The claim is patently false. There is no tiger. Yet you are not deceived and neither is anyone else. So the FTC does not flinch.

Examples of literal truth that actually deceive are equally easy to come by. In 1971 the FTC found deception in nonfalse television ads showing Hot Wheels and Johnny Lightning toy racers speeding over their tracks. To the TV viewer, the racers seemed to move like bullets. But this was merely a "special effect," which was achieved by filming the racers at close range from clever angles. The representation was technically accurate but nevertheless misleading.[2] Many further examples relate to "half-true" advertisments that, although literally true, leave an overall impression that is quite incorrect. Thus, in the late 1940s the makers of Old Gold cigarettes boldly proclaimed: "Old Golds found lowest in nicotine, Old Golds found lowest in throat-irritating tars and resins," citing research published in *Reader's Digest.* The claim was true in the sense that Old Golds did happen to be lowest of the brands tested. But the point of the *Reader's Digest* article was contrary to the ad's innuendoes. To quote the article, "The differences between brands are, practically speaking, small, and no single brand is so superior to its competitors as to justify its selection on the ground that it is less harmful." The FTC and appellate court found deception, saying that "To tell less than the whole truth is a well known method of deception; and he who deceives by resorting to such method cannot excuse the deception by relying upon the truthfulness per se of the partial truth."[3]

Who Is Deceived?   Given that deception lies in the mind of the observer rather than in the body of the advertisement, the next question is who among observers is to be protected? If one gullible person is misled, does that constitute illegal deception? What about 3%, or 15%, of the population? When reviewing a case in 1927 the Supreme Court held that Section 5 was "made to protect the trusting as well as the suspicious." Accordingly, the FTC and the appellate courts have adopted a fairly stringent standard, one that protects the ignorant, the unthinking, and the trusting as well as the suspi-

[2] *Mattel,* 79 FTC 667 (1971); *Topper* 79 FTC 681 (1971).
[3] *P. Lorillard Co.* v. *FTC,* 186 F. 2d 52 (4th Cir. 1950).

cious and hard headed.[4] The authorities have decided, for example, that a hair coloring could not claim that it colored hair "permanently." The FTC is especially protective of the ignorant, unthinking, and trusting when it comes to claims of safety or health. Were an advertiser to intimate falsely that cleaning solvent "X" was nonflammable, he would ignite a blast of official rebuke.

Still, the authorities have not gone so far as to protect the "foolish or feeble minded." They permit obvious spoofs, such as love-starved girls feverishly attacking a defenseless boy (who uses Hai Karate recklessly), and a rampaging bull that is released merely by uncorking a malt liquor (Schlitz). Moreover, as already noted, the authorities permit generous amounts of puffery, not to mention "minor" sleight of hand and tongue.

B. Intent and Capacity

Prior to the FTC Act, misrepresentation and deception could be successfully prosecuted only with great difficulty. The common law was rigged in favor of the con artist because conviction could be obtained only if the injured buyer could prove in court that

1. He understood the seller's claim to convey a fact (not a puff).
2. He had relied upon the claim.
3. He was justified (and not just stupid) in relying on the claim.
4. He had suffered financial or other injury by so relying on the claim.
5. Most difficult of all, the seller *knowingly intended* to deceive him (the buyer).

In brief, conviction required a showing of *actual* deception in the mind of the buyer and *deliberate* intent in the mind of the seller. Common law cases were consequently very rare. Perhaps the only justification for this approach was the fact that sellers could suffer harsh penalties if convicted.

The FTC Act changed all this. No component of this maze of proofs now has to be shown to exist by the FTC in order for it to reach a guilty verdict. The Commission's decision hinges solely on whether or not a sales claim possesses the *capacity or tendency to deceive.* Proof of intent is not required. The Commission attacks the ad, not the advertiser. Likewise, proof of actual deception is not required. The Commission may examine an advertisement and determine on the basis of its own expertise whether there is a *potential* for deception. The Commission need not poll consumers, nor hear from complaining witnesses.[5] Even if suspected deceivers defend themselves by providing a parade of witnesses who say they have not been misled, the FTC can still find a violation.[6]

Despite the power of the FTC to rely upon its own expertise, it has nevertheless tended in recent years to supplement its own intuitive understanding with consumers' testimony, public opinion polls, and outside experts. Whereas prior to 1955, 92% of all FTC cases were decided solely on the basis of Commission expertise, between 1955 and 1973 no more than 57% of all cases were so decided. And over the years 1970–1973, only 36% of all cases were so decided.[7] Greater reliance on outside experts' and consumers' views may be due to the Commission's recent attempts to stem more subtle forms of deception and to counter criticisms that its traditional methods were too presumptive, too shoddy, and too arbitrary.

---

[4] *Charles of the Ritz Dist. Corp.* v. *FTC,* 143 F. 2d 676 (2d Cir. 1944). See also Ira M. Millstein, "The Federal Trade Commission and False Advertising," *Columbia Law Review* (March 1964), pp. 457–465.

[5] *Montgomery Ward & Co.* v. *FTC* 379 F. 2d 666 (7th Cir. 1967).

[6] *Double Eagle Lubricants, Inc.* v. *FTC,* 360 F. 2d 268 (10 Cir. 1965).

[7] M. T. Brandt and I. L. Preston, "The Federal Trade Commission's Use of Evidence to Determine Deception," *Journal of Marketing* (January 1977), pp. 54–62.

Given the FTC's fairly free hand, what of punishment and remedy? Does a guilty verdict bring fines, damage payments, and jailings, as could happen under pre-FTC common law? . . . No. As we shall see more thoroughly later when we discuss remedies, lenient standards of offense are coupled with lenient measures of penalty. Reprimands plus orders of "cease and desist" are, in the main, what face the two-faced (except in certain cases where the consumer's physical well being is at stake[8]). As Ivan Preston puts it, the present "strategy is one of prevention rather than punishment and remedy. The goal is to give maximum aid to consumers at the sacrifice of less than maximum punishment to offenders, rather than the opposite."[9]

What of Competitive Effects? The original FTC Act made no specific mention of deception. It simply said: "Unfair methods of competition in commerce are hereby declared unlawful." As a result, early FTC assaults on deception were grounded on the theory that deceivers gain unfair competitive advantages over their more honest rivals. This approach was only partially successful and severely limited. After 1929, when the FTC moved against the blatantly fake claims of Raladam Company (that its "desiccated thyroid" obesity cure was completely safe and effective), these limits materialized. Reviewing the case in 1931, the Supreme Court ruled in favor of Raladam, saying that the FTC must prove competition "to have been injured, or to be clearly threatened with injury," in order to find a violation.[10] Injury to

consumers, or potential injury to consumers, did not count. To rectify this shortcoming, Congress passed the Wheeler-Lea Amendment in 1938. The Amendment removed the FTC's obligation to demonstrate injury to competition by outlawing "deceptive acts or practices" as well as "unfair methods of competition." It was this legislation, then, that made "capacity and tendency to deceive" the sole criteria. (Actually, it is deceptive for me to say that "capacity and tendency" are the *sole* criteria. A misleading claim is not illegal unless it is "material," that is, affects the consumer's decision. Thus we all know Joe Namath is fibbing when, in the midst of plugging Hamilton Beach popcorn poppers, he leeringly tells us that his favorite off-the-field pleasure is making popcorn. But this misrepresentation is "immaterial.")

II. Examples of Deception

There is a rich variety of illegal deceptions. Unfortunately, we have space for only a few broad classes:[11] (1) claims of composition, (2) claims of function of efficacy, (3) endorsements, and (4) mock-ups.

A. Claims of Composition

The Fair Packaging and Labeling Act, and similar acts governing textiles, furs, and woolens, now regulate ingredient claims for many products. Those claims not so covered are subject to a host of FTC precedents under Section 5. Naked lies, such as calling pine wood "walnut," are out. Many more slippery representations are now explicitly defined by the FTC. Here is a sampling:

[8] In Section 14 of the FTC Act, Congress provided criminal penalties in certain cases of deception involving food, drugs, or cosmetic devices: "Any person . . . who violates any provision of Section 12 (a) shall, if the use of the commodity advertised may be injurious to health . . . , or if such violation is with intent to defraud or mislead, be guilty of a misdemeanor." Criminal prosecutions under this section are not brought by the FTC but may be recommended by the FTC to the Justice Department.

[9] Preston, *op. cit.*, p. 136.

[10] *FTC* v. *Raladam Co.,* 258 U.S. 643 (1931).

[11] For more complete surveys see E. W. Kintner, *A Primer on the Law of Deceptive Practices* (New York: Macmillan Publishing Co., 1971), and G. J. Alexander, *Honesty and Competition* (Syracuse, N.Y.: Syracuse University Press, 1967).

"Down" indicates feathers of any aquatic bird and therefore excludes chicken feathers.

"Linoleum" designates a product composed of oxidized oil and gums mixed "intimately" with ground cork or wood flour.

"Vanilla" unqualified, describes only that which is obtained from the vanilla bean.

In 1977, General Motors found itself confronting more than one hundred private suits for deceptively using Chevrolet engines in its Oldsmobiles. There was nothing wrong with the Chevy engines. Indeed, GM had mixed engines amongst its models for years. The problem arose because GM's advertising for the Olds "Rocket V-8" had been particularly effective. As the *Wall Street Journal* explained it, "GM's advertising for years has stressed the purported merits of individual models, including the superiority of Oldsmobile's Rocket engine." But now, customers "find there is little difference in the engines involved" and they therefore feel deceived. GM has been forced to compensate upset customers for what it calls a "breakdown in communications." ("It just didn't occur to us," GM's chairman said, that "people were interested in where the engines were built.") More interesting, GM has now changed its advertising. Instead of plugging the supposed merits of any given engine, it is advertising its "great family of engines."[12]

B. Claims of Function or Efficacy

During the late 1960s, Firestone advertised that its "Super Sports Wide Oval" tires were

built lower, wider. Nearly two inches wider than regular tires. To corner better, run cooler, stop 25% quicker.

When sued by the FTC, Firestone presented evidence that cars with these tires traveling 15 miles per hour *did* stop 25% quicker than

those with ordinary width tires. However, the tests were done on very low-friction surfaces, equivalent in slickness to glare ice or waxed linoleum. Thus "Wide Ovals" might enable some poor soul who crashes through the end of his garage to stop short of the kitchen refrigerator. But slippery surfaces and slow speeds are obviously not typical of United States highway conditions. Hence the FTC decided that Firestone's ads were deceptive.[13]

Deceptive claims of efficacy or function may even run afoul of the law when they are less explicit, when, that is, they enter the realm of innuendo and suggestion. Indeed, it could be argued that this is an area where puffery is rather limited. Thus, a drug treatment for delayed menstruation was said to violate the law for advertising with such phrases as "at last—it CAN BE SOLD" and "Don't Risk Disaster," which falsely implied the product induced abortion.[14] Another example concerns "Vivarin," a simple but costly tablet containing caffeine and sugar in amounts roughly equivalent to those in a half-cup of sweetened coffee. The offending ad, which ran in 1971, had a middle-aged woman speaking as if she had just discovered a sure-fire aphrodisiac:

One day it dawned on me that I was boring my husband to death. It wasn't that I didn't love Jim, but often by the time he came home at night I was feeling dull, tired and drowsy. [Then I began taking Vivarin.] All of a sudden Jim was coming home to a more exciting woman, me. We talked to each other a lot more. . . . And after dinner I was wide-awake enough to do a little more than just look at television. And the other day—it wasn't even my birthday—Jim sent me flowers with a note. The note began: "To my new wife. . . ."[15]

[13] *Firestone Tire and Rubber Co.*, 81 FTC 398 (1972).
[14] *Doris Savitch v. FTC*, 218 F. 2d 817 (2d Cir. 1955).
[15] *Advertising of Proprietary Medicines, Hearings*, U.S. Senate, Subcommittee on Monopoly of the Select Committee on Small Business, 92nd Congress, First Session (1971), Part 1, pp. 24, 229.

[12] "Bizarre Backfire," *Wall Street Journal*, July 27, 1977, p. 1.

More mundane but equally misleading in the judgment of the FTC was a "Wonder Bread" campaign of the 1960s, which, among other things, included compelling TV commercials showing bread-eating children growing from infancy to adolescence before the viewer's very eyes while a narrator intoned that since Wonder Bread was "enriched," it "Helps build strong bodies 12 ways." The FTC charged that the ads deceptively represented Wonder Bread as an "extraordinary food for producing dramatic growth in children."[16] (Though no different and no cheaper than other common breads, Wonder built a strong market share in this way, ranking number one nationally and accounting for as much as 30–40% of bread sales in some states.)

C. Endorsements

Mention of endorsements brings to mind athletes like Joe Namath, Billy Jean King, Jack Nicklaus, and O. J. Simpson. These are certainly very important people in advertising, and the FTC has several rules of thumb governing star testimonials. Thus, for example, an endorser must be a "bona fide" user of the product unless such would be clearly inappropriate (as was true of Joe Namath's peddling pantyhose). Moreover, the Commission urges that *ex*-users not be represented as current users, although this is obviously difficult to enforce.

But celebrity endorsements are not the only kind, or even the most important kind. There are "lay" endorsements, "expert" endorsements, "institutional" endorsements, "cartoon character" endorsements, and more, all of which have at one time or another reached the FTC's attention. The flavor of the Commission's thinking in these and related matters may be tasted by quoting Section 255.3, Example 5,

[16] *ITT Continental Baking Co.*, 83 FTC 865 (1973).

from the FTC's "Guides Concerning Use of Endorsements and Testimonials in Advertising":

> An association of professional athletes states in an advertisement that it has "selected" a particular brand of beverages as its "official breakfast drink." [The] association would be regarded as expert in the field of nutrition for purposes of this section, because consumers would expect it to rely upon the selection of nutritious foods as part of its business needs. Consequently, the association's endorsement must be based upon an expert evaluation of the nutritional value of the endorsed beverage [rather than upon the endorsement fee]. Furthermore, . . . use of the words "selected" and "official" in this endorsement imply that it was given only after direct comparisons had been performed among competing brands. Hence, the advertisement would be deceptive unless the association has in fact performed such comparisons . . . and the results . . . conform to the net impression created by the advertisement.[17]

D. Mock-ups

When filming TV commercials, technicians often substitute whipped potatoes for ice cream, soap suds for beer foam, and wine for coffee. The "real thing" melts under the hot lights, or fades, or looks murky on TV screens. Such artificial alterations and substitutions for purposes of picture enhancement are called **mock-ups.** Although these mock-ups are obviously innocuous (indeed, they may often reduce deception rather than produce it), advertisers have not confined their "doctoring" to innocent, nondeceptive, and prudent dimensions:[18]

• When Libby-Owens-Ford Glass Company wanted to demonstrate the superiority of its

[17] *Code of Federal Regulations*, Vol. 16, "Commercial Practices," p. 347.

[18] Quoting from Preston, *op. cit.*, pp. 235, 243. The cases referred to are *Libby-Owens-Ford* v. *FTC*, 352 F. 2d 415 (6th Cir. 1965), and *Carter Products* v. *FTC*, 323 F. 2d 523 (5th Cir., 1963).

automobile safety glass, it smeared a competing brand with streaks of vaseline to create distortion, then photographed it at oblique camera angles to enhance the effect. The distortionless marvels of the company's own glass were "shown" by taking photographs with the windows rolled down.

• Carter Products promoted its Rise shaving cream with a mock-up that was equally fair to poor old Brand X. A man was shown shaving with an "ordinary" lather, which dried out quickly after application. He then switched to Rise and demonstrated how it fulfilled its slogan, "Stays Moist and Creamy." Unbeknownst to the TV audience, the substance he used on the first try was not a competing brand nor a shaving cream at all. It was a preparation specially designed to come out of the aerosol can in a big attractive fluff and then disappear almost immediately.

In 1965, the Supreme Court voiced its opinion of such behavior in *Colgate-Palmolive Co. v. FTC*.[19] The TV commercial in question purported to show that Colgate's Rapid Shave shaving cream was potent enough to allow one to shave sandpaper with an ordinary blade razor. The ad's action and words went together: "apply . . . soak . . . and off in a stroke." But it was a hoax. What appeared to be sandpaper was actually loose grains of sand sprinkled on plexiglas. And the soak was a 2-second pause. Curious consumers who tried real sandpaper informed the FTC that it couldn't be done. So the Commission asked Colgate to come clean. In its defense, Colgate claimed that you *could* shave sandpaper with very small grains of sand, soaked for over an hour. It said the mock-up was necessary because such fine grain sandpaper looked like plain paper on TV, and the true soak could not be captured in a few seconds. Indeed, Colgate felt so adamant about defending its ad that it fought the FTC all the way

to the Supreme Court. The key questions addressed by the Court were as follows:[20]

1. Were undisclosed mock-ups of *mere appearance* acceptable? That is, could whipped potatoes stand-in for ice cream? The Court said yes.
2. Were undisclosed mock-ups demonstrating *un*true performance acceptable? That is, could Rapid Shave be "shown" shaving the ribs off a washboard? The Court said no, clearly not.
3. Were undisclosed mock-ups demonstrating *true* performance acceptable? That is, assuming Rapid Shave *could* easily shave any sandpaper, was an undisclosed mock-up of this acceptable? The Court again said no. When the appearance is *central* to the commercial, and the clear implication is that we are seeing something real when, in fact, we are not, then the mock-up is illegal unless disclosed by saying "simulated" or something similar. Of course, if the real performance is possible and a real performance is shown, there is no problem.

Absolute truth is thus not required. Inconsequential mock-ups for appearance's sake are permitted without an admission of fakery to the audience. Simulations are also allowed with disclosure. But mock-ups that materially deceive cannot be defended. Now, given your newly acquired knowledge of the law, let's test it. How would you react if you were an FTC Commissioner and you caught Campbell's Soup Company putting marbles in the bottom of its televised bowls of soup, thereby making the vegetables and other solid parts of the soup appear attractively and abundantly above the surface? Is this mere appearance? Or is it a material deception? (Your test is not a mock-up test. The case actually came up in 1970. For the FTC's answer see footnote 21.)

[19] *Colgate-Palmolive Co., v. FTC*, 380 U.S. 374 (1965).

[20] Preston, *op. cit.*, p. 238.

III. Federal Trade Commission Procedures[22]

When attacking problems of deception (or other problems within its jurisdiction), the FTC may proceed in one of three ways: (1) complaint plus prosecution, (2) guides, or (3) trade regulation rules.

A. Complaint Plus Prosecution

This is a case-by-case approach in the sense that a particular ad or ad campaign is assailed. The complete chain of formal process is as follows: The advertiser is issued a "complaint"; his case is tried before an "administrative law judge"; the judge renders an "initial decision"; the initial decision is reviewed by the full FTC; the Commission's decision may then be appealed by the "respondent" to federal courts of appeal on questions of law, perhaps even ending up like the *Colgate-Palmolive* case in the lap of the Supreme Court. This procedure may be cut short at the outset by consent settlement, in which instance a remedy is reached without formal trial. The consent decree binds the advertiser to its provisions.

B. Guides

Whereas such case-by-case proceedings are ad hoc, piecemeal, and particular, industry guides and trade regulation rules are broader, more general, and less judicial. Their more sweeping scope often improves the efficiency and efficacy of enforcement. Industry guides are distillations of case law, usually promulgated without formal hearings. They are issued to summarize and clarify case law for the benefit of the indivuals regulated. These guides are nonbinding; they do not directly affect case-by-case procedure.

In short, industry guides are merely an expression of the FTC's view as to what is and what is not legal. There are guides for advertising fallout shelters, advertising shell homes, advertising fuel economy for new autos, advertising guarantees, and many others—a number of which are not directly related to advertising at all. In all, there were approximately one hundred guides as of 1980. One of the more recent is *Guides Concerning Use of Endorsements and Testimonials in Advertising*, from which we quoted earlier.

C. Trade Regulation Rules

These are, in contrast to guides, much more serious. Like legislation, they embody the full force of law. Respondents may be prosecuted for violating the rule itself, rather than for violating the vague prohibitions of Section 5. Rules ease the burden of proof borne by the FTC's prosecuting attorneys because, once a transgression is detected, the respondent's only defense is to prove that the rule does not apply to his case. Since trade regulation rules carry so much force, the Commission formulates them by following an elaborate set of procedures:

> Rule-making proceedings consist of two parts— a preliminary private study conducted by the Commission and the final formulation of the rule with public participation. At the first stage, the Commission gathers through investigation, studies, and discussion information sufficient to support the rule, and then formulates a tentative ver-

---

[21] Consent settlement, *Campbell's Soup*, 77 FTC 664 (1970). The FTC thought this was deceptive.

[22] Much of this and the next section is based upon M. J. Trebilcock, A. Duggan, L. Robinson, H. Wilton-Siegel, and C. Massee, *A Study on Consumer Misleading and Unfair Trade Practices*, Vol. 1 (Ottawa: Information Canada, 1976), Chapter III; U.S. Congress, House, *Oversight Hearings into the Federal Trade Commission—Bureau of Consumer Protection, Hearings*, Committee on Government Operations, 94th Congress, Second Session (1976); and G. G. Udell and P. J. Fischer, "The FTC Improvement Act," *Journal of Marketing* (April 1977), pp. 81–85.

sion of the rule. Upon completion of these preliminary steps, a hearing is initiated: the procedures provide for notice of the proposed rule-making to be published in the Federal Register and for opportunity to be given to interested parties to participate in the hearing through submission of written data or views or oral argument. After due consideration has been given to all relevant matters of fact, law, policy and discretion . . . a rule or order is adopted by the Commission and published in the Federal Register.[23]

Since these rule-making procedures were first established in 1962, more than 20 rules have been enacted. The first few were simple, even trivial, governing such matters as size labeling of sleeping bags and use of the word "leak-proof" for dry-cell batteries. More recently, the FTC has grown confident, some would even say aggressive. Rules now govern door-to-door sales, grocery store stocking of sale merchandise, gasoline octane disclosure, mailorder merchandise, and warranty disclosure.[24]

The Magnuson-Moss Federal Trade Commission Improvement Act of 1975 greatly strengthened the FTC's authority to issue trade regulation rules. The FTC's efforts prior to 1975 were challenged by litigation, but Section 202 of the Act of 1975 gave the FTC express authority to devise rules defining specific acts or practices as unfair or deceptive. The first rule issued under the Act was the "Eyeglass Rule," of 1978, which among other things prohibits restraints on the advertising of optometrists. Such restraints (many imposed by state regulation) were found to *increase* the price of eyeglasses to consumers.[25]

On the other hand, as we shall see in a mo-

ment, the Federal Trade Commission Improvements Act of *1980* weakened FTC authority. In particular, Congress may now veto FTC rules.

IV. Remedies

The product of these and other procedures is a variety of remedies designed to quash current violations, discourage future violations, and, in rare instances, erase the ill effects of past violations. The remedies include cease and desist orders, affirmative disclosure, corrective advertising, advertising substantiation, and restitution.

A. *Cease and Desist Orders*

The traditional, and in most instances of trial settlement the *only*, remedy applied is an order to cease and desist. This simply prohibits the offender from engaging further in practices that have been found unlawful or in closely similar practices. Thus Firestone was ordered to stop advertising that its tires could stop 25% quicker; and Colgate was ordered to cease "shaving" sand off plexiglas amidst ballyhoo about sandpaper. By themselves, such orders are of course little more than slaps on the wrist. No penalties are levied. Penalties may be imposed only if the errant behavior persists *after* the order is issued. (Under the FTC Improvement Act of 1975, the Commission may ask a federal court to impose civil penalties of up to $10,000 per day of violation against those who breach its cease and desist orders.) But since penalties do not apply to original violations, it is often argued that advertisers are not significantly deterred from dealing in deception.

In support of the argument, it has been estimated that *one third* of the members of the

---

[23] Trebilcock, et al., *op. cit.*, pp. 153–54.
[24] Leaf through *Code of Federal Regulations*, Title 16.
[25] In re FTC Trade Regulation Rule, Advertising of Opthalmic Goods and Services, *Trade Regulation Rep.* No. 335 (June 1978). For background see Lee Benham, "The Effect of Advertising on the Price of Eyeglasses," *Journal of Law & Economics* (October 1972), pp. 337–352.

Pharmaceutical Manufacturers Association have at one time or another engaged in illegally deceptive advertising.[26] Moreover, recidivism is common. Once one deceptive campaign is stopped, another with different deceptions may be launched. Firestone's 25% quicker claim, for instance, was Firestone's third violation in 15 years. These considerations illuminate a major advantage of relying more on the other remedies mentioned, as they are harsher.

B. Affirmative Disclosure

This remedy is especially appropriate for two particular types of deception—misrepresentation by silence and exaggerated claims of brand uniqueness. To check the problem of deceptive silence, an affirmative disclosure order prohibits the advertiser from making certain claims unless he discloses at the same time facts that are considered necessary to negate any deceptive inferences otherwise induced by silence. Perhaps the most familiar example of affirmative disclosure is the FTC's requirement that cigarette advertisers disclose the dangers inherent to smoking: "Warning: The Surgeon General Has Determined That Cigarette Smoking Is Dangerous to Your Health." Another noteworthy example concerns Geritol, which ran into trouble for representing its iron tonic as a cure for tiredness, loss of strength, wan appearance, and associated afflictions. The Commission's order for affirmative disclosure specified that if Geritol was going to sell its tonic as a cure for tiredness, it then had to disclose the fact that there is really very little connection between tiredness and iron deficiency, and that the vast majority of people who are tired are not tired because of iron deficiency.

[26] R. Burack, "Introduction to the Handbook of Prescription Drugs." in *Consumerism*, edited by Aaker and Day (New York: Free Press, 1974), p. 257. The regulations referred to here are actually those of the FDA, not the FTC, but they are similar.

C. Corrective Advertising

Whereas affirmative disclosure may prevent the *continuance* of misleading claims into the future, the purpose of corrective advertising is to wipe out any *lingering ill effects of* deception. What do we mean by lingering ill effects? There are several possibilities. From a purely economic point of view, deceptive advertising continues to generate sales even after it has stopped because of the "lagged effect" of advertising. So long as the ill-gotten gains in sales continue, the deception will return a profit and the deceiver's more truthful competitors will suffer a disadvantage. Moreover, deceptive claims may be dangerous to consumer welfare where issues of health and safety are involved. If some folks continue to believe their tires stop 25% quicker, even after this claim is taken out of circulation, there is a problem of lingering ill effect. Accordingly, the typical corrective advertising order comes in two parts:

1. Cease and desist making the deceptive claim.
2. Cease and desist *all* advertising of the product in question unless a specified portion of that advertising contains, for a specified time period, a statement of the fact that prior claims were deceptive.

Until 1977, the legal status of corrective advertising was shaky. Although the remedy was imposed in several pre-1977 consent settlements, the FTC did not apply it in a contested case and the appellate courts did not pass on its legality until the *Listerine* litigation. Listerine, presently the nation's largest selling mouthwash (with about 40% of the market), was for decades promoted as a cold preventative as well. From 1938 to late 1972 Listerine labels declared that the stuff "KILLS GERMS BY MILLIONS ON CONTACT . . . For General Oral Hygiene, Bad Breath, Colds and resultant Sore Throats." Moreover, countless TV commercials showed mothers extolling the medicinal virtues of gargling with Listerine twice a day. "I think," they would crow, "we've cut down on colds, and those we do catch, don't seem to last as long."

Although the makers of Listerine deny that their ads ever suggested that Listerine would prevent colds, millions of folks got that message. The company's own polls showed that nearly two out of every three shoppers thought Listerine was a help for colds. Medical experts testifying at the FTC trial thought otherwise. Except for some temporary relief from sore throat irritation more easily achieved by gargling with warm salt water, Listerine was, in the experts' eyes, worthless. Believing the experts and taking into account the magnitude, duration, and prevalence of this particular deception, a unanimous Commission ordered the company to include the following statement in a portion of its future ads: "Contrary to prior advertising, Listerine will not help prevent colds or sore throats or lessen their severity."

Arguing that this order infringed their rights of free speech and exceeded FTC authority, the makers of Listerine (Warner-Lambert) appealed to high federal court. In its opinion of August 1977, the Court of Appeals generally favored the FTC's side of the case. Unlike the FTC, however, the Court thought a "softer" correction would do. It said the words "contrary to prior advertising" should be dropped from the correction because they would serve only to "humiliate" the company. Warner-Lambert remained disgruntled, appealed to the Supreme Court, and lost. Corrective advertising should thus become a well-established, if seldom used, FTC remedy.[27]

D. Advertising Substantiation[28]

In 1971 the FTC announced that from time to time it would thereafter drop a net into selected industries in hopes of fishing out schools of deceptions. The net? . . . a requirement that advertisers in the target industries *substantiate* their current claims by submitting to the FTC, on demand, such tests, studies or other data concerning their advertising promises as they had in their possession *before* their claims were made. Moreover, the Commission makes these submissions available to the public, so consumers or consumer groups who are interested may see for themselves the support, or lack of support, for advertising assertions. The program's goals are threefold:

1. *Education*—to assist consumers in making a rational choice between competing claims and in evaluating those claims.
2. *Deterrence*—to discourage advertisers from rashly making unsupported claims.
3. *Enforcement*—to aid the FTC in detecting and proceeding against unfair and deceptive claims.

Understandably, the program has so far focused on objectively verifiable claims regarding such things as product performance, contents, efficacy, safety, and price. Purely emotional and noninformative appeals have been, for obvious reasons, ignored.

The first substantiation orders were lowered on manufacturers of automobiles, air conditioners, electric shavers, and television sets. Subsequent orders have been issued against producers of hearing aids, acne preparations, pet foods, and underarm deodorants among others. The orders *specify* questioned claims, such as Gen-

---

[27] *Wall Street Journal*, August 3, 1977 and December 19, 1975; "Back on the Warpath Against Deceptive Ads," *Business Week* (April 19, 1976) pp. 148–151.

[28] Besides Trebilcock, et al., *op. cit.*, this section draws upon *Advertising 1972*, U.S. Senate, Committee on Commerce, 92nd Congress, Second Session (1972), pp. 336–483, and Dorothy Cohen, "The FTC's Advertising Substantiation Program," *Journal of Marketing* (Winter 1980), pp. 26–35.

eral Motors' assertion that the Chevrolet Chevelle had "101 advantages" designed to keep it from "becoming old before its time," and Fedders' claim of unique air-conditioning potency: "RESERVE Cooling Power—only Fedders has this important feature."

The first wave of submissions covered 282 claims made by 32 different firms. The FTC's analysis of these 282 revealed some good news and some bad news. First, the good news: a majority of the claims were adequately substantiated. Next the bad news: "serious questions" arose with respect to substantiation "in about 30% of the responses." To quote some examples from the FTC Staff Report:[29]

Automobiles: General Motors' advertising announced "101 advantages" designed to keep Chevrolet Chevelle from "becoming old before its time." As documentation for the claim General Motors listed such advantages as "full line of models," "Body by Fisher," and such safety items, already required by law, as "two front head restraints" and "back up lights". . . .

Air Conditioners: Fedders, ordered to document its claim that its model ACL20E3DA alone had "extra cooling power," admitted that the claim was incorrect and stated that the claim would not be made in future advertising.

Abetted by such discoveries as these, the program has led to numerous formal complaints of violation. And in this light ad substantiation might not, strictly speaking, be considered a "remedy" at all, for these formal proceedings result in the same kind of remedies as already mentioned—that is, cease and desist orders, corrective ads, and disclosures. Still, this program places an affirmative responsibility on advertisers where none existed before, a responsibility to have prior documentation for their

claims. It might thus be regarded as a preventive remedy serving to improve the efficiency and efficacy of FTC enforcement.[30] As regards the program's other two objectives—education and deterrence—consumers have not exploited the opportunity to probe the substantiation materials, and misrepresentation continues to be a problem.

E. Restitution

The FTC Improvement Act of 1975 empowered the FTC to seek equitable relief for consumers through (1) recision or reformulation of contracts, (2) refund of money, or (3) payment of compensatory damages. If effectively used, such measures of restitution can reduce the economic incentive for behaving badly because they can extract the ill-gotten gains from offenders. They obviously can also help to make victims whole. Thus, for example, some of the FTC's largest awards of restitution to date have involved misrepresentation and fraud in land sales, one case yielding $8 million in refunds to more than 7,600 people who bought lots in Colorado. A less sizeable but perhaps more interesting case involving an acne medication extracted restitution money from the product's celebrity endorser, famed singer Pat Boone (whose daughters allegedly used it).[31]

Several limitations apply to restitution. For one, there is a three-year statute of limitations. For another, punitive damages are not allowed. Beyond these statutory limitations, there are some practical constraints that make this remedy most applicable to especially fraudulent and corrupt business practices.

Having reviewed remedies, you can now

[29] Reprinted in *Advertising 1972, op. cit.,* pp. 412–442. It may be noted that many if not most of the questioned claims of the 1970s appear to represent "experience" qualities rather than "search" or "credence" qualities.

[30] Indeed, substantiation was an explicit remedy to curb the repeatedly blatant misrepresentations of Jay Norris, Inc., a mail-order firm. *Jay Norris, Inc., et al.* v. *FTC,* CCH para. 62,623 (CA–2, May 1979).

[31] In re Cooga Mooga, Inc., et al., CCH para. 21,417 FTC File No. 722 3051 (May 1978).

more fully appreciate our earlier assertions concerning lenient treatment of offenders. Although even the harshest of these measures may seem rather light, it can be argued that none should be heavier as long as the burden of proof borne by prosecutors is rather light.

V. Miscellaneous Unfair Practices

A. Consumer Protection

The FTC's enforcement of Section 5 extends considerably beyond "advertising" and "deception." Misleading claims may be dispersed toe-to-toe, just as easily as over the airwaves or on the printed page. Furthermore, our emphasis on deception should not obscure the fact that many practices are banned for being "unfair," even if not deceptive. In the abstract, the FTC has said that "unfair" cannot be narrowly defined, that a number of factors would influence its judgment—such as, whether the questioned act or practice is immoral, unethical, oppressive, unscrupulous, or financially injurious to buyers. In the concrete, the FTC frowns upon:

1. *Bait and switch,* in which the seller lures the buyer into the store with some kind of "bait," like a sale price for a cheap model, then "switches" the buyer to something else.
2. *Merchandise substitution,* like the sale of 1980 model trucks as 1981 model trucks.
3. *High pressure,* door-to-door sales without a three day "cooling off" period for buyer cancellation.
4. *Silent warranties,* where a manufacturer follows a secret policy of extending warranties to some but not all customers.

The last of these arose when in the late 1970s the FTC accused auto makers of waging so-called "secret warranty" campaigns as a means of paying for repairs to troublesome cars on an individual basis (for individuals who were troublesome in their complaints), without formally notifying the general public. Ford's alleged campaign was especially massive, involving more than 6 million Ford cars and trucks produced between 1974 and 1978 that were susceptible to premature engine wear and cracked blocks. Under a consent order in 1980, Ford agreed to (1) notify affected car owners by mail whenever it offers extended warranty coverage; (2) offer customers "technical service bulletins" describing in plain English the existence of any engine or transmission problems that could cost over $125 to repair; and (3) set up a toll-free 800 telephone number for owners to use in requesting service bulletins. FTC action to end Ford's secrecy prior to this order reportedly saved consumers more than $30 million in repairs.[32]

Other recent FTC efforts to erradicate unfairnesses sparked stormy protests from the affected industries. A proposed trade regulation rule to restrict advertising aimed at young children, particularly TV advertising of sugared cereals and candy, provoked shrill opposition from cereal and candy manufacturers, TV networks, grocers, and others in the business community. They derided the FTC for brazenly becoming a "National Nanny." They maintained that, as easy as it might be to sell candy to a baby (or, more accurately, to the baby's parents through the baby's prompted appeals), it was not "unfair."

Equally controversial was a proposed rule regulating funeral parlors. After lengthy and costly study, the FTC's staff accumulated substantial evidence indicating that funeral homes frequently if not regularly took financial advantage of bereaved survivors. They apparently did this by (1) refusing to provide adequate price information, (2) embalming without permission, (3) needlessly requiring a casket for cremation, (4) harrassing "discount" funeral homes, (5) misrepresenting local health re-

[32] *Wall Street Journal,* February 22, 1980, p. 12.

quirements, (6) refusing to display inexpensive caskets, (7) disparaging customers who showed a concern for funeral costs (which now average over $2,000) and by other means.[33]

Waging an intense lobbying campaign against the FTC, the Commission's business foes succeeded in securing congressional passage of the Federal Trade Commission Improvements Act of 1980. The Senate version of this bill would have terminated the FTC's investigation of children's advertising while the House bill would have killed the funeral proceedings. The final version did not go this far, but some shackles were imposed.

For example, the final bill trimmed the scope of any FTC rule regulating funeral home practices. As of this writing (1982) the FTC's revised funeral industry proposals would merely:

· Require the availability of price lists, including price quotations over the telephone.
· Prohibit funeral directors from saying that a deceased person must be embalmed (unless local law requires embalming).
· Prohibit claims that a casket is required for cremation.

More important, the final bill included among its other FTC constraints one of a very broad nature—the so-called "legislative veto." Now, before *any* trade regulation rule can go into effect, it must be presented to Congress for a period of 90 days. If within that 90 days both the House and the Senate vote against the proposed rule, it cannot go into effect. This two-house veto provision represents a rather novel step, one first applied in 1982 to squash a proposed used car rule and one so novel that it may even be unconstitutional.[34] Of course final determination about constitutionality resides in the high federal courts.

This legislation of 1980 and the furor surrounding it have had repercussions not reflected in the law itself. The FTC grew weak in the knees, aborting the development of new trade regulation rules that were not fueling the controversy. Robert Reich, director of FTC policy planning, may have put it best when he said, "Big Brother Consumer Protection is dead."[35] The irony of this turn of events is that, just a few years before the FTC Improvements Act of 1980, the FTC was being lambasted with criticism that it was *not* doing enough for consumer protection. Indeed, it was this criticism that eventually resulted in the proconsumerist FTC Improvements Act of 1975.

B. Businessperson Protection

While hostility stunted the growth of FTC trade regulation rules protecting *consumers,* an important new rule protecting *business* people had clear sailing. This was the rule on "Disclosure Requirements and Prohibitions Concerning Franchising," which became effective in late 1979. The feverish growth of franchising during the 1960s and 1970s, especially in such fields as fast food, real estate, motels, hotels, hair salons, and rental services, resulted in total franchise sales of about $338 billion in 1980 from approximately 488,000 franchise establishments.[36] It also resulted in much fraud and misrepresentation by businessmen against other businessmen as many franchisors bilked franchisees.

Under the franchise system, one party (the franchisor) grants another party (the franchisee) the right to distribute or sell certain branded goods or services. In turn, the franchisee pays the franchisor for this privilege and agrees to operate his business according to the marketing plan of the franchisor. Duping pro-

---

[33] *Funeral Industry Practices,* Final Staff Report to the Federal Trade Commission, June 1978.

[34] Antonin Scalia, "The Legislative Veto: A False Remedy for System Overload," *Regulation* (Nov./Dec. 1979), pp. 19–26.

[35] "Slowing Down the FTC," *Wall Street Journal,* July 30, 1979.

[36] U.S. Department of Commerce, *Franchising in the Economy 1978–1980* (Government Printing Office, 1980), p. 1.

spective franchisees became commonplace during the 60s and 70s, prompting the attorney general of New York to complain that "franchising literally abounds with deceptive selling practices." These practices include franchisors

> (1) misleading prospective franchisees about the potential profitability of their franchises, (2) refusing to show actual profit and loss statements to potential franchisees, (3) having "hidden charges" in the prices franchisees are charged for services and supplies, (4) using a celebrity's name to deceptively promote the franchise, (5) overpromising on their aids to franchisees, and (6) using high pressure tactics in closing the sale of a franchise.[37]

The FTC's trade regulation rule was patterned after sixteen state laws in existence at the time. It calls for the *disclosure* of such information as the business experience of the franchisor; the financial health of the franchisor; the total funds which must be paid to the franchisor; the recurring obligations of the franchisee; the rights of franchisees in contract terminations, cancellations, and renewals; and the restrictions franchisees face in purchasing supplies, selecting locations, and selling their goods and services. In addition, the rule *prohibits* the franchisor from making claims of potential earnings such as "make $50,000 profit" or "earn $70,000 per year" *unless* those claims are backed up by material facts sufficient to substantiate their accuracy, facts that are relevant to the prospective franchisee's business. Such supporting material must be disclosed to prospective franchisees before they commit themselves.[38]

Although at this writing the FTC's rule is too new to assess, study of the antecedent state laws suggests substantial improvement. Noting that Wisconsin's law reduced the apparent incidence of exaggerated prospective earnings from 37 to 15 per cent, and noting other examples of heightened honesty in Wisconsin, S. D. Hunt and J. R. Nevin concluded, "The overall benefits of the full disclosure laws seem to outweigh their costs.[39]

Summary

In April, 1972, the American Association of Advertising Agencies released the results of a poll of some 9000 students from 177 universities and colleges. The students took a dim view of advertising. Fifty-three per cent told the AAAA that they considered advertising believable only "some of the time."[40] Was their skepticism unfounded?

Section 5 of the Federal Trade Commission Act (as amended by the Wheeler-Lea Act of 1938) bans "Unfair methods of competition in commerce, and unfair or deceptive acts or practices in commerce . . ." The key criterion for determining violation by deception is whether a claim has the capacity and tendency to deceive. Truth and falsity are relevant but not conclusive, for true claims may deceive and false claims may not. As deception lies in the mind of the observer, some standard must be set as to who will be protected from deception. United States authorities supposedly protect the ignorant, the hasty, and the trusting as well as those less easily deceived. Still, the authorities have not gone so far as to protect the pathologically credulous and feeble minded. Likewise they allow abundant amounts of "puffery."

Of the many specific types of deception that have collided with this criterion, four were presented—those concerning (1) claims of composition, (2) claims of function or efficacy, (3) endorsements, and (4) mock-ups. A never ending chain of cases under Section 5 has, over the years, outlined certain standards or rules in each of these areas. With respect to mock-ups, for instance, the Colgate Rapid Shave case is

---

[37] Shelby D. Hunt and John R. Nevin, "Full Disclosure Laws in Franchising: An Empirical Investigation," *Journal of Marketing* (April 1976), p. 54.

[38] *Code of Federal Regulation,* Title 16, FTC, Part 436.

[39] Hunt and Nevin, *op. cit.,* p. 62.

[40] *Business Week,* June 10, 1972, p. 48.

a particularly important link in the law. The Supreme Court reaffirmed what advertisers already believed—that undisclosed mock-ups of mere appearance were acceptable, and that undisclosed mock-ups demonstrating *un*true performance were unacceptable. The Court broke new ground also by ruling that undisclosed mock-ups demonstrating *true* performance were unacceptable insofar as the demonstration was central to the commercial. Ever since, the word "simulated" has appeared frequently on TV.

The FTC relies on three main procedures and four principal remedies to enforce the Act. The procedures are (1) complaint plus prosecution or consent decree, (2) advisory guides, and (3) compulsory trade regulation rules. The first is a case-by-case approach. The latter two are broader in scope, reaching entire industries or complete categories of deceptive acts.

The principal remedies are (1) cease and desist orders, (2) affirmative disclosure, (3) corrective advertising, (4) advertising substantiation, and (5) restitution. The first is the traditional mainstay. The other four are recent innovations that may be considered a little more stringent.

Finally, the FTC's zealous efforts to curb "unfairnesses" during the late 1970s sparked angry charges from industry that it was being overbearingly unfair to business. The agency's staff was developing some of the most far-reaching proposals on record just at the time deregulation generally was coming into vogue. The result was the FTC Improvements Act of 1980, which directly curbed existing FTC activities, indirectly dampened the agency's ardor, and introduced the legislative veto for trade regulation rules.

Postscript

President Reagan's chairman of the FTC, James C. Miller, Jr., has vowed to achieve further deregulation at the FTC. Therefore, by the time you read this chapter, much of it may be outdated. Advertising substantiation in particular will probably end, and consumer protection generally will probably be reduced substantially for budgetary and philosophical reasons.

Questions and Exercises for Chapter 13

1. Distinguish between the policies of this chapter and those of the previous chapter in (a) purpose, (b) approach, and (c) nature of remedies.
2. The line between that which is legal and illegal is drawn between that which is true and false. True or False? Explain.
3. According to the text, the FTC "attacks the ad, not the advertiser." Explain.
4. How might deception occur in claims of efficacy? In endorsements?
5. Explain *Colgate-Palmolive* v. *FTC* (1965) in (a) facts, (b) issues, and (c) decision.
6. What is the main remedy in deceptive advertising cases and why?
7. Compare and contrast "guides" and "trade regulation rules" in (a) purpose, (b) formulation procedure, and (c) legal clout.
8. Why might corrective advertising be an appropriate remedy? Inappropriate?
9. How can something be "unfair" but not "deceptive"? Illustrate with examples.
10. If some cost-benefit analysis happened to show that all the policies of this chapter were inefficient, would that mean that they should, in fact, be ended? How would value judgments influence your answer? (You may refer back to Chapter 1.)
11. There were *two* recent FTC Improvement Acts, 1975 and 1980. Compare and contrast them.

Part IV

Economic Regulation

Source: Reprinted with permission of George Basset.

Chapter 14

Introduction to Economic Regulation

Regulation is like growing old: we would rather not do it, but consider the alternative.
—William G. Shepherd

Economic regulation is an industrial halfway house. Its residents are sheltered from the cruelties of all-out competition, yet they are not crushed by total government control. Private firms own and operate enterprises, while state and federal governments police structure, conduct, and performance for purposes other than maintaining competition.

This chapter introduces Part IV by answering five questions:

  I. *What* is economic regulation?
 II. What *industries* have been so governed?
III. *Why* has economic regulation occurred?
IV. *Who* does the regulating?
 V. What are regulation's *basic problems?*

This chapter is thus an overview.

I. What Is Economic Regulation?

Under free markets, the forces of supply and demand determine product price, product quality, firm profitability, entry, and exit. Antitrust and information policies do not greatly interfere because they operate at the periphery of markets. They remove imperfections to competition, not supplant it.

Under economic regulation, however, we find that price, product, profitability, entry, and exit are determined by *administrative processes* rather than by free market forces. Such regulation originated centuries ago under Roman law. It then progressed in the Middle Ages to Church admonitions against charging anything other than a "just price." Growth continued in English common law, which established the notion that certain enterprises were "affected with a public interest." That is to say . . .

certain occupations—such as baker, brewer, cab driver, ferryman, innkeeper, miller, smith, surgeon, and tailor—came to be viewed as closely connected with the well being of society. Practitioners of these professions were not allowed to act solely in their self-interest, but were required to set prices and render service in a socially responsible manner. For example, an innkeeper whose establishment was far from the next resting spot was expected to refrain from exploiting his monopoly position and to keep rates at a reasonable level.[1]

This English common law tradition of obligation to serve at reasonable rates came to America with the colonists. Its problems came too— namely, the private plaintiff's heavy burden of proof and the common law's loose enforcement. Efforts to find substitute legal mechanisms eventually led to charters, franchises, and direct legislative control. These efforts had to conform to constitutional limitations on what the government could and could not actively do. So the evolution of regulation in the United States includes numerous opinions of the Supreme Court, chief arbiter of what is constitutional.

The single most important case in this evolution was *Munn* v. *Illinois,* decided in 1877. *Munn* was the Supreme Court's first approval of the government's right to regulate private business that is "affected with a public interest."[2] The Illinois legislature had boldly set a maximum price that Chicago warehouses could charge for grain storage. Warehouseman Munn challenged the constitutionality of this official price-fixing, but lost when the Supreme Court, looking to the common law for guidance, found that . . .

> . . . when private property is "affected with a public interest it ceases to be *juris priviti* only" . . . When, therefore, one devotes his property to the use in which the public has an interest, he, in effect, grants to the public an interest in that use and must submit to be controlled by the public for the common good to the extent of the interest he has thus created.

[1] H. C. Petersen, *Business and Government* (New York: Harper & Row, 1981), p. 182.
[2] *Munn* v. *Illinois,* 94 U.S. 113 (1877).

After the legislature's maximum price in *Munn* v. *Illinois,* the saga of economic regulation eventually branched and rebranched until it produced three broad characteristics that distinguish it from other forms of public policy toward business, three characteristics that provide the basis for the remaining portions of this section—(1) specific industry coverage, (2) the economic variables controlled, and (3) administration by commission.

Specific Industry Coverage.   Unlike antitrust, which enjoys sweeping application, economic regulation singles out certain industries for attention, namely, those "affected with a public interest." This of course implies that some decision must be made as to what is and what is not in "the public interest," a catchy phrase so vague as to include possibly everything except widget manufacturing. Electricity, natural gas, telephone service, and railroading, have, along with a few other things, dominated the list of the elected. These industries display certain characteristics that tend to set them apart for this special treatment, characteristics we discuss shortly.

Economic Variables Controlled.   Economic regulation entails administrative determination of one or more of the following variables:

1. Overall *price level* (or rate level) is a prime focus. Traditionally, this takes the form of *maximum* price level allowed, as suggested by *Munn,* but it also includes *minimum* price level allowed and even *specific* price setting. The basis for determining overall price level is typically producer's cost plus a "reasonable" rate of profit return, so price level regulation may also be called *profit level* regulation.

2. If regulated firms sold only one product or service to only one class of customer, then price level, once determined, would settle matters. But most firms' offerings and customers vary widely, as illustrated by the tele-

phone company's local versus long-distance service and its residential versus business clientele. Accordingly, *price structure* is also regulated. That is to say, the price of one service relative to all others is often set, and the price of that service may further differ depending on who is doing the buying and when.

3. Price regulation may be evaded by deliberate product deterioration, so *product quality* frequently becomes a part of economic regulation. If so, regulators may judge whether service is "unjust, unsafe, improper, inadequate or insufficient," as when for instance utility commissions set standards for the voltage of electricity, the heating value of natural gas, and the accuracy of meters.

4. *Entry* is often controlled by licenses, exclusive franchises, or certificates of "convenience and necessity." Such doorkeeping was especially important in the past when transportation was more thoroughly regulated than it is now. Newcomers to common-carrier trucking and airline transport were kept off the roads and runways, lessening competition in many ways.

5. *Exit* control takes two forms. One is the obligation to serve individual paying patrons, an obligation that differs substantially from a nonregulated firm's right of refusal to sell. The second is regulatory control over abandonments, in which case the authorities may compel continued service to an entire class of customers or to a region that the firm would prefer to abandon. Exit from nonprofitable railroad service has been an especially hot issue for several decades now.

It must be stressed that economic regulation need not involve all these variables, nor involve them to equal degrees. Entry into radio and TV broadcasting is tightly controlled, but pricing is not. Conversely, the field price of natural gas was tightly regulated during the 1960s and 1970s, but entry into field production was not. Of all the economic variables on the list, the one that is typically least attended to by officials is product quality. As Alfred Kahn explains:

> The reasons for this are fairly clear. Service standards are often much more difficult to specify by the promulgation of rules. Where they can be specified, they are often essentially uncontroversial. Where they cannot—and this is particularly the case when it comes to innovations, to the dynamic improvements of service—in a system in which the private companies do the managing and government the supervision, there is no choice but to leave the initiative with the company itself.[3]

Thus product quality will tend to get short shrift in what follows as compared to price level, price structure, entry, and exit.

Administration by Commission. A final distinguishing characteristic of economic regulation relates to governmental mechanism—independent commissions dominate the scene. Indeed, it could be argued that commissions would not exist were it not for economic regulation. Reliance on city councils, state legislatures, franchise contracts, and other such mechanisms to do the job of continually manipulating and monitoring the above variables proved to be unsatisfactory as the country grew increasingly complex and dynamic. If done right, the job of economic regulation requires moderate expertise, persistent attentiveness, and considerable flexibility—qualities not usually found either in charters, which suffer the rigidities of contracts, or in legislative bodies, which suffer the distractions of other governmental duties and the handicaps of ignorance. Thus the job fell to commissions comprised of several members, vested with fairly broad powers, and subjected to judicial review.

In 1869 Massachusetts established the first

[3] Alfred E. Kahn, *The Economics of Regulation,* Vol. I (New York: John Wiley & Sons, 1970), p. 22.

state commission to regulate railroads, an innovation premised on the inability of cities to regulate the railroads effectively. In turn, the broad geographic expanse of the railroads proved to be too much for the states individually, so the first federal commission—the Interstate Commerce Commission—was created in 1887 to oversee the interstate activities of the railroads. Later, in 1907, electric power first came under state commission control in New York. Other states followed, but their geographic limitations again prompted an extension of federal authority with the founding of the Federal Power Commission.

Economic regulation is not strictly the preserve of commissions. Much energy regulation does not fit that mold. But as we shall see, commissions dominate.

II. What Industries Are Regulated?

A. Legal Background

After *Munn* v. *Illinois* authorized economic regulation as a constitutional government activity in 1877, the key legal question became "What industries so qualify?" The courts gave two answers—one for the period 1877–1934, another from 1934 to the present.

During the six and a half decades spanning 1877–1934, the Supreme Court took upon itself the job of sorting out those industries that could legally be regulated from those that could not. The Court felt confident that it could distinguish industries "affected with a public interest" from others when statute laws were challenged. But the job became heavily tangled in argument and opinion. No clear criterion presented itself. Gas, electricity, water, and transport services qualified fairly easily. Grain elevators, banks, and insurance companies likewise cleared but less assuredly. In contrast, sharply

divided opinions of the Supreme Court kept food, apparel, and ice manufacturing from being regulated. You can appreciate the difficulties in such sorting by simply asking yourself, Why is insurance affected with a public interest while food is not?

Finally, in 1934, the Supreme Court quit trying to pick and choose among industrial candidates. *Nebbia* v. *New York* was the decision, and state regulation of the price of milk was the issue. A grocer named Nebbia violated the milk law but argued in his defense that the law was improper, that milk was not a business "affected with a public interest." The Supreme Court replied that it would no longer try to decide this sort of thing. It turned legislatures loose, saying that "a state is free to adopt *whatever* economic policy may reasonably be deemed public welfare." The only condition "due process" required thereafter would be that the laws passed "have a reasonable relation to a proper legislative purpose and are neither arbitrary nor discriminatory . . ."[4] Thus, ever since *Nebbia,* the government has been fairly free to regulate any industry it pleases.

B. The Roster of Industries

Despite this sweeping constitutional leeway, government has not run amok. The roster of the regulated, as shown in Table 14–1, is long but not endless. Indeed, several of the industries included on the list are no longer regulated at all or are in the midst of being *de*regulated—namely, trucking, airlines, railroading, crude oil, and natural gas production. Nevertheless, we shall discuss those in the throes of deregulation because the deregulation is either very recent or incomplete and the industries are very important. Moreover, many lessons are taught by the regulatory experiences of those industries.

[4] *Nebbia* v. *New York,* 291 U.S. 502 (1934).

Table 14–1. Principal Regulated Industries in the United States, 1980

Industry	National Income Accruing (in billions $)	Percentage of 1980 National Income
Electricity, gas, and sanitary services	$ 21.3	1.3%
Communications (Telephone and telegraph, radio and TV broadcasting)	34.9	2.2
Transportation		
Railroads	13.3	0.8
Trucking	28.7	1.8
Water	4.9	0.3
Other transport*	21.3	1.3
Crude oil and natural gas mining	15.7	0.9
Total	140.1	8.6

* Includes local and interurban passenger transit, airlines, and pipelines.

Source: Department of Commerce, *Survey of Current Business* (July 1981), pp. 32.

Though heavily regulated, banking, finance, insurance, and agriculture are not included here because of certain uniquenesses.

C. Characteristics of Regulated Industries

Several characteristics of these industries set them apart from most others. First, they are usually considered **vital** industries. To be sure, food and clothing (and books) are equally vital yet unregulated, but transportation, communications, and energy are necessities not to be sneezed at.

Second, nearly all regulated industries sell services rather than commodities. The movement of goods from here to there is a service, as is a phone call or a kilowatt-hour of electricity. Unlike commodities, services cannot be stored. Their production and consumption coincide inseparably, like a coin's two sides. Most regulated industries must therefore maintain excess capacity to meet peak periods of con-

sumption. In many cases they must also maintain direct connections by wire or pipe with their customers.

Third, most regulated industries are **capital intensive.** The guts of their operations are cables, turbine generators, switches, steel rails, and road beds rather than mill hands, raw materials, or merchandise. This capital intensity can be measured by the value of assets relative to annual sales revenue. It is not at all unusual for assets to be 300 or 400% of annual sales revenue in regulated industries (airlines and trucking excepted). Three or four years of sales are then necessary to match asset value. In contrast, most asset values in manufacturing are much lower, averaging about 80% of annual sales receipts. Wholesale and retail trade figures are still less, at roughly 35%. Food stores have asset/sales ratios of merely 20%, so for them a single year's sales receipts cover assets five times over.

Finally, and perhaps most important, many regulated industries manifest **market failures** and **imperfections,** such as those mentioned earlier in Chapter 2, Table 2–2. "Natural" monopoly heads the list, and others are explored following.

III. Why Regulate?

There is no easy answer to the question of why regulation has come about. The industries regulated differ substantially despite their many common characteristics. The historical conditions surrounding the advent of regulation likewise differ from industry to industry. Moreover, the reasons regulation gets started for an industry need not be the same as the reasons for its continuation. As a result, scholarly opinions also differ, as each scholar approaches regulation from a different point of view (much like the proverbial blind men inspecting the elephant, one holding the tail, another an ear, and so forth).[5] In short, generalizations are hazardous.

One way to hazard our own generalizations would be to build upon the discussions of Chapters 2 and 3. Chapter 2 suggests an *optimistic* or *public interest* explanation for regulation. That is to say, regulation may be viewed as a means of solving many of the free market's problems outlined in Table 2–2 on page 24, most notably the problems of natural monopoly (local telephone service for example), common property resources (radio and TV broadcasting), instability (railroading), short-run protection for growth (airlines), and equity in income distribution (crude oil). To say this is an optimistic or public interest view implies the achievement of laudable, broadly based objectives. Widely held value judgments are supposedly served, even allocation efficiency.

On the other hand, Chapter 3 suggests *pessimistic* or *private interest* explanations. Given

that government action is often flawed by the shortcomings outlined in Table 3–4 on page 52, the public interest explanation could well be wrong. Economic regulation may originate and continue because of official ignorance, special interest effects, dynamic problems of delay and myopia, and even perhaps distributional inequity. The so-called "capture" theory of regulation is one of the most commonly voiced along these lines. Regulatory commissions are said to be "captured" by the industries they regulate. The result is cartelization, with floors under prices and barriers against new entry, all for purposes of serving the private interest of those regulated at the expense of the public at large.[6] An even more cynical private interest theory holds that nobody but the bureaucrats who do the regulating really gain by regulation.

In truth, neither the optimist's public interest view nor the pessimist's private interest view can carry the full load of explaining economic regulation, broad though each of those views may be. Taken individually, each is too extreme to depict reality accurately. Yet each has too much validity to be discarded.

Various *blends* of these two views have therefore been offered by commentators. One blend argues that regulatory commissions go through a "life cycle," whose periods combine these explanations in varying degrees. According to Marver Bernstein, for example, commissions (1) begin during a period of *gestation,* typified by a fervor for reform and a legislative mandate that reflects the public's needs; (2) progress into a *youthful* stage of halting policy and program development but zealous enforcement; (3) enter *maturity,* a time of lethargy and political isolation, during which "the commission finally becomes a captive of the regulated groups;" and (4) eventually end up in *old*

---

[5] For a lengthy review see Barry M. Mitnick, *The Political Economy of Regulation* (New York: Columbia University Press, 1980).

[6] George J. Stigler, "The Theory of Economic Regulation" *Bell Journal of Economics* (Spring 1971), pp. 3–26; Gabriel Kolko, *Railroads and Regulation, 1877–1916* (Princeton, N.J.: Princeton University Press, 1965).

age, when the commission's primary mission becomes maintenance of the status quo for itself and its regulated industry.[7]

Another blend sees various explanations behind singular regulatory developments, such as the establishment of the Interstate Commerce Commission in 1887. Customers of the railroads supported regulation in hopes of ending what they perceived as harsh price discrimination; the railroads themselves advocated regulation in hopes of achieving cartelization; and so on. In this view, many diverse groups in combination sought to protect their interests through railroad regulation for many different reasons.[8] Still other blends emphasize interindustry diversity. As Thomas McCraw has written:

> Neither "public interest" nor "capture," nor the two in combination adequately characterize the American experience with regulation over the last century. Sometimes regulation materialized with the support or even initiative of the industry involved (as with broadcasting), sometimes with the reluctant assent (as with the ICC), and sometimes against the rigid opposition (as with the Granger commissions and the SEC). Commissions often came into existence with broad popular support, sometimes amid obvious public apathy, but never in the face of mass-based, articulate opposition.[9]

The blend of explanations that seems most instructive to the present writer centers on what may be called, for lack of a better word, "fairness."[10] Of course the notion of "fairness"

is very slippery and ill-defined. What is "fair" to one group may be "unfair" to another. What is "fair" in one era may be "unfair" in another. And attempts to achieve "fairness" often generate "unfair" side effects, as when for example, as a result of airline regulation, those flying coach subsidized the luxury treatment of those flying first class. For all these reasons I hesitate to use "fairness" to explain regulation's purposes, but a concept is needed that reflects diverse economic, political, and social values. And "fairness," unfortunately, is it.

Using fairness as our touchstone, then, Table 14–2 outlines the main purposes of regulation in terms of (A) fairness to buyers generally, (B) fairness to sellers generally, (C) fairness to certain *classes* of buyers as opposed to other buyers, (D) fairness to certain *classes* of sellers as opposed to others, and (E) fairness as an administrative process. The specific problems addressed—*whether real or imagined, logical or illogical*—are mentioned within each division, such as the classic problem of natural monopoly (A1) and the problem of price discrimination (C1). In addition, the regulatory tools referred to previously are distributed throughout Table 14–2 together with handy examples of the industries subjected to their use.

Before elaborating on Table 14–2, we should summarize the summary. It should be noted, for instance, that *maximum* price level control is the main tool of regulation aimed at fairness for buyers, whereas *minimum* price level control fosters fairness for sellers. When it comes to consideration of fairness *among* different buyers or sellers, price *structure* takes center stage, because price structure reflects the rate one buyer pays as compared to another, or the rate one seller can charge as compared to another. *Entry* limitations are protective of established sellers, so they are most important when the purpose of regulation is to achieve some notion of fairness for sellers, however unfair the results might be for buyers. Conversely, *exit* limitations tend to serve the interests of buy-

[7] M. Bernstein, *Regulating Business by Independent Commission* (Princeton, N.J.: Princeton University Press, 1955), pp. 74–102.

[8] Mitnick, *op. cit.*, pp. 173–191.

[9] Thomas K. McCraw, "Regulation in America," *Business History Review* (Summer 1975), pp. 179–180.

[10] For related views see Bruce Owen and Ronald Braeutigam, *The Regulation Game* (Cambridge, Mass.:, Ballinger, 1978); Ann Friedlander and Richard de Neufville, "The Political Rationality of Federal Transportation Policy," in R. O. Zerbe, Jr., (ed.) *Research in Law and Economics*, Vol. 1 (Greenwich, Conn.: JAI Press, 1979), pp. 97–114; Donald Dewey, "Regulatory Reform," in W. Shepherd and T. Gies (eds.), *Regulation in Further Perspective* (Cambridge, Mass.: Ballinger, 1974), pp. 27–40.

Table 14–2.   Outline of Answers to the Question Why Regulate?

A. FAIRNESS TO BUYERS GENERALLY
   1. *Problem:* natural monopoly
      Tools: maximum price level, exit control, product quality
      Examples: local electricity, local telephone service
   2. *Problem:* excessive "rent" or "windfall profit"
      Tools: maximum price level
      Examples: crude oil and natural gas production during the 1970s
B. FAIRNESS TO SELLERS GENERALLY
   1. *Problem:* destructive competition or instability
      Tools: minimum price level, entry control, product quality
      Examples: railroads, trucking, airlines
   2. *Problem:* common property resource, conservation
      Tools: entry and output control
      Examples: radio and TV broadcasting, crude oil 1930–1970
   3. *Problem:* promotion of industries
      Tools: minimum price level, entry control, subsidy
      Examples: airlines and radio broadcasting during the 1930s.
C. FAIRNESS AMONG DIFFERENT BUYERS
   1. *Problem:* "unfair" price discrimination
      Tools: price structure regulation
      Example: long-haul/short-haul in railroads
   2. *Problem:* need for cross-subsidy
      Tools: price structure regulation, entry and exit control
      Example: small-town air service, life-line energy rates
D. FAIRNESS AMONG DIFFERENT SELLERS
   1. *Problem:* diversified sellers versus specialized sellers (cream skimming)
      Tools: entry control, price structure regulation
      Example: AT&T versus long distance specialists
   2. *Problem:* new sellers versus old (intermodal rivalry)
      Tools: entry control, minimum prices, and price structure
      Examples: trucking versus railroads, cable TV versus broadcasting
E. FAIRNESS AS AN ADMINISTRATIVE PROCESS
   1. *Problem:* disruptive transitions
      Tools: all regulatory tools plus administrative delays
      Examples: railroad abandonments, energy shortages
   2. *Problem:* opportunities for complaints
      Tools: administrative procedures
      Examples: rate hearings

ers, as sellers are then compelled to offer their services against their will. These generalities should not be lost in the thicket that follows.

A. *Fairness to Buyers Generally*

1. NATURAL MONOPOLY
In some situations, economic or technical conditions permit only one efficient supplier, leading to "natural monopoly." The most obvious cause of natural monopoly is substantial economies of scale relative to demand. That is, cost per unit of output declines continuously as scale of operations increases. This is shown in Figure 14–1, where, throughout the range of quantity demanded, long-run average and marginal costs fall for a single firm. Two firms

Figure 14–1. Decreasing Cost Industry

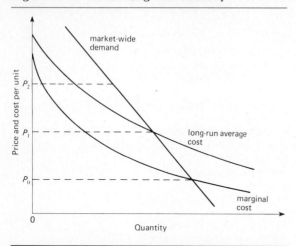

could supply the market's requirements at high price P_2, but only at lofty unit costs. A competitive duel between two such firms could be won handily by the largest rival because greater size brings lower cost, enabling the larger firm to price below its competitor's cost. At price P_1 in Figure 14–1, a sole survivor could meet *all* market demand at a point where the unit cost curve is still falling as a function of output. There is, then, room for only one efficient enterprise, whose monopoly power could be exploited to raise price to P_2.

Among regulated industries, costs decline as scale increases for local water, electric power, gas, telephone, and cable TV. The technology of transmission and the physical fact of direct connection are the main causes of this cost effect. Cables, pipelines, and other conduits have transmission capacities that grow *more* than proportionately to size or material make-up. As a consequence, the least expensive way to transmit electricity, gas, water, or telephone communications is through large lines. Furthermore, local distribution of these services requires direct connection to customers. Compe-

tition would therefore entail redundant line duplications, something obviously inefficient and wasteful—not to say damned inconvenient, ugly, and disruptive, given the excessive ditch digging, pipe laying, and wire hanging in which competition would entangle us.

The main tool of regulation in these instances is maximum price level control. Monopoly is permitted, even encouraged. But to prevent excess profits, price is held down to a level covering no more than cost plus a "fair" profit. For example, regulation of electric utilities was first initiated in New York in 1907 after it was discovered that the New York Gas and Electric Light Company sold current to residential consumers at an average price of 8.042 cents per kilowatt hour, with some paying as much as 15 cents, while the cost of production was only 3.664 cents.[11] Obligations to serve and quality surveillance accompany price level regulation.

Viewed in terms of Figure 14–1, the objective is to hold price down to P_1, below monopoly price level P_2. Moving beyond simple "fairness," efficiency could be served by a price set equal to marginal cost, as indicated by P_0. While such a single price yields insufficient revenues to cover total costs, a multipart price structure could be devised to achieve the same efficiency yet cover total costs.

2. WINDFALL PROFIT

Maximum price level regulation has been applied outside the natural monopoly context to limit "windfall" profits. Figure 14–2 simplifies the issue by assuming that supply of the product is fixed at quantity Q. If demand is D_1, the free market price would be P_1 and total revenue for sellers would be price times quantity, or area OP_1AQ. In economic jargon this revenue is called "rent" because quantity Q would be available even if price were zero. The supply

[11] Douglas Anderson, "State Regulation of Electric Utilities," in J. Q. Wilson (ed.), *The Politics of Regulation* (New York: Basic Books, 1980), p. 14.

Figure 14–2. Windfall Profit Problem

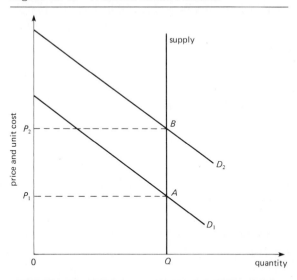

of land for instance does not vary with price, thereby providing a classic example. If demand increased to D_2, price would jump to P_2, increasing owner rental income by the added amount P_1P_2BA.

Although these "rents" certainly gladden the hearts and fill the pocketbooks of sellers, those on the demand side may think the "rents" are unfair because they are "windfalls" rather than rewards for increased productive efforts. Maximum price level regulation might seem to be the answer, and indeed this explains a major motive behind the price regulation of crude oil and natural gas production during the 1970s.

When the Organization of Petroleum Exporting Countries (OPEC) lifted the price of foreign oil by fantastic amounts in 1973 and later years, demand shifted to domestic energy sources and hiked the value of domestic oil and gas immensely. By one estimate the capitalized value of the increased domestic rents amounted

to a whopping $800 billion.[12] So the question became, who gets this? Consumers or energy resource owners? The case for fairness to consumers held out the image of poor old folks in cold New England paying their last pennies to the rich oil and gas barons of Texas and Oklahoma. This image was convincing enough to prompt temporary price controls, which because of the shortages they caused may have been unfair to consumers denied supplies. Policy has since been modified to release price level from bondage. Instead, a "windfall profits" tax now serves the cause of equity in the distribution of income, a tax that operates as an excise tax.

B. Fairness to Sellers Generally

1. DESTRUCTIVE COMPETITION OR INSTABILITY

Certain characteristics of many regulated industries—their ponderous capital intensity and susceptibility to excess capacity in particular—expose them to dangers of "destructive" competition. At least that is what some defenders of regulation contend. Excess capacity is said to induce reckless price cutting. And heavy capital intensity translates into high fixed costs as a proportion of total cost. So once prices start to fall they can plummet deeply before bottoming at average variable cost. The argument concludes, therefore, that such industries will be plagued by periodic price wars financially destructive to producers and disruptive for consumers.

Notice that this argument cannot rationalize regulation in natural monopoly markets, because natural monopolies, once established, face no competition. Notice, too, that the argument is designed to justify *minimum* price regulation, not *maximum* price regulation (as in

[12] Robert Stobaugh and Daniel Yergin, *Energy Future* (New York: Random House, 1979), p. 217.

the case of natural monopolies). Once a price floor is in place, entry restrictions are needed to prevent its collapse. Hence, this is an argument that has been invoked to justify minimum price and entry regulation in transportation.

Historically, sharp competition did precede the advent of transportation regulation. The railroads experienced price wars in the 19th century, and the railroads hoped that regulation would stem that price competition. During the Great Depression severe competition plagued trucking and airlines, ushering in regulation of those carriers. Nevertheless, these historical circumstances were rather unique. Overbuilding hampered 19th century railroading. And macroeconomic policy now shields us from further depressions. Under normal circumstances, in other words, the argument of destructive competition has limited application.

2. COMMON PROPERTY RESOURCE

A second rationale that fits the mold of fairness to sellers is best illustrated with reference to radio and television broadcasting. The radio spectrum used by broadcasters is a "common property resource" in the sense that no one really owns it and anyone could use it. But it is also a limited resource, with a limited number of band widths or channels. If broadcasters were granted free and unrestricted entry, they could very well flood the air waves, interfering with each other and garbling the reception of listeners and viewers. They could, in other words, destroy a common asset. Accordingly, access to the spectrum is limited by licensing. Broadcasters, however, are not subject to price or profit control, only to entry restrictions. The arbitrary selection of licensees now in force is supposed to favor those broadcasters who best serve the "public interest," but it is not clear that it actually does.

Another example of regulation based on conservation is crude oil from 1933–1973. As will be explained later, oil reservoirs became common property resources under the "rule of capture." State commissions therefore regulated production through well spacing and prorationing.

3. PROMOTION OF INDUSTRIES

In times past the regulation of ocean shipping, nuclear power, and energy has been linked to promotion of those industries, often for national defense reasons. The classic case, however, is the airlines. When the Civil Aeronautics Board was established in 1938, airline service was too new to be profitable, a condition aggravated by the Great Depression. Government subsidies for carrying the mail were provided, but only through a system of competitive bidding that threatened the airlines with bankruptcy. Thus protection and promotion were the major purposes prompting airline regulation. The ensuing minimum price restraints and entry restrictions lasted much longer than could be justified by these considerations, however, suggesting a shift to other rationales such as fairness among buyers.

C. Fairness Among Different Buyers

1. "UNFAIR" PRICE DISCRIMINATION

Last century's clamor for railroad regulation arose more from price discrimination than anything else. Indeed, the Interstate Commerce Act of 1887 made no explicit provision for the ICC to fix maximum overall rate levels. Instead, the Act directed that rates approved by the Commission be "just and reasonable" in structure.

As shown in Figure 9–1 on page 191 of Chapter 9, price discrimination can occur when different buyers have different elasticities of demand. These differences typically arise in regulated industries for two main reasons—(1) big buyers often have higher elasticities than small buyers because big buyers have opportunities for self-supply or monopsony power; (2) some buyers may be able to choose from among a number of sellers offering close substitutes, in which case these buyers' demand appears elastic to sellers, while other buyers have only one source of supply, something which lowers elasticity as seen by the seller. In both cases low elasticity invites a high price; high elasticity a low price.

In railroading, circa 1880, large shippers were able to extract lower rates than small shippers. Moreover, some routes experienced intense competition while others were served by only one railroad. As a result, towns without rail competition were charged higher rates than those blessed with two or more railroads. Indeed, in many instances, prices on noncompetitive *short hauls* exceeded those on competitive *long hauls*, despite one's common sense expectation that rates should rise rather than fall with distance. This was considered unfair, not to mention potentially inefficient.

2. NEED FOR CROSS-SUBSIDY

Just as regulation can *prevent* "unfair" price discrimination, it can also *impose* what some might consider "fair" price discrimination. In other words, regulators have occasionally held prices to certain buyers *up*, well above cost, so that the resulting excess profits could then be used to keep prices to other buyers *down*, well below cost.[13]

This *cross-subsidy* has usually benefited small towns at the expense of big cities because small towns tend to have "thin" demands and high unit costs while big cities have "thick" demands and low unit costs. Under CAB regulation, for instance, unprofitable airline service to small communities was subsidized using profits from the heavily traveled trunkline routes between major cities. Similarly, the ICC has

often required railroads to provide red-ink service on branch lines to country hamlets and to cover the losses using black-ink earnings on busier routes. Critics of such cross-subsidization argue that if subsidies are deemed desirable they should not be achieved by such hidden redistributions. Rather, they should for reasons of efficiency come directly from government coffers.

D. Fairness Among Different Sellers

1. DIVERSIFIED SELLERS VS. SPECIALIZED SELLERS

When cross-subsidization is viewed from the sellers' side instead of the buyers' side, special problems arise that have been exploited to justify regulation. In particular, cross-subsidization opens opportunities for *"cream skimming."* That is, the high profits on the creamy segments of the business (highly traveled routes for instance) attract the entry of firms wanting to provide *only* the highly profitable service (leaving the unprofitable business to the regulated firm). In telecommunications, for example, new private-line microwave companies have entered high-density long-distance service between major cities and ignored the less profitable low-density connections between small cities. Regulated firms offering diversified services thus plead for protection from new entrants who specialize in lucrative segments, arguing that if such regulatory protection is denied, cross-subsidization will have to cease as competition eats up the excess profits that provide the subsidy. Regulated firms also plead for protection by arguing that they generate "economies of scope," that is, efficiencies from diversified as opposed to specialized service offerings.

It can now be seen that cross-subsidization is not always forced on regulated firms, as suggested above when considering fairness among buyers. It may be instigated by regulated firms

---

[13] R. A. Posner, "Taxation by Regulation," *Bell Journal of Economics* (Spring 1971), pp. 22–50.

themselves as a means of gaining protection against "unfair" competition. This has been especially true in transportation.

2. NEW SELLERS VERSUS OLD SELLERS

In some cases regulation has been imposed on new industries because they competed against old industries already subject to regulation. ICC regulation of trucking, for example, resulted when trucks became potent competitors of the railroads. The railroads lobbied strenuously for truck regulation during the 1920s and 1930s. Truckers resisted until the Great Depression changed their minds about the desirability of federal protection. Regulation followed despite the fact that, economically speaking, truck regulation makes little or no sense.

To cite another example, the advent of cable television threatened over-the-air broadcasters who were regulated by the Federal Communications Commission. Although spectrum scarcity may properly justify the regulation of over-the-air broadcasting, it cannot justify similar regulation of cable broadcasting. Nevertheless, the FCC restricted the growth of cable TV during the 50s, 60s, and 70s to protect the over-the-air broadcasters.

E. Fairness As an Administrative Process

The essence of economic regulation is simply this: *administrative procedures* replace the free market forces of demand and supply. Thus a final possible explanation for regulation might well be this: people prefer administrative procedures to market forces at least in some instances, *not* because they believe that administrative procedures can improve upon the free market in obtaining good economic performance, but because they believe that the procedure *itself* is somehow "fairer." As Bruce Owen and Ronald Braeutigam say, "It is the procedure as much as the ultimate outcome that matters. Or rather, the procedure *is* the outcome."[14]

1. TO TEMPER DISRUPTIVE TRANSITIONS

Features of economic regulation that might further procedural fairness are the delay inherent in regulation and "due process" for buyers. Given that peoples' lives are often built around particular configurations of utility and transportation services (where they live, size of home, type of heating, and so forth), it may well be true that they place some value on the delays that regulation entails. Rail passenger services therefore linger long after they are economically obsolete, and low-priced natural gas is made available long after its value has skyrocketed. Stated differently, the world is risky, and regulation may reduce risks by delaying disruptive changes. Changes are necessary for efficiency, though, so this also delays efficient adjustments.

2. OPPORTUNITY TO VOICE COMPLAINTS

Another feature of the administrative process is that it provides a forum for buyers and sellers to express their views. Of course the voices of sellers may often drown out those of buyers, but regulation may nevertheless gain much public support for this procedural reason. As Donald Dewey puts it:[15]

> [First] we expect group therapy—a release of tension and frustrations. . . . Fortunately, plenty of angry people in this world would rather testify at a public hearing—preferably before a TV camera—than blow up buildings or beat their kids.
>
> Second, we expect regulation to protect us from the kind of sharp commercial practice that is generally impossible in competitive industries . . . The Penn Central Railroad will never refund a nickel for a breakdown in service unless it is compelled to do so by a Utility Commission.

[14] Owen and Braeutigam, *op. cit.*, p. 26.
[15] Dewey, *op. cit.*, pp. 35–37.

Third, we expect regulation to mitigate some of the consequences of the bureaucratization that comes with great size. To say the obvious, in any organization mistakes are made, and the larger the organization, the more difficult it is to pinpoint the responsibility for error. A complaint to a regulatory body is one way that the consumer has of striking back. . . .

One problem with placing value on the administrative process is that it requires administrators. The interests of those administrators may not coincide with the interests of either buyers or sellers.

IV. Who Regulates?

This brings us to the question of who does the regulating. The vast bulk of regulatory power rests with independent regulatory commissions. They are neither legislative, judicial, nor administrative. Rather, the duties of these commissions run the gamut of governmental classifications. They make rules and thereby legislate; they hold hearings or adversary proceedings and thereafter adjudicate; they enforce regulatory laws and thereby administer.

A. Jurisdiction

Although commission duties are thus typically broad, their scope of jurisdiction is often narrow. One major division of jurisdiction concerns geography. State regulatory commissions govern *intra*state commerce, whereas federal agencies oversee *inter*state commerce. Product or service determines a second division. Many commissions regulate only one type of utility, or a limited class of utilities. As shown in the top half of Table 14–3, which lists the main federal commissions, the Interstate Commerce Commission regulates interstate land transportation (and some waterway carriers); the Federal Energy Regulatory Commission (until 1977

the Federal Power Commission) regulates interstate transmission and wholesale price of electricity, rates and routes of natural gas pipelines, and the wellhead price of gas destined for interstate shipment (although this last authority is being phased out); the Federal Communications Commission licenses broadcasters and regulates interstate (long-distance) telephone and telegraph rates and levels of service; and the Civil Aeronautics Board has jurisdiction over all interstate air passenger service (until its demise in 1985).

State commissions are less narrowly specialized. With varying scope their main concerns are *local* gas, electric, telephone, water, and transit utilities, as suggested in the bottom half of Table 14–3. State or federal, the U.S. Supreme Court summarized the commission concept when it said that these agencies were "created with the avowed purpose of lodging functions in a body specifically competent to deal with them by reason of information, experience and careful study of the business and economic conditions of the industry affected."[16]

B. Commission Structure and Personnel

Commission panels usually consist of three to eleven members appointed to fixed terms by either the President (for federal posts) or the Governor (for state posts, although several states *elect* commissioners). Appointments usually must be approved by legislative bodies, the U.S. Senate in the case of federal commissions. With but few exceptions, the commissioners so selected do not fit the ideal image of objective experts. They tend to be lawyers and businessmen whose sympathies often lie with the industry they regulate, or obscure politicians (still wet behind the ears and climbing, or washed

---

[16] *Federal Trade Commission* v. *R. F. Keppel and Bros. Inc.,* 291 U.S. 304, 314 (1934).

Table 14–3. The Main Federal Commissions and Selected State Commissions (Circa 1980)

Commission (and year of origin)	Number of Members	Number of Staff Members	Jurisdiction
Federal Commissions			
Interstate Commerce Commission (1887)	11	2024	Railroads; some water shipping and trucking (with powers diminishing)
Federal Energy Regulatory Commission (formerly the Federal Power Commission, 1934)	5	1813	Electric power; some gas and pipelines
Federal Communications Commission (1934)	7	2088	Telephone; television; radio; telegraph
Civil Aeronautics Board (1938)	5	745	Airlines (with powers phasing out completely by 1985)
Selected State Commissions			
California (1912)	5	900	Electric, gas, telephone, railroads, buses, docks, water carriers, and more.
Colorado (1913)	3	95	Electric, gas, telephone, telegraph, water, buses, taxis, railroads.
Flordia (1887)	5	434	Electric, gas, telephone, telegraph, water, sewer, buses, trucks, railroads, and more.
Indiana (1907)	3	103	Electric, gas, telephone, water, buses, railroads, and more.
Massachusetts (1885)	3	122	Electric, gas, telephone, railroads, buses, trucks, taxis, water.
Pennsylvania (1908)	5	599	Electric, gas, telephone, telegraph, water, sewer, docks, airlines, buses, taxis, railroads, and more.

Source: R. J. Penoyer, *Directory of Federal Regulatory Agencies* (St. Louis: Center for the Study of American Business, Washington University, 1980); National Association of Regulatory Utility Commissioners, *1978 Annual Report on Utility and Carrier Regulation* (1979).

up and on the way out). Some appointments are even humorous. A nominee for the Federal Communications Commission was asked during his Senate confirmation hearing about his qualifications in communications. "Senator," he replied, "I don't know anything about communications. I came to Washington expecting to be appointed to the Federal Power Commission."[17]

Commissioners are aided by staffs of civil servants comprising mainly accountants, engineers, lawyers, and economists. Many critics of regulation contend that commissions cannot do an adequate job because both staffers and commissioners are underpaid and overworked. The companies they regulate can afford good personnel in plenitude. Hence, control of corporate giants with this feeble machinery has been called herding elephants with flyswatters.[18]

In any event, a skeletal example of this machinery may be found in Figure 14–3, which shows the organization chart for the Public Utilities Commission of Ohio.

C. Procedures

Important regulatory decisions are made by quasi-judicial proceedings, much like those in ordinary courts of law. Company attorneys are pitted against commission staff attorneys or outside "intervenor" attorneys. As Leonard Weiss and Allyn Strickland explain:

> Cases may be initiated by the staff and/or affected firms. The full commission may hear a case, but more commonly it is heard by a trial examiner. . . . The trial examiner is a lawyer appointed by the commission to hear evidence presented by the staff, the affected firms, and any intervenors admitted to the proceeding . . .
>
> The hearing is similar to a court proceeding

with prepared testimony, cross-examination of witnesses, and the usual rules of procedure. The participants complete the case by submitting briefs, which summarize their arguments, the relevant evidence, and appropriate precedents. The trial examiner then prepares a proposed decision, which he turns over to the commission. The commission reviews the case record and reaches its own decision, which may or may not be the same as the trial examiner's. Commission decisions are reached by majority vote [and] may be appealed on questions of law or procedure to the courts . . .[19]

This list of procedures may create the illusion that commissions are truly "independent," but that is only an illusion. Many commentators argue that commissions tend to be more responsive to corporate than to consumer interests. Commission appointment and funding are controlled by politicians in the legislative and executive branches of government. In turn, these politicians are frequently beholden to the regulated firms, their trade associations, and their unions for political support of various kinds (including campaign contributions, of course). In addition, "commissioners are commonly courted on an informal basis by representatives of the regulated industries. The big broadcasting and airline companies maintain high-paid lobbyists in Washington who regularly socialize with commissioners. Occasionally the press or congressional committees uncover stories of commissioners enjoying golfing weekends in Bermuda as guests of the airlines or travelling to Florida in private railroad cars provided by the railroads. After serving on the commissions, many commissioners and staff members are subsequently employed by regulated firms."[20] On the other hand, the dire financial straits

---

[17] Louis M. Kohlmeier, Jr., *The Regulators* (New York: Harper & Row, 1969), p. 48.

[18] B. C. Moore, Jr., "AT&T: The Phony Monopoly," in *Monopoly Makers*, edited by M. J. Green (New York: Grossman, 1973), p. 82.

[19] L. Weiss and A. Strickland, *Regulation: A Case Approach* (New York: McGraw-Hill Book Co., 1976), pp. 8–9.

[20] Ibid., p. 10. For elaboration on the causes of proindustry bias, see Roger G. Noll, *Reforming Regulation* (Washington, D.C.: Brookings Institution, 1971), pp. 15–46.

294

Figure 14-3. Organization Chart: Ohio Public Utilities Commission

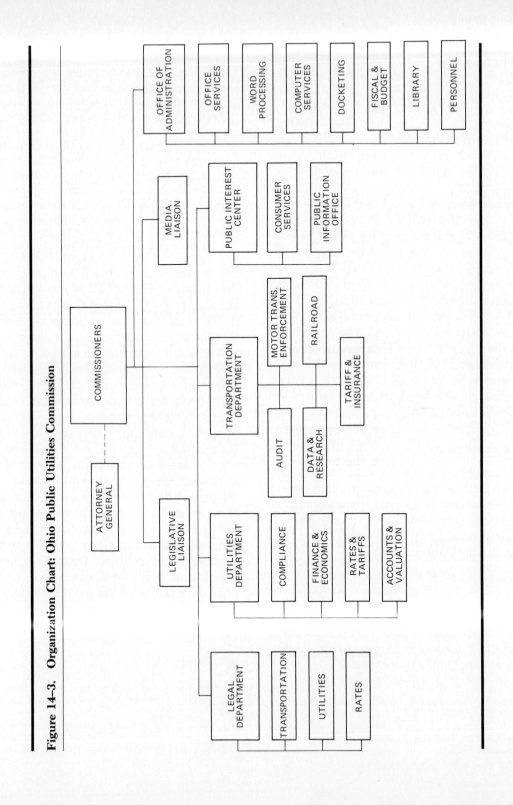

many public utilities currently face suggest that commissions can be less beholden to regulated firms than this characterization implies.

It is probably a symptom of the importance attached to independence that commissions occasionally recruit from academia on the assumption that professors are, on the whole, genuine experts and persons of integrity. Many such appointments have been particularly successful, notably those of Professors Alfred Kahn and Nicholas Johnson, two of regulation's brightest stars. Thus, some commissioners serve outstandingly.

V. Basic Problems

Regulation has received much bad press of late, as suggested most dramatically by the recent trend toward *de*regulation in airlines, trucking, and railroads. Problems of personnel and procedures do not deserve all the blame for regulation's shortcomings. There are several basic problems of concept and execution. Although these problems can be fully appreciated only after studying the details of following chapters, this introduction to the topic would be incomplete without brief mention of the main ones.

First, many legislative mandates under which commissions work are vague or misguided. This is because the purposes of regulation are often vague and misguided—especially those concerning destructive competition and cross-subsidy.

Second, the task of regulation is *inherently* difficult. There is no regulatory cookbook with recipes for every occasion, no utility child-care guide. There are a few principles, plus plenty of questions lacking pat answers.

A third problem is what James McKie aptly calls the "tar-baby" effect.[21] Each swipe regulators take at some supposed sin seems to ensnare

regulators in ever deeper difficulties. The innocent and well meaning souls who first devised regulation imagined it to be a rather simple matter. What could be easier, they must have asked, than restricting a natural monopolist's profit to some "just" percentage? Yet it is not so easy. Taking a punch at profit may mean a bulge in costs; striking at excess cost may hurt quality; close control of quality entails sticky details demanding nearly one bureaucrat for every hard-hat; and so on. Pretty soon regulators are attempting to cover everything from plant purchases to billing frequencies, and in the process they get covered with tar.

Fourth and finally, regulation is generally a poor substitute for competition (even though it may be a lesser-of-two-evils substitute for unregulated natural monopoly). No one has expressed this sentiment better than Clair Wilcox:

> Regulation, at best, is a pallid substitute for competition. It cannot prescribe quality, force efficiency, or require innovation, because such action would invade the sphere of management. But when it leaves these matters to the discretion of industry, it denies consumers the protection that competition would afford. Regulation cannot set prices below an industry's costs however excessive they may be. Competition does so, and the high-cost company is compelled to discover means whereby its costs can be reduced. Regulation does not enlarge consumption by setting prices at the lowest level consistent with a fair return. Competition has this effect. Regulation fails to encourage performance in the public interest by offering rewards and penalties. Competition offers both.[22]

In short, free-market competition should be preferred wherever and whenever it can be secured.

Summary

Under economic regulation, administrative processes rather than free market forces of de-

---

[21] James W. McKie, "Regulation and the Free Market: The Problem of Boundaries," *Bell Journal of Economics* (Spring, 1970), pp. 6–26.

[22] Clair Wilcox, *Public Policies Toward Business* (Homewood, Ill.: Irwin, 1966), p. 476.

mand and supply determine price, product, profitability, entry, and exit. The seeds of this policy were sown in English common law and took root in the U.S. after *Munn* v. *Illinois* was decided in 1877. This case established the constitutionality of such regulation for industries "affected with a public interest."

For over sixty years after *Munn* the Supreme Court attempted to judge on a case-by-case basis which industries qualified for regulatory treatment. However, from *Nebbia* v. *New York* in 1934 to the present the Court has given legislators a fairly free hand. As a result we have an impressive list of important industries subjected to economic regulation—chief among them being electric power, natural gas, telephones, radio and TV broadcasting, railroads, and (until recently) airlines, trucks, and crude oil. Except for the last ones mentioned, these industries tend to be more capital intensive than others. Moreover, they provide "vital" services, often reaching consumers directly through pipes, wires, and conduits. Finally, they tend to manifest market imperfections and failures.

As outlined in Table 14–2, economic regulation is grounded on several rationales, all of which may be expressed in terms of "fairness." (A) Fairness to buyers is of primary concern in dealing with natural monopoly or windfall profits (instances prompting maximum price level control). (B) Fairness to sellers is invoked to warrant treatment of three problems—destructive competition, common property resource, and industry promotion (in which cases regulation becomes official cartelization, with price floors and entry restrictions). (C) Fairness among different buyers motivates price struc-

Table 14–4. Summary of Chapters on Economic Regulation

Chapter	Industry	Explanation	Major Focus of Regulation	Commission
15	Local electricity and gas	Natural monopoly	Price ceiling (profit level), and price structure	State utility commissions
16	Telecommunications	Natural monopoly, cross-subsidy	Price ceiling (profit level), price structure, entry and access	FCC and State commissions
17	Broadcast communications	Common property resource	Entry licensing	FCC
18	Transportation	Price discrimination, cross-subsidy, stability	Entry, exit, price structure, price floor	ICC, CAB
19	Crude oil and natural gas production	Stability, conservation, windfall profit	Price level (floor and ceiling)	Federal Energy Regulatory Commission, Economic Regulatory Administration, and State agencies

ture regulation to end "unfair" price discrimination or to impose cross-subsidies. (D) Fairness among different sellers is the focus of regulation when diversified sellers are pitted against specialized "cream skimmers" and when new sellers vie against older regulated sellers. Entry control and price structure are the key tools for these cases. (E) Finally, regulation may be favored by some who perceive greater fairness in administrative processes than in free-market forces.

Who does the regulating? Commissions primarily. They have been called the fourth branch of government because they combine legislative, judicial, and executive powers. The jurisdiction of state commissions tends to be broad in industry coverage but narrow in geographic coverage. The jurisdiction of federal commissions follows an opposite form, with industry coverage tending to be narrow but geographic reach extending nationwide to encompass interstate commerce. In structure, the commissions are headed by a panel of several members and supported by a staff of legal, technical, and economic civil servants. Though purportedly "independent," these commissions are political creatures with political sensitivities. They thus respond to pressures from both consumers and companies, but the latter are often said to know the best pressure points.

Some of regulation's basic problems may be seen from this general survey. Two are perhaps most important. One is the problem of questionable rationale in many instances. The other is that competition has no really close substi-

tute. The remaining chapters of Part IV, as outlined in Table 14–4, elucidate.

Questions and Exercises for Chapter 14

1. What characteristics of economic regulation distinguish it from antitrust policy?
2. What, legally and economically, sets regulated industries apart from other industries?
3. Why does either a purely *public* interest explanation or a purely *private* interest explanation for regulation seem inadequate?
4. Use a diagram (derived from Figure 14–1) to explain the "natural monopoly" problem (with inefficiency and excess profit).
5. Compare and contrast "unfair price discrimination" and "need for cross-subsidy" as explanations for regulation.
6. Some people say oil and gas "windfalls" are no different than homeowner "windfalls" on house values, and therefore should be of no concern to public policy. Discuss, giving consideration to such factors as (a) dispersion of ownership, (b) production versus consumption, and of course (c) fairness, or equity.
7. What are the likely economic consequences of trying to secure "fairness" for sellers?
8. Compare state and federal commissions.
9. Why is it often said, as in the opening quote of Shepherd, that regulation is unattractive and even evil (but not as bad as the alternatives)?

Chapter 15

Electric and Gas Utility Regulation

Price regulation is the heart of public utility regulation.
—Alfred E. Kahn

Public utility regulation was a dull subject when things went smoothly. During the 1940s, 1950s, and 1960s the price of electricity declined more than 50 per cent relative to prices generally. Electricity output grew briskly at about 7 per cent per year. Machinery hummed. Much the same could be said of natural gas.

But the 1970s brought drastic changes. Electric and gas prices skyrocketed because of the industry's especially heavy dependence on two inputs whose costs soared—fuel and capital. Blackouts hit the eastern states. Three Mile Island threatened nuclear disaster and brought financial disaster. Utility consumers and owners everywhere organized armies of lobbyists for battle. And the turmoil has persisted.

The preceding chapter outlined the *what*, *why*, and *who* of electric and gas utility regulation:

- *What* . . . mainly price level and price structure regulation plus, to a lesser degree, product quality, entry, and exit.

- *Why* . . . natural monopoly and price discrimination.
- *Who* . . . independent commissions—state public utilities commissions for intrastate sales, the Federal Energy Regulatory Commission for interstate sales.

After a brief description of the industry in Section I, this chapter delves into two further questions: *How* is utility price regulation actually accomplished? *How well* has it served the interests of society? Sections II and III answer the "how" question with discussions of price level and price structure regulation. It will be recalled that *price level* refers to *overall* revenues, costs, and returns, whereas *price structure* refers to the *specific prices* charged to specific customers for specific services at specific times. Section IV addresses the "how well" question by reviewing empirical studies of the impact of regulation and by surveying current problems. Space limitations force us to neglect other issues like product quality.

Thumbnail Sketch 3:   Federal Energy Regulatory Commission

Established: 1977 (taking over for the Federal Power Commission, which was established in 1920)

Purpose: To regulate interstate aspects of the electric power and natural gas industries.

Legislative Authority: Federal Water Power Act of 1920; Federal Power Act of 1935; Natural Gas Act of 1930; Energy Policy and Conservation Act of 1975; Department of Energy Organization Act of 1977; and other legislation.

Regulatory Activity: Regulates rates charged for interstate transmission and sale of electricity and gas and oil pipeline services. Governs interconnections, mergers, and security issues of electric utilities.

Organization: The FERC is an independent agency within but separate from the Department of Energy. Its five members are appointed by the President, and its staff divisions include the Office of Pipeline and Producer Regulation and the Office of Electric Power Regulation.

Budget: 1982 Estimate, $76.2 million.

Staff: 1982 Estimate, 1648.

I. Industry Description

More than 2,000 billion kilowatt-hours (KWH) of electricity power the U.S. every year. *Generation* comes first, mostly at large plants burning fossil fuels but also at nuclear and hydro facilities. *Transmission* to population centers follows. *Distribution* to homes, factories, office buildings, and other end-points concludes the chain. Regulation covers all segments.

Natural gas goes through a similar three-stage journey. *Production* in the field entails discovery and extraction. *Transportation* to cities and towns occurs by pipeline. *Distribution* to ultimate users employs extensive local pipeline networks. Utility regulation as defined in this chapter applies only to the last two of these stages. Regulation of the field price of natural gas is relegated to Chapter 19 because its motives and methods differ markedly from traditional public utility regulation.

Electric and gas utility regulation is further limited by the fact that some utilities are owned and operated by governments. For example, the federal government accounts for about 10% of all electricity generated in the United States (TVA and Bonneville Power Administration being the most famous sources of this current). State and local governments and cooperatives account for another 10% or so nationally (Nebraska being the most prominent among these producers). This leaves approximately 80% of all electric power in the hands of several hundred private, investor-owned companies that are dealt with individually by regulatory commissions. (Many commissions have jurisdiction over municipals and cooperatives too, a topic we must neglect.)

II. Price Level Regulation

A. *Objectives and Overview*

There are any number of objectives that *could* guide price level regulation. Among the more obvious possibilities are speedy growth in service, conservation of energy, or optimal allocation of resources in the strict economic sense. For one reason or another, however, *none* of these is the main objective applied in practice. The main objective is to allow the utility sufficient revenues to pay its "full" costs plus a "fair" return on the "fair" value of its capital. Stated differently, *the main objective is to strike a reasonable balance between the interests of consumers* (who should not be gouged by monopoly exploitation) *and the interests of the utility investors and operators* (who should not be ripped off by overzealous commissions, or who, in more legalistic language, should not be deprived of their property without "due process of law"). As a Connecticut commissioner recently put it, "We're the buffer between the company and the consumer. If you're the buffer, you're going to get buffeted."[1]

This effort is captured in a simple equation:

$$TR = OE + CD + VA \cdot r$$

where

TR is total revenue
OE is operating expenses (including taxes)
CD is current depreciation
VA is value of assets (less accumulated depreciation)
r is rate of return

Note that, on the right-hand side, operating expenses, OE, and current depreciation, CD, are both *annual dollar flows.* Capital or asset value, VA, is not a dollar flow. It is the asset value

[1] *Wall Street Journal,* May 23, 1978, p. 40.

of the utility firm at a *given point in time,* also called the **rate base.** However, once this capital value is multiplied by the allowed rate of return (such as 0.10, for 10% per year), the result *is* an annual dollar flow. Thus, the basic problem of price level regulation is to see to it that the annual flow of total revenue covers the annual flow of "full cost," including depreciation, plus a "fair" or "reasonable" return on asset value, no more and no less. Generally speaking the owners or operators would like to see "more," which means that their interests lie with *high* estimates of the elements on the right hand side. Consumers, on the other hand, would like to see "less" because their interests are generally served by *low* figures for these elements. It is the job of the commission to balance these conflicting interests—to determine that operating expenses, current depreciation, capital value, and rate of return may be neither too high nor too low, and then to permit a price level that generates the necessary total revenue. Note that if prices are pressed *too* low, service could suffer and the firm could go bankrupt, injuring everyone involved.

A first step in estimating these elements is the selection of a "test year," from which data may be derived. The last twelve months for which data are available has usually served commissions in the past. With rapid inflation, however, such data quickly grow old. So some commissions now accept data based on projections for a *future* test year. Such future data are by nature more speculative than historic data, but the price level to be set is for future periods, so a future test year has the advantage of placing prices and costs in the same time frame.

Now, to appreciate fully how regulators determine permitted total revenue TR, each item of price level decision making must be discussed. We begin with operating expenses OE, and continue with current depreciation CD, rate base VA, and rate of return r.

B. *Operating Expenses* (*OE*)

Operating expenses are to some degree the easiest of all items for a commission to determine. They include such things as fuel costs (for coal, oil, gas, and uranium), workers' wages, managers' salaries, materials expense, advertising, and taxes. Of these, fuel, wages, and taxes are by far the largest components. Together, all operating expenses typically absorb about 75% and 90% of electric and gas operating revenue, respectively, as shown in Figure 15–1, which is based on data from twelve major states in 1978.

These expenses are relatively easy to determine because few such expenses can be padded or fudged. Taxes, for example, are beyond the utility's control and therefore unquestioned. Similarly, the costs of fuel are usually shaped in open markets, and workers' wages are often settled by collective bargaining, so these too are rarely questioned by commissions.

Still, there are snarls, and mention should be made of several.

Affiliate Dealings.   When a utility owns the company from which it buys, or when both the utility and the supplier are jointly owned by the same holding company, arms-length bargaining no longer prevails and the utility may try to evade profit regulation by paying exorbitant prices on the purchases it makes from these affiliated suppliers. As of 1979, for example, 37 electric utilities owned coal mines, with the result that more than 12% of all utility coal came from "captive" sources rather than open-market suppliers. A recent audit of these captive dealings disclosed that in the late 1970s American Electric Power Co. and Duquesne Light Co. had paid their mining subsidiaries about 30% above the going market price for coal. Thus some major companies may be using their coal operations to reap profits otherwise denied in the rate-making process.[2]

Automatic Pass-Throughs.   When the cost of oil and other fuels began soaring during the 1970s, utilities felt pinched as the slow regulatory process caused their utility prices to lag

[2] "Captive Customers?," *Wall Street Journal*, May 10, 1979, pp. 1, 21.

Figure 15–1.   Use of Revenues for Electric and Gas Utilities in 12 States, 1978

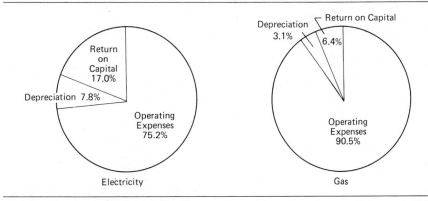

Source: National Association of Regulatory Utility Commissioners, *1978 Annual Report on Utility and Carrier Regulation.* (Washington, D.C.: 1979), pp. 596, 62.

behind their fuel costs. To meet this problem most commissions began granting utilities the opportunity to pass higher fuel costs on to their customers immediately. The amounts involved in such automatic pass-throughs have been enormous. In the 43 states that had such provisions in 1974, for example, the amount automatically passed along to customers exceeded $8 billion. The problem is that automatic pass-throughs remove incentives for shrewd purchasing and open up opportunities for abuse.[3] As a result, some commissions have tried *partial* pass-throughs, which grant immediate and unchecked price increases for only a large fraction of the cost increase.

Wages and Salaries.   Given the monopoly power of utilities and the nature of regulation, it has often been argued that wages and salaries of utility employees would tend to be excessive as increases could be passed on to consumers fairly easily. In fact, empirical evidence does not bear this out. Utility workers' wages do not seem too far out of line with those of comparable workers elsewhere.[4] And utility executives apparently earn considerably less, about 60 per cent less according to one estimate, than executives at comparable manufacturing firms.[5] Of course the problem here is determining what is comparable. In the past, managing utilities was thought to be a relatively "easy" job, but the turbulence of recent times may well have changed that.

Judgment Calls on Minor Expenses.   The problems continue as commissioners move down the list of expenses into minor categories. How much should be allowed for advertising? Does a monopolist need to advertise at all? What about public relations advertising, which

[3] For examples see "Reining in Utilities," *Wall Street Journal,* January 13, 1976, pp. 1, 27.
[4] Wallace Hendricks, "The Effect of Regulation on Collective Bargaining in Electric Utilities," *Bell Journal of Economics* (Autumn 1975), pp. 451–465.
[5] *Wall Street Journal,* May 18, 1981, p. 25.

tells us that Giant Electric is doing everything possible to clean up the environment but smokestack scrubbers ought to be scrubbed? Does the tab for these ads belong to consumers or investors? How much should be allowed for executive expense accounts, executive jets, and executive travel? Should the gasoline expenses of corporate Cadillacs be approved when economical Datsuns would do? And what about the costs of company lawyers and accountants who represent the utility before the commission? Should consumers or investors pay the company's costs of coping with regulation? What about donations to charities? Does not "good corporate citizenship" require that community causes be supported? If it does, what worthy causes should be blessed, in what dollar amounts, and what share of this burden should be borne by consumers?

Commissions' answers to these and similar questions vary widely, as you might guess.

C. Current Depreciation (CD)

Current depreciation is an important item of cost because most utilities tend to be capital intensive. As shown in Figure 15–1, current depreciation of electric utilities amounts to almost 8% of total sales, well over twice the level for all manufacturing.

No one disputes the necessity of including depreciation as a cost. In one sense, depreciation accounts for the "using up" of capital assets through wear and tear or obsolescence. In another sense, depreciation may be thought of as a payment to capital investors, much as wages, salaries, and materials expenses are payments to other factor suppliers. This means that, of the elements in the summary equation, *both* current depreciation *and* capital value times rate of return go to the investors. As Alfred Kahn explains, "The return to capital . . . has two parts: the return *of* the money capital invested over the estimated economic life of the investment and the return (interest and profit) *on* the portion of the investment that remains outstanding."[6]

Although no one disputes depreciation's inclusion as a cost, its computation is often more controversial than the computation of operating expenses. First, the allowance for depreciation is quite different from operating expenses. Whereas operating expenses entail *actual money outlays,* depreciation does not. It is an *imputed cost.* The portion of total revenues depreciation "permits the company to earn does not, as is the case with normal operating expenses, go out in payments to outside parties— suppliers of raw materials, workers and so on."[7] It goes instead to investors.

Second, since current depreciation is an imputation, there are no hard rules for its reckoning. The actual figure arrived at for any asset in any one year depends on three things: (1) the depreciation base, (2) the asset's estimated life span, and (3) the method of write-off during its life. Each element is judgmental; each is therefore open to dispute.

The depreciation base is the original cost of the asset less any salvage value at life's end. Although original cost is straightforward, salvage value is a matter of estimate. Life-span, too, is a matter of estimate. A short life with no assumed salvage value would tend to favor investors over consumers because it would lead to large, early write-offs. Conversely, a long life with high salvage value favors consumers because it leads to small annual write-offs.

As for possible write-off methods, they are too numerous and too complex to summarize here. The most common are called straight line, sinking fund, and retirement reserve. The major source of difference among them rests with whether the depreciation base is spread *evenly*

or *un*evenly over the estimated life-span. Most commissions use the straight line method, which has an even spread.

D. Capital Value or Rate Base (VA)

Far and away the most controversial part of price level regulation concerns asset value times rate of return (or rate base × per cent return) because this is the computation that determines profit. The Supreme Court's legal guide to commissions is about as solid as natural gas. Specific estimates or formulas are not so important, says the Court. It's the *end result* that counts. The end result must be "just and reasonable." What is "just and reasonable"? Earnings "which enable the company to operate successfully, to maintain its financial integrity, to attract capital, and to compensate its investors for the risks assumed . . . even though they [the earnings] might produce only a meager return."[8]

This nebulous guide gives commissions great leeway in determining both capital value and rate of return. As regards **capital value,** there is a wide range of choice concerning (1) accounting devices, and (2) what is counted as real investment.

1. ACCOUNTING DEVICES

At least four methods for computing the rate base have been adopted or proposed:

1. *Original cost* values assets at their "actual" or "book" cost.
2. *Reproduction cost* is the estimated cost of buying, building, and installing the same equipment at today's prices.
3. *Replacement cost* is the estimated cost of replacing the present plant and equipment, much of which may be outdated, with the most efficient and reliable technology availa-

[6] A. E. Kahn, *The Economics of Regulation,* vol. 1 (New York: John Wiley & Sons, 1970), p. 32.
[7] Ibid.

[8] *Federal Power Commission* v. *Hope Natural Gas Co.,* 320 U.S. 591 (1944).

ble, in amounts sufficient to supply the same service.

4. *Mixed method,* or "fair value," which is some combination, or rough averaging, of the items 1 through 3.

Subtractions for *accumulated* depreciation must be made under any of the options, which expands the horizon for judgment still further.

As suggested by Table 15–1's sample data,

Table 15–1.   Method of Rate-Base Valuation and Rate of Return Allowed by Selected State Commissions, 1978

State	Rate-Base Valuation	Electric Return	Gas Return
Alabama	Original cost	7.33%	7.34%
Alaska	Original cost	12.16	10.83
Arizona	Fair value	8.32	7.94
California	Original cost	9.60	9.73
Colorado	Original cost	9.10	9.34
Florida	Original cost	8.25	11.27
Georgia	Original cost	9.36	9.57
Illinois	Original cost	8.93	8.79
Indiana	Fair value	7.35	7.00
Iowa	Original cost	8.79	8.79
Louisiana	Original cost	9.15	11.00
Maryland	Fair value	9.11	9.11
Michigan	Original cost	8.90	8.31
New Hampshire	Original cost	10.19	10.50
New Jersey	Other	8.83	8.83
New York	Original cost	9.44	9.44
North Carolina	Fair value	9.47	8.63
Oklahoma	Fair value	8.50	7.75
Oregon	Original cost	10.53	10.51
Pennsylvania	Fair value	8.59	8.23
South Dakota	Original cost	8.83	8.75
Utah	Original cost	10.25	9.40
Washington	Other	8.96	10.13
Wyoming	Original cost	9.71	9.41

Source: National Association of Regulatory Utility Commissioners *1978 Annual Report on Utility and Carrier Regulation* (Washington, D.C.: 1979), pp. 386–87, 414.

most state commissions and the Federal Energy Regulatory Commission apply the original cost approach, followed in popularity by fair value. Replacement cost is shunned by all. Still, future changes are possible, and the pros and cons of these techniques are endlessly debated. Among the major issues are (1) ease of estimation, (2) inflation, and (3) economic efficiency.

It should be obvious that original cost is the easiest of all methods to estimate (a fact that partly explains its great popularity). The replacement cost approach is undoubtedly the most difficult, because it amounts to little more than a playground for opinion. Reproduction cost lies somewhere in between.

Although original cost is most convenient, it is least competent in accounting for changes over time, especially plant and equipment price changes. During periods of inflation, consumers prefer and investors oppose original cost because it yields a *lower* rate base than the other techniques. On the other hand, during periods of deflation (now about as dated as dinosaurs), producers prefer original cost because it yields a *higher* rate base than the other techniques. What is correct? There is no secure answer, but it can be argued that reproduction cost, which does take inflation into account, might be better economically. Why? Because under the "ideal" of pure competition, industry price will move in the long run to a level that just covers costs plus a normal return on a *new* plant. Moreover, during periods of astounding inflation, original cost valuation might sink the rate base so low as to threaten the firm's viability.

Actually, on grounds of allocation efficiency, the replacement cost approach seems most attractive because the *new* plant alluded to should be one *incorporating the latest in new technology.* Although certainly favorable to replacement cost, this argument is undercut by the fact that the main purpose of regulation is *not* allocation efficiency. Commissions make no attempt to see that utility prices always match marginal cost. They only seek a "fair" balance between opposing parties.

These considerations indicate that the different methods do produce different estimates of the rate base, *VA,* with original cost now being lowest. But *VA* is multiplied by *r* to determine ultimate return, so commissions might in practice make up for a low *VA* by allowing a high *r,* or vice versa. In fact, some evidence indicates just such an effect, so there is apparently no substantial difference in *realized* earnings of firms regulated by original cost, fair value, and reproduction cost jurisdictions.[9]

2. ASSET INCLUSION

Regardless of accounting technique, there remains the equally important question of what is to be included in the rate base. Buildings, cables, trucks, dams, generators, switches and the like obviously qualify. But what about the $1 billion nuclear power plant completed only a year ago but now shut down because geologists have just discovered an earthquake fault within a half mile of it? Who ought to pay for it? If the dead plant is included in the rate base, consumers will howl. If excluded, it would hurt investors. How would you decide as a commissioner? This question confronted regulators of General Public Utilities Corp. when its Three Mile Island nuclear plant closed indefinitely after partial meltdown in 1979. The commission yanked the plant out of GPU's rate base, pressing the company into poverty.

The most controversial issue of asset inclusion at present concerns treatment of facilities under construction. They obviously cost money and represent assets, but they are not yet actu-

ally producing. In essence, there are basically two ways of treating construction—(1) include plant under construction in the rate base, or (2) exclude it, but account for it using an "allowance for funds used during construction." Inclusion in the rate base is most favorable to utilities but also the method least commonly used.

Prior to 1970 such exclusion did not matter much because construction costs were relatively low and construction lead times were short. But the cost of a coal plant jumped from $144 per KWH in 1970 to $1,096 per KWH in 1980.[10] Moreover, lead times are now over ten years. As a consequence, the amount of investment tied up in electrical plant under construction rose to an amazing 20% of utilities' total net plant by the end of the 1970s.[11] Regulators who oppose inclusion of construction in the rate base claim that it is unfair to saddle current consumers with the cost of building a plant that will benefit future consumers. If current consumers were given an ownership interest for their contribution to future plants, then charging them would be fair. But they are not. Only investors get ownership interests, and they are also supposed to get some risk exposure with that interest. Thus the argument for exclusion. Nevertheless, it can be argued with equal conviction that exclusion is unfair to utility companies and investors, that exclusion will do so much financial damage that quality of service will be injured.

Aside from inclusion questions concerning concrete plant and equipment, there is the further question of what to do about *intangible* assets? Would you as a commissioner permit the cost of patents, franchise papers, licenses, and purchase options to enter the rate base? Many commissions do permit them—to some extent.

---

[9] Walter J. Primeaux, Jr., "Rate Base Methods and Realized Rates of Return," *Economic Inquiry* (January 1978), pp. 95–107. On the other hand see H. C. Petersen, "The Effect of 'Fair Value' Rate Base Valuation in Electric Utility Regulation," *Journal of Finance* (December 1976), pp. 1487–1490.

[10] For nuclear plants the difference is even greater —$165 per KWH in 1970 to $1,861 per KWH in 1980. These 1980 plants would be on-line in 1985.

[11] *Business Week,* May 28, 1979, p. 120.

E. Per Cent Rate of Return (r)

Utility investors own utility bonds, preferred stock, and common stock. Keeping these investors contented is important because they supply funds for plant and equipment. And given the capital intensity of utilities, these funds are truly immense, accounting for as much as one-quarter to one-half of all new securities issued by nonfinancial corporations in a given year. Thus if the allowed rate of return is too low, utilities may be unable to finance their facilities. On the other hand, if the rate of return is too high, then consumers will pay needlessly high prices.

The per cent rate of return referred to in the regulatory equation, r, is actually a *weighted average* rate, averaged over the several securities just mentioned—bonds, preferred stocks, and common stocks. Thus r is determined by a two step process: (1) determination of the individual security rates of return and (2) computation of the average.

1. INDIVIDUAL RATES

Although there are many methods of determining the individual rates of return, the most commonly used by commissions is the *cost-of-capital* approach. The cost of bonds is taken to be the interest rate that contractually must be paid, a rate that for new bond issues must be comparable to the interest rates on new bonds of comparable risk in the capital market. Risk scoring is determined by rating services like Moody's and Standard & Poor's. In December 1980, for example, the interest on an AAA bond was 13.75% and on a more risky BAA bond it was 16%. In turn, regulatory climate influences these ratings, with generous commissions being considered "favorable" to utilities or "low risk," and stingy commissions being considered "unfavorable" to utilities or "high risk."[12] For an overall interest rate on various

bond issues the commission merely divides the annual dollar flow of interest obligations by the value of the bonded debt outstanding.

The cost of capital for preferred stocks is similarly determined. Preferred stocks earn a fixed dividend much like the fixed interest earnings of bonds. This dividend runs at a higher percentage rate than bond interest, however, because preferred stocks are a bit more risky than bonds. In the event of default (and regulation does not prevent defaults), the claims of bond holders are met before the claims of preferred stock holders. Thus the cost of preferred stock capital is higher than bond capital but less than common stock capital.

Common stock capital (or "equity" capital) is the most risky and most difficult to cost because dividends on common stock are not fixed. Indeed, hard times may prevent dividend payments altogether, as happened when New York's massive Consolidated Edison skipped a dividend payment in 1974 (a first for the venerable company and a shock for all utility investors). In other words, the "cost" here is the rate that will be permitted *if* it can be earned. The problem is made all the more difficult by the fact that there is no simple, universally agreed upon method for determining the cost of equity capital. Economic experts testifying in the same rate case come up with widely differing estimates—14%, 11%, 12.5%, and so on.

Perhaps the best way to appreciate this problem is to imagine yourself as the typical investor whose capital the utility is trying to attract. What rate of return would the company have to pay (and the commission have to approve) to get you to bite? If you are shrewd, that rate would depend on at least the following: (1) the rate you could earn if you put your money elsewhere, (2) the risk of the utility's stock, and (3) the leniency of the commission in other matters, such as the rate base computation.

R. L. Hagerman and B. T. Ratchford conducted an empirical analysis of factors influencing officially allowed rates of return on electric

---

[12] Peter Navarro, "Electric Utility Regulation and National Energy Policy," *Regulation* (Jan/Feb, 1981), pp. 20–27.

utility equity capital and found that these considerations apparently do influence commissions:

1. Allowed rates rose as AAA corporate bond rates rose, indicating official awareness of investor options elsewhere.
2. Allowed rates were higher for utilities with high debt/equity ratios, a measure of risk.
3. Allowed rates were higher for utilities whose rate base was determined by original cost method as compared to fair value method, indicating that commissions make up for a low *VA* by allowing a higher *r*.

In addition, Hagerman and Ratchford found that the allowed rate rose with company size, suggesting that "larger utilities have more expertise in dealing with rate-making bodies and hence can get a higher return." Among "political variables," lengthy terms of office for commissioners lifted the allowed rate, but nothing else seemed to matter much.[13]

2. COMPUTING AVERAGE RATE *r*

Once the cost of each component of capital is determined, the weighted average cost of capital is computed to estimate *r* in the equation on page 300. The weights come from the utility's capital structure. Say, for example, that the utility's capital is 50 per cent bonded debt, 10 per cent preferred stock, and 40 per cent common equity capital. Suppose further that the estimated cost of capital for each is 9%, 11%, and 15%, respectively. Then the weighted average rate of return will be computed by multiplication and addition:

Bonds (50% at 9%)	$.5 \times .09 = .045$
Preferred stock (10% at 11%)	$.1 \times .11 = .011$
Common stock (40% at 15%)	$.4 \times .15 = \underline{.060}$
Weighted average (*r*)	.116 or 11.6%

Moving from the hypothetical to the real, Table 15–1 reports overall rates of return allowed by a sample of commissions in 1978. Again it must be stressed that these *allowed* rates do not necessarily correspond to rates actually *realized* by the companies, especially when it comes to equity capital. Nationally for instance, the average allowed return on equity was 13.3 per cent in 1978, but the average realized return was only 11.5 per cent.

F. Conclusion: Translating TR into Price Level

One of the reasons realized rates may differ from allowed rates is that price level does not follow directly from the foregoing computations. Estimates of *OE, CD,* and *VA · r* yield an estimate of the target total revenue *TR* needed to cover these outlays, but they do not tell the commission exactly what *price level* will generate the needed total revenue.

Simply stated, *realized* total revenue will be price times quantity, i.e., TR = P × Q (as 100 sandwiches at $2 each would fetch you $200 if you ran a lunch counter). This suggests an easy translation: if total revenue needs to be 10% higher to cover costs, then price needs to be 10% higher too. Although commissions often act in just this way, it incorrectly assumes a zero elasticity of demand. That is, it assumes that the 10% higher price level will not reduce quantity at all.

In fact, demand is such that quantity does change with price, muddling the linkage between price level and total revenues. What is more, the resulting changes in quantity may alter the costs that justified the target total revenues in the first place, adding further complications. Thus price level regulation is anything

[13] Robert L. Hagerman and Brian T. Ratchford, "Some Determinants of Allowed Rates of Return on Equity to Electric Utilities," *Bell Journal of Economics* (Spring 1978), pp. 46–55.

but precise. Allowables and realizations differ. About the only really solid answer a rate case provides relates to direction. If costs are rising, or realized return is less than allowed return, price level should move up. If opposites hold, price level should move down.

III. Price Structure Regulation

A. Introduction and Overview

Until recently the issue of price structure took a back seat to the issue of price level. Once price level was determined, commissions would usually let utilities devise their own price structure. Rapidly rising price levels and growing criticism from consumers and economists have buried this benign neglect. Now, price structure is a highly charged issue that commands a big chunk of official attention.

According to judicial and legislative instructions, commissions may permit prices that jump around with time, place, type of buyer, and size of transaction. However, the jumps cannot be "unduly discriminatory." The differences in prices charged various classes of service must be "just and reasonable." In carrying out this vague mandate, commissions have permitted prices to vary with *cost-of-service* and *value-of-service*.

Cost-of-service. Prices based on the cost-of-service principle would, as the name implies, fully reflect the costs associated with a particular service or product. Stated differently, profit markups would not vary; all price/cost ratios would be the same across customers.

This is an easy principle to follow when costs can be broken down customer-by-customer. The cost of a meter, for instance, can be directly assigned to the customer using it. But this is a difficult principle to follow when there are "common" costs that cannot be directly assigned.[14] For example, an electric utility's coal plant generates power for both residential and industrial buyers. How, then, is the capital cost of the plant going to be assigned to homes versus factories?

Coping with these considerations has created two branches of the cost-of-service approach. One branch uses *fully distributed costs* to guide price setting. This method begins by assigning clearly identifiable costs to the particular customers responsible for those costs, then adds common (nonidentifiable) costs for different customers according to some arbitrary distribution formula. Physical proportions of output provide one such formula, in which case residential customers would be assigned 40 per cent of the common costs if they accounted for 40 per cent of the electricity output, industrial customers would be assigned 30 per cent of the common costs if they bought 30 per cent of the electricity, and so on.

The other branch of cost-of-service uses *marginal cost* as the basis for pricing. Simply stated, marginal cost is the additional cost of producing additional units of output. Simply measured, marginal cost corresponds to clearly assignable costs and ignores common costs. But this is *too* simple and misleading. In fact, marginal costs vary widely depending on (a) the volume of additional units of output considered and (b) the time perspective assumed (i.e., short run or long run). The result is that arbitrary formulas or assumptions enter the estimation of marginal costs just as much as they enter the estimation of fully distributed costs, a result that leads to heated debate over which method is better.[15] In practice, utility regulators have stuck pretty

---

[14] A further type of cost is "joint" costs. The distinction between "common" and "joint" costs is often important, but we cannot pursue it here. See A. E. Kahn, *op. cit.*, pp. 77–83.

[15] See e.g., Harry M. Trebing (ed.), *Issues in Public Utility Regulation* (East Lansing: Division of Research, Graduate School of Business Administration, Michigan State University, 1979), pp. 197–266.

close to the fully distributed cost method, but marginal cost pricing is making large inroads, as we shall see.

Value-of-Service. When costs do not guide pricing, elasticities of demand often do. Customers with a low elasticity can be hit with a high price, those with a high elasticity require a low price if their patronage is to be held (as suggested in our earlier discussion of price discrimination at the beginning of Chapter 9). The name "value-of-service" derives from the notion that differing elasticities signal differing "values" to customers.

Because value-of-service pricing constitutes price discrimination, it may seem "unfair." But it can be argued that, under certain regulatory circumstances, such pricing is *desirable* because it promotes economic efficiency, that is, optimal allocation of resources. The theoretical ideal for efficiency would require that all prices match their marginal cost. But as we have just seen, prices matching marginal costs may not be high enough to cover undistributed common costs. Without coverage of all costs the utility would go bankrupt. Thus a "second best" formula furthering efficiency has been developed by economists, a formula that makes use of demand elasticities to get prices high enough to cover overall costs. Simply stated, this formula says that welfare is best served when prices exceed marginal cost to a degree that varies *inversely* with elasticity of demand. Thus for customers with high elasticity, price should be close to marginal cost. For customers with low elasticity, price should be higher relative to marginal cost. No commission has the precise information needed to impose these so-called Ramsey prices (after economist Frank Ramsey).[16] Even if the information were availa-

ble, commissioners might not follow the formula, given their other value judgments. In any event, the prices actually approved by commissions deviate from Ramsey prices but often reflect the spirit of Ramsey prices.[17]

Applications of the cost-of-service and value-of-service principles may be seen in the following three-part review of actual price structures. Three characteristics of purchases stand out—(1) who buys, (2) how much, and (3) when.

B. Who Buys? Customer Classes

Electric and gas utilities serve three broad classes of ultimate customer:

- residential—about one-third of the energy.
- commercial (e.g., banks and stores)—roughly one-fifth of the energy.
- industrial (e.g., steel plants)—over two-fifths of the energy.

As shown in columns (1) and (2) of Table 15–2, which reports average prices for each class in 1978, residential and commercial buyers pay considerably more on average than industrial buyers, and as suggested by the gas prices, residential customers often pay the highest prices of all.

There are two rationales for this pattern. First, from a cost-of-service perspective industrial buyers may be cheaper to supply, given their fewness, their great volumes per customer, and their willingness to provide some of the utility equipment needed at their factories. Second, from a value-of-service perspective, these prices apparently reflect differences in elasticity of demand. The quantity demanded by residential customers tends to be relatively *un*responsive to changes in price, yielding elasticity estimates for electricity in

[16] F. P. Ramsey, "A Contribution to the Theory of Taxation," *Economic Journal* (March 1927), pp. 27–61. The modern version is in W. J. Baumol and O. F. Bradford, "Optimal Departures from Marginal Cost Pricing," *American Economic Review* (June 1970), pp. 265–283.

[17] Robert A. Meyer and Hayne E. Leland, "The Effectiveness of Price Regulation," *Review of Economics and Statistics* (November 1980), pp. 555–566.

Table 15–2. Price Discrimination by Class of Customer, 1978

Customer class	(1) Electricity: average revenue per KWH sold	(2) Natural gas: price per million BTU	(3) Electricity: price/cost ratio
Residential	4.03¢	$2.53	4.46
Commercial	4.10¢	$2.28	4.52
Industrial	2.59¢	$1.91	2.41

Sources: Columns (1) and (2), U.S. Department of Commerce, Statistical Abstract of the United States, 1979, pp. 613; 614; column (3) Primeaux, Jr., and R. A. Nelson, "An Examination of Price Discrimination and Internal Subsidization by Electric Utilities," Southern Economic Journal (July 1980), pp. 84–99. These data are for 1973.

the neighborhood of 1. Their ability to substitute other sources of energy or to supply their own needs is rather limited. At the other end of the spectrum, industrial customers are quite responsive to changes in price because they enjoy greater options for substitute energy sources and self-supply. Accordingly, estimates of their elasticity of demand for electricity range higher at around 1.7. In between, commercial customers generally have fewer options than industrial buyers but more options than residential buyers, so their elasticity of demand is probably somewhere between 1 and 1.7. Indeed, by one estimate it is 1.36.[18]

To what extent can the observed price differences be explained by value-of-service as opposed to cost-of-service? To answer this we would need accurate estimates of just how much costs actually differ by customer classes to see whether the price variations correspond closely to the cost variations. If prices and costs moved together so that price/cost ratios were the same for all buyers, then cost-of-service pricing would prevail and price discrimination based on value-of-service would be absent de-

spite the elasticity differences. Column (3) of Table 15–2 reports price/cost estimates to the contrary, however. The price/cost ratios for residential and commercial customers are way above the price/cost ratio for industrial customers, indicating that value-of-service pricing is indeed practiced in the same direction that elasticities of demand would dictate. Of course these estimates depend on arbitrary assumptions for the distribution of common costs and they average over numerous companies, so they are only suggestive.[19]

C. How Much Is Bought? Quantity Structures

When Thomas Edison first wired New York City one hundred years ago he had not yet invented meters, so he charged his customers a fixed price regardless of the quantity they purchased. A remnant of that practice remains today as some utilities levy a fixed monthly "customer charge" that is independent of quantity

[18] For a survey of elasticity estimates, see L. D. Taylor, "The Demand for Electricity: A Survey," Bell Journal of Economics (Spring 1975), pp. 74–110.

[19] Big industrial power users deny that they are favored in this way, and they have sponsored a study showing that utilities make more profit off of industrial customers than residential customers. See Business Week, February 28, 1977, pp. 29–30.

Figure 15–2. Alternate Price Structures as a Function of Quantity Purchased

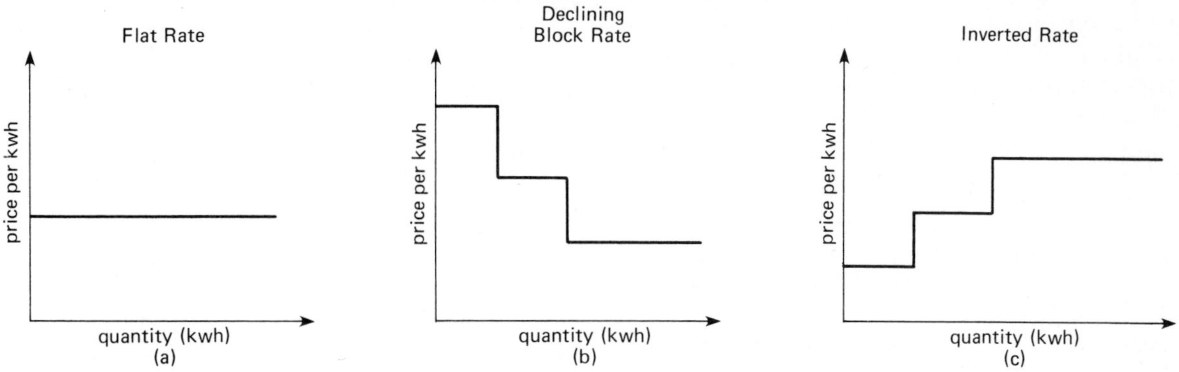

consumed. But the advent of metering brought a variety of price structures keyed to quantity as well as to customer class.

The main possibilities for quantity structures are indicated in the three panels of Figure 15–2. The first of these, the *flat rate* of panel 15–2(a), imposes a charge per unit of use that remains the same over all units. In terms of one's monthly bill, a doubling of consumption doubles the amount due.

Although commonly used after meters first became available, the flat rate was replaced by the *declining block rate* structure of panel 15–2(b) for most utilities during most of this century. Price per unit is constant within stated blocks of units, blocks such as 0–500 KWH, 501–1000 KWH, 1001–2000 KWH, and so on. But the unit price falls in each successive block until the final open-ended block. In terms of one's monthly bill, a doubling of consumption here would likely result in *less* than a doubling of the total amount due. For obvious reasons, this structure has occasionally been dubbed "promotional pricing" because it encourages large-quantity consumption. To the extent economies of scale cause utility costs per unit to fall with added output, such a structure has cost-of-service justifications. To the extent customers take care of necessities like lighting first and luxuries like air conditioning second, this structure may also conform to value-of-service principles because the high-priced blocks would be associated with inelastic (necessary) demands and the low-priced blocks would be associated with elastic (luxury) demands.

Recently, however, these rationales for declining block rates have been increasingly called into question. Economies of scale in electricity, for instance, are not nearly as pronounced as they once were. They still occur at distribution stage, but they no longer occur for most electricity generation because output in most locales has grown to the point where an efficient sized thermal plant is small in comparison to total output and because present technologies grant fewer advantages to greater generating size.[20] As regards demand considerations, it is now argued that energy use should no longer be promoted, especially not for lux-

[20] John F. Stewart, "Plant Size, Plant Factor, and the Shape of the Average Cost Function in Electric Power Generation," *Bell Journal of Economics* (Autumn 1979), pp. 549–565.

ury purposes, because we are entering an era of acute energy shortages.

Folks wanting to curb energy use for conservation or environmental reasons advocate adoption of *inverted rate* structures, as illustrated in panel 15–2(c). In this case unit price *rises* in successive blocks rather than falls, with the result that a monthly bill would rise at an increasing rate as added energy is consumed. Only a handful of states have tried inverted rates, and some of these have used them for only a few utility companies. For obvious reasons inverted rates are not very popular among consumers, so flat rates and block rates remain most common.[21]

A variant of the inverted rate structure that has recently been tried in a few states is the so-called *lifeline* rate. Here the first 300 kilowatt-hours per month or thereabouts are priced at a below-cost price per unit, with price per unit thereafter rising into a flat or inverted rate structure. The purpose of the lifeline design is to help poor people pay for a "subsistence" quantity of electricity or gas. This is only a recent pricing innovation propelled by soaring costs of energy and concerns for equity.

Figure 15–2's panels depict quantity in kilowatt-hours. There is an additional measure of quantity in electricity consumption, however, one that is particularly important in the quantity rate structures facing industrial buyers. This second measure of quantity does not gauge the amount of current consumed *over* a given time period, as does the kilowatt-hour. Rather it measures the *instantaneous* rate of consumption *at* a particular point in time as expressed in *kilowatts* (not kilowatt-*hours*). Given that an electric utility must have the capacity to meet this instantaneous demand as well as duration demand, the cost of maintaining that capacity should be borne by the customers responsible for it. This is the rationale behind the *demand* or *kilowatt charge* imposed on industrial buyers, above and beyond the regular kilowatt-*hour* quantity charges. These demand charges often follow block rate designs, such as $4.00 per kilowatt for the first 100 kilowatts, $3.80 per kilowatt for the next 300 kilowatts, and $3.20 for all additional kilowatts. (Note that special meters are needed for this.)

The traditional method of pricing industrial buyers thus involves two elements—(a) a kilowatt-hour price and (b) a kilowatt price. Hence the name two-part tariff (or Hopkinson tariff, after its originator). There is a key problem with the kilowatt price, however. Its rationale and measurement do not coincide. Its rationale is to pin the utility's peak capacity costs on those responsible. But its measurement refers solely to the peaks of *individual* industrial buyers at *any time*, not to the *utility's* system-wide peak, which may or may not occur at the same time as an individual buyer's peak. In other words, the traditional kilowatt or demand charge is not really peak load pricing at all because it does not vary with time of day or season of the year as utility capacity utilization varies. Such timing has now been introduced into price structures (in addition to class and quantity distinctions), revolutionizing electric and gas pricing.

D. When? Peak-Load Pricing[22]

Figure 15–3 illustrates the timing of electricity use in Omaha. The hourly timing over the day is typical of utilities everywhere, with use reaching a peak in late afternoon and falling into a gully at night. The solid line for summer lies above the dashed line for winter disclosing that Omaha is in a region of the country where

---

[21] For a summary of rate structure practices across states, see the *Annual Report on Utility and Carrier Regulation* published by the National Association of Regulatory Utility Commissioners.

[22] For a thorough and advanced discussion see Michael A. Crew and Paul R. Kleindorfer, *Public Utility Economics* (New York: St. Martin's Press, 1979).

Figure 15–3. Omaha Public Power District, Typical Hourly Consumption of Electricity

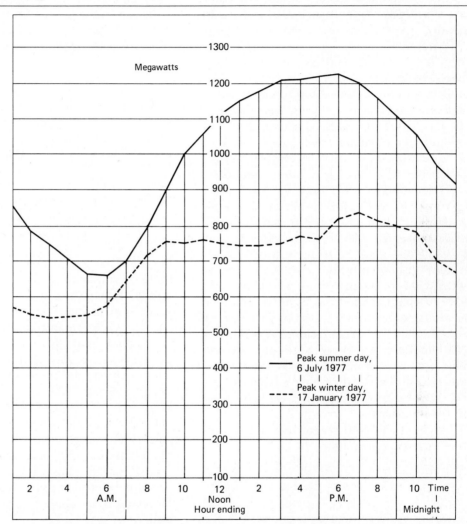

Source: Harry Trebing (ed.), *Assessing New Pricing Concepts in Public Utilities* (East Lansing: Division of Research, Graduate School of Business Administration, Michigan State University, 1978), p. 278.

summer peaking prevails. This is typical where hot summers boost air conditioning demand appreciably. In New England and certain other areas *winter peaking* occurs because electricity is needed more against the winter than against the summer. (Gas peaking centers on winter everywhere, as space heating is one of gas's greatest blessings.)

For years now we have had to pay more to telephone long distance during weekday daylight hours than to phone during nights and weekends. Traditionally, such *peak load pricing* has not been practiced by electric and gas utilities, but now there is a definite trend toward "time-of-day" and "season-of-year" price structures. In 1977, for instance, Wisconsin Power & Light Company began charging commercial customers 2.03 cents per kilowatt-hour between 8 A.M. and 10 P.M. and just 1.013 cents per kilowatt-hour at other times. Although the high costs of special metering have kept time-of-day pricing confined mostly to commercial and industrial accounts, season-of-year pricing is easy enough to include residential customers in its adoption, as many readers may already know from experience. By 1980 most states were giving peak load pricing trial runs, and now many have passed beyond the trial stage into lasting reliance.

Charging peak users more than off-peak users serves many purposes:

- It improves a utility's capacity utilization or "load factor," which is the ratio of average demand over the year to peak demand.[23] It does this by discouraging peak demand while encouraging off-peak demand.
- In turn, better capacity utilization reduces cost. Long run average cost per KWH may be as much as 13% lower for a load factor of .8 as compared to a load factor of .5.

[23] For example, if a utility runs at 300 megawatts on the average but demand gets up to 400 megawatts sometime during the year, its load factor is 300/400 or 75%.

- Peak load pricing tends to slow the growth in peak demand, reducing the need for utility capital outlays.
- It can reduce a utility's oil and gas use, thereby promoting conservation.
- It serves the principle of cost-of-service pricing.

To summarize before elaborating, higher prices during peak periods make sense because the costs of providing peak service are greater than those of providing off-peak service, maybe as much as three or four times greater.[24]

One such cost is plant and equipment. Because a utility must have on hand capacity to satisfy total peak demand, capacity costs can be blamed mainly on those who tap into the utility during peak hours. As for off-peak customers, *the plant and equipment are already there for the peak,* so capacity costs of serving them do not apply, although off-peak users do create costs for fuel and other variable inputs. Indeed, even fuel costs per unit tend to vary with time of demand because utilities usually fire up their least efficient, high-cost plants only during peak periods. The differences between plants can be substantial. In 1973, for instance, a major eastern electric company experienced fuel costs of 3.3 mills/KWH in its most efficient plant and 9.51 mills/KWH in its least efficient plant.[25] (Note that these cost experiences do not contradict the economies of scale mentioned earlier. These are *short-run* cost comparisons, not long-run scalar comparisons. Moreover, they apply to generation, not distribution.)

Figure 15–4 shows peak and off-peak demands set against the short-run marginal cost curve of a hypothetical utility. If a uniform

[24] Charles R. Scherer, "Estimating Peak and Off-Peak Marginal Costs for an Electric Power System," *Bell Journal of Economics* (Autumn 1976), pp. 575–601.

[25] E. Berlin, C. J. Cicchetti, and W. J. Gillen, *Perspective on Power* (Cambridge, Mass.: Ballinger Publishing Co., 1975), p. 35.

Figure 15–4.   Peak-load Pricing

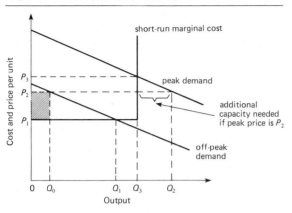

price of P_2 were charged to both peak and off-peak demands, capacity would have to equal OQ_2, which is peak quantity demanded at P_2. Off-peak demand would be OQ_0 given price P_2. Since OQ_2 greatly exceeds OQ_0, it is easy to see that peak demand would be responsible for the plant necessary to produce OQ_2 (even if off-peak demand were nonexistent). Moreover, a uniform price of P_2 would cause inefficient plant usage, because there would be tremendous excess capacity during off-peak periods. In short, such a uniform price is *too low* for peak demand (producing a state of overbuilding) and *too high* for off-peak demand (causing off-peak underutilization). Indeed, off-peak demand is to some extent subsidizing peak demand, since the shaded area in Figure 15–4 indicates the amount by which off-peak revenues exceed off-peak costs.

With a more sensible rate structure, peak customers would be charged P_3 and off-peak customers would be charged P_1. At P_3, peak demand would be curtailed to OQ_3, eliminating the need for capacity over the Q_3—Q_2 range. (It has been estimated that $13 *billion* of electric utility capital spending would be

avoided over the years 1977—1985 if all United States electric companies were using such peak-load pricing.[26]) Conversely, off-peak demand would expand to OQ_1 under a reduced price of P_1. Off-peak excess capacity would be cut appreciably, thereby achieving more efficient plant usage. Price for off-peak demand could not fall below P_1, however, without falling below marginal cost. And it is only "fair" and economically "proper" that off-peak users pay those marginal costs.

One consequence of this scheme is that, over time, peak customers may adjust their consumption patterns and become off-peak purchasers. The result would be a leftward shift of the peak demand curve and a rightward shift of the off-peak demand curve. But these shifts raise no horrendous pricing problems. As off-peak demand grows to the point of full capacity utilization, off-peak price should be raised to reflect *some* capacity costs. The distribution of capacity costs among users would then depend on the relative intensities of these demands.

One problem with time-of-day peak load pricing is that manufacturing workers' lives can be seriously disrupted as their employers step up nighttime operations to save millions in energy costs. Workers moved to "graveyard" shifts because of peak-load pricing have complained of strained marriages, stunted social calendars, and injured health.[27]

E. Summary of Price Structure

When the many foregoing factors are taken into account, the result is that price structures vary substantially from state to state and utility to utility. Moreover, the result for any one utility can be quite complex, with price schedules running several pages of fine print. Still, the

[26] *Wall Street Journal*, August 12, 1977, p. 1.
[27] "Blues in the Night," *Wall Street Journal*, October 18, 1977, pp. 1, 19; and "Shifting the Load," *WSJ*, August 12, 1977, pp. 1, 23.

essence of the matter may be appreciated by perusing Table 15–3, which shows excerpts from the 1980 price schedules of one of the country's largest utilities, Pacific Gas and Electric Company of California. The residential customer schedule shown includes a fixed monthly fee of $1.75 and quantity charges that combine lifeline, inverted block, and seasonal peak-load pricing. The lifeline and inverted block effects are achieved by successively higher unit charges across three tiers. The seasonal peak-load effect is achieved by shortening the KWH range of the tiers in the "summer" months (May–October) as compared to the "winter" months (November–April). Thus the price of 1,000 KWH is much higher in the summer than in the winter.

Large industrial customers under the schedule shown faced a hefty demand or kilowatt charge plus a declining block "energy" charge. (Note that the industrial energy charges per KWH in Table 15–3 are way below the residential KWH charges.) Finally, industrial customers got a break in their demand charges by using electricity at night and on Sundays and holidays because of peak-load pricing.

IV. Evaluation: Plaudits and Problems

A. Plaudits (?)

How well has public utility regulation worked? Has it kept prices at "reasonable" levels, prevented "unfair" price discrimination,

---

Table 15–3.   Excerpts From Pacific Gas and Electric Company's Electricity Price Structure, 1980

Residential Service Per Month

		Winter Months	Summer Months
Customer Charge (fixed fee)		$1.75	$1.75
Quantity Charge		KWH Range	KWH Range
Tier I (lifeline)	4.04¢ per KWH	0–790	0–240
Tier II	6.39¢ per KWH	791–1580	241–480
Tier III	8.82¢ per KWH	1581–over	481–over

Industrial Service Per Meter Per Month

Demand Charge	
First 1,000 KW	$2,658.00
Each KW over 1,000, per KW	2.12
Energy Charge (in addition to demand charge)	
First 100 KWH, per KWH	1.45¢
Next 200 KWH, per KWH	.99¢
All excess KWH, per KWH	.79¢

Off-peak Demand: Customers under contract over 5 years may have maximum demands ignored which occur between 10:30 P.M. and 6:30 A.M. and on Sundays and holidays.

Source: PG&E.

and promoted adequate service? Pat answers are not possible. Some commentators castigate utility regulation. Others applaud it. Some state commissions seem to do a good job. Others falter. More conclusive answers might be reached if we could compare utilities with and without regulation. But opportunities for such comparisons are curbed by the fact that virtually *all* investor-owned utilities in the United States are regulated. Comparisons with other countries are likewise limited because most foreign utilities are government owned and operated.

Still, several studies have attempted to reach general conclusions about regulation's effects. Confined mainly to the question of price level, the best of these studies suggest that electric and gas prices are on average probably lower as a result of regulation's check on monopoly power. How much lower is not clear, maybe 5 to 10 per cent.

Two main methods have been used to reach this conclusion. One compares utility prices with and without regulation under the limited circumstances in which such comparison is possible, such as early in the history of utility regulation when some states had regulation and others did not.[28] The other and more imaginative approach uses assumptions from economic theory and data from real world observations to calculate estimates of what profit-maximizing utility prices would be like in the absence of regulation. These fictitious unregulated prices are then compared to real regulated prices to measure regulation's impact. The most recent

and most thorough study of this sort yields favorable results for regulation.[29]

It is important to note that this generally laudatory verdict for utility regulation cannot be stretched to support all other areas of economic regulation. As we shall see, regulation of transportation has apparently caused price levels to rise rather than fall. Moreover, it must be stressed that utility regulation is not without its serious problems. Measured by criteria other than price level, regulation may well warrant low grades. Quality of service, though, seems good.

B. Problems and Prospects

Some of the problems are of long standing. Two of these—incentives and input efficiency—lead off this concluding section of woe. Other problems have more recent origins. Two of these—endangered earnings and conservation—round out the analysis.

1. INCENTIVES

It would be nice if commissions could reward utilities that operate efficiently and progressively while penalizing those putting out poorly. Competition contains such incentives. But no tidy incentive techniques have been devised for regulation. Traditionally, the only source of incentive has been regulatory "lag." Earnings that rise inordinately from efficiency remain with the firm until regulators act to reduce rate levels, but they act only after a long lag. Conversely, earnings that fall with inefficiency must be borne by the firm until requests for rate increases are answered, which likewise entails some lag. Thus the lag imperfectly and temporarily rewards "goodness" and punishes "badness."

Recently, a number of commissions have become more deliberate in their attempts to in-

[28] The leading study of this type is G. J. Stigler and C. Friedland, "What Can the Regulators Regulate? The Case of Electricity," *Journal of Law and Economics* (October 1962), pp. 1–16. They interpreted their data very pessimistically, leading subsequent analysts to conclusions more favorable to regulation. See e.g., William Comanor, "Should Natural Monopolies Be Regulated?" *Stanford Law Review* (February 1970), pp. 510–518, and H. C. Petersen, *Business and Government* (New York: Harper & Row, 1981), pp. 237–239. See also, R. Jackson, "Regulation and Electric Utility Rate Levels," *Land Economics* (August 1969), pp. 372–376.

[29] Meyer and Leland, *op. cit.,* pp. 555–566.

still proper incentives. For example, the automatic pass-through of fuel costs removes regulatory "lag," but the Michigan Public Service Commission has devised a formula of partial pass-through that embodies incentives. For another example, the New York Public Service Commission has begun monitoring utility efficiency and has penalized Consolidated Edison as a result.[30]

Still greater improvement in incentives could be achieved if more competition could be achieved. Although economies of scale limit the opportunities for such competition quite severely in transmission and local distribution, there are opportunities in electricity generation and *bulk* supply that have yet to be fully exploited. Electric power grids, such as that shown in Figure 15–5 for California, now link major population centers with numerous possible sources of bulk supply. The main purpose of these grids is to provide back-up capacity and smooth out capacity use at any one generating facility. But they offer the additional prospect of increased competition at generation stage because distant generators of electricity can now more readily compete with local generators. Just how far these limited prospects will be probed remains uncertain.[31]

2. INPUT EFFICIENCY

Some regulatory theorists argue that profit regulation contains some particularly unfavorable incentives. Because profit is keyed to the rate base, *there is an incentive to expand the rate base* (to substitute capital for labor) beyond the point that would be optimal in the absence of regulation.[32] Just how serious this so-called "Averch-Johnson effect" actually is no one can say. Empirical tests of the hypothesis have been mixed, half confirming and half refuting it.[33] Even if the effect does exist, it may not be as bad as it might seem. Although in *static* terms the bias favoring capital over other inputs may lift costs undesirably, the *dynamic* result may be *lower* costs through *improved technological progress*, given that most technological change tends to favor capital intensity.[34]

3. ENDANGERED EARNINGS

A number of adversities piled up during the late 1970s and early 1980s to crush many electric utilities financially. Record high interest rates, expensive environmental controls, towering fuel costs, slackening demand, and inept regulation all made their contributions to the crisis. As this is written, realized profits are well below allowable profits. Cash flow has dropped precipitously relative to interest obligations. Whereas previously the industry could boast of bond ratings at AAA and AA levels, it now falls increasingly into the A and BBB categories. According to the head of Chicago's Commonwealth Edison, "The patient is in critical condition."[35]

To many analysts, remedy requires that tight commissions become more like lenient commissions, adopting measures favorable to utili-

---

[30] Carson W. Bays, "Utility Productivity and Regulatory Incentives," *Quarterly Review of Economics and Business* (Summer 1980), pp. 51–56.

[31] Leonard W. Weiss, "Antitrust in the Electric Power Industry," in A. Phillips (ed.), *Promoting Competition in Regulated Markets* (Washington D.C.: Brookings Institution, 1975), pp. 135–173.

[32] Harvey Averch and Leland L. Johnson, "Behavior of the Firm Under Regulatory Constraint," *American Economic Review* (December 1962), pp. 1052–69; Stanislaw H. Wellisz, "Regulation of Natural Gas Pipeline Companies: An Economic Analysis," *Journal of Political Economy* (February 1963), pp. 30–43.

[33] See L. L. Johnson's survey, "The Averch-Johnson Hypothesis after Ten Years," in *Regulation in Further Perspective*, edited by Shepherd and Gies (Cambridge, Mass.: Ballinger Publishing Co., 1974), pp. 67–78; plus Charles W. Smithson, "The Degree of Regulation and the Monopoly Firm," *Southern Economic Journal* (January 1978), pp. 568–80; and Robert W. Spann, "Rate of Return Regulation," *Bell Journal of Economics* (Spring 1974), pp. 38–52.

[34] A. E. Kahn, *op. cit.*, Vol. II, pp. 106–107.

[35] *Business Week*, February 23, 1981, p. 76.

Figure 15–5. California's Electric Grid

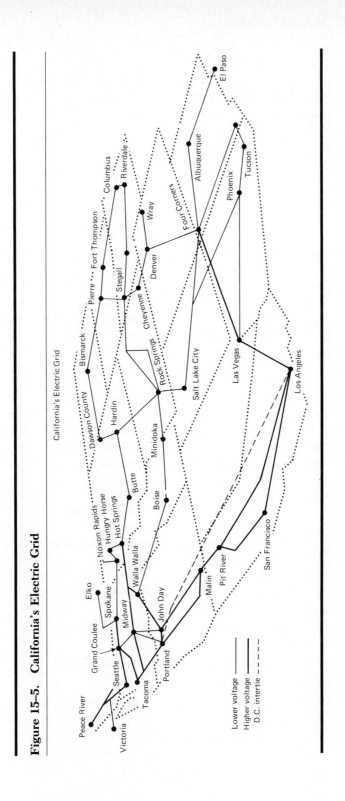

ties—(a) future test years, (b) automatic pass-throughs, (c) construction cost in the rate base, (d) high allowed rates of return, and (e) fair value rate bases.[36] Warnings abound that if something isn't done we face a dark future (literally). But the amounts of money involved—$5 to $8 billion a year *in addition* to the current $8 billion annual price increases—raise doubts that "political realities" can be overcome, given that utility consumers are already up in arms.[37]

4. CONSERVATION

Although electric utilities cannot raise capital easily now, conservation may stave off utter disaster. Less consumption would mean less need for capital.

The main impetus toward conservation has thus far come from government. As already noted, many declining block rate schedules have been scrapped in favor of flat or inverted rates, and peak-load pricing has become commonplace. State commissions were nudged in these and related directions when the federal government passed the Public Utility Regulatory Policies Act in 1978. The Act encouraged these price structure reforms to promote increased conservation of electric energy and increased efficiency in plant usage.[38] Moving beyond rate reform, a number of state commissions have pushed utilities into additional conservation programs to provide customers (a) free energy audits, (b) convenient financing for added home insulation, and (c) load management inducements. Less commonly but more intriguingly a few commissions launched efforts to encourage solar power and cogeneration, both of which tend to put utilities out of the energy business. It is too early to assess these recent changes, but one thing is certain: they give utility regulation a whole new slant, causing commissions to slide in directions never before dreamed of.

Summary

Investor owned electric and gas utilities are subjected to economic regulation in the classic sense. Price level regulation centers on finding numbers for the equation:

$$TR = OE + CD + VA \cdot r$$

Thus, when done properly, price level will generate sufficient total revenues *TR* to cover operating expenses *OE* and current depreciation *CD* plus a fair return *r* on the value of the utility's assets *VA*. Doing a halfway decent job of this is not impossible, but almost. Commissions act as arbitrators or buffers between the interests of customers and companies.

Operating expenses are usually rather easy to monitor because they typically entail payments to "outsiders." Fuel, wages, and taxes account for the lion's share. Still, there are troubles. Payments to affiliated firms for coal or other inputs are not payments to outsiders, raising opportunities for evasion. Rapidly escalating fuel costs have forced the adoption of automatic pass-throughs, which likewise may open loopholes. Smaller portions of the expense budget call for judgment calls, and so on.

Current depreciation represents the return *of* the investors' capital. Wear and tear, obsolescence, and other factors warrant this expense, which in the case of utilities looms especially large. The estimate of annual depreciation for any asset depends on (1) the depreciation base, (2) estimated life span, and (3) method of write-off. Of the methods, commissions favor straight line.

The rate base *VA* is usually estimated by

[36] Peter Navarro, "Electric Utility Regulation and National Energy Policy," *Regulation* (Jan/Feb., 1981), pp. 20–27; *Business Week*, May 28, 1979, pp. 108–124.

[37] "Plunging Power," *Wall Street Journal*, February 2, 1981, pp. 1, 12.

[38] Paul L. Joskow, "Public Utility Regulatory Policy Act of 1978: Electric Utility Rate Reform," *Natural Resources Journal* (October 1979), pp. 787–809.

the original cost approach, but fair value and reproduction cost approaches have sufficient merit to capture advocates, both official and unofficial. Of late, the added question of what can be included in the rate base has provoked barbed debate. Because of soaring construction costs and lengthening lead times, "plant under construction" now accounts for a big chunk of utility assets but most commissions do not allow it in the rate base.

The tail of the price level equation—rate of return r—wags many a rate case. This is a composit or weighted average of the returns granted on bonds, preferred stock, and common stock. The "cost" of each of these securities is sought, a fairly easy job for the first two, much less easy for the last. Alternate earnings, risk, and a blend of other factors influence the outcome.

Once price level is settled, price structure needs attention, a need of swelling intensity lately. Two principles summarize the possibilities—(1) cost-of-service, and (2) value-of-service. They often yield similar price structures, but they need not. They vie for application in three main contexts—(a) who's buying, (b) how much, and (c) when. As for who, it appears that, on average, residential and commercial buyers pay substantially higher price/cost ratios than industrial buyers, implying value-of-service pricing. As for how much, price patterns vary as widely as the options available—fixed charge, flat rate, declining block rate, and inverted rate. Cost-of-service and value-of-service both enter here. As for when, peak-load pricing is an old idea whose time has come. Firmly grounded on cost-of-service principles, such pricing serves several laudable objectives.

Finally, our overall evaluation has pluses and minuses. On the plus side, empirical studies of price-level impact suggest that, on balance, utility regulation is an improvement over unregulated monopoly, at least for consumers. On the minus side, two problems with regulation have

long been recognized—the lack of adequate incentives and the bias toward capital intensity. Two other problems spring from current events—inadequate earnings and conservation. The latter might alleviate the former; the former might force the latter. Either way, it will be interesting to see how the industry gets out of its present pickle.

Questions and Exercises for Chapter 15

1. Rearrange the equation on page 300 so that r is the unknown on the left-hand side. Why might utility regulation be considered an exercise in determining r instead of TR?
2. Identify the problem of "affiliate dealings." What policy solutions would you propose?
3. Why is current depreciation (a) large, (b) necessary, and (c) a source of controversy?
4. How is r determined? Why might r and the actual rate of return differ?
5. Compare and contrast value-of-service pricing and cost-of-service pricing.
6. What are the two branches of cost-of-service pricing? Which is intended to further economic efficiency and why?
7. Compare declining block rates and inverted rates in (a) definition, (b) consumption incentive, (c) purpose, and (d) frequency of use by commissions.
8. What are the advantages of peak-load pricing?
9. Explain why the kilowatt (demand) charge in the industrial two-part "tariff" is not really peak-load pricing.
10. What is good about regulatory lag? What is bad about it?
11. Comparing Moody's 24 Electric Utilities with Standard & Poor's 400 Industrials, profit return on average equity was about the same for both in 1960. However, in

1979 the electricals' return was 11.1% to the industrials' 17.3%. What happened to electricals?

12. The text says that wider adoption of the following would *help* utilities: future test years, automatic pass-throughs, construction cost in the rate base, and fair value rate bases. Explain why in each case.

Chapter 16

Telecommunications

With one stunning decision, American Telephone & Telegraph Co. has placed a mammoth bet on the future—by turning its back on its past. —James A. White (*January 1982*)

The story of telecommunications divides into B.F. and A.F.—Before Friday and After Friday. On Friday January 8, 1982, AT&T and the Justice Department announced the most historic antitrust consent settlement of all time. In order to end a monopolization suit halfway through trial, and in order to break the shackles of a previous, 1956 consent decree, AT&T agreed to divest itself of its 22 local operating companies worth $87 billion in assets. AT&T would remain immense—retaining its Long Lines Department, Western Electric, and Bell Laboratories, altogether worth $49 billion in 1981—but the colossus planned to split.

AT&T's consent to wholesale dismemberment was a radical break with its past. For years, AT&T spent millions to advertise "The System is the Solution." And upon announcement of the *dis*solution, AT&T president William Ellinghaus admitted, "I've been in the Bell system for 41 years and was raised with the idea that we should provide universal and end-to-end service. It's hard to pull away from that."[1]

---

[1] *Newsweek*, January 18, 1982, p. 59.

What was AT&T like in the past? How did it achieve its vast power? What pressures caused it to agree to division? What are the likely economic consequences for the future? Where does regulation fit in all this? These are the central questions of this chapter. To answer them we shall expand upon the following outline:

I. TECHNICAL, STRUCTURAL, AND HISTORICAL BACKGROUND
   A. Technical Background: Equipment and Connections
   B. Structural Background: Telecommunications On Friday
   C. Historical Background: The Bell System Before Friday
II. THE LOCAL OPERATING COMPANIES (STATE REGULATION)
   A. Before Friday
   B. After Friday
III. AT&T (FCC REGULATION AND DEREGULATION)
   A. Before Friday: Price Level and Structure

Figure 16–1. Summary of Telecommunications Developments and AT&T's Split

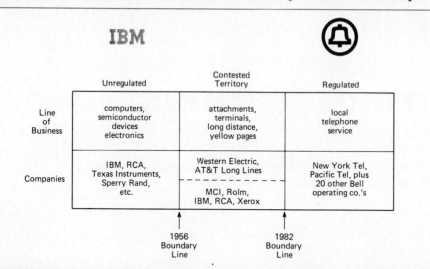

B. Before Friday: Entry and Access

C. After Friday: Competition

Aside from the B.F.–A.F. distinction, another runs throughout the discussion, namely, the economic distinction between that which is naturally monopolistic (warranting regulation) and that which is potentially competitive (warranting no regulation). AT&T built its power by blending *both* types of business and by using regulation as a shield against interlopers in potentially competitive areas. AT&T therefore thought nothing of signing an antitrust consent decree in 1956 that confined it to regulated lines of business (and the authorities sought such a decree on the theory that, without such confinement, AT&T could use its secure regulated monopoly profits to cross-subsidize nonregulated businesses and thereby monopolize them). However, as pictured in Figure 16–1 the boundary line between regulated-monopoly businesses and nonregulated-nonmonopoly businesses shifted during the ensuing years as new technologies (like microwave) and new

regulatory decisions (like *Carterphone* and *MCI*) gave outsiders the capability of competing against the Bell System in such areas as terminal equipment and long-distance service. The Bell System thus began to feel pinched—on the one side by new competitors and on the other side by the 1956 consent decree (plus new legislative proposals designed to regulate Bell's response to its competitors). Pressed still further by a government antitrust suit filed in 1974, AT&T agreed to a structural split reflecting the boundary of 1982 in exchange for an end to the 1956 decree and the 1974 suit. As AT&T Chairman Charles Brown explained it:

> The 1956 consent decree provided what we would say is a fence. The unspoken but assumed corollary to that was that the fence would stay there. But unilaterally the fence was opened with a hole (allowing competitors to sell telephones and provide long-distance service) where everybody could get in, but we couldn't get out.[2]

---

[2] *Wall Street Journal*, January 11, 1982, p. 4.

Once the split is achieved through AT&T's withdrawal from regulated local telephone service, AT&T will continue to compete in the "contested territory" of Figure 16–1, and what is perhaps even more important, it will be free to expand into wholly unregulated lines of business like computers, thereby providing competition for firms like IBM.

I. Technical, Structural, and Historical Background

A. Technical Background: Equipment and Connections

Four main elements make up the telecommunications system, as shown in Figure 16–2.

(1) *Terminal equipment* is the most visable part, as it includes the 170 million telephones we use every day. Also included are private branch exchanges, or PBXs, which serve as switchboards for hotels, offices, and countless other businesses. Indeed, terminals now run the gamut from teletypes to computers, sending and receiving everything from pictures to data. (2) A *local loop* connects terminals to the rest of the system. (3) In turn, the local loops meet at a hub known as the *central switch*. Here a local call is routed from one local loop to another. Although there are now thousands of such switching facilities, there were none when telephony first started. Callers had to have direct wire connections to those on the receiving end. (4) Long distance calls are switched into

Figure 16–2. The Telecommunications Network

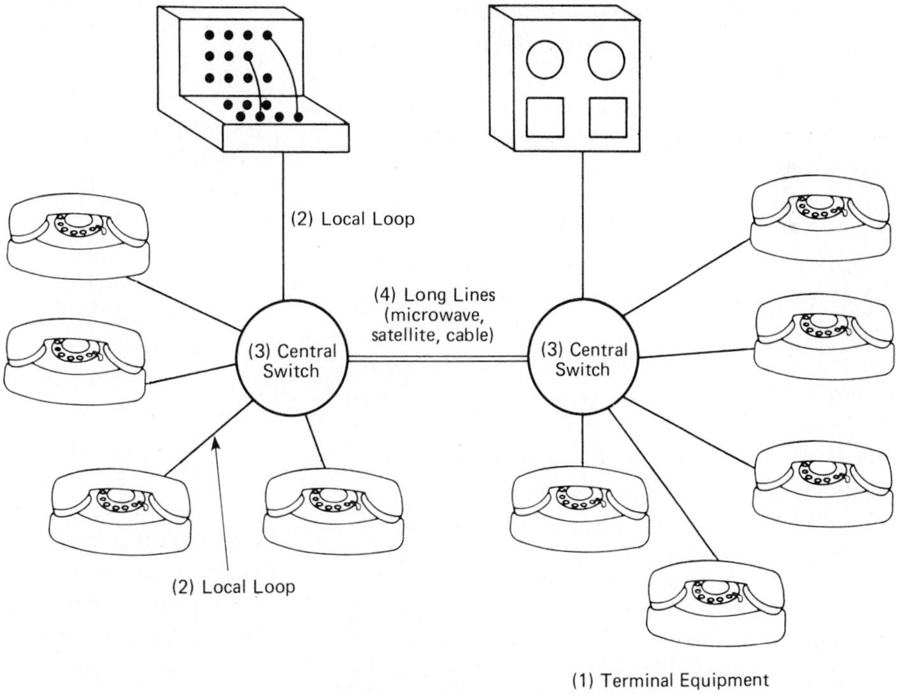

long lines for transmission to another central switch and further relay. Cables comprised these long lines until the advent of microwave and satellite communications, which now dominate the long-distance field.

A major exception to this four-part pattern is "private line" service, for which there are about 20,000 business customers. Private lines bypass the central switch even for long-distance communications because all the equipment and circuitry is fully dedicated to private line customers. Television networks, banks, airlines, and other heavy users each spend tens of millions of dollars a year for such services. And once again "lines" is largely a misnomer given the surge in microwave stations and satellites.

Local loops and their associated central switch generate sufficient economies of scale to create natural monopoly at the local level. Complete connection to two competing local companies would call for two local loops for each customer plus two central switches, with higher multiples for more rivals and with higher costs to boot.

Long-line technologies also have costs per unit that fall with added scale, but these cost reductions end at scales that are small relative to the large volumes of business flowing between major cities. For example, dozens of separate microwave systems could efficiently link New York and Chicago.[3] So monopoly is *not* natural for long lines. The same could be said with even greater force about terminal equipment manufacturing, which has cost characteristics much like electronics manufacturing generally. Thus there are serious limits to arguments invoking natural monopoly to justify regulation of this industry, limits that will become especially important later when we discuss re-

cent competitive developments in long lines and terminal equipment.

B. Structural Background: Telecommunications On Friday

1. THE BELL SYSTEM

On Friday January 8, 1982, the Bell System was a collection of diverse companies headed by AT&T. As shown in Figure 16–3, AT&T enjoyed controlling stock ownership of twenty-two separate "operating companies," whose main duty was regulated local telephone service and whose diverse geographic names divulge that the system resembled a quilted spread, with patches of regional companies varying in size coast to coast. These companies are the ones scheduled for spin-off. As this is written the consent decree has not been finalized and specific plans have yet to be laid, so it is uncertain whether the twenty-two operating companies will in the future become twenty-two separate regulated utility companies. Nevertheless, preliminary plans indicate that, prior to divestiture, the twenty-two operating companies will be reorganized into seven regional firms of fairly equal economic size, as shown by the differently shaded zones in Figure 16–4. (Geographically, the largest of the planned regional companies is made up of Mountain Bell, Pacific Northwest Bell, and Northwestern Bell.) The spin-off can then be accomplished by giving AT&T stockholders seven new shares of stock in the seven new companies for each share of AT&T stock they hold.[4]

AT&T has been and continues to be itself a regulated operating company because its "Long Lines" department furnishes long-distance telephone service subject to Federal Communications Commission regulation. Headquartered in Bedminster, N.J., the Long Lines department handles twenty million inter-

---

[3] Leonard Waverman, "The Regulation of Intercity Telecommunications," in A. Phillips (ed.), *Promoting Competition in Regulated Markets* (Washington, D.C.: Brookings Institution, 1975), pp. 201–239.

[4] *Wall Street Journal*, February 22, 1982, p. 4.

Figure 16–3.   The Bell System Divestiture

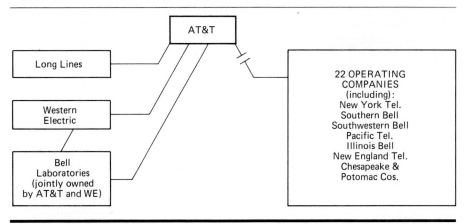

Figure 16–4.   The Bell System Operating Companies Grouped by Shading into the Seven Proposed Regional Companies that Will Be Spun-off*

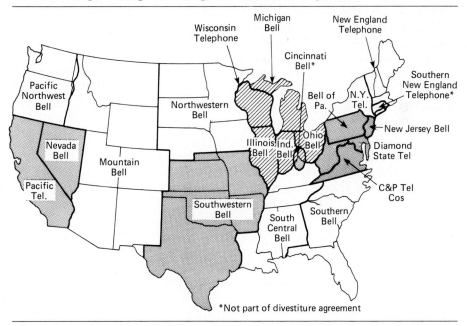

*Not part of divestiture agreement

* Note: AT&T owned minority shares of Cincinnati Bell and Southern New England Bell, so they were, in a sense, already divested.

state calls on a typical weekday, routing them through regional switching stations (by detour if necessary to avoid conjestion). Long Lines also maintains six operating rooms for overseas communications, the biggest of which is in Manhattan.

AT&T will also continue to be a holding company because it retains its subsidiary Western Electric. Owning and managing dozens of plants around the country, Western Electric manufactures and distributes the cables, switches, terminals, and other telephone equipment used by AT&T and its regional operating companies. Befitting the gargantuan scale of things in the Bell System, Western Electric ranked 22nd in sales in 1980 among the nation's largest industrial corporations (over $12 billion worth), and ranked 8th in employees (with 177,000).

Western Electric and AT&T will continue to share ownership in yet another important branch of the system—Bell Telephone Laboratories. World renown for their research prowess, Bell Lab scientists and engineers can take credit for many marvelous inventions, including the transistor.

The AT&T controlled threesome of Long Lines, Western Electric, and Bell Labs is likely to undergo future reorganization to achieve clearer delineation between regulated and nonregulated businesses. The regulated segment of the new AT&T would be made up mainly of the Long Lines department. The unregulated segment, now called Baby Bell, would be chiefly a manufacturing arm that sold or leased all AT&T terminal equipment *directly* to telephone customers, rather than, as in the past, having Western Electric supply local operating companies who in turn supply customers. By this plan Baby Bell would also get into new areas on the fringe of communications, especially areas akin to data processing and computer manufacturing.[5]

[5] *Wall Street Journal*, February 23, 1981, p. 16, and June 12, 1981, p. 3.

2. INDEPENDENTS

Though certainly formidable, AT&T shares the industry with others. So-called *"independent" telephone companies* hold the local service monopolies in many areas, such that AT&T has not accounted for 100% but rather about 82% of all telephones nationally. The largest of the more than 1000 independents is General Telephone & Electronics, or GTE. Like all independents, GTE is dwarfed by the Bell companies and it must rely on interconnection to AT&T's Long Lines department to provide long-distance service to its customers. Nevertheless, GTE is quite formidable, with over 17 million telephones in service, over 200 thousand employees, and over $10 billion in annual sales revenues. Moreover, like AT&T, GTE has its own equipment manufacturing and research facilities.

Aside from independents grounded on regulated local utility service, the industry is now populated by two other groups: (1) those supplying long-distance service, like MCI and Satellite Business Systems, and (2) equipment suppliers like ITT and Rolm. Many of these are newcomers to the industry who have, during the past two decades, crawled through the "fence" formerly protecting AT&T from competition in long-distance services and terminal equipment. Others in these groups, like GTE and Western Union, are companies of long standing who have filled various niches in the industry but are now branching out to challenge AT&T in these big markets. Indeed, with further growth in competition in these areas, there may come a day when the *only* area of telecommunications needing continued regulation is local utility operations controlling local loops and central switches. Signs of this future make sense of the split between AT&T (with Long Lines and Western Electric) on the one hand and the operating companies on the other.

The major *independent long-distance service companies* are mentioned in Table 16–1.

Table 16–1. Communications Services and Major Companies, 1981

KEY: D = PUBLIC DIAL-UP SERVICE
      L = PRIVATE LEASED CIRCUITS

Company	Long-distance Telephone	Satellite Networks	Telex and TWX	Data Communi-cations	Facsimile
AT&T	DL	D		L	
GTE	D	D		DL	
International Telephone & Telegraph	DL		DL	DL	D
MCI Communications	DL			L	
RCA	L	L	D	L	L
Satellite Business Systems*	DL	DL		DL	DL
Southern Pacific Communications	DL	DL		D	D
Western Union	D	L	D	L	L
Xerox			D	L	DL

* Joint venture of IBM, Comsat, and Aetna Insurance.
  Source: Business Week, April 6, 1981, p. 90.

The table distinguishes between public dial-up service such as that associated with your own home phone but not necessarily offered everywhere (D), and private leased circuits (L). Independent public dial-up services would be impossible if the Bell System operating companies refused to connect their dial-up users to the independent long-distance suppliers through the Bell System's local loops and central switches. For many years they did refuse (so as to protect AT&T Long Lines), but such connection was legally forced upon AT&T before January 1982. Once the Bell operating companies are severed from their parent AT&T, they will have no reason nor right to refuse connection to any independent long-distance service company. Independent offerings of private leased circuits have always been less dependent on AT&T for their success because they can often bypass the local service monopolies, connecting directly to large business customers.

Among *independent terminal equipment companies,* some 50 suppliers now compete with AT&T's Western Electric. The most notable are GTE, ITT, TRW, Rolm, and Northern Telecom. At this writing AT&T is still king of the terminal equipment hill, but its dominance is dwindling and its share in certain areas is already remarkably low compared to what it was just a few years ago. Of all new PBXs sold or leased in 1980, for example, AT&T accounted for only 54% of the revenues, down from 80% five years before.[6] The reasons for this dramatic change even before January 1982 will occupy us shortly.

In sum, telecommunications were in the past heavily dominated by the Bell System in every area. Once division of the Bell System is com-

[6] *Business Week,* April 13, 1981, p. 122. The 1980 market was worth $1.94 billion.

plete, the industry itself will become more clearly divided between (1) local operating companies subject to state commission regulation, most such companies being former AT&T subsidiaries, and (2) national long-distance services companies and equipment suppliers lacking ownership connection with the local operating companies, but often working through the local operating companies. AT&T will continue to have considerable power in these latter areas. But the immense advantages it formerly enjoyed as a *fully integrated system,* will wither with the planned restructuring. Just what those advantages were and how they were used can be seen in the history that follows. History, in other words, suggests to us that competition in long-distance and equipment could never reach its full potential as long as the Bell System remained intact.

C. Historical Background: The Bell System Before Friday

Four periods highlight the history of AT&T previous to January 1982—(1) monopoly by patent, (2) open competition, (3) monopoly by regulation, and (4) partial deregulation.[7]

1. MONOPOLY BY PATENT, 1876–1894

Patent number 174,465 may well be the most valuable patent of all time. Awarded to Alexander Graham Bell slightly over one hundred years ago, it was the foundation of the Bell Telephone Company, predecessor to AT&T. Although the validity of the patent was seriously questioned, it was narrowly upheld by the Supreme Court, thereby granting monopoly power until 1894.

From its roots in New England, the business

[7] For an excellent overview see Gerald W. Brock, *The Telecommunications Industry: The Dynamics of Market Structure* (Cambridge: Harvard University Press, 1981). For a popular account, John Brooks, *Telephone: The First Hundred Years* (New York: Harper & Row, 1975).

spread briskly despite the fact that early telephone users had to string their own connecting wires. To encourage expansion with little capital commitment, the Bell Telephone Company entered into arrangements similar to modern franchises, licensing local telephone companies who paid for their rights by giving the Bell Company large blocks of stock ownership interest. In this manner of business lay the seeds of the holding company arrangement now ending. The original patent and its exploitation through franchising proved to be extremely profitable, returning 46 per cent annually.

Correctly anticipating that these handsome profits would attract new entry upon expiration of the original patent, the Bell system pressed several strategies during this period to perpetuate its power later:

- *Further Patenting:* The company's conscientious research effort produced 900 patents by the expiration of the original patent in 1894.
- *Long Lines:* In 1885 a long-lines subsidiary was born. It was named American Telephone & Telegraph and premised on the idea that a national telephone system would have a distinct advantage over a collection of isolated independent local companies.
- *Equipment Self-Supply:* Dropping the original policy of buying from independent equipment manufacturers, the Bell system acquired Western Electric from Western Union and entered into an agreement that Bell would buy only from WE and WE would sell only to Bell.

2. COMPETITION, 1894–1913

Despite these several efforts, massive entry did occur after 1894 because of the rich profit potential and because the Bell system had failed to follow one additional strategy that would have cemented its power—namely, extensive geographic spread of local telephone service.

The Bell system had ignored many small cities, backwater towns, and isolated hamlets. They were therefore open to invasion by independent telephone companies. Folks in many cities were in fact wooed by more than one company.

The competition of newcomers led to sharply reduced prices and an explosive expansion of telephone coverage. What is more, the independents introduced many significant innovations, including the dial telephone.[8] By 1902 Bell's national market share slipped to just over 50 per cent.

The Bell system tried to stifle the competition by buying up many independents and denying others connection to its long-distance lines. These efforts eventually diminished under threat of antitrust prosecution, but not so far as to prevent Bell from being in a position to increase its market share to 79 per cent by 1932.

3. MONOPOLY BY REGULATION, 1913–1956

Another prong in Bell's attack on competition was its promotion of regulation. In the early days, Bell vigorously opposed regulation. But fear of antitrust action, concern over the possibility of government ownership as in Europe, and appreciation that regulation could offer protection against competitors brought a change of heart. Desire for regulation was not limited to Bell. Many independents favored it too, as did many in the general populace. Where monopoly prevailed, there were the typical dreads. Where competition prevailed, there was displeasure with the problems of multiple wiring and a lack of interconnection among systems.

In 1907 only a handful of states had commissions regulating the industry and federal control did not exist. Regulation grew rapidly at both levels, however, during the next thirty

years. And at both levels the Bell system was able to win favorable treatment at little cost to itself. State commissions endorsed the idea of exclusive service areas for local telephone companies. Authorities at the Interstate Commerce Commission, the first federal agency to oversee AT&T, did little more than require standardized accounting practices and periodic reports. Later, when the Federal Communications Commission took over in 1934, federal regulation did not appreciably improve, at least not for several decades. At both state and federal levels, effective regulation was hampered by fractured jurisdictional reach and by Bell's policy of purchasing hardware from its unregulated equipment subsidiary Western Electric. In short, regulation apparently served Bell's interests more than the public's for many years. As Gerald Brock says, "It gave the Bell system a powerful weapon to exclude competitors and justification for seeking a monopoly, as well as reducing chances of outright nationalization or serious antitrust action."[9]

Indeed, regulation provided AT&T with a screen that deflected antitrust action during the 1950s, action aimed at the divestiture of Western Electric. AT&T won the right to keep Western Electric by signing a consent decree in 1956 that restricted AT&T to regulated lines of business. At the time, it appeared that AT&T got something for nothing, and critics complained that the government had caved in to political pressures mustered by AT&T. Yet, in the end, as we have seen, the burden of this 1956 decree proved to be too great for AT&T. Freedom from it motivated AT&T's 1982 agreement to divest the operating companies.

4. PARTIAL DEREGULATION, 1956–1982

Two areas where regulation grew particularly protective were long lines and terminal equipment. As we have seen, these areas now

---

[8] R. Gabel, "The Early Competitive Era in Telecommunications, 1893–1920," *Law and Contemporary Problems* (Spring 1969), pp. 340–359.

[9] Gerald Brock, *op cit.,* p. 161.

witness considerable competition and more is promised for the future. But this is only a recent development, one that had to overcome formidable regulation hurdles.

In long lines, significant competition was first made possible by the advent of microwave technology during the 1940s. Competition was delayed, however, by the FCC's long standing insistence that the Bell system retain priority over microwave's use. In terminal equipment, competition was first made possible by the expiration of the original patents in 1894. Competition was delayed, however, by AT&T's refusal to allow any "foreign equipment" attachments to its system, a refusal endorsed by regulatory commissions for many decades until recently.

The events that broke down these regulatory barriers, opening the "fence" in long lines and terminal equipment, will be detailed later in Section III, which discusses AT&T's national operations. Meanwhile we must survey the areas where regulation continues unabated—namely regulation of the local operating companies.

II. Local Operating Companies (State Regulation)

A. *Before Friday: Price Level and Price Structure*

1. PRICE LEVEL

The basic monthly charge for residential phone service varies substantially from place to place—$9.50 in Detroit, $10.70 in Boston, and $6 in Los Angeles, to take examples from the late 1970s. A main reason for this is that *intra*state phone operations are regulated by state commissions. As in the case of electric and gas utilities, overall price levels for local service are set so as to generate total revenues that will cover operating expenses and current depreciation plus a "fair" rate of return on an appropriately valued rate base (asset value). Thus most of the issues that were discussed for electric and gas utilities reapply here.

For example, the method of rate base valuation (original cost, fair value, etc.) adopted by a state commission for electric and gas utilities applies to telephone companies as well. Allowed rates of return likewise tend to move together, as may be seen by comparing the following figures for telephones with those in Table 15–1 on page 304 for electricity and gas: Alabama 8.55%, Alaska 12.21%, Arizona 7.38%, California 8.85%, and Colorado 9.40%.

For another example, a few state commissions have introduced new procedural techniques for phone regulation designed to cope with the problem of rapidly inflating costs. Although telephone companies escaped the soaring fuel prices that jolted electric and gas utilities during the 1970s, they have nevertheless felt pinched. The Michigan Public Service Commission therefore granted permission in 1980 for Michigan Bell to increase its rates automatically over three years depending on increases in the government's consumer price index. Whereas rate requests previously took at least a year to process, this "indexing" of prices simplified things.[10]

Still, telephone service had one major uniqueness. *Two* price levels were at issue, one level for *local calling,* which was regulated by state authorities, and one level for interstate *long-distance calling,* which was regulated by federal authorities. Given that the local operating companies' terminal equipment and central switches were used for both types of service, a thorny question arose: What portion of these assets should be used as the *rate base* in computing the price level of *local calling,* and what portion should be added to long-lines assets for a *rate base* from which *interstate* price level could be computed? A landmark Supreme

---

[10] *Wall Street Journal,* April 3, 1980, p. 33.

Court case in 1930 held that the interstate rate base must include *some* portion of local exchange costs because local equipment is used for long-distance calls as well as for local calls.[11] But the question of how much this should amount to touched off a lengthy feud between state and federal authorities. State regulators would look good with a large shift of assets to the interstate level because the local prices for which they are responsible could then be lower because local costs would then be lower. Conversely, federal regulators would look good with a small interstate rate base. *Resolution of the dispute led interstate prices to be quite high relative to true cost, yielding a subsidy for local phone service (including even the local service provided by independent phone companies connected to AT&T's long lines).*

2. PRICE STRUCTURE

In 1877 the first telephones were leased at $40 per year for business use and $20 per year for personal use. Thus, from the very start local price structure reflected "value-of-service" as well as "cost-of-service." The traditional practice of charging business customers more than residential customers probably has some basis in costs because business users tend to place especially heavy demands on the system. But businesses also have demands that are *less elastic* than those of residential customers, paving the way for price discrimination. Just how much price discrimination has actually occurred is impossible to tell because major portions of total costs are common costs that cannot easily be delineated by service and by customer. Indeed, the difficulty of estimating costs is itself a prime reason that cost-of-service pricing has traditionally been neglected in the local service industry.

In addition to the business-residential price differential, another differential has been cus-

[11] *Smith* v. *Illinois Bell Telephone Company,* 282 U.S. 133 (1930).

tomary. This distinguishes between basic and nonbasic service. *Basic service* amounts to mere access to the system, as achieved by a single telephone and use of a local loop. *Nonbasic service* is everything beyond, including extension phones, data transmission, and long-distance toll calls. For as long as anyone can remember promotion of basic service has been a guiding philosophy of both the Bell system and government regulators. Hence the price of basic service has been kept low relative to nonbasic services, so low as to entail apparent subsidy. A major portion of this basic versus nonbasic differential was mentioned above, namely, the high price of long-distance service versus the low price of local service.

The amount of this subsidy for basic service is subject to sharp dispute because cost allocations are, at bottom, largely arbitrary. According to AT&T, however, the subsidy has been quite substantial in the past. As indicated by AT&T's data for 1975 in Figure 16–5, the average monthly price for basic local service was only $9.00, but the total cost of that basic service was $16.15. This implies a subsidy of $7.15 from other, nonbasic services. (Notice that this is not value-of-service pricing because it is not based on a high elasticity for basic service and a low elasticity on nonbasic service. The actual elasticities are probably the reverse. It is instead *cross-subsidization.*)

Past divergence in prices and costs can be further seen in the fact that, with few exceptions, local service prices have not been keyed to time of day, frequency, duration of call, and distance. Change is on the way, however. Such pricing for local service has now been introduced for about 10% of all telephones, a percentage that is rising slowly.

Change is also reflected in another form of cost-of-service pricing introduced in the mid-1970s—charging for directory assistance calls that were formerly free. When free to customers, such calls yielded some interesting statis-

Figure 16–5.   AT&T's 1975 Residential Cost Study

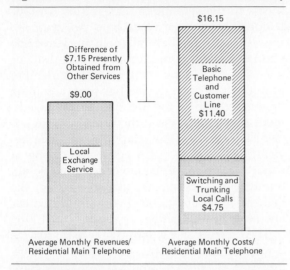

Source: Lawrence Garfinkel, "Network Access Pricing," in H. Trebing (ed.), *Issues in Public Utility Regulation* (East Lansing: Division of Research Graduate School of Business Administration, Michigan State University, 1979), p. 155.

tics. In New York, for instance, the 1971 cost of directory assistance was $82.2 million for 500 million calls, or about 16.5¢ per call. Nearly 80% of these assistance calls asked for local numbers, and 78% of these numbers were in fact listed in the local directory. Furthermore, and of particular interest, over 90% of all directory assistance calls came from only 30% of the customers, while half of all customers made no such calls during the period studied.[12] This means that when directory assistance calls are free, the service is abused and overused by a few customers who are subsidized by the rest. Now about half the states have approved charges for directory assistance. The typical ap-

proach is to permit five free calls per month, then charge 10 to 20 cents for each additional call. Where imposed, such charges have cut directory assistance calling by half, saving more than $60 million in costs annually nationwide.[13] Thus the impact of cost-of-service pricing can be substantial.

B. After Friday: Price Level and Price Structure

What will happen to local service price levels and structures once the operating companies are disentangled from AT&T by the 1982 decree? At this writing the answer is very uncertain, so wild speculations circulate. Many people predict that local rate levels will skyrocket. John Bryson, chairman of California's Public Utility Commission, claims that telephone rates paid by Californians will "triple by 1985" because of the divestiture. This could lead to a "social revolution," he says, where "one person in four who currently has a phone would not be able to afford one."[14] Neil Swift of the New York State Public Service Commission says, "This is an abomination. The stockholders will be better off and AT&T competitors will be better off, but the customer is the forgotten man."[15] The proposed antitrust settlement triggers these alarms because it limits the local operating companies to offering local exchange service and access to local networks. It strips them of AT&T's long-distance subsidy .

Fearful that state commissions will attempt to help common consumers by shifting most of the burden to business customers, some critics predict that business phone rates will soar after AT&T's breakup. These critics of the proposed settlement see the same losses to local

[12] Richard Stannard, "The Impact of Imposing Directory Assistance Charges," in H. Trebing (ed.), *Assessing New Pricing Concepts in Public Utilities* (East Lansing: Division of Research Graduate School of Business Administration, Michigan State University, 1978), p. 92.

[13] National Association of Regulatory Utility Commissioners, *1978 Annual Report on Utility and Carrier Regulation* (Washington, D.C.: 1979), p. 540.

[14] *San Jose Mercury,* February 10, 1982, p. 3F.

[15] *Wall Street Journal,* January 18, 1982, p. 21.

operating companies as just mentioned, but they are less aroused by the prospects for consumer phone rates than business phone rates. They believe that state commissions will try to help out residential consumers by placing most of the burden on business customers.

Defenders of the proposed divestiture, like AT&T Chairman Charles Brown and Assistant Attorney General Baxter, rebut by arguing that:

- Local telephone rates were moving closer to cost-of-service rates anyway.
- Operating companies will be able to charge all long-distance carriers (AT&T as well as MCI and the rest) for access to local networks, and regulators can set these access charges at lofty levels.
- To the extent long-distance rates are lowered they will better reflect true costs and benefit long-distance callers.[16]

Revision and refinement of the divestiture agreement are at present possible, so it will be interesting to see how the controversy is resolved.

III. AT&T (FCC Regulation and Deregulation)

Moving from the local operating companies to AT&T proper and the FCC, we find several interesting nuances: The rate structures have more cost-of-service characteristics. And yet the artificially high overall level of rates has stirred competition and charges of "cream-skimming," so issues of entry and access arise at this level with a vengeance. Finally, the After-Friday prospects are said to be much

brighter for AT&T than the local operating companies.

A. *Before Friday: Price Level and Price Structure*

1. PRICE LEVEL

Several factors combined to make interstate price levels relatively high in the past. One was already noted—namely, the shift of much of the local rate base to the interstate rate base, thereby elevating the apparent cost of interstate service. Another factor was listless FCC regulation. For example, after the FCC completed a formal examination of AT&T's interstate rate base in 1935–1939, more than three decades passed before another thorough investigation of the rate base was attempted. In the interim the FCC informally "negotiated" prices on long-distance service, relying on data colored by AT&T's interpretation of proprieties. Indeed, at one point, the FCC officially refused to examine AT&T's rate base closely, saying that the task was just too immense.

Finally, the FCC's allowed rate of return on AT&T's interstate business has tended to be quite adequate if not exactly generous. Most recently the FCC has taken inflation into account to raise the allowed rate of return from 8.74% in 1975 to 12.75% in 1981.[17]

Despite the foregoing factors, long-distance rate levels have had a long record of decline relative to consumer prices generally. Technological improvements and, most recently, intensifying competition have left their marks.

2. PRICE STRUCTURE

Prices that vary with time of day, frequency, duration of call, and distance have long been

---

[16] *Wall Street Journal,* January 26, 1982, p. 5; February 10, 1982, p. 25; February 24, 1982, p. 48. Indeed, AT&T may have paved the way for high "access" charges when shortly after agreeing to divestiture it asked the FCC for permission to triple then existing rates.

[17] This last overall rate includes a return on common stock of 17%. Moreover, the last increase came on the heels of a liberalization in the treatment of current depreciation. The faster depreciation boosted AT&T's annual take by about $324 million. *Wall Street Journal,* November 7, 1980, p. 4.

Thumbnail Sketch 4:   Federal Communications Commission

Established: 1934

Purpose: To regulate interstate and foreign communications by telephone, television, radio, cable, and wire.

Legislative Authority: Communications Act of 1934; Communications Satellite Act of 1962.

Regulatory Activity: Regulates rates, practices, and service offerings of telephone, telegraph, radio, and satellite communications. It also allocates radio frequency bands and licenses and regulates radio and TV broadcasters.

Organization: The FCC is an independent federal commission of seven members serving seven-year terms. Its major divisions include the Common Carrier Bureau, Broadcast Bureau, and Office of Science and Technology.

Budget: 1982 Estimate, $76.9 million.

Staff: 1982 Estimate, 1862.

---

a feature of long-distance dial-up service. Such cost-of-service pricing has been possible in part because the equipment for monitoring long-distance calling has been around a long while.

Varying price by time, or peak-load pricing, is especially noteworthy because its application in long-distance telecommunications preceded its application in electricity and gas by many decades, yet its rationale is precisely the same. Telephone companies must have the capacity to meet the demand of their customers, but that demand varies substantially with the earth's rotation. The hourly cycle of long-distance telephone demand follows a pattern pretty much like the hourly cycle of electricity demand shown earlier in Figure 15–3 (page 313), with daylight business hours holding the loftiest levels. Long-distance calling also follows a daily cycle, with twelve million calls on the typical Saturday or Sunday as compared to twenty million weekday calls. Both the hourly and daily cycles are reflected in the peak-load pricing schedule illustrated in Figure 16–6.

Outside the area of dial-up long-distance ser-

vice the FCC has faced some monumental struggles with price structure. The essense of its problem lies in finding a good answer to the question: *How low can AT&T cut its prices relative to costs when confronting competition?*

Figure 16–6.   Long-Distance Time-of-Day Discounts

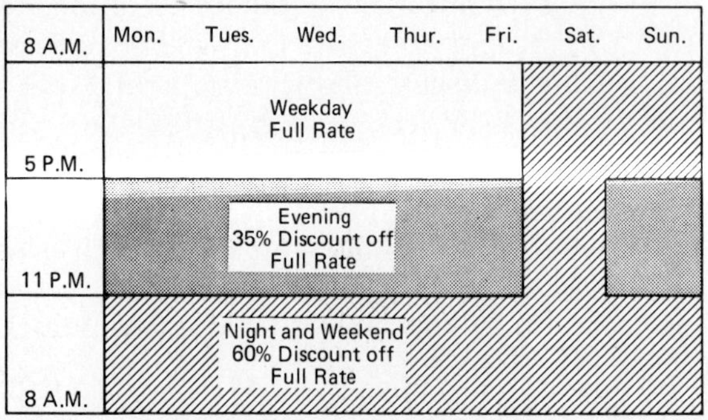

Source: Pacific Telephone Directory, 1981, San Jose CA.

The competition comes from the specialized independents mentioned earlier in Table 16–1. It also comes from the opportunity of self-supply that some heavy users of communications have. It is possible that AT&T, if left unchecked, would cut prices below cost until competitors were driven from the field or into small niches, using excess profits from its monopoly markets to finance this war against independents—predatory pricing, that is. Notice once again that value-of-service may be used to rationalize prices, but cross-subsidization is actually at issue here.

In attempting to answer this question of "fair" price structure for competitive services the FCC first had to decide the theoretical question of what "costs" were the appropriate costs to use—fully distributed cost or marginal cost. The Commission chose fully distributed cost. Next, the FCC had to obtain estimates of fully distributed costs for AT&T's many interstate services. And this horrendous exercise, culminating in the late 1970s with "Docket 18128," led the FCC into what *Business Week* has called a "journey to the center of the earth."

The FCC's investigation of AT&T's interstate prices for Telpak, which began in 1961, illustrates the difficulties. Just after non-AT&T private microwave systems were permitted, AT&T filed a price response designed to discourage competing private systems. The new prices, called Telpak, gave fantastic discounts off the old prices for leased private-line bundles:

- Telpak A, 51% discount for 12 lines
- Telpak B, 64% discount for 24 lines
- Telpak C, 77% discount for 60 lines
- Telpak D, 85% discount for 240 lines

Although AT&T's customers did not protest their new low rates, independent suppliers of microwave equipment protested because few customers would then build their own micro-

wave facilities. Western Union also protested as it was in direct competition with AT&T in providing leased private-line services. Telpak A and B discounts were lifted fairly quickly. But the issues for C and D became very complicated, and many years of hearings and studies ensued while the disputed rates were permitted on a "temporary" basis.

In 1976, after 15 years, the FCC finally decided that Telpak C and D prices were indeed unreasonably low relative to cost and therefore illegal. The FCC was upheld when AT&T appealed to federal court in 1977. But the low rates were not immediately raised because by this time large subscribers, including the U.S. government itself, began to think of the cheap Telpak prices as their legal privilege. Many of them sued to block the FCC and AT&T from abandoning Telpak, thereby touching off a further round of hearings, court appearances, and legal maneuverings. Finally, in 1981, after *20 years* of wrangling, the Supreme Court ordered an end to AT&T's Telpak discounts.[18] Customers like Associated Press, Dow Jones, ABC, NBC, and CBS now face millions of dollars in added communications costs annually.

As the FCC began to scan other services for prices unreasonably below cost, such as Wide Area Telephone Service, or WATS (which has the 800 numbers), it encountered similar difficulties. The key problem was expressed by an AT&T vice-president when he exclaimed, "Don't tell me we know our costs. We don't!"[19] In sum, long-distance price structures have followed cost-of-service criteria fairly well for dial-up toll calls, but full realization of cost-of-service pricing in other areas (and an end to cross-subsidization or value-of-service pricing) has been seriously hampered by uncertainty as to what costs actually prevail.

[18] *Wall Street Journal*, April 21, 1981, p. 4.
[19] *Wall Street Journal*, September 16, 1976.

B. Before Friday: Entry and Access

The story of entry and access regulation helps to explain why AT&T agreed to divest the operating companies because it explains what AT&T's chairman meant when he said that "the fence was opened." It is a story of *de*regulation and competition, sometimes but not always instigated by the FCC. What is perhaps even more intriguing, the story helps to explain why the 1974 monopolization suit that ended on January 8, 1982 was launched in the first place. The Justice Department felt that AT&T's responses to deregulation and competition were restrictive and anticompetitive, thereby warranting a Section 2 Sherman Act suit. In short, AT&T was suddenly and unwillingly thrust into an era of competition even before Friday. We take up long-distance service first and equipment second.

1. THE LONG-DISTANCE MARKET[20]

Background, 1945–1958. As we have seen, AT&T traditionally charged prices well above cost on long-distance service. The differential was great enough to attract profit-minded entrants as early as the late 1940s when microwave technology offered an alternative to AT&T's cables. But entry was delayed as AT&T was able to pursue several strategies barring entry. In order of AT&T's preference, these strategies were—(1) persuade regulators to block entry, (2) deny entrants interconnection to AT&T's switches and local loops, and (3) drop price below cost where entry occurs, using profits from monopoly areas to finance the subsidies.

Regulation could serve as a barrier because microwave occupies a segment of the radio frequency spectrum and the FCC licenses users of that spectrum. Moreover, if a potential entrant wanted to sell communication services to others as a "common carrier" rather than simply provide services for its own use, further FCC approval would be necessary. In fact, the FCC used these powers to protect AT&T when the microwave market first opened up in the late 1940s:

> First, the commission set aside certain portions of the microwave spectrum for use by common carriers only. Second, the commission implicitly accepted the Bell System's existing policy of refusing to interconnect with the facilities of other companies. Third, the FCC determined that only common carriers could furnish service over the so-called video frequencies. Other firms were required to abandon their systems when common carrier service became available.[21]

To some extent the FCC's restrictive policies could be excused because of technological uncertainties. In particular, the FCC thought that the microwave band might be quite limited.

Above 890 Decision (1959).[22]   Prompted by two North Dakota television stations requesting permission to build microwave facilities for their own use, and also by independent microwave equipment manufacturers who could not break the AT&T-Western Electric tie, the FCC began a broad review of its microwave policy in late 1956. Over two hundred parties participated in the hearings. Those opposed to freer use of the spectrum above 890 megacycles were led by AT&T, whose main arguments were technical and economic. On the technical front, Bell argued that multiplication of microwave facilities would foul up existing facilities with interference, causing "irreparable harm to the telephone company's ability to provide a basic nationwide communication service."[23] On the economic front, Bell argued that entrants would engage in cream-skimming. They

---

[20] For details see Brock, *op. cit.*, pp. 198–233.

[21] H. Craig Petersen, *Business and Government* (New York: Harper & Row, 1981), p. 309–310.

[22] Alfred E. Kahn, *The Economics of Regulation*, Vol. II (New York: John Wiley & Sons, 1971), pp. 129–132.

[23] Brock, *op cit.*, p. 203, quoting from the FCC report.

would enter only lucrative, high-volume markets between major cities, thereby ending AT&T's high profits there and ending the source of AT&T's subsidy to unprofitable markets in the hinter lands and in basic phone service. Tragedy would ensue, said AT&T, as this would "increase the cost of communications to the Nation's economy as a whole [and] would cast an added burden upon the individual and the small businessman who would continue to rely on common carriers."[24]

Those favoring freer use of the microwaves rebutted these points, but we need not delve into their counter arguments and contrary evidence. The FCC found in their favor in 1959 with its landmark "Above 890" decision.[25] Yet the dire consequences predicted by AT&T did not follow. Though major, the decision was really quite limited. It merely opened the way for *private* (self use) microwave systems where space was available. It did not authorize new common carrier systems. Moreover, it did not require AT&T to offer interconnection to the private systems. Yet for a few heavy communicators the breakthrough was enough because at the time AT&T was charging $75,600 per month for large-scale services that cost only about $17,141 per month to supply (240 lines of 100 mile distance).

AT&T's regulatory barrier thus fell as far as fully *private systems* were concerned. It could still deny interconnection, but that was a weak weapon against much private entry because private users have little need for switching and local loops. Left with one weapon against entry—price cutting—AT&T filed its Telpak rates. These, as we have seen, were discounts of up to 85% that were eventually found by the FCC to be unreasonably below cost.

The MCI Case (1969, 1971). The regulatory barrier against *common carrier* microwave

service lasted another ten years. It was finally knocked down at the instigation of pint-sized Microwave Communications, Inc. (MCI). MCI had an opening through which to run because AT&T's Telpak rates gave no break to small users who could not build their own systems. Thus MCI requested common carrier status from the FCC in 1963, proposing to build a microwave system between Chicago and St. Louis that would compete with AT&T by offering privately *leased* lines (capable of conveying voice, data, and facsimile), *at half the price.* Aside from the problem of winning common carrier status, MCI also faced the problem of securing interconnection with AT&T's local telephone companies. Interconnection was important because MCI's potential customers were relatively small communications users who needed local connections to reach MCI's long-distance lines.

AT&T vigorously opposed MCI's license before the FCC. AT&T argued once again that the scheme was technically foreboding. AT&T argued once again that this would be cream-skimming, with costly consequences for subsidized markets. Moreover, AT&T argued that MCI was incompetent, unqualified, and financially unfit to provide such a service. Finally, AT&T argued that authorization would be meaningless because AT&T would refuse local interconnection to MCI.

The legal battle reached partial resolution in 1969 when the FCC decided in favor of MCI.[26] A flood of similar applications followed, prompting the FCC to issue its "Specialized Common Carrier Decision" in 1971, which announced a general policy in favor of competition and approved interconnection to effectuate that policy. MCI began operation[27] but was hampered by AT&T's continued refusal to in-

---

[24] Ibid., from the FCC report.
[25] *Allocation of Microwave Frequencies Above 890 Mc.,* 27 FCC 359 (1959).

[26] *In the Matter of Microwave Communications Inc.,* 18 FCC 953 (1969).
[27] Construction cost MCI $2 million and seven months, whereas the legal fight cost $10 million and seven years.

terconnect. So the legal battle was not over on this until 1976, when MCI finally gained complete interconnection rights. Once the regulation and interconnection barriers to entry were down, AT&T again cut price to discourage further entry. Still, MCI grew to serve 70 cities by 1980.

Dial-up Service (1978).   Emboldened by its victories in leased private lines, MCI introduced a dial-up long-distance service in 1975 called "Execunet." The service was limited to areas served by MCI, which though growing were still spotty. Moreover, the service was chiefly for business, not residential, customers. Still, MCI was getting a foot in the door of the biggest long-distance market of them all, worth over $17 billion annually in total revenue.

Once again AT&T stridently protested. And once again the FCC had to decide. But this time the FCC decided against MCI in favor of AT&T. Fortunately for MCI, however, the appelate courts, including the Supreme Court, returned verdicts favorable to MCI in 1977 and 1978. The upshot is that "discount" long-distance service is now available for many dial-up users. After MCI pioneered, others followed—Southern Pacific, ITT, and Western Union among them. Benefits also followed. A 1980 survey of direct-dial daytime prices on calls from New York to Chicago disclosed discounts ranging up to 27% as compared to AT&T's rates.[28] Thus long-distance competition has spread from private systems, to private leased lines, to dial-up service, bringing lower prices in its wake.

2. THE TERMINAL EQUIPMENT MARKET

Background.   We think nothing of plugging any old toaster or TV set into our electric utility system. The utility does not manufacture or distribute these appliances. A similar degree of independence between hardware and system service is now approaching maturity in telecommunications. But for decades this was not the case. AT&T was "untouchable." *All* attachments had to be supplied by AT&T itself (i.e., Western Electric).

Bell's defense for this was technical integrity. If just anything could be attached to the system, damages would surely ensue, ruining the communications network. Given the network's elegant interdependencies, Bell would have difficulty diagnosing and correcting problems. Moreover, Bell would be blamed for virtually every failure, justified or not. Or so it was argued.

However valid these arguments may have been in the past, they could not support the absurd diligence with which Bell attacked attachments, nor the idiotic support Bell received from most commissions. For example, Bell persuaded North Carolina's Utility Commission to ban plastic phone-book covers that were not furnished by the Bell system. Thus, evolution to competition in terminal equipment had to climb a steep trail running parallel to that for long-distance service.

Hush-A-Phone (1956).   The Hush-A-Phone was a cuplike device that snapped onto a telephone's mouthpiece. The effect it achieved was the same as if a caller cupped his or her hands between mouth and mouthpiece, namely, the muffling of background noise and privacy for what was said. Bell railed against Hush-A-Phone, claiming that it distorted the speaker's voice a bit and questioning whether there was any real demand for the product.

The FCC sided with Bell, but a federal appeals court sanely reversed the commission and favored Hush-A-Phone.[29] The court noted that users of Hush-A-Phone could only harm themselves (if indeed any harm was done), and do so in a way that they could easily duplicate with their hands. As for the absence of demand, well

---

[28] *Wall Street Journal,* July 9, 1980, p. 27.

[29] *Hush-A-Phone Corporation* v. *U.S. and FCC,* 238 F.2d 266 (1956).

over 100,000 Hush-A-Phones had been sold before AT&T's assault, and that was in any case a problem for Hush-A-Phone's manufacturer not AT&T or the FCC. In short, the Hush-A-Phone case set the important precedent that some public harm must be shown in order to thwart an attachment.

Carterphone (1968). Shortly after Hush-A-Phone was decided, a tiny electronics company began selling what was called a Carterphone. This device contained a cradle that would hold an ordinary telephone handset. Without direct wire connection, the Carterphone could transmit a telephone voice into a radio broadcast for reception on mobile radios. This way someone could call a radio dispatcher by telephone and talk over the mobile radio network.

In arguing against Carterphone, AT&T suggested a number of ways that the Carterphone might harm the telephone system, but offered no evidence or example of any actual harm. The FCC therefore had little difficulty in finding against AT&T in 1968 (after lengthy legal skirmishing). This opened the door to competition a bit further.

Connecting Arrangement (until 1977). Not one to yield monopoly power easily, AT&T answered the Carterphone loss by permitting attachments only on condition that its system be protected from damage by a "connecting arrangement" that AT&T itself would supply. This device, interposed between Bell and the foreign attachment, had circuitry that would shield the telephone system against faulty customer attachments. Priced very high and installed only at Bell's convenience, customers were still discouraged from using non-Bell equipment. In PBXs, where equipment expenses were high enough to inspire customer defection to independents, Bell continued to dominate, yielding only 3.7% of its market to independents by 1974.[30]

Dissatisfied with AT&T's continued restraint of the equipment trade, the FCC probed the scientific necessity of protective connecting devices. After three years of study, the FCC decided in 1975 that the devices could be scrapped. Instead, the technical integrity of the system could be protected by a program of equipment testing and prior clearance. Attachments could qualify for attachment by meeting the FCC's technical standards. Thus FCC certification would replace AT&T constipation. AT&T protested shrilly all the way to the Supreme Court, only to suffer still another loss.

Mandatory Phone Purchases (1980). For reasons too complex to explain here, the FCC delivered yet another blow to AT&T's control of the terminal equipment market in a 1980 decision. The ruling, if fully implemented, will end the traditional practice of customers renting their telephones and other equipment from the phone company, with the cost buried in the monthly bill. Beginning in March 1982, all terminal equipment is to be sold or leased through equipment subsidiaries operating separately from the phone service companies. The market for terminal equipment is, in other words, supposed to become completely *de*regulated.

The requirement that AT&T and GTE conduct their sales through new subsidiaries has the good intention of putting AT&T and GTE on an equal footing with rival equipment suppliers who offer no phone service. The new subsidiaries are supposed to maintain "arms-length" relations with their parents to minimize the possibility of predatory pricing or other "unfair" tactics.[31]

It is too early to tell whether, once implemented, this deregulation will bring full-fledged competition to terminal equipment.

---

[30] Brock, *op cit.*, pp. 244–245.

[31] Readers who doubt that AT&T would do such a thing should consult the *Wall Street Journal* of April 4, 1981, which on pages 1 and 21 reports extensively on AT&T's "migration" policy.

One thing is certain, however, the competition that was achieved during the 1970s sparked a dazzling improvement in the rate of technological advance. Whereas terminal equipment used to be typified by drab, heavy, dial telephones that came in only one color (black), the market is now alive with models featuring Mickey Mouse, automatic dialing, and countless other innovations. In office equipment, PBXs now seem to do everything except empty trash baskets. With innovation, the total market has taken off toward $10 billion annual sales.[32]

C. After Friday: Toward More Competition and Deregulation

1. THE STATUS OF AT&T

AT&T's loss of its operating companies and loss of monopoly status in long-distance service and equipment supply might imply that AT&T faces a grim future after Friday. But such is not the case. To be sure, the operating companies accounted for two-thirds of AT&T's assets and four-fifths of its employees just before Friday. But the operating companies accounted for only 44% of AT&T's total revenues and only 40% of its total earnings, so AT&T actually retained the most lucrative parts of the overall business. Moreover, despite the inroads of independents during the late 1970s, AT&T entered the A.F. era providing nearly 97% of all long-distance communications services in the U.S.— a $30 billion business.[33] In equipment, a dwindling share of PBX sales is only part of the story. AT&T hit the ground running with all but a few million of the 140 million home telephones in the U.S. and with 1800 Phone Center Stores

---

[32] See *Business Week*, February 13, 1978, pp. 68–75; April 13, 1981, pp. 122–123; *Fortune*, February 25, 1980, pp. 134–146; Manley R. Irwin, "The Telephone Industry," in W. Adams (ed.), *The Structure of American Industry* (New York: Macmillan, 1977), pp. 328–329.

[33] *Business Week*, January 25, 1982, pp. 22–23; Bro Uttal, "Life After Litigation at IBM and AT&T," *Fortune*, February 8, 1982, pp. 59–61.

in operation.[34] As Walter Hinchman, former Chief of the FCC's Common Carrier Bureau, assessed the antitrust settlement: "Philosophically, it was a cave-in to the government. Economically, it's beautiful for Bell."[35]

2. THE LONG-DISTANCE MARKET

The FCC still regulates AT&T's long-distance services and will continue to do so for quite awhile. But the big divestiture is supposed to put AT&T on the same procedural footing as MCI and the other long-distance service suppliers, namely, they will all gain access to local exchanges on equal terms. MCI Chairman William G. McGowan was delighted by the decree. "We got what we were after: and divestiture," he said. "I'll love being able to talk with the local companies and get what I want."[36]

Long-distance price levels seem likely to fall relative to what they would have been otherwise. Both increased competition and reduced cross-subsidies from long-distance to local service point in this direction. Even so, this is pure speculation. As mentioned earlier, the fees local companies charge long-distance suppliers for access may be high enough to perpetuate some of the cross-subsidy. Moreover, AT&T's continued dominance of the main part of the long-distance market may temper its urge to cut prices, given the large loss of revenues and profits such behavior might entail (assuming a fairly inelastic demand for the company). An MCI spokesman expressed such a view: "Given the revenue penalty involved, it wouldn't seem wise business to me for AT&T to do much long-distance rate-cutting."[37]

3. THE EQUIPMENT MARKET

AT&T's Western Electric can no longer simply fill the orders of its captive customers, as

---

[34] *Wall Street Journal*, January 15, 1982, p. 25.

[35] Quoted by Uttal, *op. cit.*, p. 60.

[36] *Business Week*, January 25, 1982, p. 23; Uttal, *op. cit.*, p. 61.

[37] *Wall Street Journal*, January 21, 1982, p. 21.

they will no longer be captive. AT&T must develop marketing skills to battle rivals who now have a vastly greater opportunity to bid against it for equipment sales. As in the past, the resulting competition will probably have a greater impact on product development than prices. Cordless phones, super digital PABX switching systems, home information centers—the new gadgetry will revolutionize communications.

4. NEW MARKETS

The antitrust settlement gives AT&T the freedom to move into any market it finds attractive. At first, AT&T will probably expand into fields closely related to telecommunications—electronic mail, satellite networks for sending computer information, facsimile, and the like. Later it might well move into broadcasting, cable television, publishing, and computers. These speculations portend future competition between AT&T and another giant—IBM. Indeed, these two are already vying with each other to a limited extent, so future rivalry seems inevitable:

> The competition between the two behemoths has been brewing since IBM entered the satellite-communications business in 1974. Each company has entered the other's territory as the disciplines of communications merged. . . . Over the next decade, developing technology will fundamentally alter the way consumers and businesses communicate, receive news and other information, and create and manipulate the documents and data with which they run their affairs.[38]

The speculative nature of these ruminations must be acknowledged, for as this is written the consent settlement has yet to be finalized and Congress could legislate changes.

[38] *Business Week*, January 25, 1982, p. 22. Although the government's massive monopolization suit against IBM was dismissed the same day the AT&T consent settlement was announced, Assistant Attorney General Baxter has said that there was no connection between the two events. For details on how the AT&T settlement was reached see the *Wall Street Journal*, January 19, 1982, pp. 1, 12.

Summary

Government policy in telecommunications has been complex and confusing. On the one hand, it has encouraged monopoly power with patents and regulatory restrictions. On the other hand, it has encouraged competition with antitrust actions and regulatory relaxations. The reasons for this turmoil are several. (1) Economically, some parts of the industry are conducive to natural monopoly (local loops and central switches), while other parts can be served by competition (long lines and terminal equipment). (2) Historically, technology has changed, so policy that may have been proper for one era grew obsolete for another. (3) Politically, AT&T has seen its influence swell and contract. (4) Structurally, AT&T has been fully integrated, a condition that arguably may have been based on genuine efficiencies, yet a condition that permitted AT&T to follow such anticompetitive strategies as refusing interconnection and denying attachments.

Our survey of this convoluted terrain began with an anatomical outline of telecommunications. Its main parts are (1) terminal equipment, (2) local loops, (3) central switches, and (4) long lines. Market structure varies within each of these segments, but the overall picture is dominated by AT&T—an operating company by virtue of its Long Lines division, but also a holding company that owns an equipment subsidiary (Western Electric) and, until divestiture, local operating companies. In areas where Bell companies do not have the local monopoly, independents do. The largest of these is GTE, which is integrated, but not to the same extent as AT&T.

The industry's segments most susceptible to competition are long lines and terminal equipment. Competition in long lines first became possible with the advent of microwave technology in the late 1940s and became even more possible with the development of satellite communications. Now more than a dozen companies offer a variety of long distance services to the public as common carriers. This happy state of affairs came about slowly, however, as AT&T was able to delay new entry by employing several tactics—(1) securing regulatory restrictions, (2) denying interconnection, and (3) predatory pricing. Thus, competitive inroads had to grow by stages. Freedom to private, self-supply systems came with the "Above 890 Decision" in 1959. Competition in common-carrier offerings of private leased lines emerged after MCI won clearance in 1969 and others won clearance through the FCC's "Specialized Common Carrier Decision" in 1971. Finally, the immense dial-up market opened up in 1978 after the Supreme Court approved MCI's "Execunet" service over the objections of both AT&T and the FCC.

Terminal equipment went through similar stages, beginning with items that could hardly be considered attachments at all (Hush-A-Phone and Carterphone) and progressing to the point of permitting all "plug-ins" that meet technical standards. Indeed, after 1982, terminal equipment is supposed to be deregulated, with AT&T selling or leasing equipment *directly* to customers through an "arms-length" subsidiary.

Continued regulation of the traditional kind is likely for most telecommunications services, especially those offered to residential customers. State commissions set *price levels* for intrastate operations in ways quite similar to those governing energy utilities. FCC surveillance of price levels for interstate operations has on the whole been fairly lenient. All price level regulation has been hampered by the intrastate/interstate dichotomy, by AT&T's ownership of affiliated suppliers, and by the sheer immensity of the task.

Price structures regulation is notable for its traditional value-of-service orientation plus heavy doses of cross-subsidization. Price/cost ratios have in the past been (1) relatively high for business as compared to residential customers, (2) relatively high for long-distance as compared to local calling, and (3) relatively high for nonbasic as compared to basic service. There is, however, some trend toward more cost-of-service pricing. Locally, this is illustrated by charges for directory assistance. Nationally, this is illustrated by a long-standing policy of peak-load pricing for long-distance calling, and by the FCCs recent effort to determine costs for different classes of long-distance service. This latter effort was triggered by the torturous Telpak proceedings.

As a result of a consent settlement to a government antitrust suit on January 8, 1982 this trend toward more cost-of-service pricing is likely to be hastened, as cross-subsidies of yesteryear are cast overboard after AT&T divests the local operating companies. Indeed, many critics of the proposed settlement will seek revisions, perhaps even through new legislation, that will maintain some of those subsidies.

Certainly the greatest potential benefits of this restructuring will come in long-distance services and equipment supply, where AT&T's rivals have won "equal opportunities" to sell to residential consumers, business buyers, and the local operating companies themselves. These markets may witness further deregulation in the future. Still other, already nonregulated, markets may also witness more competition in the future as a slimmed down AT&T moves wider afield.

Questions and Exercises for Chapter 16

1. Describe the relationship between AT&T and the local operating companies before and after Friday in (a) ownership, (b) pricing policy, (c) regulation, and (d) buying and selling.

2. Why did AT& T agree on January 8, 1982 to divest the local operating companies?

3. What characteristics that are important to economic policy distinguish local telephone service from long-distance and equipment?

4. AT&T used (a) regulation, (b) denial of access, and (3) price cutting to keep potential competitors at bay. Explain each strategy with the aid of an example.

5. To what extent has cost-of-service guided long-distance price structure? To what extent not?

6. To what extent has cost-of-service guided local telephone service price structures?

7. Why were private lines the first area of competitive intrusion in the long-distance field?

8. Explain the relevance and importance of AT&T's battles with MCI. Give facts, issues, and decisions.

Chapter 17

Broadcast Communications

While we make our media, our media make us.
—Erik Barnouw

The average television set is on nearly seven hours a day. Youngsters grow up spending more time in front of the TV than in the classroom. Oldsters watch TV more than thirty-two hours a week. Thus TV has a tremendous influence on our lives.[1] In turn, the Federal Communications Commission influences TV because it regulates broadcast communications.

The story of this regulation is told in four episodes, which may be summarized in *TV Guide* fashion:

I. *Technical Background:* The radio spectrum has limits which raise havoc when exploited by the free market.

II. *Cast of Characters:* The TV industry has more actors than a mini-series. Local stations, networks, advertisers, program producers, regulators, and cable companies all play major parts.

III. *FCC Regulations:* The "cops," operating under broad legislative mandate, license broadcasters and urge good behavior.

IV. *Main Issues:* Often protecting established interests from innovative "robbers," the

FCC encounters big problems—(1) network power, (2) cable TV, and (3) pay TV.

Although TV is our main focus, radio broadcasting will often enter the picture as TV's forerunner and fellow traveler.

I. Technical Background

In November 1920, radio station KDKA went on the air in Pittsburgh, giving birth to the broadcast industry. Hundreds of radio stations followed within the next few years. The main money behind these early stations came not from advertisers but from manufacturers of radio sets—like RCA and Westinghouse—who wanted to boost the sale of sets. Colleges and universities also contributed, putting about seventy stations on the air in 1922.

Unfortunately, the radio spectrum is a limited resource, with a limited number of wavelengths. This explosion of broadcasters crowded the dial. Interference ensued. Tuning one's set demanded exceptional skill. And early regulatory efforts were consequently "much like those of a lone traffic policeman trying to untan-

---

[1] G. Comstock, S. Chaffee, N. Katzman, M. McCombs, and D. Roberts, *Television and Human Behavior* (New York: Columbia University Press, 1978).

Table 17–1. Selected Radio Frequency Allocations

Megahertz (MH$_z$)		Frequency	Allocation
.003–	.03	Very Low	Navigation; Sonar
.03 –	.3	Low	Navigation
.3 –	3.0	Medium	AM radio; amateur
3.0 –	30.0	High	Amateur; short-wave
30.0 –	300.0	Very High	VHF television; FM radio
300.0 –	3,000.0	Ultra High	UHF television; radar; CB
3,000.0 –	30,000.0	Super High	Satellite; microwave

Source: U.S. Congress, Senate Committee on Commerce, Science and Transportation, Subcommittee on Communications, *Amendments to the Communications Act of 1934,* Hearings, 96th Cong., 1st Sess. (1979), Part 1, pocket chart.

gle a mass of stalled vehicles in a rush-hour traffic jam."[2]

The first such effort was the Radio Act of 1927, which established a Federal Radio Commission to organize the spectrum and license access to it. This law set two precedents that continue to this day. First, no licensee could *own* the channel assigned to him.[3] Second, each channel was supposed to be used for "the public interest, convenience, and necessity," a vague guide whose details had to be worked out.

The duties of the Radio Commission were later transferred to the Federal Communications Commission, created by the Communications Act of 1934. The resulting organization of the radio spectrum as it stands today is indicated by Table 17–1, which summarizes the spectrum's divisions and their assigned uses.

The television portion of the spectrum has a total of 68 channels—VHF channels 2 through 13, and UHF channels 14 through 69. The number of possible stations using these channels is much larger, however. A broadcast signal can travel only a limited distance depending on the power of its transmission. As a consequence, broadcasters in different geographic areas can use the same channel. Through control of geographic separation, the total number of VHF station assignments in the U.S. is now 658 and the total number of UHF station assignments is nearly double that. These station assignments merely represent possibilities, however, because some station assignments go unused, especially UHF assignments. Moreover, many of the assignments are reserved for noncommercial uses such as educational TV.

Table 17–1 also hints at the wide range of other spectrum concerns. As this is written, for example, a debate rages over channel spacing on the AM radio dial. The question is whether the spacing should be reduced from the current 10 kilohertz to 9, which is the number used elsewhere in the world. At a more mundane

[2] *Federal Regulation and Regulatory Reform,* Report by the Subcommittee on Oversight and Investigations of the Committee on Interstate and Foreign Commerce, U.S. Congress, House, 94th Cong., 2nd Session (1976), p. 250.

[3] Some have argued that the sale (or give away) of spectrum spaces would eliminate the need for regulation. The idea is that spectrum ownership would, through economic incentives, lead to the best use of this scarce resource. See R. H. Coase, "The Federal Communications Commission," *Journal of Law and Economics* (October 1959), pp. 1–40. For a brief critique of this view see, W. H. Melody, "Radio Spectrum Allocation: Role of the Market," *American Economic Review* (May 1980), pp. 393–397.

level, the FCC must approve any device that broadcasts radio signals, even though those signals travel only a few feet. This includes things like "Sonic Scrub," a device that cleans false teeth placed in water by sending out ultrasonic waves that agitate the water to loosen debris on the dentures. Another is "BouMatic," which monitors the sexual needs of cows.[4]

In addition to VHF and UHF broadcasting, there are two more ways television signals can be carried into one's home—by satellite and by cable. These are important alternatives because they are not nearly as limited in channel capacity as VHF and UHF broadcasting. Direct home reception from satellite is now too new to be of interest to us here. Cable, however, is old and booming, so it deserves close attention.

With cable, TV signals are piped into one's home by a wire connected to a local grid. The grid can pick up those signals from a variety of sources—local live production, tape replay, local over-the-air broadcast, distant transmission via satellite, and distant transmission via ground based microwave. Because local wire carriage does not use the radio spectrum, cable has escaped much of the FCC's regulation of VHF and UHF broadcasting. Still, the FCC did assert authority over cable for quite a while, hampering its growth.

II. The Cast of Characters

Regulation of the television industry cannot be understood without an understanding of the industry's participants and their roles—the viewers, advertisers, local stations, networks, program producers, cable companies, and regulators.[5] While surveying these parties two things should be kept in mind. First, it is helpful to distinguish four crucial functions that are performed by these parties—(1) program *production,* (2) program *packaging,* (3) program *delivery* to home sets, and (4) the *funding* of production, packaging, and delivery. Some participants perform more than one of these functions, but there is substantial specialization. Second, it will be helpful if Figure 17–1 is kept in mind, as it puts each party in place. The left side of Figure 17–1 depicts the "Old System" prevailing largely undisturbed from the mid-1940s to the mid-1970s. The right side incorporates the addition of cable, which has introduced a "New System" that promises to be the wave of the future. Because the "New System" represents an addition to the "Old" and is not yet dominant, we shall focus chiefly on the "Old System" until arriving at consideration of the cable companies.

A. Viewers and Advertisers

Over 97 per cent of all households have television sets. As measured by viewing time per week, the people most fascinated by TV tend to be relatively uneducated, old, and low-income. The rest of us watch less often but nevertheless to a degree that in some ways astounds. The average viewing time for all individuals taken together is around *28 hours per week.*[6]

This audience is the *ultimate* source of funding for all commercial TV. This is true even of the Old System, where advertisers are the ones actually writing the checks and viewers watch for "free." The viewers pay indirectly through their purchase of the advertisers' prod-

[4] Whimsical though these examples may be, the interference problem can be serious. Some electronic heating machines used to make plywood and plastic goods are as powerful as large AM radio stations. *Wall Street Journal,* October 1, 1980, p. 1.

[5] James Rosse and James Dertouzos, "Economic Issues in Mass Communication Industries," *Proceedings of the Symposium on Media Concentration* (Washington, D.C.: Federal Trade Commission, 1978), pp. 87–110; Harvey J. Levin, *Fact and Fancy in Television Regulation* (New York: Russell Sage Foundation, 1980), pp. 25–47.

[6] Comstock, et al., *op. cit.,* p. 94.

Figure 17–1. Outline of TV Industry Participants and Their Relationships

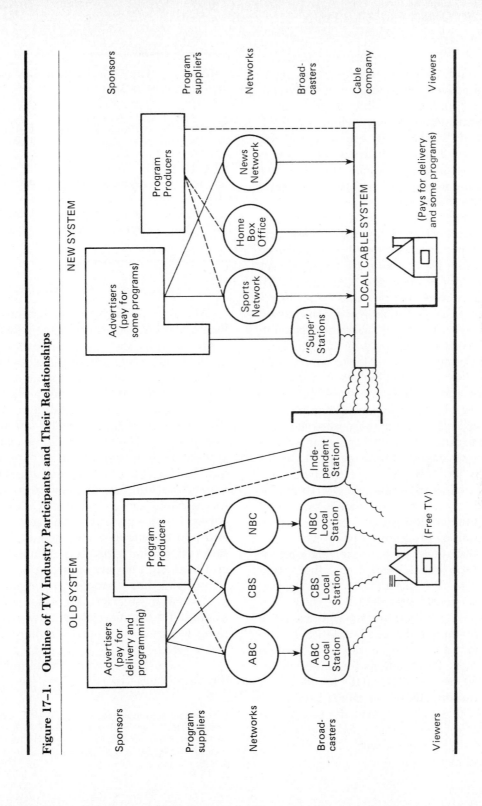

ucts. The advertisers are, in turn, the *proximate* source of funds for program production, packaging, and delivery. Spending on television advertising accounts for roughly 20 per cent of all advertising and now runs well over $10 billion annually. In short, the orientation of the Old System is one in which the audience is "sold" to advertisers. Stations and networks compete for audiences whose attention is then marketed to marketers.

The monetary contributions of viewers are more direct when served by cable. "Basic" cable service is purchased for a hook-up charge and a monthly fee of about $9. To the extent this basic service provides VHF and UHF broadcasts by wire (and presumably better reception), the fee essentially covers the added costs of delivery by cable. Program production and other costs are still paid by advertisers as in the Old System. "Pay" cable service provides *additional* pay-TV channels such as Home Box Office at an additional fixed monthly fee to cable viewers. Thus, in the case of pay TV, the audience *directly* funds all or most of the costs of program production, packaging, and delivery, thereby avoiding advertising interruptions as often as on "free" TV. For the most part programs are sold to the audience, whereas under the Old System the audience is sold to advertisers. In some cases viewers can be charged on a program-by-program basis.

Table 17-2 summarizes these relationships and roles. Over-the-air pay TV, or "subscription TV," is yet another possibility that is like pay cable except for its over-the-air delivery. (Unscramblers are attached to sets.) This possibility is not mentioned in Table 17-2, however, because it now serves only a very tiny fraction of TV homes. The fractions for other modes as of 1980 were: VHF-UHF broadcasting, 100% (either directly or via cable); basic cable 25%; pay cable 12% (i.e., half the basic cable group). By 1990, basic cable is expected to jump to 50% of all TV homes, with more than half also getting pay cable.

Table 17-2. The Financial Roles of Viewers and Advertisers in Commercial TV

Type of System	Cost of Program Production/ Packaging	Cost of Delivery
VHF-UHF Broadcasting	Advertiser pays	Advertiser pays
Basic Cable	Advertiser pays	Viewer pays
Pay Cable	Viewer pays (all or part)	Viewer pays

B. Local Broadcast Stations

The chief task of broadcast stations is to deliver programs to viewers. Some programming is produced by stations (local news in particular), but most programming is fed to the broadcasters by the networks or supplied by independent program producers, and syndicators.

Of the 638 commercial stations reporting to the FCC in 1976, 547 were affiliated with networks.[7] Affiliation entails a contractual agreement between station and network requiring the station to carry a minimum amount of network programs. Stations are compensated for carrying network programs when the networks pass on a portion of their advertising revenues to the stations. The amount of this portion varies from station to station and depends on the amount of network programming a station carries, but it ranges from about 20 to 40 per cent.[8] In addition, a portion of the time set aside for commercials in network programming is given to stations for them to sell to advertisers.

It is important to note that all but a few of the largest local markets like New York City

[7] Federal Communications Commission, *43rd Annual Report/Fiscal Year 1977*, p. 143.

[8] Roger Noll, "Television and Competition," *Proceedings of the Symposium on Media Concentration, op cit.*, p. 248.

and Los Angeles have no more than three commercial stations. These three tend to occupy the VHF band and enjoy network affiliation. Stated differently, nonaffiliated VHF independents are a very rare breed found mainly in places like New York, Los Angeles, Chicago, and San Francisco. The implication is that, from the individual viewer's point of view, television broadcasting is a highly concentrated business.

Even from a national vantage point broadcasting is more highly concentrated than would be suggested by the fact that there are more than six hundred broadcast stations. Each of the three networks *owns* five of its affiliate stations located in prime markets (the FCC allows no more). And most of the main remaining stations are clustered by chain ownership. Metromedia, Westinghouse, Cox Broadcasting, and Storer are prominent among these chains.[9]

C. Networks

ABC, CBS, and NBC produce programs, package programs produced by others, and perform some delivery services. As regards *program production,* the networks can be credited for world news, most daytime programming, and most athletic coverage. In contrast, the situation comedies, detective stories, miniseries, movies, and dramas familiar to all prime-time evening viewers are not produced by the networks. Rather, they are purchased from independent program producers and *packaged* in the network schedule. Thus ABC, CBS, and NBC have traditionally performed a middleman function, producing or buying programs, packaging them into a schedule, and then selling pieces of the package to national advertisers along with the air time of their affiliate stations. Figure 17–1's Old System depicts this situation by sandwiching the networks between the advertisers and program producers on the top and the local broadcast stations on the bottom. Net-

works may thus be likened to merchandise wholesalers who bridge the gap between manufacturers and retailers.

Simple economics explains the existence of networks. Programs that are too expensive to produce locally can be produced nationally with affiliate stations sharing the cost. With each network affiliate showing a program and sharing the cost, the cost per station is lower than it would be if each station produced its own programs. Of course, numerous stations could deal with program suppliers outside the network context, and indeed to some extent they do. But even in this case networking offers efficiencies:

> One reason is that the negotiations over the price of programs are simpler and less costly, if a single agent, such as a network, represents two hundred or more stations than if each station negotiates separately. Another reason is that networks can solve the complicated problem of scheduling programs for all affiliates, rather than have each attack the scheduling problem separately.[10]

Although these factors explain networking, they do not explain the dominance of just *three* networks, a problem we turn to shortly.

Aside from their production and packaging activities, the major networks also perform some *delivery* services. First, they each own five broadcast stations. These stations are located in the nation's largest cities, with the result that 20 per cent of the population lives in markets served by one or more of these owned affiliates. Second, the networks bear the costs of delivering programs to local stations on microwave relay, coaxial cable, and satellite. Their long-distance delivery systems—mainly leased from AT&T—accommodate live national programming such as the Super Bowl.

D. Program Producers

The logos flashed on the screen at the end of most prime-time entertainment programs in-

[9] Rosse and Dertouzos, *op. cit.,* p. 102.

[10] Noll, *op. cit.,* p. 245.

dicate their independent origins. Hollywood film companies are prominent among these program producers, but there are also dozens of others such as MTM Productions that have been enormously successful. Independent producers not only supply networks with programs, they also supply them to independent, nonaffiliated stations.

Nonnetwork programming is in part the preserve of syndicators, who purchase programs from independent producers for subsequent resale to stations or to advertisers who place the programs with stations. In addition, many of the larger stations deal directly with independent producers. Much of the programming in this nonnetwork market is original, but a great deal of it is simply reruns of former network series.

E. Cable Companies

Cable television, the linchpin of the New System depicted in Figure 17–1, is relatively small but growing rapidly. Cable's ad revenues for 1981 were less than $50 million, compared with the more than $10 *billion* garnered by the broadcast side of the system.[11] Yet cable TV is burgeoning, and its large subscriber revenues lessen the need for advertising revenues.

Cable started during the 1950s merely as an amendment to the delivery system of broadcast television. Small communities not served by local stations and too distant to pick up clear signals from big city stations were wired to large and lofty antennas that could catch those signals for the entire community. Cable also helped improve reception in urban areas where tall buildings or hills created the "fuzzies." From this start based on *picture clarity,* cable grew because of an additional advantage over conventional broadcast delivery, namely, immense *channel capacity.* Although early cable systems

[11] *Wall Street Journal,* March 31, 1981, p. 46.

carried only twelve channels, later ones were built to carry up to a hundred. This vast capacity offered the opportunity of greater program diversity and viewer choice. In 1975, exploitation of that opportunity was given a great boost with the advent of satellite relay of television signals. The broadcast signals of local *stations* could thereafter be beamed all around the country at a small fraction of the cost of microwave relay, the previous method (and the networks' main method).

Now, as suggested in Figure 17–1, cable TV has matured into a complex system of its own. At the base are the cable companies responsible for wire delivery. Cable franchises are awarded to these companies for particular areas by local governments. These franchises are usually exclusive, much like the local telephone monopolies, and in most cases local governments regulate the rates the cable companies charge their subscribers. Local governments also charge the cable companies "franchise fees" for the right to operate.[12] Although an FCC rule presently prohibits NBC, CBS, ABC, and AT&T from owning cable systems (a rule soon to be dropped), the companies with the largest accumulations of local systems and subscribers are among the giants of the communications industry. Teleprompter (a Westinghouse subsidiary), American TV & Communications (Time Inc.), and Warner Amex Cable (Warner Communications) are examples.

As indicated in Figure 17–1, a portion of cable's channels are devoted to the Old System's over-the-air signals. Additional programming is supplied by nonnetwork "superstations," the most famous of which is Ted Turner's WTBS

[12] Bidding among competing cable companies for the local franchise often centers on the amount of the franchise fee. But by FCC regulation that fee cannot exceed a fixed, fairly low limit, so the bidding also centers on other factors. Special product or service offerings, local advertising campaigns, and even bribery have been a part of the bidding wars. *Newsweek,* August 4, 1980, pp. 44–45; *Business Week,* December 8, 1980, pp. 62–68.

of Atlanta, beamed by satellite to more than 10 million cable subscribers in 48 states. Turner also pioneered with CNN in 1980, a cable news network. Other specialized cable networks offer an alluring variety of programming—sports, movies, "black" entertainment, and so on. Some of these are strictly pay-TV, like Home Box Office and Showtime. Others accept advertising. Several of the cable networks are subsidiaries of cable companies, so these companies are not limited to delivery systems. (Time Inc., for instance, owns Home Box Office.) Moreover, ABC and CBS have also recently jumped into the act.[13] Where this proliferation of cable networks will end, nobody knows.

F. The Federal Communications Commission

Operating from the sidelines is the FCC. A thumbnail sketch of the agency was given earlier on page 336, so further identification is not needed here. As for the FCC's regulatory activities in broadcasting, a special section is warranted.

III. FCC Regulation

Table 17–3 outlines the focus and purpose of FCC television regulation. Because this regulation differs markedly from the regulation of utilities, the table includes an outline of what is *not* regulated.

A. Access to the Spectrum

As we have seen, spectrum overcrowding was the main illness the FCC was created to remedy, and licensing was the medicine prescribed. No one may own or operate a broadcast station without a license designating frequency

[13] Though prevented from stringing cable by regulations, the networks are free to offer cable programming.

Table 17–3. Focus and Purpose of FCC Regulation in Brief

What *IS* regulated by the FCC:	Purpose:
Access of broadcasters to the radio spectrum.	To keep signals clear; localism.
Ownership structure, locally and nationally.	To achieve diversity of ownership; localism.
Quantity of program types.	To serve the public interest; inform.
Miscellaneous: payola; employment balance.	To keep things "fair."

What *IS NOT* regulated by the FCC:	Rationale:
Prices and profits of stations, networks, or program producers.	They are not common carriers.
Prices and profits of cable companies.	Jurisdiction rests with local authorities.
Program content.	Protected by the First Amendment.

assignment, call letters, operating power, and sign-on/sign-off times. In this connection the Commission does not license local cable TV systems because they do not transmit over the air. (It does, however, issue certificates of compliance to cable systems that have won franchises from local governments.)

Given the limited nature of spectrum openings, the FCC is often forced to choose one of a number of applicants for the same frequency. This choice could be based on competitive bidding with the proceeds going into the public's coffers or to support educational TV, but it is not. It could be based on lottery, but is not (although this is legally possible for new, low-power VHF "drop-in" stations). Rather, the choice is based on arbitrary judgment following a number of criteria: (1) diversification of ownership of the media, (2) integration of ownership and management, (3) proposed programming service, (4) past broadcasting record on other frequency assignments, (5) efficient use of the frequency, and (6) character.[14]

Moreover, these licenses terminate automatically every five years (three years prior to 1982). Renewal is customary but not necessarily automatic. Renewal is based on continued compliance with "public interest" criteria such as those just listed and with the presence or absence of rival applicants challenging the renewal. In other words, licenses, many of which are extremely valuable, may be yanked by the FCC to punish wayward licensees. Indeed, this power is the Commission's greatest enforcement weapon, a weapon that may be used to gain compliance with any of the regulations outlined in Table 17–3.

Stiff though this may sound, experience indicates that unchallenged renewal applicants are rarely scrutinized closely and challenged applicants rarely lose out to challengers. As a former FCC Commissioner rather cynically put it: "In general . . . licensees may violate FCC rules with impunity so long as they do not misrepresent facts to the Commission."[15]

A mildly amusing measure of this general laxity in wielding the licensing weapon is the surprise and outrage expressed in the business press whenever the Commission acts so boldly as to actually terminate someone's license. A recent case in point was the reaction greeting the FCC's 1980 decision to strip RKO General Inc. of three prime television licenses. RKO was found to have lied to the Commission. Moreover, its parent company, General Tire, was found to have pressured companies to advertise on RKO stations and made "questionable" bribery payments abroad. The *Wall Street Journal* editorially blasted the FCC for its harshness, mockingly calling it the Federal Character Commission.[16]

It must be stressed that only broadcast stations are licensed—not networks, program producers, or others. If the FCC wants to influence the behavior of these others it must do so indirectly through its control of station licensing.

B. Ownership Structure

The Commission restricts the number of broadcasting stations that any one individual or company may own to a total of seven TV stations (only five of which can be VHF) and seven AM and seven FM radio stations. Moreover, a given individual or company cannot own more than one station of the same kind in the same place, precluding the possibility that two of your local TV stations are jointly owned.

Further ownership restrictions curb ownerships across media. Local newspapers and local TV stations are by and large kept separate. ABC, CBS, and NBC could not in the past own local cable companies, although nothing has prevented them from cable networking. Telephone companies cannot own cable systems in areas where they hold the local telephone franchise, and so on.[17]

The purpose behind these rules is fairly obvious. They promote a diversity and decentral-

[14] The most important criteria seem to be followed. Margaret F. Barton, "Conditional Logit Analysis of FCC Decision Making," *Bell Journal of Economics* (Autumn 1979), pp. 399–411.
[15] Nicholas Johnson and John Dystel, "A Day in the Life: The Federal Communication Commission," *Yale Law Journal* (July 1973), p. 1605.
[16] *Wall Street Journal*, February 1, 1980, p. 16; June 24, 1981, p. 28. A main argument was that other delinquents had not been so punished, but of course that is precisely the point here. See also *Fortune*, April 21, 1980, pp. 128–136.
[17] For a survey see *Proceedings of the Symposium on Media Concentration, op. cit.*, Vol. II, pp. 378–428, 472–497.

ization of ownership in an area crucial to the maintenance of democracy—namely, mass communications. As the FCC once said, "The premise is that a democratic society cannot function without the clash of divergent views."[18]

C. Quantity of Program Types

The FCC insists that licensees engage in some minimum amount of "public service" or "merit" programming. In the main, this includes news, documentaries, political discussions, religious programs, and the like. All locally produced programming is to some extent also considered merit programming. To enforce its policy the Commission now requires that stations tally their merit programming during an annual sample of seven days chosen at random. Moreover, each station is supposed to ascertain and serve its community's programming "tastes, needs, and desires."

The main rationale behind these regulations is that democracy requires a well-informed citizenry. In the course of informing us, stations are supposed to comply with several related regulations. A documentary on, say, air pollution, or an hour's airing of a political speech would not necessarily be enough. The "Fairness Doctrine" requires that controversial issues receive balanced treatment and that reply time be offered for countering editorial views. In addition, political candidates are supposed to be granted "equal time" for use of the airwaves.

D. Miscellaneous Regulations

A number of additional regulations carry hopes of furthering various kinds of fairness. For one example, the FCC promotes equal employment opportunity in broadcasting. For an-

other, the FCC attempts to curb "payola"—that is, undisclosed payments which are made to get material on the air. Payola is most commonly associated with disc jockeys who take "bribes" to play certain records. But it extends to television with its abundant opportunities to "plug" products. Payments as such are not banned because they support commercial broadcasting. It is, rather, *undisclosed* payments that rub the wrong way.[19]

E. What Is Not Regulated

1. PRICES AND PROFITS

No segment of the broadcast industry is subject to FCC regulation of prices or profits. Broadcasters are not considered common carriers or public utilities. Most *local governments* police the prices of cable systems because they display characteristics of natural monopolies. But this treatment is an industry exception.

While noting this general absence of a public utility approach, it is interesting to observe that the main thrust of FCC policy is, if anything, to *boost* broadcasting profits rather than cap them. In particular:

- The FCC restricts entry by licensing access to the spectrum.
- The FCC created a few prime channels in each locality by its geographic spacing of VHF broadcasters and its mishandling of the UHF band.
- The FCC has delayed the development of competing technologies with large channel capacities, cable especially.
- The FCC charges no more than a nominal fee for its licenses, thereby *giving* to licensees the use of valuable public properties (i.e., scarce channel assignments).

---

[18] FCC, Second Report and Order in Docket No. 18110, January 31, 1975, par. 111, as quoted by Levin, *op. cit.*, p. 165.

[19] R. H. Coase, "Payola in Radio and Television Broadcasting," *Journal of Law & Economics* (October 1979), pp. 269–328.

The result of these policies is, in brief, monopoly "rent"—that is, excessively high profit from restricted competition. The economics of this were explained earlier in Figure 14-2 on page 287 of Chapter 14, although in this case the government is *creating* rather than curbing those "rents."

The numbers demonstrating this are amazing. In 1975 the annual rate of pretax return on tangible capital invested for all VHF television stations was about 67 per cent. In large cities where large audiences attract large advertising outlays, pretax profits regularly exceed 100 per cent of tangible investment and sometimes exceed 200 per cent. When sold to new owners, prime stations go for prices many times the cost of their physical assets, a phenomenon explained by the fact that the intangible license rights are worth millions of dollars. In short, television broadcasting is one of the most profitable of all industries, if not the most profitable.[20]

You might reasonably ask, "Does the Commission know what it is doing? Does it realize it's creating monopoly profits?" The answer is, "Yes, it does." But it rationalizes its protective policies on grounds of *cross-subsidization*. That is, the FCC acts on the belief that unprofitable merit programming (like religious shows) is financed by these excess profits. There is, in other words, an implicit exchange between the FCC and the industry: the FCC limits competition among broadcasters in exchange for a commitment from broadcasters to use the resulting excess profits to finance unprofitable programs that are assumed to be of great social value. Unfortunately, experts studying this exchange have concluded that it is a very bad bargain, that broadcasters (and networks) come out far ahead in the deal at the expense of the public. In particular, it has been found that: (1) much merit programming, the evening news included, is not unprofitable; (2) that which is unprofitable is not so unprofitable as to justify the enormous excess profits earned; and (3) licensing limitation has virtually no effect whatever on program composition because most of these merit programs would apparently be aired regardless.[21]

2. PROGRAM CONTENT

Although the FCC regulates the *quantity* of program types, it *cannot censor* program content. It is prohibited from doing so by the First Amendment's protection of free speech and by the Communications Act of 1934.

This is not to say, however, that the FCC has no influence whatever on content. In pursuit of audience ratings, the television industry has frequently served up abundant sex, violence, and other offensive fare. And from time to time the FCC has engaged in government by raised eyebrow, mildly pressuring the industry to clean up. Bolstering the FCC's scowl is Congress's occasional threat of more serious regulation, a threat usually voiced in congressional hearings.[22] In turn, these official bodies are pressured into pressuring the industry by

[20] Levin, *op. cit.*, pp. 111–120. See also Paul W. Mac-Avoy, *Deregulation of Cable Television* (Washington, D.C.: American Enterprise Institute, 1977), p. 35. As Robert Crandall points out, television performers *also* gain monopoly revenues from FCC policies: "Actors often earn $100,000 per hour of filming in a continuing series and local newsmen may earn as much as $100,000 per year—prices greatly in excess of their earnings potentials elsewhere. These large salaries are greatly enhanced by the lack of channel choice in television." "Regulation of Television Broadcasting," *Regulation* (January/February, 1978), p. 39.

[21] Levin, *op. cit.*, pp. 137–156; Crandall, *op. cit.*, pp. 34–39. Another complaint is that merit programming lacks merit. Like entertainment programming, it dances to the tune of audience ratings. The alleged result is distorted news, noncontroversial documentaries, and assorted pap. Erik Barnouw, *The Sponsor* (New York: Oxford University Press, 1978), pp. 123–147.

[22] Comstock, et al., *op. cit.*, pp. 467–473; Marc J. Roberts, "How Should the Content of Entertainment Television Be Determined?" in R. E. Caves and M. Roberts (eds.) *Regulating the Product: Quality and Variety* (Cambridge, Mass.: Ballinger Publishing Co., 1975), pp. 97–122.

offended citizens groups. Whether any of this moral suasion has had appreciable effect in purifying the screen is uncertain. It may be noted, however, that in 1981 the industry seemed to jump higher to please the Coalition for Better Television than it had ever jumped for anyone before. Unlike prior pressure groups, this one, made up of four hundred citizens groups like the Moral Majority, had planned an extensive boycott of sponsors of TV programs it considered objectionable. Their threatened punch in the pocketbook thus did wonders.

IV. Main Issues: Case Studies

Digging beneath this list of FCC powers to see how they have been employed in addressing specific issues, we find a recurrent theme, namely, the FCC has on balance tended to protect the industry's established interests against the intrusion of new competitive elements. This happened in (1) the FCC's allocation of VHF and UHF to television, a policy that solidified the power of ABC, NBC, and CBS against competitive networks, (2) the FCC's delay of cable competition, and (3) its adverse treatment of pay TV.

A. Network Power and Spectrum Allocations

In 1980, roughly 90 per cent of the television industry's viewers, revenues, and profits were accounted for by the three leading networks and their affiliate stations. Indeed, the three networks and the fifteen stations they own accounted for more than half of the revenue of the industry. These national statistics disguise the fact that in most local markets the networks and their affiliates have had virtually 100% of the business for quite some time. Even in the two largest markets, Los Angeles and New York, where the networks compete with a small crowd of independents, the networks usually capture 75 to 80 per cent of the audience.[23]

One consequence of this concentration of power is the huge excess profit mentioned previously. Another consequence is the reduced number of channel *options* from which viewers in any one locality can choose. With reduced options, there also tends to be a reduction in program *diversity*—that is, the number of program categories offered (situation comedy, drama, sports, detective, and many others). Diversity is lost because broadcasters, when few in number, try to gain high audience ratings by programming to suit "mass" tastes. It takes added numbers of broadcasters to cater to the preferences of "narrow" audiences, such as those who enjoy opera, science documentaries, and classical theater.[24]

That these several adverse consequences follow from a concentration of power may be seen by comparing television to radio. Radio is blessed with dozens of stations locally and over 8600 nationally. As a result, profits are at more competitive levels; listener options are abundant; and diversity runs the gamut from all-news to black and Hispanic oriented stations to every brand of music.[25]

Why do ABC, CBS, and NBC rule the video roost? The FCC has been a main factor, especially in its past pursuit of two related policies: (1) use of VHF for television, and (2) preservation of localism in apportioning the VHF band. Use of the VHF band began in the 1940s, when television was just getting started and when the leading equipment manufacturer of the

[23] Noll, *op. cit.*, pp. 243, 250; Crandall, *op. cit.*

[24] Peter O. Steiner, "Program Patterns and Preferences, and the Workability of Competition in Radio Broadcasting," *Quarterly Journal of Economics* (May 1952), pp. 194–223.

[25] Indeed, data collected by the FCC indicate that most radio stations now exceed substantially the FCC's minimum guidelines for merit programming, apparently because of the force of competition. *FCC News Release*, September 6, 1979, reporting on BC Docket No. 79–219.

day, RCA, was promoting VHF technology. The FCC approved thirteen VHF channels despite its recognition at the time that they would be "insufficient spectrum space . . . to make possible a truly nationwide competitive system."[26] If these VHF channels had been allocated to high powered *regional* broadcasters, the total number of broadcasters nationally would have been limited to less than one hundred or so, but the number of channels received by any individual viewer could have been six or more. Here is where localism came in, however. Rejecting the idea of having regional broadcasters, the FCC opted *to maximize the number of local broadcasters.* This meant that the total number of VHF broadcast stations in the country could be fairly large, but because of interference problems in their use of only a dozen channels, most localities could get no more than three VHF stations. Accordingly, the FCC dispersed VHF assignments across the country in such a way that *70 per cent of all viewers can now get no more than three commercial VHF stations over the air* (without cable). It is not surprising, then, that there are no more than three major broadcast networks.

At various times the FCC tried to rectify this situation, but only half-heartedly and never effectively. Protection of the established VHF stations and the three networks seems to have precluded vigorous remedy. In 1952, for instance, the FCC allocated the UHF space to television, multiplying local channel capacity considerably. But by that time the VHF system had become entrenched, and technical problems made UHF inferior to VHF, further hampering its success. A number of policy measures followed, all with the intent of bolstering UHF broadcasting. Ownership limits were changed to allow networks two UHF stations each in futile hopes that the networks would develop

UHF. Television sets were by law required to have UHF tuning capacity. And so on. But none of the steps taken was bold enough to endanger the toes of the established VHF interests.

Hand in hand with its feeble efforts to encourage UHF competition the Commission has tried to lessen the networks' power by regulating the networks' contract relations with affiliate stations and independent program producers. Among other things, these FCC rules prevent networks from contracting for exclusive station affiliations or sharing in the off-network rerun revenues of programs produced by independent producers. Another rule—the "prime time access rule" of 1970—prevents affiliates in the top fifty markets from airing more than three and a half hours of network entertainment programming during the four hours of evening prime time. But these contract regulations did not increase the number of broadcast networks or the number of competing outlets available to viewers. All they did was increase the number of sources supplying programs to the industry and alter programming a bit. "Prime time access," for instance, brought us the low-budget game shows that dominate early evening television.[27]

In short, the Commission has followed ambivalent policies concerning network power. It has tried to check that power with policies on ownership, contracts, and UHF development. Conversely, it has acted in ways that nurtured that power. On balance, the latter effect has prevailed.

B. Cable Television

With its massive channel capacity and high quality picture, cable television offers lush opportunities for achieving competition in pro-

---

[26] FCC Final Report, May 25, 1945, FCC Docket No. 6651, pp. 99–100.

[27] Stanley M. Besen and Thomas G. Krattenmaker, "Regulating Network Television," *Regulation* (May/June 1981), pp. 27–34. See also *Business Week*, August 31, 1981, p. 82.

gram fare (if not local delivery). Indeed, as our earlier discussion of cable indicates, cable has already brought about the advent of numerous new cable networks offering viewers greater channel options and richer diversity than ever before. Not mentioned, but no less pertinent, are the competitive profits and even losses these cable networks are currently experiencing.[28]

Unfortunately, FCC policy retarded cable's contribution for nearly two decades.[29] At first, during the 1950s, cable was welcomed by broadcasters because it was complementary rather than competitive, merely bringing clear signals to remote areas and thereby increasing the broadcasters' audience. Reflecting this chumminess, the FCC declined in 1959 to regulate cable, saying it was neither a "broadcaster" nor a "wire common carrier." The attitudes of both broadcasters and commissioners changed radically, however, when during the 1960s cable companies discovered that they could increase demand for their services by "importing" distant TV signals using microwave relay. This created competition for local broadcasters and indirectly threatened the big networks. Hence these noncable interests pressured the FCC into curbing cable, a task the FCC accepted in 1962 and asserted vigorously with policy pronouncements in 1965 and 1972.

Many rules emerged to mire cable development. Among the more important were (1) restrictions on the number and type of imported signals; (2) requirements for original cable programming; (3) provision of free cable channels for local government, public use, and education; and (4) minimum capacity requirements. The goal of these regulations was "to prevent cable growth from causing serious economic harm to broadcasters and to promote public interest objectives with respect to the services offered by cable systems themselves."[30]

Some of these rules were relaxed shortly after their inception. But cable TV was not fully freed until after 1980, when the FCC lifted two major restraints over the strident objections of the broadcasters. One limited the number of imported signals. The other gave local TV stations the right to bar cable companies from carrying a syndicated show from a distant station if the local station already had a contract to broadcast the show. In thus recently deregulating cable, the FCC has done much to rectify its previous errors.

C. Pay TV

Restraint and then relaxation is also the main plot in the pay-TV story, although in both respects this story differs substantially from cable's. The forces favoring the restraint of pay TV were much broader, as many Americans valued the prevailing system of "free" television. When relaxation was eventually achieved, it was not granted by the FCC but rather by the courts over the objections of the FCC.

In the late 1950s, when over-the-air pay TV was the only pay technology available, the FCC approved very modest experiments with pay TV. The experience led the Commission to conclude that pay TV, *if restricted to protect free television,* could be a "beneficial supplement." As Stanley Besen writes:

> The commission then promulgated a series of rules severely restricting the kinds of programming that could be offered by over-the-air pay television. The rules, which limited the movies and sports that could be carried and banned series programming entirely, were eventually extended to pay-television systems that used cable to transmit programming.[31]

[28] P. T. Bernstein, "The Race to Feed Cable TV's Maw," *Fortune* (May 4, 1981), pp. 308–318.

[29] MacAvoy, *op. cit.;* Bruce M. Owen and Ronald Braeutigam, *The Regulation Game* (Cambridge, Mass.: Ballinger Publishing Co., 1978), pp. 121–157.

[30] Ibid., p. 139.

[31] Stanley M. Besen, "Deregulating Telecommunications," *Regulation* (March/April 1978), p. 34.

In 1975, the FCC eased these restrictions a bit, but not enough to satisfy Home Box Office, one of the major firms in the pay-cable sector of the industry. Home Box Office asked the courts to rule on the legality of the FCC's restrictions on pay-cable programming. And in 1977 the Court of Appeals for the District of Columbia abolished all the rules.[32] The court questioned the Commission's jurisdiction over pay cable and held that even if the Commission did have jurisdiction it had not shown the need for such restrictive rules. In so deciding the court rejected the FCC's unsubstantiated argument that pay television would "siphon" programs away from free television, harming program quality and depriving poor people of free entertainment. Arm-waving and assertion were thus not enough for the court. It demanded evidence, and the FCC had none.

The Supreme Court later refused to accept the FCC's appeal of the circuit court's opinion in *Home Box Office* v. *FCC.*[33] Thus, for now, pay TV is free (of restraint). Future restrictions must come either from firmly substantiated FCC action or Congress.

Summary

Federal Communications Commission regulation of broadcasting is grounded on a genuine physical phenomenon—the limits of the radio spectrum relative to the demands for its use. This hiatus between nature's skimpiness and man's enthusiasm is bridged by two principles originating in early policy: (1) spectrum spaces are licensed, and (2) they are to be used for "the public interest, convenience, and necessity." The FCC's allocation of space to television now includes twelve VHF channels and fifty-six UHF channels. Cable television is a nonbroadcast medium.

[32] *Home Box Office* v. *FCC*, 567 F. 2d 9 (D.C. Cir, 1977).
[33] *Home Box Office* v. *FCC, cert. denied,* 434 U.S. 829 (1977).

The television industry is home to a diversity of participants—viewers, advertisers, local stations, networks, program producers, cable companies, and regulators. Funding of the industry comes from viewers, either indirectly through the purchase of advertised goods (as prevailed in the "Old System" of Figure 17–1) or directly through pay TV (now a part of the "New System"). Despite the recent rise of pay TV, advertiser supported TV still dominates, even in cable. Local broadcast stations are the heart of the traditional delivery system. Most stations are affiliated with one of the three major networks, which produce programs, package these and other programs into a schedule, and perform some delivery services. In the main, ABC, CBS, and NBC may be thought of as middlemen, bridging the gap between national advertisers and independent program producers on the one hand, and stations and viewers on the other. The independent program producers supply programs to networks (prime time entertainment especially) and to local stations and syndicators as well. The cable companies offer wire delivery, which has the advantages of clear signals and large channel capacity. Their technology yields characteristics of natural monopoly at the local level, so they are franchised and regulated by local governments. Cable programming now includes the offerings of many cable networks, some of which are pay networks.

FCC regulation centers on the broadcast stations, as they are the ones actually using the radio spectrum. They are tethered by five-year renewable licenses that are issued on various arbitrary "public interest" criteria. In addition, the FCC enforces certain ownership limitations designed to achieve diversity and localism. Although program contents are not expressly regulated, program types are, with minimum merit programming a condition for license perpetuation.

In exercising its regulatory authority the

FCC has tended to protect the industry's established interests against upstarts. The result has been less competition than there could be, and a consequent cost in reduced viewer options, stifled program diversity, and excess profits. Three specific cases of FCC concern illustrate the point—(1) network power stemming from the VHF allocation decision, (2) cable's delayed development, and (3) pay television's containment. Fortunately, recent deregulation by the FCC and the courts promises to promote greater competition in the future.

Questions and Exercises for Chapter 17

1. Compare and contrast the rationales for, and focuses of, FCC regulation of broadcasters and local regulation of cable TV systems.

2. Why are there only three broadcast networks but many cable networks?

3. Explain ownership regulation in purpose and approach.

4. What have been the economic consequences of the prevailing method of licensing?

5. Many have proposed licensee selection based on competitive bidding. Why?

6. The FCC does not regulate price and profit; yet cross-subsidization is an FCC rationale. Explain and assess.

7. At one time the broadcast industry welcomed cable systems. Later it opposed them. Why? What was the FCC's response?

8. What are the relevance and significance of the FCC's UHF decisions?

Chapter 18

Transportation

Americans have been a people on the move—rootless, restless, expansive.
—James Thomas

Whereas regulation is the main theme of previous chapters, *de*regulation is the main theme of this one. Whereas market imperfections and failures are stressed in previous chapters, *government* imperfections and failures are the stuffings of this one.

Almost one hundred years ago railroading became the first industry to be regulated by the federal government. That regulation was good at the outset, but its persistence, its growth, and its spread to other areas of transportation were bad. The error was recognized by many economists three decades ago. But only recently, at the close of the 1970s, did the government begin to back off.

Matters of industry identification are settled in Section I below. Section II outlines the basic economics of the industry. Sections III and IV explain the origins and nature of transport regulation. The adverse effects of this regulation are covered in Section V, followed in Section VI by a rundown of deregulation and its effects.

I. Industry Identification

Of transportation's various modes, railroads have a central place. When federal regulation began in 1887, railroads virtually monopolized intercity *freight* traffic. Waterways provided some competition, but only on certain routes. Now, as shown in Table 18–1, the dominance of the railroads has dwindled markedly with the growth of trucking and oil pipelines. Railroads are also distinguished by the fact that, until recently, *all* rail freight was federally regulated. Federal regulation never covered more than 45 per cent of truck freight, 85 per cent of oil pipeline volume, and 20 per cent of inland water traffic.

Private automobiles account for the lion's share of intercity *passenger* traffic, roughly 85 per cent. The remaining 15 per cent is handled by formerly regulated modes—airways, buses, and railroads. By far the largest of these is the airways, which account for over 12 per cent of all passenger-miles traveled.

II. The Basic Economics of Transportation

A. *Demand Side*

The demand for transportation services is essentially a *derived* demand. That is to say, trans-

Table 18–1. Intercity Freight Traffic by Type of Transport (Percent of Total Ton-Miles)

Year	Railroads	Trucks	Oil Pipelines	Inland Waterways	Airways
1940	61.3	10.0	9.5	19.1	.00
1950	56.2	16.3	12.1	15.4	.03
1960	44.1	21.8	17.4	16.7	.07
1970	39.7	21.3	22.3	16.5	.17
1979	35.8	24.7	23.3	15.9	.21

Source: Transportation Association of America, *Transportation Facts and Trends* (July 1979), p. 8.

portation is not sought as an end in itself. Its demand derives from the demand for *other* goods and services that rely on transportation for their provision and distribution. Thus the demand for electricity creates a demand for coal, which in turn creates a demand for the shipment of coal from mines to power plants. The demand for Hawaiian vacations creates a demand for passenger travel from the mainland to Hawaii. And so forth.

This derivation of transportation demand heavily influences price elasticities of demand. For one thing, price elasticity varies substantially depending on the ultimate end served. If, for example, transportation cost is a large portion of the final cost of a product—as it is for steel—then the price elasticity of demand for transportation is likely to be relatively high as compared to cases where the transportation cost is a very small portion of the final cost of the product—as it is for semiconductor devices. In passenger transport, vacationers have a relatively high price elasticity of demand for air travel as compared to businessmen (see Figure 18–1).

Demand for a specific mode of transport, say railroads, is influenced by more than the price of that mode. It is also influenced by the price of alternative modes—trucks, barges, pipelines, and so on. This gives rise to *intermodal* competition as distinct from in*tra*modal competition. It is important to note that intermodal competition is likewise influenced by numerous *nonprice* factors, the most significant of which are speed of service, flexibility, reliability, and susceptibility of freight to damage. These nonprice factors determine the total costs borne by shippers and travelers. For example, slow movement of freight raises the shipper's cost of inventory. And slow movement of people raises the traveler's cost of time in transit. (Both confirm the old saying, "time is money.") Indeed, in some cases, speed is of the essence, as when a spare machine part is *air* freighted to minimize the time a crippled machine is shut down, idling workers and stopping production. In short, transportation entails much more than getting item X from point A to point B for price Y. It is a multidimensional service, and demand varies across the modes accordingly.

This helps to explain why, as shown in Table 18–1, the share of freight volume going to trucks and airplanes has been rising for three decades despite the fact that, on average, the price of truck and air service is much higher than that of railroad service. As compared to

Figure 18–1. Differing Elasticities of Demand in Transportation

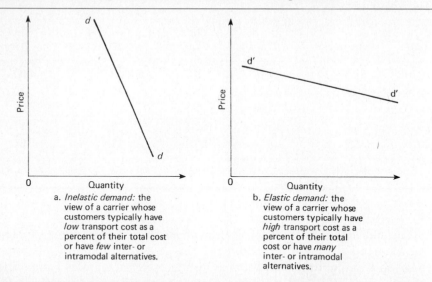

a. *Inelastic demand:* the
view of a carrier whose
customers typically have
low transport cost as a
percent of their total cost
or have *few* inter- or
intramodal alternatives.

b. *Elastic demand:* the
view of a carrier whose
customers typically have
high transport cost as a
percent of their total
cost or have *many*
inter- or intramodal
alternatives.

the railroads, average revenue per ton-mile has been nearly *five* times greater for trucks and over *fifteen* times greater for airplanes.[1]

When translating the demand for a given mode into demand facing a given carrier, int*ra*modal competition intervenes importantly. A monopolist in railroading would have a demand matching the demand for rail services, as influenced by int*er*modal substitutes. However, a railroad that vied with five other railroads would face demand that could switch to other railroads as well as to other modes. It follows that both intramodal and intermodal competition may be present. When both arise, the elasticity of demand, *as viewed by a carrier,* can be quite high, something that, absent collusion, prompts price competition and efficiency. (See Figure 18–1).

Of course these observations apply mainly to specific routes, because shippers' demands are route specific. There are, in other words,

dozens of major railroads, thousands of interstate truckers, and more than a few airlines in the United States today, implying substantial intramodal competition in each case. But these are nationwide numbers, and they need not imply intramodal competition between, say, Eugene, Oregon and Ithaca, New York. With this observation we bump squarely into supply side considerations.

B. Supply Side

Three supply side elements deserve special attention—(1) concentration, (2) condition of entry, and (3) costs.

As suggested by the fairly large number of transportation firms, *concentration* in transportation is quite low when all modes are combined nationally. Generalizations are more difficult to come by, however, when the scope of the "market" is narrowed to more relevant dimensions of specific routes and, where appropriate, specific modes for specific services. Nar-

[1] Transportation Association of America, *Transportation Facts and Trends* (July 1979), p. 7.

rowing yields many "submarkets," and the only safe generalization for them is that concentration tends to be lower (and the number of competitors higher), the heavier the volume of traffic. Thus concentration in air passenger service is lower between Chicago and Los Angeles than it is between Omaha and Santa Fe. Likewise the number of trucking companies serving Baltimore-Boston is considerably larger than those serving Boise-Butte.

As for the *condition of entry,* in the absence of regulation trucking is by far the easiest of the modes to enter. It is even easy as compared to other lines of business such as manufacturing. No special skills are required. The capital costs of buying a truck are paltry. Use of the highways is freely "leased" through the payment of road taxes. And so on. Airline entry is more difficult, given the higher costs of initial equipment (whether leased or purchased), the greater scarcity of skilled personnel, and the difficulty of obtaining airport berth assignments at many major airports. But even in the case of airlines, entry is no more than moderately difficult in purely economic terms, as best illustrated perhaps by the remarkable recent success of a number of new airlines—like Midway, New York Air, and People Express. In contrast to both truck and airline conditions, railroad and pipeline entry is much more difficult. Roadbeds for these modes are not publicly provided, necessitating their development from scratch and thereby requiring immense capital cost outlays for rights of way and construction. Moreover, these two modes display some characteristics of natural monopoly on lightly traveled routes, further hampering the prospects of new entrants. All of this was nicely summarized by a transportation analyst when he remarked:

> Anybody can buy a truck and get into the trucking business on the nation's highways; and only the number of airport gates restricts what companies can do with airlines. But you aren't likely to find any company that would build a new major railroad.[2]

Conditions concerning both concentration and entry are in part determined by the behavior of transportation *costs.* Costs may vary importantly along three dimensions: (1) the scale of a firm's operation, (2) distance, and (3) type of freight.

The first of these, *scale,* is particularly important in determining intramodal concentration and entry. Scale may be measured either by *overall firm size* or by *route density.* Size is self-evident. Density refers to the volume of traffic moving between two points, as indicated, say, by ton-miles per mile of road. Studies show that, for railroads and pipelines, costs generally fall with added scale as measured by firm size and route density, the latter especially. Diagrammatically, this is illustrated in Figure 18–2 (a). Numerically, this is illustrated by 1973 estimates of railroad costs that fall from 3 cents to 1 cent per ton-mile as density increases from 1 to 6 million ton-miles per mile of railroad.[3] Table 18–2 gives numbers for pipelines. Thus economies of scale are to some degree present in rail and pipeline operations, leading to intramodal natural monopoly where traffic volume is thin and to natural oligopoly where traffic volume is fat enough to support several carriers. In contrast, there are no appreciable economies of scale in trucking, implying constant cost behavior such as depicted in Figure 18–2 (b).[4] Airlines rest somewhere between railroads and trucking because airline costs fall a bit with overall firm size and traffic density, but not enough to justify natural monopoly except on the most lightly traveled routes (and these tend

---

[2] *Wall Street Journal,* September 15, 1980, p. 6.

[3] Robert G. Harris, "Economies of Traffic Density in the Rail Freight Industry," *Bell Journal of Economics* (Autumn 1977), pp. 556–564. On pipelines see Leslie Cookenboo, Jr., *Crude Oil Pipelines* (Cambridge: Harvard University Press, 1955).

[4] Richard H. Spady and Ann F. Friedlaender, "Hedonic Cost Functions for the Regulated Trucking Industry," *Bell Journal of Economics* (Spring 1978), pp. 159–179.

Figure 18–2.   Unit Cost as a Function of Scale of Operations (Overall Firm Size or Route Density

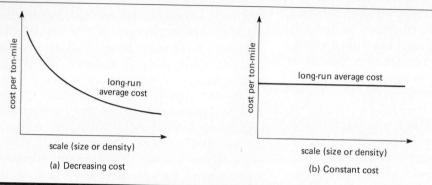

(a) Decreasing cost

(b) Constant cost

to be short-hops, with good bus and auto options).[5]

As regards the influence of *distance* and *type of freight*, they are crucial in determining intermodal relative costs. Table 18–3 summarizes the situation.[6] In distance, the lowest cost carriers for long-haul traffic tend to be railroads, pipelines, barges, and (for passengers) airlines. The lowest cost carriers for short-haul traffic tend to be trucks for freight and buses for passengers.

A chief element influencing these tendencies for distance is the level of terminal costs as compared to line-haul costs. Terminal costs are the costs of sorting and loading freight, ticketing

passengers, and the like. In total, these costs are fixed in that they do not vary with distance. Line-haul costs are the costs of actually moving a load from one place to another—that is, the cost of fuel, labor, equipment depreciation, and the like. In total, these costs are variable in that they rise with distance. When translated into

Table 18–2.   The Relationship Between Pipeline Diameter, Pipe Costs, and Flow Capacity

Diameter (inches)	Pipe Cost Factor	Capacity Factor
4	1.0	1
8	1.9	6
12	2.4	15
16	3.5	28
20	4.3	48

This says, for example, that 20 inch diameter piping costs 4.3 times as much as 4 inch diameter piping, yet has a capacity *48 times* that of 4 inch piping. The main reason for this is that capacity depends on cross section area, and the area of a circle is *pi* times the radius *squared*.

Source: George S. Wolbert, Jr., *U.S. Oil Pipelines* (Washington, D.C.: American Petroleum Institute, 1979), p. 99.

[5] Richard E. Caves, *Air Transport and its Regulators* (Cambridge: Harvard University Press, 1962), pp. 55–83; Theodore E. Keeler, "Domestic Trunk Airline Regulation: An Economic Evaluation," in *Study on Federal Regulation,* Appendix to volume VI, Committee on Governmental Affairs, U.S. Senate, 96th Congress, 1st Session. (1978), pp. 107–109.

[6] Sources include Ann F. Friedlaender, *The Dilemma of Freight Transport Regulation* (Washington, D.C.: Brookings Institution, 1969), John R. Meyer and others, *The Economics of Competition in the Transportation Industries* (Cambridge: Harvard University Press, 1959), and T. H. Oum, "A Cross Section Study of Freight Transport Demand and Rail-Truck Competition in Canada," *Bell Journal of Economics* (Autumn, 1979), pp. 463–482.

Table 18–3. Low Cost Carriers As Classified by Distance and Type of Freight

	Type of Freight			
Distance	Bulk Liquid	Bulk Dry	High Value Commodities*	Passenger Service
Short haul	truck, railroad	truck, railroad	truck	bus
Long haul	pipeline, barge	railroad, barge	truck, rail, air	airline

* Mainly manufactured goods.

per-unit terms, such as cost per ton-mile, terminal costs fall sharply with distance whereas line-haul costs do not. This means that modes with relatively high fixed terminal costs and low line-haul costs, like railroads and airlines, will be relatively efficient on long hauls. But a mode with relatively low fixed terminal costs and high line-haul costs, like trucks and buses, will be relatively efficient on short hauls. This helps to explain why, in 1978, the average length of freight haul was 301 miles for trucks, 587 miles for railroads, and 1,115 miles for air carriers. And also why the average length of passenger haul was 126 miles for buses and 719 miles for airlines.[7]

Commodity type is equally important. Large

[7] Transportation Association of America, *op. cit.*, pp. 14–15.

Table 18–4. Percentage Distribution of Freight Ton-Miles by Mode for Selected Commodity Groups, 1965

Commodity	Railroads	Trucks	Pipeline	Water	Air
Agriculture	53.3%	27.4%	0.0%	19.1%	0.2%
Coal mining	79.6	3.0	0.0	17.4	0.0
Chemicals	67.9	15.1	0.0	16.9	0.1
Iron ore	23.7	0.7	0.0	75.6	0.0
Petrol & products	2.3	3.6	49.5	44.6	0.0
Textiles and apparel	21.1	77.8	0.0	0.2	0.9
Industrial machinery	30.6	62.2	0.0	6.1	1.1
Scientific instruments	8.2	87.3	0.0	0.8	3.7

Source: Paul O. Roberts and James. T. Kneafsey, "Traffic Diversion and Energy Use Implications of Surface Transport Reform," in MacAvoy and Snow (eds.), *Regulation of Entry and Pricing in Truck Transportation* (Washington D.C.: American Enterprise Institute, 1977), pp. 166–167.

shipments of bulk liquids, like crude oil and gasoline, are most cheaply moved by pipeline or water barge. Large shipments of dry bulk commodities, like coal, iron ore, and wheat, are most cheaply moved by train or barge. Highly valued (and fragile) manufactured goods, like computers and glassware, are most cheaply shipped by truck. Further examples may be derived from Table 18–4, which shows how the freight of several commodity classes is distributed among the various modes. Railroads dominate the first three commodity classes; trucks the last three; with pipelines and water carriers covering the middle two.

C. Summary of Economics

Taken alone, these several economic features of transportation cannot explain or justify economic regulation of the industry. The derived demand is commonplace. The low to moderate concentration and barriers to entry in trucking and airlines signal rich opportunities for intramodal competition, a richness confirmed by an absence of large economies of scale. The intramodal prospects for competition in railroading and pipelines are less abundant, but intermodal competition frequently makes up for this. Indeed, it is these economic considerations that have prompted economists to question the wisdom of transportation regulation and spearhead the drive toward deregulation.

Still, there are economic features which, when combined with historic circumstances, help to explain if not justify the fact of past regulation. Elasticities of demand vary widely across shippers and commodities. Coupled with varying competitive conditions, this paves the way to stark discriminations in price, discriminations that could arouse shippers to press for regulation. Furthermore, the competitive forces may have been at certain places and times *too* great, causing the carriers themselves

to cry out for regulatory protection. These and other possibilities will be discussed next.

III. The History and Purposes of Regulation

It must be stressed that, in its heyday from 1920 to 1975, transportation regulation was quite different from public utility regulation. Whereas the main purpose of utility regulation was to *substitute* for nonexistent competition, a main purpose of transportation regulation became the *suppression* or *supplementation* of competition through cartelization. Whereas a main focus of utility regulation was maximum price *level*, a main focus of transportation regulation was price *structure*. Movement beyond these broad generalizations entails details of history.

A. History of Transportation Regulation

In 1887 there were 149,214 miles of railroad track in the U.S., about 325 per cent more mileage than existed just 22 years earlier. These statistics intimate two things. First, railroads were far and away the dominant means of transportation of the day. They bound the country together. And on routes not also served by water carriers, this prominence brought with its prospects of substantial monopoly power. Second, however, the rapid expansion of railroads meant that on some routes railroads competed vigorously with each other, even where water competition was absent. This mixture of monopoly and competition in an area where buyers themselves represented a mixture of varying demand elasticities led to sharp price discrimination among shippers, localities, and commodities. Prices were high for small-lot shippers, for isolated communities with no alternative means of transport, and for high-valued commodities. Conversely, prices were low for big shippers, for communities served

---

Thumbnail Sketch 5: Interstate Commerce Commission

Established: 1887 (making it the granddaddy of federal commissions)

Purpose: To regulate interstate surface and water transportation by railroads, trucks (except agricultural and private trucking), buses, water carriers (except bulk freight), and pipelines carrying commodities other than oil, water, and natural gas.

Legislative Authority: Act to Regulate Commerce, 1887; Transportation Acts of 1920, 1940, and 1942; Motor Carrier Act of 1935; Railroad Revitalization and Regulatory Reform Act of 1976; Staggers Rail Act of 1980; and Motor Carrier Act of 1980 (the last two of which brought deregulation).

Regulatory Activity: Regulated (1) numbers of firms with entry and exit authority, and (2) price levels and structure. Its powers have diminished, however, since 1980.

Organization: Eleven member independent commission. Presidential appointments. Numerous divisions.

Budget: 1982 Estimate, $70.1 million.

Staff: 1982 Estimate, 1653.

---

by water or competing railroads, and for low-value commodities.

This discrimination became glaringly obvious in the many instances where long hauls were charged less than short hauls. The long haul between New York City and Chicago, for example, had numerous railroads competing on price. But each railroad took a different route between New York and Chicago, meaning that many short-haul communities along the way, such as Scranton and Akron, would be served by only one railroad. With low-priced competitive long hauls and high-priced monopolistic short hauls, prices frequently seemed out of whack. The resulting outcry for regulation was bolstered by the surging "populist" sentiments of the day, for it was one further grievance of the little folks against the big.

The long-haul and water-carrier competition did more than just produce price discrimination. It produced intermittent price warfare

and rate instability. This led some railroads to support regulation in hopes of curbing "destructive" competition.[8] Whatever contribution this motive may have had at the outset, the objective of stabilization was not fully served until 1920, when minimum price regulation was introduced. The Act to Regulate Commerce of 1887 established the Interstate Commerce Commission (ICC) and gave it the power to stem price discrimination, but nothing more. The Act required that railroad rates be "just and reasonable," specifically outlawing "undue" discrimination between persons, companies, or communities and banning higher prices for short hauls than long hauls along the same tracks.

Despite popular support for the Act of 1887,

---

[8] Paul W. MacAvoy, *The Economic Effects of Regulation: The Trunk-Line Railroad Cartels and the Interstate Commerce Commission Before 1900* (Cambridge: M.I.T. Press, 1965).

it was quickly emasculated by the Supreme Court in a series of opinions instigated by the railroads.[9] To restore the ICC's lost powers, Congress passed a series of subsequent laws addressed to the specific problems motivating the original legislation:

· The Elkins Act of 1903 banned personal discrimination, that is, discrimination between shippers.
· The Hepburn Act of 1906 gave the ICC power to fix maximum rail rates and to regulate oil pipelines.
· The Mann-Elkins Act of 1910 struck at long- and-short haul discrimination.

Shortly after this shoring up was completed, Congress took significant additional steps toward regulation with its Transportation Act of 1920. In a word, this Act *cartelized* the industry. It gave the ICC power to set minimum rates, which, when coupled with earlier authority to set maximum rates, gave the ICC power to fix specific rates. The Act of 1920 also authorized the elimination of competition through "pooling" and the joint use of terminals. Control over abandonments of service was introduced at this time as well.

These steps to protect the railroads from intramodal competition were grounded on the belief that the railroads had fallen on hard times. Reprehensible buccaneering had given way to financial floundering. Yet, however bad things may have been for the railroads in 1920, they grew considerably worse thereafter with the rise of trucking and the arrival of the Great Depression. The pinch from trucking caused the railroads to begin lobbying for truck regulation in 1925. Passage of the necessary legislation was delayed ten years until the hardships of the Great Depression had fostered broader,

nonrailroad support for the idea that cartel-like regulation of trucking was a good policy. This broader support for the Motor Carrier Act of 1935 came from the Interstate Commerce Commission, many state regulatory commissions, bus operators, and a few of the largest trucking companies. Those opposed to this expansion of ICC authority included a majority of the truckers and numerous organized shippers. The forces of opposition succeeded in keeping large chunks of trucking free from regulation—private (noncommon-carrier) and agricultural trucking in particular. Still, the Act of 1935 treated common-carrier truckers as if they were railroads. Further protection for the railroads was provided when, in 1940, water carriers were partially placed under ICC jurisdiction.

For a short time during the 1930s the ICC also had a hand in regulating domestic airlines. Given their infancy at the time, the airlines were heavily dependent on government airmail contracts for their solvency. When snags disrupted the airlines' bidding for this business, they fell dangerously close to bankruptcy. Events led to passage of the Civil Aeronautics Act of 1938, which transferred regulatory authority to the newly created Civil Aeronautics Board (CAB) and thereby brought about official cartelization of the airways. Given the dire circumstances of the airlines at the time, it could be argued that the main purpose of this new branch of regulation was to prevent "destructive" competition. A collateral motive, however, was promotion. The Act of 1938 provided subsidies to nurture the airlines in hopes that they would grow strong enough to give "adequate, economical, and efficient service" on a nationwide scale, something helpful to the military, the postal service, and the country at large. Finally, a concern for airline safety also played a part. If pressed too hard by competition, airlines might try to cut costs by neglecting maintenance, hiring untrained personnel, and following other hazardous strategies. Al-

---

[9] *Counselman* v. *Hitchcock*, 142 U.S. 547 (1892); *Interstate Commerce Commission* v. *Cincinnati, New Orleans and Texas Pacific Railway Co.*, 167 U.S. 479 (1897); *ICC* v. *Alabama Midland Railway Co.*, 168 U.S. 144 (1897).

Thumbnail Sketch 6: Civil Aeronautics Board

Established: 1940 (due to expire 1985)

Purpose: Originally, to regulate interstate air travel (passenger and freight). Now, to proceed with deregulation in orderly fashion.

Legislative Authority: Civil Aeronautics Act of 1938; Federal Aviation Act of 1958; Airline Deregulation Act of 1978.

Regulatory Activity: Control of entry and prices until scheduled deregulation occurs by 1983. Representation in international aviation.

Organization: An independent agency headed by a five-member commission, appointed by the President. Bureaus for Consumer Protection and Economic Analysis.

Budget: 1982 Estimate, $25.5 million.

Staff: 1982 Estimate, 505.

---

though the CAB initially controlled safety, that duty passed to the Federal Aviation Administration (FAA) in 1958. Among other things, the FAA operates air traffic control centers, certifies the competence of pilots, and supervises the manufacture, operation, and maintenance of aircraft (duties unaffected by deregulation).

This pattern of multi-mode regulation that developed during the 1930s endured until the deregulation movement of the late 1970s. In railroading, deregulation began timidly with the Railroad Revitalization & Regulatory Reform Act of 1976. It was later expanded by the Staggers Rail Act of 1980. In airlines, the CAB itself began deregulation in 1977 by giving fresh interpretations to its then existing authority. Those liberalized interpretations were formally affirmed by Congress in the Airline Deregulation Act of 1978. Congress then lessened government control of the trucking industry by passing the Motor Carrier Act of 1980. Oil pipelines experienced no deregulation, but control of them passed from the ICC to the Federal Energy Regulatory Commission in 1977.

B. The Purposes of Regulation

When the history of regulation is stripped of its many dates and cumbersome legislative titles, we find an outline of several purposes served by regulation. As suggested earlier in Chapter 14, these purposes may be categorized as various sorts of "fairness."

1. FAIRNESS TO SELLERS GENERALLY

The protective nature of much regulation was no accident. Railroads and airlines won the sympathy of Congress by arguing that regulation was needed (a) to prevent the instability caused by "destructive" competition and (b) to promote the growth and solvency of their industries.

2. FAIRNESS AMONG DIFFERENT BUYERS

(a) Prevention of price discrimination was the main purpose of the ICC Act of 1887 and a subsidiary purpose of much regulation that followed. (b) More recently, regulation has been defended as a means of cross-subsidization—that is, using the profits of high-density routes to subsidize the losses of low-density routes.

3. FAIRNESS AMONG DIFFERENT SELLERS

If railroads were regulated, it was only "fair" that common-carrier trucks and water carriers likewise be regulated. At least that was the rationale of many officials in the 1930s.

4. FAIRNESS AS AN ADMINISTRATIVE PROCESS

History teaches that the market can be a harsh and volatile decision making process. Some saw in regulation a slower, more benign method. This rationale is especially pertinent to abandonments of service.

However accurate this list of specifics may be, the sweep of surrounding economic circumstances adds to our understanding. It should be stressed, for instance, that the crisis conditions of the Great Depression contributed substantially to the flurry of protectionist regulatory activity of the 1930s. Note, too, that deregulation proceeded in the 1970s almost as quickly as regulation was introduced in the 30s. The inflationary crisis of the 1970s impelled a search for ways to quell prices through enhanced competition.

IV. The Nature of Regulation

Generalizations about the nature of transportation regulation are possible because the main modes faced very similar controls before deregulation. Two exceptions should be noted, however. First, pipelines have been and continue to be treated very much like public utilities, and since we discussed utility regulation earlier in Chapter 15, we can now drop pipelines from further consideration.[10] Second, several major segments of transportation have never been subject to appreciable regulation.

[10] For details on oil pipelines see Edward J. Mitchell (ed.), *Oil Pipelines and Public Policy* (Washington, D.C.: American Enterprise Institute, 1979).

Most notable among these exempt segments are private (shipper owned) trucking, agricultural commodity trucking, and intrastate airline services in California and Texas. These exemptions are notable because, previous to federal deregulation, they gave economists information on the way the industry might work without regulation.

These exceptions aside, transport regulation focused most intently on two economic variables—(A) the number of firms, and (B) prices. Safety has also been regulated, but we shall concentrate on these economic variables.

A. *The Number of Firms*

Control of the number of firms extended to control of both entry and exit. *Entry* restrictions protected existing firms and were thereby looked upon as a means of preventing destructive competition or promoting solvency and growth. *Exit* restrictions furthered the causes of cross-subsidization and procedural fairness, as they prevented or delayed withdrawals of unprofitable service.

Entry Control. Entry restrictions applied to all modes but were most important in common-carrier trucking and airlines because these were this century's most rapidly growing modes. To serve the public, a carrier first had to obtain a certificate of "public convenience and necessity," that is, a license to operate. Moreover, the certificates issued by the ICC and CAB were not for entry generally. They were, rather, quite narrowly restrictive. In trucking, for instance, a typical certificate only approved carriage of certain commodities, between certain points, over exactly specified routes. Given the many possible combinations of commodities, communities, and highways it is no surprise that ICC grants of trucking authority numbered nearly 100,000 during the 1960s and 1970s. Similarly, airline certificates specified the city pairs, or routes, that an airline could serve. Given the narrow authority represented by these certificates of convenience and necessity, or operating rights, firms of a given mode could not compete with other authorized firms except insofar as their authorizations overlapped.

If operating rights had been dispensed freely to anyone wanting to enter, they would have posed no significant barrier to entry. But this was not the case. When truck and airline regulation were first introduced in 1935 and 1938, existing carriers were issued certificates for their then existing services. They were thus "grandfathered" in. Thereafter, new approvals were very tightly controlled, so new applicants confronted horrendous hurdles. An applicant could not be assured certification even on evidence that he would provide better service at lower prices that existing carriers. The essential criterion was merely whether existing carriers had enough equipment to handle the freight or passenger load. And existing carriers routinely argued that they could handle the load.

The fact that airline entry was artificially restricted is illustrated by the experience of so-called "trunk" carriers (i.e., carriers specializing in high-density, long-haul markets). For four decades after its birth in 1938, the CAB allowed *no* new trunk carrier entry despite tremendous growth in the industry over the period and despite entry applications from over 80 firms. The CAB did allow grandfathered trunk carriers to expand into new routes. Moreover, the CAB did permit some local service carriers, like Mohawk and Ozark, to serve a few trunk-type routes. So the door to airline entry was never completely barred and sealed. Nevertheless, entry was severely curtailed.[11]

In trucking, the severity of the entry restrictions was indicated by the problem of "gypsy"

truckers, who operated without ICC approval. Numbering in the thousands, they included truckers who normally carried exempt agricultural commodities and regulated truckers who went beyond the narrow confines of their operating rights. Although hard data are lacking, the ICC studied the problem in 1963 and estimated that regulated carriers lost $500 million to $1 billion to illegal truckers that year alone. The problem was serious enough that the regulated truckers took vigilante action, financing their own efforts to capture the gypsies and turn them over to the ICC for prosecution.[12]

Exit Control. Carrier exit has been controlled by regulation of route *abandonments* and firm *mergers*. This authority has been especially noteworthy for railroads, who, unlike the airlines and truckers, have faced long-term malaise, with stagnant demand, tepid profits, and occasional bankruptcies. Since the end of World War II, the railroad industry has earned a rate of return in the 1 to 3 per cent range, far below transportation and industry generally. Eastern railroads have been especially hard pressed, experiencing deficits every year from 1975 through 1980.[13]

From its inception until 1976, the ICC approved the abandonment of nearly 70,000 miles of railroad tracks. But the abandonments were granted only grudgingly and after deliberate delay because the ICC believed that low-density deficit routes should be subsidized by high-density profitable routes. In 1974, for instance, 20 per cent of the country's railroad mileage was so little used as to account for only 2 per cent of the total freight traffic.[14] Since the Railroad Revitalization & Regulatory Reform Act of 1976, abandonments have been

---

[11] William A. Jordan, *Airline Regulation in America* (Baltimore: Johns Hopkins University Press, 1970), pp. 14–33.

[12] *Business Week*, April 23, 1979, pp. 142–144.

[13] Association of American Railroads, *Yearbook of Railroad Facts* (Washington, D.C.: 1980), p. 20.

[14] P. W. MacAvoy and J. W. Snow (eds.), *Railroad Revitalization and Regulatory Reform* (Washington, D.C.: American Enterprise Institute, 1977), pp. 157–159.

easier to obtain. Still, the subject remains touchy as railroads try to dump surplus track that shippers insist should stay in service.

Exit by merger occurs when formerly independent carriers combine or when operating certificates are sold by one carrier to another. ICC and CAB power to approve such actions further typified regulation. The criteria applied to such approvals have not been limited to the maintenance of competition (which is the antitrust criterion applied to other industries). Broader considerations of "national defense" and "efficiency" have produced more lenient standards. Indeed, the ICC has a history of encouraging railroad mergers rather than discouraging them. Exhibit A of this lenient attitude is the ICC's approval of the New York Central and Pennsylvania Railroad merger in the late 1960s, a merger that ended in massive disaster when the combination quickly tumbled into bankruptcy. Despite this debacle, railroad merging picked up steam during the 1970s.

B. Price Regulation

1. PRICE LEVEL AND PROFIT

In theory, price level regulation in transportation was supposed to match that in public utilities. In practice, however, this was never the case.[15] Whereas public utilities are essentially monopolies in their local spheres of influence, and can therefore be treated individually by regulatory commissions, transportation is populated by many firms that must be treated in groups. This clustering of numerous firms in transportation prevented the ICC and the CAB from determining "just and reasonable" price levels on the basis of a "fair" rate of return on individual company investment. Instead, price levels were determined from broad aver-

ages that included data from a number of companies within a given mode. Various factors other than fair return on investment were therefore used in assessing the need for price changes, the most important factor being the ratio of operating costs to total revenues.

The specific company clusters that drew up price proposals and represented the carriers' interests before the ICC and CAB were called *rate bureaus*. These rate bureaus were, in effect, regional cartels of truckers or railroads or airlines, as the case may be. Their power to establish price levels by joint agreement, subject to commission approval, was cemented by explicit exemption from antitrust prosecution (as provided by the Reed-Bulwinkle Act of 1948 for ICC regulated carriers). This approach produced uniformity of prices among carriers of a given mode, but widely differing individual rates of return on investment (given the individual carriers' differences in costs).

There were other reasons for a lack of consistent price level regulation. The CAB, for instance, refused to develop a consistent policy on airline prices for the first twenty years of its existence. It was not until 1961 that the CAB established general principles of cost accounting and specified 10.5 per cent as a "reasonable" rate of return for trunk carriers. Furthermore, it was not until the 1970s that the CAB tied up loose ends left dangling by the inadequacies of its 1961 rulings.[16] Still, despite these other contributing factors, the main problem seems to have been that rate of return regulation is not appropriate to instances where competition would otherwise regulate. In fact, average realized rates of return from the 50s through the 70s tended to be very low for railroads, rather high for trucks, and only moderate for airlines.

2. PRICE STRUCTURE

Two generalizations about price structure regulation in transportation are particularly

---

[15] See e.g., James R. Nelson, "Abstract of Regulation of Overland Movements of Freight," *Study on Federal Regulation,* Appendix to Vol. VI, U.S. Senate, Committee on Governmental Affairs, 96th Congress, 1st Session (1978), pp. 3–72; R. E. Caves, *op. cit.,* pp. 140–155.

[16] Theodore E. Keeler, *op. cit.,* pp. 88–90.

pertinent. *First,* value-of-service pricing usually won out over cost-of-service pricing. This meant that price discrimination was quite common even though *prevention* of price discrimination was a major purpose of regulation in the first place.

The earliest and most notorious example of authorized value-of-service pricing was used by the railroads. Low-value agricultural commodities and raw materials were shipped at prices much lower than those charged to high-value manufactured goods. These rate disparities favored western farmers and miners, thereby furthering social objectives prevalent at the turn of the century. These disparities also followed disparities in elasticities of demand because low-valued bulk freight tended to have a higher price elasticity for rail transit than high-valued manufactured goods. Competition with water carriers was keener in bulk commodities as compared to manufactured goods. Moreover, transportation costs have always been a higher portion of the total costs of bulk commodities as compared to manufactured goods.

A serious problem with this railroad structure was that it persisted long after the rise of truck competition had made it obsolete. Truck competition sharply reduced the railroads' monopoly power over manufactured-goods transit, thereby raising the price elasticity of demand as viewed by the railroads. Nevertheless, the ICC prevented the railroads from raising their bulk prices and lowering their manufactured-goods prices. As a consequence, trucks grabbed ever larger lumps of high-valued manufactures traffic over time, leaving railroads to contend with low-value bulk freight. Indeed, as late as 1969, the commodities burdening railroads with the largest deficits were sand, crushed and broken stone, fresh vegetables, fresh fruit, and field crops.[17]

Value-of-service pricing also appeared *within* given commodity classes. Intermodal competition sometimes had this effect, as illustrated by comparing the 1963 rail rate on phosphate rock shipped from Bartow, Florida to Montgomery, Alabama with the rate on an identical distance from Bartow, Florida to Pensacola, Florida. The former, without water competition, was $6.33 per ton. The latter, with water competition, was $4.25 per ton.[18] Similarly, some differences in airfares could be considered value-of-service pricing within a given "commodity" class. Thus vacation fliers, as disclosed by length of stay or presence of a spouse, would often be charged less than business fliers.

This is not to say that price discrimination under regulation was bad. As one economist put it. "Price discrimination is probably a necessary aspect of the transportation industry."[19] Indeed, defenders of regulation argue that price discrimination to achieve cross-subsidization was good.

Our *second* observation on price structure is simply that, when cost-of-service pricing *was* used by regulators, the costs that guided prices were usually average total (or "fully distributed") costs rather than marginal costs. This reliance on average total cost influenced the ICC in its effort to comply with Congress's explicit request that it act so as to "preserve the inherent advantages" of each mode. The classic case here was the ICC's "Ingot Molds" decision, which was affirmed by the Supreme Court in 1968.[20] The specific question was whether ingot molds would be shipped from Neville Island, Pennsylvania to Steelton, Kentucky by rail or by truck, as determined by the price of each mode. In turn, the price of each was to be based on costs, raising the question of which costs were the appropriate ones to use. Using marginal cost, the *rail* option was cheapest, $4.69

---

[17] MacAvoy and Snow (eds.), *Railroad . . . , op. cit.,* p. 103.

[18] Friedlaender, *op. cit.,* p. 62.

[19] Ibid., p. 63.

[20] *American Commercial Lines, Inc.,* v. *Louisville & Nashville Railroad Co.,* 392 U.S. 571 (1968).

compared to truck's $5.19 per ton. Using average total cost, however, the *truck* option was cheapest, $5.19 compared to railroad's $7.59.[21] The ICC decided that average total cost was the more appropriate and set rates accordingly, thereby delivering the ingot molds business to trucks.

Neglect of marginal cost considerations caused the ICC and CAB to disallow price discounts for off-peak periods and backhauls. Peak versus off-peak price differentials would have made economic sense for reasons explored earlier on pages 312–315. Even more important in transportation is the problem of empty backhauls. A truck shipping beer from St. Louis to San Francisco, for example, might be empty going back to St. Louis. The marginal cost of shipping wine on the return trip would be very low given that the truck must return anyway. This could justify a low "backhaul" price for wine on this carrier going from California to Missouri. But the ICC consistently denied such low backhaul prices because they would have introduced "too much" competition into transportation. The result was that empty backhauls remained empty, as the price structure was too rigidly structured.

V. The Consequences of Regulation

A. An Overview: Prices

When first applied to railroads, regulation yielded greater benefits than costs.[22] But it must be remembered that last century's economic conditions did not last. As the railroads lost their monopoly power, regulation became less and less appropriate. Nearly all studies of this century's transportation regulation show the costs greatly exceeding the benefits.

A summary index of regulation's adverse consequences is a comparison of price level with and without regulation. Economic estimates of this price level effect in trucking and airlines are possible because portions of these modes escaped regulation. In the mid-1950s, for example, fresh and frozen poultry and frozen fruits and vegetables were switched from regulated to exempt commodities in trucking. The U.S. Department of Agriculture conducted a "before and after" study of freight rates and service quality. Rates fell 33 per cent on poultry and 19 per cent on fruits and vegetables, while service quality apparently improved.[23] Other estimates, based on regulated versus nonregulated comparisons at a given point in time, suggest that deregulation would reduce truck rates by 6.7 per cent.[24]

In the air, travel within California and Texas could not be controlled by the CAB. A comparison of *intra*state air fares and *inter*state regulated air fares in 1975 is shown in Table 18–5. It does not take a pilot's keen eyes to see that, for routes of similar length and paired-city size, the unregulated *intra*state fares are far lower. More elaborate analyses of airline economics show regulation boosting prices 15 to 30 per cent.[25]

When these percentages for trucking and airlines are translated into dollar amounts, the result is striking. Regulation of them cost several billion dollars per year in the mid-1970s.

Estimates of the costs of railroad regulation

---

[21] Actually, it was a truck-barge combination rather than trucks alone, and ATC matched MC at $5.19 because of constant cost behavior, as illustrated earlier in Figure 18–1(b).

[22] Richard O. Zerbe, Jr., "The Costs and Benefits of Early Regulation of the Railroads," *Bell Journal of Economics* (Spring 1980), pp. 343–350.

[23] P. W. MacAvoy and J. W. Snow (eds.), *Regulation of Entry and Pricing in Truck Transportation* (Washington, D.C.: American Enterprise Institute, 1977), pp. 8–9.

[24] James Sloss, "Regulation of Motor Freight Transportation: A Quantitative Evaluation of Policy," *Bell Journal of Economics* (Autumn 1970), pp. 327–366.

[25] T. E. Keeler, *op. cit.*, p. 119.

Table 18–5. Comparison Between Interstate and Intrastate Air Fares, 1975

City-Pair	Miles	Fare ($)
Los Angeles—San Francisco	338	18.75
Chicago—Minneapolis	339	38.89
New York—Pittsburgh	335	37.96
Los Angeles—San Diego	109	10.10
Portland—Seattle	129	22.22
Dallas—Houston	239	13.89*
Las Vegas—Los Angeles	236	28.70
Chicago—St. Louis	258	29.63

* This is the night and weekend rate. Day-time week-day rate was $23.15.

Source: Civil Aeronautics Board Practices and Procedures, Report of the Subcommittee on Administrative Practice and Procedure, U.S. Senate (1975), p. 41.

are less solid, given the lack of nonregulated sectors and economic characteristics that differ from trucks and airlines. Some estimates are quite high, with double-digit percentages and several billions in annual dollar amounts.[26] Other estimates are rather low, running no more than a few tenths of a per cent and a few millions of dollars annually.[27] Indeed, for reasons to be explained shortly, *de*regulation of railroads could well *increase* rail prices. In any event, the numbers cannot be used to defend past railroad regulation.

[26] Anne F. Friedlaender, "The Social Costs of Regulating the Railroads," *American Economic Review* (May 1971), pp. 226–234; Thomas G. Moore, "Deregulating Surface Transportation," in *Promoting Competition in Regulated Markets,* edited by A. Phillips (Washington, D.C.: Brookings Institution, 1975), pp. 55–98; and Douglas Caves, Laurits Christensen, and Joseph Swanson, "The High Cost of Regulating U.S. Railroads," *Regulation* (Jan./Feb. 1981), pp. 41–46.

[27] James R. Nelson, *op. cit.,* Kenneth D. Boyer, "Minimum Rate Regulation, Modal Split Sensitivities, and the Railroad Problem," *Journal of Political Economy* (June 1977), pp. 493–512; Richard C. Levin, "Allocation in Surface Freight Transportation: Does Rate Regulation Matter?" *Bell Journal of Economics* (Spring 1978), 18–45.

The next question is: why did transportation regulation generally raise price levels? There are two answers: it raised *profits* in some instances. Further, and more important, it raised *costs* of operation in many instances. Thus our catalog of regulation's adverse effects must move from the summary index provided by price levels to the specifics of profits and costs.

B. Profits and Monopoly Power

A detailed study of trucking in the Rocky Mountain area showed that about one-fourth of the towns in that nine-state area were served by no more than one common-carrier trucker in 1972. Similarly, interviews of New Orleans retailers disclosed that, for more than half of their shipments, no more than two motor carriers were authorized to serve them.[28]

These examples imply that the ICC's entry restrictions in trucking artificially created instances of monopoly power. Confirmation of this suspicion is found in the very high value of many truckers' certificates of convenience and necessity, or operating rights. ICC data on transactions in operating rights during 1967–1971 show that forty-three operating rights sold for a total of $3,844,100.[29] These rights had value only because they were tickets of admission to monopoly earnings. With stiff competition, they would have been worthless. Indeed, *de*regulation had exactly this effect. In 1980, many major truckers "wrote off" the lost value of their acquired operating rights—Consolidated Freightways lost $32.1 million, Yellow Freight $34.8 million, and Roadway Express $26.8 million.[30]

[28] MacAvoy and Snow, *Regulation of Entry . . . , op. cit.,* p. 21.

[29] Milton Kafoglis, "A Paradox of Regulated Trucking," *Regulation* (Sept./Oct. 1977), pp. 27–32.

[30] *Wall Street Journal,* September 26, 1980, p. 20; October 23, 1980, p. 4. As a spokesman for Yellow Freight explained it, "the value attributable to restricted entry has been eliminated resulting in the decision to write off the investments."

The relatively low to moderate overall profits in railroading and airlines during the past half-century indicate that these modes gained less monopoly power from regulation than trucking, if any at all. Still, there may have been pockets of artificial power on specific routes. And such power as there was may have led to higher costs rather than higher profits.

C. Costs and Inefficiency

Regulation escalated costs by propagating three kinds of inefficiency—(1) intramodal inefficiency, (2) intermodal inefficiency, and (3) dynamic inefficiency.

1. *Intramodal inefficiency* occurs when there is substantial excess capacity for traffic that would move by a given mode in any event. For example, excess capacity arose from airline regulation when the airlines did not compete on price but competed instead by scheduling more flights on their routes, by offering spacious seating, and by offering sumptuous meals that required galley space (further reducing airplane seating capacity). The effect of over-scheduling can be measured by the average load factor, that is, the percentage of total seats flown that were actually occupied by paying passengers. During the late 1950s and early 1960s the load factor for regulated trunk airlines was only 59 per cent whereas the load factor for unregulated California airlines was 71 per cent.[31] Translating regulation's lower load factor into dollars and cents, it may have cost as much as 10 per cent more per passenger-mile.[32] Shucking seats to make room for first class passengers and kitchen galleys may have boosted costs per passenger-mile by a similar magnitude. In more concrete terms, it takes $47,000 to fully fuel a Boeing 747. The fewer the people on board, the higher the cost per person.

Intramodal inefficiency in trucking and railroading arose from regulation's bans on backhaul discounts and peak-load pricing. Moreover, about 30 per cent of the ICC's commodity-restricted operating rights in trucking were limited to one-way authority, thereby aggravating the problem of empty backhauls. For these and other reasons, regulation may be partially blamed for the fact that during the 50s and 60s, trucks operated at less than 50 per cent and railroads less than 76 per cent of capacity utilization, with costs in the billions.[33]

Intramodal inefficiency can take forms other than excess capacity. For example, ICC route restrictions apparently caused many trucks to take longer routes than they would otherwise. Still, excess capacity is probably the main element of intramodal inefficiency.

2. *Intermodal inefficiency* occurs when freight and passengers are misallocated among modes, that is, they are not moved by the most efficient, cheapest means. Regulation can have this effect when it distorts prices relative to costs. That is to say, thirty tons of machinery might move 1,000 miles most efficiently by train. But if the train rate exceeds the truck rate, trucks will likely get the business regardless of resource costs.

Misallocation was never very serious in short hauls, where trucks rightly carried virtually everything. Nor was it much of a problem on really heavy, long-haul loads because trains always dominated there. But between these extreme conditions, it appears that regulation overpriced rail service, thereby causing more freight to move by truck than economically warranted. Estimates of the costs of this and

---

[31] W. A. Jordan, *op. cit.*, p. 203.

[32] *Civil Aeronautics Board Practices and Procedures*, Report, U.S. Senate, Committee on the Judiciary, Subcommittee on Administrative Practice and Procedure, 94th Congress, 1st Session (1975), pp. 54–57.

[33] Friedlaender, *The Dilemma . . .*, *op. cit.*, pp. 84–88.

related misallocations of ground freight range from zero to $500 million annually.[34] Though less than the costs of excess capacity, these costs were probably not trivial.

3. *Dynamic inefficiency* refers to instances where regulation impeded progress, reducing productivity and raising costs. The ICC displayed special ineptitude when it delayed railroad innovations that would cut costs and take traffic away from other modes. In the early 1960s, for instance, Southern Railway tried to introduce "Big John" cars for bulk grain shipments. Twice as large as conventional boxcars yet considerably lighter in weight, the aluminum "Big Johns" would have permitted Southern to cut its rates 60 per cent. When put before the ICC, however, these new lower rates were denied because the ICC wanted to protect trucking. It took four years and an appeal to the Supreme Court to overcome the ICC's opposition.[35] Another example of obstructionism occurred when the ICC delayed for five years the introduction of unit coal trains in the East.[36]

D. *Consequences of Regulation: Benefits?*

In fairness, we should note that this century's transportation regulation was not totally lacking in benefits. Still, these benefits were probably minor in comparison to the foregoing costs or they were questionable benefits. Let's quickly consider three claimed benefits—(1) cross-subsidy, (2) service quality, and (3) stability.

Empirical studies of cross-subsidies in trucking and airlines have shown that, in fact, the subsidies were slight. Trucks and airlines had greater flexibility in route selection than the cross-subsidy argument assumed, and they apparently exercised their flexibility to evade many loss situations.[37] In the case of railroads, cross-subsidies were clearly present and often large. Yet in this case it can be argued (as in all cases) that subsidies, if believed necessary, are most efficient when openly and directly paid from public funds rather than buried in the price structure of businesses.

In service quality, regulation admittedly maintained good quality. Indeed, in the case of airlines, regulation spurred increased flight frequencies, spacious seating, and other non-price amenities. But the rigidities of regulation fixed quality at a given level, barring a *range* of qualities from "cheap" to "luxury" that customers might like. John Snow explained this by analogy. The regulatory system, he wrote,

> operates as if all restaurants were required to charge five dollars for a meal. This would result in an excellent choice of five-dollar meals. But the person who wanted a ten-dollar meal or a one-dollar meal would be out of luck.[38]

Finally, in furthering stability, regulation can take but small credit. The instabilities prompting regulation are now largely a thing of the past. And the economic characteristics of trucking and airlines are simply not the type that would normally provoke "destructive" competition. In short, a thumping of the alleged benefits barrel yields a hollow ring.

---

[34] MacAvoy and Snow, *Regulation . . . , op. cit.,* p. 104.

[35] *Arrow Transportation Co.* v. *Cincinnati, New Orleans and Texas Pacific Railway Co.,* 379 U.S. 642 (1965).

[36] Paul W. MacAvoy and James Sloss, *Regulation of Transport Innovation: The ICC and Unit Coal Trains to the East Coast* (New York: Random House, 1967).

[37] *Civil Aeronautics Board Practices . . . , op. cit.,* pp. 63–70; Clinton V. Oster, Jr., "The Impact of Deregulation On Service To Small Communities," *Journal of Contemporary Business* (Vol. 9, No. 2), pp. 103–121; Denis A. Breen and Benjamin J. Allen, "Common Carrier Obligations and the Provision of Motor Carrier Service to Small Rural Communities," *Quarterly Review of Economics and Business* (Winter 1980), pp. 86–106.

[38] MacAvoy and Snow, *Regulation . . . , op. cit.,* p. 11.

VI. Deregulation

A. *The Airlines*

Under the leadership of Chairman Alfred E. Kahn, the CAB began deregulating the airlines in 1977. The CAB's relaxation of entry restrictions and fare restraints was formally endorsed by Congress with passage of the Airline Deregulation Act of 1978. Under the Act, existing airlines could immediately more freely expand or abandon their operating rights, and new airlines could more easily enter. As one CAB aide put it, the agency would hand out new routes "like confetti." The Act also introduced price flexibility, immediately allowing fares to fall as much as 50% or rise as much as 5% without CAB approval. Eventually, all CAB control of routes and pricing would end in 1983, and the CAB itself would be abolished in 1985. The upshot is that we now have more experience with airline deregulation than with truck or railroad deregulation.

What has this experience shown? Any assessment is obscured by extraneous events that occurred about the same time as deregulation. Still, at least one thing is certain: Deregulation stimulated competition but not destructive competition. In turn, heightened competition seems to have produced several improvements—(1) lower and more flexible prices than otherwise, (2) easier entry, and (3) a greater variety of service options.

1. *Prices:* The average price of a major airline's ticket increased 6% in 1977, fell 2% in 1978, and rose 6% in 1979.[39] Prices on other goods and services were inflating rapidly at the time. Thus, in real terms, airline prices fell substantially with deregulation. The price competition began with "discount" fares conditioned on length of stay, advance ticket purchase, and off-peak travel times. It then branched out to include across-the-board fare reductions, such

as Continental's "Chicken feed" fares of 1978. Thereafter, prices on some routes fell temporarily to fantastically low levels as some established airlines used promotional fares to break into markets they had not served before. Eastern Air Lines, for instance, promoted its entry into the transcontinental market with $99 fares between California and New York, pulling Pan Am, TWA, and American down to $99 as well for a while.

The precise extent and duration of deregulation's downward pressure on price is impossible to calibrate. In 1980, average airfares leaped nearly 30% then half again as much the year after, implying that deregulation's impact was only temporary. But by this time other factors were jolting the industry, such as a doubling of fuel prices in 1980, muddying the waters of analysis. Still, it can be argued that deregulation's impact remained substantial. Aside from the fact that the higher average air fares of the early 1980s did not give the major airlines monopoly profits, vigorous price competition continued with the expansion of existing cutrate carriers, like Texas International Airlines and Air Florida, plus the fresh entry of brand-new cut-rate carriers—Midway, New York Air, and People Express among them. For example, in 1981 these upstart airlines caused base fare reductions to $35 from $82 for New York–Norfolk, to $59 from $135 for New York–Cleveland, and to $116 from $149 for Omaha–Detroit.[40]

2. *Entry (and Exit):* The recent entry of several new cut-rate airlines illustrates perfectly deregulation's greater freedom. How do the upstarts do it? How can they enter with prices 40 to 50 per cent off prevailing fares and still hope to make a profit? Their costs are considerably lower. Their labor is generally nonunion, with consequent wage savings. Their fleets have no more than just one or two types of aircraft, cutting maintenance costs. Their planes are packed with seats. They use their

---

[39] *Wall Street Journal,* February 6, 1981, p. 25.

[40] *Business Week,* June 15, 1981, p. 79.

personnel and planes more intently and efficiently. They concentrate on high-density, medium-haul routes to maximize their load factors and growth. Their customer service is barebones, without food, without multistop ticketing, without baggage forwarding, without coddling, and so on.[41] In other words, they follow a pattern that, previous to deregulation, could be found only among intrastate airlines serving Texas and California. This suggests that their appearance elsewhere after deregulation was more than just a coincidence.

Among established airlines, greater freedom in route selection produced many changes. Some airlines, like United, cutback sharply on routes served. Others, like Braniff, bounded blindly into new markets. Some cities, like Reno, witnessed a substantial increase in airline service. Others, like Hartford, suffered service curtailments.

Two observations are particularly important in this connection. First, contrary to the warnings of many opposing deregulation, air service to small communities has *not* evaporated. The Airline Deregulation Act provided temporary subsidies for small-town service. But more than that, small commuter airlines with cost-efficient small planes have blossomed to fill the void left by the departing majors. Second, contrary to the dire forecasts of those opposed to deregulation, the added competition has *not* caused the demise of all but the largest airlines. Indeed, as suggested by recent entry experience, the relatively small regional airlines are at present thriving.[42] The only ones really hurting are the medium-sized trunk carriers, many of which have tried to pull out of their tailspins by merging.[43] Thus freedom of entry (and exit) appears to have produced social benefits at little cost.

3. *Service Quality:* Certainly one of the biggest benefits of deregulation is the greater variety of service options offered the public, with a matching variety in prices. Those wanting no-frills service can now get it. Those with more expensive tastes can still get luxury treatment. Indeed, rumor has it that some airlines may try first-class-only service.

B. Trucking Deregulation

Following the lead of the CAB, the ICC began easing its regulation of trucking without new legislation. In 1978, for instance, the ICC began granting operating rights more freely than previously. Thus, even before President Carter signed the Motor Carrier Act of 1980 into law, competition shook the industry. Although trucking prices climbed with general inflation after 1978, it was the opinion of many analysts that they would have climbed more steeply without the ICC's rule changes. As if to confirm this, the press reported many examples of price cutting activity.[44]

Under the Act of 1980, truckers can decrease or increase their rates as much as 10% annually without ICC approval, and even more with approval. The law also made it easier for trucking companies to enter markets or expand their networks of routes. Still, the ICC retained considerable power.[45] And early experience indicates that deregulation may progress more slowly than it did in airlines. President Reagan kept campaign promises made to Teamster union and trucking company supporters that he would pick proregulatory commissioners. These appointees have applied the brakes to deregulation (but have not made a U-turn toward reregulation).[46]

[41] Ibid., pp. 78–92; *Fortune*, February 9, 1981.

[42] These include U.S. Air, Southwest, Frontier, Piedmont, Air Florida, and Texas International.

[43] These include Western, Continental, Braniff, and National.

[44] *Wall Street Journal*, May 9, 1980, pp. 1, 28.

[45] John Guandolo, "The Role of the Interstate Commerce Commission in the 1980s," *American Economic Review* (May 1981), pp. 116–118.

[46] *Wall Street Journal*, August 5, 1981, p. 48.

C. Railroad Deregulation

Railroad deregulation differs from airline and truck deregulation in three major particulars. First, *impetus*. Whereas the airlines and truckers stoutly resisted deregulation, the railroads heartily advocated deregulation. Second, *purpose*. Whereas the prime purpose in deregulating airlines and trucking was to increase competition, the prime purpose in deregulating the railroads was to increase rail profits. Indeed, this divergence of purpose explains the divergence in impetus. The railroads' very low profits, bankruptcy casualties, and declining share of the nation's traffic volume made them look like an endangered species. Third, *methods*. Whereas in airlines and trucking the main methods were downside price flexibility and easier entry, in railroads the main methods were *upside* price flexibility and easier *exit* (via merger and abandonments). These might not win railroads a greater traffic share, but they should lift profit prospects.

In 1976 Congress passed the Railroad Revitalization & Regulatory Reform Act. Its 120 pages amounted to an immense CARE package, with such items of relief as (1) a promise of $1.6 billion in government subsidies, (2) new procedures to expedite merger approvals, (3) organization and aid to ConRail, formed from the remains of the bankrupt Penn Central and several smaller lines, (4) easier abandonment of low-density, money-losing branch lines, and (5) greater pricing freedom where railroads lacked "market dominance." In short, the Act was a mix of more and less regulation.

Though promising on paper, the 4R Act of 1976 was *interpreted* by the ICC and other responsible government authorities in ways that brought little change. Indeed, the industry's profits tumbled rather than trebled. In pricing freedom, for instance, the qualifying phrase "market dominance" became a Catch-22. As interpreted, it permitted the railroads freedom to raise rates *only* on the 50% of their business where they in fact could not raise rates, where, that is, they lacked "market dominance" because they faced vigorous competition from trucks, water carriers, and pipelines. As for the rate increases allowed on the regulated 50%, they were small potatoes compared to the 25% overall increase that the Association of American Railroads insisted was necessary to give railroads a rate of return comparable to other industries.[47]

Thus the purpose of the ensuing Staggers Rail Act of 1980 was, in a sense, to do things right the second time around. The Act of 1980 authorized further subsidies and easier abandonments. Most important for our purposes, the Act of 1980 allowed railroads to boost rates freely until they reached 160% of variable costs, a percentage that would gradually increase to 180% in 1984. On top of this, rates could be raised additional amounts without ICC approval to offset inflationary cost increases. One condition attached to these new leniencies was that the railroads could no longer set their rates collusively. Their rate bureaus lost antitrust immunity.

Although experience under the new law is limited, it appears that railroad rates are indeed going up, especially on those routes and on those commodities where the railroads are so dominant that their shippers are "captives." This is now mainly large long-haul shipments of bulk items like coal, iron ore, raw chemicals, and clay. At the same time, however, rail price structures have become more flexible by more accurately reflecting peak load conditions and varying with quality of service.[48] Whether the Staggers Rail Act of 1980 will be enough to save this endangered species remains to be seen, however. Some analysts argue that it is

[47] *Business Week*, August 28, 1978, pp. 80–86.
[48] *Wall Street Journal*, October 14, 1980, p. 1, 28.

not.[49] If not, then we can expect to see still more major "deregulatory" legislation for railroads in the future.

Summary

Among transportation's several modes, trucks and airlines have been this century's sprinters. Railroads and inland waterways, the old mainstays, together still account for half of all freight volume. But the railroads have been troubled.

These developments indicate a certain degree of intermodal competition, as determined in large part by the industry's economics. Aside from price, demands for transportation are based on nonprice factors such as speed and reliability. Indeed, speed alone explains much of the success of trucks and airlines. On the supply side, we find that costs vary across modes, but they vary in such a way as to give certain modes advantages in certain traffic, such as railroads in large long-haul dry bulk shipments and trucks in relatively small short-haul high-value shipments. These conditions inhibit intermodal competition in some services, but this lack is often made up for by opportunities for intramodal competition. The economics of trucking and airlines are particularly conducive to intramodal competition. Concentration in relevant markets for these modes can usually be no more than low to moderate. Entry is fairly easy. Costs are rather constant with scale, implying no natural monopoly.

Regulation of the industry sprang from a combination of economic conditions and historic circumstances. A mixture of monopoly power and competition in railroading produced stark price discrimination, prompting establish-

ment of the ICC in 1887 to provide fairness *among* buyers. Fairness *to* sellers later motivated the cartelizing features of the Transportation Act of 1920, which followed a stressful time for the railroads. That stress deepened with the onslaught of trucking and the Great Depression, occasioning the spread of cartel-like regulation to a large portion of trucking in hopes of furthering fairness *among* sellers. Airlines were also brought under the umbrella at this time, for promotional and safety reasons as well as for fairness to sellers. Along the way, a restrictive policy toward railroad abandonments developed, illustrating fairness as an administrative process.

Regulation controlled entry, exit, and prices. *Entry* was artificially curbed by limited issuance of narrowly drawn operating rights. The effect was especially adverse in trucking and airlines, the growth sectors. *Exit* was controlled by surveillance of route abandonments and mergers. Railroads, the declining sector, hurt most from that policy. With respect to *prices,* levels of price followed no rational formula, as clustering in cartel-like rate bureaus stood in the way. Price structures mainly followed value-of-service rather than cost-of-service patterns. One adverse result was an inordinate shift of business from railroads to trucks during the first two-thirds of this century. Another was an absence of backhaul discounts and peak-load pricing.

The consequences of this regulation were higher prices in trucking and airlines due to higher profits and higher costs. The higher costs could be pinned on intramodal, intermodal, and dynamic inefficiencies. In railroads, the price effects of regulation are less clear. Low profits signaled low prices, but inefficiency may have caused high costs.

Deregulation of the airlines and trucking vastly increased competition. In turn, this competition has in both cases apparently (1) reduced prices below what they would have been

---

[49] John F. Due, "Railroads: An Endangered Species and the Possibility of a Fatal Mistake," *Quarterly Review of Economics and Business* (Spring 1981), pp. 58–76.

otherwise, (2) encouraged entry, and (3) stimulated a wider variety of service offerings. The evidence in these respects is most solid for airlines, the first to be fully deregulated.

The main purpose in deregulating railroads was, in contrast, to boost profits. This will mean substantially higher prices in areas where railroads enjoy monopoly power unless cost savings from efficiency improvements are large enough to more than offset the higher price targets. Easier abandonments are also a part of rail deregulation. Finally, it should be remembered that deregulation in railroads and trucking is so far incomplete in the sense that the ICC still retains some discretionary powers. And, unlike the CAB, the ICC faces no death sentence.

Questions and Exercises for Chapter 18

1. What is the relevance and importance of differing elasticities of demand in explaining (a) the origin of railroad regulation, and (b) the behavior of airlines after deregulation?
2. Use this chapter's early discussion of railroad costs to explain its later assertions that an easier abandonments policy should improve railroad profitability.
3. Compare and contrast railroad and truck costs in (a) long-haul versus short-haul and (b) speed.
4. Compare and contrast the origins of railroad and trucking regulation in (a) historical circumstances, (b) sources of lobbying support, and (c) economic rationales.
5. How and why did price regulation of transportation differ from price regulation of electric utilities?
6. What are the differences and similarities between value-of-service pricing and cross-subsidization?
7. Distinguish intramodal, intermodal, and dynamic inefficiencies.
8. Why was entry regulation important in trucking and airlines but unimportant in railroading?
9. What clues do we have that entry regulations in trucking and airlines were in fact restrictive? (Use evidence from regulation *and* deregulation periods.)
10. Compare and contrast deregulation in airlines and railroading with respect to (a) impetus, (b) purpose, (c) methods, and (d) economic consequences.

Chapter 19

Energy: Petroleum and Natural Gas

In an electoral system it is the rule rather than the exception that good economics will be dominated by exigencies of the moment and by transitory political concerns.
—Neil de Marchi

I. Introduction

Like much other regulation, price regulation of crude oil and natural gas originated during the economic turmoil of the 1930s. Moreover, like much other regulation, this price regulation was relaxed or abandoned during the economic turmoil of the late 1970s and early 1980s.

The importance of oil and natural gas to the U.S. economy is easy to state. In recent decades they have accounted for roughly 75 per cent of all energy consumption, with oil carrying the greater part of the burden at just under 50 per cent. The ability of free markets to arrange the production and distribution of this energy is, for an economist, just as easy to state, at least in theory. Consumer demand and producer supply would be guided by prices determined by the interaction of supply and demand. It does not matter that oil and natural gas are extracted from the earth, or that they are ex-

haustible resources valued by future generations as well as our own. Many economists argue that the laws of demand and supply can, with little modification, be relied upon to yield good results for all concerned.

Economic theory notwithstanding, oil and natural gas have until recently seen more regulation than most industries. The story of that regulation is worth telling because of its immense impact, its interesting origins, its unique features, and its continuing attractiveness to many who would like this regulation renewed. It must be stressed that in telling the story we will focus solely on price regulation, ignoring conservation measures and subsidies such as those promoting oil-shale development. Moreover, the prices of interest here are "wellhead" prices, or "field" prices. Prices at later stages of the production-distribution process have been, and to some extent remain, regulated. But that regulation is mainly public utility regulation of interstate pipelines and local gas utilities, a form of regulation covered earlier in Chapter 15.

Such as it is, our story has three main parts:

1. *Petroleum Before 1971:* Echoing the experience in transportation regulation, *price support* and stability were the main objectives of crude oil regulation from 1934 to 1971. Domestic oil was abundant. And state governments were the main regulators.
2. *Petroleum After 1971:* The pre-1971 abundance gave way to post-1971 shortage, a shortage that helped OPEC raise foreign oil prices repeatedly and astronomically. The federal government took the regulatory reins, imposing *price ceilings* on domestic oil.
3. *Natural Gas Regulation:* Federal price ceiling regulation of natural gas was legally conceived in 1938, nurtured by the Supreme Court in 1954, and reached maturity in the 1960s and early 1970s.

In discussing each division, we shall touch upon (1) regulation's main *purposes,* (2) its major *characteristics,* (3) its good and bad economic *effects,* and (4) recent *deregulation.*

In every respect, these energy regulations were extremely complicated. The reasons they were complicated are themselves complicated. For one thing, a multitude of goals were claimed for these regulations, including equity, efficiency, stability, national defense, and preservation of small independent businesses. For another, the regulations varied to fit a vast array of different suppliers—some big, some little; some vertically integrated, some not; some importing oil, some not; and so on. Conversely and correspondingly, the regulations twisted and turned to accommodate the diversity of energy buyers and end uses (then and still prevailing). Some buyers are int*ra*state while others are int*er*state. Some buyers are major oil companies while others are small indepen-

dents. Some ultimate buyers (such as teenage Saturday night "cruisers") have frivolous energy needs, while others (such as hospitals and farmers) have critical needs. Ultimate end uses range from jet fuel to naphtha, asphalt to fuel oil.

We shall simplify. Our first simplifications are found in the two panels of Figure 19–1, which diagrammatically summarizes the price *floor* regulation of oil (1934–1971) and the price *ceiling* regulation of oil (1971–1981) and natural gas (1954–1985). Assuming pure competition,[1] the supply curves labeled S have a conventional positive slope, indicating that additional supplies entail additional costs. The demand curves, D, display the usual negative slope. Equilibrium is achieved in each instance by prices and quantities corresponding to the intersection of demand and supply, that is, P_e and Q_e.

To have any impact, a price floor would have to be *above* equilibrium price, as P_f is above P_e in Figure 19–1(a). At price P_f the quantity suppliers wish to offer, Q_s, exceeds the quantity buyers demand, Q_d, creating a surplus, $Q_s - Q_d$. This surplus would normally tend to drive price down toward P_e, expanding demand and contracting supply to eliminate the surplus. Thus, in order to enforce the price floor at P_f, supply must be artificially constrained not to exceed Q_d. This constraint was achieved in oil regulation prior to 1971 by restrictions on domestic output, so-called "prorationing," and by quotas on imports from abroad.

Conversely, to have any impact, a price ceil-

[1] The assumption of pure competition is perhaps the biggest oversimplification in this analysis. At best, "workable" competition prevails, and some industry experts argue that noncompetitive oligopoly typifies oil and gas production in the U.S., primarily because of the dominance of such major firms as Exxon, Texaco, Mobil, Shell, and Chevron, but also because of extensive joint venture activity in the industry. See, e.g., John W. Wilson, Testimony, *The Natural Gas Industry,* Part I, U.S. Senate, Committee on the Judiciary, Subcommittee on Antitrust and Monopoly (1973), pp. 456–504.

Figure 19–1. Price Regulation of Oil and Natural Gas

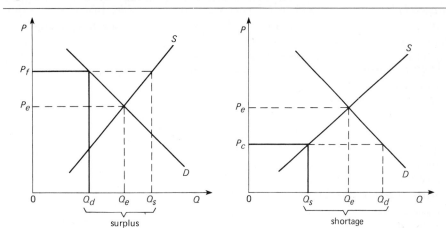

(a) Price Floor

(b) Price Ceiling

ing would have to be *below* equilibrium price, as P_c is below P_e in Figure 19–1(b). At price P_c the quantity suppliers offer is Q_s whereas quantity demanded is Q_d. Because demand exceeds supply there is a shortage of $Q_d - Q_s$. Given that price is not allowed to ration quantity among buyers, nonprice mechanisms must be employed to allot existing supply and shift the demand curve back. In oil after 1971, rationing was achieved by long lines at gas stations and official allocations. A 55 mph speed limit encouraged conservation. In natural gas, shortages during the 1970s were handled by a system of curtailments to existing gas customers and by prohibitions on new hookups.

Two key criteria for assessing the effect of these price regulations are *efficiency* and *equity*. Price floors and price ceilings are both *inefficient* because they lead to misallocations of resources. They result in too little being produced and consumed relative to the optimal amount Q_e. In technical jargon, Q_d in the floor case of 1(a) and Q_s in the ceiling case of 1(b) are outputs where marginal benefits (as indi-

cated by the demand curve) exceed the marginal costs (as indicated by the supply curve). Society gains from added output until the marginal benefits match the added costs, as they do at Q_e. This, it must be noted, is only the most obvious form of inefficiency. Oil and gas regulations have created other inefficiencies because of the particular form they have taken. To enforce the pre-1971 oil price floor, for example, the output of low-cost, efficient oil wells tended to be more heavily restricted than the output of high-cost, inefficient wells. Given that price interference in these industries has always produced inefficiency, it should be obvious that these regulations were never seriously proposed as a means of advancing efficiency. Rather, inefficiency has always been their major social cost, with alleged benefits coming from other value judgment criteria such as equity or stability or conservation.

As regards *equity*, price floors favor sellers at the expense of buyers, while price ceilings favor buyers at the expense of sellers. The "equity" of price controls thus depends on the relative prosperity of buyers and sellers. If, as many believe, owners of oil and gas properties are generally more wealthy than oil and gas consumers, the generalization most easily drawn in light of existing value judgments is that favoritism to producers is *in*equitable and favoritism to consumers is equitable. The oil price floor could thus be considered inequitable and the oil/gas price ceilings could be considered equitable. Still, there are serious complications. As regards the alleged equity of price ceilings, for example, we must note the inequity suffered by those whose supplies are seriously cut or totally denied by nonprice rationing.

Further complications in judging equity are best left to the detailed discussion following. That discussion will also acknowledge other policy objectives that have rationalized these regulations, stability in particular.

II. Oil Price Supports Before 1971[2]

A. *Purposes*

Prior to 1934 the price of domestic crude oil was highly unstable. That instability can be blamed on a combination of four main characteristics: (1) inelastic supply in the short run due to heavy sunk costs plus a "law of capture," (2) inelastic demand in the short run, (3) sharp shifts in the supply curve due to erratic results from oil exploration, and (4) shifts in the demand curve due to cyclical swings in general business activity. Given the inelasticity condi-

tions, prices had to fall abysmally low to choke off supply or stimulate demand. Conversely, prices had to climb quite high to curb demand or boost output significantly. Although inelasticity alone is no problem, the added presence of shifts in demand and supply meant that prices were frequently called upon to perform these difficult feats.

Things came to a head in the early 1930s. Discovery of the immense East Texas Field in 1930 and the country's simultaneous slide into depression combined to press the price of oil down to amazingly low levels, even as low as 10 cents a barrel. As just suggested, this kind of instability may be attributed in part to the "law of capture." Under the "law of capture" crude oil belongs to whomever gets it out first. Couple this law with (1) fragmented property ownership over a given oil reservoir, (2) the fluid nature of the stuff, plus (3) standard profit-maximizing behavior, and you have a mad rush to drain the reservoir. The goal of each owner was simply (and crudely): "get it out while the getting's good." Aside from instability the results were:

- Appalling *physical waste,* because of reckless damage to the reservoir's natural drive pressures.
- Enormous *"economic waste,"* because of extraction and consumption of crude oil when its value was low and because of excessive investment in drilling and rigging.
- Shameful *environmental damage,* both because of the ugliness of oil rig forests and the pollution of streams and soils from oil run-off.

Stability and conservation thus justified the imposition of oil price supports in the early 1930s. An added purpose became apparent with time and with ever higher prices, namely, protection and prosperity for politically powerful oil producers.

[2] Main sources for this section are M. G. de Chazeau and A. E. Kahn, *Integration and Competition in the Petroleum Industry* (New Haven: Yale University Press, 1959); Walter Measday, "The Petroleum Industry," in *The Structure of American Industry,* edited by W. Adams (New York: Macmillan Publishing Co., 1977); S. L. McDonald, *Petroleum Conservation in the United States* (Baltimore: Johns Hopkins Press, 1971); Cabinet Task Force on Oil Import Control, *The Oil Import Question* (Washington, D.C. 1970).

B. *Characteristics of the Regulation*

Price support was achieved by official cartelization. That cartelization rested on a combination of state and federal policies.

1. STATE CONTROLS

Control of oil well output was achieved by *demand prorationing*. The basic idea was to stabilize price by reducing output as demand fell and expanding output as demand rose. Moreover, a generally restrictive hold on output lifted price above what it would have been on average. First instituted by state authorities in Oklahoma and Texas, demand prorationing later spread to Louisiana, Kansas, and New Mexico, thereby including the states most bountifully blessed with oil.

Operation of the system is illustrated in Figure 19–2. In essence, supply was restricted or expanded to whatever level was necessary for price to be at or above the "administered price" level. The supply curve looked like an L lying down. This configuration meant that supply was perfectly price elastic up to full capacity use

(at the corner of the L). Not all wells were subject to regulation, the main exemptions being "discovery" wells and inefficient "strippers," the latter being wells physically incapable of producing more than a few barrels a day. Moreover, state authorities had no control over imports into the United States. Hence, exempt and import supplies were subtracted from projected demand before determining the output allowed from the regulated wells. In short, the fraction of allowed capacity utilization was reckoned monthly by the following formula:

fraction of capacity utilization for
regulated wells

$$= \frac{\text{demand} - (\text{exempts} + \text{imports})}{\text{total capacity of regulated wells}}$$

Thus, with decreased demand, or increased imports, or greater exempt output, state authorities would reduce the "allowable" for regulated wells from, say, 90 per cent to 80 per cent capacity use. Competitive drilling under the law of capture was limited indirectly but not completely through additional regulations defining "total capacity" for each producer.

Figure 19–2. **Restriction of Supply Under Demand Prorationing, Lifting Prices to "Administered Level" Above Free Market Level**

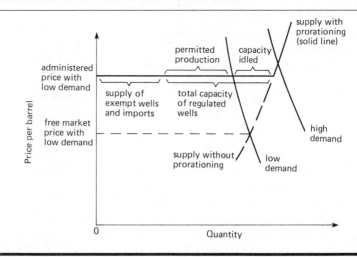

2. FEDERAL CONTROLS

The U.S. Bureau of Mines helped the states by providing the monthly estimates of oil demand used in the above formula. More important, though, three federal measures backed up state prorationing. (1) The Connally "Hot" Oil Act of 1935 prevented the interstate shipment of crude oil produced in excess of state prorationing allowables. (2) The Interstate Oil Compact Commission Act, also of 1935, provided a forum for the prorationing agencies of producing states. They could thereby collude and coordinate their supply control efforts. (3) Mandatory import quotas came much later, beginning in 1959.

During the early years of prorationing, restrictions on imports were not needed. The United States enjoyed an abundance of oil, giving its oil a low price relative to foreign oil. Indeed, as late as 1949 the U.S. accounted for 36% of the world's known reserves and 55% of its production. Thereafter, however, U.S. fortunes flagged, with the result that, during the 1950s, domestic oil came to be priced above foreign oil, in part because the domestic price was artificially supported (as described previously).

Low-priced imports gushed into the U.S., playing havoc with prorationing. In 1958, for instance, regulated wells in Texas were held to only 33% capacity use, down from 100% in 1948. Continued price support thus depended on quotas against imports, which quotas were imposed on grounds of "national defense."

C. Effects of the Price Support System

The system had the effect of redistributing real income out of consumers' pockets into producers' pockets. The import quotas, for instance, elevated the price of oil to the point of costing consumers $7 to $8 billion a year extra. Not all of these billions took the form of excess profits for producers, however, because the regulations also raised producer's costs. In particular, there was substantial excess capacity and the most efficient wells were the ones most tightly constrained. These bloated costs amounted to approximately $2 billion a year. Finally, there were still further costs associated with the welfare loss of misallocated resources.

In short, the program was both inequitable and inefficient. Its main goodness was price stability (albeit at an artificially high level).

D. Deregulation

Defacto deregulation of the price support system followed the first serious signs of our oil depletion in 1969. Ominously, United States productive capacity began a continuing decline while demand swelled to record levels. Prorationing allowables were pegged at 100% in 1972 and have remained there since. Import quotas were discontinued in 1973, as imports became the only means of meeting our voracious demands. The mechanisms and agencies for price supports remained intact after 1971, but the perceived problem shifted from a free-market price that was "too low" to one that was "too high."

III. Oil Price Ceilings After 1971[3]

A. Purposes of Ceilings: Stability and Equity

For a while stability continued to serve as a major justification for oil price regulation. But

[3] Main sources for this section include Craufurd D. Goodwin (ed.), *Energy Policy in Perspective* (Washington, D.C.: The Brookings Institution, 1981), especially the chapters by de Marchi, Cochrane, and Yager; Paul W. MacAvoy (ed.), *Federal Energy Administration Regulation* (Washington, D.C.: American Enterprise Institute, 1977); W. David Montgomery, "A Case Study of Regulatory Programs of the Federal Energy Administration," in *Study on Federal Regulation,* Appendix to Vol. VI, U.S. Senate, Committee on Governmental Affairs (December 1978), and J. M. Griffin and H. B. Steele, *Energy Economics and Policy* (New York: Academic Press, 1980).

as suggested by the shift from price floors to price ceilings, the nature of the stability problem changed dramatically. Whereas before 1971 the alleged problem was the *downside* instability associated with abundance and depression, after 1971 the problem became the *upside* instability associated with domestic shortage and price inflation.

Price ceilings were first introduced in 1971 as part of President Nixon's broader policy to curb inflation by wage-price controls. Thus, at the outset, oil was not singled out for special treatment but instead included in a general clampdown (the nature of which will be detailed in Chapter 24). Later, when oil did receive special attention, a major purpose of the price ceilings remained inflation control, or aggregate economic stability.

The shortages that made oil a threat to overall inflation were due to a number of factors besides the onset of diminishing U.S. productive capacity. The winter of 1969–70 was the coldest in thirty years, putting a burden on fuel oil supply. The Trans-Arabian pipeline was closed, cutting 500,000 barrels a day to the west via the Mediterranian. Air-pollution standards shifted demand from dirty coal to relatively clean oil and gas. Nuclear plant construction fell behind schedule. And so on. Nixon's wage-price controls apparently also contributed to the shortage in certain product categories.

The inflation threat went from bad to worse in 1973 when the Organization of Petroleum Exporting Countries (OPEC) began a quick spurt of price hikes that quadrupled the cost of imports in short order just when our dependence on imports had reached addictive proportions. As previously mentioned, our dire straits had forced the abandonment of import quotas and 100% capacity use in prorationing states. Moreover, European consumption reached an all-time high, putting OPEC in a particularly advantageous position. Then in October 1973, war erupted between Israel and the Arabs. A partial oil embargo followed, lifting the auction prices of crude oil as high as $17 a barrel, way above the existing $3 posted price (i.e., contract price). With a hop and a skip, OPEC lifted the posted price. Hopping first to $5.11, then skipping to $11.65 within a few month's time, OPEC shocked the U.S. and the world. Thereafter, OPEC escalated price by 5% to 10% annually until 1979, when it doubled price from $14 to $28 a barrel.

Events of 1973–74 raised an old problem besides inflation—the problem of equity. If the price of domestic oil were allowed to rise freely to match the price of oil imported from OPEC, there would have been a massive transfer of income from domestic oil consumers to domestic oil producers. The potential transfer has been variously estimated, but the order of magnitude is in any case huge—roughly $10 to $20 billion per year.[4]

Concern for inflation, stability, and equity mobilized political forces, swamping economic arguments that the free market should be allowed to work. Economically, the free market's soaring price would have curbed consumption (allocating oil to those most willing and able to pay for it) and would have provided incentive for increased domestic output (in the long run if not the short run). Most of President Nixon's top decision-makers—William Simon, Herbert Stein, George Shultz, and Roy Ash—were among those most ardently fond of the free market. Yet they were willing to betray their beliefs when confronted with (1) announcements of rapidly rising oil company profits, (2) embarrassing disclosures that Nixon's 1972 campaign had been financed in large part by the oil industry, (3) public and congressional suspicions that the shortage had been contrived by the major oil companies, and, of course, (4) public and congressional fears that the free market would brutalize poor consumers and

---

[4] See Griffin and Steele, *op. cit.*, p. 248.

aggravate inflation.[5] The acts emerging from these concerns were temporary but important.

B. Characteristics of the Policy

1. PRICE CEILINGS

Just before the embargo of 1973, the federal government's wage-price control policy evolved to the point of establishing a "two-tier" price system for crude oil. "Old" oil that was already flowing in 1972 was subjected to a low ceiling, while "new" oil from newly opened wells was free of any price ceiling. The idea was that the flow of "old" oil would continue at the lower price and that any price increases on that oil would give producers windfalls. However, "new" oil needed higher free-market prices because "new" oil cost more to find and produce than "old" oil. Without the incentive of higher prices, producers would not produce "new" oil nor would they invest in exploration. If viewed in terms of Figure 19–1(b), P_c would be the price of "old" oil and P_e would be the price of "new" oil.

There followed a complex series of legislative acts:

- 1973—Emergency Petroleum Allocation Act
- 1974—Federal Energy Administration Act
- 1975—Energy Policy and Conservation Act
- 1976—Energy Conservation and Production Act

Among other things, these Acts created the Federal Energy Administration (FEA), authorized oil price controls after the expiration of the wage-price program, and provided for administrative allocations of oil and oil products. FEA's implementation of the price ceiling provisions eventually led to a "three-tier" system of crude oil pricing fashioned on the "two-tier" model. In 1977, for example, "old" oil was priced at $5.19 a barrel, "new" oil went for

$11.22 a barrel, and third-tier oil made up of stripper well output and imports was freely priced at $13.59, the "world" price.[6]

Figure 19–3 gives a simplified view incorporating only two prices—a control price for domestic crude labeled $P_{control}$ and an import price labeled P_{OPEC}. The horizontal line labeled P_{OPEC} indicates that the U.S. could purchase any amount at $14.50 per barrel. The upward slope of the domestic supply curve labeled S indicates that additional domestic production requires ever higher prices. In the absence of price control, the price of imports, P_{OPEC}, would determine market price, and the supply curve combining domestic and foreign sources would trace a schedule indicated by $KDBJI$. Demand intersects that supply schedule at point J, so total free-market supply would equal Q_D, with $Q_D - Q_s$ coming from imports. In this free-market case, domestic suppliers receive total revenues of $OABQ_S$. Their costs of production are the area under the supply curve, $OKBQ_S$. Thus their "producers' surplus" or "rent" is KAB, most of which could be considered windfall.

A price ceiling on domestic oil of $9.50 transfers some of this rent or windfall to consumers as they then pay a lower average price for oil. At $P_{control}$ of $9.50, domestic producers supply Q_S^l, earning total revenues equal to $OEFQ_S^l$ of which only EFK is rent. Imports amounting to $Q_D^l - Q_S^l$ then meet the additional demand. At price P_{OPEC} the total amount spent on imports is $Q_S^l GIQ_D^l$. Combining this expenditure with the amount spent on domestic oil, $OEFQ_S^l$, yields an overall amount spent of $OEFGIQ_D^l$. If this total dollar expenditure is divided by quantity Q_D^l, the result is average price P_{avg}, which is what indicated to us the amount that would be imported to reach controlled equilibrium at point H.

---

[5] See, e.g., de Marchi, op. cit., pp. 425–468.

[6] The Energy Fact Book, U.S. House, Subcommittee on Energy and Power of the Committee on Interstate and Foreign Commerce (Nov. 1980), p. 266.

Figure 19–3.   The Effect of a Price Ceiling on Crude Oil

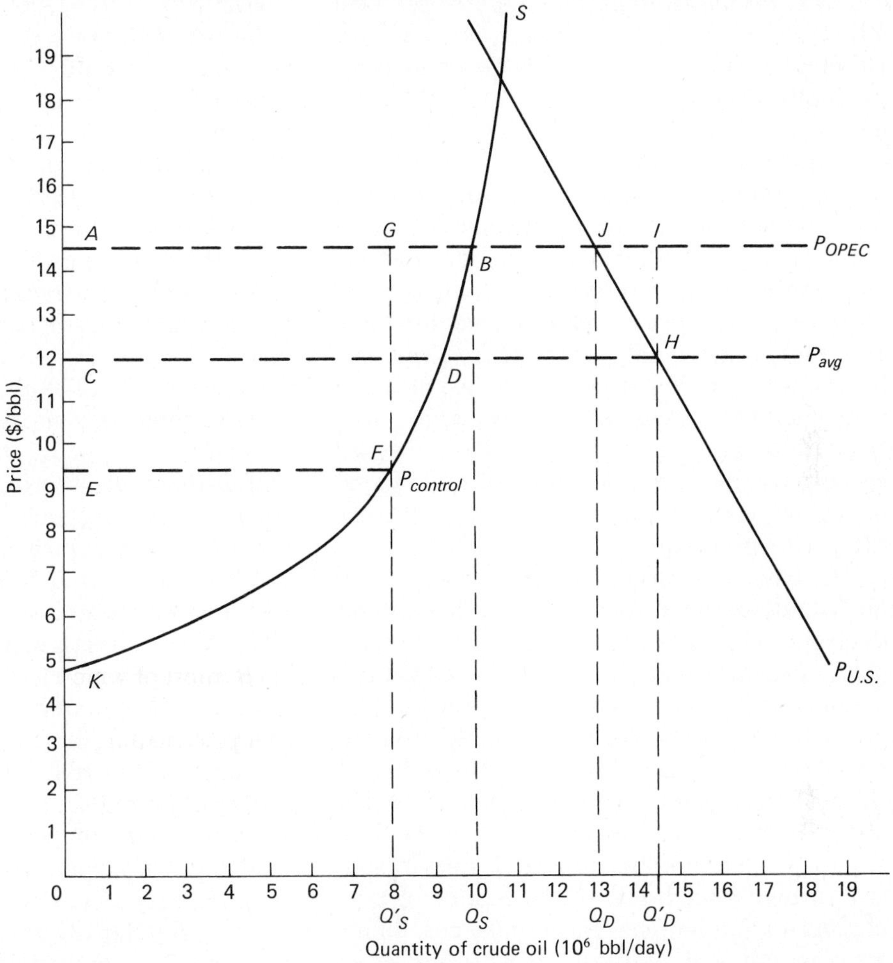

Source: J. M. Griffin and H. B. Steele, *Energy Economics and Policy* (New York: Academic Press, 1980), p. 247.

The total dollar gain to consumers from price control is equal to area *AGFE*, because that is the *difference* between the amount they pay for Q'_D oil *absent* control, namely $OAIQ'_D$, and the amount they pay *with* control, namely $OEFGIQ'_D$. The producers' loss from control is *ABFE*, which is slightly greater than the consumers' gain of *AGFE*. (It is slightly greater because *FGB* is an efficiency loss due to misallocation. Area *JIH* is also an efficiency loss.)

It should be noted that imports were greater with controls ($Q'_D - Q'_S$) than without controls

$(Q_D - Q_S)$. Thus one adverse impact of the program was that it increased rather than decreased our dependency on OPEC oil. This added demand on OPEC may have helped OPEC maintain price above what it would have been otherwise.

2. ENTITLEMENTS

A big problem with a two- or three-tier system can now be recognized. Refiners who buy crude oil for processing into consumer products compete with each other when selling refined products. If the prices refiners paid for their crude oil varied widely across tiers, then those having access to low-priced crude would have a tremendous competitive advantage over those getting high-priced crude. Thus, in order to equalize the price of crude oil to refiners, an elaborate scheme was devised called the entitlements program.

The basic idea was that a refiner had to have an "entitlement" to use a barrel of low-priced domestic oil. These entitlements were "equitably" distributed among refiners on the basis of precontrol crude purchases. Moreover, the entitlement tickets were marketable so as to avoid the physical transfer of old oil in exchange for new oil. Those refiners having access to an above-average percentage of low-priced old oil had to buy entitlements from those heavily reliant on high-priced new oil. The price of purchasing an entitlement reflected the cost difference in old and new oil, so the market in entitlements had the effect of equalizing the cost of crude oil to all refiners.

3. ALLOCATION REGULATIONS

Once price no longer rationed supplies among those demanding oil, various allocation regulations had to do the job. These were many and varied. Indeed, the entitlements program was a form of administrative rationing where the entitlements functioned as ration tickets. A more obvious form of administrative allocation was the supplier/purchaser rule, under which a supplier of crude or refined products had to continue to supply his past purchasers with what was called "base period volume." The vertical buy-sell relationships of the production-distribution process were, as a consequence, largely frozen, putting a chill on competition. A seller could not seek out the highest bidder for all his sales because he had to stand ready to supply past buyers minimal amounts. A buyer, however, was not compelled to purchase any of these allocations if he did not want to. This vertical freeze did not apply directly to ultimate consumers, like you and me or factories.

Another level of allocation regulations handled ultimate end users by classifying them into four priority groups. At the very top priority were those who were allowed all their fuel requirements without restraint—the Department of Defense, farmers, and medical and nursing facilities. At bottom priority were those who received no assured allocation whatever. This deprived class included motorists, but they were not completely abandoned because gasoline station operators were entitled to an allocation based on "base period" use. The upshot of all this was that, during several periods of severe shortage, some end users had to wait in line while others did not.

To summarize, the regulations President Nixon imposed in 1973 during the Arab oil embargo and OPEC price escalations were intended to promote domestic price stability and income equity. They applied to both crude oil and refined products, but hit crude the hardest with first a two-tier then a three-tier price formula. Entitlements were needed to equalize the price of crude to refiners. Additional allocation controls tended to lock refiners and retailers into their historical relationships.

C. Effects of Oil Price Ceilings

The major effects of the control program, both good and bad, were premiered in Figure

19–3. On the good side, controls served the causes of macro stability and equity when the price of oil was held below what it would have been otherwise. Quantification of these effects is difficult, but in raw totals macroinflation may have been a few percentage points less and oil producers may have lost $13 billion to consumers annually during the mid-1970s. It must be acknowledged, however, that these are gross estimates that by argument, assumption, and analysis may vary considerably. Some would argue, for instance, that inflation is solely a monetary problem best controlled by monetary policy. As for equity in income distribution, conservative assumptions can be used to argue that the gains were "worth" no more than about $1.4 to $1.9 billion per year.[7]

On the bad side, the artificially low prices seem to have increased consumption and reduced domestic production compared to what they would have been. The consumption effect is easiest to appreciate. The price elasticity of demand for oil is roughly −0.5, which means that a 1% increase in the price of oil reduces the quantity demanded about 0.5%. With controls, the average price consumers paid was below the free-market price. If average price was as much as 10% lower, then consumption was roughly 5% too high.

The reduced production effect is more difficult to appraise because "new" oil was granted a high price to encourage its discovery and production. That price may not have been high enough, however, as the *cost* of new oil soared during the 1970s. Drilling costs per foot of well, for instance, rose 50% in constant dollars.[8] This resulted as the search for oil moved to more hostile environments than before. By 1980 skilled drillers in the Arctic were earning $90,000 a year (even young ones with no more than a high-school education)! And unskilled

people who aided the Arctic drillers by cooking and cleaning made $40,000 per year.[9] As for the low price on "old" oil, it too may have curbed production. The output of "old" oil can be boosted, or its rate of decline can be curbed, by the application of secondary and tertiary recovery techniques, such as steam injection. But these techniques are very expensive, and they will not be employed unless oil's price is high enough to cover the high cost and a normal profit.

In technical jargon, there was a misallocation of resources because of these consumption and production effects. Consumers did not pay a price high enough to reflect accurately the economic value of a marginal, or additional, barrel of oil (regardless of whether that marginal barrel came from inside or outside the U.S.). The overall cost of inefficiency has been estimated to have been somewhere between $0.5 and $3.5 billion annually.[10] Thus, a liberal estimate of inefficiency's cost could exceed a conservative estimate of equity's benefit, yielding a negative verdict with respect to the control program's net value. (Such comparisons of inefficiency costs and equity benefits are awkward because those who pay the inefficiency costs may not be the same folks as those who receive the equity benefits. But theoretically, elimination of inefficiency's costs would provide savings that could be transferred to those who, in the process, lose their equity benefits.)

D. Decontrol and Excess Profits Tax

Setting aside the problem of macroinstability, which at best could justify no more than a temporary regime of price controls, an ideal policy toward oil would address *both* efficiency and equity. Efficiency now requires that consumers pay a high price, one covering the high cost of producing an additional barrel of domestic oil or importing an additional barrel of for-

[7] K. J. Arrow and J. P. Kalt, "Why Oil Prices Should be Decontrolled," *Regulation* (Sept./Oct. 1979), pp. 13–17.

[8] *The Energy Fact Book, op. cit.,* p. 346.

[9] *Wall Street Journal,* April 14, 1981, pp. 1, 15.

[10] Arrow and Kalt, *op. cit.,* and Montgomery, *op. cit.*

eign oil. A free-market price would thus serve efficiency.

To meet the problem of equity without disturbing the free-market price, a tax on windfall profits would be appropriate.[11] If adroitly designed, such a tax would extract producer windfalls, or rents, without damaging production incentives. The revenues collected could be funneled into relief for the poor, or subsidies for energy research and development, or any other cause deemed worthy.[12]

As it turned out, policy developments moved in these directions, bringing free-market prices and a windfall tax. President Carter initiated price decontrol in 1978 and 1979. His program gradually reclassified old oil as new oil and at the same time gradually raised the ceiling on the price of new oil to meet the world price. October 1, 1981 was the date all controls were to end. That date was advanced several months, however, when Ronald Reagan, in one of his first acts as president, lifted the lid in late January 1981.

As for the windfall profits tax, it was passed at Carter's urging in 1980. The tax resulting was not on windfall profits per se. Rather, it was like an excise tax, with varying percentage rates applying to the *difference* between the former regulated prices and free-market prices.

[11] The free-market price plus windfall tax formula has long been recognized. For recent elaboration see Robert Stobaugh and Daniel Yergin, *Energy Future* (New York: Random House, 1979).

[12] Conservative economists do not see equity as any problem at all, or argue that attempts to deal with equity are inevitably too costly in stifling investment and risk-taking. David Hale, for instance, argues that a windfall tax on oil makes no more sense than a windfall tax on firewood (*Wall Street Journal*, February 13, 1980). A. A. Alchian warns, "If past earnings or wealth are *expropriated* by confiscatory taxation, then future investments that look profitable will be ignored, because investors will believe future profits also will be confiscated." Alchian, "Big Oil Profits and Massive Analytical Confusion," (Los Angeles: International Institute for Economic Research, 1981). Query: Were *past* earnings or wealth expropriated by either the price controls or windfall tax? Read on.

The highest tax rate was 70%, which essentially applied to "old" oil. The lowest rate was zero, which applied to certain newly discovered oil.[13]

The effects of decontrol-with-tax can be summarized under headings of (1) consumption, (2) production, and (3) profits.

1. *Consumption:* During controls, U.S. consumption of oil rose from 15.2 million barrels a day in 1971 to 18.8 million barrels a day in 1978 (the latter figure being an all-time record). Imports supplied the increase, leaping from 3.9 to 8.4 million barrels a day over the same period, (the latter figure amounting to a worrisome 44.4% of domestic consumption). Dramatic reversal followed decontrol in 1979, with consumption falling nearly 10% to 17.1 million barrels a day in 1980.[14] Imports dropped accordingly by amounts nearly matching the drop in consumption. Decontrol certainly helped these favorable developments. But decontrol cannot get all the credit, as the plunges were also propelled by general recession and by a trebling of the price of OPEC oil.

2. *Production:* Regarding domestic production, there is good news and bad news. The good news is that drilling activity went into a frenzy after decontrol. Drilling in 1981 was 40 per cent more intense than in 1978. The bad news is that, despite drilling more than 60,000 wells annually, the industry will *not* be able to increase oil production substantially because the amount of oil actually discovered per well is shrinking rapidly. Whereas in 1970 the industry found nearly 40 barrels of oil for every foot drilled, the industry found only 12 barrels per foot in 1979.[15] The finding rate may fall even further in the 1980s. Translated into annual flows of oil, U.S. production will apparently fall

[13] Stephen L. McDonald, "The Incidence and Effects of the Crude Oil Windfall Profit Tax," *Natural Resources Journal* (April 1981), pp. 331–339.

[14] *Wall Street Journal*, June 6, 1981, p. 25.

[15] *The Energy Fact Book, op. cit.*, p. 351, *Fortune,* Nov. 3, 1980, p. 89.

from 10.2 million barrels a day in 1979 to something in the neighborhood of 7.9 MBD in 1985 and 6.5 MBD in 1990.[16]

In other words, the higher prices wrought by decontrol cannot change geology, and U.S. geology, while fairly rich in unconventional sources of oil like oil shale, is growing poorer by the day in conventional, liquid crude oil. As of 1981, estimates of our remaining oil stood at about 110 billion barrels (27 billion in proved reserves and 83 billion in undiscovered reserves).[17] This is not very much. Even with parsimonious consumption, this will not be enough to get us much beyond the first decade of the next century.[18] Robert Baldwin, president of Gulf Oil Corp.'s refining and marketing unit put it in economic terms when he said that "if crude oil went to $100 a barrel, we couldn't arrest the decline rate."[19] At best then, decontrol has merely *curbed the decline* is conventional crude production. It has not worked wonders.

3. *Profits:* Oil industry profits were by no means paltry during the control period. Indeed, they rose fantastically. Whereas the oil and gas industry accounted for slightly more than 20% of all nonfinancial company profits during the uncontrolled mid-1960s, it garnered well over 30% during the controlled 1970s.[20] "The magnitude of the oil industry's growth in the share of total corporate profits is," according to *Business Week,* "mind-numbing."[21] Without the windfall profits tax, decontrol would have made the industry's profits even more mind-numbing, adding an estimated extra $1 *trillion* pretax dollars during the 1980s. After taxes, however, the decade's projected net is reduced as follows:[22]

$1,000 billion decontrol profit before taxes
 −227 billion windfall tax
 −552 billion other federal, state, and local taxes
 $ 221 billion producer's net profit from decontrol

Thus the windfall tax reduces the industry's profits substantially, but those profits are so big to begin with that they remain huge.

Of course the hope is that most of these immense profits will be invested in oil exploration and other energy development. And, as we have seen, early indications from drilling show movement in this direction. There is an additional use for those profits, however, one that deserves mention because it rouses the industry's critics. Many oil companies have used their new-found wealth to finance billion-dollar conglomerate acquisitions. Mobil bought Montgomery Ward. Exxon purchased Reliance Electric. Standard Oil of Ohio acquired Kennecott. Arco bought Anaconda, and so on.[23]

E. Summary on Oil

In retrospect, the switch from price floor to price ceiling was a temporary policy reaction. Given the rather abrupt switch from oil abundance to oil scarcity, and given the severity of the ensuing problems of stability and equity, the ceilings are understandable if not wholly justifiable. Awesome political pressures favored ceilings and nonprice rationing, pressures that even staunch friends of the free market could not rebuff. While the controls did serve the ends of stability and equity, they created inefficiencies. Domestic scarcity fostered control, but control aggravated that scarcity. Decontrol has now dissipated the inefficiencies, and new taxes have been introduced to handle the prob-

[16] Office of Technology Assessment, *World Petroleum Availability 1980–2000* (U.S. Congress, 1980), p. 36.
[17] *Wall Street Journal,* February 26, 1981, p. 4.
[18] Some well-reasoned forecasts are even bleaker. See, e.g., *Wall Street Journal,* February 3, 1981, p. 14.
[19] *Wall Street Journal,* July 8, 1980, p. 16.
[20] *Business Week,* June 1, 1981, p. 69.
[21] *Business Week,* August 18, 1980, p. 84.
[22] *Wall Street Journal,* April 3, 1980.
[23] For an interesting article on Getty Oil's free-spending ways, see *Business Week,* June 23, 1980, pp. 99, 102.

lem of equity. As for macroinstability, oil's contribution to the problem was temporary, so it is appropriate that for this purpose too the controls were temporary.

IV. Natural Gas Price Ceilings

A. Purpose

Firms in the natural gas industry are of three main types: (1) field producers who find and extract natural gas from the earth then sell it to pipelines; (2) pipelines who buy gas from field producers, transport it, and then sell to local distributors and very large end users like chemical plants; and (3) local distributors who buy from pipelines and sell to end users. Price regulation of the industry began with state and local public utility regulation of local gas distributors during the 1920s. Regulation spread to interstate pipelines when Congress passed the Natural Gas Act of 1938, giving the Federal Power Commission (FPC) authority to assure that pipeline prices were "just and reasonable." The theory in 1938 was that public utility regulation of local distributors would be worthless without additional public utility regulation of the pipelines supplying them. Finally, price regulation was applied at the field-production level during the 1950s by extension of essentially the same logic, even though market structure at production level was not anywhere near as monopolistic as it was at both pipeline and local distribution levels. Thus, in contrast to oil, wellhead price ceiling regulation of natural gas sprouted from public utility origins.

Although the Natural Gas Act of 1938 made no explicit provision for wellhead price regulation, the Supreme Court gave the Act that interpretation in *Phillips Petroleum Company* v. *Wisconsin et al.*, a famous case of 1954.[24] Phillips, a producer, hiked the wellhead price of its natural gas, inciting protests from the state of Wisconsin and several major gas-consuming cities. The Federal Power Commission ruled that it lacked jurisdiction over Phillips. But on appeal the Supreme Court held otherwise, stating its belief that "legislative history indicates a congressional intent to give the Commission jurisdiction over the rates of all wholesales of natural gas in interstate commerce, whether by a pipeline company or not and whether occurring before, during, or after transmission by an interstate pipeline company." So saying, the Court instructed the FPC to see to it that wellhead prices of natural gas sold in interstate commerce were "just and reasonable." This authority passed to the Federal Energy Regulatory Commission in 1977 when bureaucratic shuffling revamped the FPC.

B. Character of the Regulation

1. PRICE LEVELS

The FPC began wellhead price regulation on an individual, case-by-case basis, patterned on the model of traditional public utility regulation. However, two terribly sticky problems bogged down the Commission.

First, the FPC had a devil of a time determining producers' costs. A key problem here stemmed from the fact that much gas is found and produced in conjunction with oil, meaning that the costs of finding and producing gas cannot easily be separated from the costs incurred for oil. Even if a well produces *only* gas, the exploration activities leading to that well often lead to the discovery and development of wells producing oil.[25]

Second, there were just too many producers

---

[24] *Phillips Petroleum Company* v. *Wisconsin et al.*, 342 U.S. 672 (1954).

[25] On other cost problems see Thomas R. Stauffer, "Liquified and Synthetic Natural Gas—Regulation Chooses the Expensive Solutions," in Caves and Roberts (eds.), *Regulating the Product* (Cambridge: Ballinger Publishing Co., 1975), 171–198.

to permit a case-by-case approach. Within six years after the *Phillips* opinion the Commission faced a backlog of 3278 producer rate filings needing decisions. Estimating that it would take eighty years to process these pending cases individually, the Commission shifted to area rate making in 1960. By this approach, wells in the U.S. were assigned to one of twenty-three geographic areas, and uniform rates were to be set for all the wells in a given area. This, too, proved too cumbersome, however. In 1974, after *fourteen years* of area rate-making, the Commission had completed rate proceedings on less than half of the twenty-three geographic areas. Thus the Commission eventually resorted to nationwide pricing beginning in 1974.[26] Such pricing could not, needless to say, be cost-based.

The prices actually arrived at by these procedures reflected the reasoning behind the "old" and "new" prices discussed previously for oil. Beginning in the 1960s with a simple two-tier system for gas from the Permian Basin Area, the Commission adopted a multi-tier system when shifting to the nationwide approach in the mid-1970s. In 1978, for instance, price per thousand cubic feet ranged from 29.5 cents for the oldest gas to $1.42 for the newest gas, with steps of 52 cents and 93 cents in between. This structure of prices suggests to us that *average* wellhead price was rising over time, and indeed it was. During the 1960s, average wellhead price rose slightly from 14.0 to 16.7 cents per thousand cubic feet. During the 1970s, average wellhead price jumped sharply from 17.1 to 114.4 cents per thousand cubic feet.[27] Consumers paid this average price instead of the higher marginal, or top-tier price, because distribution systems followed an averaging (or "roll-in") formula.

2. RATIONING

Despite the 1970s' price escalation, shortages developed. Official rationing ensued. The FPC's steps toward rationing were highlighted by Order 467–B of March, 1973. This order specified service priorities, indicating a nine category sequence that customer curtailments should follow. Those first to be cut off were buyers consuming more than 10,000 thousand cubic feet per day whose contracts provided "interruptible" service and whose energy requirements could be met by alternative fuels. Those last to be cut off were residential buyers and small commercial buyers.

These priorities reflected the regulators' judgment of who valued gas most highly. For example, those who could not readily switch to alternative fuels presumably valued gas very highly, so they were given relatively high priorities. This made sense because it tried to emulate free-market allocation based on price. But it did not silence critics of controls who argued that it would be best if the free market actually did the allocating.[28]

C. *Effects of Gas Price Ceilings*

With wellhead prices held artificially low, consumers paid less for natural gas than otherwise. One of the more reasonable estimates of this equity effect indicates a transfer from producers to consumers of about $3 billion annually during the mid-1970s.[29] Attractive though this number might be, there is a serious "catch." This benefit accrued only to those folks actually able to buy natural gas. As just noted, many eager buyers were denied gas because of severe shortages, and these buyers suffered

---

[26] Ronald Braeutigam, "An Examination of Regulation in the Natural Gas Industry," in *Study on Federal Regulation*, Appendix to Vol. VI, U.S. Senate, Committee on Governmental Affairs (December 1978), pp. 671–673.

[27] *The Energy Fact Book, op. cit.*, p. 490.

[28] Braeutigam, *op. cit.*, p. 687.

[29] Ibid., p. 699.

from the necessity of having to pay higher prices than otherwise for alternative fuels. Whether consumer losses from regulation exceeded consumer gains is impossible to say. At least one estimate, however, yields a negative balance.[30]

Development of the shortage, as estimated by James Griffin and Henry Steele, is shown in Figure 19–4. Wellhead price was held down prior to 1971, but not so low as to create deficits. Productive capacity began to decline in 1968, however, and by 1971 demand had overtaken supply. Curtailments of several trillion cubic feet followed, intermittently closing factories and frightening people dependent on gas in the colder parts of the country, particularly New England and the Midwest. Figure 19–4 indicates that the Federal Power Commission tried to alleviate the shortages by raising wellhead prices appreciably in the late 1970s. And indeed, the price hikes nearly doubled drilling activity, from 7 thousand gas wells in 1974 to 13 thousand in 1978. But normal delays in bringing the newly discovered gas on line and declining discovery rates per foot drilled stood in the way of quick relief.

Complexities prevent a precise estimate of the efficiency losses associated with the shortages, but they were probably substantial, perhaps even greater than the equity gains. These ominous inefficiencies led Ronald Braeutigam to conclude, "Even if one includes income redistribution as a benefit, it is not clear that the

[30] Paul W. MacAvoy and Robert S. Pindyck, *Price Controls and the Natural Gas Shortage* (Washington, D.C.: American Enterprise Institute, 1975), pp. 54–55.

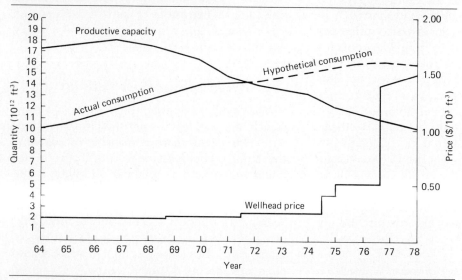

Figure 19–4.   Natural Gas Wellhead Prices, Demand, and Productive Capacity Under FPC Regulation. Estimates of Productive Capacity Are Based on a Reserves-to-Production Ratio of 11 Prior to 1972

Source: J. M. Griffin and H. B. Steele, *Energy Economics and Policy* (New York: Academic Press, 1980), p. 272.

economic case for regulation is strong or even marginal. The case for regulation is supportable only if we believe that income is in fact redistributed in a desirable way and that efficiency in resource allocation is not as important."[31]

D. Decontrol

The political fight over wellhead price decontrol was one of the hardest fought in congressional history, with representatives of consuming states battling those of producing states. Those opposed to decontrol argued that the shortage was artificially contrived, that the industry was not sufficiently competitive to assure consumers a fair shake under decontrol, and that gas supply was in any case price inelastic.[32] Those arguing in favor of deregulation contended that the shortage was a direct and natural consequence of control, that the industry was highly competitive, and that supply would gush with free-market prices.[33]

The truth probably lies somewhere between these extremes, and the decontrol legislation that actually emerged in 1978 represents a compromise. The Natural Gas Policy Act of 1978 provides complete decontrol of "new" gas more than 15,000 feet deep and phased decontrol of most other gas continuing until 1985. Just before decontrol on January 1, 1985, the average price of gas is supposed to be $2.97 per thousand cubic feet. No windfall profits tax was included in the package.

Early indications are that the first stages of decontrol have stimulated seismic work and drilling, especially in strata below 15,000 feet.

But it is still too early to tell the consequences for gas reserves and production.[34] Moreover, present decontrol policy has its problems. Most importantly, the price increases scheduled by decontrol are not great enough to put natural gas on a par with oil at time of full decontrol on January 1, 1985. As this is written (in 1982), gas's pre-1985 price of $2.97 is only half the *current* price of oil in energy equivalent. It now appears that gas prices will therefore skyrocket in 1985 unless the law is changed. Suggested changes call for immediate or accelerated decontrol. The argument favoring such changes is essentially this: Given our commitment to decontrol, the only remaining question is *how* we achieve that end. Immediate or hastened decontrol would be easier on the economy than postponed decontrol.[35] If Congress buys the argument, wellhead price lids could well be lifted earlier than presently expected.

Summary

Economic regulation of oil and natural gas at wellhead level divides into three episodes: (1) price floor regulation of oil from 1934 to 1971, (2) price ceiling regulation of oil from 1971 to 1981, and (3) price ceiling regulation of natural gas from 1954 to 1985 (or thereabouts). These experiences differ in (a) regulation's main purposes, (b) its major characteristics, (c) its good and bad economic effects, and (d) recent deregulation.

1. *Oil Price Floors:* Stability and conservation were the chief targets of oil price supports, supplemented by goals of protection and prosperity for domestic oil producers. History seemed to verify the need for such regulation when discovery of the immense East Texas Field and the Great Depression conspired to

---

[31] Braeutigam, *op. cit.*, p. 700.

[32] U.S. Congress, House, Subcommittee on Oversight and Investigations of the Committee on Interstate and Foreign Commerce, *Federal Regulation and Regulatory Reform* (October 1976), pp. 379–420.

[33] On the question of competition see Joseph P. Mulholland, *Economic Structure and Behavior in the Natural Gas Production Industry* (Federal Trade Commission Staff Report 1979) and John W. Wilson, *op. cit.*

[34] *Wall Street Journal*, March 17, 1981, pp. 1, 17.

[35] *Business Week*, September 28, 1981, pp. 123–127; *Fortune*, October 19, 1981, pp. 153–168.

cause prices to plummet. The "law of capture" also contributed.

Official cartelization characterized these regulations. Prices were supported and stabilized by supply curtailments that fluctuated with demand. This "prorationing" was the work of state officials who were supported by several federal measures, the most important of which was an import quota. The program brought stability and aided producers, but did so very inefficiently and at great cost to consumers. In the end the program fizzled out as the key condition underlying it—domestic oil abundance—evaporated during the late 1960s.

2. *Oil Price Ceilings:* As the U.S. and the rest of the industrialized world grew increasingly dependent on OPEC oil during the early 1970s, OPEC exploited that dependence with huge price increases. The consequences were inflationary shock for all consumers and massive windfall profits for domestic producers. Thus in the name of stability and equity, the federal government instituted price ceilings on domestic production, ceilings that were a natural outgrowth of the general wage-price control policy existing at the time. The Federal Energy Administration was the main agency involved.

Different prices for "old" and "new" oil were deemed appropriate on the theory that they would prevent windfalls on "old" oil while encouraging production of "new" oil. Moreover, allocation became an administrative chore once price no longer did the rationing.

Although the causes of stability and equity were served, there were large costs in inefficiency. Domestic production may have suffered. And consumption most certainly ballooned, something which aggravated our dependency on imports. These burdens were temporary, however, because the program was, as intended, temporary. Decontrol reduced the inefficiencies by slowing the decline in domestic production and curbing consumption. The problem of equity has been turned over to a windfall profits tax.

3. *Natural Gas:* Shortages and rationing also accompanied wellhead price ceilings on natural gas. Originating in 1954 under the Supreme Court's interpretation of the Natural Gas Act of 1938, these price ceilings spread from the public utility regulation of other segments of the industry.

The Federal Power Commission, however, could not apply the public utility approach. It stumbled over cost complexities and producer hordes. After severe shortages appeared in the early 1970s, the Commission abandoned cost-based pricing altogether and converted to nationwide rates that rose by steps on newer and newer gas. Rationing also proved necessary. The resulting inefficiencies may have been offset by consumer gains in equity, but this is not certain. Deregulation in natural gas is strung out until 1985, but the Reagan administration may accelerate the schedule.

Questions and Exercises for Chapter 19

1. Explain with the aid of diagrams why a price floor might be considered "equitable" to producers but a price ceiling "equitable" to consumers.

2. Is the allocation inefficiency associated with a price floor the same or different than the allocation inefficiency associated with a price ceiling? Explain.

3. Explain how the allowable production capacity under prorationing would be affected by (a) a drop in demand, (b) an increase in exempt production, and (c) a drop in imported oil.

4. Compare and contrast the "stability" rationales of the 1930s and 1970s.

5. What parallels and differences do you see in prorationing on the one hand and entitlements plus supply allocations on the other? Discuss in the context of Figure 19–1.

6. Compare and contrast two-tier price controls with *no* controls plus a windfall profits tax in (a) efficiency and (b) equity.

7. Why did the oil price controls of the 1970s increase consumption and what supply source filled the demand?

8. Why, despite good intentions of aiding consumers with a price ceiling, might many consumers be harmed rather than helped by it?

9. What difficulties did the FPC encounter while trying to regulate the field price of natural gas?

10. What have been the results of decontrol in oil? In gas?

Part V

Social Regulation

"Remember the good old days when we only had to smoke a few cigarettes and eat saccharin?"

Source: Mike Peters, Dayton, Ohio, *Daily News*

Chapter 20

Safety, Health, and Pollution Regulation: An Overview

I like life better than figs.
—William Shakespeare

Regulations concerning safety, health, and pollution date back to ancient times. Their appearance in the U.S. originated in the last century with state and local laws. Regulation spread to the federal level with the Tea Importation Act of 1897 and the Food and Drug Act of 1906. Further developments followed, but none as earthshaking as the explosion of "social" regulations in the 1960s and 1970s. That outburst had its heroes (e.g., Ralph Nader) and spectacular events (e.g., Earth Day 1970), but most importantly it produced reams of new legislation with titles like:

- 1966—Highway Safety Act
- 1970—Clean Air Act Amendments
- 1970—Occupational Safety and Health Act
- 1972—Consumer Product Safety Act
- 1972—Water Pollution Control Act Amendments

The powers of old agencies were abruptly expanded and new agencies were created.

The words "safety," "health," and "pollution" all relate to *harmful risk*, but they convey different meanings. "Safety" often refers only to protection against violent accidents, such as auto crashes or workplace injuries. "Health" usually indicates security against risk of disease, infirmity, or death as might result, for example, from exposure to carcinogenic gases or tainted food. "Pollution" refers to assaults on the environment generally. Its scope of reference thus includes amenity losses, property damage, and injury to nonhuman creatures as well as threats to human safety (as when smog reduces pilot visibility) and threats to human health (as when carbon monoxide emissions trigger angina attacks). To simplify matters we shall often use "safety" and "health" interchangeably but let "pollution" stand alone.

Three subsequent chapters discuss the details of regulation in three areas:

21. Consumer safety and health, as enforced by the Food & Drug Administration (FDA), National Highway Traffic Safety Administration (NHTSA), and Consumer Product Safety Commission (CPSC).
22. Labor safety and health, as enforced by the

Occupational Safety and Health Administration (OSHA).

23. Environmental protection, as enforced by the Environmental Protection Agency (EPA).

This chapter introduces these others with several preliminaries. First, we must recognize that the free market is capable of handling harmful risk to some degree. Second, we identify problems with the free market's provision of safety and environmental protection. The main message is that, for various reasons, the free market provides *too little* safety and environmental protection. Third, we specify policy ideals as derived from benefit-cost analysis. Finally, we outline the main policy method currently used to correct the market's failures—a method broadly referred to as "regulation" or "command and control" but more revealingly described as "standard setting and enforcement." Standards set the aim of policy and divide the critics. Some say the standards are too lenient. Others claim the standards are too harsh, providing *too much* safety and environmental protection. These latter critics have been winning most of the arguments lately. Enforcement methods also attract rebuke, so they too attract our attention.

I. Free Market Provision of Safety and Environmental Cleanliness

Setting aside all considerations of morality and equity, the market can handle the problem of risk under ideal circumstances. The two main circumstances that must hold are (1) that *the risk be known* to those in danger, and (2) that *the risk be voluntarily accepted.* When risks are known and voluntarily accepted, a properly functioning free market will make adjustments in prices and quantities such that, given people's tastes and preferences, the right amounts of risk and risk prevention will be provided.

A. Safety

Because people other than Shakespeare "like life better than figs," they typically shy away from risky, unsafe products and occupations (thereby voluntarily acting on their knowledge). However, a moment's reflection reveals that people do *not* demand absolute safety. They willingly accept the risk of dreadful injury, disease, and even death, as indicated by all sorts of everyday behavior—smoking, driving without seat belts, hang gliding, whatever. People are especially willing to accept risks when they are fully informed about the potential costs of hazards and they are compensated for them monetarily either by lower prices for hazardous products or higher wages for hazardous employment, as compared with safer alternatives.

The free market's handling of risk that is both known and voluntarily accepted is illustrated in Figure 20–1, which assumes perfect competition. In part (a) of Figure 20–1, dealing with **consumer products,** two versions of the same product, one "safe" and one "risky," generate two different demands, D_{safe} and D_{risky}. Demand for the risky version is less than demand for the safe version because of risk aversion. Nevertheless, the market could accommodate both demands by compensating those who choose the risky version with a lower price P_r, as compared to the price of the safer alternative, P_s.

In part (b) of Figure 20–1, illustrating the **labor market,** workers would not offer their labor services in the risky job except at a higher wage rate than the safer alternative, with the result that labor supply S_{risky} lies above supply curve S_{safe}. Given the demand for labor, D, equilibrium wage for risky work would be W_r, which is higher than that for safe work, W_s.

Figure 20–1. Free-Market Adjustment for Risk

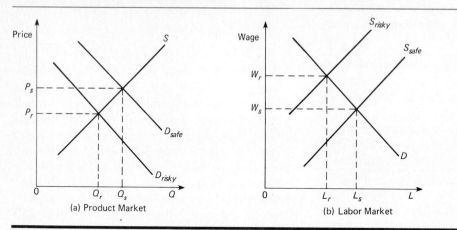

(a) Product Market   (b) Labor Market

Empirical research has verified the payment of wage premiums for high-risk occupations. Estimates of the wage premium vary, however. It ranges from a few hundred dollars per year to several thousand dollars per year for each added death per 1,000 workers annually.[1]

Indeed, under ideal theoretical circumstances, the market does more than take risk into account, it provides the optimal amount of risk, given people's preferences. The ideal market is, in other words, *efficient*.[2] In the case of *labor safety*, the wage premium for risky work acts as an inducement for the employer to provide some job safety. An employer willingly incurs costs for safety because that safety lowers the risk premium he must pay to attract workers. The added costs of added safety are accepted as long as they are offset by greater wage savings, which wage reductions measure the benefits of the added safety to workers. Once the added costs of safety exceed the wage-saving benefits, risk reduction stops.

In sum, the efficiency of the ideal market lies in its nice balance of risk and safety. There is neither too much risk (too little safety) nor too much safety (too little risk), as measured by economic benefits and costs.

B. Pollution

Economic theory can crank out similar conclusions for the problem of pollution.[3] Unfortunately, an explanation of this is more difficult than the explanation for safety, so we can do no more here than briefly state some generalities.

First, it must be appreciated that pollution abatement entails costs as well as benefits. Cleaning up the environment requires man-

---

[1] R. Thaler and S. Rosen, "The Value of Saving a Life," in N. E. Terleckyz (ed.), *Household Production and Consumption* (New York: National Bureau of Economic Research, 1976); W. K. Viscusi, "Labor Market Valuations of Life and Limb: Empirical Evidence and Policy Implications," *Public Policy* (Summer 1978), pp. 359–386.

[2] W. Y. Oi, "The Economics of Product Safety," *Bell Journal of Economics* (Spring 1973), pp. 3–28; T. R. Saving, "Welfare Aspects of Mandated Quality," in R. F. Lanzillotti (ed.), *Economic Effects of Government-Mandated Costs* (Gainesville: University Presses of Florida, 1978), pp. 157–185.

[3] R. H. Coase, "The Problem of Social Cost," *Journal of Law and Economics* (October 1960), pp. 1–44.

power, materials, and machinery—resources that could be used to produce other goods and services. Thus, getting *perfectly* clean is not necessarily desirable. Stated differently, cleanliness is not so much a technical problem as it is an economic problem. Technically, the air in Los Angeles could be purified immediately if all autos were abandoned and factories were closed, but the economic costs of these measures apparently exceed the benefits of clean air because people have not carried them out.

Second, it has been argued that, under ideal circumstances, the free market could handle pollution because those who demand cleanliness, call them pollutees, could pay polluters not to pollute. Pollutees would be willing to pay amounts reflecting the benefits they gain from cleanliness. And polluters would be willing to clean up as long as their cleaning costs were less than the payments they received from pollutees. Put on a personal level, you would be willing to pay your neighbor not to dump his trash on your property, a payment your neighbor accepts insofar as his costs of cleanliness are compensated.

Third, the ideal market principles outlined above can yield efficient results for pollution. That is to say, clean up occurs as long as benefits exceed costs. Once costs exceed benefits, however, no further cleanliness is provided because pollutees will not cover the polluters' costs of abatement. It can even be argued that a reversal of property rights, such that the polluters would then have to pay the pollutees for permission to pollute, would not affect the resulting mix of cleanliness and dirtiness. But this argument is open to serious question.[4] Indeed, as suggested by the very limited applicability of the example of your neighbor's trash, the whole theory of the free market's handling of

pollution is open to very serious question. It is, in short, more a fantasy than a theory.

II. Shortcomings in the Market: Rationales for Government Intervention

Upon leaving the pleasant world of theory and entering the harsh world of reality, we find market imperfections and failures that may warrant government intervention. In particular, the two key conditions for free-market proficiency—(1) full knowledge of risks, and (2) voluntary exposure to risk—often do not hold. Without them, the market yields inefficient results, namely, too much risk. Moreover, aside from concerns for economic efficiency, society often seems to think that the free market's results are too risky in light of certain *non*economic value judgments—morality and equity in particular. Thus we shall review four reasons for government policy—(1) morality, (2) equity, (3) ignorance, and (4) externalities causing involuntary risk exposure. Each is covered as it pertains first to safety and health and then to pollution.

A. Safety and Health: Market Shortcomings

1. MORALITY
Economic theory assumes that "optimal allocation of resources" and "consumer sovereignty" are society's supreme values, the ultimate criteria by which to judge good and bad. As we have seen repeatedly, however, folks often give higher rank to other considerations. This is especially true in matters of life and death, where notions of morality frequently overwhelm economic criteria. This seems to be a major explanation for many safety regulations that do nothing but protect individuals from

[4] Mark Kelman, "Consumption Theory, Production Theory, and Ideology in the Coase Theorem," *Southern California Law Review* (March 1979), pp. 669–698.

themselves. Motorcycle helmet laws and the provision of elaborate barriers to prevent people from jumping off bridges are examples.[5] Regarding occupational safety and health, Representative Phillip Burton once expressed the belief that all American workers have the *"inalienable right* to earn their living free from the ravages of job-caused death, disease, and injury."[6] Whether all American workers would like to see the prices of all products rise as a consequence of such a risk-free environment is another issue. Apparently some would reject economic trade-offs here as legitimate.

2. EQUITY

The free market handles risk by pricing risky products lower and risky jobs higher than safer alternatives. This means that the distribution of risk will be tilted unfavorably against low-income people as they are pushed by force of frail financial circumstances into buying riskier products and working in riskier jobs. In other words, risk acceptance in the ideal free market is more than merely a matter of taste, it is also a matter of income distribution. And the results may be considered inequitable.

Equity may even be a problem where income distribution is irrelevant. All meat eaters benefit, for example, when cattlemen use diethylstilbestrol (DES) to boost the livestock industry's productivity and thereby lower beef prices 3% or so. However, the use of DES also raises the risk of cancer to consumers, a risk that horribly collects its due from only a relatively few families despite the widespread benefits bestowed in the bargain. Millions gain a little benefit and run a little risk, but only a

few are actually forced to pay the dreadful costs of contracting cancer. Many folks might think that these are serious mismatches of getting and deserving, that the imbalances are unfair or inequitable to the few unlucky souls who encounter the Grim Reaper earlier than expected.

3. IGNORANCE

The foregoing value judgments might be dismissed as maudlin or irrelevant. However, the problem of ignorance is not so easily dismissed. Even though press, TV, radio, and government agencies pour out massive amounts of information concerning product hazards, the public remains uninformed. Test yourself. As one who is above-average in attentiveness and intelligence, how much do you know about diethylstilbestrol, Red Dye No. 2, saccharin, and zirconium, to name just a few substances given ample recent press coverage. Could you compute the marginal cost of added risk from using products laced with these chemicals? Are you even aware of which products formerly contained them? Probably not.

If one assumes that the experts know the risks, there is in other words still the problem of *informing* consumers and workers. As A. Nichols and R. Zeckhauser point out, "This information must be available, transmitted to the affected parties, and understood."[7] Yet the free market often falls short on all three counts. Those with most of the information—namely producers and employers—have little incentive to make such information available because it could damage their marketing or hiring prospects. Once available, transmission becomes a problem because of imperfections in the markets for information. Buyers of information are necessarily uninformed, and sellers' incentives suffer from piracy of their information by word of mouth. Finally, there is a problem of under-

[5] Tibor Scitovsky, *The Joyless Economy* (New York: Oxford University Press, 1976), Chapter 10.

[6] Quoted by A. Nichols and R. Zeckhauser, "OSHA after a Decade: A Time for Reason," in L. W. Weiss and M. W. Klass (eds.) *Case Studies in Regulation: Revolution and Reform* (Boston: Little, Brown & Co., 1981), p. 212. (emphasis added).

[7] Ibid., p. 207.

standing once the problems of availability and transmission are whipped. People have difficulty processing information about complex technical matters, about small probabilities, and about myriads of things, all of which characterize consumer and worker safety and health.

Going beyond risk, there is the additional problem of uncertainty. **Risk** simply refers to a situation in which sufficient statistical evidence exists to allow experts to predict the probability that a particular event will occur. Thus experts tell us that failure to wear seat belts more than doubles frequency of death in auto accidents. Similarly, fatal blood clots strike women who use "The Pill" at a rate of about 30/1,000,000, whereas nonusers run a considerably lower risk of 5/1,000,000. As with the flip of a coin, the outcome in any particular instance of auto wreck or "Pill" use is unknown, but its *probability* is known.

In contrast, **uncertainty** is a black abyss. The statistical *probabilities are unknown* as well as the particular outcomes. Thus experts may be able to establish a causal link between a hazard and bodily harm, but the linkage may elude numerical expression of risk:

> Giving mice a massive exposure to a chemical and observing that in a short period of time the mice develop cancer establishes that a substance is carcinogenic. It does not establish the extent to which the carcinogenic effect depends on dosage, the type of tissue exposed, the method of exposure, and the other features of the environment in which the dosage was administered. One may conclude that the experimental results make it more likely that the same substance in dosages comparable to human exposure levels causes human cancer, but the extent to which the likelihood has been increased is not even roughly quantifiable.[8]

[8] N. W. Cornell, R. G. Noll, and B. Weingast, "Safety Regulation," in Owen and Schultze (eds.) *Setting National Priorities* (Washington D.C.: Brookings Institution, 1976), p. 468.

Uncertainty not only baffles consumers, it also befuddles experts, as indicated by the endless string of health and safety experts who appear before Congress every year with testimony that takes the form of "Well, on the one hand . . . but then, on the other hand. . . ." Senator Muskie expressed everyone's frustration with this when, after listening to a lot of "one hand . . . other hand" testimony, he quipped, "What I need is some one-armed scientists."

N. W. Cornell, R. G. Noll, and B. Weingast argue that uncertainty engenders a political demand for public controls more stringent than would otherwise be justified. They argue in particular that we should "minimax regret" by adopting "strategies that avoid the worst logically possible outcomes, thereby minimizing the maximum possible loss, no matter what the likelihood that the maximum loss will actually occur."[9]

4. INVOLUNTARY RISK EXPOSURE, OR EXTERNALITIES

All of the foregoing considerations relate to risks to which individuals expose *themselves* in the course of consumption or employment. Morality, equity, and ignorance may thus persuade some folks that government regulation is needed to protect people from *voluntary* exposure to hazard. But there is an added flaw in the market system, namely, externalities, or adverse third party effects, which impose risks on people involuntarily.

For an example from consumer product safety, Hot Rod Charlie may willingly buy and drive a cheap car with faulty brakes and flimsy tires (perhaps even reveling in its risky prospects), but the car poses a hazard to *other* people traveling the same roads as Charlie. Similarly, some people may willingly save a few cents by purchasing soda pop in bottles susceptible to explosion, and the market could fill their

[9] Ibid., p. 469.

needs. However, what about those who want nothing to do with flying glass? They are exposed to risk when searching grocery shelves for safer brands. The free market thus yields less than satisfactory results, a conclusion equally applicable to occupational safety and health.

Aside from the *physical* externalities just alluded to, there is the further problem of *financial* externalities. The *costs* of these accidents and illnesses are not always confined to the individual consumer or worker but also inflicted on society at large. As A. Nichols and R. Zeckhauser explain with respect to occupational safety and health:

> The family of a worker killed on the job, for example, is likely to qualify for survivor benefits under Social Security. More generally, the whole medical care system is laced with subsidies, so that when a worker seeks medical care, a substantial portion of the cost is borne by taxpayers as a whole. The retired worker who develops cancer as a result of earlier occupational exposures to a carcinogenic chemical, for example, is likely to have his medical bills paid by Medicare.[10]

In short, whenever there are physical or financial externalities, the uninhibited market system tends to yield too much risk because transacting parties do not confront the full gravity of their acts.

B. Pollution: Market Shortcomings

The foregoing topic titles may be recycled to outline the market's ineptitude in handling pollution.

1. MORALITY

It can be argued that the market system cannot adequately protect the environment because the market system serves only *human* interests. The well-being of grizzly bears,

brown pelicans, and redwood trees is thus given no account whatever by the market except insofar as that well-being can be marketed to humans. Yet by the ethics of many environmentalists, nature's creatures ought to be protected by further rights that only the legal system can provide. Lest this notion seem utterly bizarre, it may be recalled that once upon a time slaves were, like redwoods, subhuman market merchandise unprotected by today's ethics and laws. Moreover, it has been argued before the Supreme Court that trees and rivers should have legal "standing," just as other inanimate objects (ships and corporations) already have "standing."[11]

2. EQUITY

Although the hazards and costs of pollution are not distributed equally among society's members, the main problem of equity in this context is not one of present-day distribution. Rather, it is a problem of equity and fairness to future generations who obviously lose as species of flora and fauna are exterminated, as lakes are killed by eutrophication, and as soils are contaminated by toxic wastes. To be sure, the market takes the future into account (otherwise no buildings would ever be erected). But the future is "discounted," with the result that the present generation is favored at the expense of future generations. In the eyes of many environmentalists, "the standard technique of 'discounting' the future with a negative exponential function lays waste to the real future."[12] The implication is, then, that the market slights future generations in the limited extent to

[10] Nichols and Zeckhauser, *op. cit.*, p. 208.

[11] For more on this see, e.g., Aldo Leopold, *A Sand County Almanac* (New York: Oxford University Press, 1949), pp. 201–226; Christopher D. Stone, *Should Trees Have Standing?* (Los Angeles: William Kaufmann, Inc., 1974); and almost any issue of the scholarly journal *Environmental Ethics*.

[12] Garrett Hardin, "Dr. Pangloss Meets Cassandra," *The New Republic* (October 28, 1981), p. 34.

which environmental resources are pre-served.[13]

3. IGNORANCE

To what extent is acid rain caused by sulfur dioxide emissions from coal-fired electric power plants? How far can the sulfur dioxide be carried by the weather? Is the atmosphere's rising carbon dioxide content causing a dangerous "greenhouse" effect? The answers to these and countless other environmental questions are unknown, illustrating that the problem of igno-rance has scope beyond product and occupa-tional safety and health.

4. EXTERNALITIES OR INVOLUNTARY RISK

To economists, the free market's main flaw in causing pollution is externalities. As ex-plained earlier on pages 29 and 30, the problem arises because producers do not themselves pay the costs of disposing of their wastes cleanly. Rather, they impose these costs on *others* by fouling air, water, and land with their filth. Be-cause these costs are external to the firm, they are called *external costs*. Such external costs arise from consumption as well as production, illustrated best perhaps by automobile pollu-tion or pop bottle litter. The free market gives polluters a free ride via externalities. And just as you would take advantage of free rides in an amusement park, so too polluters take ad-vantage of their free ride. The result is more pollution than economically warranted—misal-location.

Lest you doubt that pollution actually creates external costs, stop and reflect. Think of the added laundry bills borne by people living around smoky steel mills. Think of crop dam-age, houses being painted every five years in-stead of ten, days of labor lost to bronchitis or early death, medical expenses, dead fish, and so on. Tens of billions of dollars are involved annually.

The problem of externalities can be viewed as resulting from poorly defined property rights. Neighbors solve their weekly trash prob-lem by respecting each others' property rights. But no one owns our clean air or water, they are *common property resources*. As a result there is no price placed on them, no market mechanism to limit and ration their use effi-ciently. As Larry Ruff puts it:

> Clean air, clean water, wilderness areas, and the earth's ozone layer are resources that provide na-ture and human society with a whole array of indispensable services, supporting recreation, in-dustry, agriculture, health, and the very life-sustaining processes of the earth. When human society makes few demands on these resources, the supply is adequate for all. But as human num-bers, concentrations, and activities grow, these demands begin to compete and interfere with one another, subjecting the environmental re-sources to more demands than they can meet. For most valuable resources, such conflicts are mediated by supply and demand in a market. *But for most of the resources affected by pollution, no natural markets exist and the market failure is total.*[14]

If we ask not why pollution occurs, but rather why pollution, once out there, is not cleaned up by market processes, we have still another way of looking at the problem. Clean air and water are *public goods*, provision of which, like national defense, benefits all simultaneously. As pointed out previously on pages 30–31, collec-tive, governmental action is often necessary to provide such public goods.

---

[13] Talbot Page, *Conservation and Economic Efficiency* (Baltimore: The Johns Hopkins University Press, 1977). See also R. C. D'Arge, W. D. Schulze, and D. S. Brookshire, "Carbon Dioxide and Intergenerational Choice," *American Economic Review* (May 1982), pp. 251–256.

[14] Larry E. Ruff, "Federal Environmental Regulation," in Weiss and Klass, *op. cit,* p. 236. (Emphasis added.)

III. The Goal of Government Intervention: Efficiency?

A. Benefit-Cost Analysis

In light of the foregoing analysis, there are several possible goals for government intervention in these areas of safety, health, and pollution. In the past, ill-defined goals relating to morality, equity, and health generally held sway. Preambles to legislation have touted such aims as "fishable, swimable rivers" and employee protection against "material impairment of health or functional capacity" without substantial regard for the costs of control.

Now, however, after the heavy costs of control have become apparent with a decade of implementation efforts, goals have shifted somewhat toward efficiency as guided by benefit-cost analysis, especially since Ronald Reagan became president. His Executive Order 12291 of February 1981 directed regulatory agencies in the executive branch (like EPA and OSHA)

to demonstrate, to the extent permitted by statutory laws, that the potential benefits of their major regulatory proposals outweigh the potential costs. As we shall see, some agency statutes can be construed as prohibiting benefit-cost analysis, so the Order is less earthshaking than it might appear. Still, it represents a major change over former procedures.

The basic economics of this objective are sketched in Figure 20–2, which refers to pollution but could equally well refer to safety and health with an appropriate change of labels. The horizontal axis ranges between two origins, one representing perfect dirtiness, the other perfect cleanliness. Society must obviously be at some point on that axis. At any such point, the marginal cost of pollution and the marginal cost of pollution abatement are measured vertically. For example, at dirty origin O, the marginal cost of pollution is very high while the marginal cost of abatement is zero. With market failure and no government intervention, society ends up somewhere close to the dirty

Figure 20–2.   Efficiency in Pollution

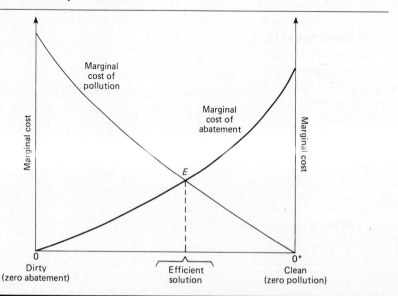

origin. Moving from dirtiness toward cleanliness under the press of government policy, the marginal cost of pollution falls and the marginal cost of abatement rises. How far toward cleanliness should we go? If we went all the way to O^*, the marginal costs of abatement would be very high relative to the reduction in pollution costs obtained. The efficient solution thus falls short of perfect cleanliness; it occurs where the marginal cost of abatement equals the marginal cost of pollution.

In terms of benefit-cost, the *benefits* of abatement are the *reduced costs* of pollution while the *costs* are the *increased costs* of abatement. The negatively sloped curve thus depicts the benefits and the positively sloped curve depicts the costs. Efficiency occurs where they cross at E. Indeed, *if* there were an ideal market for environmental cleanliness, the negatively sloped curve would reflect demand for cleanliness and the positively sloped curve would reflect supply. Their intersection at E would be the equilibrium and efficient solution. To the left of that point not enough cleanliness is provided; to the right too much is.[15]

Conceptually, if Figure 20–2 were referring to safety, the O origin could reflect extreme danger; the O^* origin could depict perfect safety. The negatively sloped curve would then depict the marginal cost of risk and the positively sloped curve would then represent the marginal cost of risk reduction. Accordingly, the benefits and costs of moving toward safety would meet at efficient solution E.

However attractive this efficiency objective might be, there are serious hurdles to its practical application. Certainly the most sensational of these practical problems is the problem of finding a dollar value for the human lives saved by safety, health, and pollution control. Some people believe that putting a dollar value on human lives is impossible or morally repugnant. Others, mainly economists, reply that dollar values are placed on human lives all the time—either explicitly or implicitly, usually implicitly, when communities buy expensive fleets of ambulances, when the airforce spends $4 million per life saved to equip fighter jets with ejection seats, when the government spends billions on highway guard rails, and so on. Moreover, economists are quick to point out that the valuation of *specific* lives is not necessary. Rather, the exercise entails evaluating "statistical" lives—say, for example, the two thousand anonymous people saved annually by better auto brakes, not knowing whether John Smith and Suzy Jones are actually among those saved next year.

Still, even on the economists' own turf, practical difficulties remain. There is no consensus among economists on what the dollar value of a life is, or what method should be employed to find out. The most popular method at present translates the wage premium workers receive for risky employment into a dollar value per life saved (on the theory that this premium reflects the amount people are willing to receive in exchange for risk exposure). But there are conceptual problems with this method and the estimates vary widely from $170,000 to $3,000,000 per life saved (in 1978 dollars). Perhaps the most reasonable range is $400,000 to $500,000, but no one knows for sure.[16]

---

[15] An alternative way to appreciate the efficient solution is possible when one states the overall objective thus: to minimize the total cost of waste disposal, that is, to minimize the *sum* of total pollution cost and total abatement cost. At point O in Figure 20–2, total disposal costs are entirely in the form of total pollution costs, namely the entire area under the marginal cost of pollution curve. Conversely, at point O^*, the total cost is all abatement cost, equal to the entire area under the marginal cost of abatement curve. At the efficient solution the total cost of waste disposal is the area of the triangle OEO^*, which combines some cost of abatement (the left side area) with some cost of pollution (the right side area).

[16] Martin J. Bailey, *Reducing Risks to Life* (Washington, D.C.: American Enterprise Institute, 1980). The basic computation is as follows: If statistical estimates reveal an annual wage premium of $300 for each added death per annum per thousand workers, then 1,000 workers must be paid $300 each for accepting the risk of that one death. $1,000 \times \$300 = \$300,000$, the value of that "statistical" life.

Less sensational but no less troublesome to practical application of benefit-cost analysis are the many other areas where unknowns intrude.[17] Indeed, placing a dollar value on lives, injuries, or amenity losses is only the last step in a sequence of several steps necessary to estimate the benefit of some safety or pollution abatement device. For example, the dollar benefit from catalytic mufflers on cars depends on:

1. The degree to which auto *emissions* are actually curbed, taking into account driving conditions and other factors.
2. The impact of reduced emissions on *ambient air* conditions, taking into account interactions with other pollutants and weather patterns.
3. The relationship between improved ambient air conditions and *physical effects* such as human death and illness, crop loss, property damage, aesthetic losses, and so on.
4. The *dollar value* one places on those physical improvements, including the dollar value of human lives.

With judgment and estimation entering at each step, the results are wide-ranging. It is not surprising, then, that estimates of the annual economic benefits for *all* air pollution control in the late 1970s range from $4.6 billion to $51.2 billion.[18]

Estimates for the cost side of the benefit-cost calculus are often more solid than the benefit side. Still, the numbers jump rather wildly about. Depending on who you read, for instance, the costs of auto safety regulations in 1978 were $430 or $368 or $250 per car.[19] To some, the practical infirmities of benefit-cost analysis are totally incapacitating. After considering the matter at length, a congressional committee concluded, "The limitations on the usefulness of benefit/cost analysis in the context of health, safety, and environmental regulatory decision making are so severe that they militate against its use altogether."[20] Economists, on the other hand, tend to be more optimistic. And as a last resort many of them, like M. J. Bailey, contend that there is simply no other alternative to responsible decision making:

. . . the use of benefit-cost analysis to aid regulatory decisions should be compared not with an ideal but with the practical alternative. Reckless issuance of regulations in disregard of the costs will damage the public interest if the benefits to health and safety are too small to justify the costs.[21]

B. Cost Effectiveness

When placing dollar values on benefits is either impossible or undesirable, efficiency can still be served by following principles of *cost effectiveness*. The basic idea is to get the greatest amount of goodness per dollar spent. Two ways of achieving this end present themselves depending on whether it is the dollar cost or unvalued goodness which is fixed: (1) If the total dollar cost is set at some maximum amount available, then the objective is to save the greatest number of lives (or some similar unvalued result) with that given cost. (2) If on the other hand the unvalued objective is set at, say, a reduction of 10,000 traffic fatalities per year,

[17] This is especially true on the benefit side. For a brief survey see Nicholas Ashford, et al., *The Benefits of Environmental, Health and Safety Regulation*, U.S. Senate, Committee on Governmental Affairs (March 1980). For details in one area, see A. M. Freeman III, *The Benefits of Environmental Improvement* (Baltimore: Johns Hopkins University Press, 1979).

[18] National Commission on Air Quality, *To Breathe Clean Air* (Washington, D.C., 1981), p. 261.

[19] National Highway Traffic Safety Administration "The Contributions of Automobile Regulation" (Washington, D.C., 1978), pp. 8–11.

[20] U.S. Congress, House, Subcommittee on Oversight and Investigations of the Committee on Interstate and Foreign Commerce, *Federal Regulation and Regulatory Reform*, 94th Congress, 2d Session (1976), p. 515.

[21] M. J. Bailey, *op. cit.*, p. 21.

then the objective is to achieve this result with the least cost possible.

Safety, health, and pollution regulations usually take the second of these forms, namely, standard setting for physical results. Thus we can illustrate cost effectiveness for this kind of situation with a simple hypothetical example of cost minimization. Assume that Congress has set an objective of eliminating 30 million tons of sulfur dioxide from our atmosphere. Consultation with engineers and economists reveals six methods (or sources) of sulfur dioxide reduction, with total maximum reduction and total cost for each method as indicated in Table 20–1. The question is, then: Which method, or combination of methods, should be employed to achieve the 30 million tons reduction at least cost? The answer is: Begin with least-cost method A (which costs $1 per ton removed and eliminates 5 million tons), and then use successively higher cost methods or fractions thereof (C, F, and half of D) until the 30 million tons target is reached. Total cost by this approach will be $62 million (A = $5m, C = $15m, F = $12m, $\frac{1}{2}$D =$30m), which is much lower than the cost of relying on method B alone (30 m. tons × $3.20 per ton = $96m.) and lower than

any other possible combination of methods. The moral of the example is that low cost-per-unit techniques should be used first and most intensively.

Shifting from the hypothetical to the actual, Table 20–2 ranks selected highway safety measures by decreasing cost effectiveness, assuming a ten year time horizon for both fatalities forestalled and costs incurred. Efficiency would require that we move down the list, adopting safety measures until meeting some specific objective in total lives saved, or, if cost is the constraint, until our total cost limit is reached. Of course *non*efficiency considerations may interfere. Mandatory safety belt laws, the first measure on the list, may be rejected because it interferes with personal freedom, for example. Such other considerations explain why many if not most government measures in the area of safety, health, and pollution are *not* actually cost effective. Still, efficiency is desirable and it repays our pursuit.

C. Efficiency in Policy Design

Whereas full-blown benefit-cost analysis mainly addresses the question of *how much risk*

Table 20–1. Cost and Quantity Data for Finding Efficient Program to Reduce Sulfur Dioxide Emissions

(1) Method (source)	(2) Total reduction possible by method	(3) Total cost with full application	(4) Cost per ton of reduction: col. (3)/col. (2)
A	5 million tons	$ 5 million	$1.00
B	35 million tons	$112 million	$3.20
C	10 million tons	$ 15 million	$1.50
D	20 million tons	$ 60 million	$3.00
E	25 million tons	$ 95 million	$3.80
F	5 million tons	$ 12 million	$2.40

Table 20–2.   Ranking of Highway Safety Measures by Decreasing Cost
Effectiveness in 1976 Dollars Per Fatality Forestalled—10-Year Total

Safety measure	Fatalities forestalled	Total cost ($ millions)	Dollars per fatality forestalled
Mandatory seat belt usage	89,000	$ 45.0	$ 506
55-mph speed limit	31,900	676.0	21,200
Regulatory road signs	3,670	125.0	34,000
Guard rails	3,160	108.0	34,100
Motorcycle rider helmets	1,150	61.2	53,300
Breakaway sign and lighting supports	3,250	379.0	116,000
Median barriers	529	121.0	228,000
Periodic auto inspections	1,840	3,890.0	2,120,000
Paved or stabilized shoulders	928	5,380.0	5,800,000

Source: National Transportation Policy Study Commission, *National Transportation Policies* (Washington D.C., June 1979), p. 413.

reduction do we want, cost effectiveness mainly addresses the question of *what tool* is best to achieve a given goal of risk reduction. Policy tools are essentially of four types: (1) direct regulation, (2) information improvement, (3) taxation, and (4) subsidy. Each policy has its strengths and weaknesses, hence efficiency is best served if the policy selected fits the problem.

Direct regulation is control by decree. The government enacts laws forbidding DDT, limiting auto emissions to "x" grams per mile, prohibiting sharp-edged toys, reducing factory noise, and so on. This is the major method of U.S. government intervention in these areas of safety, health, and pollution, so it will be covered at length later. The main point to be made here is that regulation is not always the most efficient policy option available. It entails extensive meddling in the private affairs of businesses

and people. It requires an army of government snoopers for enforcement. It rarely achieves its aims by least-cost means. Indeed, its general neglect of economic considerations can result in adverse side effects. For example, forcing safety features on autos may reduce auto fatalities, but they may also increase the price of autos to the point of inducing poor people to ride motorcycles, which are considerably more dangerous than autos.

Information improvement entails the same kind of activities as discussed earlier in Chapter 12. To the extent a safety problem can be corrected by information disclosure this policy is undoubtedly superior to direct regulation. It is more efficient not only because it entails less government apparatus and less private and public resource expenditure, but also because it permits greater flexibility on the part of those who face risks. An example is provided by saccharin, an artificial sweetener. In 1977, the Food and Drug Administration took steps to ban saccharin as a food additive after Canadian scientists found it caused cancer in laboratory rats. Opponents of the ban argued that without saccharin people would consume more sugar, thereby aggravating such health risks as obesity, heart disease, and arthritis. Public outcry and subsequent congressional action forced the FDA to retreat. At present, warning labels have taken the place of prohibition.

The **taxation** approach includes a number of policy tools that might be called market simulators. The basic idea is to change behavior for the better by monetary inducements such as the market provides. Taxation of pollution offers the greatest opportunities in this respect, as we shall see. But the approach could be extended to include taxation of workplace injuries or the sale of limited pollution rights. Because this approach works by market principles, the results are usually more efficient than those obtained through direct regulation. Yet taxation and related methods can be employed where mere information improvement is either inappropriate or insufficient to the task.

Subsidies have seen very limited use in safety and health (as they are confined mainly to government provision of information), but they have seen moderate action in the fight against pollution. Whereas taxes *goad*, subsidies *entice*. The government pays polluters to install abatement equipment or to clean up. Aside from government aid to purge the nation of its most hazardous toxic waste disposal sites, most federal subsidies have financed municipal sewage treatment facilities. A main problem with subsidies aimed at private industry is that, unlike direct regulation or taxation, subsidies yield abatement without product price increases, so the costs of abatement are disguised. Consumers do not confront the true social costs of production, including the costs of cleanliness. As a result, consumers are not encouraged to shift their purchases from high-pollution products to low-pollution products. Society's misallocation of resources may therefore persist under the subsidy approach.

In the chapters that follow we shall have very little to say about information improvement and subsidies. Taxation receives substantial attention because of its attractive properties. Occupying center stage will be direct regulation, so we conclude this introductory chapter with an overview of safety, health, and pollution regulation.

IV. Regulation: an Overview

A. Historical and Institutional Contexts

To understand further why rational economics is so often slighted in these matters, it should be recognized that current policies did not derive from economic theorizing of the type imposed upon you to this point. Almost without exception these policies emerged from historical and institutional backgrounds that contained three elements.[22] First, they were usually part and parcel of a broader reform movement—the Progressive movement of 1900–1912, the New Deal of FDR, the Great Society of LBJ, and so on. Second, influential journalists and idealistic writers contributed with scathing attacks on the status quo. Upton Sinclair (*The Jungle*), Rachel Carson (*Silent Spring*), and Ralph Nader (*Unsafe at Any Speed*) occupy prominent places in the pantheon of literate crusaders. Finally, and most importantly, the policies represent responses to specific tragedies or general conditions of crisis. Killer smogs, highway death tolls of epidemic proportions, blinding eyelash cosmetics,

[22] Mark Nadel, *The Politics of Consumer Protection* (Indianapolis: Bobbs-Merrill, 1971).

and grotesquely deformed babies propel the history of regulation in these areas.

Moving beyond the question of why the government got involved at all to the question of why regulation became the chosen instrument of that involvement, two observations seem warranted. First, government tends to be dominated by lawyers, not economists or businessmen. This is true of the executive branch as well as the legislative and judicial branches of government. So when a perceived problem arises, the legalistic, regulatory response comes natural to those in power. Second, many precedents for the regulatory approach had been laid with reliance on regulations to handle public utilities, telecommunications, broadcast communications, and so on. Thus, imagine yourself in the shoes of an attorney turned United States senator, say, twenty years ago. You perceive a problem of hazardous products or annoying pollution and wonder: "What the hell can be done about it?" Creating a regulatory agency on which to dump the problem might seem a good idea.

The remaining question is what duties and powers should be invested in the agency to solve the problem? The question is a treacherous one because, hypothetically, the bad answers outnumber the good. And historically we have had our share of bad answers. Weak and halting efforts at food and drug regulation date back to 1906. Water pollution legislation goes back to the Refuse Act of 1899, but that law was not enforced until 1970. Legislators apparently learned from these bad experiences, for there has evolved a distinct pattern of fairly effective regulatory activities common to the several agencies operating in this area of safety, health, and pollution.

These regulatory activities are outlined in Table 20–3 together with the purpose of each, examples of each, and some rough indications of where each activity takes place. At first glance this looks confusing. The table's cluttered appearance seems to indicate only "red tape" and "bureaucratic hassle," but there is method to the muddiness. Notice first that virtually all major regulatory activities fall into one of three broad categories: (A) standard setting, (B) enforcement, and (C) research. Broadly speaking, **standards** are necessary so that everyone involved—both regulators and regulated—know what they are *supposed to be doing* to attain good performance. In turn, **enforcement** of these standards is necessary to assure that the regulated *actually do* what they are supposed to. Finally, **research** is necessary to *evaluate* the agency's standards and enforcement programs. This last category includes "follow through" to help assure that the regulat*ors* are doing what they ought to be doing (and not overlooking something important). Research also embraces the search for new ways of achieving old objectives. Discussion of the specific activities listed under each broad category illuminates these assertions.

B. Standard Setting

There are typically two types of standards—broad and narrow. **Broad standards** are vague, generalized concepts of what is desirable. Because they are typically set by Congress and because they are found in the legislation establishing regulatory agencies or amending established agency powers, broad standards may be viewed as the goals and limits governing the regulat*ors*, *not* the regulat*ed*. Thus, for example, the Consumer Product Safety Act says vaguely that one goal of the Consumer Product Safety Commission is "to protect the public against unreasonable risks of injury associated with consumer products." And the Federal Water Pollution Control Act of 1972 calls for "recreation in and on the water . . . by July 1, 1983." The purpose of broad standards is not limited to issuing mandates, it extends to giving time schedules and future goals.

Table 20–3. Outline of the Major Activities that Regulation Entails

Activity	Purpose	Examples	Locale of activity
Standard setting			
Broad standards	To set goals and limits for regulators	"Safe" products "swimmable" rivers	Set by Congress in legislative mandates
Narrow standards	To set goals and limits for firms and products regulated	Lead level in paint not to exceed 0.5%; dual braking systems in all autos	Usually set by agency after study and hearings
Enforcement for compliance			
Certification or permit	To approve of regulated firms' intentions and give guidance or premarket clearance	Engine design-"X" approved; effluent permit granted	Laboratory; agency offices
Sample testing	To monitor regulated firms' activities on regular basis	Antibiotics batch tested for purity; smokestack emissions measured	Assembly line; plant floor; sewage outfalls; stacks
Field surveillance (optional)	To double check compliance and catch "mistakes"	Annual inspection of autos; investigate consumer complaints	Highway; retail stores; repair shops; homes
Remedies	To bring violators into line	Seize contaminated canned goods; force recall of autos; fine violators	Warehouses; stores; courtrooms; agency offices
Research			
Technical research	To explore new possibilities	Build experimental "safety" cars; test new monitoring devices	Laboratories
General surveillance	To assess program operation and discover new problems	Collect data on accidents; measure air quality	Hospital emergency rooms; highway patrol offices, weather stations, river banks, etc.

421

Broad standards may be considered the regulators' standards for another reason. Namely, no private company or citizen can be prosecuted for violating these broad standards because they are *too* vague and *too* ill-defined to guide the actions of those who are regulated. For enforcement and prosecution **narrow standards** are necessary. These are very specific; some so much so that they fill thousands of pages in the *Code of Federal Regulations*. A simple example given in Table 20–3 is the 0.5% lead standard for paint, one purpose of which is to prevent lead poisoning in toddlers who may innocently choose to cut their teeth on the window sill. These narrow standards are usually developed by the regulatory agencies themselves, not Congress, although certain particularly earthshaking standards may be subject to congressional approval. Congress delegates this authority for a simple reason: specific, narrow standards tend to be highly technical and complex, involving tens of thousands of products, countless producers, hundreds of different problems, and other large dimensions of perplexity. Moreover, the *procedures* required to develop narrow standards are tangled snarls, involving notifications, hearings, conferences, and so on—in short, many things for which Congress has no capacity.

It should also be noted that narrow standards may be of two types: (1) performance standards or (2) design standards. **Performance standards** merely specify some specific level of performance—for example, for auto pollutants, no more than 3.4 grams of carbon monoxide emitted per mile traveled. This approach leaves it up to the regulated firm to devise some means of meeting the performance standard, and many different engine designs or exhaust control devices meet this example of auto regulation. In contrast, a **design standard** specifies the *particular designs* that are acceptable. This alternative approach is much less flexible but equally possible and frequently used.

C. Enforcement of Compliance

Certification and Permits. Once narrow standards are set, the next step is to get folks to abide by them. Implementation typically requires four distinct activities. The first, as outlined in Table 20–3, is certification or the issuance of permits. The purpose of certification is to approve the regulated firms' intentions, to give guidance *before* massive investments in plant and equipment are made and *before* any harm is done. An example is the FDA's clearance of new drugs. All new drugs have to be certified as being in compliance with standards of safety and efficacy before they can be marketed.

Sometimes certification is undertaken not so much for the benefit of consumers as it is for the benefit of regulated firms. An example of this is EPA's certification of engine designs that meet emission performance standards *prior* to actual production of those engines. Imagine the billions of dollars an auto company could lose if it invested in production facilities for an engine that it thought would meet standards only to find out later that in the view of EPA the engine did not. Where performance standards are involved, certification is particularly important.

Sample Testing or Monitoring. The second major enforcement activity is sample testing. In a word, this is monitoring. Once standards are set and certification (if any) is completed, there remains the question of what is actually going on at the factory. Do the goods coming off the assembly line comply with standards? Is the plant's sewage pure enough to be dumped into the local river? Are gases and particulates escaping in volumes greater than those specified by permit? Are foods and drugs manufactured in surroundings that are clean? The only way these questions can be answered is by extensive on-the-spot sampling, testing, inspecting, scouting, and detecting. Of course an army of enforcement personnel is required for this task, more than 20,000 or so snoopers for all the agencies under review here. Budgetary limits hold the number down, so great reliance is placed on "spot" checking and "small" sampling.

Field Surveillance. An activity that is only sometimes used (and therefore optional) is field surveillance, the third step outlined in Table 20–3. This may be considered a process of double checking or back-up monitoring. When consumer products are under scrutiny (instead of, or in addition to, production processes), sample testing at production sites often is not enough to assure compliance. Because only sample testing is involved, some goods that are not up to snuff will reach retail shelves and showrooms. There may also be a problem of post production tampering, wherein safety devices or pollution control devices are removed by retailers or consumers or employers in order to gain better gas mileage, greater convenience, lower operating costs, or some other advantage. As a result, field surveillance is necessary to (1) detect substandard goods that have slipped through sample testing and (2) assure continued compliance. Field surveillance involves observation and sample purchasing at the retail level. In the case of autos it may include the annual inspection of autos in use. Finally, and perhaps even more important, field surveillance also entails (3) the receipt and investigation of consumer and employee complaints. Swift action may be necessary even where formal standards are absent.

Remedies. Of all enforcement activities, the imposition of remedies is most readily understandable. Some remedies might be considered "light" penalties, such as seizure of the offending goods, closure of production plants, and compulsory product recalls. Yet these are not necessarily "light" at all. They can be expensively onerous in terms of lost inventories, idle plants, and replacement parts. Going one level higher in the echelon of remedies, fines and imprisonment are used under certain circumstances. The purpose served by granting regulators these various armaments should be obvious. They provide incentive. They motivate compliance.

D. Research

Major research activities may be divided into two groups. Those listed first in Table 20–3 are *scientific or technical.* Regulatory agencies conduct "in-house" research, or fund private research, to discover new and safer product designs, to devise improved testing equipment, to explore the relationship between poor air quality and human health, and so on. These activities are worthwhile for at least two reasons: (1) without official assumption or funding these areas of research are likely to be slighted, and (2) they enable regulators to keep abreast of technological developments, thereby improving the quality of regulatory effort. Indeed, this research often indicates where standards should be modified, abandoned, or imposed.

A second type of research may be called *general surveillance.* The forms of surveillance discussed earlier under compliance were "over the shoulder" types of surveillance. Their objective is to spot specific violations of specific standards. Although general surveillance may turn up specific violations, that is not the primary function. Rather, its purpose is to "keep the eyes peeled," a cliché connoting a general awareness of what is going on. Perhaps the best example of this is the National Electronic Injury Surveillance System maintained by the Consumer Product Safety Commission. This system connects the Commission to over one hundred hospital emergency rooms scattered throughout the country. The hospitals report a daily flow of information concerning product-related injuries and fatalities, thereby enabling the

CPSC to maintain an up-to-the-minute vigilance over its area of concern.

Of the several regulatory activities neglected by the preceding review perhaps none is more important than consumer education. As we have seen earlier, information disclosure can often correct the market's faults, and all the agencies of interest here have education programs. We shall not discuss these programs here, however.

Summary

Insofar as efficiency is our only concern, economic theory postulates that ideal markets produce ideal results when it comes to problems of safety, health, and pollution. These results do not entail zero risk because people willingly accept some risk and the costs of achieving zero risk would be huge. Rather, the ideal market compensates those who accept risks with appropriately lower prices on risky products or higher wages for risky occupations. The ideal market also provides environmental protection. Risk reduction proceeds in all these ideal cases until the added benefits match the added costs.

The theory is useful because it suggests that real world markets may not be complete failures and because it indicates efficient (benefit-cost) solutions. But the real world does not conform to theory's ideals. In particular, noneconomic value judgments such as (1) morality and (2) equity may cause people to call upon the government even when the market is efficient. To many environmentalists and consumer advocates, efficiency is neither moral nor equitable. Moreover, there is the added problem that real-world markets are not efficient because people frequently (3) do not know about risks or (4) face risks involuntarily.

Of these last two justifications for government intervention, ignorance is probably most pertinent to consumer and worker safety and health. When experts know of risks the information must be made available, transmitted to those affected, and understood, but this chain is often broken. Moreover, "uncertainty" often prevails, in which case the risk probabilities are unknown even to the experts.

Government action for safety and health can also be grounded on involuntary risk exposure, but this is most pertinent to pollution, where externalities run rife. Polluters use common property resources to dispose of their wastes, thereby inflicting costs on others. The result is too much pollution.

If efficiency were the goal of government intervention, benefit-cost analysis would determine how much safety, health, and environmental cleanliness should be provided. Steps in the direction of these noble aims would be desirable as long as the benefits from each step exceeded or equalled the costs. Unfortunately, benefit-cost analysis is very difficult to apply in practice. Benefit estimation is especially tough. Aside from difficulties in placing dollar values on such things as human lives, the linkages between government standards and physical effects often elude accurate estimation. Because the cost side of the calculus is typically more fathomable, and because regulation usually sets physical standards, cost effectiveness often proves useful. When evaluated by cost-effectiveness, information improvement and taxation generally rank higher than direct regulation and subsidies among policy tools.

Notwithstanding its considerable drawbacks, direct regulation dominates U.S. policy in these areas. This approach evolved to the point where, by 1970, three broad activities typified regulation in these areas—standard setting, enforcement, and research. Each of these activities divide into several subactivities, which have been summarized in Table 20–3.

Questions and Exercises
for Chapter 20

1. Explain *how* and *how well* the free market can provide an optimal degree of worker safety under ideal circumstances.

2. Compare and contrast "risk" and "uncertainty" in the context of knowledge. Which is more readily capable of rationalizing government intervention?

3. Explain why each of the following might warrant policy attention: (a) airplane noise, (b) pesticide spraying on farms; (c) gladiator battles; (d) baby crib hazards.

4. Why was information improvement not mentioned as a possible policy in the case of pollution?

5. Why might cost-effectiveness be especially appropriate (as opposed to full-blown cost-benefit) when a risk reduction objective is set by criteria of "morality"?

6. What would you need to know in order to estimate the benefits of reducing paper mill water pollution?

7. Check your understanding of Table 20–1 by (a) eliminating Method A from consideration and then (b) finding the cost-effective means of reducing 35 million tons of SO_2.

8. Compare and contrast broad and narrow standards.

9. Outline the elements of "enforcement," explaining the rationale for each element.

10. Regulation is regulation. Why, then, would research have any role?

11. What is the purpose and focus of these "social" regulations in terms of market structure, conduct, and performance?

12. Is it possible for someone to accept an existing environmental standard but argue for a tax as the means of enforcement using cost-effectiveness in support? Explain.

Chapter 21

Consumer Product Safety: FDA, NHTSA, and CPSC

By the time they have finished breakfast, most people have come into contact with twenty or thirty products that we regulate.
—Dr. Alexander M. Schmidt
(*former commissioner of the Food and Drug Administration*)

Thousands upon thousands of consumer products are regulated for safety—from your bowl of breakfast cereal to the tires on your car. The best way to approach this mountain of regulatory debris is to take each major agency in turn: (I) Food and Drug Administration, (II) National Highway Traffic Safety Administration, and (III) Consumer Product Safety Commission. Our discussion of each will be divided into three parts: (A) standards, (B) enforcement activities, and (C) chief controversies. One major regulatory activity mentioned in the previous chapter that cannot be covered here is research.

I. Food and Drug Administration

A. Standards: Broad and Narrow

The FDA's origins date back to 1906, making it the granddaddy of these agencies. Major modifications in the FDA's powers occurred in 1938, 1958, 1962, and 1976. In jurisdiction, the agency's scope of authority goes well beyond the foods and drugs of its title to include cosmetics and medical devices. Within each of these four divisions official attention spans a bewildering variety of products. Take drugs, for example; there are over 60,000 prescription-drug products and over 100,000 over-the-counter formulations, such as aspirin, subject to FDA vigilance.[1]

Although safety is the FDA's primary concern, the agency devises and enforces standards tangential to safety—standards for product purity, product efficacy, and production cleanliness. These broad standards do not apply equally to all products under FDA jurisdiction. So a summary cross-tabulation between the four product classes and four broad standards is provided in Table 21–1. Authority is indicated by the dates the FDA was given duties

---

[1] Indeed, a complete tally of FDA's scope would reveal its responsibility for laser lights at rock concerts, FDA, *Annual Report,* 1978, p. 43.

Table 21–1. FDA's Broad Standards and Product Jurisdiction, by Date of Congressional Mandate

Broad Standard	Food	Drugs	Cosmetics	Medical Devices
Safety	1906, 1958	1906, 1938, 1966	1938	1938, 1976
Purity	1906, 1938	1906	(partially)	(partially)
Production cleanliness	1938	1938, 1966	1938	1938
Efficacy	—	1962	—	1976

in these respects. A listing of more than one date indicates strengthening of the law by amendment.

Thus it may be seen that standards of "safety" and "clean production processes" now apply to all four product groups. Rigorous and complete standards of "purity" apply only to food and drugs. And standards of "efficacy" apply only to drugs and medical devices.

Why the differences in standard coverage? A partial answer may be found in the preceding chapter. That is, the inadequacies of the free market system do not strike all products equally, and government regulation of these "qualities" is not equally appropriate to all commodities. (How, for example, could you regulate the efficacy of cosmetics?) A still more complete answer hinges on a more complete understanding of what is meant by "safety," "purity," "production cleanliness," and "efficacy," which brings us to narrow standards.

1. SAFETY

In general, the FDA's narrow standards for safety in *drugs and medical devices* tend to be *relative*. They weigh risks against benefits, permitting substantial risks when the potential benefits are also great. For a hypothetical example, a drug that is known to kill ten out of every one hundred patients who ingest it may nevertheless be approved for sale if it is fairly success-

ful in curing cancer malignancies that are otherwise incurable. Unfortunately, there are no simple criteria for drawing the line in benefit-risk trade-offs because it is not always simply a matter of life and death.[2] Is substantial risk of death tolerable in exchange for such benefits as pain relief or paralysis reduction? These are obviously judgment calls. Indeed, no drug is risk-free. All have potential side effects, so crude judgments are inevitable.

Although seriously hazardous substances are permitted if the benefits they bestow are truly great, such substances are carefully controlled as prescription drugs. Prescription drugs can be dispensed only by licensed physician, dentist, veterinarian, or pharmacist. Nonprescription drugs, or over-the-counter medicines, are generally regarded as safe for the consumer to select and use when he or she follows the required directions and warnings.

Safety standards for *foods* and *cosmetics* tend to be more nearly absolute. No risk at all is permitted, but there are enough exceptions to make this less than a general rule. The most clearly absolute standard in this area is the 1958 Delaney amendment to the Food, Drug, and Cosmetic Act, which states that "no additive shall be deemed to be safe . . . if it is found,

[2] Statement of Commissioner Schmidt, *Reforming Federal Drug Regulation* (Washington, D.C.: American Enterprise Institute, 1976), p. 26–27.

after tests which are appropriate for the evaluation of the safety of food additives, to induce cancer in man or animal." In short, the Delaney clause reflects a congressional decision that *no* risk is warranted for carcinogenic food additives. Thus, when it was discovered in 1969 that the artificial sweetener cyclamate caused cancer in laboratory animals, the FDA had no choice but to ban it. Saccharin became the only remaining artificial sweetener, but that too was found to be carcinogenic in laboratory animals. So in 1977 the FDA proceeded to ban saccharin as a general food additive.

Public protest over the proposed saccharin ban caused Congress to grant an exception, permitting saccharin as an additive if accompanied by a warning label. When a food ingredient is *not* an additive and when the risk involved is *not* cancer, relative standards then apply, opening the door for many more "exceptions." For example, a known carcinogen, aflatoxin, occurs naturally in peanuts. Also, environmental pollution puts mercury in fish, and mercury attacks the human nervous system. If a no-risk standard were applied to aflatoxin and mercury, we would have virtually no peanut or fish products. Permitted levels of these substances and others like them are judged "safe enough" but not completely safe.

A cosmetic is considered "safe" when, *under normal use,* it is not hazardous. A nail polish could thus be "safe" even if drinking it would polish you off. Even when normal use is slightly hazardous (as with hair dyes), cosmetics are permitted *if* they carry clear warning of their dangers.

2. PURITY

Purity is not the same thing as safety, although the two often overlap. Pure strychnine is anything but safe. Conversely, watered down milk may be perfectly safe but it is hardly pure. Given the basic difference between purity and safety, it is possible to have *relative* standards

of safety while imposing *absolute* standards of purity. And the FDA does have fairly absolute standards of purity for foods and drugs.

The standards concern two main types of purity—composition (or "strength") and contamination. Thus for drug **composition** and **potency** the major official compendiums of specific standards are the *United States Pharmacopeia* and the *National Formulary,* which together cover some 2000 drug forms. By these standards, for example, a 5-grain aspirin tablet must contain 5 grains of "aspirin" (and all other drugs so regulated must meet their standards) within a tolerance of plus-or-minus 5%. Similarly, many foods are "identified" as to quality of contents to prevent "watering down." Tomato "paste," for instance, must contain not less than 25% salt-free "tomato solids." Such standards of composition apply only to foods and drugs.

Contamination standards prohibit filthy, putrid, or decomposed products, be they foods, drugs, cosmetics, or medical devices. Thus, for example, the FDA claims that it does not permit any variations from "absolute cleanliness or soundness in foods."

> The Act does not authorize "tolerances" for filth or decomposition in foods. It states that a food is adulterated if it consists *in whole or in part* of a filthy, putrid, or decomposed substrate.[3]

In practice, however, the standards are only "reasonably" absolute, since foreign matter is permitted "below the irreducible minimum after all precautions humanly possible have been taken to prevent contamination." This leniency is illustrated by standards governing tomato canning:

> In judging whether tomato products have been properly prepared to eliminate rot and decay, the Food and Drug Administration uses the Howard mold-count test, and refuses admission to import

[3] Food and Drug Administration, *Requirements of the United States Food, Drug and Cosmetic Act* (1972), p. 6.

Thumbnail Sketch 7: Food and Drug Administration

Established: 1931 (formerly Bureau of Chemistry in Agriculture Dept.).

Purpose: To protect the public against unsafe, impure, and ineffective drugs and medical devices, and to regulate hazards in foods, cosmetics, and radiation devices.

Legislative Authority: Food and Drug Act of 1906; Food, Drug, and Cosmetic Act of 1938 as amended in 1958 (food additives), 1960 (color additives), 1962 (drug efficacy), and 1976 (medical devices); Radiation Control for Health & Safety Act of 1968.

Regulatory Activity: (1) Sets standards for safety, purity, production cleanliness, efficacy, and labeling of the products under its jurisdiction. (2) Enforces those standards with premarket review and certification, sample testing, surveillance, and remedy imposition. Conducts research.

Organization: A division of the Department of Health and Human Services, headed by a commissioner.

Budget: 1982 estimate: $328 million.

Staff: 1982 estimate: 7142.

---

shipments and takes action against domestic shipments if mold filaments are present in more than 40% of the microscopic fields in the case of puree, paste, more than 30% in the case of catsup, or sauce, or more than 20% in the case of tomato juice.[4]

Lest the percentages that escape bother you, it should be noted that FDA standards for food purity usually go well beyond the point of assured safety.

3. PRODUCTION CLEANLINESS
Standards governing production cleanliness underscore this last statement. In fact, the mere processing of a food under insanitary conditions that may contaminate the food renders such food adulterated under the law:

The maintenance of sanitary conditions requires extermination and exclusion of rodents, inspection and sorting of raw materials to eliminate the insect-infested and decomposed portions, fumigation, quick handling and proper storage to prevent insect development or contamination, the use of clean equipment, control of possible sources of sewage pollution, and supervision of personnel who prepare foods so that acts of misconduct may not defile the products they handle.[5]

The FDA provides details in *Current Good Manufacturing Practice Regulations.* These cover even such matters as building design, lighting, and ventilation. Similar standards apply to drugs, cosmetics, and medical devices.

(All this may sound comforting. But keep in mind that standards and enforcement are quite different. As with a 55 miles per hour speed limit, compliance is sometimes short of the statute.)

4. EFFICACY
The issue of efficacy is in many ways similar to the issue of deceptive advertising. In both cases the key question is whether the product

---

[4] Ibid., p. 12.

[5] Ibid., p. 5.

performs as claimed. However, the FDA's regulation of efficacy differs markedly from ordinary curbs against deception. As we saw in Chapter 13, the FTC's fight against deception sweeps the mass media clean of most false and misleading *claims*, but it leaves even the most worthless deceptively promoted *products* on store shelves. No attempt is made by the FTC to sweep shelves clear of worthless junk. No attempt is made to restrict the use of deceptively promoted products to applications for which they are effective. Whereas regulation of sheer "deception" entails none of these measures, regulation of "efficacy" entails them all. A drug is *banned* if "there is a lack of substantial evidence that the drug will have the effect it purports or is represented to have under the condition of use prescribed, recommended, or suggested . . ."[6]

Justification for an efficacy standard rests in part on safety. Given that all drugs are to some degree poisonous, an ineffective drug would impose risk for no benefit. Risk also arises if ineffective therapies supplant effective therapies.

It was lack of effectiveness that caused the FDA to ban laetrile—an ineffective cancer cure whose strident supporters fought the FDA with such ferocity that the controversy continues to this day. Because the efficacy standard was added by Congress only in 1962, drugs on the market prior to 1962 had to be reviewed for efficacy by the FDA, which review produced some statistics even more interesting than the laetrile controversy. With the aid of over two hundred outside experts, the FDA's effectiveness review resulted in the removal of more than six thousand drug products (or brands) from the market during the 1960s and 1970s.[7]

[6] Federal Food, Drug, and Cosmetic Act, Section 505 (d).

[7] *FDA Annual Report 1975*, p. 36; 1976, p. 33. See also Sidney Wolfe and C. Coley, *Pills That Don't Work* (New York: Farrar, Straus, & Giroux, 1981), according to which, 607 ineffective drugs remained on the market in 1979, costing consumers $1.1 billion annually.

B. FDA Enforcement

1. CERTIFICATION

The 1962 Drug Amendments also imposed standards of efficacy on new, post-1962 drugs. Enforcement of the standard for new drugs involves FDA premarket clearance or certification based on research materials supplied by the drug companies to the FDA. Safety, too, must be demonstrated, but of all aspects of premarket clearance, efficacy has stirred the greatest controversy, a controversy that we will take up shortly.

Certification in other areas of FDA authority is somewhat of a hodgepodge. Medical devices are treated like drugs, with premarket clearance for safety and efficacy. Food additives are, in general, divided by a 1958 amendment into "old" additives generally recognized as safe and "new" additives that must be approved for safety prior to use. In cosmetics, prior approval for safety is not required, so enforcement is an ex-post affair.

2. SAMPLE TESTING AND FIELD SURVEILLANCE

During 1979 FDA agents inspected 32,787 establishments, ranging from food warehouses to cosmetic production plants. During the same year FDA technicians analyzed 18,683 samples of food, 6829 samples of human drugs, 2093 samples of animal drugs and feeds, 481 samples of medical devices, and 45 samples of cosmetics. But these are only *domestic* numbers. In addition, the FDA made 95,941 wharf inspections and analyzed 18,615 samples of imported products.[8]

Hidden beneath these numbers are some truly heroic efforts. Consider, for example, the case of Mr. Albert Weber, an FDA chemist with rare talents who was honored with a front-page *Wall Street Journal* article, cleverly written by Jonathan Kwitny. Some excerpts follow:

[8] *FDA Annual Report 1979*, pp. 35–36.

Who knows what evil lurks in the hearts of mackerel? Albert Weber's nose knows.

For, while a nose is a nose is a nose in most cases, Mr. Weber's proboscis stands between this country and one heck of a stomachache. Mr. Weber is the recognized dean of organoleptic analysts—food sniffers. He is one of some two dozen Food and Drug Administration chemists around the country who use their beaks instead of their beakers to check the healthfulness of suspect foods for which there aren't any convenient chemical tests. Mostly, that's rotten fish. Mr. Weber is the only one who does this work full time.

His sizable snout has been compared to Namath's arm, Heifetz's hands and Einstein's brain. His judgments are accepted almost as law in court cases involving hundreds of thousands of dollars in rejected foodstuffs. . . .

In the 32 years since [he started smelling fish], Mr. Weber hasn't grown to like his work any better. "How can you when you have to smell that stink all day?" he asks. But he has made adjustments. He will not allow friends to see him at work. He drives home alone. His wife stays out until after he has had a chance to shower and change. But the FDA needs him, and he says loyalty keeps him on the job. . . .

He smells about 4,000 fish or shrimp in a day and rates them Class I (good commercial), Class II (slightly decomposed) or Class III (advanced decomposed—or, as popularly known, "Phee-Yew!"). Some samples, he says, are "beyond Class III—you have to smell those at arm's length." Often in such cases he says he can tell by looking from across the room that a sample is bad. But visual opinions won't stand up in court if a food dealer challenges the FDA's rejection. Mr. Weber has to smell everything that comes his way.

Usually he breaks the skin of the fish or shrimp with his thumbnails and quickly sticks his nose into the crevice for a sniff. "As a rule, one sniff will do, but on the border line, maybe four. If you can't make up your mind by four sniffs, you shouldn't be doing this work," he says.[9]

By the way, Mr. Weber must rule a shipment acceptable if the portion he samples contains

[9] *Wall Street Journal*, October 7, 1975, p. 1.

no more than 20% Class II or 5% Class III. Thus, some fish and shrimp of the "Phee-Yew" variety get through. This, and similar standards, some critics claim, is too lenient. Likewise, some critics of the FDA contend that its inspectors do not canvas plants often enough or thoroughly enough. Accordingly, they would like to see *more* FDA regulation, not less. For example, in 1971 the General Accounting Office, a watch-dog agency of Congress, checked up on FDA surveillance by inspecting a representative sample of 97 food plants. The General Accounting Office found that "39, or about 40 per cent, were operating under insanitary conditions. Of these, 23, or about 24 per cent, were operating under serious insanitary conditions having potential for causing or having already caused, product contamination."[10] The FDA could apparently use more people of Mr. Weber's caliber. With about 90,000 plants, mills, and other establishments needing surveillance, the FDA has huge enforcement responsibilities.

3. REMEDIES

Table 21–2 reveals that constant vigilance is indeed necessary. Serious problems occur more often than most of us would like to think and usually end in recalls. The year reported there, 1979, was not unusual. To overcome the drabness of these statistics, one recent and especially serious case can be cited:

Under pressure from the FDA, which was threatening to order a formal recall, Procter & Gamble Company withdrew its 'Rely' tampons from the market in late 1980. The tampons were associated with toxic shock—a baffling disease that struck menstruating women and claimed 80 lives over three years. The company's after-tax loss as a result of the recall was $75 million. Other brands

[10] *Dimensions of Insanitary Conditions in the Food Manufacturing Industry,* Report of the Comptroller General of the United States, B–164031 (2), April 18, 1972, p. 2.

Table 21–2. Summary of FDA Remedial Actions During 1979

Program	Recalls	Seizures	Prosecutions	Injunctions
Foods	127	157	13	3
Human drugs	692	138	1	11
Animal drugs and feeds	58	51	0	13
Medical devices	342	20	0	3
Cosmetics	13	0	0	0
Radiological health	45	135	0	5

Source: FDA Annual Report 1979, p. 37.

of the same 'superabsorbent' type were withdrawn by other companies.[11]

In sum, the FDA's enforcement activities keep it very busy. Observers of all political stripes often contend that the agency needs a bigger budget and larger staff to do its job competently and expeditiously.

C. Major Controversies

Still another way to view and evaluate the FDA is through the controversies it ignites. Two controversies stand out—one concerning new drug certification, the other concerning risky food additives.

1. NEW DRUG REVIEW AND APPROVAL

In 1962, the Food, Drug, and Cosmetic Act was amended to raise the hurdles a new drug must clear before marketing. The changes were prompted by thalidomide, a tranquilizer developed in Germany in 1957 that was approved for use in several European countries with tragic consequences. Women who had taken

[11] *Wall Street Journal*, February 26, 1981, pp. 1, 19; June 26, 1981, pp. 1, 25; *Fortune*, August 10, 1981, pp. 114–129.

the drug during pregnancy gave birth to horribly deformed babies, about 8000 in all. The toll in the U.S. was held to only a few because the drug was circulated here only for research, as the FDA had delayed granting its approval for general marketing on suspicion that it was unsafe. Premarket safety clearance had been a part of U.S. law since 1938, but because of this tragedy two new stringencies were added to premarket clearance standards. First, the 1962 law required firms to provide scientific evidence of a new drug's *efficacy* as well as its safety. Second, the *research process* itself became subject to regulation to protect humans serving as research subjects.

The main *benefits* of the amendment are greater assurances of efficacy and safety. But these standards lengthened the time between discovery and marketing considerably, so that now the normal trip from laboratory to pharmacy shelf takes as long as nine or ten years, two or three times the previous duration. Thus the *costs* of the 1962 amendment, aside from the R&D and administrative costs, are the lives lost and suffering endured as the marketing of beneficial new drugs is delayed (or perhaps never permitted at all). There is, in short, an ominous trade-off, or dilemma. *"Simply put,"* to use the words of Upjohn's president, Dr. William Hubbard, Jr., *do the benefits of increased certainty about the drug arising from delay outweigh the benefits that might have arisen from its use during the delay?*[12] Given the large element of judgment needed to answer this question, the FDA is in a no-win situation. Any movement along the trade-off incites critics and defenders.[13] At present the critics are most vocal.

Critics of the FDA point first to the substantial drop in new drug introductions that followed the 1962 amendments, as shown in Figure 21–1. Between 1950 and 1962 an average of 54 new chemical entities were approved by the FDA each year. Thereafter, from 1963 to 1975 an average of just 16 new chemical entities were cleared each year, a tremendous drop of 70%. The critics concede that some decline was to be expected, given that ineffective drugs would no longer be approved. But the critics also have a long list of complaints associated with this trend:[14]

- Drug development costs have soared to more than $40 million per drug.
- The higher costs of drug R&D have hurt small firms severely and have boosted the four largest firms' share of innovation output from 24% in the late 1950s to 48.7% during 1967–1971.
- American drug companies are allegedly be-

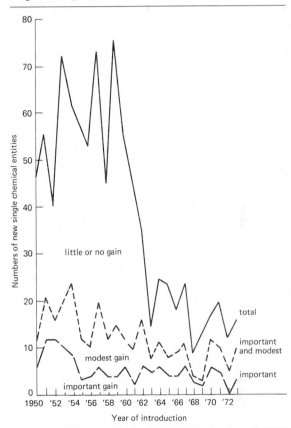

Figure 21–1.   FDA Classification of Annual New Drug Approvals by Degree of Therapeutic Importance, 1950–1973

Source: Examination of the Pharmaceutical Industry 1973–1974, Part 7, Hearings before the Subcommittee on Health of the Committee on Labor and Public Welfare, U.S. Senate, 93rd Congress, 2nd session (1974), p. 3050.

---

ing forced to move their operations abroad, costing Americans their jobs.
- Most important, critics claim that American medical care has deteriorated, that the array of effective new drugs available to American patients has been needlessly and injuriously restricted as compared to new drugs availa-

---

[12] W. N. Hubbard, Jr., in *Reforming Federal Drug Regulation, op. cit.,* p. 13.

[13] For a good summary see Denise Grady, "Bottleneck at the F.D.A.," *Discover* (November 1981), pp. 52–56.

[14] See e.g., Sam Peltzman, "An Evaluation of Consumer Protection Legislation: The 1962 Drug Amendments," *Journal of Political Economy* (September 1973), pp. 1049–91; H. G. Grabowski and J. M. Vernon, "Consumer Protection Regulation in Ethical Drugs," *American Economic Review* (February 1977), pp. 359–364; H. G. Grabowsky, *Drug Regulation and Innovation* (Washington, D.C.: American Enterprise Institute, 1976); William Wardell, "More Regulation or Better Therapies?" *Regulation* (September/October 1979), pp. 25–33.

ble in foreign countries. Chymopapain, metaproterenol, and propranolol are among the dozens of cures suffering "bureaucratic lag"—i.e., available abroad long before here.

Defenders of FDA regulations concede that the number of new drug introductions has taken a nose dive, but they argue that the post-1962 regulations cannot be blamed for all of the decline. They claim that research *opportunities* withered as the new mines opened by breakthrough discoveries during the 1940s and 1950s petered out. In support of this claim defenders point out that new drug introductions began to decline *before* the 1962 Amendments took hold, and that new drug introductions have declined in Germany, France, England, and other advanced countries as well as in the United States despite no comparable changes in their laws.[15] Moreover, the FDA's defenders deny that United States medical care has suffered under efficacy regulation. They contend that the decline in introductions is mainly accounted for by elimination of drugs representing little or no important therapeutic gain (see Figure 21–1 again). The disproportionately greater loss of trivial drugs is understandable, they say, because rising costs of new drug development would tend to cripple the profit prospects of trivial drugs before crippling the profit prospects of important drugs, given that trivial drugs ordinarily have weaker profit potential to begin with.

As for the problem of extended time lags, FDA's defenders admit to delays. But they contend that drugs in the research stage can be obtained through "compassionate approval" procedures, and that the FDA can occasionally move quickly, as it did for *l*-Dopa.[16] As if admitting to excessive past delay, however, the FDA recently introduced special efforts to gain speed.[17]

Exactly where the truth lies between the objections and rebuttals is uncertain. In any event, Congress has acted ambivalently. In 1976 Congress displayed confidence in the FDA and in efficacy regulation when it gave the FDA new power to regulate the efficacy of medical devices. This was a massive extension of FDA authority. On the other hand, Congress has revealed some misgivings by recently considering a number of legislative reforms that would, among other things, hasten the approval process generally and relax the standard of effectiveness for breakthrough drugs. A reform that seems to have broad support would significantly alter the present approach of intensive premarket research coupled with little postmarket surveillance to establish a new system of reduced premarket research coupled with greatly expanded postmarket surveillance. In short, any likely congressional reform will probably say to the FDA: keep your good safety record—but be quick about it.

2. FOOD ADDITIVES

The main bone of contention in food additives concerns the Delaney clause, which sets a no-risk standard for carcinogenic food additives.[18] Critics contend that such an absolute no-risk standard is *foolish* when carcinogens abound. Moreover, it is *inconsistent* with the relative benefit-risk standard adopted for

[15] Further support for this claim came in the late 1970s when new approaches to drug research were apparently opening vast new horizons. At about the same time a staunch FDA critic was saying, "There is a real risk that the entire system for developing new drugs in the United States may even now be grinding to a halt," (Ibid., p. 33), the business press was reporting substantial increases in R&D expenditures and quoting drug executives as saying that research was "flowering" and "will in time" produce "important new products in larger number than we have ever seen before." *Business Week,* October 29, 1979, pp. 134–145; *Fortune,* October 19, 1981, pp. 94–112; *Wall Street Journal,* January 22, 1981, pp. 1, 14.

[16] Milton Silverman and Philip Lee, *Pills, Profits, and Politics* (Berkeley, Calif.: University of California Press, 1974), p. 251.

[17] *Wall Street Journal,* August 12, 1981, p. 25; September 16, 1981, p. 8.

[18] Extended coverage of the debate may be found in *Food Safety: Where Are We?,* U.S. Senate, Committee on Agriculture, Nutrition, and Forestry (July 1979).

Table 21–3.   **Annual Risk of Death for Individual Participants or Those Subject to Exposure (Mid-1970s)**

Activity	Risk	
Drinking 1 diet soda/day (saccharin)	1 in	100,000
Eating 4 tablespoons peanut butter/day (aflatoxin)	1 in	25,000
Drinking Miami or New Orleans water	1 in	800,000
Smoking (all bad effects)	1 in	300
Taking contraceptive pills	1 in	50,000
Power boating	1 in	5,900
Motor vehicle travel	1 in	4,500
Home accidents	1 in	83,000
Breathing (air pollution)	1 in	6,700
Getting hit by lightning	1 in	2,500,000

Source: P. B. Hutt, "Unresolved Issues in the Conflict Between Individual Freedom and Government Control of Food Safety," *Food Safety: Where Are We?*, U.S. Senate, Committee on Agriculture, Nutrition, and Forestry (July 1979), pp. 296–297.

aflatoxin, mercury, and other harmful substances that enter the food supply naturally or inadvertently. Moreover, critics favor a benefit-risk or benefit-cost approach as a matter of *principle*, not just of consistency. They point out that food additives often have tremendous benefits—extending product shelf life, preventing food-borne disease (like botulism), providing convenience, improving nutrition, and enhancing appeal through taste and color. For a concrete example, it has been estimated that bread without additives would cost 17 per cent *more* than bread made with additives, mainly because of the increased distribution and selling costs that greater perishability would entail.[19] As for the risks, advocates of a benefit-risk approach cite numbers such as those presented

in Table 21–3 to argue that the risks associated with cancerous substances in food are no greater, and in many cases much smaller, than the risks people willingly face daily.

Defenders of the Delaney clause rebut, first, by making the factual observation that, contrary to popular misconception, not all additives tested prove to be cancerous. Second, they claim that a distinction between risks that are natural or inevitable on the one hand, and those that are deliberately introduced into food on the other, is a meaningful distinction to make for policy purposes because the latter are *manageable* risks. Third, defenders say that a benefit-risk approach is fraught with too many uncertainties and dangers to be acceptable. "Any program," they say, "that assumes the ability to identify, quantify, and evaluate risks present in food will lead to serious damage to individual members of the population."[20] Finally, and not altogether consistent with the foregoing, defenders claim that there is enough flexibility in the present system to handle special cases, as when Congress exempted saccharin in response to public protest.

Where do you stand?[21]

II. National Highway Traffic Safety Administration

A. Standards

1. BROAD STANDARDS

The compelling need for the strong automobile safety legislation . . . lies embodied in these statis-

[19] Ibid., p. 636.

[20] Ibid., p. 366.

[21] In case you are swayed by expert opinion, you should know that in 1979 the National Academy of Sciences recommended an entirely new system that would move in the benefit-risk direction. Under the proposal, the FDA would classify substances as high-risk, moderate-risk, or low-risk. From there the FDA would have wide-ranging regulatory options: complete ban, restricting sale or use, requiring warning labels, public education campaigns, or no restriction, selection being based on benefit-risk judgment. Ibid, pp. 194–203.

tics: 1.6 million dead since the coming of the automobile; over 50,000 to die this year. And, unless the accelerating spiral of death is arrested, 100,000 Americans will die as a result of their cars in 1975.[22]

With these words Congress justified its establishment of NHTSA in 1966. Congress could have abolished automobiles or (as in the early days in England) required each moving auto to be preceded by a pedestrian carrying a red flag. But these policies defy practical consideration. So, instead, Congress ordered NHTSA to devise and enforce specific standards in furtherance of "motor vehicle safety." Such are the vague, broad standards guiding NHTSA policy.

2. NARROW STANDARDS

Upon getting the green light in 1966, NHTSA got quickly into high gear. The agency, which is housed in the Department of Transportation, issued 29 specific equipment standards in its first 4 years. Since that time NHTSA has more or less coasted, issuing fewer and fewer new standards each year while concentrating on enforcing and modifying its old standards. As of 1981, a total of 51 specific standards had been issued.

A simple list of the equipment covered—such as tires, windshields, child restraints, steering columns, brakes, and motorcycle helmets—reveals nothing more systematic than the jumbled contents of an average private garage. Nevertheless, all standards have one prime criterion: they must meet "the need for motor vehicle safety." Moreover, all standards may be classified, analyzed, and organized in three groups.[23]

100 Series, Precrash Standards. These standards improve the capacity of drivers to *avoid* crashes and reduce the capacity of cars to *cause* crashes. Examples include No. 101, which re-

quires that clearly identified, well illuminated essential controls be within easy reach of a driver restrained by safety belts; No. 105, which requires split braking systems, incorporating emergency features capable of stopping the car under certain specified conditions; and No. 109, which requires that tires meet minimum standards of quality, endurance, and high-speed performance.

200 Series, Crash Standards. These are aimed at protecting auto occupants and highway pedestrians *during* a crash. Their implementation softens blows, holds riders snug, and cuts down on flying debris. Examples include No. 202, which requires head restraints hindering "whiplash"; No. 203, which requires padded, collapsible steering systems; No. 205, which requires shatter-proof glass; and No. 206, which requires especially strong and reliable door latches.

300 Series, Postcrash Standards. The purpose of these standards is to keep injuries and losses to a minimum in the period *after* the crash has occurred. As of 1981 only two such standards had been issued—No. 301, which tries to minimize fire hazards by specifying certain features of fuel tanks, fuel tank filler pipes, and fuel tank connections; and No. 302, which requires that flame resistant materials be used in auto interiors.

In addition to these equipment standards, a number of nonequipment standards govern manufacturing and distributing practices. The most important of these concern product identification and record keeping. They enable manufacturers and retailers to track down purchasers of autos, tires, motorcycles, and other equipment long after purchase in the event a recall is necessary.

B. Enforcement

1. CERTIFICATION

NHTSA's certification efforts are minor in comparison to its other enforcement activities.

---

[22] Senate Report No. 1301, 89th Congress, Second Session (1966), pp. 1–2.

[23] For a more detailed and more interesting excursion through these standards the reader should look into the *Code of Federal Regulations* Title 49.

Thumbnail Sketch 8:   National Highway Traffic Safety Administration

---

Established: 1966 (called the National Highway Safety Agency 1966–1970).

Purpose: Administers federal programs designed to increase motor vehicle safety (and fuel economy).

Legislative Authority: National Traffic and Motor Vehicle Safety Act of 1966; Highway Safety Acts of 1966 and 1970; Energy Policy and Conservation Act of 1975.

Regulatory Activity: Sets and enforces mandatory standards for the safety of motor vehicles and related equipment (such as motorcycle helmets). Enforces 55 mph speed limit. Regulates fuel economy. Conducts research.

Organization: A division of the Department of Transportation, headed by an "administrator."

Budget: 1982 estimate: $51.1 million.

Staff: 1982 estimate: 686.

For the most part manufacturers accept the responsibility of testing old and new equipment to check compliance with the standards. If satisfied, the manufacturers then certify to NHTSA (and often to buyers via stickers) that their products meet standards.

2. TESTING AND SURVEILLANCE

During 1979 NHTSA selected 185 motor vehicle models for 313 tests to check compliance with standards. This represented a very small sample compared to the 400 different models of the 10 million vehicles produced. But compliance testing involved 4329 separate items of equipment on these vehicles, including door locks, seat belts, brake systems, and lights.[24]

Field surveillance includes the agency's toll-free Auto Safety Hotline, which allows consumers to contact NHSTA directly to register safety-related complaints or obtain information. The Hotline averages 500 to 600 calls per day. Folks contacting manufacturers instead of NHTSA may rest assured that the manufacturers themselves must notify the agency of their knowledge of hazards. If these and other sources of information reveal disturbing signs, NHTSA launches a "defects investigation." Over 200 such investigations occur in a typical year.

3. REMEDIES

The NHTSA has a number of remedies at its disposal, including fines (which totaled only $1.7 million up through 1980). Recalls, however, are by far the most familiar and most commonly used remedy. The majority of recall campaigns are initiated "voluntarily" by manufacturers (under threat of compulsory recall). Moreover, recalls have resulted in some of the most astounding statistics passing through these pages. Between NHTSA's founding in 1966 and early 1980, approximately 83.7 million vehicles were recalled for safety defects in 2942 separate campaigns.[25] Because 155.8 million cars were sold in the U.S. during that time, this suggests that one out of every two cars was recalled! But some cars were recalled more than once, so it is not literally true that 50% of all

---

[24] NHTSA, *Motor Vehicle Safety,* 1979, p. 45.

[25] Ibid., p. 46.

cars leaving the showroom proved faulty. For a recent example, Ford recalled Escort and Lynx *eight* times shortly after their introduction to fix safety and other defects (despite touting these cars as "the highest quality products in Ford history").[26]

The recall record for tires has been cheerier, representing a small fraction of all tires sold. Through 1979, 15.9 million tires had been recalled in 160 separate campaigns. The most notable of these campaigns involved the Firestone "500" steel-belted radial tire, whose tendency to fall apart apparently caused 41 fatalities. Approximately 7.5 million of these tires were faulty, costing Firestone $155 million to recall.

C. Controversies

1. RESULTS OF REGULATION

The estimated costs of mandated safety features vary from a few hundred to many hundreds of dollars per car. Given these costs, and given that our own necks are at stake, more than idle curiosity compels us to ask about the benefits these standards bestow. Have they made any difference? Some observers claim that they haven't, arguing that as cars get safer people drive more recklessly.[27] Others claim

otherwise. NHTSA, for instance, claims that its efforts "have saved more than 55,000 lives between 1966 and 1978, and . . . this figure will amount to 150,000 by 1987."[28] Where, then, does the answer lie?

In this writer's opinion the best studies reveal substantial gains.[29] One of the most thorough was undertaken by the General Accounting Office in 1976:

> The GAO analyzed information on more than 2,000,000 cars in crashes in North Carolina and New York, comparing driver death and injury rates and model cars. The GAO found that the 1966–70 standards may have saved 28,230 lives between 1966 and 1974 nationwide. Compared to pre-1966 models, it found from 15% to 25% fewer deaths and serious injuries occurring in 1966 to 1968 model cars and 25% to 30% fewer in 1969 and 1970 models. GAO found little further improvement, however, from standards introduced in 1971–1973 model cars.[30]

The results of a second study are shown in Figure 21–2.[31] It compares occupant fatalities per 100,000 cars in Maryland during 1972–1975 across three classes of cars: (1) unregulated models, (2) belt equipped 1964–1967 models, and (3) post-NHTSA era models from 1968–1975. Comparing the last category with the first reveals an overall 39% reduction in fatality rates. Figure 21–2 also shows the impact of the 55 miles per hour speed limit beginning in 1974. It is estimated that this speed limit saves about 4500 lives per year nationwide.

---

[26] *Wall Street Journal*, August 25, 1981, p. 22. Incidentally, the record largest safety recall to date is GM's recall of 6.7 million 1965 through 1969-model Chevrolets with faulty engine mounts. Ford narrowly missed this dubious distinction when in late 1980 the government let Ford off the hook on a proposed campaign that would have recalled 20 million 1970–1979 Ford vehicles for faulty transmissions. NHTSA said the defect had resulted in 98 deaths and 1710 injuries.

[27] Sam Peltzman, "The Effects of Automobile Safety Regulation," *Journal of Political Economy* (July/Aug., 1975), pp. 667–725. The basic assumption is that people have a fairly fixed preference for risk and therefore increase driving "intensity" as the inherent risks of autos falls. This contrasts with the assumption underlying regulation which is that there is a fairly fixed driving "intensity" and safety features thereby reduce overall risk. Query: Does the fact that accidents rise markedly in rainy weather, during holiday periods, and on certain obviously hazardous stretches of road indicate fixed risk preference or fixed driving intensity in varying risk situations?

[28] NHTSA, *Traffic Safety* '78, p. 6.

[29] For a critique of Peltzman see Leon S. Robertson, "A Critical Analysis of Peltzman's, 'The Effects of Automobile Safety Regulation,'" *Journal of Economic Issues* (September 1977), pp. 587–600.

[30] U.S. House, Committee on Interstate and Foreign Commerce, Subcommittee on Oversight and Investigations, *Federal Regulation and Regulatory Reform*, 94th Congress, 2nd Session (1976), p. 169.

[31] Ibid., p. 170.

Figure 21–2.   Car Occupant Fatalities per 100,000 Registered Cars, by Type of New-Car Safety Regulations, Maryland, 1972–1975

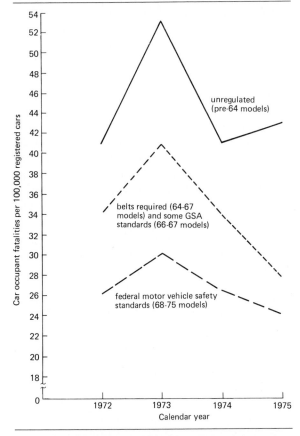

Source: *Federal Regulation and Regulatory Reform,* Subcommittee on Oversight and Investigations of the Committee on Interstate and Foreign Commerce, U.S. House of Representatives, 94th Congress, 2nd session (1976), p. 170.

2. PASSIVE RESTRAINTS

Of all proposed safety standards, none has kindled sharper dispute than the "passive restraint" standard that was promulgated by the Carter administration in 1977 but was rescinded by the Reagan administration in 1981, just prior to its actual implementation during the 1982–1984 model years. The problem is that no more than about 12% of all auto travelers use safety belts, which are "active restraints" because people must consciously buckle-up. If lap and shoulder belts received 100% usage, an estimated 16,300 lives would be saved each year. The inactivity of active restraints, however, led safety proponents to advocate compulsory inclusion of *automatic* belts or *automatically* inflating air cushions in all new cars—i.e., passive restraints that would save approximately 10,000 lives annually. As for cost, NHTSA estimated that automatic belts would raise the price of a car by $75 to $100 and that air bags would add $300 to $1,100.

A favorable benefit-cost computation for passive restraints supported official approval of passive restraints in 1977.[32] But opponents of the standard were neither passive nor restrained, and they eventually won the battle with some interesting arguments. First, there were a number of technical problems, such as the inconvenience and discomfort inherent in the designs of passive belts and the tendency of air bags to set-off inadvertently. Second, there was a problem of equity. The few who *do* wear safety belts would have been forced to pay heavy costs just so those who stupidly choose *not* to wear safety belts could be automatically protected. Is this fair? Finally, there is an issue of individual freedom here. Why force passive restraints on people? No adverse third party effects are present so long as "active" belts are available to all passengers who want to wear them.

Aside from these antiarguments, passive restraints were dropped because of an additional factor. Scrapping the standard was part of a general drive by the Reagan administration to aid the auto industry through relaxation and removal of safety and environmental regula-

[32] Secretary of Transportation, *Public Notice Concerning Motor Vehicle Occupant Crash Protection,* June 9, 1976.

tions. Despite this recent deregulation, the auto industry still faces many more restrictions than it did before 1966.

III. Consumer Product Safety Commission

A. Standards

1. BROAD STANDARDS

Created on October 27, 1972, the CPSC is the youngest of the three agencies reviewed here. The legislation establishing CPSC states that its primary purpose is "to protect the public against unreasonable risks of injury associated with consumer products." To this end, CPSC administers five laws:

1. The Consumer Product Safety Act
2. The Federal Hazardous Substances Act
3. The Flammable Fabrics Act
4. The Poison Prevention Packaging Act
5. The Refrigerator Safety Act

The last four of these preceded CPSC's creation, and were therefore formerly administered by other agencies, such as FDA and FTC. The overall significance of these regulations may be measured in round numbers thus:

> An estimated 20 million consumers are injured each year through the use of consumer products, of which 110,000 are permanently disabled and 30,000 are killed. The Commission also estimates that there are more than 10,000 different consumer products and more than 2.5 million manufacturers, importers, packagers, distributors, and retailers who are subject to Commission regulations.[33]

The only consumer products not included under CPSC's umbrella are those covered by other agencies: foods, drugs, cosmetics, medical devices, firearms, pesticides, motor vehicles, aircraft, and boats.

2. NARROW STANDARDS

Most mothers do not know it, but 2.375 inches is a very important measure to them. Before 1973 about 150 babies died annually in a rather bizarre fashion. When playfully dangling their feet between two slats of their cribs, these babies slipped out—their hips and torso following their feet toward the floor. However, their naturally large heads would not clear the slats, causing the babies to strangle or hang to death. The industry's crib slat spacing of 3.5 inches was clearly too great. But what spacing was proper? Formal research into the question led to studies of babies' buttocks, because buttock bulk could protect babies from passing beyond the threshold of danger. Of particular interest was the anterior-posterior measurement of baby buttocks when compressed between two slats by the downward force of a baby's weight. It was concluded that slat spacing of 2.375 inches would protect 95% of all infants from self-strangulation. Hence, the Commission's standard for baby cribs reads in part: "the distance between components (such as slats, spindles, crib rods and corner posts) shall not be greater than 6 centimeters ($2\frac{3}{8}$ inches) at any point."[34]

This was one of the first and easiest to formulate of all the Commission's narrow standards. As Steven Kelman comments:

> The CPSC's crib safety standard represents something like an ideal case of product safety regulation, displaying all the potential advantages of such regulation and none of the pitfalls. The decision to intervene in the marketplace with mandatory rules involved a hazard of which most consumers are totally ignorant, and the risks of which are assumed involuntarily by an infant unable to

[33] *Better Enforcement of Safety Requirements Needed By the Consumer Product Safety Commission*, Report by the Comptroller General of the United States (GAO), HRD–76–148 (July 26, 1976), p. 1.

[34] *Federal Code of Regulations*, Title 16, Chapter II, Section 1508, 4, p. 174.

Thumbnail Sketch 9:   Consumer Product Safety Commission

Established: 1972

Purpose: To protect the public against unreasonable risks of injury or death associated with consumer products (not covered by FDA or NHTSA).

Legislative Authority: Consumer Product Safety Act of 1972; Flammable Fabrics Act of 1954; Refrigerator Safety Act of 1956; Hazardous Substances Act of 1960; and Poison Prevention Packaging Act of 1970.

Regulatory Activity: Sets and enforces standards for the safety (and labeling) of consumer products. Bans certain products. Conducts research.

Organization: A five-member independent commission, appointed to seven-year terms by the President, with Senate advice and consent.

Budget: 1982 estimated: $31.7 million.

Staff: 1982 estimated: 631.

---

protect itself. The cost of making the product safe was minimal. The safety change did not reduce the utility or attractiveness of the product, and the likelihood that the standard would indeed reduce injury and death was extremely high.[35]

Were all CPSC standards as ideal as this, the Commission would be one big continuous picnic. Unfortunately, that is not the case. Most standards relate to complex problems and may take years to formulate. For this reason CPSC relies mainly upon "voluntary standards" as opposed to "mandatory standards." Whereas

mandatory standards are developed by CPSC itself, voluntary standards are developed by industry groups acting under the guidance and prodding of CPSC, which retains rights of final approval. Use of voluntary procedures saves CPSC's resources, broadens CPSC's scope, and improves the chances of self-enforced industry compliance. Still, the voluntary procedure offers no panacea. Proposed ladder standards consumed tens of thousands of man-hours, reams of paper, and hundreds of thousands of dollars belonging to both industry and government.

Given the difficulties of standard formulation and given the thousands of products subject to CPSC jurisdiction, the Commission has set some vague priorities to guide its endeavors. The main criteria have been (1) frequency and severity of injuries, (2) causality of injuries, and (3) chronic illness and future injuries. Product data concerning these criteria are obtained through an information gathering network that connects CPSC to hospital emergency rooms.

In the late 1970s and early 1980s the Com-

[35] Steven Kelman, "Regulation by the Numbers—A Report on the Consumer Product Safety Commission," *Public Interest* (Summer 1974), p. 86. Kudos may also go to CPSC's poison prevention packaging standards, which are *performance* rather than design standards. They are phrased in terms of how *difficult* it is for a large sample of children between the ages of 12 and 51 months to open containers and how *easy* it is for adults to open these same containers. They require: "(1) Child-resistant effectiveness of not less than 85 per cent without demonstration and not less than 80 per cent after a demonstration of the proper means of opening . . . (2) Adult-use effectiveness of not less than 90 per cent . . ." where the adults are "age 18 to 45 years inclusive, with no overt physical or mental handicaps . . ." CFR Title 16, Chapter II, p. 330–331.

mission began to weigh its standards by benefit-cost criteria. It defended its power mower rules, for example, by saying that they would benefit consumers $211 million in avoiding injury expenses while costing $190 million annually in equipment and implementation. This benefit-cost orientation was a radical change for an agency of this type, but heavy pressure by agency critics brought it about.

In round numbers the CPSC had about 30 standards on the books at the end of 1980, half of which were bans of various types. In addition, the agency was enforcing 80 special packaging and labeling regulations.[36]

B. Enforcement

1. CERTIFICATION

CPSC's certification activities are, like NHTSA's, minimal. Section 14 of the Consumer Product Safety Act puts the onus on manufacturers to certify that their products meet CPSC standards. Any certification testing procedures not explicitly set by standards may be set by the Commission.

2. SAMPLE TESTING AND FIELD SURVEILLANCE

During 1980 CPSC conducted over 4000 inspections and nearly 3000 sample collections. Compliance is also monitored by: (a) The agency's National Electronic Injury Surveillance System, which feeds data from a large sample of hospital emergency rooms to CPSC on a regular basis; (b) its review of death certificates in cases where a consumer product may have been at fault; (c) a consumer Hotline; and (d) mandatory reports from manufacturers who learn of hazards in their products.

3. REMEDIES

When establishing CPSC, Congress gave the agency a wide variety of remedial weapons,

including product seizures, recalls, injunctions, cease and desist orders, and civil and criminal penalties. Until 1978 these weapons were rarely used. Thereafter the Commission grew bolder. In 1980, for instance, 132 separate campaigns were conducted to recall a total of 23 million units of hazardous products. This activity included several million hair dryers that sprayed asbestos fibers and 180,000 toy blow guns with mouthpieces that were deemed choking hazards. In the same year the CPSC attacked delinquent business behavior with 13 injunctions, 6 seizures, 12 civil penalties, and 5 consent agreements.[37]

C. Controversy

The greatest controversy surrounding CPSC is whether the agency itself should continue to live, and, if so, what powers it should retain. When created, CPSC's life span was regulated by a "sunset" provision, which automatically killed the agency after a fixed duration unless Congress deliberately revived it. In 1981, when the agency's budget and continued existence were up for review, the Reagan administration called upon Congress to kill CPSC, or if not kill it at least cut its budget and powers considerably. Backing the administration was an army of business lobbyists representing the National Association of Manufacturers, the National Mass Retailing Institute, the Toy Manufacturers of America, and others who felt oppressed by the

---

[36] Consumer Product Safety Commission, *Annual Report 1981*, Part II, pp. 176–190.

[37] Ibid., pp. 214–216. A major problem with CPSC's recalls (and those of NHTSA as well) is that quite frequently, relatively few of the offending products are ever actually replaced or repaired. A CPSC 1978 study revealed that in 36 recall campaigns involving nearly $2\frac{1}{2}$ million small electrical appliances, an average of only 12% of the items were repaired or replaced. This understates the success rate because the 12% makes no allowance for products retired from service or repaired independently of the campaigns. Still, the rate is low, apparently because of (a) inadequate publicity, (b) inadequate consumer incentive, and (c) a "numbness" to hazards brought on by so many recalls. *Consumer Reports* (January 1981), pp. 45–48.

Commission. The Commission had, according to its enemies, grown overzealous, unreasonable, incompetent, unnecessary, and redundant.

An informal coalition of consumer, labor, and environmental groups rushed to the agency's defense. CPSC officials also came to the agency's defense by claiming a variety of agency achievements, including:

- Voluntary industry standards that prevent an estimated 200 deaths and 125,000 injuries annually.
- Prevention of more than 1 million injuries through recalls.
- Benefit-cost justifications of regulations.
- A 90% reduction in child poisoning fatalities (which previously took 500 lives annually) as a result of rules requiring child-proof caps on drugs, pesticides, cleaning solvents, and other toxic substances.

What will eventually become of the agency is at this writing uncertain.[38] Significant change seems to be in store, however. At the very least the agency's budget is likely to be slashed 30% or so. And the commissioners Reagan is likely to appoint will be committed to some degree of deregulation. This of course will not end the controversy, as whatever the compromise result there will be advocates for either more or less regulation.

Summary

Until fairly recently in our history the government was largely reactive rather than preventative in the area of consumer safety. As former commissioner Statler of the CPSC once put it, government was "the ambulance at the bottom of the cliff instead of the fence atop."[39] Even the original Food and Drug Act of 1906 was reactive, as it made no provision for pre-market safety certification. Beginning in 1938, however, this changed. After 107 people died from Elixir Sulfanilamide, Congress gave the FDA power to build a preventative safety fence for drugs, a fence that has since been extended to protect against hazards in consumer goods generally.

The FDA imposes standards for safety, purity, production cleanliness, and efficacy in foods, drugs, cosmetics, and medical devices. Safety standards for drugs and medical devices tend to be relative. That is, the greater the benefits, the higher the risks that will be permitted. Safety standards for foods and cosmetics tend to be more absolute, as illustrated most sharply by the Delaney clause banning carcinogenic food additives. Leeway is allowed, however, for other hazards that would be very costly to remove completely. Such partial relativity extends beyond safety standards to include purity, production cleanliness, and efficacy.

FDA's enforcement activities include pre-market certification, sample testing, and plant inspections. Given the many thousands of products and plants involved, the task is immense. Among remedies, recalls are the mainstay, backed up by seizures and even the possibility of criminal penalties.

Stormy controversies have raged over the 1962 drug amendments and the Delaney clause. The premarket hurdles of the 1962 amendments yield benefits of assured safety and efficacy, but they do so at the cost of considerable delay in getting new drugs to market (not to mention other costs like higher R&D expense). Critics pooh-pooh the benefits and stress the costs while defenders of the policy have an opposite placement of emphasis. Some kind of compromise seems likely, with expe-

---

[38] *Wall Street Journal*, April 30, 1981, p. 48, Richard I. Kirkland, Jr., "Hazardous Times for Product-Safety Czars," *Fortune* (June 15, 1981), pp. 126–134.

[39] *Wall Street Journal*, April 30, 1981, p. 48.

dited procedures granted to new breakthrough drugs. The Delaney dispute has already produced compromise in the form of a saccharin exemption.

The National Highway Traffic Safety Administration implements vague broad standards with over 50 narrow standards. These set design and performance specifications from bumper to bumper. Compliance is checked by agency testing and by surveillance systems of various kinds. Certainly the most graphic measure of the agency's impact lies in its recalls, which constitute the chief remedy. By early 1980, 83.7 million vehicles had been recalled for hazards in 2942 campaigns.

Just how much NHTSA has preserved life and limb is subject to dispute, but the best evidence shows a significant impact, especially from the agency's early standards. Among specific proposed standards, by far the most controversial was the "passive restraint" standard issued in 1977 and rescinded in 1981. Though defensible on benefit-cost grounds (only because people shun safety belts), the standard posed problems of technical inconvenience, economic inequity, and interference with personal freedom.

The Consumer Product Safety Commission was established "to protect the public against unreasonable risks of injury associated with consumer products." Probably the best narrow standards evolving from this mandate relate to child safety—toys, baby cribs, and protective caps on containers of toxic substances. Another plus is the agency's increased reliance on benefit-cost analysis in standard formulation.

After a timid start, CPSC's enforcement effort grew some teeth in the late 1970s and early 1980s. Annual tallies of recalled products mounted into the tens of millions of units. Partly because of this increasing bite, opposition to the agency has billowed as business interests have increasingly lobbied for the agency's demise or curtailment. Given the hostile political climate, it seems doubtful that the agency can protect itself from injury.

Questions and Exercises for Chapter 21

1. Compare and contrast the narrow safety standards for drugs and for foods. Why do they differ?
2. Why are there no efficacy standards for food and cosmetics?
3. Why is the FDA in a "no win" situation on the issue of premarket clearance of drugs? Do you think less stringent premarket study coupled with closer postmarket surveillance would be a good compromise? How would this shift the focus of enforcement among the categories of Table 20–3 of the last chapter?
4. Explain how value judgments might influence one's opinion on the issue of food additives.
5. Where, among enforcement activities, has NHTSA placed its greatest effort? What defenses and criticisms might be made of this approach?
6. What value judgments would influence your assessment of auto passive restraint policy?
7. Why has the CPSC's baby crib standard been uncontroversial?
8. Pick a pro or con position on continuation of CPSC and argue your case.

Chapter 22

Labor Safety and Health: OSHA

In the 10 years that have passed since the Occupational Safety and Health Act was enacted, its implementation has aroused very deep felt reactions of all sorts. On the one hand, it has been praised by workers as a program that has provided the protections needed to make workers safe. On the other hand, it has been denounced by employers as creating a petty bureaucracy whose inspectors are asked to enforce ridiculous regulations and harass employers for minor infractions.
—Senator Alan Cranston

In 1970 Congress overwhelmingly approved the Occupational Safety and Health Act in hopes of cutting workplace casualties. At the time, job-related accidents were producing 15,000 deaths and 2.2 million disabling injuries annually, and job-related health hazards were causing perhaps as many as 100,000 deaths and 400,000 new cases of occupational disease each year. The good intentions behind the OSH Act still win everybody's blessing. But congressional support for the Act's design and execution has crumbled. The Occupational Safety and Health Administration (OSHA), which implements the Act, has become the most controversial agency in Washington D.C.

Business organizations like the Chamber of Commerce and National Association of Manufacturers applaud the idea of reduced worker risk but vilify OSHA for:

- Perpetrating misguided, nitpicking, "Mickey Mouse" standards not related to safety and health.
- Workplace inspections not targeted on where the need is greatest.
- Arbitrary and inconsistent enforcement actions, often amounting to harassment.
- A lack of results, a complete failure to reduce death, injury, and disease despite enormous compliance costs.[1]

Unionized labor stands staunchly in defense, saying that the OSH Act "is a sound law; it is an effective law, and it is a law which is absolutely essential to the future well-being of

[1] U.S. Senate, Committee on Labor and Human Resources, *Oversight on the Administration of the Occupational Safety and Health Act,* Hearings (1980), Vol. 1, pp. 766–805, Vol. 2, pp. 1271–1309.

American workers and their families."[2] Yet even these friends of OSHA voice qualms, complaining that standards are too lax, that inspection personnel are too sparce, that delays in enforcement are all too common.

Our review of OSHA will cover standards first and enforcement activities second, followed by discussions of controversies and proposals for reform. A distinction between safety (against accidents like falls) and health (against diseases like cancer) is maintained throughout.

By way of preliminary clarification, it should be noted that states can set up their own programs of worker protection which, if approved by OSHA, receive federal funding and supplant federal authority. Moreover, OSHA efforts do not detract from workman's compensation programs, which compensate victims and their families for job-related casualties while at the same time protecting employers from costly negligence suits. The OSHA approach attempts to prevent loss in the first place rather than smooth its aftermath.

I. Standards

A. Broad Standards

Congress stated OSHA's goal in very general terms: "to assure so far as possible every working man and woman in the Nation safe and healthy working conditions."[3] To guide OSHA in determining what is "safe and healthy," the OSH Act goes on to say that OSHA can impose standards "reasonably necessary or appropriate to provide safe or healthful employment and places of employment." For toxic substances, the Act calls for protection "to the extent feasible," which is a bit more specific than the "reasonably necessary" language applicable to all

risks, but not much.[4] These vague broad standards have touched off intense legal battles, as we shall see shortly.

B. Narrow Standards

To assist OSHA's launching, Congress ordered OSHA to adopt existing "national consensus standards." These were voluntary safety and health standards developed prior to the OSH Act by industry trade associations or research organizations such as the National Fire Protection Association. When arguing against the establishment of OSHA, business lobbyists claimed these consensus standards made government intervention unnecessary. So, assuming they were sound, OSHA's first director gave little thought to adopting thousands of them hastily. Unfortunately, these consensus standards were riddled with obsolete, inane, irrelevant, and even stupid provisions, leading OSHA into a concern for such things as the shape of toilet seats and the presence of hooks on restroom walls. The resulting ridicule heaped upon OSHA lingers to this day, even though OSHA purged these standards of over 900 faulty provisions in 1978.

Two characteristics further marred OSHA's early standards, characteristics that to some extent remain. First, the standards were dominated by *design* standards rather than *performance* standards (in part because of their "consensus" origins). That is, they were specification-oriented rather than performance-oriented. Ladders had to have rungs one inch thick rather than support capacity of 500 pounds. There are advantages to design standards, such as ease of inspection enforcement and clarity for compliance. But there are also big disadvantages, such as interference with safety innovations, a frequent failure to achieve the desired result, and greater expense as com-

---

[2] Statement of Steelworkers President, Lloyd McBride, ibid., p. 700.

[3] Occupational Safety and Health Act, Section 2(b)

[4] Ibid., Section 6(b)(5).

Thumbnail Sketch 10:   Occupational Safety and Health Administration

---

Established: 1970

Purpose: To develop and enforce workplace safety and health standards.

Legislative Authority: Occupational Safety and Health Act of 1970.

Regulatory Activity: Sets and enforces safety and health standards; engages in liaison, education, and consultation activities with employers, employees, and trade associations. OSHA's decisions are subject to review by the Occupational Safety and Health Review Commission (OSHRC). The National Institute for Occupational Safety and Health (NIOSH) conducts research and recommends standards to OSHA.

Organization: A division of the Department of Labor headed by a Deputy Assistant Secretary of Labor. (OSHRC is an independent commission, and NIOSH is housed in the Health and Human Services Department.)

Budget: 1982 estimate: $192.6 million.

Staff: 1982 estimate: 2354.

---

pared to cheaper but equally safe alternatives. Only recently, starting with the Carter administration, has OSHA moved to rectify this bias by converting many of its design standards into performance standards.

The second further failing of OSHA's early standards was their emphasis on *safety* to the neglect of *health*. One of the major justifications for regulating worker protection is workers' ignorance of hazards. But the ignorance problem arises most starkly in connection with health, not safety. If a fork-lift truck lacks a driver's canopy to catch falling objects, or if a section of guard rail is missing from a catwalk 100 feet above a plant floor, the hazard is readily apparent to workers. But what about those who handle betanaphthylamine, or those who breathe small amounts of vinyl chloride gas when manufacturing plastic pipe? The danger is less apparent and the unhealthy consequences may emerge only after considerable delay.

Severe shortages of professional industrial hygienists and persistent legal challenges by businesses contributed to OSHA's early slowness in dealing with health hazards. But now these obstacles have withered. During OSHA's first five years only three health-related rulemakings were completed, resulting in standards for asbestos, vinyl chloride, and fourteen carcinogens. During OSHA's next five years, eight health-related rulemakings were completed, leading to standards for hazards like benzene, inorganic arsenic, lead, acrylonitrile, and cotton dust.

OSHA may set a permanent standard for safety or health on its own initiative, in response to the appeals of employees or employers, or in response to the recommendations of the National Institute for Occupational Safety and Health (NIOSH), which was also established by the OSH Act. Whereas OSHA is housed in the Department of Labor and concentrates on setting and enforcing standards, NIOSH is housed in the Department of Health and Human Services and concentrates on research.

Regardless of where a standard's impetus originates, the procedures for developing standards are, as in the case of NHTSA, CPSC, and other such agencies, quite complex and protracted. Notices, hearings, and even judicial appeals are involved. The first appellate authority to rule on questions concerning OSHA's standards is the Occupational Safety and Health Review Commission (OSHRC), which is an independent agency comprised of three commissioners appointed by the President.[5] After OSHRC, which was established by the OSH Act for the express purpose of reviewing OSHA decisions, appeals may be pursued in the federal courts. The Supreme Court's rulings on standards for benzene and cotton dust will occupy us momentarily.

After following the tortuous procedures case-by-case, substance-by-substance for health standards for ten years, OSHA broke new ground with its Cancer Policy in 1980. The cumbersome substance-by-substance approach had produced very few standards despite the fact that there are over 2000 potential carcinogens in American workplaces. Thus the Cancer Policy is supposed to streamline standard setting for potential carcinogens by treating them in two broad classes—confirmed and suspected. Those falling into the *confirmed* class (as determined by the policy's procedures) will earn expedited standards reducing worker exposure to the lowest "feasible" level. Those classified as *suspected* will receive less restrictive standards and further study. Whether the Cancer Policy wins Reagan administration approval and survives judicial review remains to be seen.[6] If it does endure, it could pave the way

for other comprehensive "generic" standards, such as might be appropriate for pesticides.

II. Enforcement

Like those of police parking patrols, OSHA's enforcement activities center on inspections and citations. Consultations with employers and education programs for employees play a growing but still tangential part. Certification and permit activities, so prominent in activities of FDA and EPA, play no part at all.

A. Inspections

Robert Stewart Smith once quipped that "the typical establishment will see an OSHA inspector about as often as we see Halley's comet."[7] Notwithstanding its considerable truth, the metaphor is somewhat misleading. OSHA has approximately 2800 inspectors, including those working under OSHA state plans. Their inspections are, as suggested in Table 22–1, of four types:

1. *Programmed inspections*, by far the largest in number, are scheduled on the basis of sample selection. The sample is not random, as every OSHA administration has made an effort to target its inspections on high hazard industries such as construction, logging, longshoring, and metal fabricating. Early administrations were less successful in this than recent administrations, partly because data deficiencies hampered target sampling. Inspections of small fruitcake bakeries with forty years of totally harmless operation were not uncommon. Rather than risk the wrath of such businesses, the Reagan administration recently drew its focus more narrowly than any previous administration by announcing a sweeping ex-

---

[5] Nicholas A. Ashford, *Crisis in the Workplace: Occupational Disease and Injury* (Cambridge: MIT Press, 1976), pp. 144–145, 167–173.

[6] *Business Week*, February 4, 1980, p. 76; *Wall Street Journal*, January 17, 1980, p. 2.

[7] Robert S. Smith, *The Occupational Safety and Health Act* (Washington, D.C.: American Enterprise Institute, 1976), p. 62.

Table 22–1.   OSHA Inspections by Type, 1979

Type	Federal OSHA Inspections	State OSHA Inspections
Programmed inspections	23,763	70,762
Accident investigations	2,304	5,181
Employee complaints	20,170	15,285
Abatement follow-up	11,700	16,408
Total	57,937	107,636

Note: Federal OSHA inspections averaged 113 man-hours per inspection, as contrasted to 10 man-hours per state-plan inspection. The twenty-two states include California, Indiana, Iowa, Maryland, Michigan, Oregon, South Carolina, Tennessee, and Washington.

Source: Oversight on the Administration of the Occupational Safety and Health Act, U.S. Senate, Committee on Labor and Human Resources (1980), pp. 286–87, 409.

emption for nearly three-fourths of all U.S. manufacturing companies. The 70,200 concerns remaining subject to routine safety inspection sampling were above-average in injury incidence, accounting for 78% of the nation's 1.2 million annual serious manufacturing injuries.[8]

2. *Accident investigations,* the second class mentioned in Table 22–1, are inspections triggered by fatalities and catastrophies. Some states also respond to reports of amputations, permanent disfigurements, and lengthy hospitalizations.

3. *Employee complaints* also trigger unscheduled inspections. Given that workers are OSHA's main constituency, unionized workers especially, it is not surprising that in times past OSHA responded to virtually every employee complaint it received, stretching its

[8] *Wall Street Journal,* September 24, 1981, p. 17.

limited inspection resources thin in order to probe very minor problems like dimly lit washrooms, thereby unconsciously helping many employees to "get back" at their employers for assorted grudges. Recently, OSHA has grown circumspect about complaint investigations, inspecting only where hazards appear serious while handling other complaints by mail or telephone.

4. Finally, OSHA conducts *follow-up inspections* in situations where citations for serious, willful, or repeated violations have been issued, or where a court has issued a restraining order in an imminent danger situation. Follow-up inspections for nonserious violations are discretionary and rare.

To round out this statistical survey, it may be noted that there were over 9 million employees in the establishments inspected in Table 22–1. Moreover, 88 per cent of the inspections mentioned were for safety while 12 per cent were for health, revealing a continuing tilt in favor of safety.

B. Citations and Other Remedies

In recent years slightly more than half of all inspected work places have been found in compliance. Citations greeted the violations of the remainder, multiple citations in instances of multiple offenses. In particular, the inspections itemized in Table 22–1 resulted in 128,544 federal citations and 275,442 state citations.

Monetary penalties put bite in these citations, varying in average severity from several thousand dollars for "willful" violations to several hundred dollars for "serious" or "repeat" violations to only a few dollars for "nonserious" offenses. The proposed penalties emerging from the inspections of Table 22–1 totaled over $30 million.

Just as parking tickets stimulate people's frustration and irritation, so too OSHA's citations have often proved annoying, provoking charges of harassment and worse. For example, small businessmen Irvin Dawson attracted some press attention when in 1974 he closed his Cleveland business for one day to protest "the loss of rights of [American] citizenry under the so-called OSHA." An OSHA inspector had cited him for such nonserious violations as:

> Failing to post a copy of the act (which he never received).
> Failure to maintain a separate OSHA folder even though he had all necessary records.
> The presence of an 'insufficiently' guarded fan, which was dust-covered, its cord wrapped around the base, without brushes, and obviously not in use.[9]

Still, examples at the opposite end of the spectrum readily avail themselves. The largest tally of offenses ever charged against a single firm occurred in 1980 against Newport News Shipbuilding & Dry Dock Company. The inspection produced 617 alleged violations, including 54 "willful" and 37 "repeat" violations. Among other things, the shipyard's workers were allegedly exposed to excess levels of lead, asbestos, chromate, silica, and cadmium, and ominously endangered by scaffolding openings, unguarded machinery, and fire hazards. Proposed penalties for this one case came to $786,190.[10]

Fines are not the only remedy. OSHA's equivalent of a recall is the *imminent danger* citation. This applies when there is reasonable certainty that the hazard threatens death or serious physical injury before it can be corrected by normal procedures. If the employer fails to rectify the violation immediately, OSHA can go directly to the nearest federal district court for legal action.

Firms taking offense at being accused of of- fenses can appeal to the Occupational Safety and Health Review Commission (OSHRC). Past appeals, which run into the thousands, reveal that employers can be just as "nitpicky" as OSHA. For example, violators have argued that their inspections or citations should be invalidated on grounds that nonemployees had notified OSHA of the discovered dangers and that a roof needed no railing because it was not, strictly speaking, an "open-sided floor or platform."[11] Many cases get into the federal courts, and those are fortunately meritorious.

C. New Directions in Enforcement

To encourage voluntary compliance and cooperation, OSHA has developed a number of programs that make it seem less like a club wielding policeman. These include maintaining liaison activities, providing technical services and information, consulting with employees, and operating a wide variety of training programs for employers and employees. Consulting, for instance, includes on-site visits by *non*enforcement personnel to (1) survey workplaces, (2) inform employers of hazards, and (3) suggest corrective measures. Consultations are of greatest benefit to small businesses lacking the where-with-all to hire in-house safety and health experts or to buy the services of private consulting firms. The highly technical nature of many OSHA regulations necessitates expert interpretation, and OSHA consultation can inexpensively provide that expert interpretation for those who want to comply without simultaneously risking citations and penalties.[12]

The most innovative recent break from normal enforcement procedures is the "labor-management committee." The idea is to have rep-

---

[9] As related by Murray L. Weidenbaum in *Business, Government, and the Public,* 2nd ed. (Englewood Cliffs, N.J.: Prentice-Hall, 1981), pp. 82–83.

[10] *Wall Street Journal,* February 28, 1980, p. 4.

[11] *The President's Report on Occupational Safety and Health* (1974), pp. 95–97.

[12] Though not included in the OSH Act, on-site consultation began in 1975 after amendment. The program was greatly expanded under the Carter administration.

resentatives of both labor and management form in-plant committees to formulate safety and health programs, respond to worker complaints, conduct monthly inspections, and see to it that hazards are eliminated. OSHA approval of a committee program wins exemption for that plant from OSHA's normal inspection-citation procedures. First tried experimentally in California during the late 1970s in cooperation with the Bechtel Corporation, the method has attracted favorable attention and will see much wider application in the future.

III. Key Controversies

A. *Benefit-Cost Analysis*

1. THE ISSUE
The OSH Act's history reveals no recognition by Congress or by those testifying before Congress that there is a trade-off between benefit and cost—that is, added benefit from risk reduction requires added cost. As John Mendeloff summarized his review of the record . . .

the most striking characteristic of the testimony and the congressional commentary was their idealism and their silence on the costs of regulation. In the whole legislative history, I found only two brief statements by Republican conservatives that point out that intervention can do more harm than good. In contrast, the idea that even one injury or fatality is too many is frequently repeated, along with assertions about the infinite value of human life.[13]

In the end, Congress gave only implicit recognition to the problem of cost by vaguely saying in the Act that standards need go no further than *"reasonably necessary"* and *"to the extent feasible."* OSHA interpreted these qualifiers to

mean that, in general, costs need *not* be weighed against benefits. Costs would be considered relevant only when they were so high as to seriously jeopardize the financial condition of the industry or its companies—when, that is, plant doors would be closed and workers would lose their jobs. OSHA's refusal to weigh benefits and costs was repeatedly challenged by business, but the issue was not resolved until the Supreme Court ruled in OSHA's favor in *American Textile Manufacturers Institute* v. *Raymond Donovan, Secretary of Labor* (1981).

To prepare the ground for our discussion of this important case, we must first explore some of the reasons behind Congress's and OSHA's aversion to benefit-cost analysis.

2. COST ESTIMATION
Rough estimates put the annual cost of health and safety regulation somewhere between $0.5 and $2.5 billion.[14] These can be no more than very rough guesses because the cost of specific individual standards is itself typically speculative. The classic example concerns vinyl chloride, which causes a fatal form of liver cancer. In 1974, after discovering the problem, OSHA proposed a standard that would reduce the allowable level of vinyl chloride gas exposure from 500 parts per million parts of air to 1 part per million (ppm). Industry studies predicted the strict standard would shut down all polyvinyl chloride plants and severely cripple the entire plastics industry, costing the economy $65 to $90 *billion* in lost GNP and eliminating between 1.7 and 2.2 million jobs. OSHA did not flinch and imposed the 1 ppm standard anyway.

What happened then? It turned out that the total cost did not exceed $250 million, few workers actually lost their jobs, and the prod-

[13] John Mendeloff, *Regulating Safety: An Economic and Political Analysis of Occupational Safety and Health Policy* (Cambridge: MIT Press, 1979), p. 20.

[14] Ibid., p. 88. *Oversight* Hearings, Vol. 2, *op. cit.*, p. 1283.

uct's price rose only about 6 per cent.[15] These costs were substantial, but they were hardly as bad as the industry's dire projections.

The example indicates the practical difficulty of projecting a proposed standard's costs. Those who have the best data—industry members—also have an incentive to exaggerate costs. Even when costs are not deliberately exaggerated, they may be inflated from a failure to account for technological change. In the case of vinyl chloride, for example, the industry's credibility was never questioned. But technological developments after the standard was set saved the day, the standard, and the industry. In short, it was a "technology-forcing" standard that happened to pay off. Its great success has undoubtedly fed OSHA's doubts about relying heavily on benefit-cost analysis.

OSHA's rather casual attitude toward costs is further explained by its bias favoring engineering controls and opposing personal protective equipment. Guarding workers against excessive noise, toxic fumes, and other health hazards can often be achieved much more cheaply by means of earmuffs, respirators, and other personal protective equipment than by insulating partitions, ventilation systems, and other engineering alterations to production processes. Yet OSHA has shown persistent partiality for engineering controls on grounds that "personal protective equipment can be as effective as engineering controls only if it is carefully implemented (for example, to assure proper fit and maintenance.)"[16] Critics of the agency pooh-pooh this rationalization, pointing instead to political and ideological reasons, such as workers' general dislike for respirators and

earmuffs plus union opposition. Moreover, economists argue that physical effectiveness alone is not the issue but rather *cost-effectiveness*. And judged by cost-effectiveness, personal protective equipment should receive the favorable bias, not engineering controls. For example, one study estimates that the total cost of achieving an industrial noise limit of 85-decibels by personal protective gear would be $2.4 billion, considerably less than the $19.4 billion cost of engineering controls.[17]

Business interests, it need hardly be said, favor personal gear, countering labor's position and putting OSHA in a bind. OSHA's solution has been a sort of compromise. Its health standards have mandated engineering controls "to the extent feasible," thereby appeasing its labor constitutents. At the same time, however, OSHA has eased industry's burden by allowing very gradual implementation of those controls. Its lead standard allows a phase-in over ten years. And its cotton dust standard has a four-year grace period.

3. BENEFITS

Even though the vinyl chloride standard proved to be economically "feasible," its costs were nevertheless high relative to the risk reduction—$9 million per life likely to be saved, by one estimate.[18] This means that, *by implication*, OSHA puts an extremely high value on human life when considering benefits. Many economists critically point out that OSHA's implicit values greatly exceed the $200,000–$500,000 values estimated by economists and used by other agencies, such as NHTSA and CPSC. Business interests criticize OSHA without specifying their benefit values.

Rather than criticize OSHA's high implicit

[15] For accounts of the story see David D. Doniger, *The Law and Policy of Toxic Substances Control: A Case Study of Vinyl Chloride* (Baltimore: Johns Hopkins University Press, 1978); and H. R. Northrup, R. L. Rowan, and C. R. Perry, *The Impact of OSHA* (Philadelphia: Industrial Research Unit, University of Pennsylvania, 1978), pp. 291–418.

[16] Mendeloff, *op. cit.*, p. 163.

[17] John F. Morrall, III, "Exposure to Occupational Noise", in Miller and Yandle (eds.) *Benefit-Cost Analyses of Social Regulation* (Washington, D.C.: American Enterprise Institute, 1979), pp. 33–58.

[18] Northrup, Rowan, and Perry, *op. cit.*, pp. 390–405.

values, John Mendeloff asks "why?" and then comes up with some interesting answers:[19]

- Workers are not perceived as choosing their risks as freely as consumers choose theirs because of occupational and geographic immobilities. Thus what is appropriate for NHTSA and CPSC may not be appropriate for OSHA.
- Spending great amounts to save identifiable victims, such as workers trapped in a coal mine cave-in, is commonplace. Quite often the potential victims of occupational hazards are in a relatively small, identifiable group.
- Unionized labor is OSHA's chief client, and labor leaders give tremendous weight to protection. Thus for political reasons, OSHA's benefit values are high in comparison to cases where those protected are less well organized and vocal.

As a matter of *principle,* then, OSHA tends to treasure immensely *any* perceived benefits. Probing further, we find that OSHA resists explicit benefit computation as a *practical* matter also. As former labor secretary Ray Marshall once said, "Uncertainty involved in assessing the health benefits of regulations renders precise cost-benefit analysis difficult."[20] Indeed, OSHA used "uncertainty" to excuse itself from reckoning even the nonmonetary benefits of its benzene standard and the result was a major Supreme Court case (*American Petroleum Institute* v. *Marshall*).

Benzene is used to make solvents, pesticides, detergents, and other petrochemical products. High exposure, well above 10 parts per million parts of air, has been associated with leukemia. In 1977, OSHA ordered a sharp reduction in exposure limit from the old 10 ppm standard to a new 1 ppm standard without evidence that the old 10 ppm was in fact unsafe. The petroleum industry challenged the new standard's

benefits, arguing in federal court that it would prevent, at most, only one case of leukemia every 15 to 38 years. OSHA defended itself by arguing that the evidence was "too imprecise" to establish risk below the old 10 ppm standard. It was enough to know, said OSHA, that benzene caused leukemia at high levels of exposure, because that established the absence of a "safe level" below which exposure would be assuredly risk-free.[21]

The Supreme Court's 1980 judgment of the benzene case is itself somewhat uncertain because five of the nine Justices wrote opinions. Nevertheless, the Court struck down the strict new benzene standard largely because it was based more on speculation than scientific fact.[22] Justice Stevens, writing for four members of the Court, said that OSHA failed in issuing the benzene standard to establish that it was "reasonably necessary and appropriate" to remedy a "significant risk." OSHA had not obtained any "empirical evidence" or "opinion testimony" that "exposure to benzene at or below the 10 ppm level had ever in fact caused leukemia." As a result of this case, then, OSHA can no longer blithely *assume* that, once a substance has been shown to cause cancer at some (high) level of exposure, it can require employers to reduce exposure to the lowest "feasible" level. Benefits must be based on actual estimates, not assumptions.

4. BENEFITS AND COSTS TOGETHER

Although the Supreme Court ruled in benzene that benefits could not be merely assumed, it did not go so far as to say that benefits must be weighed against costs. That issue was addressed in *American Textile Manufacturers Institute* v. *Donovan,* the landmark "cotton dust" case of 1981.[23] Approximately 800,000

[19] Mendeloff, *op. cit.,* pp. 71–79.
[20] *Oversight* Hearings, *op. cit.,* p. 1016.

[21] *Wall Street Journal,* January 9, 1980, p. 42.
[22] *Ray Marshall, Sec. of Labor* v. *American Petroleum Institute,* 65 L Ed 2d 1010 (1980).
[23] *American Textile Manufacturers Institute, Inc.* v. *R. J. Donovan, Sec. of Labor,* 69 L Ed 2d 185 (1981).

textile workers are exposed to cotton dust, which causes byssinosis, or "brown lung," a disease that produces breathlessness, chronic cough, and occasionally death. OSHA's standard set a ceiling of 0.2 milligrams of dust per cubic meter of air. The standard's benefits and costs were hotly disputed by OSHA and the textile industry. OSHA claimed that brown lung afflicted 20% of the textile workers, whereas the industry said the proportion was only 2%. OSHA estimated the cost of compliance to be $656.5 million, whereas the industry's estimate was $2 billion, or three times as much. The key issue before the Court, however, was not whose numbers were correct. Rather, it was whether benefits had to be weighed against costs in order to establish a health standard's validity. OSHA said "no." Industry urged "yes."

The Supreme Court decided "no." After noting that Congress can expressly call for benefit-cost analysis when it wants to (as it has for dams and other water projects), the Court went on to point out that the OSH Act is devoid of benefit-cost language. Moreover, the Court felt that requiring a benefit-cost test for workplace health standards "would inevitably" lead to less protection and would violate the law. By using the word "feasible," which means "capable of being done," Congress "defined the basic relationship between costs and benefits by placing the 'benefit' of worker health above all other considerations save those making attainment of this 'benefit' unachievable." Thus the Court, like OSHA, defined "feasibility" in technical rather than economic terms.

Of course Congress can change its directive by amending the OSH Act. And at this writing there are rumblings that the Reagan administration will urge Congress to do so. But for now benefit-cost analysis need not back standards. Notice: the Court did not say that benefit-cost *cannot* be used, so the Reagan administration could move in the direction of benefit-cost even without congressional action.

B. Effects of OSHA

Another hot controversy centers on the question of whether OSHA has in fact made any headway in reducing job-related casualties. Business spokesmen argue that "the available data on workplace injuries suggest that OSHA activities have not brought about demonstrable reductions in the incidence of injuries and illnesses in the workplace."[24] Union spokesmen argue otherwise, saying that . .

fatalities have decreased 10% during the program's history; that means the lives of thousands of workers have been saved. Similarly, thousands of workers have been spared serious injuries with a 15% overall decline in total injuries during the program's history.[25]

Academic researchers are also divided, but their work merits closer attention. The problem with raw data on injury and illness rates, such as those alluded to above, is that injuries and illnesses are affected by many factors other than OSHA. These other factors are especially important in assessing trends in job-related illnesses as opposed to injuries. Illnesses like cancer are caused by such nonoccupational factors as smoking, air pollution, and food impurities. Thus, for example, it is often impossible to tell whether an asbestos worker's lung cancer is job-related or not, and correspondingly whether a decline in lung cancer among asbestos workers is due to reduced exposures on the job or improved conditions among other possible causes. Good studies of OSHA's impact would take these other factors into account in order to isolate the role of regulation. Academic studies typically attempt to do this through multiple-regression analysis. Unfortunately, such analysis has been conducted only for the safety side of OSHA's efforts. For health, there is too much muddling by other factors and too many impurities in the available data to permit a ret-

---

[24] *Oversight*, Hearings, Vol. 1, *op. cit.*, p. 779.
[25] Ibid., Vol. 2, p. 1215.

rospective estimate of OSHA's impact on illness. Moreover, health analysis is severely hampered by the fact that occupational illness often strikes only after *accumulated* exposure and a *long lag*. Liver cancer of the type caused by vinyl chloride, for instance, has a latency period of 10 to 30 years.

What, then, do academic studies of OSHA's safety performance show? They show little if any aggregate impact, looking at overall injury rates at industry wide levels. In an early study, Robert S. Smith analyzed pre- and post-OSHA injury rates across industries to see if those industries receiving OSHA's special attention improved relative to those not targeted by OSHA. There was no significant difference.[26] W. Kip Viscusi tested the impact of two OSHA policy variables: (1) the intensity of inspection activity and (2) the magnitude of citation penalties. Comparing 61 industries over several years he found no significant reduction in injury rates in response to OSHA's activities.[27] Finally, John Mendeloff constructed a statistical model of factors causing temporal variations in aggregate U.S. injury rates *prior* to OSHA (including such factors as percentage of males in the workforce 18 to 24 years of age, a factor that increases injuries because these fellows tend to be careless). He then checked to see if observed injury rates *after* OSHA were in fact lower than could be accounted for by these other, non-OSHA factors, and he found that they were not.[28]

The only studies that show significantly reduced injury rates from OSHA are those using disaggregated data, that is, data on specific types of injuries or data on specific plants inspected by OSHA. Mendeloff, for instance, applied his before-and-after technique to check the trend in injuries where workers were caught in or between machinery. These injuries, he argued, were of the type most likely to be affected by OSHA standards. Using data from California, which keeps good records on injuries by type, Mendeloff found that post-OSHA injury rates were as much as 30% lower than they would have been otherwise.[29] Because these caught-in-between injuries account for fewer than 10% of all injuries, extrapolation of these and related results to an aggregate level led Mendeloff to some small but not negligible numbers:

> Perhaps the total effect of OSHA on the manufacturing rate has been to reduce it by 3 to 5 percent. For the construction industry the range might be similar, but for most sectors the effects would almost certainly be smaller . . . For the entire private sector, the reduction might be on the order of 2 to 3 per cent—approximately 40,000 to 60,000 out of the two million disabling injuries that occur nationally each year.[30]

Robert S. Smith undertook a different disaggregated study, looking at the impact of OSHA's 1973–1974 inspections on the injury experience of specific industrial plants. He found a statistically significant 16% reduction in injury rates for the 1973 inspections and a nonsignificant reduction of 5% for 1974.[31]

Thus, if one believes these disaggregated studies, OSHA has indeed had a favorable impact. But the impact is so minimal as to fuel critics' charges that "OSHA has not affected injury rates significantly in either a statistical or a practical sense."[32] It is natural, then, that we ask, "Why are the results so small?" And a search for answers reveals many reasons why

---

[26] Robert Stewart Smith, *The Occupational Safety and Health Act: Its Goals and Its Achievements* (Washington, D.C.: American Enterprise Institute, 1976).

[27] W. Kip Viscusi, "The Impact of Occupational Safety and Health Regulation," *Bell Journal of Economics* (Spring 1979), pp. 117–140.

[28] Mendeloff, *op. cit.,* pp. 102–105.

[29] Ibid., p. 111.

[30] Ibid., p. 117.

[31] Robert Stewart Smith, "The Impact of OSHA Inspections on Manufacturing Injury Rates," *Journal of Human Resources* (Spring 1979), pp. 145–170.

[32] Albert Nichols and Richard Zeckhauser, "OSHA after a Decade: A Time for Reason," in Weiss and Klass (eds.), *Case Studies in Regulation: Revolution and Reform* (Boston: Little, Brown & Co., 1981), p. 217.

OSHA *should not be expected* to have much of an impact on overall injury rates.

First, and most important, a large proportion of injuries are apparently caused by human error or human recklessness instead of faulty tools, unguarded machinery, or other environmental factors controllable by standards. Still another large proportion is caused by some interaction of human and environmental factors. Exactly what these proportions are is difficult to determine. But an official of the National Safety Council estimated on the basis of workman's compensation cases that 19 per cent of occupational accidents are caused solely by human factors, 63 per cent are caused by some combination of human and environmental factors, and only 18 per cent are caused wholly by environmental elements.[33]

A second reason for doubting that OSHA, at best, could not generate dramatic results is that many hazards arise from temporary circumstances—such as wet floors or trash-blocked isles, which precipitate falls. Given the intermittence and in many plants the nonexistence

[33] Ibid., p. 215.

Table 22–2.   Projected Benefits of Selected Occupational Health Regulations

Regulation	Benefits	Comments
Asbestos (Settle, 1975)	630 to 2,563 deaths avoided per year (United States) from asbestosis and cancer. Social cost of disease avoided is $164 to $652 million per year.	Benefits do not occur until many years after imposition of regulation. Estimate includes medical costs plus cost to workers from lost life expectancy.
Vinyl Chloride (Ashford, Zolt, et al., 1979).	Approximately 2,000 deaths from all types of cancer avoided in the period 1976–2000 as a result of OSHA vinyl chloride standard.	Takes into account worker mobility, job tenure, exposure variations.
Cotton dust (Research Triangle Institute, 1979).	Imposition of exposure limit of 0.2 mg/m^3 would avoid 1,749 cases of byssinosis per year initially. Eventually, imposition of 0.2 mg standard would result in decrease in total number of cases of byssinosis by 21,674.	Using the number of cases of byssinosis (brown lung) may be misleading, because it fails to differentiate between the different grades and severities of the disease.

Sources: R. Settle, "Benefits and Costs of the Federal Asbestos Standard," U.S. Department of Labor, 1975; N. A. Ashford, E. M. Zolt, et al., "Evaluating Chemical Regulations," U.S. Council on Environmental Quality, 1979; Research Triangle Institute, "Inflationary Impact Statement: Cotton Dust," U.S. Department of Labor, OSHA, 1979; all as reported by Center for Policy Alternatives at the Massachusetts Institute of Technology, *Benefits of Environmental, Health, and Safety Regulation,* U.S. Senate, Committee on Governmental Affairs (1980), p. 32.

of OSHA's inspections, such hazards are resistant to the OSHA approach. Taking this temporary element and the human element together, President Carter's Interagency Task Force on Workplace Safety and Health concluded that no more than "perhaps 25 per cent of injuries are preventable by enforcement of present OSHA standards."[34]

A third and rather obvious possible reason for OSHA's ineffectiveness is that, until recently, compliance may have been lax. The penalties levied in the past were piddling in all but a few instances, averaging just a few dollars per violation. Moreover, inspections have been, from the typical employer's view, rare, if not as rare as Halley's comet.

In sum, the OSHA approach to injuries is inherently handicapped. Large aggregate results from it are simply not to be expected. This negative conclusion is probably less appropriate for *health* standards, given that human error and transient conditions probably contribute less to illness than to injury. Exposure limits backed by monitoring might have more potency here, once again underscoring the fact that OSHA's strong suit is really in health rather than safety. Unfortunately, full verification of these optimistic presumptions for health is impossible, given the grave difficulties in conducting retrospective tests of OSHA's impact on illness noted earlier. However, estimates of the prospective impact of health standards are available. Table 22–2 outlines forecast estimates of the benefits associated with three health standards mentioned previously, those for asbestos, vinyl chloride, and cotton dust.

Although to this point we have measured OSHA's impact in terms of injury, illness, and death rates, it is important to note in closing that these merely summarize benefits taking many alternative forms, some easily quantifiable, others not. A reduction in workplace casualties reduces workmen's compensation liabilities, disability and other income maintenance costs, medical expenses, and health insurance. Moreover, curbing casualties increases worker productivity by improving worker health, shrinking absenteeism, and diminishing worker turnover. Intangible benefits include lessened pain and suffering for workers and their families. Thus, even if OSHA's success is limited, the ramifications of that success might be considerable.[35]

IV. Policy Improvements

In light of what has been said, the goal of proposed policy changes should be sharper reductions in workplace casualties or greater economic efficiency or both. Proposed changes fitting this description can be divided into two classes depending on how the main problems with present policy are perceived.

The *first* class of proposed changes might be called reforms in the *execution* of the present approach. Examples of previous changes along this line include (1) the abolition of over 900 "consensus" standards that were ridiculously obsolete, petty, and irrelevant, (2) the trend toward targeting inspections on industries and plants with the worst casualty records, and (3) OSHA's shift of emphasis away from safety toward health. These reforms never questioned the standards-inspection-penalty approach of direct regulation in concept or principle. Rather, they represented improvements in the execution of that approach. Critics urge further such changes, three of which we shall review following: (1) greater use of cost-effectiveness in designing standards; (2) greater reliance on benefit-cost analysis in designing standards; and (3) a shift to more cooperative enforcement.

The *second* broad class of proposed changes

---

[34] *Oversight* Hearings, *op. cit.*, p. 3.

[35] An optimistic and upper bound extrapolation of the Smith and Mendeloff estimates yields an annual benefit of $4.6 billion. See the last source of Table 22–2.

covers those that do question the standards-in-spection-penalty approach of direct regulation. These might be called *conceptual* changes because they assume that the present approach is inherently flawed. They imply abandonment of the present concept and urge movement toward rather radically different policies, such as an injury tax.

A. Changes in Execution of the Present Approach

1. COST EFFECTIVENESS

If a thousand lives can be saved by either method A or method B, but method A is much cheaper, then why not use method A? This is the essence of cost effectiveness. And this is essentially the query of economists when they question the wisdom of design standards and engineering controls. OSHA has acknowledged the faults of design standards, and has made an effort to replace many of them with performance standards. But OSHA's critics contend the agency could do more. "We recommend," the U.S. Chamber of Commerce recently stressed, "the adoption of a performance-oriented approach to *all* new and existing standards, recognizing that performance standards must have elements of specificity to be effective."[36] As for engineering controls, OSHA has never visibly wavered from its insistence that engineering controls are preferable to personal protective equipment despite the fact that engineering controls are typically many times more costly and sometimes less protective of workers. Thus a very commonly recommended change is that OSHA forsake its infatuation with engineering controls and adopt a more flexible stance toward personal protective equipment.

On a broader scale, economists have pointed out that cost per life saved varies widely among different standards—a few hundred thousand dollars per life saved for one standard as compared to tens of millions of dollars for another.[37] The implication is that regulation is not cost-effective in a broad social sense. For example, spending $50 million of society's resources to save *one* life from acrylonitrile exposure would be foolish if the same $50 million could instead save *thirty* lives from lead exposure. It would of course be nice if we had unlimited resources, Aladdin's lamps galore, for we could then spend $50 *billion* in *both* directions without blinking. But, as economists like to remind us, scarcity rudely forces us to choose, to allocate, to suffer trade-offs; so we had better choose, allocate, and suffer wisely.

A change toward greater reliance on cost effectiveness on a broad scale is not without its problems. We noted earlier the practical difficulties of estimating the costs of standards. Moreover, there is the problem of ranking or weighting different sorts of casualties. Confining the calculus to lives saved per dollar cost, as assumed above, simplifies the problem greatly. But how are we to include consideration of amputations, respiratory incapacities, hearing loss, and sterility? How many arms equal one life? How many cases of 30% hearing loss would it take to justify a standard that detracted resources from a 1 ppm benzene standard? At this level, cost effectiveness loses its punch, but that is precisely why many economists go beyond recommending cost effectiveness, which at best only answers rather narrow questions concerning techniques, to urge adoption of benefit-cost analysis.

2. BENEFIT-COST ANALYSIS

The Supreme Court's "cotton dust" opinion said that OSHA *need not* weigh benefits against costs in formulating standards. The court did not go so far as to say that OSHA *could not*

---

[36] *Oversight* Hearings, *op. cit.,* p. 1293.

[37] M. J. Baily, *Reducing Risks to Life* (Washington, D.C.: American Enterprise Institute, 1980), pp. 26–27.

do so. Thus a change toward greater reliance on benefit-cost analysis may be possible within the present regulatory framework. If OSHA were to follow the recommendations of many economists and business organizations, this greater reliance would ensue. However, given unionized labor's traditional opposition to benefit-cost, the agency is unlikely to move voluntarily in this direction without some substantial modifications in the technique. Giving greater values to human life than other agencies, for example, would for reasons given earlier probably be defensible. Still, political realities being what they are, a significant shift by OSHA toward benefit-cost seems doubtful without congressional amendments that would reverse the Supreme Court's cotton dust ruling.

3. COOPERATIVE ENFORCEMENT

OSHA's critics doubt that a marked reduction in occupational casualties will ever occur without a marked reduction in the animosity business displays toward OSHA and its labor constituency. To this end a number of recommended changes have been offered in hopes of securing warm yet effective cooperation among all concerned. One major previous change, for instance, brought in-plant government-business consultations. A major future change would be to expand greatly the use of labor-management committees tried experimentally with Bechtel in California. Other proposed changes, such as complete elimination of "first instance" penalties and less reliance on general duty clause citations, amount to little more than relaxed enforcement. But some prospective strides toward "cooperation" have merit, and may help quell what the National Association of Manufacturers calls a "rebellion" against "OSHA's impudence and imprudence."[38]

B. Changes in Concept: Diminishing Direct Regulation

When choosing its method of intervention, Congress gave no consideration to any approach other than the enforcement of standards. Thousands of occupational safety and health standards were already used to some degree by industry—the so-called consensus standards in particular, voluntarily developed and deployed. Moreover, the idea of *enforcing* standards had previously been tried for federal contractors and for a few industries receiving special congressional attention, coal mining in particular (not to mention the experience of FDA and NHTSA). Thus the precedents were there. The standard-enforcement approach fit experience and ideology. Legislators and lobbyist alike consequently ignored other options.

1. INFORMATION AND EDUCATION

One other option that received last minute recognition and secondary inclusion was the information and education option. Given that the main source of market failure in this area is the workers' ignorance of hazards, the provision of more information and training to workers would greatly help and would lessen the need for an elaborate standards-enforcement effort. As workers learn about hazards, they can demand higher, risk adjusted wages or press for elimination of the risk, or adopt strategies to avoid it. Indeed, the OSH Act's provisions to keep workers informed and trained resulted from the efforts of Ralph Nader's staff, "whose skepticism toward both union and government bureaucrats led it to favor strengthening workers' capabilities to protect themselves."[39] Moreover, education and information help reduce the many casualties attributable to human error or carelessness.

Thus current government efforts in this area exist. The National Institute of Occupational

---

[38] *Oversight* Hearings, *op. cit.*, p. 803.

[39] Mendeloff, *op. cit.*, p. 25.

Safety and Health (NIOSH) sponsors and conducts research. OSHA sponsors and conducts seminars, publishes literature, and so on. But in the past these programs have been miniscule. In 1976, for example, only seven-tenths of one per cent of OSHA's budget was allocated to education, information, and training. The budget share has since grown, and innovative programs like "New Directions" have been instituted. But still more could be done.

2. INJURY TAXES

Rather than set standards and police them, the government could induce employers to reduce casualties by taxing injuries. The higher the tax, the greater the incentive to reduce injuries. Robert S. Smith, for example, estimates from 1970 data that an injury tax of $2,000 per injury would reduce the manufacturing injury rate an average of about 8.2 per cent, whereas an injury tax of $4,000 would curb injuries about 16.3 per cent.[40] The basic idea is that employers would improve safety to avoid these levies as long as the added cost of such improvement were less than the cost of the prospective taxes.

In theory, there are a number of advantages to the tax approach as opposed to the standards-enforcement approach:[41]

• *Ease of Administration:* Regular and detailed inspections of workplaces would no longer be necessary (though accident and complaint inspections could continue). Firms would have to report injuries to the "tax" authorities, but such reporting is already in place for workman's compensation and OSHA.

• *Sweep of Incentive:* The current approach cannot reach the 75% or so injuries caused by human factors or temporary conditions. A tax on *all* injuries would induce employers and employees to work on the *whole range* of factors causing injuries, not just the physical conditions specified by standards. We could expect closer attention to work practices, employee training, and safety related personnel policies.

• *Prices Reflecting Social Costs:* If for technical reasons the injury tax had *no* effect on the injury rate of a high-risk industry, it would still be beneficial. The cost of the tax would raise the product's price, which in turn would shift consumer demand toward goods produced by safer means.

• *Cost Effectiveness:* With a tax, it is left up to the employers (and employees) to determine the best way to curtail injuries. Such flexibility will yield a variety of methods among different firms and industries, as employers seek out what for them are the most efficient ways of gaining safety. If, in other words, a tax achieved the same level of safety as the present standards, it would probably do so more cheaply than the present standards.

• *Innovation:* The inflexibilities of standards tend to stifle safety innovations. Thus another possible advantage of an injury tax is that it would not block any avenues of technological change.

(These last two advantages will be more fully explored in next chapter's discussion of environmental policy because the tax approach has actually been tried in that context).

The tax approach is not without its weaknesses. For one thing, it would not work well for illnesses because of the difficulty in linking specific cases of illness to workplace conditions and because of the long latency periods of many illnesses. A tax not on illnesses but rather on toxic emissions themselves might be possible, but then many of the advantages mentioned

[40] Robert S. Smith, "The Feasibility of an 'Injury Tax' Approach to Occupational Safety," *Law and Contemporary Problems* (Summer–Autumn 1974), p. 741.
[41] Nichols and Zeckhauser, *op. cit.*, pp. 228–229.

above would be lost. Emission fees are, as we shall see, quite an attractive approach for curbing pollution generally, but they seem less attractive in the workplace, given that personal protective equipment could make emissions per se somewhat irrelevant.

Among other weaknesses of the tax approach, certainly the most crucial are political. No support for the tax approach comes from businessmen, labor leaders, or politicians. Businessmen apparently fear that their total cost burden (abatement costs plus tax costs) would be greater under a tax approach than at present. Labor leaders would probably lose some of the powers they presently enjoy as OSHA's prime political supporter. Moreover, as Mendeloff points out, "By allowing employers to choose the methods for reducing injuries, the injury tax could lead to difficult problems for unions: replacing or firing workers with bad accident records; stricter discipline for violation of safety rules; requiring workers to wear safety shoes or safety glasses."[42] As for politicians, they are unlikely to move unless pushed by either businessmen or labor leaders. Moreover, the injury tax is so passive and automatic in comparison to the active and deliberate standards-enforcement approach that it gives appearances of being a "license to maim," an image that might be exploited by the enemies of any politician who advocated an injury tax. Finally and most fundamentally . . .

> one should not expect the Congressional decision-making process to accord with the analytic ideal of reviewing policy options to see which rank highest in achieving specific objectives. Politicians are more interested in finding issues that meet their political needs than in finding policies that meet analytic needs.[43]

There is thus, perhaps, a governmental failure in coping with this market failure. Dramatic departure from the OSHA approach, however attractive the injury tax might be to economists, does not appear in the offing.

Summary

A poster popular among western state industrialists depicts "The Cowboy After OSHA"— he wears a hard hat and goggles; his horse sports a safety net to guard riders against falls; and a box beneath the horse's rear catches slippery emissions. It's a wonder that labor unions have not retaliated with a poster of "Mr. Blue-Collar Before OSHA?"—his blue collar is not visible beneath the full-body cast.

OSHA is, in short, the most controversial of government agencies. With good intentions acceptable to everyone, Congress set forth vague broad standards urging safe and healthy working conditions "so far as possible" and "to the extent feasible." OSHA's implementation generated narrow standards that were more "technically" than "economically" possible or feasible, thereby ignoring cost-effectiveness or benefit-cost justifications. OSHA's early standards were particularly ill-conceived, as they were (1) drawn largely from consensus standards, (2) design-oriented instead of performance-oriented, and (3) focused on safety rather than health. Time has brought improvements, in part because of the inputs of NIOSH, but critics remain vocal.

Enforcement of these standards centers on inspections and citations, the results of which are subject to review by the Occupational Safety and Health Review Commission, an independent agency created by the OSH Act. Scheduled inspections are most numerous, with sampling targeted on the riskiest firms and industries. Accident investigations are prompted by very serious mishaps. Employee complaints trigger still another class of inspections. And follow-up inspections check on the remedial ef-

[42] Mendeloff, op. cit., p. 29.
[43] Ibid., p. 156.

forts of employers. Citations result from detected violations, with penalties ranging from pocket change to moderately ponderous amounts.

Responding to past criticism, OSHA has shifted its enforcement efforts toward consultation, education, and cooperation. But many critics remain dissatisfied.

Two key controversies hit OSHA—(1) the question of whether benefit-cost analysis should guide standard development, and (2) the question of whether OSHA has actually reduced workplace casualties. Opposition to benefit-cost analysis stems from allegiance to value judgments other than economic efficiency and from skepticism that the practical difficulties of benefit-cost estimation can ever be overcome. Advocacy of benefit-cost elevates economic efficiency above other value judgments and discounts the practical difficulties. Looking at the word "feasibility" in the OSH Act, the Supreme Court decided in the cotton dust case that health standards *need not* pass a benefit-cost test. Safety standards presumably escape as well.

By nature, health casualties defy easy measurement and most safety mishaps have causes beyond OSHA's reach. Tests of OSHA's impact thus breed controversy. At best, OSHA has had slight overall impact, most of the improvement coming from injury categories sensitive to the standards approach.

What improvements might be made without abandoning the standards approach? Advocates may be found espousing (1) greater reliance on cost-effectiveness, especially as it relates to personal protective equipment in lieu of engineering controls; (2) benefit-cost tests for all standards; and (3) a shift toward "cooperative" enforcement. What of different methods? Information and education efforts could be considerably expanded. And if Congress wanted to be really daring (yet rational), it could do worse than pass an injury tax.

Questions and Exercises for Chapter 22

1. Compare and contrast safety versus health in (a) OSHA's emphasis, (b) strength of regulatory rationale, and (c) appropriateness for a tax.
2. Compare the engineering approach versus protective equipment approach in (a) OSHA's emphasis, and (b) typical cost effectiveness.
3. What controversies surround OSHA's inspections?
4. How has OSHA assessed the benefits of its proposed regulations?
5. Explain the relevance and importance of the "cotton dust" case in (a) facts, (b) issues, and (c) results.
6. What has been the impact of OSHA in actually increasing safety?
7. Why is the OSHA approach limited in what it can be expected to achieve?
8. Is there room for improvement within the present OSHA framework? Explain.
9. What are the advantages of an injury tax? Disadvantages?

Chapter 23

Environmental Protection

There is no such thing as a free lunch in nature.
—Barry Commoner

Throughout this book we have encountered the old economic axiom, "There is no such thing as a free lunch." When discussing the markets' ability to allocate scarce resources, we found that more steel for cars meant less for railroads. While rummaging through energy regulations we discovered that low price ceilings on natural gas caused shortages. When studying cotton dust control we learned that worker health could be bought only at the expense of hundreds of millions of dollars in resources that could have been used elsewhere, for hospitals or schools perhaps. The economic world is thus a Rubik's cube: getting one red square in place simultaneously displaces blue, green, and yellow squares.

In nature there is likewise no such thing as a free lunch. Nature's laws of conservation of mass and energy tell us that we never really "consume" anything. When we use minerals, fuels, gases, and other materials we merely change their form, extract their services, and push them around a bit. When ultimately discarded as trash, sewage, exhaust, or other waste, they remain in our environment. Natural dissipation and chemical conversion make some of these wastes harmless. Others, how-

ever, become costly hazards, as when for example an electric power plant that uses river water for cooling must pay the expense of cleaning that water before reuse because it has been polluted by an upstream paper mill. More dramatically, 20 people died and 6000 others became seriously ill when in 1948 the industrial town of Donora, Pennsylvania was blanketed by thick smog laced with sulfur dioxide. In England a smog attack killed 300 Londoners in December 1962. One's waste can thus literally become another's woe.

It is the task of environmental policy, then, to contend with the fact that there is *no free lunch either in nature or economics*. What goes up, must come down, often hitting us. And procuring protection diverts economic resources from other things worth tens of billions of dollars per year.

Our review of environmental policy answers four questions:

I. What is pollution?
II. What has been done about it?
III. What is the impact of current policy?
IV. What policy improvements might be made?

I. What Is Pollution?

Our environment—the air, water, and land around us—serves us in three ways. First, it provides a *habitat*, that is, life support surroundings. Destruction of our habitat or the habitat of other creatures is not merely inconvenient or uncomfortable, it is deadly. Second, the environment provides natural *resources* useful for the production of goods and services. Clean air, for instance, is a handy source of oxygen for combustion and a convenient place to dispose of combustion wastes. River water quenches thirst, yields fish, floats transport, powers electric generators, and irrigates crops. Minerals like coal and oil give energy. And so on. Third, environmental *amenities* make life pleasant. Swimming, boating, fishing, skiing, hiking, picnicking, and sight seeing—the list of nature's pleasant offerings is truly copious.

In a physical sense, pollution occurs whenever man alters the environment. In an economic sense, *pollution occurs when one use of the environment diminishes other service capabilities of value to mankind.* Typically, resource exploitation injures habitat and amenity properties, as when use of the atmosphere as an exhaust repository creates smog that kills people, hides picturesque mountains, and blots out beautiful sunsets. However, pollution also occurs when one resource use hurts another resource use. Chemical waste disposal competes with commercial fishing and strip mining interferes with farming. Furthermore, amenity uses may even produce pollution, as when thoughtless hikers and picnickers litter the landscape with beer cans and pop bottles, diminishing the pleasure of other hikers and picnickers. Pollution is, in short, a problem of scarce environmental capacities relative to man's demands. Misuse is equivalent to misallocation; *there is too much pollution when the environment is used too much for waste disposal relative to cleaner endeavors.*

A. Air Pollutants

The wastes dumped into the air are certainly the most obvious, as they impair breathing, burn eyes, cloud visibility, and worse. The main chemicals at fault and their total annual emission tonnage during the 1970s are given in Table 23–1:

- *Total Suspended Particulates* (TSP): In addition to soot and dust, particulates are composed of organic compounds containing metals, sulfur, and nitrogen. Industrial processes and fuel combustion in stationary sources are the main sources of particulates, which lessen visibility and cause respiratory ailments.
- *Sulfur Dioxide* (SO_2): Coal and oil combustion in stationary sources like electric power plants are the main sources of sulfur dioxide, which in high concentrations is associated with acute and chronic respiratory disease. Moreover, SO_2 reacts in the atmosphere to form sulfuric acid, thereby contributing to the infamous "acid rain" that harms vegetation and fish.
- *Nitrogen Dioxide* (NO_2): This stuff plays a major role in the atmospheric reactions that produce smog. Its effects on health remain uncertain except that high level exposure can cause pulmonary edema. Motor vehicles and electric generating plants are chief sources.
- *Hydrocarbons* (HC): These are vapors of gasoline, chemical solvents, and various burned fuels. Atmospheric reactions convert them into *ozone*, which as everyone in Southern California knows severely irritates mucous membranes, hampers breathing, and aggravates the symptoms of people suffering asthma, heart disease, and other ailments.
- *Carbon Monoxide* (CO): Primarily a product of auto and truck exhaust, and a favorite means of dispatch for many suicides, carbon monoxide can concentrate in urban air to

Table 23–1. National Emissions Estimates, 1970–78
(million metric tons per year)

Year	TSP	SO_2	NO_2	HC	CO
1970	23.2	29.8	19.9	28.3	102.6
1971	22.0	28.2	20.6	27.8	103.1
1972	21.0	29.3	21.6	28.3	104.4
1973	20.3	30.4	22.4	28.4	103.5
1974	17.9	28.5	21.8	27.1	99.6
1975	14.6	26.2	20.9	25.3	97.2
1976	14.1	27.4	22.5	27.0	102.9
1977	13.6	27.2	23.4	27.1	102.4
1978	12.5	27.0	23.3	27.8	102.1
Percentage change, 1970–78	−46.1	−9.4	+17.1	−1.8	−0.5

1 million metric tons = approximately 1.1 million short tons.

Source: U.S. Environmental Protection Agency, *National Air Pollutant Emission Estimates, 1970–1978,* EPA–450/4–80–002 (Washington, D.C., 1980), p. 2.

the point of affecting mental function, visual acuity, and alertness among normal people. Sufferers of anemia, emphysema, and other lung diseases suffer more.

Overall, energy use is clean air's greatest enemy. In 1978 fossil fuel combustion accounted for approximately 41% of national TSP emissions, 85% of SO_2 emissions, 95% of NO_x emissions, 40% of HC emissions, and 85% of CO emissions.[1]

Less pervasive but in many ways more hazardous to the few people at risk are a number of pollutants like asbestos, lead, mercury, and beryllium. Airborne asbestos fibers, for instance, can congregate around asbestos mills, freshly demolished buildings, and mining areas.

B. Water Pollution

Ground water and surface water are both susceptible to a confusing variety of pollutants. For our purposes these pollutants may be classi-

[1] National Commission on Air Quality, *To Breathe Clean Air* (Washington, D.C.: 1981), p. 284.

fied as either *degradable* or *nondegradable*. Once in the water, degradable pollutants change through chemical and biological processes. They are, in short, subject to nature's self-cleansing capabilities as long as they do not concentrate to the point of clogging those capabilities. Domestic sewage (like wildlife sewage) is among these degradable wastes along with the organic waste materials of food canneries, paper mills, and oil refineries.

Bacterial degradation of organic wastes consumes the oxygen dissolved in water, so a common measure of these pollutants is biochemical oxygen demand (or BOD). As organic waste discharges increase, BOD increases. Conversely, an increase in BOD *reduces* the dissolved oxygen in water, so dissolved oxygen is a measure of water quality important to fish as well as to humans. Low levels of dissolved oxygen ruin fish habitat.

Nondegradable pollutants do not change in the water, or change only very slowly. Mercury, lead, cadmium, PCBs, and DDT persist in nature long after emission. They can be directly poisonous or more deviously dangerous. Some, like DDT, can concentrate in animals highly placed in nature's food chain, harming their reproductive capacities or doing other damage. Some nondegradable pollutants are so persistent that they even elude water purification processes, as illustrated by the fact that drinking water derived from the Mississippi River has been linked to cancer fatalities in Louisiana.[2]

The several panels of Figure 23–1 show the recent national trend in surface water pollution as measured by dissolved oxygen, fecal coliform bacteria, total phosphorus, cadmium, lead, and mercury. Except for mercury, which shows a substantial rise, median concentration levels seem to be holding steady or improving markedly. Of course these national averages hide wide divergences in local conditions. Your nearby rivers and lakes may be following much happier or sadder courses.

Toxic chemicals pose the most ominous present danger to *ground* water supplies. There are some 30,000 hazardous waste disposal sites in the U.S., hundreds and maybe thousands of which seep acutely poisonous substances like benzidene, vinyl chloride, C–56, polychlorinated biphenyls (PCBs), and DDT. Cancer, genetic alteration, neurological damage, and sterility threaten those exposed. The Love Canal tragedy of the late 1970s epitomized the problem.[3]

[2] T. Page, R. H. Harris, and S. S. Epstein, "Drinking Water and Cancer Mortality in Louisiana," *Science,* (July 2, 1977), pp. 55–57.

[3] After abandonment by the Hooker Chemical and Plastics Company, which had used Love Canal as a dumping site from 1947 to 1953, several hundred homes and an elementary school were constructed in the area, which is in Niagara Falls, N.Y. After residents complained of abnormal numbers of miscarriages, birth defects, cancer, and a variety of other illnesses, the area was checked by health authorities who found what they called a "grave and imminent peril." Contaminated ground water was seeping into basements and rising to the surface. The air contained pollution 5,000 times maximum safe levels. More than 260 families had to be evacuated and the area quarantined. Damage suits top $3 billion and have yet to be settled.

Figure 23–1. Trends in National Average Water Pollution, 1975–1979

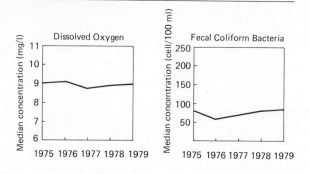

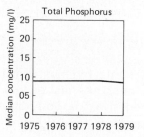
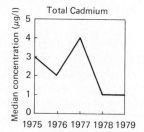

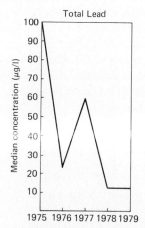
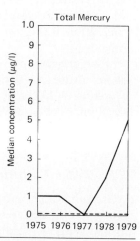

Source: Council on Environmental Quality, *Environmental Quality 1980* (Washington, D.C.: 1980), pp. 102–107).

C. Land Pollution

Unsound hazardous waste disposal also pollutes the land because it reduces the capacity of the land to render environmental services. Moreover, millions of tons of solid wastes—ranging from highway litter to scrapped automobiles and appliances—have their adverse effects as well. Aside from dumping, the earth's surface is marred by strip mining, highway construction, off-road vehicle recreation, and other acts of gouging, tearing, grading, and paving. The damage is not limited to the amenity losses suffered by hikers, campers, and sightseers. Agriculture and forestry can also be dented.

D. Why Does Pollution Occur?

We need not repeat the discussions on pages 29 to 32 of Chapter 2 and pages 412 and 413 of Chapter 20, which give explanations of why pollution occurs. But it might be helpful to quickly recollect three concepts that lie at the heart of the matter: (1) **External costs** arise when individuals or firms or government facilities impose costs on others by emitting wastes burdening others. Polluters will naturally reduce their own costs of waste disposal if they can by shifting the costs to others. (2) **Common property resources,** like the air, are open to exploitation by everybody. Each individual's use diminishes the usefulness of the property to others, but individuals do not confront these costs because they are not obliged to compensate others. The result is an overuse of common property resources. (3) **Public goods** are, for our purposes, goods jointly consumed. The mere *existence* of species, the *opportunity* to visit national parks, and the *cleanliness* of air and water are public goods whose free-market provision is seriously hampered by the free-rider problem. Free riding is a plausible strategy in the case of public goods because, for them, paying and receiving are severed. Unlike private goods, where paying and receiving are

inextricably linked, people might pay for a public good yet not receive it, or they might *not* pay and actually get it.

There is, in short, too much pollution from a free-market system because the polluters do not have to pay. The intent of policy should be, then, to make polluters pay.

II. What Has Been Done About Pollution?

There are many possible approaches to environmental policy—moral suasion, direct regulation, subsidies, and taxation among them.[4] Practically all have been tried at one time or another here and abroad. Our experience with moral suasion, for instance, includes publicity campaigns featuring cartoon characters who urge us not to be "litter bugs" or chirp "give a hoot, don't pollute." Although some ardent environmentalists have faith that the rest of us can someday be converted to their staunch ethical views and clean behavior, moral suasion has had little impact to date. It works best only during crises (like serious smog attacks) and among souls atuned to nature's wonders (backpackers, for instance). William Baumol and Wallace Oates thus have every right to be skeptical when they say, "Unfortunately, if greater moral commitment is the prerequisite for a better environment, it may wait indefinitely. As in the case of the Victorian gentleman who refused to remove his clothing to save a drowning person, morality may be preserved even though the cause is lost."[5]

The approach tried most persistently in the United States has been direct regulation. This

---

[4] For a review see William J. Baumol and Wallace E. Oates, *Economics, Environmental Policy and the Quality of Life* (Englewood Cliffs, N.J.: Prentice-Hall, 1979), pp. 217–366, or J. J. Seneca and M. K. Taussig, *Environmental Economics* (Englewood Cliffs, N.J.: Prentice-Hall, 1979), pp. 211–291.

[5] Baumol and Oates, *op. cit.*, p. 5.

Thumbnail Sketch 11:   Environmental Protection Agency

Established: 1970

Purpose: To protect and improve the physical environment.

Legislative Authority: Clean Air Act Amendments of 1970 and 1977; Water Pollution Control Act Amendment of 1972 and 1977; Federal Insecticide, Fungicide and Rodenticide Act of 1972; Noise Control Act of 1972; Safe Drinking Water Act of 1974; Toxic Substances Control Act of 1976; Resource Conservation and Recovery Act of 1976.

Regulatory Activity: In league with state and local governments, EPA controls pollution through standard setting, enforcement, and research in six areas: air, water, solid waste, toxic substances, radiation, and noise.

Organization: An independent agency, located in the Executive branch, headed by a Presidentially appointed administrator.

Budget: 1982 estimate: $555.1 million.

Staff: 1982 estimate: 9243.

---

is true despite the fact that regulations prior to about 1970 were abysmal failures.[6] Why the failures? Key elements of the overall regulatory strategy outlined earlier in Table 20–3 on page 421 were always left out of those earlier efforts. The Refuse Act of 1899 required a permit for the discharge of refuse into navigable waters, but standards were never set to guide permit provisions and enforcement was absent until 1970. Air and water legislation of the late 1940s and early 1950s authorized research but little else. Slight progress was made in the 1960s when Congress provided broad ambient standards, but without narrow standards limiting the *emissions of specific sources,* enforcement to achieve those broad ambient standards proved impossible. As the environmental movement reached its pinnacle in 1970, these

futile federal efforts became the butt of scathing criticism and even ridicule.[7]

Government finally "got tough," greatly modifying its half-baked earlier efforts with the Clean Air Amendments of 1970 and the 1972 Water Pollution Act Amendments. As subsequently further amended in 1977, these Amendments remain the basis of present policy, supplemented by the Toxic Substances Control Act of 1976, the Resource Conservation and Recovery Act of 1976, the Noise Control Act of 1972, and the Safe Drinking Water Act of 1974. How could Congress be confident that these new regulatory efforts would succeed when earlier efforts failed? They were more comprehensive, less riddled with gaps. They incorporated all the major elements of Table 20–3—standards, enforcement, and research. Still, critics have not been so confident, as we shall see.

---

[6] Allen V. Kneese and Charles L. Schultze, *Pollution, Prices, and Public Policy* (Washington D.C.: Brookings Institution, 1975), pp. 30–50.

[7] David Zwick and Mary Benstock, *Water Wasteland* (New York: Grossman, 1971), and John Esposito, *Vanishing Air* (New York: Grossman, 1970).

Printing these measures would make a fat book over four hundred pages long, so our survey must be considerably condensed. We shall cover air, water, and toxic substances. Standards and enforcement are outlined for each.

A. Air Pollution Regulation

1. BROAD STANDARDS FOR AIR

Congress acted, it said "to protect and enhance the quality of the Nation's air resources so as to promote the public health and welfare and the productive capacity of its population." This vague pronouncement might seem sufficient for a broad standard, but Congress elaborated with specifics. It called for the attainment by 1975 of a set of national "primary ambient-air quality standards" and later attainment of "secondary" ambient standards. The "primary" ambient standards were to be set by the Environmental Protection Agency (EPA) so as to protect human health, while the "secondary" standards were intended to protect against all other damage (property, animals, vegetation, materials, visibility, and aesthetics). EPA re-

sponded with an early version of these standards in 1971 for so-called "criteria" pollutants. Now modified, these standards set maximum ambient thresholds for particulate matter, sulfur oxides, carbon monoxide, nitrogen dioxide, ozone, hydrocarbons, and lead, some of which are given in Table 23–2.

Three characteristics of these broad standards for "criteria" pollutants deserve special notice. *First,* they are ambient standards, *not emission* standards. They specify air quality thresholds. They do not place emission limits on particular polluters, a task that is left to narrow standards and the issuance of permits under those narrow standards. The distinction is underscored by the fact that Congress took a different approach for "hazardous air pollutants," which (by its broad standard) "may reasonably be anticipated to result in an increase in mortality or an increase in serious irreversible, or incapacitating reversible, illness." Ambient standards would not do for these horrors, so Congress directed EPA to identify such "hazardous air pollutants" and set *emission* standards providing "an ample margin of safety to

Table 23–2. Selected National Ambient Air Quality Standards (Maximum Levels)

Pollutant	Averaging Time	Primary Standard (micrograms per cubic meter of air)	Secondary Standard (micrograms per cubic meter of air)
Particulates	Annual (average)	75	60
	24 hours*	260	150
Sulfur oxides	Annual (average)	80	—
	24 hours*	365	—
	3 hours*	—	1300
Ozone	1 hour	240	240
Lead	3 months	1.5	1.5

* Not to be exceeded more than once a year.

Source: Council on Environmental Quality, *Environmental Quality-1980* (Washington, D.C.: 1980), p. 172.

protect public health." Asbestos, beryllium, mercury, vinyl chloride, and several other noxious substances have received such attention.

Second, the ambient air standards for regular, "criteria" pollutants are based on a *threshold* concept, implying an absence of adverse effect from pollution levels below the specified threshold. Exposure-effect function *A* in Figure 23–2 illustrates this threshold concept. Greater exposure to air pollution (moving to the right horizontally) does not cause higher mortality (vertical movement) until after a threshold is crossed. This is contrasted to the *continuous* exposure-effect function labeled *B,* which shows adverse effects starting with very low pollution exposure. Since passage of the 1970 Clean Air Act Amendments, growing evidence suggests that the continous function as the best picture of reality. Retention of the threshold concept has therefore elicited sharp criticism, especially from those who advocate a larger place for benefit-cost analysis in standard setting. They say that the continuous function implies *zero* pollution if the Act's "health and welfare" objective is to be honored. But because

zero pollution could be obtained only at horrendous cost (closing down Los Angeles, for instance), critics contend that we must weigh benefits and costs along the continuum indicated by the empirical evidence.[8]

The *third* thing to notice about the national ambient air quality standards is that they are *national,* not regional or local. This uniformity produced a tricky problem. Areas not meeting standards would obviously have to cut back emissions to comply with the thresholds. But what about the many areas that already enjoyed air quality *better* than the standards? Would their air be allowed to deteriorate to the level of the national standards? What would this mean for national parks like the Grand Canyon where visibility is especially important?

Prompted by environmentalists, Congress amended the Act in 1977 to meet this problem, with the result that, in practice, *special* broad ambient standards now apply to "attainment" areas to "prevent significant deterioration." Congress directed that attainment areas be subdivided into three classes:

Class I: Crucial areas such as national parks where virtually *no* deterioration would be permitted (only about 1% of U.S. land area).

Class II: Areas where moderate deterioration would be permitted (most of the U.S.).

Class III: Areas which could deteriorate to the point of equalling threshold standards.

An interesting irony in this approach is that it creates a contradiction in policy because the resulting gradations imply a *continuous* exposure-effect function contrary to the *threshold* exposure-effect originally assumed. Either the

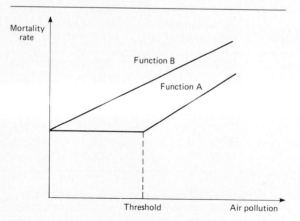

Figure 23–2.   Threshold (A) and No-Threshold (B) Exposure-Effect Functions

Mortality rate

Function B

Function A

Threshold   Air pollution

[8] A. Myrick Freeman III, "Air and Water Pollution Policy," in P. R. Portney (ed.) *Current Issues in U.S. Environmental Policy* (Baltimore: Johns Hopkins University Press, 1978), pp. 31–34.

threshold concept is right, and these gradations in ambient standards are wrong, or the threshold concept is wrong and these gradients are right (and indeed further gradations should be adopted). Some critics maintain that benefit-cost gradations should be developed that vary by region because benefits and costs vary by region.[9] Such would serve consistency but add complexity.

2. NARROW STANDARDS FOR AIR

Narrow standards for the "criteria" pollutants are outlined in Table 23–3. Because their purpose is to restrict *emissions* from specific sources, these standards fall into two main divisions: (A) Stationary sources, like factories and electric power plants, and (B) mobile sources like autos, trucks, and buses. Stationary sources are further subdivided by area, by old versus new source, and by state versus EPA formulation. State environmental protection agencies have major responsibilities under the Clean Air Act because they must formulate plans, set narrow standards, and enforce those standards with permits and surveillance, all so as to achieve the broad ambient air standards mentioned earlier. To guide the states in setting their narrow standards the law offers technical catch-phrases like "reasonably available control measures" and "lowest achievable emission rate," which standards are the most stringent among all the stationary standards because they apply to old and new sources in nonattainment areas (see A.1.a. and A.1.b. in Table 23–3). EPA sets some stationary standards itself, however, under its authority to set so-called "New Source Performance Standards" for certain new sources, most notably new electric generating plants that burn coal. Thus states share new source authority with EPA, and the states' new source standards in nonattainment areas

[9] David Harrison, Jr. and Paul R. Portney, "Making Ready for the Clean Air Act," *Regulation* (March/April 1981), pp. 24–31.

Table 23–3. Narrow Emissions Standards under the Clean Air Act, by Source and Area

A. STATIONARY SOURCES (LIKE POWER PLANTS)
  1. *Nonattainment Areas: State Standards*
     a. Old Sources—"reasonably available control measures."
     b. New Sources—"lowest achievable emission rate" plus an offset with old sources, cost considered.
  2. *Attainment Areas: State Standards*
     a. Old Sources—no alteration needed unless source is "modified," in which case it becomes "new."
     b. New Sources—"major" sources must adopt "best available control technology for maximum degree of pollution reduction achievable, taking into account cost."
  3. *EPA New Source Performance Standards*
     For certain new source categories, the "best technological system of continuous emissions reduction that has been adequately demonstrated, considering costs and other environmental impacts."
B. MOBILE SOURCES (VEHICLES)
  Differ by type of vehicle and model year. 1981 autos and later model years have standards set by Congress:
  Carbon Monoxide   3.40 grams per mile
  Hydrocarbons   0.41 grams per mile
  Nitrogen Oxides   1.00 grams per mile

(A.1.b.) are quite similar to EPA's New Source Performance Standards despite differences in the guideline language.

More concretely, the typical narrow standard calls for a certain percentage of abatement as guided by technological possibilities, ambient air conditions, and other considerations. For example, in areas of New York, New Jersey, and Connecticut that do not meet the ambient ozone standard, controls call for 40 to 50 per cent reductions in the hydrocarbons emitted by 15 categories of stationary sources.

This percentage reduction approach reached a peak of sorts when Congress itself

set narrow standards for automobiles in the 1970 Clean Air Act Amendments. Those original standards called for 90 per cent reductions in hydrocarbons, carbon monoxide, and nitrogen oxide emissions below the levels of 1970–71 model cars. The 90% curtailments were to be achieved by steps culminating with 1975–76 model cars, but economic difficulties and technical trouble caused Congress to bow repeatedly to industry demands that the 90% standards be postponed. Thus the 1981 standards mentioned for hydrocarbons and carbon monoxide in part B of Table 23–3 happen to be the original 90%-off standards for 1975, and the nitrogen oxides standard of 1.0 gram per mile amounts to 70%-off instead of 90%-off.[10]

Consideration of economic cost has influenced narrow standard setting, either implicitly or explicitly. Implicit consideration of cost motivated the repeated postponement of auto emission deadlines, for instance. Honda and Volvo were able to produce virtually pollution-free cars by the mid-1970s, signifying the *technical* feasibility of the early deadlines. But American manufacturers could not shoulder the costs of converting to these technologies and shrunken car sizes, so they won delays by threatening shutdowns. Implicit consideration of cost is also allowed by the word "reasonably," which qualifies narrow standards for old stationary sources in nonattainment areas (category A.1.a. in Table 23–3). Explicit consideration of cost is provided for in all other narrow standards, as study of Table 23–3 will reveal.

3. ENFORCEMENT FOR AIR

Enforcement entails (1) certification or permit at least for new sources, mobile and stationary, (2) monitoring, and (3) remedies. In the case of autos, *certification* carries the main burden. Manufacturers deliver prototype vehicles to EPA for certification, and these vehicles must meet the emission standards for their model year before any others like them can be marketed. The analogous process for stationary sources is *permitting*, authority for which is divided among all three levels of government. Before a new petroleum refinery can be built, for example, its owners must obtain a pollution permit that sets emission limits and grants operating clearance.

Monitoring of mobile sources entails assembly-line testing and on-the-road testing to assure that compliance carries beyond the prototype stage. Implementation of assembly line testing was long delayed because of bureaucratic in-fighting and manufacturer foot-dragging, but now about 20,000 autos are sampled annually before shipment to buyers.[11] On-the-road testing is needed as well as assembly line auditing because poor maintenance or tampering can neutralize or damage the control equipment. Indeed, cars are supposed to meet standards for their first 50,000 miles. Yet implementation of on-the-road testing has stumbled over more delays than assembly line testing. By 1981 EPA had directed twenty-nine states to have vehicle inspection and maintenance programs under penalty of federal funds withdrawals and other sanctions, but only seven states had active programs at that point. Among the laggards, California was the biggest and the most truculent, failing even to make plans for such a program.

As for stationary sources, EPA inspects or

---

[10] Because 1970–71 cars were already under control as compared to earlier cars, the 90% reduction standard was actually more than 90% when compared to pre–1968 uncontrolled cars. Compared to pre–1968 cars (with CO 90, HC 8.2, and NO_x 3.4), the 1981 standards of Table 23–3 amount to reductions of 96%, 96% and 76%, respectively.

[11] Regulations provide a lenient threshold of acceptance. A particular class of car is considered acceptable if as few as 60% of the cars sampled in that class meet standard. As originally proposed, the regulations specified a more stringent 90% threshold, but EPA changed its mind, explaining that it did not want the testing program to be "unreasonably burdensome to the auto companies." U.S. Congress, House, Subcommittee on Oversight and Investigations of the Committee on Interstate and Foreign Commerce, *Federal Regulation and Regulatory Reform*, 94th Congress, 2d Session (1976), p. 125.

Table 23–4. Compliance Status of Major Stationary Air Pollution Sources, 1980

Industry	Number of Stationary Sources	Number Complying with Emissions Limitations	Per cent Complying with Emissions Limitations
Electric plants (coal/oil)	700	559	80%
Iron & steel (integrated)	60	8	13
Iron & steel (other)	144	102	71
Primary smelters	28	13	46
Pulp and paper	475	417	87
Municipal incinerators	72	60	83
Petroleum refineries	214	170	79
Aluminum reduction	49	37	76
Cement	200	176	88
Sulfuric acid	262	246	94
Phosphatic fertilizers	69	62	90
Coal cleaning	409	395	97
Grey iron	433	381	88
Asphalt concrete	2,862	2,752	96
Total	5,977	5,378	90

Source: Council on Environmental Quality, *Environmental Quality 1980* (Washington, D.C.: 1980), p. 181.

monitors only about 10 per cent of the major sources annually, so it must rely on state and local authorities to cover most emitters. A wide range of surveillance activities is involved—stack tests, source inspections, and opacity readings among them. In some cases fuel samples are analyzed for sulfur content because such is the chief source of sulfur dioxide.

Remedies include auto recalls, civil fines, and in serious cases even criminal penalties. The least burdensome and most common of remedies is the "notice of violation," which amounts to little more than a warning ticket and which in the late 1970s numbered 10,000 or so annually (counting both EPA and state citations). Civil and criminal legal actions are more serious but less frequent, numbering in the high hundreds and low thousands each year (again combining EPA and state efforts.)[12]

[12] Council on Environmental Quality, *Environmental Quality 1980* (Washington, D.C.: 1980), pp. 182–183.

Table 23–4 shows the compliance status of nearly 6,000 major stationary sources in thirteen key industries as of 1980. Except for steel and related ferrous metal industries, compliance seems fairly good. The leading delinquent in steel happens to be U.S. Steel, who in 1976 was singled out by EPA Director John Quarles as the country's worst offender ("most wanted" as it were). "U.S. Steel has compiled a record of environmental recalcitrance second to none," he said.[13]

Except for an occasional recall the auto industry has been able to comply with its stan-

[13] *Wall Street Journal,* February 6, 1976, p. 4. Compliance figures can be misleading, however, and steel may not be the only problem. In particular, *continuing* compliance has been spotty, with one in-depth study revealing that, of 180 sources reported to be in compliance, 71% had documented incidents of excess emissions that resulted in a cumulative annual excess of 25% over allowed emissions level. National Commission on Air Quality, *op. cit.,* p. 230.

dards, but only because the timetable for achievement has regularly been extended by Congress. Had the timetable not been stretched, the auto industry would have long ago closed down, given that the penalty for delinquency has been, since the 1970 Amendments, a fine of $10,000 per "dirty" car.

B. Water Pollution Regulation

1. BROAD STANDARDS FOR WATER

The 1972 Water Pollution Amendments state that their goal is "to restore and maintain the chemical, physical, and biological integrity of the Nation's waters." More specifically, the 1972 Act called for an amazing feat when it urged ". . . that the discharge of pollutants into the navigable waters be *eliminated* by 1985." The elimination of all discharges was to be preceded by attainment of two interim broad standards, both of which were technically oriented but tempered slightly by cost considerations:

- 1977 was the deadline for achieving the *Best Practicable Control Technology* (BPT) in industry and secondary treatment for municipal sewage.
- 1983 was the deadline for achieving the *Best Available Control Technology* (BAT) in industry and best practicable technology for municipal systems. "Fishable and swimmable" waters was the ambient goal here.

The 1977 deadline saw only 81 per cent of all major industrial dischargers and 58 per cent of all municipal dischargers in compliance.[14] There were several reasons for the substantial failure, one of which was unrealistic stringency in the 1977 BPT standards. It then dawned on Congress that complete elimination of discharges by 1985 was likewise an unrealistic objective, so late in 1977 Congress amended the

1972 Act, postponing the BPT standards until 1979 for polluters deemed to have made a "good-faith" effort to meet the old 1977 deadline and substantially altering the best available control technology standards (BAT). Three different classes of pollutants were given different deadlines and different definitions of BAT:

1. Most stringent was a 1984 BAT standard without qualification for toxic pollutants like mercury, arsenic, and zinc.
2. A 1984 BAT standard tempered by "reasonableness" of control cost was set for "conventional" pollutants like human waste and organic debris (BOD).
3. Least stringent was a call for controls by 1987 on "unconventional" pollutants such as ammonia and commercial solvents.

Lest these relaxations give appearances of a "sell-out" to industrial and municipal lobbyists, it should be noted that total elimination of all discharges would not only have been *extremely* costly (running into the hundreds of billions of dollars), it would *not* have assured "fishable-swimmable waters" because these strict standards would have applied only to *point* sources of pollutants, like factories and sewage plants. They would not reach *nonpoint* sources of pollution such as urban storm runoff or agricultural runoff. All told, nonpoint sources account for hefty portions of several pollutant discharges—suspended solids 92%, fecal coliforms 98%, and total phosphates 53%.[15] So complete control of point sources would have still left many water bodies degraded.

2. NARROW STANDARDS FOR WATER

Emission levels for tens of thousands of specific point sources have been derived from the broad BPT and BAT standards. For example, the majority of effluent limitations under BPT take the form of a maximum allowable dis-

---

[14] Council on Environmental Quality, *Environmental Quality 1978* (Washington, D.C.: 1978), pp. 108–110.

[15] Freeman, *op. cit.*, p. 52.

charge quantity of a specific pollutant per unit of production—say, two pounds of suspended solids per 1,000 lbs. of product. The allowables are usually expressed in averages for 30 days with a 24 hour maximum. And the specific pollutants controlled vary from industry to industry, but just about all include BOD and suspended solids.[16]

3. ENFORCEMENT FOR WATER

These discharge limits for specific pollutants are incorporated into source-by-source *permits* that also establish schedules for upgrading controls to meet such limits and require monitoring and periodic reports on compliance. By 1980 nearly 60,000 permits had been issued, as *every* public or private facility that discharges wastes directly into U.S. waters is required to obtain a permit.

EPA focuses most of its *monitoring* activities on "major" permit holders, roughly 12 per cent of the total. Definition of "major" is based chiefly on effluent volume, so this 12 per cent of permit holders accounts for well over 50 per cent, by volume, of all discharges. Small dischargers qualify for "major" status and close surveillance if their effluent is particularly toxic.

In hopes of *remedying* violations, EPA issues "notices of violations" and "administrative orders" backed up by the possibility of fines. In 1979, for instance, approximately $7.5 million in fines were levied. Data for the late 1970s indicate that municipalities are more frequent offenders than industries. Indeed, as late as February 1980 nearly 40 per cent of all major municipal treatment facilities "were not yet in compliance with the original July 1, 1977 statu-

tory deadline requiring secondary treatment or more stringent treatment necessary to meet water quality standards."[17] Government failure thus emerges once again.

C. Toxic Substances Regulation

Aside from toxic air and water pollutants, EPA has substantial additional authority to regulate toxic substances. This authority may be conveniently divided into two broad areas of responsibility—(1) control of hazardous *products*, or components of products, and (2) control of hazardous *wastes* other than those directly entering the air or water.[18]

1. HAZARDOUS PRODUCTS OR COMPONENTS

Hazardous products include, most prominently, pesticides, which are subject to EPA control by authority of the Federal Insecticide, Fungicide, and Rodenticide Act (1947, as amended in 1972 and 1978). Hazardous components of products include a wide variety of chemical substances used as insulators, refrigerants, aerosol propellants, and what not. These chemical components and many hazardous substances serving as final products are subject to EPA regulation under the Toxic Substances Control Act of 1976. Of course EPA must share its authority in these realms with the FDA, CPSC, and OSHA, something which lends confusion to the matter.

Broad standards to guide EPA in this area were never clearly enunciated by Congress, but they can be inferred from the statutory language defining toxic or hazardous substances. The basic idea is to protect people and the environment from "unreasonable" risks of injury,

---

[16] Two contrasting cases illustrate the point: Canning industry pollutants are BOD, suspended solids, fecal coliform, pH, oil and grease. Inorganic chemical industry pollutants include these (except fecal coliform) and also ammonia, fluoride, sulfite, sulfide, cyanide, bromide, arsenic, barium, cadmium, chromium, copper, iron, lead, manganese, and other metals.

[17] Council on Environmental Quality (1980), *op. cit.,* p. 131.

[18] For another summary see P. R. Portney, "Toxic Substance Policy and the Protection of Human Health," in Portney (ed.), *op. cit.,* pp. 105–143.

ill health, or destruction while at the same time giving due consideration to the economic cost of doing so. Narrow standards defy such simple summary because they vary case-by-case, as the hazards vary from cancer to genetic alteration to species annihilation to destruction of the upper atmosphere. The specific activities EPA pursues to fend off "unreasonable" risks are fairly easy to summarize, however, because they mirror those of the Food and Drug Administration discussed earlier:

- *Burden of Proof:* EPA may require the manufacturers of hazardous substances to prove through appropriate tests that those substances are "reasonably" safe for their intended uses. In all other areas, EPA bears the burden of showing harm before acting.
- *Premarket Notification and Registration:* EPA must be notified of new pesticides and new chemical concoctions *prior* to their manufacture and marketing. As a corollary, EPA maintains an inventory of all pesticides and hazardous substances with information on their properties, structures, and uses. EPA's initial inventory of commercial chemicals subject to the Toxic Substances Control Act listed 43,000 unique formulations reported by almost 7400 manufacturers and importers.[19]
- *Regulatory Options:* The restrictions EPA can impose range widely from rather mild labeling requirements to partial or complete prohibitions. EPA has, for instance, banned the use of DDT on crops and prohibited the manufacture or use of chlorofluorocarbons as aerosol spray propellants.
- *Remedies:* Seizures and recalls are weapons in EPA's arsenal of remedies here, along with others mentioned previously.

[19] Council on Environmental Quality (1979), *op. cit.*, p. 216.

2. HAZARDOUS WASTES

Hazardous wastes come from hospitals, research facilities, and government installations, but industry is their most prolific source. Besides toxicity, the hazards of concern are inflammability, corrosivity, and reactivity (e.g., spontaneous explosion). The tragedy of Love Canal tipped everyone off to the problem, and subsequent study has revealed that over 50 million metric tons of such wastes are generated annually in the U.S. As of 1980 approximately 90 per cent of them were being disposed of in environmentally dangerous ways—by improper burning, by deposit in unsecured landfills, and by illegal "midnight dumping."

The Resource Conservation and Recovery Act of 1976 requires safe disposal of hazardous wastes. EPA's regulations under the Act define hazardous wastes and establish a "cradle-to-grave" management system to track the movement of wastes from point of generation to point of proper disposal. The system includes standards for generators of hazardous wastes, standards for transporters, and standards and permits for owners and operators of facilities that store, treat, or dispose of hazardous wastes.

Enforcement of the 1976 Act is still in its infancy, but if the past is prologue this area of the law should produce some sensational cases. Dumping at the Love Canal predates the new law, but under old laws the Department of Justice and EPA have filed the largest environmental enforcement action ever against Hooker Chemical Company and its parent company Occidental Petroleum Corporation. The amount sought for cleanup and compensation to victims is at least $125 million.[20]

[20] Council on Environmental Quality (1980), *op. cit.*, p. 221. Although those responsible for Love Canal are identifiable and financially viable, such is not the case for hundreds of other hazardous dump sites in the U.S. Thus in 1980 the Comprehensive Environmental Response, Compensation, and Liability Act was passed, which among other things establishes a $1.6 billion fund that will be used to finance the cleanup of "orphan" dump sites.

III. What Is the Impact of Policy? Costs and Benefits

A. The Costs of Abatement

A typical 1981 model car carries $582 worth of pollution control equipment. That may not sound like much, but the manufacture and sale of nearly 9 million 1981 autos converts that few hundred dollars into more than $5 billion, demonstrating that the costs of pollution abatement equipment can be towering. Moreover, such capital costs are only part of the story; additional abatement outlays go for operation and maintenance—that is fuel, labor, repair, and the like.

Table 23–5 shows the combined capital, operating, and maintenance costs due to pollution regulation in the U.S., as estimated by the Council on Environmental Quality for the years 1979 and 1988 and the decade of 1979–1988. Slightly over half of the $36.9 billion total expenditure for 1979 funded capital equipment as opposed to operating and maintenance expenses, a rough 50–50 split that shifts toward capital cost as the 1979–88 decade progresses. Among abatement programs, it is easy to see that air pollution control is by far the most costly, accounting for nearly 60 per cent of all outlays annually and cumulatively. Water pollution control comes in a respectable second, with $12.7 billion in 1979 and $169.7 billion over the decade. Roughly half of these amounts for water finance municipal waste treatment projects and other public endeavors; the rest support private efforts.

To put these figures in perspective it may be noted that 1979's total of $36.9 billion was about three-fourths the size of all federal spending on health care in that year and 62 per cent the size of our oil import bill. It was also about $168 per person, a tidy sum. The total did not, however, exceed 1.6 per cent of GNP in 1979, and the forecast total of $69.0 billion for 1988 should be somewhere near 2 per cent of GNP.[21]

Unfortunately, there are still further possible costs or adverse economic impacts not reflected in Table 23–5. *Inflation* may be aggrevated when the costs of abatement show up in higher product prices. *Productivity growth* may be cut as investment resources are diverted from plant and equipment that would produce goods and services into capital expenditures for pollution abatement hardware. *Unemployment* may rise at the local level because of plant closings and at the national level because of adverse macroeconomic effects. *Foreign trade balances* might tilt against us as the heavy costs of abatement put our domestic producers at a disadvantage vis-a-vis their foreign competitors, many

Table 23–5. Estimated Incremental* Pollution Abatement Expenditures, 1979–1988 (Billions of 1979 Dollars)

Program	1979 Annual Costs	1988 Annual Costs	Cumulative 1979–88 Costs
Air pollution	22.3	36.7	299.1
Water pollution	12.7	24.4	169.7
Toxic substances	.3	1.1	8.2
Pesticides	.1	.1	1.2
Solid waste	.05	2.3	15.4
Noise	.1	1.6	6.9
Drinking water	.05	.4	2.7
Land reclamation	1.4	1.5	15.3
Total	36.9	69.0	518.5

* Incremental costs are those made in response to federal regulation beyond those that would have been made absent that regulation.

Source: Council on Environmental Quality, *Environmental Quality 1980* (Washington, D.C.: December 1980), p. 394.

[21] Paul R. Portney, "The Macroeconomic Impacts of Federal Environmental Regulation," *Natural Resources Journal* (July 1981), p. 468.

of whom may face more lenient regulations or may have their abatement costs covered by government subsidies.

Estimates of these additional impacts are very tough to calculate. At the macroeconomic level there are many more factors influencing inflation, productivity growth, unemployment, and export-import performance than pollution abatement efforts. Nevertheless, estimates incorporating these sundry other influences show that the macroeconomic impacts of pollution control are very slight—fractions of percentage points up and down, here and there.[22] To cite just one example, U.S. productivity growth fell from a 3 per cent annual rate in the 1960s to zero in 1980. Yet only about 8 to 15 per cent of this drop, or .24 to .45 percentage points, can be pinned on environmental regulations.[23] The main reason macroeconomic impacts are muted is that, though large in absolute dollar terms, the costs are small as a percentage of GNP.

This is not to say that specific industries are not hit hard. Many are. The costs of air pollution abatement hit the auto and electric power industries forcefully. In water, the blows fall heaviest on steel, metal finishing, and pulp and paper. The chemical industry, for its part, must feel clubbed black-and-blue by toxic substance controls. Certain geographic localities could likewise be singled out for their sacrifices, as plant closures and production cutbacks have economically battered surrounding cities and towns. Figure 23–3 shows, for instance, that most plant closings due at least partially to environmental regulations over the period 1971–1977 were centered in the industrialized northeastern and Great Lake states. In all, 118 plants

[22] For surveys see Ibid, and Council on Environmental Quality (1979), *op. cit.*, pp. 655–664.

[23] Robert H. Haveman and Gregory B. Christiansen, "Environmental Regulations and Productivity Growth," *Natural Resources Journal* (July 1981), pp. 489–509.

Figure 23–3.   Plant Closings Allegedly Resulting in Part from Pollution Abatement Costs, April 1978

	▱ 4 Plants	⬆ 400 Employees		
Region	Number of plant closings	Number of affected employees	Labor force (thousands)	Regional unemployment rate
I	▱	⬆⬆	5,871	8.4
II	▱▱▱▱▱	⬆⬆⬆⬆⬆⬆⬆⬆⬆⬆⬆⬆⬆⬆	7,830	9.2
III	▱▱▱▱	⬆⬆⬆⬆⬆⬆	13,906	7.4
IV	▱▱	⬆⬆⬆⬆	15,884	6.7
V	▱▱▱▱▱▱▱	⬆⬆⬆⬆⬆⬆⬆⬆⬆⬆⬆⬆⬆⬆⬆⬆⬆⬆	20,905	5.9
VI	▱▱	⬆⬆⬆⬆⬆	10,251	5.6
VII	▱▱	⬆⬆	5,550	4.4
VIII			2,974	5.7
IX	▱▱▱▱	⬆⬆⬆⬆⬆	12,242	8.5
X	▱▱▱	⬆⬆⬆⬆⬆	3,443	8.5

Source: U.S. Department of Labor, Bureau of Labor Statistics News, June 12, 1978, letter from Douglas Costle, Administrator, U.S. Environmental Protection Agency, to Ray Marshall, Secretary of Labor, May 9, 1978. As printed in Council on Environmental Quality, *Environmental Quality 1978*, p. 433.

affecting over 21,900 employees were closed during those years.

Disheartening though these adversities may be to particular industries and individuals, it must be recognized that, from a broad social perspective, they represent desirable or at least defensible symptoms of change. If in the past there was too much pollution, then adjustment to less pollution requires that relatively "dirty" products be priced higher than before to reflect *all* the costs they impose on society, including external costs. It also requires that "dirty" plants be made cleaner or closed, and that employees be shifted from relatively "dirty" industries and occupations to relatively cleaner undertakings. Indeed, many costs of abatement represent temporary transition costs rather than permanent equilibrium costs. A laid-off steel worker cannot become a stack-gas technician or water-filter designer overnight, but the gap narrows in the long run. In fact, employment in environmentally positive pursuits has burgeoned, running into the hundreds of thousands and numerically offsetting the job losses depicted in Figure 23–3.

Furthermore, abatement yields benefits, redeeming most if not all these costs.

B. The Benefits of Abatement

The benefits of pollution abatement are much harder to estimate than the costs of abatement, largely because those benefits take the form of *reduced pollution damage and avoidance costs,* costs which by the very nature of the pollution problem are not solidly registered in any marketplace but are instead "external" costs. Reduced *damage* costs include (1) reduced cost of ill health (hospital and medical bills, job absenteeism, pain, suffering, and early death), (2) lessened crop damage, (3) diminished deterioration of materials like rubber and paint, (4) reduced cleaning expenses, (5) enhanced aesthetic enjoyment of vistas, parks, or everyday neighborhoods, and so on. Reduced pollution *avoidance* costs include (1) less travel expense to reach fishable-swimmable waters, (2) reduced commuting time and cost as cleaner city centers attract dwellers, and (3) curbed air conditioning use. Stated differently, economists define the benefits of environmental regulation as the total amount people would be willing to pay for pollution control. And that amount

Figure 23–4. Estimated Annual Air Pollution Damage Costs 1970–86

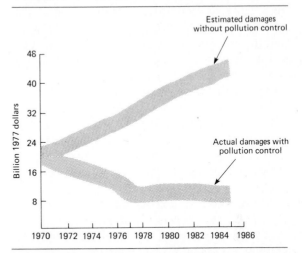

Source: Thomas E. Waddell, "Preliminary Update and Projections of Selected Categories of Damage Cost Estimates," prepared for the Council on Environmental Quality, May 1978.

should correspond to the curtailments in pollution costs associated with abatement.

Table 23–1 and Figure 23–1 showed earlier that policy has made some headway against pollution.[24] Modest success can even be claimed in the many instances where emissions or ambient conditions are merely holding steady because without controls, conditions would apparently be much worse. When the monetary costs of air pollution damage with and without control are estimated over the years 1970–1986, the result is Figure 23–4. Uncertainties and alternative assumptions make the cost estimates for each year a range rather than a single point, hence the shaded bands.

[24] For qualitative evidence see Environmental Protection Agency, *National Accomplishments in Pollution Control: 1970–1980, Some Case Histories* (Washington, D.C.: 1980).

Still, it can be seen that, *without* pollution control, damage costs would by now be well over $35 billion annually. *With* controls, however, these costs are contained to a range around $10 billion annually. The *difference*, which in these rough numbers would be $25 billion annually, is an estimate of air pollution policy benefits because it represents the amount air pollution damage costs are reduced by control.

Different estimates of the benefits of air pollution control are reported in the top half of Table 23–6. The time is a year in the late 1970s, say 1979, and benefit sources are distinguished. Improved human health scores most highly.

The overall benefits of water pollution control have been subject to only scant research, but the bottom half of Table 23–6 gives some idea of the possibilities. The numbers there are actually estimates of the total yearly damage from water pollution as of 1973, so they are quite different than those for air. They represent the potential benefits from reducing all water pollutants to "threshold" levels (not necessarily eliminating them completely). Note that roughly half of the benefits would be in the form of enhanced recreational opportunities.

The temptation to compare these several benefit estimates with the earlier cost estimates should be resisted. Both sets of numbers are mere approximations. Moreover, both are too aggregated to be very meaningful—that is, benefit-cost estimates are best when viewed for *individual* pollutants, policies, and projects, such as automobile carbon monoxide control. Indeed, our next section will demonstrate that the benefit-cost performance of specific policy areas could be vastly improved by modifying present policy to incorporate greater use of economic incentives. Still, when such broad comparisons of overall costs and benefits are made, they suggest that a stern commitment to a

---

Table 23–6. Estimated Annual Benefits from Air Pollution Control and Potential Benefits from Water Pollution Control, 1970's (Billions of Dollars)

Air Pollution Control Benefits (1979)	*Range of Estimates*
Human health	3.0 to 40.0
Vegetation (crops)	0.7 to 1.7
Materials	0.9 to 3.9
Soiling and visibility	1.0 to 2.8
Total benefits	5.6 to 48.4
Potential Water Pollution Control Benefits (1973)	
Recreational opportunities	2.5 to 12.6
Aesthetic and ecological improvements	0.6 to 2.8
Reduced water-borne disease	0.3 to 1.0
Industrial water use	1.1 to 2.3
Total potential benefits	4.5 to 18.7

Source: Adopted from A. Myrick Freeman III, *The Benefits of Air and Water Pollution Control* (1979) and A. Hershaft *et al.*, *Critical Review of Estimating Benefits of Air and Water Pollution Control* (1978), as reported in R. Halvorsen and M. G. Ruby, *Benefit-Cost Analysis of Air-Pollution Control* (Lexington, Mass.: Lexington Books, 1981) and Center for Policy Alternatives at MIT, *Benefits of Environmental, Health, and Safety Regulation* (Washington, D.C.: Committee on Governmental Affairs, U.S. Senate, 1980); and National Commission on Air Quality, *To Breathe Clean Air* (Washington, D.C.: 1981).

cleaner environment may after all be worth some staggering costs.

IV. Policy Alternatives: Economic Incentives

A. *Problems with the Present Approach*

As we have seen, the present standards-enforcement approach is technologically and bureaucratically oriented. It has, to be sure, produced some desirable results. But it suffers many deficiencies, including the following.

1. TECHNICAL KNOWLEDGE

Technology-based standard setting, if done properly, requires that bureaucrats understand production and abatement technologies as well as or better than industry insiders. What are "best practicable" and "best available" technologies? What is the "lowest achievable emission rate"? Can autos with internal combustion engines really be expected to emit no more than 3.4 grams of carbon monoxide per mile?

If only a few pollutants, polluters, and industries were involved, this depth-of-knowledge problem would be trifling. But there are dozens of pollutants emitted by countless polluters in thousands of industries. Once consideration of control costs is included in the standard setting, as often called for by legislation and practicality, the knowledge problem is compounded substantially. Little wonder, then, that EPA, with its staff at times reaching over 10,000, is far and away the single largest federal agency reviewed in this book, not to mention the vast numbers involved in state programs.

2. ARBITRARY DECISIONS

The statutory qualifiers guiding EPA decision making—"practical," "feasible," "available," and "reasonable"—call for judgments, *arbitrary* judgments. In turn, polluters can and

do challenge these judgments in federal courts. Shortly after BPT water standards were developed, for instance, 250 of them were challenged, bogging the program down for years. Distinguishing between sources stirs similar conflicts. When, for example, does a modification to a production process transform an "old" source into a "new" source under the Clean Air Act? Does a new boiler do it? Or conversion from coal to residual fuel oil? Or expanded output?

3. BENEFIT-COST

Why require autos in Fargo, North Dakota to be as pollution-free as those in Los Angeles? The $600 cost per car is the same, but the benefits gained are worth nickels in Fargo while probably exceeding $600 in Los Angeles. A "two-car" policy of strict controls in major metropolitan areas and relaxed controls elsewhere would attain most of the benefits of reducing auto emissions without saddling residents of clean-air areas with heavy costs. Opportunities for benefit-cost strategies such as this abound but go neglected by EPA.

4. COST EFFECTIVENESS OR EFFICIENCY

We can discard the above criticism if we assume that the benefits of abatement are too elusive to justify adoption of full-fledged benefit-cost criteria (with both benefits and costs variable in monetary terms). However, once we accept EPA's ambient environmental standards as given (for their nonmonetized desirabilities), we can still criticize current policy for not being cost effective. The same degree of abatement presently achieved could, in other words, be achieved at less cost to society. Although data do not exist to estimate the total cost savings for all programs nationally, some studies suggest cost savings for certain regions and pollutants to be over 80 per cent.[25] Possible

[25] W. Harrington and A. J. Krupnick, "Stationary Source Pollution Policy and Choices for Reform," *Natural Resources Journal* (July 1981), p. 543.

savings of 30 to 35 per cent, which have been found for water policy nationally, are more typical and probably more realistic but no less impressive.[26]

The main reason the standard-enforcement approach lacks cost effectiveness is that it usually requires all polluters of a given class to abate by more-or-less *equal* percentages, ignoring the fact that the cost of abatement varies substantially by source. If sources with low-cost abatement could be curbed more than sources with high-cost abatement, then a given level of abatement could be achieved most cheaply.

Table 23–7 illustrates the point. The hypothetical data are the same as those used in Table 20–1 on page 417, and the problem here is the same: How can we eliminate 30 million tons of sulfur dioxide pollution? The most efficient way, as we saw when discussing Table 20–1, is to use lowest-cost abatement first (source A), second lowest-cost next (source C), and so on until the 30 million ton target is reached. Total cost by that approach would be $62 million. Note that some sources of pollution (A, C, and F) are required to abate *completely*, another to abate only *partially* ($\frac{1}{2}$ D), and the remainder *not at all* (B and E).

Alternatively, we could achieve the 30 million tons target by calling for 30 per cent abatement by each source, because, as shown in column (2) of Table 23–7, all sources together emit 100 million tons. The tonnage reduction of each source is then given in column (3) of Table 23–7 (1.5m for A, for instance). And the total cost of each source's abatement effort is given in column (4), where the tonnage reduction is multiplied by the abatement cost per ton of reduction (as computed earlier in column (4) of Table 20–1). Adding the costs of all sources yields a total cost for this 30 per cent across-the-board 30m ton cutback of $89.7 million, which is nearly *45 per cent higher* than the

$62 million cost of relying on low-cost abatement more heavily than high-cost abatement.

5. INCENTIVE TO ABATE

Compliance delays and failures such as those mentioned earlier suggest that many polluters find it cheaper to challenge regulations in court, to violate established standards, and to weedle and waffle in negotiating with EPA as long as they can. Recently EPA has elevated fines to eradicate the gains of noncompliance. But even if we assume this particular problem of incentives is now solved, there still remains another. All a polluter need do is meet his standard. There is *no* incentive to do better and abate more if the opportunity avails itself through newly discovered low-cost technologies.

6. INNOVATION

The standards-enforcement approach can be faulted also for not encouraging innovation in control technologies. As A. V. Kneese and C. L. Schultze put it:

Auto emission controls pay no attention to the potentialities of new engine developments. The law that stipulates water effluent limits based on the "best available technology economically achievable" discourages innovation because that would put firms in the ironic position of handing the regulatory authorities the means of imposing on them new and more costly standards of pollution control.[27]

Other problems with the standards-enforcement approach could be mentioned, but these are the main ones.[28] To correct or alleviate most if not all these deficiencies, economists advocate a shift toward policies embodying economic incentives. These include marketable permits and effluent taxes. These alternatives

---

[26] A. M. Freeman III, *op. cit.*, p. 56.

[27] Kneese and Schultze, *op. cit.*, pp. 82–83.
[28] For a full discussion see Baumol and Oates, *op. cit.*, pp. 230–245, 323–366.

Table 23–7. Cost of 30% Abatement by All Sources of SO₂ Using Data from Table 20–1 (Page 417)

(1) Source of Pollution	(2) Emissions in Millions of Tons	(3) 30% Reduction, Each Source	(4) Cost in Millions of Dollars
A	5	.3 × 5m = 1.5m	1.5m × $1.00 = $ 1.5m
B	35	.3 × 35m = 10.5m	10.5m × $3.20 = $33.6m
C	10	.3 × 10m = 3.0m	3.0m × $1.50 = $ 4.5m
D	20	.3 × 20m = 6.0m	6.0m × $3.00 = $18.0m
E	25	.3 × 25m = 7.5m	7.5m × $3.80 = $28.5m
F	5	.3 × 5m = 1.5m	1.5m × $2.40 = $ 3.6m
Totals	100	.3 × 100m = 30m	$89.7m

are not panaceas. They too have faults, and, indeed, many economists believe they are inappropriate for controlling highly toxic pollutants, whose environmental dangers are so serious as to warrant tight regulation and virtually 100% abatement. Still, policies imposing economic incentives could supplant the vast bulk of standards-enforcement regulation, Congress willing.

B. Bubbles and Offsets: First Steps

To introduce our discussion of such policies we can acknowledge two steps in the desired direction already taken by EPA. In 1979 its "**bubble**" policy was introduced. Whereas before EPA regulated discharges "stack-by-stack," calling for near equal percentage emission cutbacks at each physical source, the bubble policy now places an imaginary bubble over an entire plant, allowing the plant to meet its overall emission standards by putting extra controls on discharge points that have low control costs and relaxing controls on discharge points having high control costs. Because plant managers make the decision as to where in the plant abatement will be greatest, the plant's overall abatement cost is minimized without EPA

having to acquire detailed knowledge of technology and expense. The large potential cost savings from the "plant-by-plant" bubble approach are illustrated in a study of fifty-two DuPont plants having a total of 548 sources of hydrocarbon emissions. Source-by-source reduction of 85 per cent of the emissions cost $105.7 million annually (in 1975 dollars). In contrast, the same 85 per cent reduction on a plant-by-plant basis would have cost only $42.6 million, a remarkable 63.1 per cent saving.[29]

As of February 1981, there were 68 plant bubbles in EPA's reporting system. And later that year, EPA moved to expand the bubble concept to a company-by-company basis. So expanded, two or more plants in a given region are treated as if they are a single pollution source, and extra emission reductions at one plant (with low-cost abatement) can be used to compensate for emission increases at another plant (with high-cost abatement).

Even before bubbles became fashionable, "**offsets**" were being tried, as provided under the 1977 Clean Air Act Amendments. These offsets arose because without them, industrial

[29] M. T. Maloney and Bruce Yandle, "Bubbles and Efficiency," *Regulation* (May/June 1980), pp. 49–52.

growth in nonattainment areas would have been completely shackled, as growth would have brought new sources of pollution where pollution already exceeded ambient standards (see item A.1.b. in Table 23–3 for reference). The idea of the offset is to permit a new source to pollute insofar as that new source offsets the new pollution by getting old sources in the area to reduce their pollution commensurately. In one case under the program, a cement company wanting to build in New Braunfels, Texas, entered into an agreement to pay for the installation of dust collectors at another local company. In another instance the Times Mirror Company was able to expand greatly a paper mill near Portland, Oregon after purchasing the right to emit about 150 tons of extra hydrocarbons into the air annually, which tonnage was previously emitted by local dry cleaning and wood coating establishments. The purchase price? About $50,000.[30]

Why would new sources want to pay others to abate instead of abating themselves? Because it would be cheaper that way. Why would an old source agree to abate? Because the compensation received would cover the cost of abatement and maybe more. It is the combination of these questions and answers that reveals the social cost savings in the offset approach. Overall abatement remains unchanged or increases as the low-cost abaters are induced to carry the abatement burden for high-cost abaters.

C. Marketable Pollution Permits

Many economists urge that the bubble and offset policies be expanded until full-fledged **markets for pollution rights** are established to protect both air and water.[31] Guided by ambient air-conditions, for instance, total allowable emissions of sulfur dioxide in the northern Ohio area could be set at, say, 100,000 tons annually. One hundred permits of 1,000 tons each could then be auctioned off to the highest bidders among those who want to pollute. Those facing relatively high abatement costs would bid high for permits because they would rather pay to pollute than pay to abate. Those facing relatively low abatement costs would bid low because for them, rights to pollute would not be worth much given their relative ease of abating. Low-cost abaters would thus abate more than high-cost abaters for a cost effective result. The General Accounting Office estimated in 1981 that a "viable market in air pollution rights" could cut pollution control costs *at least* 40 per cent.[32] That would be nearly $9 billion off the cost in 1979. Substantial savings for water could be expected as well.

There are, aside from cost-effectiveness, a number of other good qualities that recommend the marketable pollution permits approach. Implementation of this approach would probably be much simpler than the standards-enforcement approach, as the knowledge required of the regulators would be greatly reduced, and fewer arbitrary judgments subject to court challenge would have to be made. There would be, in a word, less *meddling* in the affairs of business people, as they would then assume most of the burden of deciding the where, the who, and the how of abatement. Another bonus of this approach is that it would encourage rather than stifle innovations in abatement technology. Abaters would not be wedded to specific technologies, and they would be constantly on the lookout for new ways to abate at lower costs.

One potential drawback to marketable permits is that they give appearances of being *inequitable*. The standards-enforcement ap-

---

[30] For further examples see National Commission on Air quality, *op. cit.*, pp. 136–137.

[31] The idea originates with J. H. Dales, *Pollution, Property, and Prices* (Toronto: University of Toronto Press, 1968).

[32] *Wall Street Journal*, June 18, 1981, p. 25.

proach tends to call for equal percentage curtailments from all sources, which sounds "fair." By comparison, marketable permits would cause low-cost abaters to abate more and allow high-cost abaters to abate less, giving low-cost abaters a greater share of the overall financial burden than before. Whether or not this is in fact "unfair," however, depends on one's definition of "fairness." With standards-enforcement the physical percentages tend toward equality, but the financial burden falls heaviest on the high cost abaters. (Check column (4) of Table 23–7 again.) With marketable permits, the physical percentages diverge substantially but the financial burden is spread more evenly as the share of low-cost abaters rises and that of high-cost abaters falls. Value judgments differ among people, but most folks might find this latter result more fair than the former. Note, too, that with permits the costs are not merely more evenly distributed, they are, through efficiency, *lower overall*, which seems fairer to society as a whole. Finally, staunch environmentalists might even find fairness in this approach. They could enter the bidding to keep some permits out of the hands of polluters, thereby reducing the level of pollution even below EPA authorized levels.

D. Effluent Taxes

Effluent taxes (or emission fees) work on the same principle as marketable pollution permits. The main difference in concept is that, whereas the permit approach sets the *quantity* of pollution allowed and lets the market determine the price of pollution rights, the tax approach sets the *price* polluters must pay to pollute and lets the ultimate quantity of pollution be determined by abatement costs relative to the tax. Any quantity of abatement achieved by marketable permits could be realized through a tax by raising the tax on pollution high enough to discourage an equal amount of pollution.

Figure 23–5 illustrates the tax approach with familiar data taken from Tables 20–1 and 23–7. The cost of abatement rises by steps: source A at \$1.00 per ton of SO_2 removed; source C at \$1.50; and so on. With a tax on SO_2 emissions, each source would have to decide whether to pollute and pay the tax or abate and avoid the tax. Cost minimization determines the choice. So if the tax were \$2.00 per ton of SO_2 emitted, sources A and C, whose abatement costs are \$1.00 and \$1.50 per ton, would find it in their interest to abate and avoid the tax, with the result that 15 million tons of SO_2 would be removed from the air. Remaining sources accounting for 85 million tons would choose to pollute and pay, as their costs per ton of abatement exceed the \$2.00 tax per ton. (Their total tax bill would be $\$2 \times 85$ million = \$170 million, but their total abatement bill would be \$279 million.) Raising the tax to \$3.10 per ton would, however, induce abatement from sources F and D as well as A and C because \$3.10 exceeds their abatement costs of \$2.40 and \$3.00, respectively. With A, C, F, and D abating, 40 million tons of SO_2 would be removed from the air. It follows that still higher taxes would bring still greater abatement.

Development of taxes requires (1) selection of a *basis* for each tax, such as the tonnage of SO_2, the poundage of BOD, or the volume of hydrocarbons, (2) methods of *monitoring* the flow of pollutants under the selected bases, and (3) specification of the tax *rate*. According to economic ideals, the tax rate should correspond to the marginal costs of pollution, for it would then generate a degree of abatement where the marginal cost of pollution would just match the marginal cost of abatement (as shown earlier in Figure 20–2 on page 414). In reality this cannot be done because we do not know the marginal costs of pollution with accuracy. The implication of the ideal is, however, that tax rates would be highest where pollution is most concentrated, where the pollutant is most

Figure 23–5. Effluent Tax Approach to Abatement

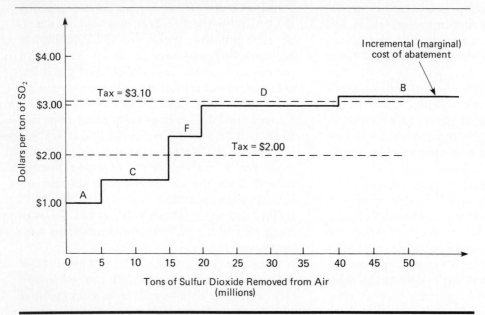

harmful, and where the greatest number of people are threatened.

Given the great conceptual similarity between emission taxes and marketable permits, it is hardly surprising that the qualities of the two approaches are similar. The tax requires no more than a modicum of technical knowledge and relatively few arbitrary decisions on the part of government officials, qualities that minimize intrusion into the affairs of businesses. The tax is cost-effective because low-cost abaters curb their pollution more than high-cost abaters. The tax imposes economic incentives to innovate new and cheaper abatement technologies. Finally, the equity implications are similar, too.

Permits and taxes do differ, however. Theoretically, the marketable permit approach might be superior to a tax on grounds that the quantity of abatement achieved is more certain in advance of program implementation. The permit approach is also more insulated against inflation, for tax rates would have to be raised with inflation to maintain a constant degree of abatement.[33]

Among the tax's advantages, the tax presses polluters to abate more and more as innovation reduces the cost of abatement. Figure 23–6 illustrates this for a single polluter. Two curves for the marginal cost of abatement are shown—one for old, high-cost technology, MC_{old}, the other for new, low-cost technology, MC_{new}. (Both rise with greater abatement, which is more realistic than the constant abatement cost per polluter assumed earlier.) At the tax rate indicated, cost minimization would cause the firm to abate to point J (M) under the old technology and to point K (N) under the new technology. The reason for this is that the total cost of abatement plus tax is reduced from area

[33] Baumol and Oates, *op. cit.*, pp. 250–53.

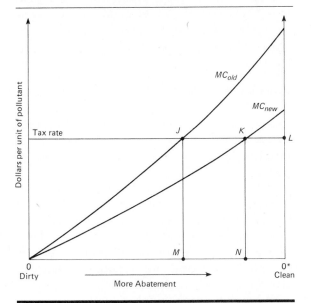

Figure 23–6. **Incentive to Abate Further Under a Tax, Given an Innovation**

OJLO* to area OKLO* by such "good" behavior.[34] Notice that these savings also induce greater innovation in abatement methods than otherwise.

The tax approach has won widespread adoption in European water pollution control efforts.[35] It has also been used against air pollution abroad, such as to control sulfur dioxide emissions in Japan. However, proposals for

emission taxes in the U.S. have been rebuffed, primarily for political reasons. For example, an unsuccessful Pure Air Tax Act proposed by President Nixon in 1972 would have taxed sulfur emissions, with the tax rate varying depending on regional air quality. The proposed tax was 15¢ per pound of sulfur in regions where primary ambient air standards were violated, 10¢ in areas where secondary ambient air standards were violated, and zero where all standards were met.

The closest thing to a large-scale pollution tax presently in force in the U.S. is the mandatory deposit on beverage containers that seven states currently impose. Oregon's "Bottle Bill" of 1971 introduced the idea by imposing a mandatory refundable deposit of 5¢ on standard beer and soda pop containters plus a larger deposit on unique containers. The purpose of the program was to encourage the use and reuse of reusable containers so as to cut down on solid waste, reduce litter, and save energy. By all accounts the program has been resoundingly successful on all counts. Yet stiff opposition by beverage industry interests and container manufacturers has prevented the spread of this policy to the national level or even beyond the seven states currently in the unlittered lot.[36]

In short, the tax approach represents more than the ivory-towered theorizing of economists. It has been tried both here and abroad in various ways that illuminate its promise. But that promise has only begun to be tapped, and it is hoped that experiments with it will be greatly expanded in the future.

Summary

What is pollution? It occurs when one use of the environment, waste disposal in particu-

---

[34] To break this down, at the J solution total abatement cost will be the area under the marginal cost of abatement curve, OJM, and the total tax bill will be the tax rate MJ times the amount of pollution MO*, which is area MJLO*. Both together are total combined cost area OJLO*. At the K solution, total abatement cost is area OKN, and the tax bill is area NKLO*. The combined total is then area OKLO*.

[35] Organization for Economic Co-Operation and Development, *Pollution Charges: An Assessment* (Paris: 1976) and *Pollution Charges in Practice* (Paris: 1980); Blair R. Bower et al., *Incentives in Water Quality Management: France and the Ruhr Area* (Washington, D.C.: Resources for the Future, 1981).

[36] For analysis of a national policy see Resource Conservation Committee, *Committee Findings and Staff Papers on National Beverage Container Deposits* (Washington, D.C.: 1978).

lar, diminishes other environmental service capabilities of value—habitat and amenity services especially. The waste substances of greatest damage to the air are particulates, sulfur dioxide, nitrogen oxides, hydrocarbons, and carbon monoxide. Water pollutants are more varied, ranging from simply BOD to highly toxic metals. Land pollutants include solid wastes and toxic chemicals. Many pollutants can be neutralized by the environment's dissipation and purification processes, suggesting that 100% abatement of all pollutants is neither necessary nor desirable. On the other hand, complacency is not warranted either, as even the most innocent of pollutants can become injurious through concentration.

What has been done about pollution? The U.S. strategy has been direct control through the development of elaborate emission standards and their enforcement. The standards have been technologically based, tempered slightly by cost considerations. The result is that emitters of a given class (say coal burning electric power plants producing SO_2 along with electricity) are typically pressed to curb their discharges by some fairly common percentage figure, like 60%. In turn, enforcement follows a bureaucratic-legalistic course entailing (1) certifications or permits, (2) monitoring, and (3) remedies of assorted types and severity.

Broad standards for ambient *air* conditions incorporate a threshold concept at primary and secondary levels presumed to be protective of humans first and other things second. Modified to prevent substantial deterioration in relatively clean areas, these broad standards have been translated into narrow emission standards that vary by mobility and age of emitting source, by enforcement agency, and by attainment status (see Table 23–3). Enforcement effort has yielded a level of compliance distorted upward by shifting standards and incomplete monitoring, with the result that ambient standards in many areas will not be achieved even as late as 1985.

Broad *water* standards originally aimed at complete elimination of point-source discharges by 1985. Best "practicable" (BPT) and best "available" (BAT) technologies were steps along the way. Stumbling on the very first step (BPT by 1977), officials revamped policy to postpone BPT standards for some, modify BAT standards for all, and drop the idea that emissions be eliminated. Narrow standards under these guidelines set emission limits for specific sources, as enforced by nearly 60,000 permits, extensive monitoring, and threatened penalties. Municipalities have proven to be the most persistent offenders.

Toxic substances, both as products and wastes, have most recently attracted the attention of EPA. Regulations are tighter here than elsewhere, incorporating such features as a burden of proof of safety on proponents of new chemical substances and cradle-to-grave control of hazardous wastes.

What is the impact of these policies? For one thing they perpetrate costs running more than $40 billion annually. Though indeed large these costs are a tiny fraction of GNP, so macroeconomic impacts on unemployment, inflation, productivity growth, and trade balances tend to be slight. Still, certain industries and localities are hit hard.

The benefits of pollution control can be measured, at least theoretically, by the amount pollution costs are reduced, which should broadly correspond to people's willingness to pay for a cleaner environment. Practical difficulties reduce measurement to guesswork, but that guesswork has succeeded in demonstrating that abatement is worth tens of billions of dollars a year in improved health, broadened recreation opportunities, reduced property damage, and so on.

What policy improvements could be made? Greater reliance on instruments imposing economic incentives—that is, marketable pollution permits and emission taxes—would seem to be wise. They have the advantage of (1) requiring less technical knowledge, (2) minimizing bureaucratic meddling, (3) promoting cost-effectiveness or efficiency, and (4) accomodating and even encouraging innovation in abatement technology. Their cost-effectiveness is a particularly attractive point, as studies indicate that immense cost savings, 80 per cent in some cases, could be realized without compromising environmental ideals.

These alternatives have their own drawbacks, and they therefore should not take over the entire burden of policy. What seems best is a mix of instruments, including even moral suasion in the mix. The standards-enforcement approach seems particularly well suited to handling the problem of toxic substances, which in many instances must be banned. Marketable permits and emission taxes seem most appropriate for emissions that are generated regularly and fairly easily monitored—BOD and SO_2, for example.

Questions and Exercises for Chapter 23

1. The *economic* definition of pollution differs from the *physical* definition. How does the economic definition relate to optimal allocation of resources? How does "scarcity" influence problem assessment here?

2. What has been the trend in air and water pollutants over the past decade?

3. Why is it important to distinguish between pollutants in their severity and persistence?

4. Why do present regulations embody the entire range of regulatory activities—i.e., broad and narrow standards, permits, certification, and so forth?

5. Characterize the broad standards for "criteria" air pollutants.

6. To what extent have costs been taken into account, either systematically or haphazardly, in developing and amending air and water standards?

7. Compare and contrast hazardous substance control with water pollution control of "conventional" pollutants.

8. What types of costs arise from abatement? Benefits?

9. Identify "bubbles" and "offsets," explaining how they help lessen regulatory costs.

10. Compare and contrast the regulatory approach with the marketable permits approach.

11. What is similar about marketable permits and effluent taxes? What is different?

Part VI

Miscellaneous Policies

"It has something to do with sex-discrimination law
. . . for every bull he fights he has to fight a cow!"

Source: The Wall Street Journal. Used py permission of Cartoon
Features Syndicate.

Chapter 24

Wage and Price Controls

We have learned a lot about wage and price controls but not how to control wages and prices.
—Sidney L. Jones

Panic, chaos, disillusion—all are possible if inflation gets out of hand. Rapid inflation drastically reshuffles people's real incomes, as some keep up and others fall behind. It ambushes savings, disrupts corporate finance, and undermines long-term projects.

Wage-price control is an attempt by governments to deal directly with inflation. It has been tried at various times in the U.S. and Europe, and is likely to be tried again in one form or another. Our review of wage-price control covers several questions. How might wage-price control help fight inflation? What does wage-price control entail? What has experience taught us? What improvements might be made in the policy if it is ever tried again?

I. The Problem

A. The Causes of Inflation

There are essentially three causes of inflation: (1) demand-pull, (2) exogenous shock, and (3) market-power push (also called cost-push in some forms). The price effect of each may be seen in Figure 24–1, which shows simple shifts in demand and supply.

1. *Demand-pull* operates on the principle of excess aggregate demand. As demand increases from D_1 to D_2 in Figure 24–1, price level is pulled up from P_1 to P_2 and equilibrium shifts from point F to point E. A jump in the supply of money could cause such a demand-pull inflation. This is immortalized in the old saying that inflation is just "too much money chasing too few goods."

2. *Exogenous shocks* are severe shocks that crimp an economy's productive power, or, in economic jargon, lessen real income potential (where "real income" is money income deflated by price level). If California slid into the sea, its agricultural capabilities would be lost to the nation, forcing up the price of food. If earthquakes wiped out our coal resources, fuel would suddenly become more expensive. More realistically, OPEC hiked the price of imported oil four-fold in 1973–74, jolting the U.S. economy. In Figure 24–1 such shocks would shift the supply curve from S_1 to S_2 because they increase the cost of production. For given demand D_1, price then leaps from P_1 to P_3. These losses in real income can be called exogenous because they are due to forces outside our economy.

3. *Market-power push* likewise operates on

Figure 24–1. Inflation from Shifts of Demand and Supply

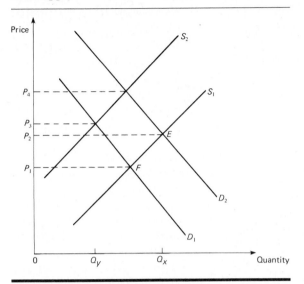

B. *The Ultimate Role of the Money Supply*

It should be noted that exogenous shocks and market-power pushes erupt from certain sectors of the economy, say food in the case of a drought or steel in the case of excessive steel-worker wage increases. These sectoral jumps in prices need not result in overall inflation of the *average* price level if elsewhere in the economy prices are falling. Thus exogenous shocks and market-power pushes do not generate general inflation unless "endorsed" at the aggregate level by money supply expansion, responsibility for which rests with the Federal Reserve Board. Stated differently, virtually all aggregate inflations are *accompanied* by money supply expansion but not all inflations are *caused* by it. Exogenous shock and market-power push stand as separate causes.

The critical role of aggregate money supply works in the opposite direction as well. Virtually all inflations can be stopped dead in their tracks by sufficiently stringent money supply curtailment. This works through lessened aggregate demand, and may be illustrated simply by referring again to Figure 24–1. If at the start demand is D_2, a market-power push that shifted supply from S_1 to S_2 would lift price from P_2 to P_4. But a drop in demand from D_2 to D_1 by monetary restraint could press price level back down to P_3, nearly wiping out the inflationary effect.

The great importance of money supply to inflation has spawned an entire school of economic thought, members of which are called *monetarists*. Monetarists are the chief critics of wage-price controls because, as they see it, monetary restraint is both necessary and sufficient to achieve price and wage stability. Moreover, in this view, direct controls are not merely worthless. They are oppressive, wasteful, and economically deadly. They create artificial

the supply side, but not from a decline in productive capability or lost real income. Rather, prices are pushed up by wage escalations that exceed productivity growth or by higher profit markups. The guilty parties here are obviously powerful labor unions and/or large corporations.

A simple example of the wage effect may help: If the hourly wage of tee shirt painters doubled from $3.00 to $6.00, the cost (and price) of painted tee shirts *need not* also rise if a new application of stencils doubled the hourly output of each painter from 2 to 4 shirts per hour. Labor cost per tee shirt both before and after is $1.50 ($3/2 and $6/4). However, with *no* added productivity in output, labor cost per tee shirt would double with the doubled wage rate ($3/2 to $6/2). In Figure 24–1, the higher cost per tee shirt would shift supply up from S_1 to S_2, which relative to D_1 boosts price from P_1 to P_3.

shortages and black markets, crimp freedom, and lead to misallocations of resources.[1]

C. The Problem: Where Controls May Help

Those who advocate the use of wage-price controls concede that money supply is crucial. Indeed, they even concede that tight monetary constraint could stop any inflation if sufficiently tight. Where, then, do advocates of controls differ from the monetarists? First, they draw a distinction between demand-pull inflation caused by excess money supply growth and other kinds of inflations. Second, they believe that money supply reductions *alone* are a proper remedy to cure only excess demand inflation. Third, they argue that combat against market-power push inflation is best conducted by a two-pronged attack—monetary restraint *plus* wage-price control. Fourth, they contend that in this context monetary curtailment alone is too blunt an instrument, one that creates very high costs in unemployment and excess capacity. Thus, in short, procontrols people arrive at their position by weighing perceived benefits and costs. They advocate controls as a low-cost means of countering market-power push inflation.

In terms of Figure 24–1, the basic idea can be appreciated by looking again at what happens when demand is pressed down from D_2 to D_1 in the effort to counter the shift of supply from S_1 to S_2. Price, as we noted, falls from P_4 to P_3. At the same time, however, quantity falls toward Q_y, resulting in an overall drop in quantity from Q_x to Q_y. With quantity down, unemployment rises and idle capacity emerges—the costs of concern to advocates of controls. Would it not be better, procontrols people ask, if instead of shifting demand from D_2 to D_1, we simply shifted supply from S_2

to S_1 through the application of wage-price controls?

Monetarists concede that when money supply curbs depress demand, unemployment and idle capacity ensue. But they are not overly concerned about these costs because they consider them to be mild and temporary. Moreover, monetarists scoff at the theory of controls, saying that the shift from S_2 to S_1 would occur even without controls if monetary restraint substantially raised unemployment for a sufficient spell. (Granting this, a more sophisticated theory of controls would hold that controls can achieve a *quicker* shift than monetary policy alone can attain.) In short, the monetarists do not see powerful unions and large corporations as being much of a problem. If those possessing market power do not respond immediately to recessionary forces, they will *eventually* be beaten into submission by the penalties of low profits and high unemployment.

D. The Problem: Concrete Examples

However lightly monetarists may regard it, there is enough of a problem with market-power push inflation to cause politicians to take wage-price controls seriously. Some evidence indicates that highly unionized and highly concentrated sectors of the economy occasionally cause inflation directly. Even if this evidence is discarded, there is other evidence indicating that inflations started by other causes are perpetuated and aggravated by market power.[2] Market power seems to make prices and wages unresponsive to downward demand pressures.

The steel industry provides several classic examples. Between 1955 and 1958 capacity usage in steel fell sharply from 92.1% to 59.1%; at the same time the price of steel mill products rose roughly 23%. Between 1973 and 1976 capacity usage dipped markedly again; yet prices

---

[1] For a good statement of the monetarist position, see Samuel Brittan and Peter Lilley, *The Delusion of Incomes Policy* (New York: Holmes & Meier, 1977).

[2] For a review see D. F. Greer, *Industrial Organization and Public Policy* (New York: Macmillan Publishing Co., 1980), pp. 508–550.

simultaneously soared over 60%. A major contributing factor to these and similar experiences was ever rising steelworker wages and fringe benefits. Between 1952 and 1977 average hourly employee costs in steel rose 450%, which was much more than the 297% increase in all of manufacturing.[3]

A broader example comes from the Nixon era. Shortly after taking office in 1969, President Nixon announced that he would bring price and wage inflation down from their lofty Vietnam War levels by reducing aggregate demand through balanced budgets and curtailed monetary growth. Money supply was cut back from an annual growth rate of 10% in 1968 to 2% during the first half of 1970. As a consequence, the unemployment rate advanced from 3.3 to 4.8% over the same period, advancing thereafter to 6.0%. Nevertheless, frustration followed. Union wages not only *continued* to increase, their *rate of increase increased* from an annual inflation rate of 6.7% in early 1969 to 12.9% in late 1971. Nonunion wages also continued to increase, but they did not accelerate like union wages. Thus the Vietnam War inflation, which was caused by demand-pull forces, was perpetuated by market-power forces. In the end, President Nixon, a staunch free-market supporter, turned to direct wage-price controls.

II. Wage-Price Controls

A. Background

Monetarists like to point out that wage-price controls have a long and unclean record. They contend that all control efforts have been failures since as early as Roman times, when the Emperor Diocletian fixed the value of 900 goods, 130 grades of labor, and 41 freight rates. The death penalty was prescribed for breaches, of which there were apparently many. According to one historian of the day, Lactantius, much blood was shed "upon very slight and trifling accounts." Even so, failure of the policy lay more in the shortages and disruptions it seems to have caused than in the official savagery. People stopped bringing goods to market "because they could not get a reasonable price for them."[4] History is littered with hundreds of further attempts at direct control that monetarists consider no more than temporary successes (unless one wants to count totalitarian control programs as long-term successes). Of course procontrols people disagree with this interpretation. They argue in rebuttal that success often needs to be no more than "temporary," as in time of war. They argue further that crude ancient schemes imposed to counter money supply inflations cannot be fairly compared to our more sophisticated modern versions, which are designed to check market-power push inflations.

In fact, there is a spicy variety of "control" policies. Their common element is some form of **direct government supervision** of wages, salaries, prices, and perhaps profits, interest rates, and rents as well. The usual purpose of such controls is to stem inflation, although they have also been aimed at balance of payments improvement and income redistribution. Of present interest are control policies designed to check market-power push inflation.

Such control policies vary in four major respects: (1) coverage, (2) the nature of wage-price standards, (3) methods of enforcement, and (4) duration.[5] The scope of **coverage** may be very broad, in which case the program includes virtually all industrial sectors and most income variables—wages, salaries, prices, rents,

[3] Council on Wage and Price Stability, *Prices and Costs in the United States Steel Industry* (October 1977); R. M. Duke, R. L. Johnson, Hans Mueller, P. D. Qualls, R. T. Roush, and D. G. Tarr, *The United States Steel Industry and Its International Rivals* (Federal Trade Commission, 1977).

[4] Brittan and Lilley, *op. cit.*, p. 73.

[5] Arnold R. Weber, *In Pursuit of Price Stability* (Washington, D.C.: Brookings Institution, 1973), pp. 10–14.

and so on. Conversely, a program of limited coverage may focus on just a few industries (especially those thought to be sources of inflation) and a few economic figures (wages and prices, say). Between these extremes are countless combinations.

As for **standards,** every control policy must define what behavior is "proper." Standards may be simple or complex, vague or specific. An example of a fairly simple standard is a wage-price freeze. Usually, control policies have rather simple and vague *overall* standards, such as "wage restraint" or "increases matching productivity," applying to everyone covered. These standards are then augmented in the course of enforcement by more *specific* standards applying to certain industries or companies.

One extreme of **enforcement** has already received mention—Diocletian's death penalty. At the other extreme are official "urging," "jawboning," and "exhortation." These latter means of compliance obviously play on peoples' feelings of patriotism or fairness as opposed to their fear of oblivion. They are also the means western democracies rely on most heavily; so voluntary compliance is essential to the success of their control. Even where fines, or worse, serve as penalties, widespread support or acquiescence is necessary. (Otherwise the authorities would quickly run out of jail space.) As you might guess, there are some strong links between compliance method and program coverage. Jaw-boning can only work with limited coverage because it works on the spotlight principle, wherein public opinion is mobilized against offenders. Just as it is impossible for everyone to be famous, it is impossible to spotlight every corner grocer and auto repair shop. Programs of broad coverage consequently require specific legal sanctions.

Regarding **duration,** most control policies have no set lifespan. A few, however, do, most notably policies that freeze wages and prices.

In such cases the duration is always short—60 to 90 days or so. Longer freezes would petrify the economy until brittle.

With this background we are prepared to survey two United States control programs—Kennedy's wage-price "guideposts" and Nixon's Phases I through IV. A brief rundown of European experience then follows.

B. The Guidepost Program (1962–1966)

Well aware of the wage-price antics in steel and other power-laden industries during the late 1950s, President Kennedy's Council of Economic Advisors introduced an informal "guidepost" program in 1962. As stated in the *Economic Report of the President* the standard for noninflationary wage behavior was that wage increases in each industry should not exceed the rate of *overall* productivity increase.[6] Later, the vagueness of "overall productivity increase" was removed by specifying one number for wage increases, 3.2%, which was an average estimate of the previous 5 years' productivity growth. The theory underlying this standard derives from conditions pictured in Figure 24–2. Regardless of what happens to hourly compensation in dollars and cents, *real* income follows a narrow path cleared by output per worker hour, that is, productivity. Hence the growth of *money* income might as well match the growth of *real* income as determined by productivity improvement. Moreover, if these two figures do match, producers' labor cost per unit will not increase on average because additions to labor cost will be offset by additions to output. With unit labor cost steady, *prices need not climb* (unless pushed up by raw materials costs). In short, the guideposts were designed so the productivity dividend could go to consumers (everybody) without rising prices.

---

[6] *Economic Report of the President,* 1962, p. 189.

Figure 24–2. Indexes of Output per Worker and Real and Nominal Compensation, Private Nonfarm Business, for All Persons*

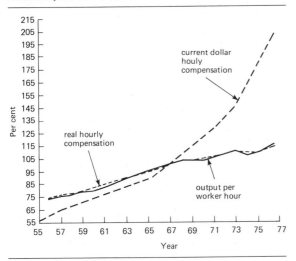

Source: U.S. Department of Labor, Bureau of Labor Statistics.
* 1967 = 100.

Prices, that is, need not rise *overall*. The guidepost standard for *individual* industry price changes could not be zero because productivity advance *varies* from industry to industry. Given wage increments of 3.2% for all workers, unit labor costs will *fall* in those industries experiencing above average productivity growth and *rise* in those industries languishing with below average productivity growth. Accordingly, the guidepost standard for prices was that prices fall where productivity improvement was unusually brisk and rise where it was unusually slow. Given uniform wage increases, this price behavior would prevail under competitive conditions. Figure 24–3 conveys the idea because it shows price changes plotted against productivity changes in 139 industries over 1958–1968. On average, prices rose, so declines did not offset increases. But the broadly negative relation is plain to see. If price changes had averaged out to zero, the price reductions would clearly have come chiefly from particularly progressive industries.

These general wage and price standards were qualified by certain "exceptions." Wage increases, for example, could be above standard if necessary "to attract sufficient labor." And prices could rise above an industry's standard if necessary "to finance a needed expansion in capacity." Although economically defensible, these exceptions offered loopholes that complicated enforcement.

Jaw-boning, ear-stroking, and related anatomical incantations provided the main firepower of enforcement, although President Kennedy and later President Johnson were by no means averse to harsher measures. Various threats—ranging from prospective antitrust suits to massive sales from government stockpiles—were occasionally brought in for reinforcements. Still, the program was "voluntary," so the focus of its coverage remained rather narrowly fixed on the biggest, most highly concentrated, and most thoroughly unionized industries. Moreover, no bureaucracy was created to implement the program.

Because most control policies are based on the same economic principles as those guiding the guideposts, the problems arising under this program carry special significance.[7] High on the list of difficulties was the necessity of relying on *past* productivity performance to channel *future* wage settlements. In fact, productivity growth in 1963–65 exceeded the 3.2% standard while wages generally met the standard. As a consequence, profits ballooned, angering organized labor. The Council of Economic Advisors considered raising the wage standard to 3.6%, which union leadership advocated, but stuck with 3.2% in the end. A measure of the delicacy of labor's support is the explosion of tempers

[7] For a thorough discussion, see John Sheahan, *Wage-Price Guideposts* (Washington, D.C.: Brookings Institution, 1967).

Figure 24–3.   Per Cent of Change in Output Per Man-hour and Prices, for 139 Manufacturing Industries, 1958–1968

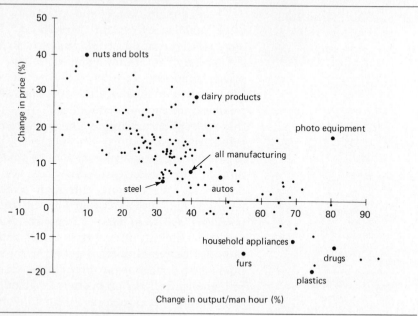

Change in output/man hour (%)

Source: Bureau of Labor Statistics Bulletin 1710, Productivity and the Economy (1971), p. 29.

caused by this little 0.4 percentage point difference of opinion. Unfortunately, it is not possible to solve the problem of finding a correct standard by adopting a short-run estimate based on current experience because productivity is whipped about rather wildly by the short-run business cycle. The problem is thus endemic to all control programs.

A major problem concerning prices lay in getting price reductions in industries experiencing especially favorable productivity growth. Competition would normally *force* price reductions in such cases, but of course competition was (and is) lacking in many industries. In particular, the auto industry gained substantial profit increases by refusing to cut prices in the face of above average productivity growth. Auto workers then felt free to press for wage increases that would break the 3.2

ceiling, and their success undermined the program. A similar situation arose in the airline industry in 1966. This latter breach in the ceiling damaged the program's foundation, heralding collapse shortly thereafter.

The guideposts might have been able to outlast these difficulties. They could not, however, endure the forces of economic boom that began building in 1966 and 1967 with the escalating war in Vietnam. As demand-pull inflation raised prices in competitive sectors outside the guidepost program, the 3.2% wage standard, which was barely acceptable to organized labor even assuming zero inflation, became intolerable. The moral is simple: *strong demand-pull pressure will crush any such voluntary program.* By extension, a substantial exogenous shock inflation would also have destroyed the modicum of social consensus sustaining the program.

It is of course impossible to "prove" whether or not a given controls policy successfully stems inflation (or reduces unemployment) because one can never be sure what conditions would have been like without the policy. Nevertheless, deviations from prepolicy trends can be estimated statistically. A number of tests by this method show that, despite their several failings, the guideposts were moderately successful, at least temporarily. Overall wage and price inflation were trimmed by 1 or 2 percentage points between 1962 and 1966.[8] Moreover, the bulk of curtailment seems to have been achieved in those sectors receiving greatest policy attention—that is, highly unionized and highly concentrated industries such as machinery, chemicals, rubber, and petroleum.[9]

C. The Wage-Price Freeze of 1971, or Phase I[10]

The guideposts were just a teaser. They were so informal that Council economists learned of price increases through the newspapers. The guideposts likewise had no congressional authorization, no biting sanctions. It could be said, then, that on August 15, 1971, the United States really lost its virginity in this area of peacetime wage-price controls. On that day President Nixon, acting under standby authority granted by Congress in 1970, imposed a 90-day wage-

price freeze. The freeze replaced his unsuccessful two and a half year effort to curb inflation by monetary restraint and deliberate recession. Most folks were by that time growing weary of inflation *plus* unemployment. There was consequently tremendous pressure on Nixon to "do something." Immediately after the freeze began, opinion polls showed 75% approval, including several expressions of near ecstasy from businessmen.[11]

The freeze was supposed to be a short and simple surprise. It was short because it was meant to be no more than a stopgap until a more elaborate Phase II control program could be devised. The element of surprise was necessary because prices and wages in power-laden sectors would have gone up like a gas tank inspected by match illumination had everyone known in advance that controls were in the offing. As for simplicity, a zero rate of change implies a clarity and purity unequalled by any other standard imaginable.

Yet, the freeze was anything but simple. A listing of its complexities could fill a big book. Such a book would be instructive, however, because its message would be (quite simply) that even the simplest of control programs is a rat's nest. No less than four government agencies got their fingers in the enforcement stew. In the short span of 90 days, these agencies had to answer no fewer than 800,000 inquiries at field office level, 2435 special exemption requests, 400 executive-level questions, and 75 key policy issues. Among the policy issues were the following:

1. What should be covered besides wages and prices? Rents, interest rates, dividends, and profits? What about country club dues, college tuition, social security payments, and the like? Raw agricultural products were exempt from the start, but when are honey and peanuts transformed from raw to pro-

[8] Ibid., pp. 79–95; Norman Keiser, *Macroeconomics* (New York: Random House, 1975), pp. 324–333; Otto Eckstein and R. Brinner, *The Inflationary Process in the United States,* U.S. Congress, Joint Economic Committee Study, 1972. On the other hand, see S. W. Black and H. H. Kelejian, "A Macro Model of the U.S. Labor Market," *Review of Economics and Statistics* (September 1970), pp. 712–741.

[9] Stanley S. Wallack, "Wage-Price Guidelines and the Rate of Wage Changes in U.S. Manufacturing 1951–66," *Southern Economic Journal* (July 1971), pp. 33–47; D. F. Greer, "Market Power and Wage Inflation: A Further Analysis," *Southern Economic Journal* (January 1975), pp. 466–479; George L. Perry, "Wages and the Guideposts," *American Economic Review* (September 1967), pp. 897–904.

[10] This section is based largely on Arnold Weber, *op. cit.*

[11] *Business Week,* August 21, 1971, pp. 21–22.

cessed? What about exports and imports? Are their prices to be frozen?

2. The freeze applies in comparison to what? Prices and wages prevailing on August 15, 1971? If so, what about the many items that were "on sale" that day? What about goods whose prices are seasonal—normally rising or falling during the freeze period? Given an exemption for seasonal goods (which was granted), is Halloween candy a seasonal good?

3. There has to be some means of preventing evasion through quality change, but what is a quality change? Are grocery store trading stamps part of quality? And so on, ad infinitum.

4. What about price and wage changes that are by contract due to occur during the freeze? Should they be allowed? What about price increases that were posted and paid for *prior* to 8/15/71, but on goods and services not yet delivered? For example, should those who in July bought season tickets to see the Atlanta Falcons play football in the fall be reimbursed for the increase over prior year's prices?

The actual answers were stringent enough to decelerate prices and wages substantially. Between August and November 1971 the consumer price index rose at an annual rate of 1.6%, well below the 4.0 rate of increase during the 6 months preceding the freeze. Greater reductions were registered in the wholesale price index and various wage indexes. Whether the freeze had any lasting impact, however, is debatable. A big "bulge" of increases occurred just after the thaw on November 14.

D. Phase II (November 1971 to January 1973)

The freeze gave way to what turned out to be protracted controls of varying coverage and stringency. Table 24–1, which is a terse summary, conveys the content and complexity of these regulations.

During Phase II, statutory controls limited price increases on a firm-by-firm basis to a per cent pass-through of cost increases, meaning, for example, that prices could rise 10% if costs rose 10%. Since *increases* rather than *absolute levels* were being controlled, there had to be some base period against which the current costs could be compared, and the period varied. It could be either the time of the "last" price increase or January 1, 1971, whichever was more recent. But there was a catch. Price increases by this standard could not be such as to generate "excess" profits, which were defined in historic terms particular to each firm. The *overall* goal was to hold price inflation to 2.5% per year.

The general standard for wage increases was 5.5% per year. This standard was based on the theory that, assuming a 3% rate of productivity advance, 5.5% wage inflation would attain the 2.5% target level of price inflation. The ghost of the old guideposts should be obvious here. Unfortunately, organized labor was disenchanted with this standard (thinking it was too low, of course), so an additional 0.7 percentage point was added for fringe benefits, resulting in a total compensation standard of 6.2%. Furthermore, a major exception for additional increments was granted to workers earning "substandard" wages. Interpretation of "substandard" proved a problem because the Cost of Living Council, whose administrative responsibility carried over from the freeze, wanted a threshold figure of $1.90 per hour, whereas organized labor insisted it be higher. A compromise of $2.75 settled the dispute.

While the Cost of Living Council had overall policy authority, responsibility for direct supervision of prices and wages was split between a Price Commission (for prices) and a Pay Board (for wages and salaries), both of which ranked below the Cost of Living Council. To aid their enforcement efforts, these agencies developed rules for business notification of intended changes and for reporting of actual changes. Their basic scheme divided all covered firms into three tiers:

1. **Tier I firms** had sales exceeding $100 million or collective-bargaining units of 5000 or more employees. These firms had to obtain *prior approval* before implementing price and wage increases.
2. **Tier II firms** had sales between $50 million and $100 million or collective-bargaining units of 1000 to 5000 employees. These firms did not need prior approval for their actions, but they had to *submit regular reports* of behavior.
3. **Tier III firms,** with sales and employees below those of tier II firms, had no prenotification or reporting requirements.

Beyond these generalities lay hordes of exemptions, special treatments, and individual cases. Major exemptions were raw agricultural commodities, exports, imports, and small firms. One of the main special treatments concerned public utilities. Rather than duplicate the efforts of public utility commissions, the Price Commission delegated its authority to control prices in those areas to existing regulatory authorities. A memorable hint of the program's burial beneath detail arose in this regard when the Price Commission received a letter from a legal brothel in Nevada that was regulated by health authorities. The letter asked whether the Pay Board considered prostitution a service industry or regulated utility.[12]

Problems with Phase II.   Administrators of the Phase I freeze passed a 400 page book of problems on to the officials who took over for Phase II. On top of this, Phase II produced its own brands of perplexity.

A problem now acknowledged even by former price control officials might be called the "great grocery gaffe." During the Phase I freeze grocery stores were required to post prices conspicuously so that shoppers could compare posted prices with actual prices and blow the whistle on any grocer with gross discrepancies. However, the freeze was so short and the signs so difficult to compile that the signs could not be posted until a few days before the end of the freeze. Rather than rub grocers the wrong way by scrapping the signs at the start of Phase II, they were kept for reporting "base prices." But the main technique of Phase II was to allow price increases for cost increases, not to freeze prices. So, as grocery prices climbed above posted prices, great confusion ensued. Many consumers thought the posted prices were the only legal prices, but unless the consumer knew specific margins of markup above cost, he could detect no violations by the signs, even if he understood what the signs represented. Hence the signs provoked many groundless complaints, and led many folks to think that Phase II was fake.[13] Indeed, it was probably a mistake to try to regulate retail food prices in the first place because raw agricultural products were exempt and grocery retailing is largely competitive.

The fundamental method of percentage cost pass-through has also been attacked. With few exceptions, price increases were permitted to cover increased costs *plus* a customary profit margin on those added costs. By this method profits could increase with added cost, leading to charges that inefficiency was rewarded. It has been argued in defense of the program that the adverse effect was not as bad as it might

[12] Jackson Grayson, "A View from the Outside of the Inside of Upside Down," in *The Illusion of Wage and Price Control,* edited by M. Walker (Vancouver, B.C.: The Fraser Institute, 1976), p. 169.

[13] Robert F. Lanzillotti, Mary T. Hamilton, and R. Blaine Roberts, *Phase II in Review* (Washington, D.C.: Brookings Institution, 1975), pp. 54–55.

Table 24–1. Regulations of the Controls Program, Phases II, III, and IV

Program	Phase II 14 November 1971 to 11 January 1973	Phase III 11 January 1973 to 13 June 1973	Phase IV 12 August 1973 to 30 April 1974
General Standards			
Price increase limitations	Percentage pass-through of allowable cost increases since last price increase, or 1 Jan. 1971, adjusted for productivity and volume offsets. Term limit pricing option available.	Self-administered standards of Phase II.	In most manufacturing and service industries dollar-for-dollar pass-through of allowable cost increase since last fiscal quarter ending prior to 11 Jan. 1973.
Profit margin limitations	Not to exceed margins of the best 2 of 3 fiscal years before 15 August 1971. Not applicable if prices were not increased above base level, or if firms "purified" themselves.	Not to exceed margins of the best 2 fiscal years completed after 15 August 1968. No limitation if average price increase does not exceed 1.5%.	Same years as Phase III, except that a firm that has not charged a price for any item above its base price, or adjusted freeze price, whichever is higher, is not subject to the limitation.
Wage increase limitations	General standard of 5.5%. Exceptions made to correct gross inequities, and for workers whose pay had increased less than 7% a year for the last 3 years. Workers earning less than $2.75 per hour were exempt. Increases in qualified fringe benefits permitted raising standard to 6.2%.	General Phase II standard, self-administered. Some special limitations. More flexibility with respect to specific cases. Workers earning less than $3.50 per hour were exempted after 1 May.	Self-administered standards of Phase III. Executive compensation limited.
Prenotification			
Prices	Prenotification required for all firms with annual sales above $100 million, 30 days before implementation, approval required.	After 2 May 1973, prenotification required for all firms with sales above $250 million whose price increase has exceeded a weighted average of 1.5%.	Same as Phase II except that prenotified price increases may be implemented in 30 days unless CLC requires otherwise.
Wages	For all increases of wages for units of 5000 or more; for all increases above the standard regardless of the number of workers involved.	None.	None.
Reporting			
Prices	Quarterly for firms with sales over $50 million.	Quarterly for firms with sales over $250 million.	Quarterly for firms with sales over $50 million.
Wages	Pay adjustments below standard for units greater than 1000 persons.	Pay adjustments for units greater than 5000 persons.	Same as Phase III.
Special Areas	Health, insurance, rent, construction, public utilities.	Health, food, public utilities, construction, petroleum.	Health, food, petroleum, construction, insurance, executive and variable compensation.

Table 24–1. (Continued)

Program	Phase II *14 November 1971 to 11 January 1973*	Phase III *11 January 1973 to 13 June 1973*	Phase IV *12 August 1973 to 30 April 1974*
Exemptions	Raw agricultural commodities, import prices, export prices, firms with 60 or fewer employees.	Same as Phase II plus rents.	Same as Phase III plus public utilities, lumber, copper scrap, and long-term coal contracts, initially with sector-by-sector decontrol of prices and wages until 30 April 1974.

Source: Cost of Living Council and *Economic Report of the President, 1974,* p. 91.

seem.[14] Still, it can also be argued that a scheme of *partial* cost pass-through might have served better.[15]

Economic distortions provide the most sensational problems of any controls program, including Phase II. The lumber industry, where distortions stemmed from evasion efforts, is perhaps the best example to emerge from Phase II:

First, since the regulations permitted higher prices when services were added to products, plywood producers performed the "service" of cutting 1/8 inch off plywood sheets and sold the sheets for substantially higher prices. The dimensions of lumber products were also shaved as a device to obtain effective price increases.

Second, since the Price Commission could not control foreign producers and import prices were thus uncontrolled, producers in the Pacific Northwest exported lumber to Canada and reimported it at substantially higher prices.

Third, Price Commission regulations that permitted normal markups at each stage of distribution spawned shipments of lumber from one wholesaler to another; each added a normal markup but did not perform all of the usual wholesaler functions.

[14] Ibid., pp. 80–97.
[15] A. Bradley Askin, "Wage-Price Controls in Administrative and Political Perspective," in *Wage and Price Controls: The U.S. Experiment,* edited by John Kraft and Blaine Roberts (New York: Praeger, 1975), pp. 26–27.

Finally, at least for a time, the regulated price on two-by-fours was relatively high as compared with boards; thus, logs were turned into two-by-fours and a shortage of boards developed.[16]

On the *wage* side of Phase II, the biggest problem with the Pay Board was that it leaned toward leniency, especially where strong unions were involved. As compared to the 5.5% wage standard, the average rate of approved increases in major collective bargain agreements was 7.0% during 1972. Nonunion wage increases were considerably lower, however, largely as a result of continued slack in aggregate demand during 1972. These substandard increases in the nonunion sector permitted overall average hourly earnings to rise at a 5.6% rate during the year, running just shy of the 5.5 target.

These many sour spots in Phase II would leave less aftertaste today if it could be shown that Phase II allayed wage-price inflation significantly. But econometric studies yield no consensus that it did. Several estimates reveal absolutely no effect for either prices or wages. Several others suggest a downshift of 0.5 to 2.0 percentage points in price inflation plus some

[16] William Poole, "Wage-Price Controls: Where Do We Go From Here?" *Brookings Papers on Economic Activity,* No. 1 (1973), p. 292.

lesser consequences for wage inflation. The one thing that seems certain is that *if* there was any effect at all, prices were restrained more than wages.[17]

E. Phases III and IV, Plus Another Freeze

President Nixon terminated Phase II on January 11, 1973, replacing it with Phase III. As shown in Table 24–1, Phase III retained the standards of Phase II but removed most prenotification and reporting requirements. The Pay Board and Price Commission were abolished, leaving only the Cost of Living Council. In addition, exemptions were broadened to free rents and free more workers earning "substandard" wages. (Remarkably, the new low-wage exemption was set at $3.50, which was only slightly below average hourly earnings for *all* nonfarm workers.[18]) The stated purpose of the changes was to reduce administrative burdens while continuing controls. Compliance was to be "voluntary." In fact, most people saw Phase III as a *relaxation* of controls rather than a mere *reorganization*.

Price behavior during the next six months seemed to confirm people's impression of an economic dam-break: the wholesale price index leaped to a 22.3% annual rate of increase, and the consumer price index rose to an 8.0% annual pace of advance. Actually, conversion to Phase III had little to do with this surge, for it came mainly from sectors uncontrolled from the beginning. In particular, wholesale prices of farm products exploded, elevating at close to a 60% annual rate of increase during the first six months of 1973. This jump was due to domestic shortages of agricultural commodi-

ties relative to an extremely strong surge of worldwide demand for our exports. Prices for timber and petroleum leaped for similar reasons.[19] On top of these exogenous shocks, the aggregate economy moved into high gear, responding to expansionary monetary and fiscal policies launched with the Phases. Unemployment fell from 6.0% at the start of Phase II in November 1972 to 4.8% in June 1973. In short, the timing of Phase II's demise was a public relations catastrophe.

Amid public pressure to reinstate tough controls, Phase III was abandoned while still in its infancy. A second freeze descended over the land. Like the first freeze, this one hit during the summer, lasting from mid-June to mid-August. *Unlike* the first one, this one hit just when the main inflationary forces at work were chiefly exogenous shock and demand-pull. What is more, this freeze was followed by Phase IV, which, as shown in Table 24–1, was in many respects even more stringent than Phase II. In particular, the new price standards permitted pass-through of cost increases only on a dollar-for-dollar basis, not on a percentage basis. (That is, if one's cost rose by 50¢ a widget, price per widget could rise only 50¢, not 50¢ plus some percentage markup.)

The results of Freeze II and Phase IV added up to more than a public relations catastrophe. Their inappropriateness produced some genuine economic catastrophes, many for reasons disclosed earlier in our discussion of Figure 19–1(b) on page 387, which showed the impact of price ceilings.

When prices of more and more commodities were held below market clearing levels in late 1973, symptoms of inefficiency became increasingly widespread and diverse. Curtailment of domestic supply was sometimes threatened by increased exports, reduced production to avoid

---

[17] For reviews, see Kraft and Roberts, *op. cit.*, pp. 143–149; Jerry E. Pohlman, *Inflation Under Control?* (Reston, Va.: Reston Publishing Co., 1976), pp. 221–226; Brittan and Lilley, *op. cit.*, pp. 146–150.

[18] Albert Rees, *Wage-Price Policy* (General Learning Press, 1974), p. 16.

[19] Ross E. Azevedo, "Phase III—A Stabilization Program That Could Not Work," *Quarterly Review of Economics and Business* (Spring 1976), pp. 7–21.

losses, and failure to expand production through use of marginal production capacity. Lack of availability and wide differences in prices of material inputs complicated production planning and threatened to disrupt production schedules. Distribution and purchasing operations were complicated by multiple prices and instances of bartering in order to reduce costs or obtain scarce materials, and black markets were frequently reported. Shortages were perhaps the most commonly reported symptom of inefficiency . . .[20]

Under these burdens, folks quickly became weary and disenchanted. Phase IV officially died on April 30, 1974. Whereas controls were greeted with rousing cheers in August 1971, no wailing over Phase IV's death could be heard the first day of May 1974. The contrast of public emotions seems odd when set against the fact that consumer prices were rising *three times faster toward the end of Phase IV than they were rising before imposition of Phase I.* Of course the explanation is very simple. People began to look upon controls as a sham and a burden. That is, folks learned two lessons: (1) controls cannot suppress a chronic inflationary trend, especially not one "goosed" by exogenous shocks, and (2) if controls are given an earnest try, they create distortions, inefficiencies, and inequities that may even aggravate the inflation in the long run.

F. European Experience

European experience with controls, usually called "incomes policies," is greater than the United States experience. Although a few observers look favorably on European policies,[21]

most agree that on balance they have failed.[22] Thus, Lloyd Ulman and Robert Flanagan conclude their study of seven European countries by saying that "in none of the variations so far turned up has incomes policy succeeded in its fundamental objective, as stated, of making full employment consistent with a reasonable degree of price stability."[23] Walter Galenson's view is also representative: "Great Britain, Sweden, and Holland have had indifferent success with bouts of formal incomes policy."[24] Even proponents of controls, like Jerry Pohlman, admit that the European record is bleak:

> Certainly, one who attempts to find strong support for the effectiveness of wage and price restraints by looking abroad will be disappointed. Without exception, market controls have broken down at some time or another in all the free economies that have tried them.[25]

It may seem odd, then, that experience has not discouraged advocates of controls. They argue that controls are sound in principle; that failures occur only because of faulty application. They explain away failures as results of (1) inadequate sanctions, (2) lack of public support, (3) failure to constrain money supply in the course of control effort, (4) inappropriate application to money supply inflations, (5) over ambitious coverage and duration, and (6) unsatisfactory supervision of relative income shares.

---

[20] Marvin Kosters, *Controls and Inflation* (Washington, D.C.: American Enterprise Institute, 1975), pp. 94–95.

[21] For example, Organization for Economic Co-operation and Development, *Socially Responsible Wage Policies and Inflation* (1975); Ann R. Braun, "The Role of Incomes Policy in Industrial Countries Since World War II," *International Monetary Fund Staff Papers* (March 1975), pp. 1–36.

[22] For example, Brittan and Lilley, *op. cit.;* Lloyd Ulman and Robert J. Flanagan, *Wage Restraint: A Study of Incomes Policies in Western Europe* (Berkeley, Calif.: University of California Press, 1971); David C. Smith, *Incomes Policies* (Ottawa: Economic Council of Canada, 1966); Walter Galenson (ed.), *Incomes Policy: What Can We Learn from Europe?* (Ithaca, N.Y.: Cornell University School of Industrial and Labor Relations, 1973); Michael Parkin and Michael T. Sumner (eds.), *Incomes Policy and Inflation* (Toronto: University of Toronto Press, 1972).

[23] Ulman and Flanagan, *op. cit.,* p. 216.

[24] Galenson, *op. cit.,* p. xiv.

[25] Pohlman, *op. cit.,* p. 187.

III. Proposed Improvements

Can controls be patched up? Can they be made to succeed? Mention of a few proposed improvements (short of totalitarianism) concludes this review.

Limited coverage is one of the most common corrections called for. The idea is to focus stringent controls solely on big business and big labor, ignoring competitive areas, such as food and lumber, which have been reduced to chaos by past control efforts. There is a problem here, however. Defenders of limited coverage have yet to explain why this narrow lunge at largeness is politically more realistic than a policy of competitive restructuring, or why, if it is equally realistic, controls are superior to competition.

Another modification would be to keep controls temporary, to apply them only occasionally. Although this view has its merits, it seems tantamount to applying a band-aid to cure a malignant tumor. Temporary application of controls may even have the adverse side effect of delaying implementation of more effective long-lasting treatments.

Others see past controls as not being permanent enough. If controls collapse because of disputes over relative income shares, then the solution is to draw up a massive schedule of formulas "fairly" fixing everyone's wage relative to everyone else's wage. There are two problems with this approach, however. First, if the wage-relatives decided upon do not correspond to those that would be cranked out by the market (and there is no reason to think that they would so correspond), economic chaos will ensue. Second, the approach is politically unrealistic. As explained by Samuel Brittan and Peter Lilley:

> However resentful they are about it, people will in the last resort accept a relatively low position in the pecking order if it is due to the luck of the market. . . . If, on the other hand, their low position seems to result from a moralistic eval-

uation of their merits made by their fellow citizens through some political process, they will stop at nothing to get the judgment withdrawn. No one likes being consigned to the rubbish heap by a body of wise men appointed to express the supposed moral evaluations of society.[26]

Finally, a number of economists, most notably Sidney Weintraub and Henry Wallich, advocate a "taxed-based incomes policy," or TIP.[27] The basic ideal is to stiffen the backbone of businessmen against labor's inflationary wage demands. This would be achieved by heavily taxing those businesses that grant wage increases above some specified standard. An alternative approach would provide tax breaks for those who voluntarily limit their wage increases to a specific amount. In essence, these plans provide streamlined enforcement mechanisms for a guidelines policy. They have the advantage of relying on market forces more than most incomes policies. Yet they, too, are not without deficiencies and distortions.[28]

Assuming market-power push inflation is a problem, this analysis paints a rather bleak picture. Our alternatives seem to be limited to (1) trying a tax-based incomes policy, which at least theoretically is the best of the wage-price control policies, (2) going through the wringer of tight monetary restraint now and again with every substantial exogenous shock, or (3) learning to live with inflation, nasty though it is. Actually, there is another alternative. We could strike at the root of the problem by lessening market power itself. This would be achieved by curbing union power and restructuring industry through more vigorous antitrust. Greater competition would also follow from less anticompetitive government intervention, as

---

[26] Brittan and Lilley, op. cit., p. 186.
[27] Henry Wallich and Sidney Weintraub, "A Tax-Based Incomes Policy," Journal of Economic Issues (June 1971), pp. 1–19.
[28] Perhaps the best plan is the invention of Abba P. Lerner and David C. Colander, MAP: A Market Anti-inflation Plan (New York: Harcourt Brace Jovanovich, Inc., 1980). But it is too complex to describe here.

occurred in transportation deregulation. Unfortunately, political realities seem to bar significant achievements in these respects, so alternatives (1), (2), and (3) above probably exhaust the possibilities.

Summary

Inflation has essentially three causes—(1) demand-pull, (2) exogenous shock, and (3) market-power push. Under the last of these, prices are pushed up by wage escalations that exceed productivity growth or by higher profit markups—the work of powerful labor unions and/or large corporations.

The chief purpose of wage-price controls is to curb inflations that are either caused or aggravated by market-power forces *while at the same time* minimizing the adverse effects on unemployment and idle capacity. Advocates of wage-price controls agree with monetarists that monetary restraint is also desirable. Indeed, they generally concede that inflation could be halted by monetary policy alone. But they look upon controls as a means of minimizing the economic casualties inflicted by monetary restraint alone. Review of specific evidence indicates that the advocates of controls may well be right in that there *is* a problem. But review of past control policies indicates that these policies may not be the best solutions.

Such policies vary in their coverage, standards, enforcement method, and duration. In coverage, they can broadly include most everything from dog license fees to ballplayer salaries, or they can focus narrowly on sectors where problems of market power are most pronounced. In standards, the growth rate in labor productivity has served as a key benchmark because if wages on average rose no faster, they would not be inflationary. In enforcement, programs have been voluntary and compulsory, with blends in between. In duration, they have been brief when harsh and long when lax.

Aside from wartime, controls in the U.S. first blossomed in the 1960s and 1970s. The Kennedy administration launched wage-price "guideposts" in 1962. Though casual, with little bureaucracy and rubbery enforcement, the program was partially successful until demand-pull pressures pulled the program apart in 1966.

Nixon's multiple "Phases" began with a 90-day freeze in 1971 and evolved into a program of protracted controls of varying coverage and stringency. The massive complexity of this effort is nicely illustrated by the freeze because that would intuitively seem to be the easiest of all kinds of control programs. The freeze was anything but simple, however. The adverse consequences of the Nixon effort are perhaps best illustrated by the experience of lumber under Phase II. Shortages, distortions, evasions, and other unsavory effects arose. Overall, the benefits of the "Phases" were less than outstanding.

European experience with controls has not been notably better than ours. A key problem in the failure of many of these attempts is their tendency to shatter when hit by exogenous shocks, such as fuel shortages.

Improvements have been proposed. Of these, tax-based incomes policies are most favored by economists who favor controls. Whether these will ever be tried is uncertain. But the problem will not go away as long as monopoly power and anticompetitive government policies endure. Thus we may one day witness a tax-based incomes policy or some first cousin of such.

Questions and Exercises for Chapter 24

1. Money supply stringency could stop inflation in its tracks. Why, then, has government been reluctant to apply this policy to the extent necessary?

2. What is the basic rationale behind wage-price control policies?
3. Why does productivity growth provide a commonly used basic standard for allowable wage increases under control policies?
4. Why are monetarists skeptical of wage-price control policies?
5. Compare and contrast Kennedy's "guideposts" and Nixon's first wage-price "freeze" in (a) coverage, (b) standards, and (c) duration.
6. Trace organized labor's disruptive influence in both Kennedy's and Nixon's programs.
7. How and when did "demand-pull" and "exogenous-shock" inflations hamper American experience with controls?
8. What problems plagued Phases III and IV?
9. How might wage-price controls be improved?

Chapter 25

Patents and R&D Funding

The patent system added the fuel of interest to the fire of genius.
—Abe Lincoln

From the first squawky telephone to the latest supersonic airplane, technological change has done more than anything else to shape our modern economy and everyday life. Innovation spurs growth, boosts productivity, lifts profits, lengthens lives, generates jobs, and enriches experiences. Nearly half of all this century's gains in real income can be attributed to technological progress. The lion's share of the products we now use and take for granted simply did not exist as little as three generations ago—television, frozen food, zippers, computers, air conditioning, penicillin, nylon, refrigerators, synthetic detergents, Frisbees, and so on.

Two government policies promoting technical progress are the concern of this chapter—patents and R&D funding. To be sure, invention and innovation would exist without these policies. The wheel is evidence of that. But there would be considerably less invention and innovation. Thus the main purpose of these policies is to stimulate more technical progress than the free market would provide.

Our discussion of patents answers such questions as: What is a patent? What can be patented? Why have patents? What are the benefits and costs of patents? Our discussion of government funding of research and development covers two basic questions: What amounts of money are involved? Why is such funding needed?

I. The Patent System: Nature and Scope

A. Background

A patent is a **monopoly right** to make and sell some product, or use some process, that is governmentally granted for a limited number of years as a reward for invention. The character and duration of this right differs from country to country. United States law grants "for the term of seventeen years [from the patent's date] . . . the right to exclude others from making, using, or selling the invention throughout the United States."[1] The right is a form of private property that can be bought and sold, traded, given away, and leased or licensed for the use of others (who pay a "royalty" for the privilege). The invention covered can even go unused if the owner wishes. Moreover, although only individuals can be awarded patents, corporate employees typically "assign"

[1] U.S.C. Section 154 (1970).

their patents to their employers, and independent inventors often sell or license their patents to others for commercial application.

Regardless of ultimate ownership, roughly half of all patents go unused because the inventions they cover are too far ahead of their time, too costly to develop relative to the potential profit, or too unsettling to the ultimate owner's old way of doing things. Many go unused because close substitutes for the invention are available. Thus, the monopoly granted may be only a measly one.

Indeed, more than four million patents have been issued since inception of the system. Of late, the annual flow tops 70,000. If these figures are not big enough to suggest to you that many if not most patented inventions are rather pedestrian, consider the following: Patent 2,-882,858, awarded in 1959, covers a diaper for parakeets. A vibrating toilet seat won patent No. 3,244,168 in 1966.[2]

Fortunately, enforcement of any patent is left up to the patent holder. Accused infringers must be hauled into court by patentees. The original Bell telephone patents, for instance, were enforced with more than six hundred infringement suits initiated by Bell interests. What is more, the patent office does not have final say as to what constitutes a valid patent. The federal courts have final say. So, once in court, an infringer almost always defends himself against a patentee's attack by claiming the patent is invalid. This defense is by no means futile because court judges generally hold more stringent standards of patentability than the patent office. Approximately 60% of all patents coming under court review are declared invalid and unenforceable. In three out of four cases the chief cause for rejection is a lack of "inventiveness."[3] The remaining reasons for invalidation can be understood only after an explanation of what can and cannot be patented.

---

[2] Stacy V. Jones, *The Patent Office* (New York: Praeger, 1971), pp. 64–69.

[3] Ibid., pp. 43–44.

B. Patentability

According to statute law, "Whoever invents or discovers any new and useful process, machine, manufacture, or composition of matter, or any new and useful improvement thereof, may obtain a patent therefor." Embedded in the language are four criteria for patentability: (1) inventiveness, (2) novelty, (3) utility, and (4) subject matter.

To cross the threshhold of **inventiveness** the discovery must be "nonobvious" at the time "to a person having ordinary skill in the art." There must, in other words, be some creativity. Just how much creativity is required and how much creativity went into any claimed invention are often difficult to judge. What is "nonobvious" to one patent examiner may not be to another. The uncertainties in the "nonobvious" standard are, in fact, almost vague and various enough to call for discriminating "creativity" on the part of patent examiners. To restate the problem more concretely, do you think the following should qualify? Putting a rubber erasure on the end of a pencil? Making doorknobs of clay rather than metal or wood? Devising a motorized golf-bag cart? All three were in fact awarded patents, but when tested in court two were found wanting. Given the nature of the problem, it is hard to disagree with Judge Learned Hand, who once grumbled that the test of invention was little more than a vague and fugitive "phantom."[4]

As for **novelty**, the invention must not be previously known or used. This standard is fairly straightforward, but it takes patent examiners a long time to review past patents and published scientific papers in search of duplication. Of all standards, **utility** is certainly the least demanding. As the extravagant examples given above illustrate, many approved inventions are empty of all but the most fantastic applications.

---

[4] *Harries* v. *Air King Prods. Co.*, 183 F. 2d 158, 162 (2d Cir. 1950).

Because patentable **subject matter** is limited to mechanical or chemical processes and compositions, much is excluded. Discovery of fundamental laws of nature, such as $E = mc^2$, may not be patented, however brilliant or useful their discovery may be. The same holds for mathematical formulas, managerial strategies, teaching methods, and the like. Products of nature are likewise unpatentable, although this rule has exceptions. One patentable exception is new asexually reproducing plants—that is, those cultivated by grafts, or cuttings, or such. These are not to be confused with sexually reproducing plants, which cannot be patented (for reasons other than moral turpitude, of course).

In 1980, the Supreme Court made headlines by deciding that manmade living organisms could be patented. The organism at issue was a new bacterium capable of "eating" crude oil, making it useful in cleaning up oil spills. But the decision had broad implications because it opened the door for patents on all kinds of newly created microbes. Indeed, shortly thereafter, the first U.S. patent covering techniques of recombinant DNA, or genesplicing, was awarded for work done at Stanford University and the University of California. These developments sparked controversy because to some folks they gave birth to a Brave New World. One overwrought group claimed that such patenting "lays the groundwork for corporations to own the processes of life in the centuries to come."[5]

C. Obtaining a Patent

The rules and regulations of patentability give appearances of an imposing thicket, blocking all but a privileged few. But of the more than 100,000 patent applications filed annually, 50% or so gain patent office approval. Appli-

cants are aided not only by lenient standards of invention and utility but also by an army of clever, well-healed patent attorneys. Indeed, these attorneys are often more crucial to obtaining a patent than an invention is.[6]

The point is driven home by citing Patent 549,160, which a patent attorney obtained for himself in 1895, and which covered what later proved to be the wonder machine of our modern age—the automobile. According to legend, George Selden stole ideas from genuine auto engineers and bluffed his way far enough along to see his auto patent earn $5.8 million in royalties and gain the approval of a U.S. District Court. The only person willing and able to challenge the validity of Selden's patent was Henry Ford, who eventually won his case in Circuit Court.[7]

II. Two Case Studies

At its best, the patent system stimulates progress, rewards deserving inventors and innovators, and arouses competition. At its worst, it fosters opposite tendencies. Each extreme may be vividly depicted by a case history.

A. United States Gypsum and Wallboard[8]

There is nothing especially clever about wallboard, looking at it with today's familiarity. It

---

[5] *Wall Street Journal,* June 17, 1980, p. 3; December 31, 1980, pp. 1, 8.

[6] Specific evidence is provided by F. M. Scherer, "Firm Size, Market Structure, Opportunity, and the Output of Patented Inventions," *American Economic Review* (December 1965), p. 1111, note 20. See also Corwin D. Edwards, *Maintaining Competition* (New York: McGraw-Hill Book Co., 1964 edition), p. 218.

[7] Jones, *op. cit.,* pp. 77–79; Irene Till, "The Legal Monopoly," in *The Monopoly Makers,* edited by M. J. Green (New York: Grossman, 1973), pp. 293–294.

[8] This section is based primarily on *United States* v. *United States Gypsum Co.* 333 U.S. 366 (1947); and Clair Wilcox, *Competition and Monopoly in American Industry,* Monograph No. 21 of the Temporary National Economic Committee, U.S. Congress (1940), pp. 161–163.

is plaster sandwiched between two sheets of paper. At the turn of the century, all wallboard was produced with open edges that exposed the plaster filler. Exposure caused the edges to chip and crumble when bumped in transit. The obvious remedy for this problem—paper covering for the edges as well as the body of the wallboard—was hit upon in 1912 and won for its discoverer, one Utzman, patent No. 1,034,746. This patent covered the process of closing the edges of wallboard by folding the bottom cover sheet over the edge and then affixing the top cover sheet.

Realizing its great value, United States Gypsum Corporation (called U.S. Gypsum), the leading wallboard producer of the day, acquired the Utzman patent and then used it as a springboard to four decades of industry dominance. On the face of it, the odds against U.S. Gypsum's conquest were rather large, for it was based on a brittle springboard. Aside from the fact that the Utzman patent lasted only seventeen years, competitors could easily "invent around" it by closing wallboard edges in other, equally obvious ways. The top cover sheet could fold toward the bottom; the two cover sheets could *both* fold to overlap the edge; the two cover sheets could be imbedded in the center of the plaster edge; a separate sheet could cap the edge, and so on. U.S. Gypsum, however, was able to control the competition these options offered its smaller rivals by tenaciously suing for infringement at every fold. After thus "softening" up its competitors, U.S. Gypsum bought their renegade patents.

In exchange for the cooperation of its rivals, U.S. Gypsum licensed them to use its accumulated patents through agreements that fixed the prices all parties charged for their wallboard. While building these arrangements, U.S. Gypsum seems to have avoided court and favored nontrial settlements as often as possible, perhaps out of fear that its patents would be found invalid if ever truly tested. In other words, com-

petitors were sufficiently strong and U.S. Gypsum's patents were sufficiently weak that the company could not monopolize the trade. At best, it attained a 57% market share. Even so, U.S. Gypsum was resourceful enough to construct a network of license agreements that effectively cartelized the industry. "According to the plans we have," an optimistic executive said at one point, "we figure that there is a possibility of us holding the price steady on wallboard for the next fourteen or fifteen years which means much to the industry."[9] How much it meant is measured by the fact that in 1928, U.S. Gypsum reportedly earned a profit of $11.09 per 1000 square feet of wallboard over the manufacturing cost of $10.50.

Subsequent patents on wallboard became the basis of subsequent cartelization. But the cartel's life was cut short by action of the Antitrust Division of the Department of Justice. Attacked for violating the Sherman Act, the cartel was dissolved after the Supreme Court decided in 1947 that "regardless of motive, the Sherman Act bars patent exploitation of the kind that was here attempted."[10]

B. Chester Carlson and Xerox[11]

Born to the wife of an itinerant barber and raised in poverty, Chester Carlson invented xerography. Various family tragedies compelled Carlson to work unceasingly from age twelve to support his family and his education. His dire

---

[9] *U.S.* v. *U.S. Gypsum, op. cit.*, 374.

[10] Ibid., p. 393.

[11] This section is based on J. Jewkes, D. Sawers, and R. Stillerman, *The Sources of Invention* (New York: Norton, 1969), pp. 321–323; D. V. DeSimone, Testimony, *Economic Concentration*, Part 3, U.S. Senate Subcommittee on Antitrust and Monopoly, (1965), pp. 1108–1111; E. A. Blackstone, "The Copying-Machine Industry: Innovations, Patents, and Pricing," *Antitrust Law & Economics Review* (Fall 1972), pp. 105–122; and F. M. Scherer, *The Economic Effects of Compulsory Patent Licensing* (New York: New York University Graduate School of Business Administration, 1977), p. 9.

boyhood circumstances induced dreams of escape. In his own words:

> At this stage in my life, I was entranced by the accounts I read of the work and successes of independent inventors and of the rewards they were able to secure through the patents on their inventions. I, too, might do this, I thought; and this contemplation gave stimulus and direction to my life.

After working his way through to a physics degree at the California Institute of Technology, Carlson accepted a research position at Bell Telephone Laboratories in 1930, a position made temporary by the Great Depression. Though plagued by financial difficulties during the depression, he found a job in the patent department of another company. His tasks there impressed upon him the need for quick, inexpensive copies of drawings and documents. Thus it was that in 1935 Carlson began a spare-time search for a copy machine. Although he was working full time and attending law school at night (in hopes of becoming a patent attorney!), his research and experimentation were extensive, leading eventually to his key idea of combining electrostatics and photoconductive materials. The first successful demonstration of Carlson's ideas took place in a room behind a beauty parlor in Astoria, Long Island, on October 22, 1938. He used a crude device to copy the message "10–22–38 Astoria."

Four patents awarded to Carlson between 1940 and 1944 covered his basic concepts. During the same years he tried to find a firm that would develop his invention for commercial use, but he encountered a stream of rejections, including those of twenty large firms—IBM, Remington Rand, and Eastman Kodak among them. The project was finally picked up for experimentation by Battelle Memorial Institute, a nonprofit research outfit, which thereby gained partial rights to any future earnings on the patents. Battelle devised a number of major patentable improvements, including use of a selenium plate, which allowed copies to be made on ordinary as opposed to chemically coated paper. But Battelle did not have the resources to manufacture and market the machine.

Quest for a commercial innovator led to another round of rejections from big companies, whereupon, in 1946, the task was undertaken by Haloid Company, a small firm earning an annual net income of only $101,000. Motivated by partial rights to potential earnings and led by a bright, enthusiastic fellow named Joseph Wilson, Haloid pushed the project to fruition. Among the landmarks on the long road that followed were (1) the first marketing of an industrial-use copier in 1950; (2) a change of company name from Haloid to Xerox; (3) first profit earnings in 1953; (4) development by 1957 of a prototype office copier, the cost of which nearly bankrupted the company; and (5) commercial introduction of the famous 914 console copier in 1959, more than 20 years after Carlson began his initial experiments.

All told, over $20 million was spent on the development of xerography before 1959. It is doubtful whether such a large financial commitment would ever have been made by the people who made it without patent protection. Besides Carlson's first four patents, the project generated well over one hundred improvement patents for various machine designs, selenium drums, paper feeding devices, copy counters, powder dispensers, and so on. The significance of patents to Xerox is summarized by Joseph Wilson:

> We have become an almost classic case for those who believe the (patent) system was designed to permit small, weak companies to become healthy. During the early years of xerography we were investing almost as much in research as we were realizing in profit. Unless the first faltering efforts had been protected from imitators, the business itself probably would have foundered, thus oblit-

erating opportunities for jobs for thousands throughout the world.[12]

(Carlson, Battelle, and Wilson were each eventually rewarded with eight-digit earnings.)

III. Why Patents?

The Xerox story implies several justifications for the patent system that now ought to be openly stated. At bottom, support rests on three legs: "natural law" property, "exchange-for-secrets," and "incentives."

A. *Natural Law*

The natural law thesis asserts that inventors have a natural property right to their own idea. "It would be a gross immorality in the law," John Stuart Mill argued, "to set everybody free to use a person's work without his consent and without giving him an equivalent."[13] Although this view appeals to our sense of fairness, it is not without its practical problems. For one thing, it implicitly assumes that invention is the work of a single, identifiable mind, or at most a few minds. But today invention is usually the product of a faceless corporate team, and any resulting patent rights rest with the corporation, not with the deserving inventors, individual or otherwise. Of course corporations may fund the research and thereby accept the risks, so the property argument could be extended to corporate research on grounds of "just" compensation.

This extention does not square with the fact that corporations doing research for the U.S. Department of Defense get exclusive patent rights on their defense work without bearing any financial risk. The property rationale is further undermined by the fact that patents pro-

tect only a few classes of ideas. If one is seriously concerned about the fair treatment of thinkers, why forsake those who push back the frontiers of knowledge in areas excluded from patent eligibility—such as pure science, mathematics, economics, and business administration? Is the inventor of parakeet diapers more deserving than the inventor of double-entry bookkeeping?

B. *Exchange-for-Secrets*

Patent law requires that inventors disclose their invention to the public. Without patent protection it is a pretty safe bet that inventors would try to rely on secrecy more than they now do to protect their ideas from theft. Thus the exchange-for-secrets rationale "presumes a bargain between inventor and society, the former surrendering the possession of secret knowledge in exchange for the protection of a temporary exclusivity in its industrial use."[14] Widespread public knowledge is assumed to be more beneficial than secret knowledge because openness fertilizes technological advance. One discovery may trigger dozens of others among many inventors. And, although the initial discovery cannot be used freely for seventeen years, secrecy might prevent full diffusion of its application for an even longer duration. Just how well society comes out in the bargain is impossible to say. The benefits of openness and the costs of temporary monopoly defy accurate estimation, especially the former. About all that can be said with confidence is that abolition of the patent system would cause the burial of *some* knowledge currently revealed in patent applications.[15]

---

[12] DeSimone, *op. cit.,* p. 1111.
[13] Cited by Floyd L. Vaughan, *The United States Patent System* (Norman, Okla.: University of Oklahoma Press, 1956), p. 27.

[14] Fritz Machlup, *An Economic Review of the Patent System,* Study No. 15, U.S. Senate, Subcommittee on Patents, Trademarks, and Copyrights, 85th Congress, Second Session (1958), p. 21.
[15] C. T. Taylor and Z. A. Silberston, *The Economic Impact of the Patent System* (Cambridge, U.K.: Cambridge University Press, 1973), p. 352.

C. Incentive

The justification most solidly illustrated by the story of Xerox, and the justification most supportive of the patent system, is that it provides incentive to invent and innovate. This rationale rests on two propositions: first, that more invention and innovation than would occur in the absence of some special inducement are desirable, and second, that giving out patents is the best method of providing such special inducement. In other words, discoveries would surely occur without patents, but it is believed that their unearthing will be appreciably hastened, or that more of them will be obtained, if the vast profit potential exclusive patents provide is used to lure inventors and innovators into action.

There can be no doubt that many inventions and innovations depend on patents for their existence or early arrival. Stories of people like Chester Carlson tell us that garrets and garages shelter thousands of inventors so inspired. As for innovation, which is the commercial application of an invention rather than the invention itself, evidence shows patents providing further incentive. A good test of this incentive would compare the commercial development of inventions *with* and *without* patent protection. The inventions that emerge from government funded research and development yield data for such a test because those doing the research sometimes get exclusive patent rights and sometimes not. (When not, the patent is publicly available to anyone.) These data show that commercial development of inventions (i.e., innovation) is two to three times more common *with* exclusive patent protection than without.[16] Results like these prompted a change in policy in 1980. Amendments to patent law now allow universities and small busi-

nesses to patent all technology developed with federal funds.

Still, the incentive thesis needs qualification at two levels. First, social benefits of cost savings and added consumer surplus may be rightly credited to the patent system for fathering "patent-dependent" inventions and innovations, but patent protection of these discoveries also creates social costs. These costs are the usual ones associated with monopoly—such as higher prices than otherwise. When these costs are deducted from the social benefits provided by these patent-dependent discoveries, the *net result* is considerably smaller than that suggested by brash talk of the gross benefits. This qualification of the incentive thesis is nevertheless not very serious because theory can demonstrate that the social benefits of these patent-dependent discoveries nearly always exceed those social costs to yield a positive net social benefit.[17] (See Appendix to this chapter.)

The second and higher level qualification is critical, however. We may comfortably assume that patent-dependent inventions and innovations are always, on balance, beneficial. But we *cannot* jump from there to conclude that the *patent system itself* is, on balance, always beneficial. Inability to make this leap weakens the incentive thesis. Thus a more thorough discussion of the patent system's costs and benefits is needed.

IV. Benefits and Costs of Patents

If the net social benefits of patent-dependent discoveries and developments were all that counted, the value of patent systems could not be questioned. However, patents are extended to *all* inventions that meet the legal qualifications, including inventions that are *not* dependent on the patent system for their existence.

---

[16] U.S. House of Representatives, Subcommittee on Domestic and International Scientific Planning and Analysis, *Background Materials on Government Patent Policies*, Vol. II, 94th Congress, 2nd Session (1976), p. 97.

[17] For a review, see Scherer, *op. cit.*, (1977), pp. 25–34.

Whatever social benefits may be claimed for these *non*patent-dependent inventions, they cannot be attributed to the patent system for the simple reason that their existence does not hinge on patent protection. Patent protection for these nondependent inventions does create social costs, however, costs of the monopoly kind. So in such cases there will *always be net social costs* from patents. Given that (1) patent dependency always yields net social benefits and (2) *non*patent dependency of patented inventions always yields net social costs, economists have devised the following criterion for judging the value of the patent system. As stated by F. M. Scherer, one "must weigh the *net* benefits associated with inventions which would not have been available without patent protection against the *net* social losses associated with patented inventions that would be introduced even if no patent rights were offered."[18]

Unfortunately, balance scales capable of this weighing have not yet been invented (patentable or otherwise). Some have even said the task is and always will be impossible because there is no sure way of telling whether a given invention is, or is not, patent dependent. Still, the major considerations that would guide educated guesswork on the issue have been sketched, and they include the following.

A. Tallies of Patent Dependency

Rough approximations have occasionally been made about the number of patent-dependent versus nonpatent-dependent inventions, on the assumption that, if the former number falls considerably short of the latter, the net benefits of the former are also likely to fall short of the net costs of the latter. For example, these two figures have been crudely estimated by classifying discoveries of individual inventors (and perhaps those of small firms too) in the

patent-dependent group and relegating those of corporations (or *large* corporations) into the nonpatent-dependent group. Questionnaire surveys of patentees rather consistently reveal that, in general, individual inventors rely heavily on patent protection to sustain their efforts, whereas most corporations claim that patents are neither the chief goal nor principal determinant of their innovative efforts.[19]

By this broad measure it would appear that *non*patent-dependent inventions easily outnumber patent-dependent inventions by a ratio somewhere in the neighborhood of 3 or 4 to 1. However, the very rough nature of this approximation is underscored by substantial differences of patent-dependency across industries. Chemical and pharmaceutical companies claim to lean more heavily on patents than do other corporate classes. A West German study arrived through opinion surveys at the following estimates of patent-dependent inventions as a per cent of all patented inventions in West Germany: chemicals and drugs, 36%; electrical equipment, 21%; instruments and optical, 21%; machinery, 3%; and iron and steel, 0%.[20]

Patent dependency has also been examined by study of situations in which patents have not been available. Neither Switzerland nor the Netherlands had patent systems during the latter half of the nineteenth century and the first decade of this century. According to Eric Schiff, who assessed the evidence provided by these countries, the absence of patents failed to petrify industry in either. On the contrary, industry thrived. As regards inventive activity itself, the evidence for the Netherlands is mixed, meaning that substantial growth was apparently based on technological change borrowed from foreign countries with patent systems. On the other hand, Swiss inventive activity appears to have been totally unaffected by a lack of

---

[18] F. M. Scherer, *Industrial Market Structure and Economic Performance* (Chicago: Rand McNally, 1970), p. 384.

[19] For a survey of the surveys, see Scherer, *op. cit.*, (1977), pp. 50–56.

[20] Ibid., p. 53.

patents, inasmuch as it was vigorous both during and after the patentless period.[21]

If, on the whole, patents are no more forceful in stimulating invention and innovation than is indicated by these items of evidence, obviously there must be other sources of incentive, other factors propelling progress. In the first place, to the extent *secrecy* can be maintained, it provides protection in lieu of patent protection. Second, many companies engage in progressive activities to remain *competitive* or gain competitive leadership. Introduction of new products or product improvements is a form of product differentiation, much like advertising. Natural lags, including temporary secrecy and retooling requirements, prevent immediate imitation of these efforts, gaining prestige and customer loyalty for the innovators. With all or most firms in an industry competing in this fashion, average industry price level will normally be high enough to cover the industry's R&D costs, just as price level covers advertising costs. Third, even where imitation is not substantially delayed, innovative investments are not always or even usually flushed down the drain by the price competition of imitators. High concentration, stiff barriers to entry, and similar sources of *market power other than patents* furnish a basis for postimitation price discipline in many industries. Finally, even when R&D does not on average pay its own way, it may nevertheless persist. Like gamblers, inventors and innovators often have distorted visions. They tend to see the Chester Carlsons more clearly than the Feckless Floyd failures. They *overrate their chances* of winning the spectacular treasures, and, as a consequence, they often subsidize their R&D efforts from unrelated earnings.

Note that most of these nonpatent inducements probably apply most strongly to medium-sized or large firms. Secrecy cannot be maintained by a small individual inventor who must go around displaying his ideas in hopes of finding a firm that will commercialize them. A small, newly entering enterprise that dares to threaten the established position of existing behemoths cannot count on the restraint of their price discipline should they elect to crush the newcomer. A small company cannot gain much of a jump on its rivals if its brand name is less entrenched and its distribution channels are shallower and thinner than those of its larger rivals. A small company likewise tends to be less diversified than its larger foes, so it may have fewer opportunities to subsidize its R&D during periods of financial drought. Perhaps these considerations explain why individual inventors and small firms profess greater reliance on the patent system, and claim a keener interest in its perpetuation, than big firms. (This does not necessarily mean that the patent system is, on balance, procompetitive. The story of U.S. Gypsum should dispel hasty conclusions of that kind.)

To summarize, various empirical tallies of patent dependency indicate that the system provides life-support for only a minority of inventions and innovations, a minority whose origins are of usually humble size. This minority wins credit for the system. But since patents are also showered indiscriminately on the nonpatent-dependent majority of inventions, it would appear from tally-type evidence that the net costs of the majority exceed the net benefits of the minority, and the system should therefore be reformed or abolished. However, we must hold off the executioners, at least momentarily.

B. The Economic Significance of Patent-Dependent Inventions

Although the weight of numbers suggests the patent system is economically unfit, that measure may be misleading. What if the relatively few inventions that are patent-dependent in-

[21] Eric Schiff, *Industrialization without Patents* (Princeton, N.J.: Princeton University Press, 1971).

clude the relatively few inventions that are truly revolutionary, whereas, at the same time, the relatively numerous nonpatent-dependent inventions include only simple improvements or inanities? It has been argued that, to some extent, there is a direct relationship between the economic significance of inventions and their patent dependency. F. M. Scherer speaks for this view:

It is conceivable that without a patent system some of the most spectacular technical contributions—those which effect a genuine revolution in production or consumption patterns—might be lost or (more plausibly) seriously delayed. . . . Such innovations may lie off the beaten paths of industrial technology, where no firm or group of firms has a natural advantage, and the innovator may be forced to develop completely new marketing channels and production facilities to exploit them. They may entail greater technological and market uncertainties, higher development costs, and longer inception-to-commercialization lags than the vast bulk of all industrial innovation. Entrepreneurs may be willing to accept their challenge only under highly favorable circumstances—notably, when it is anticipated that if success is achieved, it can be exploited to the fullest through the exercise of exclusive patent rights.

That such cases exist is virtually certain. Black-and-white television and the development of Chester Carlson's xerographic concepts are probable examples.[22]

Undoubtedly it is this possibility, coupled with notions of "natural law" property, that persuades politicians to keep the patent system intact. At a bare minimum, such crude *qualitative* accounting raises serious doubts about the accuracy of negative conclusions derived from simple *quantitative* tallies.

[22] Scherer, *op. cit.*, (1970), p. 388.

C. The Social Cost of Nondependent Inventions

But the qualifications cannot end there, not in fairness to those critical of patents, anyway. Just as the net benefits of dependent cases need qualification, so too the net costs of granting patents in nondependent cases need amplification—an exercise that tips the balance back in the negative direction, especially where revolutionary innovations of this nondependent stripe are concerned. First, granting monopoly rights over knowledge that is not dependent on patents artificially restricts use of that knowledge below what is socially optimal. The marginal cost of using technical knowledge is zero in the sense that knowledge can be used over and over and over again, by one person or many, without even the slightest danger of exhaustion through wear and tear. No one is compelled to get less of it when anyone else gets more.

Ideally, therefore, technology should be *freely* available to all potential users because the "pure" marginal cost of its dissemination and application is zero. But the grant of monopoly leads to exclusions, either directly or by the extraction of a royalty-price that exceeds zero.[23] A second social cost, one stemming from that just mentioned, is a blocking effect. Potential inventors who might like to use a patented invention to further their research in different or related fields may be blocked from doing so, in which case the patent would not be fostering progress but rather inhibiting it. Third, if a patent is extended to a firm with a preexisting monopoly position, then suppression of the patented invention is possible under certain circumstances.[24] Fourth, patents give rise to monopoly powers and restrictive practices that

[23] Wassily Leontief, "On Assignment of Patent Rights on Inventions Made Under Government Research Contracts," *Harvard Law Review* (January 1964), pp. 492–497.
[24] For a review of suppression cases, see Vaughan, *op. cit.*, pp. 227–260.

go well beyond those inherent in patents themselves.

It is at this last point that patent policy collides with antitrust policy. Pure and simple patent monopoly escapes antitrust attack for obvious reasons. But, as seen earlier in the story of U.S. Gypsum, patents may be cleverly accumulated and manipulated to construct fortresses of monopoly power or networks of price-fixing agreements. The line between proper use and malevolent abuse of patent rights is difficult to draw, but the antitrust authorities and federal courts have over time made the attempt. As a result, the following practices, among others, have been declared illegal:

Restrictive licensing. If a number of patent licensees are restricted to charging prices specified by the patent holder, or if a number of licensees collude to allocate markets using patent licenses to formalize their agreement, violation is likely, as in the *Gypsum* case.[25]

Cross-licensing. Two or more patent holders may exchange rights of access to each other's patents, something which is often desirable in light of the fact that several firms may contribute to the technology of a single item, such as a TV set. However, patent "pools" that exclude others, or fix prices, or otherwise restrain trade are illegal.[26]

Acquisition of patents. Monopoly power built on the acquisition of many patents (as opposed to relying on one's own inventiveness) may be attacked under Section 7 of the Clayton Act.[27]

Tying. Tying the sale of an unpatented product (like salt) to a patented product (a salt dispensing machine used in food processing) is virtually per se illegal.[28]

In brief, antitrust policy permits patent holders to earn their "legitimate" reward for invention, a reward that may be monopolistically plump. But patent rights cannot be stretched beyond "legitimate" rights. Tight interpretation of legitimacy has held down the social costs of the patent system, but not to the point of quieting cries for reform.

V. Proposals for Reform

A. Proposals to Weaken the System

Ideology and evidence lead few folks to advocate complete abolition of the United States patent system. The natural law property thesis rests on strongly held value judgments unrelated to economic benefits and costs. There is also enough incentive provided by the system to produce some social benefits. Whether these benefits exceed the social costs is, as we have seen, uncertain, but the benefits are large enough that abolition of the system might give appearances of throwing the baby out with the bath water. Hence critics who want the system weakened usually advocate reform, not abolition.[29]

One of the most obvious improvements that could be made in the system is the elimination of improvident patent grants. The test of inventiveness could be tightened substantially.

A number of other proposed changes would lessen the monopoly power of patents. These include such things as shorter patent life and compulsory licensing. Reducing patent life below seventeen years would reduce monopoly's

---

[25] *U.S.* v. *United States Gypsum Co.* 333 U.S. 364 (1948); *U.S.* v. *Masonite Corp.,* 316 U.S. 265 (1942); *Newburgh Moire Co.* v. *Superiors Moire Co.,* 237 F.2d 283 (3d Cir. 1956).
[26] *U.S.* v. *Line Material Co.,* 333 U.S. 287 (1948); *U.S.* v. *Singer Manufacturing Co.,* 374 U.S. 174 (1963).
[27] *U.S.* v. *Lever Bros. Co.,* 216 F. Supp. 887 (S.D.N.Y. 1963); *Kobe, Inc.* v. *Dempsey Pump Co.,* 198 F.2d 416 (10th Cir. 1952).

[28] *International Salt Co.* v. *U.S.,* 332 U.S. 392 (1947).
[29] Patent systems in less-developed countries are an entirely different matter, though: D. F. Greer, "The Case Against Patent Systems in Less-Developed Countries," *Journal of International Law and Economics* (December 1973), pp. 223–266.

duration. Compulsory licensing would simply require patent holders to license their patents to all who wanted to use them at a "reasonable" royalty fee. This would reduce monopoly power because it would end the exclusiveness that patents presently bestow. Empirical studies of compulsory licensing indicate that it would also substantially deflate the system's incentives, but by less than abolition would.[30]

B. Proposals to Strengthen the System

As the U.S. economy grew sluggish in the late 1970s, our technological superiority was called increasingly into question. This spurred proposals to *strengthen* the patent system rather than weaken it. The result was a new patent law in December 1980. The law gives small businesses and universities exclusive patent rights to products invented with federal research funding. Some government agencies had insisted that patents from federally funded research be subject to compulsory licensing.

Another provision of the new law reduced the likelihood that courts would declare patents invalid. Unlike before, the Patent Office can now recheck on the validity of a challenged patent. The results of the recheck, if favorable to the patent, solidify its validity.

As this is written, another piece of strengthening legislation seems to be moving toward passage. This bill would, in effect, lengthen the life of many patents, especially those covering drugs, chemicals, and medical devices. The problem addressed by the bill is this: some products, like drugs, cannot be marketed without prior government approval. But that approval can take a long time, as long as ten years. Thus new product "X" might be patented shortly after invention in 1980, but not be sold until after 1990. With the patent expiring in 1997, there would be only seven years of legal

monopoly in the market instead of the seventeen accorded products not needing premarket clearance. The intent of the proposed legislation, then, is to extend patent life by the amount of time the product is under premarket regulatory review.[31] If this proposal gives any indication, the prevailing mood portends future reforms that would build up rather than tear down the patent system.

VI. Federal Funding of R&D

A. Trends

The federal government has seated itself at the dining table of technology, supped gluttonously, and has begun picking up the tab. Back in 1940 federal expenditures on R&D amounted to no more than $74.1 million, which was 0.8% of the total federal budget and barely 0.07% of GNP. A further mark of that era is the fact that federal spending on *agricultural* R&D exceeded *defense* R&D spending. World War II, the Cold War, the Space Race, and the Vietnam War conspired to change all that. By the mid-1960s federal R&D spending had soared to exceed $14 *billion,* which relative to total federal spending of all kinds topped 12%, and compared to GNP exceeded 2%. Defense R&D spending exploded to 41 times the size of agricultural outlays.[32]

Since the mid-1960s things have slackened off a bit. Total federal R&D funding has continued to climb to ever higher absolute dollar levels, exceeding $27 billion in 1979. Yet price inflation exaggerates these dollars, and, as a proportion of the total federal budget or relative to GNP, federal R&D funding has recently

---

[30] Taylor and Silberston, *op. cit.;* Scherer, *op. cit.,* (1977).

[31] *Business Week,* February 16, 1981, p. 29.

[32] National Science Foundation, *Federal Funds for Research, Development, and Other Scientific Activities* (NSF 77–301, 1977), p. 4; Edwin Mansfield, *The Economics of Technical Change* (New York: Norton, 1968), p. 163.

fallen to about three fifths of what it was during the mid-1960s.

Recent trends in the composition of this expenditure are depicted in Table 25–1. National defense and space head the list of allocations. In 1979 their combined total of $17 billion accounted for about 62% of all federal R&D money. But this proportion was down from 77% in 1969, a drop of 16 percentage points. Quite clearly there has been a substantial revision of priorities, with military and space losing ground to a wide range of civilian R&D programs. Note especially the massive rise in energy R&D funding, from $328 million, or 2.1%, in 1969 to $2827 million, or 10.1% of the total R&D budget, in 1979. By far the

biggest chunk of energy money has gone to support the development of nuclear power—projects like the liquid metal fast breeder reactor, uranium enrichment processing, magnetic fusion, and laser fusion. In 1969 these efforts took 93% of the energy outlay. In 1979 these still took a hefty 38%, but other energy sources were then getting much greater attention, including coal gasification, oil shale, and solar power.

Three other areas enjoying rapid relative growth in funding are environment, natural resources, and "science base." The first is self-explanatory. The second entails research in such areas as mineral reserve estimation, watershed management, and forestry protection.

Table 25–1.   Federal R&D Funding by Function: Fiscal Years 1969 and 1979

Function	Millions of Dollars		Per Cent of Total	
	1969	1979*	1969	1979*
National defense	$ 8,354	$13,833	53.4%	49.5%
Space	3,732	3,383	23.9	12.1
Energy	435	2,827	2.1	10.1
Health	1,127	3,034	7.2	10.8
Environment	285	1,082	2.0	3.9
Science base	436	1,061	3.3	3.7
Transportation and communications	458	838	2.9	3.0
Natural resources	201	644	1.3	2.3
Food, fiber, agriculture	225	543	1.4	1.9
Education	155	146	1.0	0.5
All other (crime, housing, social services, etc.)	233	581	1.5	2.1
Total	15,641	27,972	100.0	100.0

* Estimates based on President's 1979 budget to Congress

Source: National Science Foundation, An Analysis of Federal R&D Funding by Function (NSF 78–320, 1979), p. 5.

"Scientific base" refers chiefly to basic research that has no obvious or immediate application in either commerce or government. Much of it is "glamorous" science, such as high-energy physics, molecular biology, and oceanography. But it stretches from mathematics to materials-processing to anthropology.

B. The Reasons for Federal Funding

Why has the government opened its purse so widely to these pursuits? Why has the distribution of money moved around so much? What guides Washington in these matters? There are no really solid answers because noneconomic value judgments play a crucial role in the decision making. Which will reduce the threat of death more—a billion dollars spent for a new military weapon or for a cure for cancer? Which will do more to relieve the energy crisis by the year 2000—a billion dollars spent on nuclear or on solar power? No one knows for sure; speculation reigns amidst the inherent uncertainties. Hence, value judgments are inescapable, and these shift under the press of political, social, international, and technical developments.

Still, there are a few broad economic foundations for this effort.[33] To begin with, most federal R&D is allocated to areas where the federal government stands as the sole or chief consumer of the ultimate product. National defense and space are the most obvious instances. Because the federal government has prime responsibility for provision of these "public goods" (a responsibility recognized by even the most miserly conservatives), it is strongly felt that the government should also take responsibility for technological advance in these areas.

Other R&D programs are grounded on the belief that private incentives are lacking. That is, the social benefits of advancement greatly exceed the benefits that can be privately captured, or if they can be privately captured, such would be undesirable. Research in basic science, health, environmental protection, and crime prevention probably fit this justification. Still other programs can be defended as offsets to market imperfections of somewhat different sorts. Single R&D projects in such areas as nuclear power and urban mass transportation couple costs of billions of dollars with risks of ominous magnitudes, so much so that even our largest and most courageous private companies are scared to undertake them without government support. The necessity for government R&D funding in agriculture, housing, construction, and coal is often defended because these industries tend to be populated with firms too small and too scattered to shoulder the burdens of even medium-sized R&D projects. As concentration in these industries has increased over time, and as firm size has likewise grown, this justification has lost some of its punch. Still, it remains persuasive to many politicians, and it probably remains valid at least in some areas.

Whatever the reason, federal R&D outlays now exceed those of private industry by a fat margin. Accordingly, our survey of policy would have been woefully lacking had it concealed this contribution.

Summary

The United States government's promotion of technical progress dates from the days of the Founding Fathers. Patents originate in the Constitution, which authorizes legislation to "promote the progress of science and useful

---

[33] For details see Mansfield, *op. cit.*, pp. 186–187; *Priorities and Efficiency in Federal Research and Development*, A Compendium of Papers, Subcommittee on Priorities and Economy in Government of the Joint Economic Committee, U.S. Congress, 94th Congress, Second Session (1976); and John E. Tilton, *U.S. Energy R&D Policy* (Washington, D.C.: Resources for the Future, 1974).

arts, by securing for limited times to authors and inventors the exclusive right to their respective writings and discoveries." Under present law, patents last seventeen years and cover discoveries that pass fairly lenient standards of inventiveness, novelty, and utility. With few exceptions, admissible subject matter is limited to mechanical and chemical products or processes, thereby excluding fundamental laws of nature and other worthwhile discoveries.

At its best, the patent system stimulates progress, rewards deserving inventors and innovators, and arouses competition by nourishing small firms. The history of Xerox illustrates these beneficent effects. On the other hand, deserving and getting do not always coincide under the system, with the result that patents protect discoveries that would be available anyway. Moreover, patents often provide hooks on which to hang restrictive practices, and they occasionally even stifle technical progress. Many of these blemishes in the system were underscored by the story of wallboard.

The main justifications for the patent system are "natural law" property, "exchange-for-secrets," and "incentives." Each has appeal; each has problems. As the law presently stands, too much is arbitrarily excluded to make the natural law argument natural, and society gets in on too few of the secrets it bargains for. That patent incentives pull some discoveries from the nether world cannot be doubted, but this effect is easily exaggerated.

Ideally, a benefit-cost analysis would compare the net benefits of patent-dependent inventions with the net costs of extending patents to nonpatent-dependent inventions. Unfortunately, data deficiences permit no more than speculation on this score. What little evidence is available indicates that net benefits have the best chance of exceeding net costs on those patents that are extended to individual inventors and small firms. Chemicals and pharmaceuticals might also enjoy favorable balances.

Recent reform proposals have urged a strengthening of monopoly rights instead of a weakening. It may be no accident that these reforms have especially favored those whose incentives are most stimulated by patents, namely, small businesses generally (who now have exclusive patent rights under federally funded research) and those producing chemicals and pharmaceuticals (who may gain greater patent longevity).

Federal funding of R&D has grown from little more than a teenager's weekly allowance to amounts in excess of $27 billion. For a while, defense and space R&D were deemphasized in favor of civilian R&D, but Reagan may change that. Noneconomic value judgments play a particularly prominent role in this policy area.

Questions and Exercises for Chapter 25

1. In each case, why wouldn't the following be patentable? (a) a vampire protection kit, (b) the discovery of a cure for inflation, (c) the shoe.
2. Why was U.S. Gypsum attacked under the antitrust laws when its monopoly power was based on patents?
3. Identify and assess the natural law property rationale for patents.
4. Which rationale for patents most convincingly supports the award of exclusive patents from government financed R&D?
5. Conceptually, how would one conduct a benefit-cost analysis of the patent system?
6. What evidence indicates that the number of patent-dependent inventions is actually quite small?
7. Why does the story of Xerox support the patent system despite the fact that patent dependent inventions seem to be a rather small fraction of all patented inventions?

8. What policies bolster the "incentive" effect of patents?
9. Why might federal funding of R&D be warranted?

Appendix to Chapter 25: The Economic Benefits of Cost-Reducing Inventions

In cases where patents bring forth new *products,* the net social benefits are easy to imagine because new products yield new consumer surpluses even when priced at monopoly levels. Less intuitively plausible are the net benefits associated with *production process* innovations, where no new product is involved and where the monopoly control granted by the patent can convert a purely competitive industry into a monopoly. Figures 25–1 (a) and (b) illustrate the two possibilities in this regard.

If, as in Figure 25–1(a), production costs per unit drop substantially from C_1 under pure competition to C_2 under monopoly, then buyers will gain an immediate benefit from the invention—namely, a price reduction from P_1 to P_2, which increases quantity from Q_1 to Q_2. Under pure competition, price equals marginal cost, as P_1 equals C_1 in Figure 25–1 (where marginal cost is assumed constant and therefore also equal to average cost). When cost falls from C_1 to C_2 because of the invention, price will not fall as much because patent monopoly prevails as well as cost C_2, and the monopolist's price, P_2, will be above C_2. Still the price reduction increases consumers' surplus from AEP_1 to ABP_2.

Aside from the price reduction, society also gains by the fact that, after the invention, fewer resources are used to produce Q_1, a savings represented by the area JP_1EH. Although most of these savings are pocketed by the monopolist in the form of excess profits, they are nevertheless genuine and the monopolist is, after all, a member of society, not a Martian. Once the patent expires the industry could return to a purely competitive structure (assuming favorable conditions), at which time price will drop to C_2 and all gains then pass to buyers (consumers).

The cost reduction in panel (b) of Figure 25–1

Figure 25–1.   The Economic Effects of Patent-Dependent Cost-Reducing Inventions

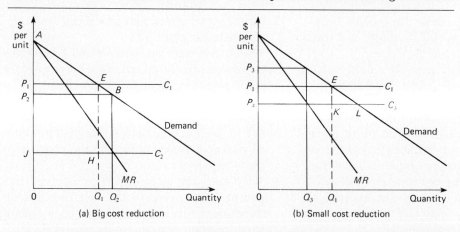

(a) Big cost reduction

(b) Small cost reduction

is smaller, C_1 to C_3. Indeed, it is small enough to suggest that, with conversion to monopoly, price could actually rise from P_1 to P_3, given that marginal revenue MR equals marginal cost C_3 at quantity Q_3, which is less than Q_1. However, the monopolist's price cannot rise above P_1 because the pure competitors can sell at P_1, and they would be encouraged to do so at any price above P_1. Thus in this case price is likely to remain at P_1, implying no immediate gain for buyers. All the immediate social gains take the form of reduced resource use in the production of Q_1, a reduction represented by area P_1EKP_4. These savings go to the monopolist (still a member of society). If pure competition

returns after expiration of the patent, buyers then reap the benefits when price falls to P_4 from P_1. The gain in consumer surplus then equals P_4P_1EL, because triangle ELK is added to the cost savings of P_1EKP_4 just mentioned. Thus in this case, too, a patent dependent invention yields net social benefits even though the patent creates a seventeen year monopoly.[34]

[34] For further discussion, see Dan Usher, "The Welfare Economics of Invention," *Economica* (August 1964), pp. 279–287; William D. Nordhaus, *Invention, Growth and Welfare* (Cambridge, Mass.: MIT Press, 1969); F. M. Scherer, *Industrial Market Structure and Economic Performance* (2nd ed.) (Chicago: Rand McNally, 1980), pp. 442–444.

Chapter 26

Promotion and Protection Policies

We're pro free enterprise—but often the business community isn't.
—Robert Bartley
Editor, Wall Street Journal (*referring to the business community's pursuit of government subsidies, tariffs, and other favors*)

Making financial history, General Motors, Ford, and Chrysler racked up combined losses of $4.01 billion in 1980. Chrysler's share, $1.71 billion, was the largest annual loss ever recorded by a single company. The federal government had helped the Big Three during 1980 by giving Chrysler a massive loan guarantee and hiking the tariff on light-truck imports from 4% to 25%. Yet a worried Detroit appealed to Washington, D.C. for still more aid—a quota on auto imports.

These numbers and actions caught the tenor of the times. As other industries also sank into trouble, people cried out for "The Reindustrialization of America." Such was the title, for instance, of a special issue of *Business Week* in 1980 and a 1981 book by the Business Week Team. Pundits proclaimed that the economic malaise of the 1970s could be replaced by prosperity in the 1980s if only business, labor, and government committed themselves to the task, and if the last of these groups, government,

instituted bold new policies of promotion and protection.

The Reagan administration resisted most appeals for new special favors, preferring instead to keep free enterprise "free" and stimulate our weakened economy with enormous tax and budget cuts. "We intend to create a climate in which business can flourish," said Treasury Secretary Donald Regan. "But having created this climate, we then expect businesses either to thrive or not on their own." The administration could not resist all pleas, however. Among other things, the auto industry won new restraints on auto imports and relaxed safety, energy, and environmental regulations worth billions. The ocean shipping industry was allowed to cartelize more than before. And most of the old promotions and protections survived the onslaught of President Reagan's free-enterprise ideology, albeit in withered forms.

There is thus still quite enough promotion and protection around to hold our attention for a full chapter. Indeed, the variety of such policies is bewildering. U.S. shipping lines are aided by a law requiring that all Alaskan oil be moved by American tankers. Cotton, wool, apple, and potato interests are served by advertising campaigns financed from special taxes. Books and magazines enjoy unusually low postal rates. The patent and R&D funding policies discussed in the previous chapter likewise qualify.

Here we shall focus on four major classes of such policies, each of which may be illustrated by the experiences of important industries:

I. Direct Subsidies: Transportation and Energy
II. Loans and Loan Guarantees: The Chrysler Bailout
III. Import Protection: Steel
IV. Price Supports: Agriculture

While reviewing these policies of promotion and protection it will be noted that the reasons for such policies range widely. National defense, income equity, stability, efficiency, conservation, progress, economic growth, national prestige—the list of alleged benefits is so long that one wonders how a pennant for the hapless Chicago Cubs misses mention. Though some of these laudable purposes are indeed served by policies of promotion and protection, the plain fact is that much if not most of the motivation is simply special interest politics, whereby a few are able to benefit at the expense of the many. Because the few who benefit usually benefit a great deal per capita or per firm, they press their political representatives hard with lobbying efforts and campaign funding. Because the many who consequently pay higher taxes or higher prices pay relatively little per capita or per firm, their countervailing pressures are weak and diffuse by comparison. Thus one reason special interest politics can succeed is a *disparity* in the concentration of benefits relative to costs. A second reason is *logrolling*, which is simply the exchange of political favors. This explains how minorities can gain at the expense of the majority. Detroit's representatives in Congress vote for federal tobacco subsidies benefiting rural Southerners because those representing rural Southerners vote loan guarantees for Chrysler Corporation. Representatives from Wyoming and Colorado vote for shipping subsidies benefiting coastal states because coastal-state representatives support synthetic fuel subsidies bound to benefit Wyoming and Colorado. And so on. Little wonder, then, that presidents, with broadly based political constituencies, have time and again proposed the abolition or substantial curtailment of special favors only to be rebuffed by Congress.

I. Direct Subsidies

A. Theory

Nearly every economist has his own definition of subsidies. According to one they are "Government programs that modify the operation of the market mechanism or of the tax laws for limited sectors of the economy or limited groups of the population."[1] According to another, subsidies work "through the private market, by altering certain market prices" in order to "induce someone to increase or decrease his purchases, or his production, or use of some particular thing or group of things."[2] Such general definitions typically have two features in common. First, they stress that subsidies merely *modify markets* rather than totally supplant them. This excludes from the realm of subsidies government activities like equipping an army, floating a navy, or issuing cur-

[1] Hendrik S. Houthakker, Testimony, *The Economics of Federal Subsidy Programs,* Hearings, U.S. Congress, Joint Economic Committee, 92nd Congress, 1st Session (1972), p. 14.
[2] Carl S. Shoup, ibid, p. 5.

rency. Second, they specify the *limited scope* of subsidies, thereby stressing sectoral favoritism. This excludes such broad or common benefits as investment tax credits and social security.

At this level of generality, every policy reviewed in this chapter could be considered a subsidy. But the *mechanisms* by which these subsidies operate, and their immediate *impact* on the market place differ enough to allow categorized treatment. The so-called **direct subsidies** of this section include, in ascending order of government involvement:

1. *Tax breaks* for favored goods and services, such as the tax deferral exporters receive under the DISC program, or the 4¢ lower federal fuel tax on gasohol as compared to gasoline.
2. *Direct payments* to producers or consumers to help cover the costs of producing or consuming certain favored commodities or services. Examples include the federal government's payment of half the costs of building ships in U.S. shipyards and its funding of railroad passenger service through Amtrak.
3. *Government ownership and operation* of certain kinds, such as government ownership and operation of the Synthetic Fuels Corporation, which promotes synfuels development. Much government ownership is not for purposes of subsidy (it is for instance an alternative to regulation in the field of public utilities). But much of it clearly is.

The impact of such direct subsidies on the favored markets may be seen in Figure 26–1. Assuming pure competition for simplicity, S_1 represents supply without subsidy and embodies all per-unit costs of producing various quantities of the commodity in question, including tax costs and a normal return to investors. Free-market price and quantity will then be P_1 and Q_1, where S_1 intersects demand. A subsidy has the effect of lowering cost per unit, thereby shifting the supply curve down from S_1 to S_2.

The vertical distance between S_1 and S_2 is the amount of subsidy per unit, and any given quantity, say Q_1, will be supplied at an equivalently lower price. The subsidy thus lowers the price charged to buyers below that necessary to cover full unit cost. Given Figure 26–1's demand, the result is a lower price of P_2 (despite real unit costs at C), and a larger quantity at Q_2. For a concrete example from Amtrak in 1981, the typical rail passenger paid $25 for his or her trip, but Amtrak's cost of supplying that trip was $60. Subtracting $25 from $60, we see that the average subsidy was $35 per passenger.[3]

Recognizing that a direct subsidy increases quantity above the free-market level, we can now note that such subsidies may serve legitimate economic purposes. If the free-market result is for some reason flawed, so that too little quantity is provided, then a subsidy would be warranted insofar as the benefits of the added quantity exceed the costs of the added quantity. If for example railroad passenger travel yielded such external benefits as reduced pollution, curbed fuel consumption, and less highway congestion as compared to auto travel, it might well be that a subsidy for Amtrak of $35 per average passenger is warranted. Still, these external benefits would have to be worth at least $35 per passenger to be warranted by economic efficiency criteria. In other words, we who do not ride trains should be willing to pay some of the costs of those who do *to the extent* we benefit by their train travel.

We should hasten to add, however, that relatively few subsidies probably serve such laudable purposes, and among these few the subsidy magnitudes are not as finely determined as economists would like. During the first ten

---

[3] *Wall Street Journal*, June 25, 1981, p. 48. Average subsidy on the Washington–Cincinnati run was much higher at $137 a ticket, so high that it would have been cheaper for the government to close that line and buy airline tickets for the rail travelers affected.

Figure 26–1. The Impact of Direct Subsidies

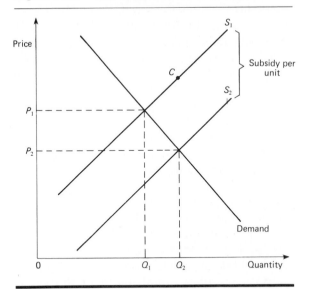

years after its inception in 1971, for instance, Amtrak gobbled up a total of $5 billion in government subsidies keeping its 24,000-mile system in operation. Yet analysis reveals very few external benefits for the money. In fuel consumption per passenger-mile, most of Amtrak's system performs no better than the average private car. In pollution performance, Amtrak is not significantly better than cars, buses, or airplanes.[4] Facing the facts, the Carter administration proposed in 1979 to eliminate 43 per cent of the most heavily subsidized mileage in the Amtrak system while retaining service to over 90 per cent of the people traveling the original routes. Congress, however, consented to no more than a 15% cutback. Then in 1981 the Reagan administration urged that the annual subsidy be pared one-third further from $900 to $613 million. But once again Congress resisted, approving $735 million for fiscal 1982.

[4] For a brief survey, see "A Subsidy for Sentiment," *New Republic,* April 21, 1979, pp. 5–8.

Western-state senators and representatives, aided by their governors and abetted by thousands of riders who protested the loss of such trains as the Chicago–San Francisco "Zephyre" and the Seattle–Salt Lake City "Pioneer," led the movement to retain sizeable subsidies. Aside from self-interest, broad-based public opinion lends support to passenger train subsidies for no other apparent reason than sentiment.[5]

B. Direct Subsidies in Practice: Transportation and Energy

Historically, government has probably poured more direct subsidies into transportation and energy than any other sectors of the economy save perhaps education. Beginning with last century's railroad land grants and continuing with this century's oil depletion allowances, airline subsidies, nuclear power assistance, and much more, the total figure, if ever computed, would surely be in the hundreds of billions of dollars. Our brief review of recent subsidies for these two sectors divides into three parts: (1) tax breaks, (2) direct payments, and (3) government ownership.

1. TAX BREAKS

The tax system can be manipulated to grant subsidies by lowering the tax liability of favored firms or individuals who, by virtue of their special identity or behavior, thereby benefit relative to others. Stanley S. Surrey explains that these tax subsidies substitute for direct government expenditures, so they could also be called "tax expenditures:"

> The Federal Income tax system consists of really two parts: one part comprises the structural provisions necessary to implement the income tax on individual and corporate net income; the second part comprises a system of tax expenditures

[5] Ibid., p. 5.

under which governmental financial assistance programs are carried out through special tax provisions rather than through direct government expenditures. The second system is simply grafted on to the structure of the income tax proper; it has no basic relation to that structure and is not necessary to its operation. Instead, the system of tax expenditures provides a vast subsidy apparatus that uses the mechanics of the income tax as the method of paying the subsidies.[6]

These subsidies take a variety of forms, including exclusions from income, deductions from income, preferential rates of tax, and deferrals of tax. One of the most popular forms for recent energy subsidies is the so-called tax credit. This permits the tax payer to treat a portion of the purchase price of energy related equipment as if it were a tax payment. A 50% tax credit on your purchase of a $4,000 solar heating system would, for instance, reduce your tax bill by $2,000, so the price of the system would in effect be one-half off. The Energy Tax Act of 1978 offered tax credits to individuals equalling 15 per cent but not more than $300 of the cost of outfitting their homes with energy-saving items like insulation, storm windows and doors, weather stripping, and clock thermostats. Solar credits were larger, and related credits were showered on businesses. In 1980 these several tax credits were extended and expanded to the point of saving consumers an estimated $600 million and businesses an estimated $5 billion during the decade following.

Other parts of the tax system, besides those pinching income, have likewise been used for subsidies. Gasohol's four cent per gallon waiver from the federal excise tax on gasoline caught our notice earlier. Honoring the fuel efficiency of buses (which is roughly twice as good as autos

on average), Congress has exempted buses from federal gasoline taxes altogether and from an excise tax that used to be collected on purchases of bus parts. The bus subsidy amounts to $50 to $100 million annually.

Of course the purpose behind these many tilts in the tax system is to curb energy consumption or redirect it toward new and cleaner energy sources such as solar and wind. Because the combustion of oil and coal is presently the single largest contributor to air pollution, such objectives seem sound. The subsidies encourage behavior having substantial external benefits. In addition, conservation and conversion enhance our security against the interruption of oil imports and benefit future generations with less costly energy supplies than otherwise. (An obvious by-product of these social benefits is the billions in private benefits gained by those in the new and expanding industries that result, such as solar energy.)

2. DIRECT PAYMENTS

Estimates of the federal government's direct subsidies to the nuclear power industry vary widely depending on where one draws the line. If one counts spending on early military reactors which provided the technological basis for later commercial reactors, plus government outlays for research on nuclear waste disposal, plus the cut-rate prices the government charges private parties for enriching uranium fuel, then the total subsidy from 1950 through 1980 comes to a whopping $37 billion. If on the other hand one excludes all forms of support other than money spent directly on civilian reactors, then the government's contribution amounts to "only" $12.8 billion.[7]

In transportation, Amtrak's subsidies could be considered direct payments because Amtrak is technically a private, not a government, corporation. Another railroad heavily dependent

[6] S. S. Surrey, "Tax Subsidies as a Device for Implementing Government Policy," *The Economics of Federal Subsidy Programs*, U.S. Congress, Joint Economic Committee, 92nd Congress, 1st Session (1972), p. 49.

[7] *Wall Street Journal*, March 12, 1981, p. 10.

on federal largesse is Conrail. Not to be confused with Amtrak, Conrail is primarily a freight railroad that operates (as of this writing) 17,000 miles of track in 16 Eastern and Midwestern states. Created by Congress in 1976 out of the remains of six bankrupt railroads, the largest of which was the Penn Central, Conrail issued common stock to the estates of the bankrupt precursor railroads and gained debt and preferred stock financing from the federal government. Most of the government's $3.3 billion subsidy to date is actually in the form of loans. But prospects for the repayment of those loans plus interest are currently so dim as to warrant their classification as direct subsidies. The Reagan administration is vigorously seeking an end to all Conrail subsidies, something that would likely force the sale of Conrail's assets at distressed prices.

Ocean shipping has likewise a hand in the government's purse, extracting hundreds of millions annually to support ship building and ocean shipping operations. Because national defense allegedly justifies these subsidies to a greater extent than those for railroads, they may prove more resistant to Reagan's budget cutting.

3. GOVERNMENT OWNERSHIP

Figure 26–2 inventories the extent of government ownership in eighteen noncommunist countries as of 1978. It reveals one of the most striking features of government ownership of business, namely its pervasiveness in energy and transportation sectors. Aside from postal service and telecommunications, government ownership is concentrated in such industries as electricity, gas, oil production, coal, railways, and airlines. The reasons for this are *not* all related to subsidies. Government ownership is, for one thing, an alternative to price and profit regulation in dealing with natural monopolies (and this helps to explain the prevalence of nationalization in electricity and gas). There may

also be some slight ideological element in the selection of these industries (even though the countries surveyed are for the most part in the capitalist camp, and the few with socialist leanings profess no doctrinaire beliefs that airlines must be state possessions). Still, many of the reasons for this particular pattern *are* related to subsidies, and those reasons are of interest to us here.

First, many governments use subsidized nationalization as a politically popular way to bolster employment in depressed or declining industries and localities. This was a major motivation behind the Tennessee Valley Authority here at home (during the 1930s) and a factor influencing take-overs in coal and shipbuilding abroad. Of course industries other than transportation and energy are afflicted with setbacks or offer means of spurring regional development. But transportation and energy are often considered "key" industries to national defense and national self-sufficiency, so they offer attractive targets for take-over.

Second, enterprise undertakings in energy and transportation often entail massive capital commitments or very risky prospects, two features that tend to discourage private investment and give pretexts for government ownership. Large scales and considerable risks not only seem to sway people to the notion that nationalization is needed (whether justified or not), they also seem to feed notions that a full return on the government's investments in these undertakings is not necessary, thereby leading to subsidies.

Third, subsidies to energy and transportation through the device of nationalization can be used to subsidize certain *consumers* of energy and transportation, be they other industries of crucial importance or common folk. Given that practically everyone depends in one way or another on energy and transportation, government ownership of enterprises in these sectors offers great versatility in subsidizing

Figure 26–2. Scope of State Ownership in Noncommunist Countries, 1978

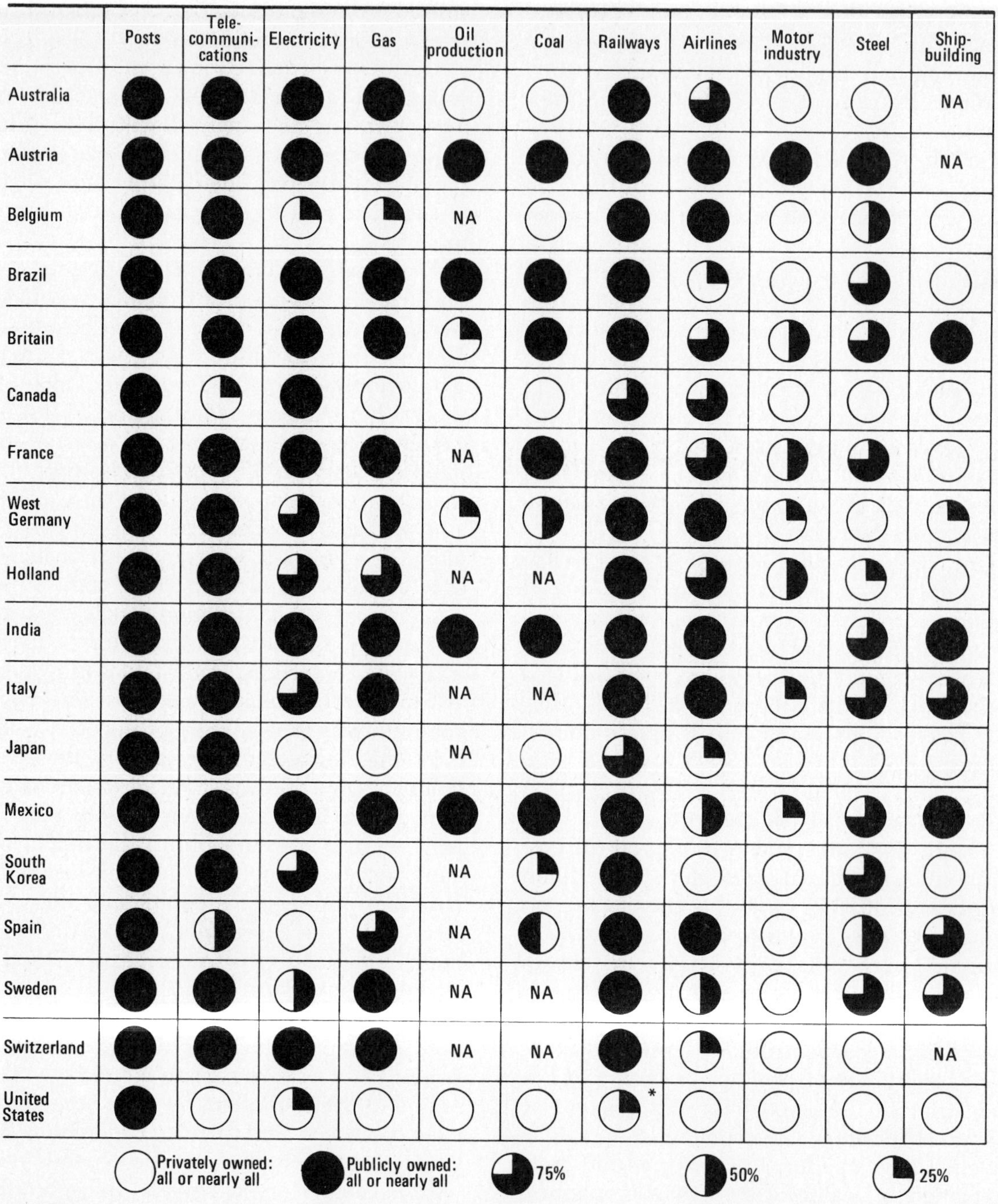

	Posts	Tele-communi-cations	Electricity	Gas	Oil production	Coal	Railways	Airlines	Motor industry	Steel	Ship-building
Australia	●	●	●	●	○	○	●	◕	○	○	NA
Austria	●	●	●	●	●	●	●	●	●	●	NA
Belgium	●	●	◔	◔	NA	○	●	●	○	◐	○
Brazil	●	●	●	●	●	●	●	◔	○	◕	○
Britain	●	●	●	●	◕	●	●	◔	◐	◕	●
Canada	●	◔	●	○	○	○	◐	◕	○	○	○
France	●	●	●	●	NA	●	●	●	◔	◐	◕
West Germany	●	●	◕	◐	◕	◔	●	●	◔	◔	◔
Holland	●	●	◔	◕	NA	NA	●	◕	◐	◔	○
India	●	●	●	●	●	●	●	●	○	◕	●
Italy	●	●	◔	●	NA	NA	●	●	◔	◕	◕
Japan	●	●	○	○	NA	○	●	◔	○	○	○
Mexico	●	●	●	●	●	●	●	◐	◕	◕	●
South Korea	●	●	◔	○	NA	◔	●	●	○	●	◐
Spain	●	◐	○	◔	NA	◐	●	●	○	◐	◔
Sweden	●	●	◐	●	NA	NA	●	◐	○	◕	◕
Switzerland	●	●	●	●	NA	NA	●	◔	○	○	NA
United States	●	○	◔	○	○	○	◔*	○	○	○	○

○ Privately owned: all or nearly all   ● Publicly owned: all or nearly all   ◕ 75%   ◐ 50%   ◔ 25%

Source: From a chart in *The Economist* (London), December 30, 1978, p. 39, and reprinted with permission.

farmers or exporters or whomever else one might want to help. Thus ownership is often a subsidy for achieving other subsidies.

These explanations assume that the association between subsidization and nationalization developed because perceived needs for subsidization brought about the nationalization, at least in capitalist countries. Of course the causal flow could be the reverse: nationalization, for whatever reason, could have led to subsidization. But the above explanations receive the backing of K. D. Walters and R. J. Monson who write, "The biggest advantage of state-owned companies is their ability to succeed and even thrive without earning profits."[8]

In 1980 Congress established the U.S. Synthetic Fuels Corporation (SFC), a subsidized government enterprise whose express mission in life is to subsidize the commercial development of "synfuels"—that is, oil from shale rock and gas and other fuels from coal. Originally authorized to spend $20 billion over its first five years and to seek as much as $68 billion more in future years, the Synthetic Fuels Corporation launched an entirely new industry with its nose in the federal trough. When signing the legislation President Carter exclaimed, "Its scope, in fact, is so great that it will dwarf the combined efforts expended to put Americans on the Moon and to build the entire Interstate Highway System of our country."[9] In round numbers the original objective was to foster the production of the equivalent of 500,000 barrels of oil a day by 1987, and 2 million barrels a day by 1992, about 10% of expected oil consumption.

Although Synthetic Fuels Corporation can legally build and operate its own synfuel plants in joint ventures with private companies, its main objective is to rear an industry of private enterprises, nursing them to maturity with direct government loans, guarantees of private loans, product purchase agreements, and product price guarantees. In deciding which private synfuels projects to support, SFC is supposed to consider the diversity of available technologies, the overall production potential of each technology, and the potential of each project for compliance with environmental regulations. The entire orientation is commercialization of known technologies, not fresh research and development. Two typical early shale oil projects in the same neck of the woods near Parachute, Colorado: Union Oil Company got a $400 million purchase agreement and price guarantee; Tosco Corporation received a $1.1 billion loan guarantee and purchase commitment. In short, we have in SFC a subsidized government corporation in the business of banking, buying, and brokering for the benefit of private oil, gas, coal, and chemical companies producing nonconventional energy.

Two arguments provide the main rationale for this endeavor:

> The first says that the United States is becoming more and more dependent on imported energy from sources that are increasingly insecure and that we can reduce this dependence by accelerating the production of new domestic energy supplies . . .
> The second argument says that projects to produce these energy sources are of a special nature that makes it difficult or impossible for them to be undertaken by the private sector without government assistance . . . In effect it is argued that there are significant imperfections which make nonconventional technology *look* unprofitable to private firms, even though its social value is considerable, and that it is these imperfections which justify intervention.[10]

[8] Kenneth D. Walters and R. Joseph Monsen, "State-Owned Business Abroad: New Competitive Threat," *Harvard Business Review* (March–April 1979), pp. 160–170.
[9] U.S. Senate, Committee on Energy and Natural Resources, *Synfuels from Coal and the National Synfuels Production Program: Technical, Environmental, and Economic Aspects*, 97th Congress, 1st Session (1981), p. 21.

[10] Paul L. Joskow and Robert S. Pindyck, "Synthetic Fuels: Should the Government Subsidize Nonconventional Energy Supplies?" *Regulation* (September/October 1979), pp. 19–20.

Critics of the Synthetic Fuels Corporation assault the first of these arguments by contending that the best way to curb imports is to tax imports and allow domestic prices of oil and gas to rise freely—thereby simultaneously discouraging energy consumption, encouraging conventional domestic production, and indirectly encouraging nonconventional synfuels production to the extent warranted by the higher prices. It is argued that people could then choose to avoid paying higher energy prices by limiting their consumption in contrast to being forced to pay higher income taxes for subsidies.

The problem of market imperfections is also questioned by critics of synfuels subsidies. One alleged imperfection is the unusually large-scale nature of most synfuel projects. But critics contend that the investments contemplated "are not significantly larger than the amounts the energy industry has raised in the past." Another possible imperfection in the private free market is that technological information will be generated by these projects, information with a social value exceeding its privately appropriable value. Keyed only to the private value, free markets would be stunted. Critics rebut by saying that while "this argument is generally true for R & D activities that produce basic scientific and technical knowledge, it is not applicable to the *commercialization* of new energy technologies."[11]

Early indications are that synfuels development will move more slowly than originally planned, not because the critics have succeeded in killing the Synthetic Fuels Corporation but because private energy companies have been, despite the subsidies, less than enthusiastic about building synfuel projects. Much of their current hesitancy is due to a fear that the glutted condition of the oil market in 1981 and 1982 will continue into the late 1980s.[12]

[11] This paragraph's quotes come from ibid., pp. 22–23.
[12] *Wall Street Journal,* December 28, 1981, pp. 1, 16.

Still, synfuels are becoming a reality, illustrating that direct subsidies can do more than lower price and boost output for existing industries. They can also create new industries from scratch.

II. Loans and Loan Guarantees

A. Theory

Our mention of government loans and loan guarantees for railroads and synfuels revealed only the tip of an iceberg. Government credit programs loom immensely. Uncle Sam's loans and loan guarantees resemble direct subsidies because they reduce costs to recipients and thereby influence the market in the fashion of Figure 26–1. Here, however, the cost savings are somewhat hidden. Government **direct loans** are simply loans granted by the government itself, usually at interest rates much below those of private lenders. The loans issued under government **loan guarantees** are the loans of private lenders such as banks, but the government guarantees that the loans plus interest will be paid off even if the borrower defaults. In this case the main cost savings to borrowers is again a reduced interest rate because the guarantee reduces the private lender's risk. In short, defaults under any of these programs leave the government holding the bag.

Since the borrowers benefiting from government loans and loan guarantees *are* expected to repay, it may appear that these forms of subsidy are costless to taxpayers except for the occasional defaults and administrative burdens. But this is not true. These particular costs comprise only one class of government costs that may be called *"ultimate fiscal costs."* Another class of government costs emerges from the fact that these credit activities raise the government's cost of borrowing, and indeed the government is a very big borrower. These may be called *"initial fiscal costs."* Finally, there are nongovernmental *"economic costs"* that arise because government loans and loan guarantees divert credit away from nonsubsidized borrowers. Murry Weidenbaum explains these classes of costs in reverse order:

1. *The economic cost.* Since they do little if anything to increase the total supply of investment funds in the economy, government credit programs take credit away from other potential borrowers. These unsubsidized borrowers might have produced more for society than the recipients of the government-supported credit. This can be the situation when the presence of federal credit encourages individuals or organizations to incur expenditures that they would forgo in the absence of the federal subsidy.

2. *The initial fiscal cost.* To the extent that government credit programs increase the total size of government-related credit, they cause an increase in the interest rates that are paid in order to channel these funds away from the private sector. Some increase, therefore, results in the interest rates paid on the public debt, which is a direct cost to the taxpayer.

3. *The ultimate fiscal cost.* When defaults occur on the part of the borrowers whose credit is guaranteed by the federal government, the Treasury winds up bearing the ultimate cost of the credit. In such cases the government credit programs become a form of backdoor spending whereby federal expenditures are incurred in the absence of direct appropriations for the purpose.[13]

Thus government credit programs permit subsidized borrowers to elbow out unsubsidized borrowers, producing hidden costs as well as visible administrative costs. The social benefits associated with this effort are the benefits gained from channeling more credit—and ultimately more real economic resources—into

[13] Murray L. Weidenbaum, *Business, Government, and the Public* (Englewood Cliffs, N.J.: Prentice-Hall, 1981), p. 194.

beneficial activities such as education, pollution control, transportation, and energy conservation.

B. The Scope of Federal Credit Activities

Figure 26–3 shows the towering growth of federal credit programs over the past decade. Beginning at just under $50 billion in 1971, new commitments for federal credit burgeoned until Carter requested $160 billion for fiscal 1981. Reagan's plans call for a cut to $140 bil-

Figure 26–3.   Growth of Total New Commitments for Federal Credit, 1971–1981

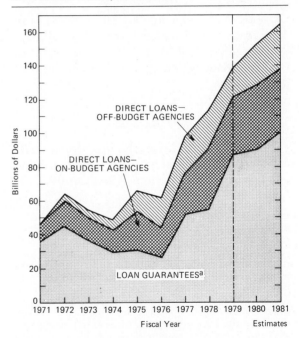

aPrimary guarantees: excludes secondary guarantees and guaranteed loans acquired by on- and off-budget agencies.

Source: Congressional Budget Office, *Federal Credit Activities: An Analysis of the President's Credit Budget for 1981* (1980), p. 3.

lion in fiscal 1981, still leaving a substantial increase over 1971 after taking inflation into account. Loan guarantees have surged the most.

Direct loans are distinguished by issuing agency in Figure 26–3. On-budget agencies are subject to traditional budget control. These include:

- The Small Business Administration, which makes loans to small businesses for expansion.[14]
- The Economic Development Administration which makes loans to businesses for commercial expansion or survival in economically distressed areas.
- The Export-Import Bank, which finances export sales, especially sales of durable goods like aircraft and computers.

Off-budget agencies include the U.S. Railway Association, which makes loans to Conrail, and the Rural Electrification and Telephone Revolving Fund, which supports public utilities in rural areas.

C. The Chrysler Bailout

In total dollar volume, the industry benefiting most from federal credit programs is housing. The Federal Housing Administration, or

FHA, is the most familiar part of this effort (with new loan guarantees of $34 billion in 1981). Nevertheless, one single loan guarantee of "only" $1.5 billion has attracted more attention in recent years than all housing credit subsidies combined—Chrysler's loan guarantee of 1980.

Chrysler's present trouble began in 1973 when OPEC quadrupled the price of oil. This hurt the entire U.S. auto industry because it sparked a deep recession and it caused auto buyers to shift from gas-guzzling American cars to fuel-efficient compact imports (see Figure 26–4). This hurt Chrysler more than GM and Ford, and forced it to cut capital spending and staff to a degree that sapped its strength against later difficulties. On top of these general economic woes, the burdens of meeting environmental and safety regulations grew heavier. And of the domestic Big Three, Chrysler's regulatory costs per car were heaviest because it was the smallest.[15]

In 1978 Chrysler suffered a $205-million loss. The following year its problems worsened when once again gasoline prices jumped, causing the public to switch further to small fuel-efficient cars. Simultaneously, another recession hit the industry (see Figure 26–4). Chrysler's subcompacts sold well in 1979, but its losses tumbled pass the billion mark for the first time. Appeals to the federal government brought help. Scary visions aroused by the prospects of Chrysler going under were enough to jolt politicians of every stripe and stature. After all, with over $100 billion in annual sales and over 800,000 employees, the domestic auto industry is immensely important to the economy. Chrysler's 140,000 employees in 1979 were backed up by hundreds of thousands more in indepen-

[14] The Small Business Administration originated in 1953 as an outgrowth of a Korean war program that funneled military supply contracts to small business. With loan guarantees of only $2.8 billion in 1981, it does not have the capacity to help more than a handful of the country's 10 million small businesses. But support for small business seems to benefit society greatly. It is a striking fact that most new employment in our economy comes not from the big GMs or GEs but rather from small businesses. A massive study by D. L. Birch of MIT shows that, during the 1970s, small firms (with 20 or fewer employees) generated *two-thirds* of all new jobs in the U.S. This was due partly to a shift in the economy toward services, away from manufactures. But it was also due to entrepreneurial spunk. D. L. Birch, "The Job Generation Process," in *Conglomerate Mergers—Their Effects on Small Business and Local Communities, Hearings*, U.S. Congress, House, Subcommittee on Antitrust of the Committee on Small Business, 96th Congress, 2nd Session (1980), pp. 649–671.

[15] This is because many of those regulatory costs were in the nature of total fixed costs, which on a per unit basis fall with greater volume. K. W. Clarkson, C. W. Kadlec, and A. B. Laffer estimate Chrysler's regulatory cost per car to be $200 above GM's and Ford's. "Regulating Chrysler out of Business," *Regulation* (September/October 1979), p. 46.

Figure 26–4.   U.S. Retail Auto Sales: Domestic and Imports

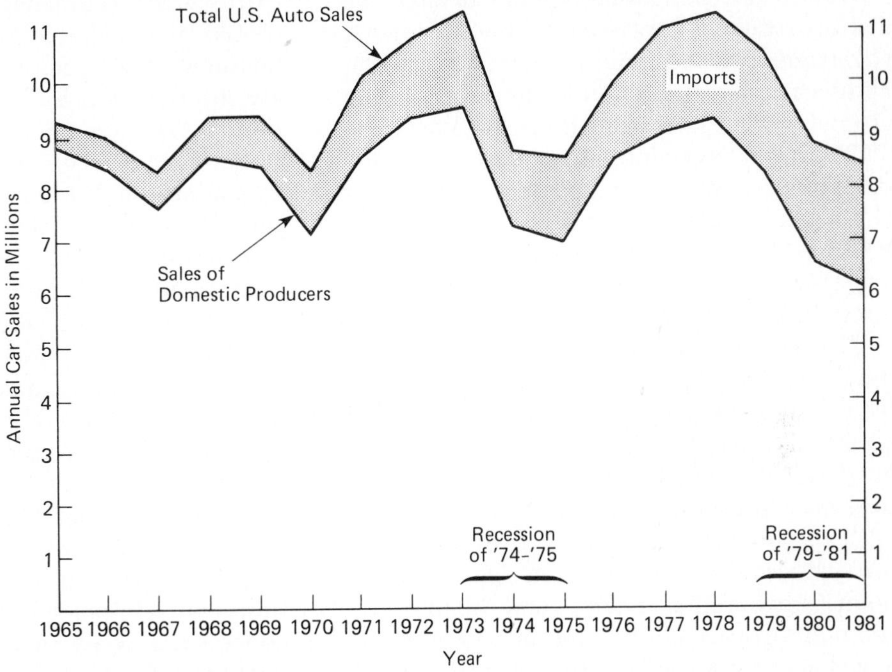

Source: *Automotive News, Wards Automotive,* and *Wall Street Journal.*

dent firms supplying parts, selling cars, and the like. Washington apparently could not turn its back on these hordes just before the 1980 elections.

Hence Congress approved a $1.5 billion loan guarantee scheme to be administered by a special Loan Guarantee Board. The law establishing the Board required that Chrysler match every chunk of loan-guarantee money with equivalent dollar-for-dollar concessions from other sources, namely, discounts from Chrysler's parts suppliers, reduced wages from employees, and partial forgiveness of debt obligations from Chrysler's existing creditors. Moreover, the law required that Chrysler for-

mulate a plan of survival—firing workers, closing plants, and developing new products—to satisfy the Loan Guarantee Board that Chrysler would be a "going concern" in the auto business after December 31, 1983.

Chrysler succeeded in satisfying the demands of the Board, but it remains to be seen whether Chrysler will eventually succeed in surviving. As shown in Figure 26–4, 1980 and 1981 proved to be very bad years for the domestic industry, so bad that it would take a spectacular recovery to improve matters appreciably. Chrysler increased its market share slightly in 1981 to 8.6 per cent, but the general state of industry depression pushed its losses past the billion-dollar mark for the third year in a row. Current forecasts look bleak.

Whatever the eventual fate of Chrysler, the main question for us here is whether the federal government should stand ready to catch stumbling corporate giants before they crash to the ground. Big rescue operations for Lockheed and Seatrain preceded Chrysler's. And many influential people advocate the establishment of a governmentally sponsored Reconstruction Finance Corporation that would bail out faltering companies on a rather routine basis. The question is thus a serious one.

The case *in favor* of such bailouts is fairly self-evident: (1) Big failures can have ripple effects, causing panic in financial markets and puncturing business confidence. (2) Bailouts need be no more than temporary, provided they have appropriate controls and incentives. (3) The government's cost of permitting failure—that is the resulting costs of unemployment compensation, welfare, and the like—exceed the government's cost of rescuing big beleaguered companies. And (4) the government may be at fault for the trouble.

On the other hand, the case *against* big bailouts is less obvious, so we should linger over the arguments. First, there are the appreciable costs of any federal credit program noted earlier. Initial and ultimate fiscal costs must be borne. And then additional economic costs will be important in this context. As big distressed companies receive guaranteed loans at less than the going market rate, they have an incentive to borrow more than they otherwise might. It may be argued that the pool of loanable funds remaining for healthy companies is thereby reduced, and the interest rates charged to healthy borrowers increased. Helping the weak at the expense of the strong weakens the economy.

Second, it is argued that bailouts adversely affect business incentives. "The possibility of bankruptcy is a necessary incentive for efficiency," explains Murry Weidenbaum. "I don't think big companies should be bailed out. After all, it's a profit-and-loss system."[16] In other words, waste, mismanagement, and inefficiency should be penalized lest they infect corporate boardrooms with sloth. Labor incentives would also be distorted by bailouts, as unions would then not face the unemployment consequences of outrageous wage demands. Indeed, a major reason auto imports have been battering U.S. producers is that domestic cars have been priced about $1,500 above comparable import models, and $700 to $800 of that price disadvantage is due to higher auto-worker wage rates here than abroad.[17] Moreover, just as Chrysler was going under for what seemed the last time in 1979, and just before Congress came to its rescue, the United Auto Workers extracted new wages from the auto industry worth an amazing 33% increase over three years. The UAW did grant a few concessions to Chrysler to help Chrysler gather matching funds for its loan guarantee. But these labor concessions were so slight that noted labor economist Herbert Northrup of the University of Pennsylvania called them "a fraud on the public."[18]

Third, bailouts favor big companies over small ones. Total corporate bankruptcies exceeded 25,000 the same year Congress approved Chrysler's bailout. In fact, corporate bankruptcies exceeded 25,000 annually during the entire last half of the 1970s. But Congress flinches only for the big ones, and all but a few

[16] *Business Week*, March 24, 1980, p. 104.

[17] This is not because of higher wages generally in the U.S., as U.S. autoworkers earn high wages even by American standards. Their average wage was 46% above the all-manufacturing average in 1979, up from 29% in 1960. For more see "Japan's Edge in Auto Costs," *Business Week*, September 14, 1981, pp. 92, 97; "Why Detroit Still Can't Get Going," *Business Week*, November 9, 1981, pp. 106–110; Office of Technology Assessment, *U.S. Industrial Competitiveness: A Comparison of Steel, Electronics, and Automobiles* (Washington D.C.: U.S. Congress, 1981), pp. 58–60.

[18] *Wall Street Journal*, January 7, 1980, p. 2.

bankruptcies involve relatively small firms. (In autos, Chrysler may be contrasted with Studebaker-Packard, which was allowed to fold, and with American Motors, which has so far survived not by loan-guarantees but by merger with a foreign sugar daddy, Renault.) Because small firms account for most of the economy's new jobs and a surprisingly large share of all technological innovations, a bias against small companies in favor of the big ones would seem unwise. It might, moreover, encourage needless big-business growth.

Fourth and finally, bailouts may not be needed because the economic trauma of big business failures is not, in the end, as horrid as it may seem. In particular, bankruptcy is *not* necessarily the same thing as liquidation. It may involve nothing more than a restructuring of the liabilities and net worth of the stricken company. To be sure, creditors and owners lose in the process, but the company's plants do not crumble into a heap. Nor do all the jobs vanish overnight.[19] Penn Central, for example, went through bankruptcy and the trains still run (albeit in the case of Penn Central's trains they are now run by subsidized Conrail). Even when bankruptcy does not provide shelter for a rehabilitating financial reorganization, but rather constitutes a last step toward liquidation, it provides an orderly exit.

As harsh as this may sound, it must be remembered that the economy regularly experiences tremendous volatility and turnover. Change is constant. Little of it should be prevented because most of it is probably for the best. By one estimate, each area in the U.S. loses an average of 50 per cent of its job base every 5 years. New jobs replace the old ones to bring stability or growth to most areas.[20]

In short, business people, the public, and influential politicians may look aghast at big corporate failures, but it is not at all clear that huge safety nets should be strung up. The problem might warrant indirect policies, such as tighter treatment of large conglomerate mergers. (These mergers elevate firms to towering sizes that do damage in the event they topple, yet on the average they yield no efficiencies or other social benefits.) But big bailouts seem unwise. If careful scrutiny were brought to bear on the myriad other federal credit programs, many of them might also lose their economic appeal. Still, *political* appeal seems to be what counts here. We should therefore not be surprised to see federal credit operations above $100 billion continuing in the future, with ample slices of the pie serving purposes other than such laudable ones as external benefits and national defense.

III. Import Protection

A. Theory

In May, 1981 Japan's minister of international trade and industry announced that Japan would limit auto shipments to the U.S. to 1.68 million cars during the ensuing year, down 7 per cent from the previous year. Restraint was promised for a second year as well. Detroit cheered.

Why would Japan want to restrict its exports? Was it stupidly shooting itself in the foot? No, Japan wasn't shooting itself in the foot so much as choosing its poison, for it acted under threats from the U.S. government. If Japan had not curbed auto exports "voluntarily," Congress and the President would have probably slapped still harsher limits on Japanese auto sales through an import quota or tariff.[21] This type of "protection racket" has become quite com-

[19] For an analysis of bankruptcy see Philip B. Nelson, *Corporation in Crisis: Behavioral Observations for Bankruptcy Policy* (New York: Praeger Publishers, 1981).

[20] D. L. Birch, *op. cit.*, p. 230.

[21] *Wall Street Journal*, April 22, 1981, p. 2; May 4, 1981, pp. 3, 8; *Fortune*, May 4, 1981, pp. 156–164.

mon in recent years—affecting TV sets, textiles, steel, baseball mitts, bicycles, and other commodities as well as autos—because genuine quotas and tariffs are all too real.

1. THE CASE FOR FREE TRADE

Although economists are notorious for their differences of opinion, they nearly all agree that free trade is generally good. This goodness can be viewed in the abstract or in the concrete, but it is a goodness for society at large, the overall economy.

In the abstract, free traders cite the theory of **comparative advantage.** Without trade, we in the United States could consume only what we produce. If we wanted to consume bananas, we would have to produce them. If we wanted to consume coffee, we would have to produce coffee. And so on for all the thousands of things that fracture our personal budgets. Given resource scarcity and technological realities, this tight connection between domestic consumption and domestic production would mean that obtaining some of the things we enjoy could prove very costly. Producing our own bananas, for instance, would take abundant land, labor, and capital away from apples, peaches, and oranges, squeezing our consumption of those delicious fruits. Our welfare would, in other words, be bounded by our limited domestic production capabilities.

With free trade these bounds are broken. Our *consumption* possibilities reach beyond our domestic *production* possibilities. We can consume what *other* countries produce as well as what we produce. Of course we must give up in trade some of the goods we produce in order to get the goods other countries produce, just as without trade we would have to give up oranges to get more bananas. But *the terms of trade internationally are better than the terms of production exchange domestically because of the principle of comparative advantage.* The quantity of, say, oranges we would have to give up in exports to get a certain quan-

tity of bananas imported would be *less* than the quantity of oranges we would have to give up in curtailed domestic production to get the same quantity of bananas domestically. Bananas simply cost less through internal trade than they do through domestic production. National productive endowments differ, and our "comparative advantage" lies in oranges while Ecuador's lies in bananas. More broadly but more realistically, international trade patterns reveal a U.S. comparative advantage in (1) capital equipment goods like airplanes and machinery, (2) high technology goods like computors, and (3) certain agricultural commodities like wheat and soybeans.

The basic idea of comparative advantage is, then, that we can buy some goods more cheaply abroad than at home. Another benefit from free trade, one a bit more concrete perhaps, it that it *provides competition* for domestic suppliers and thereby permits us to buy more cheaply *at home* than otherwise. As Richard Caves once said, "The unholy alliance between the tariff collector and the local monopolist is a long-standing one." Numerous statistical studies support Professor Caves by showing an inverse relationship between industry profits and import penetration.[22] That is to say, import competition constrains domestic pricing. Conversely, to the extent tariffs and quotas repress imports they therefore also boost domestic monopoly power.

What is more, the benefits of import competition often go beyond price. Accumulated evidence indicates that over the past thirty years foreign auto producers have been, on the whole, more innovative and more quality con-

[22] L. Esposito and E. F. Esposito, "Foreign Competition and Domestic Industry Profitability," *Review of Economics and Statistics* (November 1971), pp. 343–53; E. Pagoulatos and R. Sorenson, "International Trade, International Investment and Industrial Profitability in U.S. Manufacturing," *Southern Economic Journal* (January 1976), pp. 425–34; T. A. Pugel, "Foreign Trade and U.S. Market Performance," *Journal of Industrial Economics* (December 1980), pp. 119–29.

scious as well as more price competitive than domestic producers. Who led the way with disk brakes, fuel efficiency, diesel engines, compact styling, and better "fits and finishes"? Was it Detroit? The growth of auto imports shown in Figure 26–4, from 6.1 per cent of the U.S. market in 1965 to 26.8 per cent in 1981, suggests the answer. Datson, Toyota, Honda, and their brethren have checked the market power of GM, Ford, and Chrysler, preventing what otherwise would be tight-knit oligopoly and pushing the domestic Big Three toward better overall performance.[23]

2. THE CASE AGAINST FREE TRADE

There are of course many arguments against free trade, but they need not detain us. From the viewpoint of society as a whole, protectionism cannot be defended. As P. T. Ellsworth wrote long ago:

> The case for free trade has never been successfully refuted, nor even has an intellectually acceptable argument for long-run, enduring protection, based on economic considerations, ever been devised, though much ingenuity has gone into the attempt. The arguments for protection that do have validity are either short-run or noneconomic in character, or require the realization of very special conditions. Yet most of the arguments advanced by protectionists are unqualified, asserted with great conviction, and what is more important, are widely believed.[24]

Melvyn Krauss put it somewhat differently:

> The conflict between the economic interests of specific groups within the community and the economic interests of the community as a whole is the essence of the free trade versus protectionism controversy. Free traders argue from the standpoint of the overall economy; protectionists

argue from the standpoint of particular interest groups.[25]

It might seem, for example, that if anything could justify protection, national defense could. Self-sufficiency in such "essential" industries as aircraft, optical instruments, explosives, and electronics might be deemed necessary to self-preservation. Reliance on foreign suppliers for these goods could be considered too risky. Yet full acceptance of these judgments does not justify tariffs or quotas against imports of these crucial goods. The best means of promoting self-sufficiency in these instances is direct subsidies. Direct subsidies funded from income taxes are more *equitable* than tariffs or quotas because they spread the cost burden of supporting national defense among taxpayers at large rather than concentrate the burden on consumers of optical instruments, electrical devices, and other protected products. Moreover, it can be shown that direct subsidies are more *efficient* than tariffs or quotas in supporting crucial domestic industries.[26]

3. THE BASIC ECONOMICS OF TARIFFS AND QUOTAS

If we assume a standardized final product like textiles, produced under competitive conditions at home, and displaying perfectly elastic supply in the world market, the impact of im-

---

[23] For details see Lawrence J. White, *The Automobile Industry Since 1945* (Cambridge: Harvard University Press, 1971) and U.S. Congress, House, Subcommittee on Trade of the Committee on Ways and Means, *Auto Situation: 1980* (Washington, D.C.: 1980).

[24] P. T. Ellsworth, *The International Economy* (New York: Macmillan, 1964), p. 219 (emphasis in original).

[25] Melvyn B. Krauss, *The New Protectionism: The Welfare State and International Trade* (New York: New York University Press, 1978), p. 6.

[26] One of the most common protectionist arguments now circulating is the diversification argument, which decries the sinking competitive position of the U.S. auto and steel industries. Services are booming, but these basic manufactures are languishing. Thus AFL–CIO President Kirkland urges protection because we "must be a diversified manufacturing, agricultural and service economy." Senator Riegle of Michigan backs him up, "We cannot all be just making McDonald's hamburgers for one another." But this argument likewise suffers flaws. See the debate between Riegle and Henry Wallich in U.S. Senate, Subcommittee on Industrial Growth and Productivity of the Committee on the Budget, *Industrial Growth and Productivity*, Hearings, 97th Congress, 1st Session (1981), pp. 137–144, 160–175. See also Ellsworth, *op. cit.*, pp. 222–23.

port restraints is easily understood with the aid of Figure 26–5. S_d represents the domestic supply curve, and D_d the domestic demand curve. S_f indicates that foreign supply is perfectly elastic at world price P_w; that is, as much or as little can be purchased at price P_w as desired. With free trade domestic price would equal the world price, $P_d = P_w$, and the supply curve confronting domestic consumers would be, first, the low-cost portion of S_d below $P_d = P_w$ in the lower left-hand corner plus, second, the portion of foreign supply S_f spanning quantity range XY. Thus, with free trade, consumers are charged price P_w and they buy OX from domestic producers plus imports of XY from foreign producers for a total consumption of OY.

Tariffs. A tariff of T per unit would be like a tax on imports, lifting the price of imports above the world price P_w to P_t. This tariff inflated price P_t then establishes a new domestic price P_d' above the old domestic price P_d. The consequences of this tariff for quantity are that domestic consumption *falls* from OY to OY' while domestic production *rises* from OX to

Figure 26–5. The Effects of Tariffs and Quotas

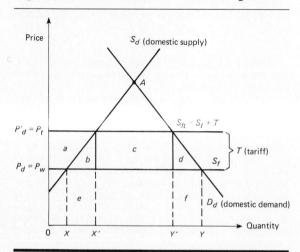

OX'. Imports are thus pinched back by the tariff from XY under free trade to $X'Y'$. Clearly, if the tariff were still higher, imports would be pinched further until in the end they could be reduced to zero at the intersection of S_d and D_d, point A.

Recalling that multiplication of a dollar-per-unit value times the number of units yields a total dollar result, we know that the economic effects of the tariff can be divided in four parts corresponding to areas a, b, c, and d in Figure 26–5:

a. The redistribution effect.
b. The loss-due-to-production effect.
c. The tariff revenue effect.
d. The loss-due-to-consumption effect.

Taken together $(a + b + c + d)$ these areas comprise a total loss to consumers corresponding to their lost consumers' surplus. Area a is called the redistribution effect because it is a transfer from consumers to domestic producers. The move from quantity X and price P_d to quantity X' and price P_d' increases the total revenue of domestic producers by amount $a + b + e$. Portion $b + e$ represents increased domestic costs of production, so a is added rent or windfall profit to producers.

Area b, the loss-due-to-production effect, depicts that portion of total added production cost, $b + e$, which is rather senseless. Quantity XX' could either be imported at total cost e, or produced domestically at higher total cost $e + b$. The difference, b, shows a sacrifice in production efficiency from the tariff, a violation of the principle of comparative advantage.

Area c is the total revenue the government gains from the tariff. Multiplying imported quantity $X'Y'$ by tariff rate T yields area c. Notice that if the tariff were so high as to cause zero imports, there would be no tariff revenue at all.

Finally, area d, the loss-due-to-consumption effect, is the lost consumers' surplus associated with the decline in consumption from Y to Y'. This is analogous to the loss in consumers' surplus resulting from monopoly pricing (or, conversely, the efficiency gain associated with elimination of monopoly) depicted many chapters ago in Figure 3–1 on page 46.

In short, two of the four areas, a and c, amount to *transfers or redistributions* from domestic consumers to others—to domestic producers in the case of a and to government in the case of c. The two remaining areas, b and d, represent *efficiency or welfare losses*. They amount to consumer losses not recouped by others in society.

Quotas. A quota works not on price directly, as does a tariff, but rather on *quantity*. A quota on steel, for instance, might say that no more than 10 million tons of steel can be imported annually. Because the effects of a quota resemble those of a tariff, Figure 26–5 can depict a quota if we imagine that the quantity of imports legally allowed is $X'Y'$, down from the free-trade volume of XY. Supply thus restricted, domestic price is again bumped up to P_d', which is above the old domestic price P_d and above the continuing world price P_w. As a consequence, consumers lose combined area $a + b + c + d$, as under a tariff.

Of this total loss, areas a, b, and d entail losses comparable to those experienced under a tariff, namely, (*a*) a redistribution effect, (*b*) a loss-due-to-production effect, and (*d*) a loss-due-to-consumption effect. The main difference between a tariff and a quota lies in the fact that, under a quota, area c does *not* represent tariff revenue. Area c might go to domestic firms in the business of importing who buy at world price P_w and sell at domestic price P_d'. Area c might be captured by the domestic government if import licenses for the amount $X'Y'$ are auctioned off to high bidders. It might go to foreign suppliers granted quota "allotments," which suppliers then price discriminate by charging us P_d' while charging everyone

else the world market price P_w. In other words, disposition of c depends on how the quota is administered. Indeed, it could be some mix of these possibilities.

Voluntary Export Restraints. Since the first half of this century, when ardent protectionism produced lofty tariff rates averaging 40, 50, and even 60 per cent, tariffs have fallen substantially here and abroad. Levered down by several "rounds" of multinational negotiations, average tariff rates now lie in the neighborhood of 5 per cent.[27] This liberalism fostered a stupendous sixfold increase in the volume of international trade between 1948 and 1978. However, partly in reaction to these swelling trade flows, a movement toward "new protectionism" has been building since 1973. In Europe, new protectionism has fostered an outbreak of regular quotas. In the U.S., new protectionism has spawned a variety of voluntary export restraints.

As illustrated by our introductory story on Japanese autos, *voluntary export restraints* are similar to quotas in that they constitute quantitative restrictions. They differ from regular quotas, however, because they are not imposed unilaterally by the *importing* country against those in the outside world. Rather, they are "voluntarily" agreed to by selected *exporting* countries, usually in the belief that such self restraint will forestall importing countries from imposing stiff tariffs or quotas. In economic impact, voluntary export restraints differ from quotas primarily by what happens to area c in Figure 26–5. Whereas the destination of those c revenues can vary under regular quotas, it ends up in the exporting country under voluntary export restraints because the exporting country is the one administering the restraint. Indeed, the inticement offered by area c's scar-

[27] A. V. Deardorff and R. M. Stern, *An Economic Analysis of the Effects of the Tokyo Round of Multilateral Trade Negotiations*, U.S. Senate, Committee on Finance, Subcommittee on International Trade (June 1979), pp. 41–44.

Table 26–1. The Economic Impact of Import Restrictions on Four Products, Late 1970's[a] (Millions of Dollars)

Economic Cost to Consumers	Radios	Sugar	Nonrubber Footwear	Apparel
Redistribution effect, a (subsidy to producers)	6.5	731	N.A.[b]	N.A.[b]
Loss due to inefficiency $b + d$	26.1	155	589	1,532
Tariff revenue effect or quota scarcity rent, c	81.8	984	436	3,541
Total consumer cost $(a + b + c + d)$	114.4	1,560	1,025	5,073

[a] The estimates are cumulative over four years except for CB radios, which are three-year estimates.
[b] Not possible to estimate.

Source: Morris E. Morkre and David G. Tarr, Effects of Restrictions on United States Imports (Washington, D.C., Federal Trade Commission, 1980), p. 197.

city rents encourages exporters to cooperate with importers. They "volunteer," in other words, in part because they are "bought off."

These voluntary export restraints can be informal, as in the case of Japanese autos, or they can be formal, as in the case of textiles. A so-called Multifiber Agreement has governed world textile trade since 1977. At present, the accord sets guidelines holding exports of major Asian producers to the U.S. and European Common Market at a growth rate not to exceed 2 per cent per year.[28]

Cost Estimates. If the total dollar cost to U.S. consumers caused by tariffs, quotas, and voluntary export restraints were ever added up, the number would probably run tens of billions. We do not really know what the sum is because estimation of areas a, b, c, and d in Figure 26–5 is difficult for even *one* product, let alone *all* the products effected by import restrictions. Nevertheless, Table 26–1 is suggestive. It gives the estimated total consumer cost of restraints on four products, broken down by the designa-

[28] *Wall Street Journal,* December 23, 1981, p. 19.

tions of Figure 26–5, and accumulated over four years in the late 1970s (except for CB radios which is a three-year estimate). The totals range from $114.4 million for CB radios to just over $5 billion for apparel. Combined, they come to $7.8 billion. We need not strain to imagine, then, that a similar sum, if calculated for all protected commodities, would indeed be a princely sum.

B. *Import Protection in Steel*

1. ECONOMIC BACKGROUND

The American steel industry's current battle against imports is rooted in the 1960s, when imports leaped from 4.7% of domestic consumption in 1960 to 16.7% in 1968. Imports dipped a bit in the mid-1970s, reaching a low of 12.4% in 1973; but they rebounded thereafter, crossing the 20% mark in 1981.

Why has the steel industry, virile symbol of our industrial might for nearly a century, withered in world stature? Why has it been reduced to whining for official protection? The *short* answer is that foreign steel, especially that of Japan, has been $100 to $150 a ton cheaper (in 1981 dollars) than the domestic version. Because steel is a standardized product, steel sheets, tubes, beams, rods, and plates from abroad are physically identical to those from U.S. mills. Competition therefore centers on price—not packaging, brand image, or even patriotism—and U.S. producers have not been fully price competitive.

The *long* answer attempts to explain *why* the American steel industry has not been fully price competitive. That answer, if wholly developed, would indeed be very long because of the many possible considerations. Among other things, it has been alleged that:

1. Foreign governments subsidize their steel producers.
2. Foreign steelworkers are paid slave wages.
3. Domestic technology lags behind foreign technology, creating a disparity in productivity.
4. Environmental regulations impose greater costs on domestic producers than foreign rivals.
5. The oligopolistic domestic firms, in attempting to gain monopoly profits, have overpriced their product.

Sifting through these possibilities, a number of in-depth studies of steel's predicament find a bit of truth in each of these accusations, but only a bit.[29] It is estimated, for instance, that foreign governments subsidized their steel industries in the late 1960s and early 1970s, but only by a few dollars a ton (i.e., less than 1% of price).[30] Lately, however, foreign subsidies seem larger. As for technology and productivity, there is some evidence that U.S. producers have lagged behind Japanese and European steelmakers in adopting several revolutionary production innovations—basic oxygen process and continuous casting in particular. But during the late 1970s the productivity of American steelworkers was about equal to that of the Japanese and considerably better than the West Germans, French, and English, so these lags have not severely damaged basic efficiency.[31]

In sum, those five possible factors are relatively minor when compared to a sixth—extraordinarily high U.S. steelworker wages. In 1970, steelworker hourly earnings were already 26% above the average for all U.S. manufacturing. By 1981 they were well over 60% above the U.S. average. High by domestic standards, U.S. steelworker earnings are also high by international standards despite the fact that foreign steelworkers are pretty well paid. When coupled with the fact that U.S. productivity is not fantastically better than that abroad, the result is comparatively lofty labor costs per ton of U.S. steel. In 1976, for which several estimates are available, U.S. labor costs were nearly $160 per ton while Japanese labor costs were only $60 per ton, a difference roughly equal to ultimate price difference per ton.[32] Such are the consequences, in large part, of a strong steelworkers' union in the United States. Indeed, steadily declining employment in steel since 1966 should have prompted wage moderation, not skyward momentum.

---

[29] These studies include Kiyoshi Kawahito, *The Japanese Steel Industry with an Analysis of the U.S. Steel Import Problem* (New York: Praeger, 1972); Council on Wage Price Stability, *Prices and Costs in the United States Steel Industry* (Washington, D.C.: October 1977); R. M. Duke, *et al.*, *The United States Steel Industry and Its International Rivals: Trends and Factors Determining International Competitiveness* (Washington, D.C.: Federal Trade Commission, 1977); U.S. Congress, Office of Technology Assessment, *Technology and Steel Industry Competitiveness* (Washington, D.C.: 1980); Douglas R. Sease and Urban C. Lehner, a series of articles, *Wall Street Journal*, April 2, 1981, pp. 1, 19; April 7, 1981, pp. 1, 19; April 10, 1981, pp. 1, 17.

[30] R. M. Duke, *et al.*, *op. cit.*, pp. 311–369.

[31] In 1978, the number of employee hours required to produce a ton of steel in the U.S. was 8.63, Japan 9.79, W. Germany 11.82, France 14.12, and the U.K. 23.21. Office of Technology Assessment, *Technology and Steel . . .* , *op. cit.*; p. 138.

[32] Ibid., p. 135.

2. PROTECTIONIST POLICY

Steelworker pay envelopes might have thinned instead of fattened if the U.S. government had been less protective of the industry. Recent protection began in 1969 when "voluntary" export restraints were added to the existing tariff of about 6 per cent. Negotiated by the Department of State, these voluntary restraints set import quotas on Japanese and European steel. It was said at the time that the voluntary quotas would be only temporary. Moreover, the rationale was that their shelter would give domestic firms an opportunity to modernize, rejuvenate, and restore competitiveness.

The voluntary quotas lasted six years, during which time domestic steel production was as much as 10 per cent above levels that would have been likely without quotas. Profits also jumped a bit.[33] Still, the promised revitalization went slowly.

In 1974, when steel's voluntary quotas expired, Congress passed the Trade Act Amendments of 1974. Although of no immediate aid to the steel industry, this legislation clarified the President's power to negotiate voluntary export restraints and tightened the legal definition of "dumping." Under the old Antidumping Act of 1921, it was unlawful for foreigners to "dump" products on the U.S. market at prices less than the *prices they charged at home.* Under the 1974 Amendments it became unlawful for foreigners to "dump" products in the U.S. at prices less than their *cost of production, including overhead costs of at least 10 per cent of direct costs, plus an 8 per cent profit margin.* This new standard placed a higher floor under import prices than before. If, for example, steel

prices in Japan are pressed down by recession to the point of yielding zero profit, the Japanese could not sell in the U.S. except at prices *higher* than at home. The consequences of illegal "dumping" are in any case the same as under the old law. If it can be shown (1) that products are in fact being "dumped" in the U.S. at "unfair" prices, and (2) that this injures domestic producers, then punative protective action may ensue. The Commerce Department and the United States International Trade Commission share responsibility for determining the facts and imposing antidumping duties against foreign goods, a responsibility that can be met only by following complex procedures.

The 1974 legislation was of no immediate use to the steel industry because world economic conditions held steel imports down during the mid-1970s. This gave the domestic industry still more time to revitalize vis-a-vis its foreign rivals, but apparently to little avail. Imports surged toward 18% of domestic consumption in 1977, up from 14% in 1976, as worldwide excess capacity encouraged worldwide price-cutting. Unable to stem the renewed tide of imports on its own, the U.S. industry turned to the government again, threatening to file a barrage of antidumping suits under the 1974 law. If successful, these suits could have contributed to inflation at home and ill will abroad, so the Carter administration made an offer to the steel industry: In exchange for the industry's withdrawal of its antidumping suits, the administration promised to protect the industry with a "trigger-price mechanism." Government offers of new loan guarantees and other aides sweetened the deal, and the industry accepted.

Thus it was that from 1978 through 1981, the government announced "trigger prices" based on Japanese costs of production plus freight to America. For example, $422.95 per ton was the trigger price for the second quarter of 1981. These prices were *minimum* price tar-

[33] Office of Technology Assessment, *U.S. Industrial Competitiveness, op. cit.,* p. 111. See also Walter Adams and Joel Dirlam, "Import Quotas and Industrial Performance," in Jacquemin and deJong (eds.) *Welfare Aspects of Industrial Markets* (Leiden, Netherlands: Martinus Nijhoff, 1977), pp. 165–172.

gets for all foreigners, not just the Japanese, because products priced below the trigger level would trigger expedited antidumping investigations. With few exceptions foreign exporters kept above trigger levels, so U.S. (and world prices) rose. Robert Crandall estimates that the trigger-price policy "raised U.S. steel import prices by about 10 per cent and domestic steel prices by about 1 per cent through 1979," for a total cost to American consumers of "about $1 billion."[34]

Even so, the domestic industry grew disgruntled. The trigger prices were set too low it said. Evasion was rampant because of poor enforcement it said. More importantly, 1981 saw steel imports running over 20% of the U.S. market for the first time. Thus, as this is written (in early 1982), U.S. Steel, Bethlehem, and the other big steel companies have 100 antidumping suits in the works against 41 steelmakers in 11 countries, apparently unconcerned that the Reagan administration will scrap trigger pricing as a result.[35] Moreover, the industry will apparently win added protection.

One interesting twist to this story is that, as with quotas, the trigger prices were supposed to provide temporary cover for American steel's modernization through investment and innovation. After four years, however, the industry is still struggling. Investments have been made, but they have not and cannot be expected to work miracles, especially not in light of the fact that the U.S. industry has been and still is one of the most (if not *the* most) productively efficient in the world. To this writer, the main problem is not so much outmoded plants as it is outlandish wages. (Maybe the industry is beginning to realize this. Rather than invest all the fruits of their trigger-price protec-

tion in steel's rejuvenation, U.S. Steel has acquired Marathon Oil Company for $6.4 billion, National Steel has been buying up savings and loan operations, and Armco has bought an insurance company. These conglomerate acquisitions raised eyebrows, even among folks whose probusiness credentials could never be questioned.)[36]

To summarize, import restrictions serve as a major protectionist instrument—costly to consumers and society as a whole, but coveted dearly by special interests. No solid economic case can be made for such protectionism, not even national defense. Yet it persists. Tariffs declined substantially after World War II, only to be partially replaced by quantitative restrictions and a newly tightened defintion of illegal "dumping." Such have been the shelters provided to American steel on the understanding that the industry could use the opportunity to revitalize, benefiting U.S. society as a whole. But the performance of the steel industry over more than a decade has yet to disprove the economic principle that protectionism can be little more than special privilege.

IV. Price Supports: Agriculture

The U.S. Department of Agriculture has one bureaucrat for every twenty-five American farms. They administer a dazzling array of promotion and protection programs for our largest industry (whose crop, livestock, and dairy sales exceed $130 billion annually). There are loans and loan guarantees for equipment, feed, seed, housing, electrical power, telephone service, emergencies, flood prevention, conservation, and even youth programs. There are direct sub-

[34] Robert W. Crandall, "Steel Imports: Dumping or Competition?" *Regulation* (July/August 1980), p. 23.

[35] *Business Week*, January 25, 1982, pp. 27–28; *Wall Street Journal*, January 11, 1982, p. 2; January 12, 1982; p. 48.

[36] See the editorials in the *Wall Street Journal*, November 24, 1981, p. 26; December 7, 1981, p. 26; and *Business Week*, December 7, 1981, p. 144.

sidies for irrigation water, agricultural research, and marketing information. Tariffs and quotas fend off imports of meat, sugar, peanuts, and dairy products. Tax breaks abound. And marketing cartels enjoy exemption from the Sherman Antitrust Act.

Of special interest to us are **price supports** and **direct income payments,** two policies of old lineage differing from those of preceding sections. We proceed by first outlining the problems these policies are supposed to cure. An explanation of the operation of these policies comes next, followed in conclusion by a critique.

A. Agriculture's Problems[37]

Today's agricultural policy represents a watered-down version of what started fifty years ago during the Great Depression. Little wonder, then, that the farm problems allegedly addressed by current policy—instability and poverty—cast especially dark shadows in those days, source of many of the following statistics.

1. INSTABILITY

Over time, farm prices and incomes trace a silhouette that looks like the skyline of a mountain range. Ups and downs in corn prices produced a wild coefficient of annual variation of 28 per cent during 1910–1949. Over the twelve recent months of 1981 cotton prices plummeted from 87¢ to 57¢ a pound. From a broader perspective, the net income of all farmers gyrated from $18.7 billion to $33.3 billion and back to $18.7 during the mid-1970s.

What causes this instability? It is a combination of what may be called internal and external conditions. The *internal conditions* determine

the *shape* of agriculture's demand and supply curves plus *location* on those curves. The *external conditions* produce *shifts* of demand and supply. Taken alone, neither the internal nor external conditions exert jolting influences. But taken together they can knock farmers around handily.

In particular, there are four internal conditions:

a. *Pure Competition:* With a very large number of producers, fairly easy entry, and standardized products, agriculture is one of the few industries that can be characterized as purely competitive. There are, for instance, over 90,000 cotton farmers in the U.S. And Grade AA white eggs are the same no matter whose chickens lay them.

b. *Gestation Period:* The time span between crop planting and harvesting or between livestock birth and maturity creates a lag between farm inputs and outputs. Cows, for example, have only one calf each year, and the calf isn't ready for market until it's almost two years old. Rough guesses about future market conditions consequently guide today's decisions, which in turn determine next season's output.

c. *Inelastic Demand:* A 10 per cent drop in the price of corn stimulates only a 2 per cent increase in quantity demanded. Quantity demanded is also unresponsive to price changes for wheat, milk, and other basic farm commodities because of their necessity to consumers. (Inelasticity also stems from the fact that, on average, farmers get only 40 cents of the consumer's dollar after transportation and processing.)

d. *Inelastic Supply:* Large swings in price likewise fail to generate large changes in quantities supplied, especially in the short run. Once a crop is planted, near-term supply is fairly fixed. Once buildings and equipment are designed for dairy farming, they cannot

[37] Basic references include Dale E. Hathaway, *Government and Agriculture: Economic Policy in a Democratic Society* (New York: Macmillan, 1963) and Leonard W. Weiss, *Case Studies in American Industry* (New York: John Wiley & Sons, 1980), pp. 21–89.

easily be converted to orchard operations. The same is true for other outputs.

To oversimplify, condition (a) denies farmers any monopolistic control over their prices or quantities, so prices and quantities tend toward equilibrium at the intersection of demand and supply. Gestation condition (b) means that movement from one equilibrium to another may not be smooth. Inelasticity conditions (c) and (d) make demand and supply curves very steep, implying that price must rise or fall markedly to close gaps in demand and supply.

Figure 26–6 partially illustrates the consequences for instability. Competition pushes price toward equilibrium points like E, E', or E^*. With inelastic supply shifting from S_1 to S_2 and back to S_1 against inelastic demand curve D_i, price lurches from P_1 to P_2, creating a choppy price pattern over time. In contrast, the same to and fro shifting of supply against elastic demand D_e generates a smoother price pattern over time because price fluctuates between P_1 and P_3 instead of P_1 and P_2.

If supply stood still at S_1 in Figure 26–6, and if demand curve D_i remained stable, there would of course be no movement away from E. *External conditions* thus contribute to instability by causing *shifts* in supply and demand:

a. *Supply Side:* Capricious weather, crop diseases, and injurious pestilence shift supply about. Freezes in January, 1982 damaged Florida's pole bean crop, lifting price from $12 to $20 a bushel within a week. Conversely, especially good weather in 1979 boosted California's artichoke output 40%, driving price down to $4 a carton from $10 the year before.

b. *Demand Side:* Domestic demand shifts with the general business cycle. Foreign demand for U.S. crops varies with the success or failure of crops abroad. Now, with about 1 out of every 3 acres of U.S. farm land producing for exports, swings in export demand pack a wallop.

Agreeing that the combination of these external and internal conditions causes sharp disturbances, you may nevertheless wonder, "Why is any government intervention needed? Aren't other industries also unstable?" To be sure they are, so our discussion should acknowl-

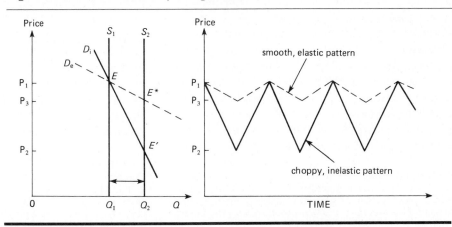

Figure 26–6. Price Instability in Agriculture

edge the fact that agriculture is more unstable than most industries. Moreover, when stabilization policies were first formulated during the Great Depression, one-quarter of the population was rural, giving farmers powerful political clout. Finally, it can be argued that stability, if achieved by policy, promotes farm efficiency and productivity. Without stability, farmers would try to protect themselves by investing in nonproductive cash reserves rather than productive buildings, machinery, and equipment. Without stability, farmers would also tend to hedge their bets through diversified farming even though specialized farming proves more efficient.

2. POVERTY

Were stability the only problem, agricultural policies could be aimed solely at price or income stabilization, but they haven't been. They have also aimed at price and income *elevation* and *maintenance*. The reason for this may be seen in a few statistics that fertilized the roots of present policy. In 1939, income per capita of the farm population averaged only 37% of nonfarm income. Two decades later farm folk were only half as well off as city folk. A large part of the problem lay in chronic output abundance, which tended to depress farm prices and incomes. Rapid productivity growth pushed crop supply curves to the right faster than demand shifted with expanding population and personal income. Cotton yield per acre, for instance, leaped from 191 to 524 pounds between the mid-30s and mid-60s. More broadly, whereas one farmer formerly produced food and fiber for nine other people, he or she now produces enough for 55 others.[38] Hybrid seeds, pesticides, fertilizers, and modern farm equip-

ment have, in short, wrought production miracles which may have contributed to economic woes.

Still, caution flags must be raised. These numbers misleadingly suggest that all farmers suffer downtrodden fates when in fact their earnings vary widely. Some face poverty, but many enjoy riches. Moreover, their fortunes as a class have improved dramatically in recent decades. Guided by the old disparity of nonfarm over farm income, farmworker population shrunk from 11 to 4 million between 1940 and 1970. The migration from country to city simultaneously reduced the income disparity to a small fraction. This in turn stemmed further outmigration after 1970. There are, to be sure, still variations in earnings across farmers and across time. But on the whole, current long-run profit performance is not as bad as farmers claim in their annual appeals to Congress for aid. As Tom Alexander observes, "The after-tax rate of return on farming assets between 1975 and 1979—a period that included both good and bad years—averaged about 9.6% a year, considerably better than the 0.59% return from stocks and a minus 4.5% from bonds during the same period."[39] But we're getting ahead of our story. We will return to agriculture's current economic health after reviewing price and income supports.

B. Government Policy

If simple stability were the sole objective of government policy, official intervention would not attempt to influence average price, only the *amplitude* of price's peaks and valleys. Government might do this, for instance, with an

---

[38] This does not take account of our large net exports which would probably boost the number past 60. For statistics such as these see any basic annual, such as the *Economic Report of the President*, or *Statistical Abstract of the United States.*

[39] Tom Alexander, "Free the Farm 2½ Million," *Fortune,* October 19, 1981, p. 117. Indeed, an interesting bit of trivia is that Idaho has more millionaires per capita than any other state, in large part because of the prominence of farmers in Idaho's economy and their valuable holdings of farm land.

"ever-normal granary," buying up part of bumper crops when price is low, storing the purchases, and then selling out of storage when crops are poor and prices are high. The buying would lift the low prices above what they would otherwise be, and the selling would hold the high prices down below what they would otherwise be. Price fluctuations would thus be reduced while average price level remained untouched. The idea is an old one, dating back to ancient China. And in theory it is a good one. In practice, however, there are problems—such as inappropriateness for perishable crops like lettuce and uncertainty in knowing exactly when to buy and sell. In any case, this is *not* the concept guiding U.S. policy because stability has not been the sole objective. Aims of income elevation and maintenance were grafted onto stability, so *price supports,* supplemented by *direct income payments,* have been the focus of U.S. policy. In turn, this focus has necessitated various *supply restrictions.*

1. PRICE SUPPORTS

Rather than be guided by estimated average equilibrium prices, as would be determined by long-run market conditions and fitting for the operation of an ever-normal granary, Congress and the Department of Agriculture have used various standards of *"fairness"* in setting price support levels. From the 1930s to the early 1970s the standard was "**parity.**" This standard assumed that farmers received "fair" prices for their crops relative to their costs during 1910–1914, when farming was particularly prosperous. This "fairness" eroded over ensuing years when prices farmers *received* for their crops did not rise as much as prices they *paid* for fuel, machinery, clothing, and other things. Hence the idea was to support farm prices near "parity" by lifting them in step with other prices. To illustrate by hypothetical example, the parity price for corn would now be $5 a bushel if in 1910–1914 corn was priced at $1

a bushel and since that time the prices corn farmers paid had gone up five-fold. Price support at parity would then require that the government guarantee $5 a bushel to corn farmers. The absurdity of pegging everything to 1910–1914 caught up with the farm program during the 1950s, forcing a modification in the parity formula, and then overtook it in the 1970s, causing government to introduce large departures from the parity standard. Now "fairness" is largely determined by simple reference to present costs of production (somewhat in the fashion of public utility pricing), although the Department of Agriculture still publishes parity prices for farm commodities, and support prices for a few products are still expressed as percentages of parity.

The mechanics of the price support program are essentially as follows. Before planting season, the Secretary of Agriculture announces a price support level for each of the covered crops—mainly cotton, wheat, rice, feed grains, soybeans, peanuts, and tobacco (less than half of all farm marketings). If after harvest the market price is low, farmers can store their output, borrowing from the government's Commodity Credit Corporation (CCC) amounts equal to the value of the goods when priced at support level. If market price later rises *above* support level, farmers can then sell their goods on the market and repay the loans from the proceeds, keeping for themselves the difference between market and support price. If market price remains *below* support level, the loan may be paid in full by turning the goods over to the government.

The simple economics of the system are illustrated in Figure 26–7 for cotton. Free-market price would be 50 cents a pound, as determined by the interaction of supply and demand. Corresponding quantity would be 7 billion pounds. Setting support price at 80 cents a pound would dislodge the market from this equilibrium, with free market demand taking no more than 5 billion pounds. If supply were not artificially

Figure 26–7.   Price Support for Cotton

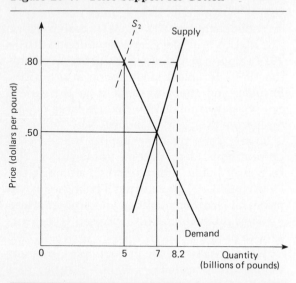

mid-1970s because free market prices were unusually high, relieving government of the burden of supporting them. But the subsidies returned to quite similar magnitudes during 1978–1980.[41] Annual outlays under President Reagan will probably be lower at roughly $3 billion from taxpayers and $2–$3 billion from consumers.

2. DIRECT INCOME PAYMENTS

Rather than go through all the rigmarole of CCC loans, surplus purchases, and the rest (which is actually so confusing as to leave even farmers perplexed),[42] the government could of course just pay farmers the difference between market price and some supposedly "fair" price. In Figure 26–7, for instance, the government could simply pay farmers 30 cents a pound on no more than 7 billion pounds (distributed proportionately among cotton farmers according to past output). If market price fell below 50 cents, the payments could expand accordingly. In comparison to price supports, such direct income payments would result in lower, market-clearing prices. In turn, lower market-clearing prices would yield many favorable effects. They would:

- eliminate consumer-paid subsidies, thereby benefiting the poor, who spend a larger portion of their income on food than the rich,
- eliminate government purchases of surpluses,
- eliminate the need for import restrictions (which have protected crops like sugar and peanuts, whose support price is usually above world market price).

One drawback with direct payments is that taxpayers would have to pay more to keep farmers

restricted, the government would then have to buy up (collect in loan payments) all output in excess of 5 billion pounds, which in this case, 3.2 billion pounds, is the difference between 8.2 and 5. At support price of 80 cents a pound, that would cost the government $2.56 billion. This subsidy would show up on the government's budget books, and come out of taxpayers' pockets. In addition there is a hidden subsidy paid by consumers through a higher market price, namely, $1.5 billion in this case, which is the price difference, 30 cents, times 5 billion pounds.

To flesh this out with some real numbers, over 1968–1970 taxpayers paid farmers about $5 billion annually while consumers paid $4.5 billion more annually in higher prices. The total subsidy thus approached $10 billion yearly.[40] These subsidies lessened substantially in the

[40] Charles L. Schultze, *The Distribution of Farm Subsidies* (Washington, D.C.: Brookings Institution, 1971) pp. 1, 22–25.

[41] *Economic Report of the President 1980*, pp. 284–285 and *Wall Street Journal* August 14, 1979, pp 1, 22.

[42] See Terri Minsky, "Farmers' Confusion on Corn Reserve Plan Could Lead to Problems at Harvest Time," *Wall Street Journal*, September 25, 1980, p. 38.

equally well off once the consumers' burden is reduced by lower prices. But that taxpayer burden would not be greater than the *combined* taxpayer plus consumer burden of price supports. Moreover, because the federal tax structure tends to be income progressive, the shift to taxpayers would likely be more equitable to society's poor.

Another drawback to direct income payments is that, despite their economic advantages, they have been opposed by farmland's politicians. With price supports, the consumer's part of the subsidy is hidden. With direct payments, the entire subsidy is in the federal budget for all to see—embarassingly so. Though perennially proposed from the late 1940s on, direct payments were always shunned by Congress until the Food and Agriculture Act of 1977, which finally introduced a timid form of direct payments for wheat, cotton, and feed grains. Still, price supports were not abandoned for these crops. Instead, support prices (i.e., loan prices) were lowered below what they would have been, and direct payments were made to cover the difference between these lower support prices and higher "target" prices. For example, the support price for wheat in 1978 was $2.35 a bushel (guaranteed by CCC loan to participating farmers) and the target price was higher at $3.40 a bushel (guaranteed by direct payments for a portion of the crop of participating farmers). Thus if market price fell to, say, $2.15 a bushel, participating farmers could get $2.35 through price support loans plus $1.05 ($3.40 − $2.35) in direct payments for the quantity of their output so covered.[43]

This rather tentative, partial acceptance of direct payments became even more tentative when the Reagan administration's policy for

1982–85 backed away from but did not abolish "target prices." The stated reason: budget cutting. The result: a return to support prices for the backbone of farm policy.

3. SUPPLY RESTRICTIONS

Depending on how high support prices are set and what market conditions prevail, the surpluses CCC might acquire could be quite high. During the 1950s these surpluses grew mountainous. At the end of 1960, for instance, CCC's pantry was bulging with enough wheat to feed all Americans for two years. Ploys to dispose of such surpluses have proliferated over the years—crop destruction, foreign aid, domestic welfare grants, and school lunch larding, some of which are still with us to some degree. In 1981 the government handed out roughly $2 billion in surplus milk products, much of it in low-priced sales abroad. (And we accuse others of dumping!)

But of course the best attack against the problem of surpluses (aside from abolishing price supports above equilibrium levels) is supply constraint. Figure 26–7 shows that the surplus of 3.2 billion pounds (8.2 − 5) would vanish if the supply curve could be held back to S_2. This is the essential idea behind various official and artificial production restraints that have from time to time graced agricultural policy:

- *Permanent acreage allotments* restrict planting to a fixed number of plots having official permits. More common thirty years ago than now, this technique is still used for tobacco and peanuts.
- *Land set-asides* induce grain farmers to restrict planting by offering rewards of price supports (and/or direct income payments) to those who participate. Farmers are given a choice—they either reduce their acreage in the support crop (by percentages that vary yearly) and receive protection, or strike out on their own, plant all they want, and forgo government guarantees.

[43] For details see USDA, *Policy Research Notes*, No. 8, July 1979, pp. 6–7 or Congressional Budget Office, *Food and Agriculture Policy Options* (Washington, D.C.: 1977).

• *Marketing agreements* are encouraged by federal laws for some dairymen, orchard owners, and vegetable farmers. These organizations may require their members to withhold or destroy some of their crop. These restrictions need not be associated with specific official price supports, although they elevate price indirectly.

Some idea of the magnitude of past supply restraints can be kindled if America's *total* crop acreage of 350 million acres is mentally compared to some annual figures on set-asides for wheat and feed grains. In each of the years 1963, 1967, and 1973 more than *60 million acres* were withheld from production. Set-asides slipped toward zero in 1975–76 because massive crop failures abroad hoisted export demand sharply. But they bounced back to the 20 million acre range as the 1980s began. Do you notice any irony in a subsidy program that discourages rather than encourages output?

C. A Critique of Farm Policy

Many harsh critics of U.S. farm policy favor *some* protection for farmers against temporary downside economic and natural disasters. Hendrik Houthakker of Harvard, for instance, advocates "a distress-loan rate set at very low support levels to temper the extreme variations in crop prices that make it so hard for farmers to plan their capital expenditures and thus to increase their efficiency."[44] As practiced, however, farm policy has been less of a safety net and more of a dole (a "rip-off," Houthakker has said). Among the program's most obvious flaws, we find the following.

1. OBSOLESCENCE
However wise price supports may have been during the Great Depression (or even the 1950s

and 1960s), they hardly seem appropriate today. Farm incomes *were* abnormally low. Output *was* perhaps overly abundant. But now, after an outmigration of farm population and other developments, farm incomes are on average quite respectable and output is eagerly bought by the world's hungry. Our exports zoomed from $7 billion in 1970 to nearly $45 billion in 1981. Yet another measure of changing conditions is the growing animosity farmers themselves express toward traditional farm policy. The American Farm Bureau Federation, a very large lobbying group, urges abandonment of production restraints and calls for lower price support levels. "If market prices are low," says AFBF's Mike Durando, "it should be a signal to farmers that too much wheat is being grown. The government is interfering with that signal system."[45]

2. INEQUITY
Although farm poverty has served as an ostensible reason for farm subsidies, the fact is that the richest farmers hog the bulk of the benefits. In 1979, for instance, farms with sales exceeding $40,000 comprised only 22 per cent of all farms, but they reaped 57 per cent of all government benefits.[46] Knowing that farm subsidies are linked to output rather than income directly, you should not be surprised by this. Don Paarlberg, former Assistant Secretary of Agriculture isn't. He says the subsidies "put nickels and dimes into the pockets of some farmers and wads of dollars into the pockets of others."[47]

3. DISTORTIONS
When cotton is overpriced by government supports, synthetic fibers like nylon, rayon, and polyester capture large slices of the textile trade

---

[44] *Business Week*, April 18, 1977, p. 111.

[45] *Fortune*, October 19, 1981, p. 129.
[46] *New Republic*, July 19, 1980, p. 13. See also C. L. Schultze, *op. cit.*, pp. 25–30.
[47] *Business Week*, February 11, 1980, p. 58.

for no good economic reason. When peanut acreage is held down by allotments to boost prices, competing oil seeds like soybeans and sunflower seeds get an artificial stimulus to sprout, grow, and cover the vegetable oil market. When government subsidies are capitalized in higher land prices, and when the subsidies encourage capital intensive farming (as they have), they might well make farming *more* risky, not less risky. Fluctuations in price now seem to cause greater fluctuations in net income than in earlier times.

These several distortions and many others arise from the farm program simply because that program pushes, pulls, props, and depresses the free market in unnatural ways. Resources are therefore misallocated; inefficiency ensues.[48]

4. CONTRADICTIONS

On the one hand government busily tries to restrict agriculture outputs with acreage allotments, land set-asides, and the like. On the other hand, government finances water projects, agricultural research, farmer education, and other means of increasing farm output. One odd result from such inconsistent policies is that something like *two-fifths* of all land made farmable by government subsidized water projects is planted in price-support crops.[49]

Would the agriculture industry collapse if the government's heaviest props were buried? Probably not. Many sectors of the industry succeed without props. Moreover, the private sector has devices for dealing with the uncertainty and risk that accompany instability. Many farmers now produce under contracts to food processors at fixed prices. (This is the way tomato farmers in New Jersey supply Campbell's Soup,

for instance.) Hedging in commodity futures markets is also possible. A farmer can therefore secure a set price for his crop by selling futures at a guaranteed price before planting.[50] Finally, plowing under the heaviest props need not imply total government withdrawal. Distress-loan rates (or direct payments) set at very low price levels need not produce the problems outlined above. International arrangements could be made to smooth export fluctuations. The collection and dissemination of agricultural statistics could continue and even grow, providing farmers with better market information and assuaging uncertainty. It would take political resolve to hold government to such lesser roles. (The government's role was greatly pruned back during the happy harvests of the mid-1970s, only to sprout again in the late 1970s and early 1980s.) But it might be possible.

Summary

At this point you may be tempted to turn Winston Churchill's famous words around and murmur to yourself, "Never has so much been done for so few by so many." Taxpayers and consumers, as we have seen, support favored business groups and activities through a wide assortment of promotion and protection policies. By broad division these interferences with free markets include (1) direct subsidies, (2) loans and loan guarantees, (3) import protection, and (4) agricultural price supports.

1. *Direct subsidies* include tax breaks, direct payments, and government ownership and operation of certain kinds. The basic idea is to have taxpayers pay some of the costs of selected goods and services. With costs reduced, prices for these goods and services are likewise trimmed, encouraging greater output and con-

[48] For an interesting detailed example of distortion see *Wall Street Journal*, April 10, 1978, p. 28.

[49] *The New Republic*, September 22, 1979, p. 6.

[50] For more on private mechanisms, see Bruce Gardner, *The Governing of Agriculture* (Lawrence: Regents Press of Kansas, 1981).

sumption than otherwise (whether justified by such laudable reasons as external benefits or not).

Tax breaks work by lowering taxes on pet sectors and activities (thereby increasing the tax burdens of others). Energy tax credits have been particularly popular of late. In contrast, direct payments amount to expenditure handouts. Energy has been blessed here, too, particularly nuclear energy. Transportation, especially railroad and ocean transportation, have also benefited by huge direct payments. Finally, much government ownership embodies subsidization. Our biggest recent example in the U.S. is the Synthetic Fuels Corporation, which acts as a banker, broker, and buyer for private synfuel companies. SFC's conceptual grounding has been undermined by critics, but its political grounding seems secure (a dichotomy common to many subsidies).

2. *Loans* grant government credit at reduced interest rates. *Loan guarantees* provide borrowers with low-interest private funds secured by government backing. The economic effects of these credit instruments are similar to direct subsidies, although the costs to the Treasury and society are less apparent. "Economic costs" arise when credit is diverted from worthy nonsubsidized borrowers to less worthy subsidized borrowers. "Initial fiscal costs" impose burdens for financing the public debt. "Ultimate fiscal costs" include default losses. Chrysler's loan guarantee illustrates the many pros and cons involved here.

3. *Import protection*—whether it be achieved by tariffs, quotas, or voluntary export restraints—benefits domestic producers at the expense of society at large. Because free trade promotes international comparative advantage and competitive discipline, the costs of import protection to consumers can be quite large, maybe tens of billions of dollars annually once all inefficiency and transfer effects are taken into account. Recent official protection for steel

began in 1969 when steel's 6% tariff was supplemented by voluntary export restraints extracted from Japanese and European producers. Those restraints ended in 1974, but a new definition of "dumping" shifted protection to "trigger pricing" and then to "dumping" suits. Steelworkers have been the major beneficiaries, as their outsized earnings seem to be the main cause of the American steel industry's vulnerability to import competition.

4. *Price supports* in agriculture grew out of the Great Depression, when instability and poverty pummelled the industry. Instability remains a problem but not poverty. Nevertheless, price supports at income boosting levels persist. The basic idea is to lift selected crop prices with guaranteed price floors, implemented by surplus purchases, land set-asides, and other methods of keeping supplies off the market. The alternative technique of direct income payments would allow market prices to fall, yielding substantial benefits over price supports. Yet direct payments have only been tried for a few crops as a supplement to price supports. Some government intervention seems warranted by the instability problem, but only a bushel and a peck.

Questions and Exercises for Chapter 26

1. Referring to broad definitions of "subsidy," the text says that "every policy reviewed in this chapter could be considered a subsidy." Explain.
2. How would external benefits be drawn in Figure 26–1 so as to justify the subsidy depicted? Explain your result.
3. Why are tax breaks subsidies?
4. In what ways are direct payments and government ownership alike? In what ways different?

5. Compare and contrast solar tax credits and synfuels subsidies in (a) methods, (b) amounts, and (c) rationales. For example, do solar subsidies have a stronger case regarding external benefits?

6. What are the economic costs of government loans and loan guarantees?

7. Argue your preferred case on the Chrysler bailout, pro or con.

8. Why do economists favor free trade?

9. Double the tariff in Figure 26–5 and indicate the resulting (a) redistribution effect, (b) loss-due-to-production effect, (c) the tariff revenue effect, and (d) loss-due-to-consumption effect.

10. What import protections have the steel industry enjoyed? Who has been the primary beneficiary?

11. Explain the causes of instability in agriculture?

12. Compare and contrast price supports as shown in Figure 26–7 with direct subsidies shown in Figure 26–1. Why the differences?

13. Critique U.S. farm policy (a) in comparison to direct income payments, and (b) in comparison to very low, safety-net support.

Chapter 27

Equal Employment Opportunity

We hold these truths to be self-evident, that all men are created equal . . .
—The Declaration of Independence

Equality, in a vague, ill-defined, abstract sense, has always been a main value in American society. Equality in specific, well-defined, concrete areas, however, has evolved in American society only by fits and starts. Freedom for slaves and voting rights for women emerged slowly. Equality in the marketplace has yet to be fully realized, but momentum has been building. Markets for housing, consumer credit, hotel accomodations, and several other goods and services have in the last few decades won the focus of new antidiscrimination policies.

Here we consider policies concerning equality in labor markets. Broadly stated, their aim is to secure for minorities equal "opportunity" regarding employment, wages, fringe benefits, promotion, and work conditions. By legal definition, the "minorities" so protected now actually comprise a majority of the population—all females, all blacks, all those of Spanish, Asian, Pacific Island, or American Indian ancestry, all those handicapped, all "old" workers between ages 40 and 64, and members of religious and ethnic groups such as Jews, Catholics, Greeks,

and Slavs. Before discussing policy, however, we shall review evidence of the problem addressed by these policies. After discussing the problem and present policies, we shall evaluate the policies, paying particular attention to so-called "affirmative action" programs.

I. The Problem of Discrimination

A. Earnings Differentials

In 1970, when equal opportunity policies were just budding, the average annual earnings of white males were $7,928. In contrast, average annual earnings of black males were $4,844, only 60 per cent as high as white earnings. How much of this large discrepancy can be attributed to racial discrimination in labor markets? Certainly not all of it, because factors other than race influence worker earnings, and blacks and whites differ in these other factors as well as in race. Earnings tend to rise with education and experience, for instance, reflecting returns to investments in "human capital" (economists' jargon for developed or refined productive skills and knowledge). Earnings also tend to be lower in southern states as compared to northern states. Thus to the extent blacks and whites differ in these and other pertinent respects, their earnings will differ, just as the earnings of various whites differ by education, skill level, and geographic location.

Once these other elements are taken into account, however, labor market discrimination remains an important influence. Broadly speaking, the 60 per cent lower earnings of black males in 1970 could be accounted for as follows:[1]

1. *Education:* If blacks on average brought educational backgrounds to the labor market equal to those of whites in both quantity (years of schooling) and quality (school equipment, teacher competence, etc.), they would have earned 80% as much as whites.
2. *Experience and Geography:* If in addition to educational equality, blacks were like whites in skills, age composition, regional distribution, and all other such factors, they would have earned 90% as much as whites.
3. *Labor Market Discrimination:* By implication, the remaining 10 percentage point residual represents racial bias. Blacks would move from 90 to 100 per cent of white earnings if labor market discrimination were eliminated.

Stated differently, fully one-half of the earnings differential (20 percentage points) could be pinned on educational differences alone. One-fourth (10 percentage points) could be attributed to all other measurable characteristics. And one-fourth is left to be explained by labor market discrimination.

[1] Bradley R. Shiller, *The Economics of Poverty and Discrimination* (Englewood Cliffs, N.J.: Prentice-Hall, 1973), pp. 125–126.

These statistics may understate the economic impact of racial discrimination because it could be argued that the lower educational attainments of blacks were in fact also due to discrimination. *Education discrimination* (as opposed to labor market discrimination) caused much of the disadvantage in quality of education experienced by blacks before the 1970s. Regarding years of schooling, blacks could not be expected to stay in school as long as whites if the economic rewards blacks gained from added schooling were severely crimped by labor market discrimination. Indeed, some observers claim that racial differences in work skills and experience, the second element of earnings difference outlined above, can be attributed to *past* labor market discrimination. If so, then racial discrimination of various kinds—education discrimination, past labor market discrimination, and prevailing labor market discrimination—might account for a very large part of the black/white earnings gap.[2] But it must be stressed that, at the time government action against *prevailing labor market* discrimination was in its infancy, prevailing labor market discrimination accounted for only a fraction of observed job market disparities.

Sex discrimination likewise shows up in earnings statistics. Historically, full-time female workers have, on average, earned only about 60 per cent as much as comparable male workers. Figure 27–1 presents data for 1971 indicating substantial differences in annual earnings when men and women of the same age and

[2] Ibid., p. 126. For more on racial discrimination and earnings, see the survey by Albert Rees, *The Economics of Work and Pay* (New York: Harper & Row, 1979), pp. 165–174. Other observers stoutly deny this. Thomas Sowell, for instance, contends, "Not only history but also economics argues against the widespread assumption that group income differences are largely a function of discrimination, rather than human capital differences or differences in age, geographic distribution and other factors." *Wall Street Journal*, December 4, 1980, p. 22.

Figure 27–1. Annual Income by Age for Male and Female High School and College Graduates

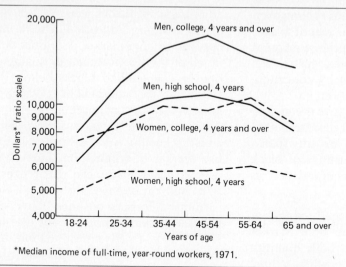

*Median income of full-time, year-round workers, 1971.

Source: U.S. Department of Commerce.

education are compared. It may be noted that men with only a *high school* education earned more, during much of their working lives, than women did with a *college* education.

Because males and females shared the same classrooms, these discrepancies cannot be accounted for by divergent qualities of education, nor, for that matter, by differences in geographic distribution. Some of the earnings discrepancies between the sexes can be blamed on the fact that women often interrupt their careers to raise children, limit their choice of work opportunities to obtain flexible hours, and otherwise meet home responsibilities in ways harmful to their incomes. But only *some*. Accounting for all such factors does not alter the conclusion that females seem to have suffered substantial discrimination, earning perhaps as much as 20 per cent less than males for this reason alone.[3]

B. *Specific Types of Labor Market Discrimination*

Average annual earnings of comparable blacks and whites or comparable females and males can diverge because of (1) hourly *wage rate differences* paid by a given employer, (2) *employment disparities* in layoffs, overtime opportunities, promotions, and job assignments, and (3) *occupational discrimination* such as

[3] Hilda Kahne, "Economic Perspectives on the Roles of Women in the American Economy," *Journal of Economic Literature* (December 1975), pp. 1259–1261; Mary Corcoran, "The Structure of Female Wages," *American Economic Review* (May 1978), pp. 165–170.

that which shunts women into nursing instead of full-fledged doctoring. In other words, labor market discrimination takes forms other than the blatant wage rate discrimination that would occur if an employer paid two equally experienced people, working elbow to elbow in exactly the same job, different wage rates. Although there was a time (in 1927) when a New York apparel manufacturer seeking laborers could unabashedly advertise "White Workers $24; Colored Workers $20,"[4] that has not been the case for quite a while, since perhaps even before such wage discrimination became illegal in the early 1960s.

Employment discrimination shows up most clearly in unemployment statistics, such as those in Table 27–1. Nonwhite males consistently experience unemployment rates twice as high as those for white males of comparable age. This is true of recession years like 1975 as well as more normal years like 1970. Notice, too, from Table 27–1 that this divergence has not lessened with time.

Occupational disparities, caused by deep-seated cultural traditions as well as more overt forms of discrimination, cause women to become clerical workers, secretaries, flight attendants, elementary school teachers, and toilers in other relatively low-paid callings. Blacks still face particularly severe difficulties breaking into the executive ranks of major corporations. Those who do reach high corporate levels tend to be public-relations or personnel directors—visible but not exactly venerable positions.[5] Indeed, this observation leads to another, namely, that blacks who do gain access to the better occupations usually end up in the lowest and least desirable jobs *within* each occupation group:

> Within the professional, technical, and managerial class, for example, white workers tend to be lawyers, doctors, engineers, and social scientists. Black workers, on the other hand, are more likely to be funeral directors, welfare workers, and teachers in segregated schools . . . [Among] clerical workers are grouped both white insurance adjusters and black postal clerks, among salesworkers both white stockbrokers and black newsboys.[6]

Much the same could be said of occupational discrimination against women. Men, for example, make up only a small fraction of elementary school teachers. Yet a disproportionate number of elementary school principals are men.[7]

C. Economic Costs of Discrimination

If we assume, for sake of simplicity, that the labor market could be divided into two similar parts, A and B, then the impact of occupational and employment discrimination can be illustrated in Figure 27–2. Without discrimination,

---

Table 27–1. Per Cent of Male Workers Unemployed, by Race and Age, 1970, 1975, and 1980

Age/Race	1970	1975	1980
16–19 years			
white	13.7	18.3	16.2
nonwhite	25.0	35.4	34.9
Over 20 years			
white	3.2	6.2	5.2
nonwhite	5.6	11.7	11.4

Source: Economic Report of the President, 1981.

---

[4] Orley Ashenfelter, "Changes in Labor Market Discrimination Over Time," *Journal of Human Resources* (Fall 1970), pp. 403–430.

[5] *Wall Street Journal*, July 9, 1980, pp. 1, 23.

[6] Bradley Shiller, *op. cit.*, p. 129.

[7] *Wall Street Journal*, February 25, 1981, p. 25. Of course sexism can operate against men who want to become secretaries, nurses, and flight attendants, as well as women who want to become truck drivers, lawyers, and engineers.

Figure 27–2. The Impact of Occupational Discrimination

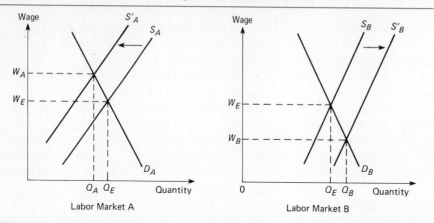

Labor Market A

Labor Market B

it is assumed that workers could shift between market A and market B fairly freely, with the result that labor supply S_A and labor supply S_B would intersect their respective labor demand curves in such a way as to yield the same equilibrium wage in both markets, namely W_E. Wage equality prevails because any difference in wage between markets A and B would cause labor to shift from the low wage sector to the high sector, restoring the original equality.

Once discrimination is introduced, barring blacks from market A, this tendency toward wage equality disappears. Barring blacks from A shifts supply in that market to S'_A. As blacks drift into market B, supply there shifts outward to S'_B. With available labor quantities reduced in A and expanded in B, equilibrium wage rates diverge to W_A on the high side and W_B on the low side. The obvious implication is that whites in market A gain by the discrimination. Less obvious is the fact that many other whites lose because of the discrimination, in particular, those who work in markets like B, which are open to blacks. While some whites gain and some lose, all blacks lose. Such theorizing can encompass sex biases also.

Aside from microeconomic consequences like these, there are aggregate efficiency losses reducing the nation's output of goods and services. Unemployed, underemployed, and inappropriately employed minority people cannot produce to their full potential. Denying them the opportunity to perform in jobs best suited to their talents, devotions, and interests deprives society of the full potential fruits of their labors. Putting some round numbers on the nation's aggregate economic loss due to racial discrimination, the President's Council of Economic Advisors estimated in 1966 that it was $27 billion annually. That is to say, if the unemployment rate and average productivity of blacks were equal to those of whites at the time, total production of our economy would have been $27 billion greater than it was.[8]

Labor market discrimination has lessened in

[8] *Economic Report of the President 1966* (Washington, D.C.: 1966), p. 10. For an updated estimate of $37.6 billion in 1978 see C. C. Ciccone and J. D. Fisk, "An Estimate of the Loss in Potential Gross National Product . . . ," in U.S. Congress, Joint Economic Committee, *The Cost of Racial Discrimination*, Hearings, 96th Cong., 1st Sess., (1980), pp. 2–5.

some respects since the 1960s, in part because of equal opportunity policies. Discussion of those improvements is postponed, however, pending our review of those policies.

II. Equal Opportunity Policies

Federal government antidiscrimination policies are enunciated in a wide variety of laws and directives, including the Fifth and Fourteenth Amendments to the Constitution and the Pregnancy Discrimination Act of 1978. Space limitations force us to discriminate against peripheral issues. Our focus is therefore confined to three broad areas: (A) equal employment opportunity *generally,* (B) more stringent policies concerning *government contractors,* and (C) *affirmative action,* which in some configurations is an extreme and controversial form of enforcement common to both the above areas.

A. Equal Employment Opportunity Generally

Prompted by massive demonstrations and violent riots, the Civil Rights Act was enacted in 1964. Under Title VII of the Act, firms, unions, apprenticeship programs, and employment agencies are prohibited from discriminating against any individual on the basis of race, color, sex, or national origin. The terms of employment so covered include hiring, training, paying, promoting, and firing workers. The 1964 Act was expanded by the Equal Employment Opportunity Act of 1972, which amended Title VII. As thus amended the Act applies to all employers with fifteen or more employees including educational institutions, plus state and local governments.

The Equal Employment Opportunity Commission (EEOC) enforces Title VII, as amended. An independent agency composed of five com-missioners, EEOC conducts its enforcement through the following procedures:[9]

1. *Complaint:* Any person, organization, or agency may file a written charge of discrimination.
2. *Informal Investigation:* Informal investigation determines EEOC's jurisdiction and the seriousness of the charges.
3. *Conciliation:* EEOC urges the opposing parties to reach voluntary accomodation. If the charges carry weight, conciliation usually entails a promise from the employer to stop discriminating, to take some "affirmative action," and to pay back-wages or other compensation to the claimant.
4. *Suit:* If attempts at reconciliation prove futile, the EEOC can conduct a detailed formal investigation and file suit against the respondent party in federal court.
5. *Remedies:* Court imposed remedies can be quite severe, including "affirmative action" of various kinds and back pay.

Besides handling individuals' complaints, 120,000 of which were in backlog at one time, EEOC may investigate and prosecute cases of "systematic discrimination." These are allegations of patterns of employment discrimination throughout an entire company or industry. The most famous of these cases involved American Telephone and Telegraph. In the early 1970s EEOC accused AT&T and its operating companies with systematic job discrimination against blacks and Spanish-Americans. As for women, AT&T was allegedly "the largest oppressor of women workers in the United States." Telephone operators, at the time 99.9% female, suffered "virtually intolerable" working conditions including "authoritarian" work rules and

---

[9] For details, see e.g., *Federal Regulatory Directory, 1979–80.* (Washington, D.C.: Congressional Quarterly, Inc., 1979), pp. 182–185, or *Promises and Perceptions: Federal Efforts to Eliminate Discrimination,* U.S. Commission on Civil Rights (1981), pp. 17–28.

Thumbnail Sketch 12:   Equal Employment Opportunity Commission

---

Established: 1964

Purpose: To enforce Title VII of the 1964 Civil Rights Act banning discrimination based on race, sex, color, religion, or national origin in hiring, firing, promotion, wages, and all other conditions of employment.

Legislative Authority: Title VII of the Civil Rights Act of 1964; Age Discrimination in Employment Act of 1967; Equal Employment Opportunity Act of 1972; and the Pregnancy Discrimination Act of 1978.

Regulatory Activity: The Commission (1) investigates charges of discrimination, (2) presses suits in federal court, (3) develops guidelines on employment discrimination.

Organization: An independent agency headed by a five member commission. The President appoints commissioners with Senate approval.

Budget: 1982 estimate: $133.9 million.

Staff: 1982 estimate: 3316.

---

limited opportunities for advancement. AT&T, whose workforce was 13% racial minority and 55% female, denied the charges but agreed to two consent decrees in 1973 and 1974, the likes of which were momentous. Back pay and salary adjustments for thousands of employees came to $68 million. AT&T also agreed to pursue ambitious percentage goals to put women and minorities into craft jobs and managerial posts (and to attract men into operator and clerical jobs).[10] Since then, "Virtually every decision that's made of a personnel nature has an EEO consideration in it," according to AT&T's director of equal employment and affirmative action, Don Liebers.[11]

The EEOC also has authority to issue regulatory "guidelines." Though not legally binding, these guidelines signal the agency's position in future litigation and thereby carry some force in business circles. Recently proposed guidelines address such issues as religious accommodation (arranging time off for those observing non-Christian holidays), reproductive hazards (the automatic exclusion of women of childbearing age from jobs involving exposure to possible reproductive hazards), and sexual harassment (the problem of male superiors forcing their lustful intentions on female underlings, or vice versa). EEOC's guidelines on sexual harassment, for instance, say that conduct that "unreasonably" interferes with someone's work performance or breeds "an intimidating, hostile or offensive work environment" is unlawful. This vague language seems to extend the definition of sexual harassment beyond the realms of hiring, promotion, and pay, which federal courts have recognized and attacked. Thus critics contend that these guidelines "invite an avalanche of questionable charges" concerning "vague, subjective encounters be-

---

[10] Lester A. Sobel (ed.), *Quotas & Affirmative Action* (New York: Facts On File, 1980), pp. 84–87.

[11] Carol Loomis, "AT&T in the Throes of 'Equal Employment,'" *Fortune*, January 15, 1979, p. 56.

tween coworkers" amounting to little more than "innocent flirtation."[12]

B. Policy Toward Government Contractors

In 1980, Firestone Tire & Rubber Company received word from Washington D.C. that it could no longer sell goods and services to the federal government. The potential cost to Firestone? About $40 million annually. The reason for purging Firestone from the roster of government contractors? A dispute over affirmative action at one of its Texas plants.[13] This made Firestone the largest of 27 companies to be denied federal contracts under antibias rules up through 1981.

Legal authority for such action against federal contractors rests not on Title VII of the Civil Rights Act, but rather on Executive Order #11246, promulgated by President Johnson in 1965 and adhered to by subsequent Presidents. Like Title VII, the Order prohibits discrimination by race, color, religion, and national origin. Unlike Title VII, this Order is enforced by the Office of Federal Contract Compliance (OFCC), a division of the Department of Labor, which has set standards for federal contractors above and beyond those of Title VII:

> It requires (1) an analysis of all major job classifications and an explanation of why minorities may be underutilized; (2) the establishment of goals, targets, and affirmative action commitments designed to relieve any shortcoming identified; and (3) the development and supply of data to government organizations . . .[14]

The specifics of these standards reached severely detailed dimensions before the Reagan administration relaxed them in 1981. The number of affirmative action steps required of construction contractors was, for example, reduced from sixteen to nine. Various paperwork and reporting requirements were scrapped or trimmed. And goals for minority hiring were made less stringent. Still, the standards exceed those of EEOC under Title VII, and the penalty for their violation—total termination of contractor status—can be especially harsh.

The importance of this niche in the law should not be overlooked. Most enterprises of any significant size are federal contractors. Those with contracts worth at least $10,000 are supposed to take affirmative action to hire and promote women and minorities (although those with fewer than 250 employees and contract business of less than $1 million are, at the time of this writing, exempt from preparing any *written* affirmative action plans). The Reagan administration's regulations, though abridged in comparison to those of previous administrations, cover 30 million workers in about 200,000 firms with federal contracts.

C. Affirmative Action

When one individual has a *"right,"* others must perform duties to honor that right. You have, for example, a right to peacefully assemble with others, a right that permits you to go to a movie theater. Others are duty bound not to detain you. Actually getting into the theater is, however, merely a "liberty," for if the theater is full, no one is obligated to give you their seat.

Similarly, the original idea behind the Civil Rights Act of 1964 was to give minorities and women the "right" to *equal opportunity*, not the "right" to a job. The duty of employers thereafter was to give no consideration whatever to race, color, and so on. Employers were not obliged to give women and minorities jobs or to promote them. As Senator Hubert Hum-

---

[12] Joann Lublin, "Guideline-Happy at the EEOC?" *Wall Street Journal,* August 28, 1980, p. 16.

[13] *Wall Street Journal,* July 22, 1980, p. 28.

[14] G. F. Bloom and H. R. Northrup, *Economics of Labor Relations* (Homewood, Ill.: Richard Irwin, Inc., 1977), p. 712. For details see *Promises . . . , op. cit.,* pp. 5–16.

phrey, a fervent champion of civil rights, explained during Senate debate on the bill:

> nothing in title VII . . . tells any employer whom he may hire. What the bill does . . . is simply to make it an illegal practice to use race as a factor in denying employment. It provides that men and women shall be employed on the basis of their qualifications, not as Catholic citizens, not as Jewish citizens, not as colored citizens, but as citizens of the United States.[15]

Obvious exceptions were allowed; Kosher butchers must, for instance, meet certain reasonable religious criteria. But the gist should be clear. Employment procedures could no longer consider groups of people, only *individuals*. And since this was merely a procedural change, there was no guarantee that results would change (that workforce composition would actually change), only that *opportunities* would improve for the disadvantaged.

Problems arose, however, in interpreting what was meant by "equal opportunity," problems associated with the fact that prevailing labor market discrimination accounted for only a fraction of observed group discrepancies. As we have seen, *educational discrimination* and *past labor market discrimination* played major roles. Thus one question to arise was this: To what extent could an employer demand of his job applicants aptitude tests, work experience, or educational prerequisites? Could a night club owner refuse to hire go-go dancers lacking two or more years of college? Could restaurant managers require passing grades on spelling tests of those seeking jobs as waitresses and cooks? In 1971, the Supreme Court ruled in *Griggs* v. *Duke Power* that seemingly "neutral" requirements for hiring, job placement, or promotion could not be used if they had a "disparate impact" on protected groups unless such requirements could be shown to have a "demonstrable relationship to successful perfor-

[15] Quoted in Sobel, *op. cit.*, p. 2.

mance" on the job. Thereafter the onus was on employers to prove that requirements like high school diplomas and acceptable exam scores were genuinely job-related.[16]

Affirmative action also evolved. This entails preferential treatment for minorities and women instead of strict neutrality. In its most innocent guise this might mean deliberate selection of the black person when choosing between a black and a white of precisely equal qualifications (rather than, say, flipping a coin). Slightly more intense affirmative action occurs when employers make special efforts to recruit minorities and women or to help them acquire training. Posting job vacancy notices in black schools or black churches that were previously ignored illustrates these possibilities. On yet a higher plateau of affirmative action, employers set goals and timetables against which to measure their efforts. Such goals might specify certain percentages of minorities and women in various job classifications, but they need not be considered "mandatory." Finally, affirmative action came to include quota systems, which assign slots in hiring, training, or promoting minorities and women in some fixed proportion to the slots assigned to unprotected job candidates, white males in particular. Proportions for either "goals" or "quotas" are usually based on some estimates of the proportions prevailing in locally available work forces. And the art of designing goal or quota systems has developed into an elaborate, complex science, now thought worthy of sophisticated statistical techniques that we cannot begin to discuss here.[17]

The main problem with affirmative action goals and quotas is that they move away from *individual opportunity* toward *group results*, thereby fostering if not exactly promoting "reverse discrimination." When Congress passed the Civil Rights Act of 1964 it stressed that non-

[16] *Griggs* v. *Duke Power Company*, 401 U.S. 424 (1971).

[17] For an entire book of techniques, see Harold P. Hayes, *Realism in EEO* (New York: John Wiley & Sons, 1980).

discrimination should not be interpreted as requiring any employer "to grant preferential treatment to any individual or to any group" on the basis of any statistical "imbalances" in its work force. Yet the Equal Employment Opportunity Commission and the Office of Federal Contract Compliance have indeed required employers to adopt specific goals and quotas to erase statistical imbalances. Strictly speaking, these official efforts have been confined to government contractors and to instances of proven past illegal discrimination. The courts have upheld these remedies insofar as they were merely "goals" or, if genuine quotas, were "necessary correctives for the employer's past discrimination." Nevertheless, such affirmative action has stirred bitter controversy.

Of all the affirmative action cases to reach the Supreme Court, none has been more controversial than the *Weber* case of 1979, which held that *employers and unions could establish voluntary programs incorporating quotas even when there was no evidence of past discrimination by the employer.*[18] The employer in question was Kaiser, whose Gramercy, Louisiana plant had a labor force of craft workers (electricians, machinists, and so on) that was only 2 per cent black, a considerably smaller number than the 39 per cent black composition of the Gramercy area labor force generally. During the 1970s Kaiser tried to recruit *already trained* black craftsmen but found very few. Escalating its efforts, Kaiser, in agreement with the local union, set up an in-plant training program that would admit one black for every one white until the percentage of black craft workers equalled 39 per cent (a goal that would take an estimated thirty years to realize). Black and white applicants were selected according to seniority within their respective racial groups. Thus it came to pass in 1974 that Brian Weber,

a white man, was repeatedly turned down for craft training even though he had more seniority than several successful black candidates.

Weber sued, challenging the 50 per cent minority quota under Title VII of the Civil Rights Act. A Supreme Court majority of five decided against Weber, however. Justice Brennan's opinion stressed three things:

1. *The voluntary and temporary nature of the program.* ". . . since the Kaiser-USWA plan was adopted voluntarily, we are not concerned with what Title VII requires or with what a court might order to remedy a past proven violation of the act." Although Congress did say that government could not *"require* any employer . . . to grant preferential treatment . . . on account of a de facto racial imbalance in the employer's work force," Congress never said that voluntary preferential treatment was *impermissible.* "The natural inference is that Congress chose not to forbid all voluntary race-conscious affirmative action."

2. *The problem of historic disadvantage:* "The purposes of the [Kaiser] plan mirror those of the statute. Both were designed to break down old patterns of racial segregation and hierarchy. Both were structured to 'open employment opportunities for Negroes in occupations which have been traditionally closed to them.' "

3. *Legislative intent:* "The prohibition of racial discrimination . . . of Title VII [a literal reading of which Weber relies upon] must . . . be read against the background of the legislative history of Title VII and the historical context from which the Act arose. Examination of those sources makes clear that an interpretation of the sections that forbade all race-conscious affirmative action would 'bring about an end completely at variance with the purpose of the statute' and must be rejected."

[18] *Kaiser Aluminum & Chemical Corp.* v. *Weber,* 443 U.S. 193 (1979).

Chief Justice Burger and Justice Rehnquist dissented. Burger accused the majority of re-writing Title VII "to achieve what it regards as a desirable result." Rehnquist vigorously complained that the majority's holding was a "tour de force reminiscent not of jurists . . . but of escape artists, such as Houdini. . . . Quite simply, Kaiser's racially discriminatory admission quota is flatly prohibited by the plain language of Title VII."

Thus the arguments written in the *Weber* opinion, pro and con, reflect the arguments surrounding affirmative action in the press, in Congress, in scholarly papers, and, indeed, in the workplace.[19] Those *favoring* strong affirmative action tend to stress fairness in results set against a backdrop of regrettable history:

[It] is fundamental that civil rights without economic rights are mere shadows.
—*Judge Charles R. Weiner*[20]

The courts have acknowledged that it is simply not enough to say, at this point in time, "all persons should have equal opportunity;" given the fact that discrimination against women and minorities was a matter of national policy and common practice, that in essence racism has been as much a part of our history in this country as the Declaration of Independence.
—*Congresswoman Shirley Chisholm*[21]

[There are reasons] to believe that our society operates so as to pass on from one generation to the next that racial inequality originally engendered by historical discrimination. [So we should not] expect the continued application of racially *neutral* procedures to lead eventually to an out-come no longer reflective of our history of discrimination.
—*Professor Glenn C. Loury*[22]

In contrast, those who *oppose* affirmative action stress fairness in procedures and impracticalities:

"Under the present bureaucratic formulation, affirmative action is, in reality, affirmative discrimination"
—*Senator Jesse Helms*[23]

What gives our government the right to decide which group is the most deserving of special treatment? And how do they make these decisions? Obviously, blacks have suffered in the past . . . But how does one decide that blacks need more special consideration than Jews, . . . or the Italians, the Irish, or the Chinese?
—*Senator S. I. Hayakawa*[24]

No one can really know what the "results" of a truly nondiscriminatory employment policy would be for any particular employer: workers do not distribute themselves among firms in a perfectly random manner, and there is no reason to suppose that job qualifications (education, experience, talent, proven integrity, or ambition) are distributed in precise, statistically even proportions across every ethnic group at every level of employment.
—*Professor Jeremy Rabkin*[25]

Depending on where you stand on this issue you will be pleased or disappointed to learn that the Reagan administration has been backing away from affirmative action. Just how far it will go remains unclear.

---

[19] For accessible yet articulate pro and con commentaries on *Weber* by two noted legal scholars see Ronald Dworkin, "How to Read the Civil Rights Act," *New York Review of Books,* December 20, 1979, pp. 37–43; Bernard Meltzer, "The Weber Case: Double Talk and Double Standards," *Regulation* (September/October, 1979), pp. 34–43.

[20] Quoted in Sobel, *op. cit.,* p. 20.

[21] Ibid., p. 5.

[22] Glenn C. Loury, "Is Equal Opportunity Enough?" *American Economic Review* (May 1981), p. 124. (Emphasis added). See also U.S. Commission on Civil Rights, *Affirmative Action in the 1980s: Dismantling the Process of Discrimination* (1981).

[23] Sobel, *op. cit.,* p. 3.

[24] Ibid., p. 6.

[25] Jeremy Rabkin, "The Stroke of a Pen," *Regulation* (May/June, 1981), p. 16.

III. Evaluation

The precise impact of equal employment opportunity policies is impossible to measure. If one looks at individual cases one can find evidence of substantial progress. For example, a 1979 study of the changes wrought in AT&T as a result of its 1973 consent decree reveals, among other things, that:

- Women increased their share of all management jobs from 22.4% to 28.5%.
- Blacks held 12% of Bell system jobs in 1979, up from 10.6% in 1973.
- Hispanic employment went from 2.5 to 3.9%.[26]

On the other hand, evidence of specific cases is not always good. Murray Weidenbaum cites experiences in St. Louis to suggest that affirmative action could have perverse effects:

> A company could avoid the entire problem [of Title VII] by locating its new plants in largely white communities, making it more difficult for minority group applicants to obtain jobs. In such an event, the EEOC's actions would hurt the very people it is trying to help.[27]

Aggregate data more reflective of the overall picture indicate progress in some respects but continued discrepancies in others. The average *earnings* of blacks *who actually have jobs* or who freshly enter the workforce *with college degrees* have been gaining on those of whites. Table 27–2 shows the changes for black males with data on black earnings as a per cent of white earnings in 1967 and 1978. Notice in particular that young black college graduates (i.e., those out of school 1–5 years) earned 98% as much as their white cohorts in 1978, up from 74% in 1967.

Table 27–2. **Black Average Annual Earnings As a Per Cent of White Earnings, Males, 1967 and 1978**

Years of School Completed	Average Annual Earnings (per cent) 1967	1978
A. All Ages		
8–11 years schooling	67%	74%
High school diploma	69	77
College diploma	63	84
B. Those Out of School 1–5 Years		
8–11 years schooling	79	69
High school diploma	81	76
College diploma	74	98

Source: Finis Welch, "Affirmative Action and Its Enforcement," *American Economic Review* (May 1981), p. 132.

Earnings improvements for those actually employed offer little solace to those who are unemployed. And, as we saw earlier, unemployment statistics indicate continuing problems for minorities. Moreover, the earnings statistics reveal very little about such things as occupation "status." A 1981 *Fortune* article, surveying progress in these respects, comments:

> Overall numbers . . . do not say much about the quality of black employment. The number of black (and women) executives remains small. At the other end of the scale, many groups of working blacks still feel the punishing effects of past discrimination. Thirty-one per cent of all the families below the poverty level in the U.S. are black. Older black males earn much less than whites, and remain locked in lower-status jobs.[28]

The trends for females likewise show great progress in some, but not all, respects.

To what extent can the progress that has been registered be credited to equal employ-

---

[26] Sobel, *op. cit.*, p. 87.

[27] Murray L. Weidenbaum, *Business, Government, and the Public* (Englewood Cliffs, N.J.: Prentice-Hall, 1981), p. 148.

[28] Walter Guzzardi, Jr., "The Right Way to Strive for Equality," *Fortune*, March 9, 1981, p. 106.

ment opportunity policies? So many factors affect labor-market decisions that the influence of policy is very difficult to isolate. Nevertheless, studies show positive contributions of various degrees. In one of the earliest and best of these studies, William Landes analyzed the impact of *state* fair employment practices acts prior to the passage of federal civil rights legislation in the early 1960s. He concluded that "relative wages were higher by about 5 per cent and discrimination lower by between 11 and 15 per cent in states with fair employment laws compared with states without these laws in 1959."[29] A more recent Rand Corporation study of earnings trends through time concluded that federal government programs have had some positive impact, especially for women. But that impact appeared to be small in comparison to other historical changes such as educational gains and the industrialization of the south.[30] Still other observers of the historical record give more credit to official policy. Bloom and Northrup contend that "the EEOC has had a profound impact on hiring practices and employment patterns, both as to race and as to sex."[31]

Whatever the importance of past government policies, the changes have been large enough to give those who oppose affirmative action a new argument—namely, the argument that affirmative action is no longer needed. Defenders of affirmative action, a substantial majority of blacks included, disagree. They apparently think that special government programs for minorities and women are still needed, and probably will be for quite some time.[32]

Summary

Data from decades past indicate substantial labor market discrimination against minorities and women. As recently as 1970, average annual earnings of blacks and females were only 60 per cent as high as white males. Factors other than labor market discrimination—such as education in the case of blacks and family responsibilities in the case of women—accounted for large portions of these discrepancies, but labor market discrimination still made itself felt.

Labor market discrimination can take three forms: (1) wage rate differences among fellow employees, (2) employment bias in terms of hiring, firing, layoffs, overtime, promotion, and the like, and (3) occupational discrimination. The first of these is easily detected and remedied, so it has not been much of a problem for quite a while. The latter two are more subtle and persistent, so it is not surprising that current policy focuses most heavily on them.

Title VII of the 1964 Civil Rights Act, as amended in 1972, crowns federal policy in this area. It prohibits all labor market discrimination based on race, color, sex, or national origin. The Equal Employment Opportunity Commission, which enforces Title VII, can right individual or systematic wrongs by force of moral suasion or court action. Government contractors face additional and more stringent standards under Executive Order #11246, which is implemented by the Office of Federal Contract Compliance in the Department of Labor.

Of all enforcement techniques employed by these agencies none has sparked more controversy than affirmative action goals and quotas.

[29] William Landes, "The Economics of Fair Employment Laws," *Journal of Political Economy* (July/August 1968), pp. 507–552.

[30] James Smith and Finis Welch, "Race Differences in Earnings: A Survey and New Evidence," R–2295–NSF Rand Corporation, 1978.

[31] Bloom and Northrup, *op. cit.*, p. 709. For recent evidence on sex discrimination, see Andrea H. Beller, "The Impact of Equal Opportunity Policy on Sex Differentials in Earnings and Occupations," *American Economic Review* (May 1982), pp. 171–175.

[32] Guzzardi, *op. cit.*, p. 102; Sobel, *op. cit.*, p. 181.

Courts have found goals legal as long as they remain mere "goals" (even if diligently pursued). Quotas were for a long time limited to instances of proven past illegal discrimination, and therefore could not be required of employers generally. Quotas voluntarily and temporarily used to correct racial imbalance were approved in the *Weber* case, prompting outcries of "reverse discrimination" and worse.

Debate over affirmative action is likely to continue. The Reagan administration has largely abandoned the pursuit of quotas, but goals and other forms of affirmative action remain. Since the economic lot of minorities and women has recently improved substantially in many respects, partly because of equal opportunity policy, some retreat on the more controversial forms of affirmative action seems desirable to opponents of affirmative action. But continued disparities fuel the arguments of proponents.

Questions and Exercises
for Chapter 27

1. To what extent can disparities in income earnings be attributed to employment discrimination?

2. How is employment discrimination manifested?

3. What are the equity and efficiency implications of employment discrimination?

4. What written authority makes employment discrimination illegal generally? Government contractor discrimination?

5. Identify EEOC and OFCC in (a) scope of authority, (b) procedures, and (c) remedies.

6. Given three types of discrimination influencing earnings disparities—educational, *past* labor market, and *prevailing* labor market discrimination—which is (are) the main concern of equal opportunity in the narrow, procedural sense? Which is (are) addressed by affirmative action?

7. Can you identify differing value judgments on the two sides of the affirmative action debate? Or differing definitions and priorities among value judgments?

8. What has been the trend in minority and sexual disparities over time? Why has the contribution of policy been disputed?

Name Index

Case Index

Subject Index